W9-ABG-499

THE ORIGINS OF CRITICISM

THE ORIGINS OF CRITICISM

LITERARY CULTURE AND POETIC
THEORY IN CLASSICAL GREECE

Andrew Ford

PRINCETON UNIVERSITY PRESS

PRINCETON AND OXFORD

PUBLISHED BY PRINCETON UNIVERSITY PRESS, 41 WILLIAM STREET,
PRINCETON, NEW JERSEY 08540
IN THE UNITED KINGDOM: PRINCETON UNIVERSITY PRESS,
3 MARKET PLACE, WOODSTOCK, OXFORDSHIRE OX20 1SY

LIBRARY OF CONGRESS CATALOGING-IN-PUBLICATION DATA

FORD, ANDREW, 1952–

THE ORIGINS OF CRITICISM : LITERARY CULTURE AND
POETIC THEORY IN CLASSICAL GREECE / ANDREW FORD.

P.   CM.

INCLUDES BIBLIOGRAPHICAL REFERENCES AND INDEX.

ISBN 0-691-07485-2 (ALK. PAPER)

1. GREEK LITERATURE—HISTORY AND CRITICISM—THEORY, ETC. 2. LITERATURE—
HISTORY AND CRITICISM—THEORY, ETC. 3. POETRY—HISTORY AND
CRITICISM—THEORY, ETC. 4. CRITICISM—GREECE—HISTORY—TO 500.
5. LITERATURE—PHILOSOPHY. 6. PHILOSOPHY, ANCIENT.
7. RHETORIC, ANCIENT. I. TITLE.

PA35.F67   2002

880.9′001—dc21   2001036925

THIS BOOK HAS BEEN COMPOSED IN SABON TYPEFACE

PRINTED ON ACID-FREE PAPER. ∞

WWW.PUP.PRINCETON.EDU

PRINTED IN THE UNITED STATES OF AMERICA

1   3   5   7   9   10   8   6   4   2

For Martine

συνεργὸν ἀμείνω Ἔρωτος οὐκ ἄν τις ῥᾳδίως λάβοι

CONTENTS

PREFACE

AT THEIR winter festival for Dionysus in 405 B.C.E., the Athenians awarded the prize for best new comedy to a play devoted to traducing literary discussion, parodying its jargon, lampooning its better-known practitioners, and even twisting familiar tragic lines upon the rack of linguistic science. To be sure, Aristophanes had leavened his *Frogs* with political farce and social satire and had seasoned it with dashes of obscenity; and he was no doubt flattering many in his audience when he described them as "veterans" in the wars of criticism who came to plays armed with texts and a knowledge of the finer points of literature (1109–18). But *Frogs* is only one among a number of Greek texts that attest to a widespread and often heated interest in innovative approaches to literature twenty-four centuries ago.

We may feel affinity with Aristophanes' audience because we have also witnessed a great burst of critical activity since the 1960's, when the relatively placid reign of New Criticism broke up and was succeeded by a series of theoretical revolutions as structuralist, poststructuralist, psychological, and sociological approaches to literature radically reconceived its nature, and in some cases rejected its coherence as a concept. These debates became quite sharp at times, and certain critical themes and slogans were heard beyond the seminar room, attracting the notice not only of other disciplines within the academy—such as law, history, and politics—but also of a wider public questioning the goals of a traditional education in literature. One of the benefits of our own critical wars has been at least that we have been forced to reconsider what literary criticism can and ought to do and what value literary study might have in education. In such a reexamination, a historical perspective on criticism may be of interest, as is suggested by recent work that has turned from the absorbing complications of theory to examine the social and institutional history of criticism. Within this perspective, which has so far focused on the rise of "modern" criticism since the eighteenth century, the period to which this book is dedicated may be of special interest, for it can fairly be described as the point when Greek, and hence Western, literary criticism was founded. The teachings ridiculed by Aristophanes came from intellectuals with widely varying avocations, none of whom was interested in poetry simply as poetry. They would have preferred to be called "wise men" (*sophoi*) or even "professors" (*sophistai*) rather than "critics" (*kritikoi*). But in the aggregate, the effect of their ideas was great: they shaped the youth of Isocrates and Plato, both of whom would write influentially about literary culture in the fourth century, and they were absorbed by Aristotle, who sometime around the middle of that century wrote up lectures "on poetics," the first theory of poetry in the West.

Searching for historical origins has come to be viewed with suspicion in many quarters, but if any of our intellectual disciplines can be said, for better or worse, to have been "founded" in ancient Greece, it is criticism—which has a Greek word at its root, as do "poetry," "metaphor," "meter," and indeed "theory" itself. Despite real difficulties that confront literary history, it seems worth noting that all these words, and a host of related terms from "heroic hexameter" and "elegiac" to "epic" and "tragedy," were either first coined or first took on their technical meanings relatively late in the visible history of Greece. We speak Greek when we speak the language of criticism because the authors studied below used such terms to approach their culture's songs, plays, and stories no longer as social, political, or religious events but as a form of language requiring its own interpretative techniques. They were, as far as we can see, the first Western thinkers to compare poems with works of visual art, to discuss the nature and uses of artistic representations, and to tie a conception of literature as a specially valuable form of language to an ideal of liberal education.

This book attempts to trace that story, differing from previous accounts in two main respects. The first is to complement what has mainly been a history-of-ideas approach by understanding criticism as a social activity. Beginning with a broad definition of criticism as any public response to a song, I examine Greek pronouncements about poetry with as much attention to the occasions and contexts in which they were made as to their theoretical implications. The second is the scope of the study, which bridges the common division of Greek criticism into pre- and post-Platonic periods. In following critical practices from the end of the archaic age in the late sixth century to the rise of poetics in the late fourth, I hope to give a richer and more precise account of how criticism became an autonomous discipline with its own principles and methods. To make room for a wider set of witnesses than is usual (including historians, natural scientists, and political theorists as well as rhetoricians and poets), I have had to be selective in my emphases. In considering Plato and Aristotle, for example, I have aimed only to indicate the essential points in which their treatments of poetry differed from previous approaches, foregoing any attempt to describe in full their rich and complex views. Happily, there are many recent works that do this job well. Similarly, in treating Aristophanes and the other dramatists chiefly as evidence for the circulation of critical ideas and terms, I have foregone trying to recover them as significant poetic theorists. I do not imply that they were not original and serious thinkers as well as artists; rather my goal has been to fill out the broader set of ideas within which their dramatic theories might be reconstructed.

After an introduction, which gives an overview of the argument, my account is organized into four chronologically sequential parts. The first enters late archaic discussions of literature though the symposium to show the close connections between social occasion and critical values. After considering other scenes of interpretation, including allegorical interpretations of epic and public debates over the meaning of oracles, I turn in the second part to define a new set of approaches to song developed among certain intellectuals in the first half of the fifth century. This "invention of poetry" was connected to the rise of a new set of terms that focused on the poet as a "maker" of texts, and encountered resistance among composers of song for public occasions, who continued to present it as inextricable from its performative context. Part III studies the dissemination of such views among a wider public in the second half of the fifth century, when adaptations and mockery of higher criticism allow us to discern some of its limitations. Because this revolution, for all its scientism and technicality, did not yet conceive of a special art (*tekhnē*) of poetry, I present it as only preparatory to the development of a properly literary criticism, which is the subject of part IV. Here, the focus is on prose writers writing about prose; in presenting their own writings as a special use of language that required its own techniques of composition and appraisal, they provided a template for defining poetry and poetics. The final chapter looks back over changing notions of the judge or "critic" of poetry through the main stages of my narrative. It draws together my argument that it is first in the fourth century that we can recognize something like the modern notions of literature as imaginative writing and of literary criticism as a special knowledge of such writings, which, in their essentials, continue to be taught in schools, disseminated in public media, and theorized (and historicized) in academies.

To follow the rise of Greek criticism in social terms is not only to clarify the roles of Isocrates, Plato, and Aristotle in transforming fourth-century Athenian literary culture into a paradigm for Western literary education, but also to highlight the social implications of classical criticism as well as its ingrained powers and limitations. The history recounted here shows what may be involved when we identify a certain set of texts as "literature" and recommend (or deplore) their study. I have accordingly written not only for classicists but for any student of critical traditions. I offer no new Platonic-Aristotelian critical theory to resolve our debates, but urge that considering how literary institutions, methods, and practices were designed at a crucial stage in the Western critical tradition may help us understand what we are asking when we charge teachers with the tasks of knowing about, understanding, and explaining these works, as Western criticism enters the twenty-fifth century of its history.

A study of the institutions of criticism should not neglect the institutional support it has itself enjoyed. I undertook primary research for this book as a junior Fellow of the Center for Hellenic Studies in 1989–90. Its superb facilities were made more rewarding by the kindness of its staff and the stimulation provided by other Fellows. I was able to draft the manuscript through a grant from the National Endowment for the Humanities in 1993–94 (FA-32088–93). I can best express my thanks for the invaluable freedom these stipends provide by saying how much I regret that they have since become available to fewer scholars.

Institutions are inhabited by people, and greater generosity hath no scholar than to read another person's work during term time. Claude Calame, Thomas Cole, and Simon Goldhill read lengthy and rough early versions of some chapters; their acute comments persuaded me to abandon several false trails, though they are not responsible for where I have erred since. A penultimate version of the whole was much improved by the learning and style of Doug Patey, friend and critic. Some of the ideas in this book, and many no longer in it, have benefited from discussion at Columbia University, Swarthmore College, and King's College, Cambridge. I have also learned much from students in my seminars on ancient literary criticism at Princeton University, especially that it is no mere cliché to say that the *Poetics* has as many interpretations as readers. The collegiality of the Classics department at Princeton has been such that I can most suitably thank them collectively for crucial support in the period when I was writing; I am, however, conscious of having had specific problems unknotted by past and present colleagues: Peter Brown, Elaine Fantham, Joshua Katz, John Keaney, André Laks, John Ma, Richard Martin, Josh Ober, Charles Segal, Christian Wildberg, and, last but not least, Froma Zeitlin. To the *équipe* CorHaLi, a band of fellow travelers in early Greek literature, I am obligated for their hospitality, friendship, and models of scrupulous inquiry. With them in mind, I thank its informal directorate, David Bouvier, Gregory Nagy, Pierre Judet de la Combe, Philippe Rousseau, and Pietro Pucci. Finally, although I have enough confidence in my reading skills to suspect that I have already named the two anonymous readers for Princeton University Press, I must thank them again for helpful comments.

ABBREVIATIONS

AS   Ludwig Radermacher, *Artium Scriptores. Reste der voraristotelischen Rhetorik* (Vienna: Rorher, 1951).

Bergk   T. Bergk, *Poetae lyrici Graeci*, 3 vols. (Leipzig: Teubner, 1914–15).

Campbell   David A. Campbell, *Greek Lyric*, 5 vols., Loeb Classical Library (Cambridge, Mass.: Harvard University Press, 1982–93).

CEG   P. A. Hansen, *Carmina epigraphica Graeca saeculorum vii–v a. Chr. n.*, Texte und Kommentare 12, 2 vols. (Berlin and New York: De Gruyter, 1983).

Chantraine P. Chantraine, *Dictionnaire étymologique de la langue Grecque*, 2 vols. (Paris: Klincksieck, 1968–77).

D   E. Diehl, *Anthologia lyrica Graeca*, 3d ed. (Leipzig: Teubner, 1949–52).

DK   H. Diels and W. Kranz, *Die Fragmente der Vorsokratiker*, 6th ed., 3 vols. (Berlin: Weidmann, 1952).

DL   Diogenes Laertius *Lives of Eminent Philosophers.*

EGF   M. Davies, ed., *Epicorum Graecorum fragmenta* (Göttingen: Vandenhoeck and Ruprecht, 1988).

FGrH   F. Jacoby, *Fragmente der Griechischen Historiker* (Leiden: Brill, 1923–).

Fraenkel   E. Fraenkel, *Aeschylus: Agamemnon*, 3 vols. (Oxford: Clarendon Press, 1950).

IEG   M. L. West, ed., *Iambi et elegi Graeci*, 2d ed., 2 vols. (Oxford: Clarendon Press, 1989–92).

Iliad   References to commentators are to G. S. Kirk et al., eds., *The Iliad: A Commentary*, 6 vols. (Cambridge: Cambridge University Press, 1985–93).

GGL   W. Schmid and O. Stählin, *Geschichte der griechischen Literatur*, 2 vols. (Munich: Beck, 1929–34).

Kern   O. Kern, ed., *Orphicorum poetarum fragmenta* (Berlin: Weidmann, 1922).

Ki   G. Kinkel, *Epicorum Graecorum fragmenta* (Leipzig: Teubner, 1877).

KRS   G. S. Kirk, J. Raven, and M. Schofield, *The Presocratic Philosophers*, 2d ed. (Cambridge: Cambridge University Press, 1983).

LfrgE *Lexicon des frügriechischen Epos*, ed. B. Snell et al. (Göttingen: Vandenhoeck and Ruprecht, 1979–).

L-M Provisional translation of the Derveni papyrus by André Laks and Glenn Most, in *Studies on the Derveni Papyrus* (Oxford: Clarendon Press, 1997), pp. 9–22.

LSJ H. G. Liddell , R. Scott, and H. S. Jones, *A Greek English Lexicon*, 9th ed. (Oxford: Clarendon Press, 1925–40).

M-W R. Merkelbach and M. L. West, *Fragmenta Hesiodea* (Oxford: Clarendon Press, 1967).

Nauck A. Nauck, *Tragicorum Graecorum fragmenta*, 2d ed. (1889). Revised with suppl. by Bruno Snell (Hildesheim: Olms, 1964).

OCD *The Oxford Classical Dictionary*, edited by Simon Hornblower and Anthony Spawforth, 3d ed. (Oxford: Oxford University Press, 1996).

Od. References to commentators are to A. Heubeck et al., eds., *A Commentary on Homer's Odyssey*, 3 vols. (Oxford: Clarendon Press, 1988–92).

PCG R. Kassel and C. Austin, eds., *Poetae comici Graeci* (Berlin and New York: De Gruyter, 1983–).

PEG A. Bernabé, *Poetae epici Graeci: Testimonia et fragmenta* (Leipzig: Teubner, 1988).

PMG D. Page, ed., *Poetae melici Graeci* (Oxford: Clarendon Press, 1962).

PMGF M. Davies, ed., *Poetarum melicorum Graecorum fragmenta*, vol. 1 (Oxford: Clarendon Press, 1991).

RE A. Pauly, G. Wissowa, W. Kroll, eds. *Real-Encyclopädie der classischen Altertumswissencschaft*. (Stuttgart: J. B. Metzler, 1893–).

Rose V. Rose, ed., *Aristotelis qui ferebantur librorum fragmenta*, 3d ed. (Leipzig: Teubner, 1886).

S-M Either *Bacchylides*, ed. B. Snell and H. Maehler (Leipzig: Teubner, 1970) or *Pindari carmina cum fragmentis*, ed. B. Snell and H. Maehler, 2 vols. (Leipzig: Teubner, 1987–89).

TrGF B. Snell, R. Kannicht, and S. Radt, *Tragicorum Graecorum fragmenta*, 4 vols. (Göttingen: Vandenhoeck and Ruprecht, 1971–85).

V E.-M. Voigt, *Sappho et Alcaeus* (Amsterdam: Polak and Van Gennep, 1971).

Wehrli Fritz Wehrli, *Die Schule des Aristoteles*, 2d ed., 10 vols. and 2 suppl. (Basel: Schwabe, 1967–78).

THE ORIGINS OF CRITICISM

INTRODUCTION

DEFINING CRITICISM FROM
HOMER TO ARISTOTLE

CRITICISM as an instinctive reaction to the performance of poetry is as old as song," writes George Kennedy in beginning the *Cambridge History of Literary Criticism*, and Kenneth Dover reminds readers of the *Frogs* that "in pre-literate cultures the composition of songs is a process in which discussion and criticism, often passionate, play an important part—and inevitably so, because aesthetic reaction implies preference and preference implies criticism."[1] As the Greeks were surely singing long before our first literary texts appear in the eighth century B.C.E., this means we cannot hope to trace criticism to its beginnings. But such broad perspectives should not lead us to neglect the fact that what Kennedy calls the "instinct" for criticism is always exercised in a social context—that the "aesthetic reaction" of which Dover speaks begins to acquire a history the moment it is uttered before a particular group on a particular occasion. Criticism may have no discernible beginning, but it does have a history, and this book is dedicated to tracing how the tradition of Western talk about stories, songs, and plays was crucially changed in Greece between the end of the sixth and the fourth century B.C.E. In speaking of this development as "the origins of criticism," I mean to highlight the emergence, within the manifold activities that might be called criticism, of a specific set of presuppositions about the nature of poetic language and ways of analyzing it that continues to shape our approaches to literature. Acknowledging that Greek song culture has continuities that reach into prehistory, we may still take notice when early statements about poetry are not assimilable to classical norms and when, and under what circumstances, these norms are first attested.[2]

One sign of the success of classical criticism is that its cornerstones—its admiration for works that marry style to content, that exhibit harmony, proportion, and appropriate ornament in effecting a special emotional and cognitive response in the audience—may seem to be valid in all peri-

[1] Kennedy 1989: ix. Dover 1993: 33, citing Finnegan 1977: 82–83, 85–86.
[2] For anthologies of problems in literary history, see Perkins 1991 and Too 1998: Introduction. For me, Too's thesis that criticism is always a discriminatory and repressive social discourse poses historical questions: Why this form of "repression"? Why there and then?

ods.[3] Histories of Greek criticism have tended, partly because of the limited evidence available, but partly, too, because of the overwhelming influence of the developed classical paradigm, to emphasize early texts that adumbrate this essentially rhetorical approach to poetry as a verbal artifact.[4] Classicizing criticism's regard for poetic form, after all, held out the promise of a perfect work of art, a formal harmony whose appreciation is independent of time and place, of party or creed. From this vantage point, Homer can stand as the father of Greek criticism (as he can for so much else) when he praises the power and pleasure of song. In his wake, the next proto-critics usually identified are the sixth-century philosophers who were concerned with language, truth, and deception. An evolving "self-consciousness" among poets is often postulated as well, especially in connection with the many references to the power of song found in the high lyric of the later sixth and early fifth centuries.[5] Around this time, on the prevailing account, Xenophanes' critiques of Homer and Hesiod, the first shot in Plato's "ancient war between poetry and philosophy," provoked defenders of Homer to respond by interpreting his texts allegorically. But a saner and more fruitful response is credited to the fifth-century sophists: their rhetorical and grammatical studies, according to a common interpretation of the sophist Gorgias, made possible a literary

[3] The broad continuities in Greek criticism are surveyed topically by Russell 1981, a companion to his collection of critical texts in translation with Winterbottom (1972). Similar in orientation are Ritoók 1989 and Verdenius 1983. I find Trimpi 1983 a too-grand synthesis that tends to swallow up the distinctive features of preclassical criticism.

[4] Of general accounts of early Greek criticism, the most recent, in Kennedy 1989, unfortunately devotes but 13 of 346 pages to the fifth century. Indispensable surveys of the period from Homer to the classical age are Lanata 1963, Maehler 1963, Harriott 1969, Pfeiffer 1968, and Svenbro 1984a. Good short accounts are Heath 1989: ch. 1 and Halliwell 1986: ch. 1; Finkelberg 1998, though devoted primarily to the notion of fictionality in Homer, offers a chapter (6) on post-Homeric developments. Perceptive overviews are Wimsatt and Brooks 1957 and Grube 1965. The accounts in Sikes 1931 and Atkins 1934 differ little from Saintsbury 1908 or Egger 1886 (first edition 1846). Other important works with a more specific focus include Walsh 1984, on the notion of enchantment; and Goldhill 1986 and 1991, on poetry and social praise. O'Sullivan 1992 is an invaluable compendium of classical critical terminology; Too 1998 tracks the theme of criticism as the repression of "polyphony" throughout ancient criticism; Dupont 1999 is stimulating, but there is a disproportion between the few texts examined and the very large claims. Indo-European antecedents are studied by Durante 1976, Pagliaro 1963, Schmitt 1967, and Nagy 1989 and 1990. Nagy's approach, cross-fertilizing Claude Lévi-Strauss and Milman Parry, is broader than my own, but I have found his anthropological account of "the social function of early Greek poetry" (1989: 1) helpful.

[5] Russell, most recently in the OCD s.v. "literary criticism in antiquity," p. 869. Kennedy 1989: ix: "Literary theory begins to emerge in Archaic Greece in the self-reference of oral bards and early literate poets and as part of the conceptualization of ideas which marked the birth of Greek philosophy." For a wide-ranging collection of passages taken to be self-referring in archaic Greek poetry, see Nünlist 1998.

appreciation for poetry's deceptions and even a theory of tragedy as therapy through art. By the time of Aristophanes' *Frogs* in 405, the art of criticism had arrived, and the main task left to Aristotle was to redeem the art of poetry after Plato's aberrant moral attacks.

A different view of each of these turning points will be given in this book by highlighting the social contexts and institutions within which criticism was practiced. In this way we can move beyond discussion of how far early Greeks anticipated the views of Plato and Aristotle on poetry and recover the broader issues their responses to song addressed. To extract from a narrow sample of earlier literature an implicit evolution toward Platonic-Aristotelian poetics turns history into a too orderly array of disembodied theoretical positions, engaging only with each other, and only on a narrow range of rhetorical concerns. Similarly, the "self" in literary "self-consciousness" is too easily reduced to a song's awareness of its rhetorical elements, neglecting many other aspects that singers were equally eager to express. My history obviously depends on how criticism is defined, and so I begin by defining, with a minimum of justification, what I will count as criticism, as literary culture, and as poetic theory. Defining literary terms is notoriously thorny, but the following definitions can at least claim not to be based on principles developed in the late classical age.

To begin this study, criticism will be any public act of praise or blame upon a performance of song. Focusing on its public character reflects the practice of criticism as carried out in the predominantly oral culture of archaic and early classical Greece; it suggests that we should consider the critic, no less than the poet, a performer before a social group. "Praise" and "blame" are the Greeks' own general terms for what one says in response to song; they remind us that interpretation need not be the primary function of criticism and helpfully separate the history of criticism from the history of aesthetic response. What people felt as opposed to what they said about poetry is not only inaccessible to the historian but should not be accorded *a priori* the same importance it may have in modern, privatized notions of aesthetic experience. The related question of how far singers and storytellers themselves should be regarded as practicing a form of criticism in their works seems to me a legitimate and rewarding inquiry, since it is impossible to retell even the most traditional tale without strategic selection and emphasis.[6] But a space must still be left for what I call "critical scenes," social occasions in which one person offered a musical performance and another the judgment upon it. I thus distinguish the artist from the critic not on the basis of a problematic

---

[6] Cf. Detienne 1981: ch. 5, esp. 131–32 on Lévi-Strauss' insistence on the ineliminable element of interpretation in retelling myth, even for participants themselves.

Romantic distinction between "creativity" and "analysis," but as distinct social roles (even if the same person may play both in turn, and even if the criticism takes the form of a new song). I call the object of criticism "song" as did the early Greeks (*aoidē, humnos, melos,* etc.): some limitation is needed, since proposals at an assembly or speeches in court were also performances calling for public praise and blame, but with different criteria from those applied to songs and with different consequences. To speak of "song" when the Greek texts do also signals the important fact that this category was significantly reconceived during the fifth century, when the words for "poetry," "poem," and "poet" (*poiēsis, poiēma, poiētēs*) rose to prominence. Finally, it is necessary to think of "performances" rather than "texts" as the objects of criticism, since Greek poetry did not become an affair of private reading until late in the fifth century (and even then only for a small minority of the population).[7]

Criticism thus defined takes place within a larger set of practices that I call literary or "musical" culture. Although neither the word nor the notion of "literature" is ancient, "literary culture" is our closest equivalent to what the Greeks called *mousikē,* a term more broad than "music" that included all the arts associated with the Muses, singing and dancing as well as music in its narrow sense. This term is needed to locate criticism within the many ways that songs were present in society—all the places where they were performed and reperformed, quoted after dinner or carried in the head, parodied or written down, on temple walls or on tombstones or scraps of papyrus. Needless to say, I cannot hope to give anything approaching a full description of Greek literary culture in this period, but I have been influenced by recent work on modern criticism that highlights the wider social arrangements within which it emerged.[8] Setting criticism within "musical" culture will help us observe that something like the eighteenth-century notion of literature was formulated in the fourth century B.C.E., when that part of musical culture that was song was examined in isolation from the rest: once the further step was taken of separating the words of songs from the music and actions they had accompanied, the particular effects of poetic language could be studied in a form of criticism one may call "literary" insofar as it was specific to the poetic art.

Finally, I use the phrase "poetic theory" quite narrowly to refer to self-conscious attempts to give systematic accounts of the nature of poetry in

---

[7] Cf. Herington 1985: ch. 1, and Kannicht 1988, on the "song culture" of early Greece.

[8] I may cite particularly Eagleton 1983: ch. 1 and 1984, as well as Graff 1987, both building on Palmer 1965. I have found Bourdieu's (1967, 1984, 1990, 1993) analyses of literary culture as a form of "social capital" enlightening, and Guillory 1993 a stimulating and penetrating analysis of the institutional tensions in current academic criticism. Cf. now Gallagher and Greenblatt 2000.

the most scientific terms available. This is what the Greek word "poetics" (*hē poiētikē tekhnē*, "the art of poetry") means, and it is a main contention of this study that Aristotle's work of that title embodied a new conception of the task of criticism and not simply the inexorable working out of tendencies that can be traced back to Homer. In putting the rise of poetic or literary theory so late, I do not forget that any response to a work of art (Homer's no less than my own) may be said to imply a theory, and it would be naive to think of the rise of poetics as a fall from a primitive, unmediated enjoyment of song into self-conscious analysis. But to generalize from any statement about song the total theory it may imply short-circuits the historical study of criticism by identifying criticism with theorizing. My view tends in the opposite direction and holds that theory's insistence that everything be viewed under its ken was itself just one strategic move within a widely varied set of ways to respond to song. Once we regard theorization as a social activity, we will be better able to understand how the self-conscious and formal theorization of poetry triumphed at a particular time and place within the traditional song-culture of Greece.

My aim in attending to social contexts is not to reduce all criticism to bids for power or prestige, but to make more of its history visible and comprehensible, including early critical responses that may seem foolish from a classical perspective. Donald Russell forewarns readers of his insightful *Criticism in Antiquity* that they may be "bewildered, disconcerted, perhaps disappointed" by the ancients' judgments about their own literature, which often appear "inadequate and unsatisfactory if we compare them to our own responses to the same texts."[9] We have a better chance of understanding such judgments on their own terms if we consider where they were proposed and what extra-rhetorical ideas might have made them important to their audiences. To illustrate my terms and approach, I take a speech from the first book of the *Odyssey* that has been called "the earliest literary criticism in Greek literature."[10]

Critical Scenes: Telemachus

The scene is the dining hall of Odysseus' palace, where Penelope's suitors sit over their wine while Phemius, a professional singer (*aoidos*), entertains them with a rendition of "The Disastrous Return of the Achaeans

---

[9] Russell 1981: 1. Harold Bloom speaks more vividly of the "dumbfoundering abyss" that separates ancient and modern aesthetics: *The Art of the Critic*, vol. 1 (New York, 1985), vii–x.

[10] S. West on *Od.* 1.346 ff., also the source of the quotation in the following paragraph.

from Troy" (1.326–27, 339–40). Penelope appears with her maids at the threshold and bids the singer to switch to some other theme because his present song is painful to one whose husband has yet to return (1.328–44). At this point Telemachus intervenes with a speech that can be said to counter Penelope's blame with praise: reproving his mother, he tells her that if anyone is to blame for the fates men receive, it is Zeus, not singers. Phemius has only been performing the latest song, which is what everyone likes to hear; Penelope should therefore steel her heart and go back to weaving with her maids. That is her place and her task (*ergon*), he concludes:

But making speeches (*muthos*) is an affair for men, one that concerns
    all the men here,
and me especially, for mine is the authority (*kratos*) in this house.[11] (1.358–59)

This exchange includes several suggestive statements about the nature of poetry, as Stephanie West remarks when she says that Telemachus is "the poet's spokesman in his plea for artistic freedom and his emphasis on the importance of novelty." One could go much further and suggest, for example, that the contrasting responses of Penelope and the suitors to the same song dramatizes the aesthetic paradox that artistic representations of painful events can give pleasure. But before converting Homer into the father of Aristotle, it is useful to put the speech in context, since it would be a reductive account of Telemachus' criticism that did not note that the most basic issue at stake in Book 1 is who shall call the tune. As Telemachus' words make clear, speaking up about poetry at a feast is a way of claiming a social role and asserting authority (*kratos*) over others. Up to this point, Telemachus has been hesitant and ineffectual before the suitors, but now he seizes his role as prince by taking command of the singer who had been performing for the suitors "under duress" (1.154; cf. 22.331).[12] The singer is answerable to the head of the house, and Telemachus has implicitly taken up this role, which he will give back to the true lord of Ithaca when he returns and summons the bard to a life-and-death critical appraisal (22.330–77).

---

[11] All translations are my own, except where indicated.

[12] See Goldhill 1991: 60–61. Svenbro (1984a: ch. 1) illuminates the "social control" over song in Homer, but puts too much stress (esp. 44) on singers' being forced to articulate the values of the dominant group (which he applies to the idealized Demodocus in happy Phaeacia no less than to Phemius in strife-torn Ithaca). If we accept Svenbro's conjecture (36–37, 50) that Phemius was singing the death of Odysseus to please the suitors, it becomes quite odd (to all but the most reflexive Freudian) that Telemachus does not change the song. Social control over the singer was doubtless real, but could be hedged in, e.g., by the notion that the singer was sacrosanct or by Telemachus' idea that any blame for painful events they recount is to fall not on them but on Zeus.

In addition, to become a man among men, Telemachus asserts himself as a man over women. His peremptory dismissal of his mother from speaking in this context is given the accents of male heroism: "This is an affair for men" is what a warrior says in setting off to battle.[13] Publicly pronouncing on song will remain a male prerogative from the time Penelope retires with her maids through the fourth century, when, in Plato's version of an ideal dinner party, a gentleman dismisses the flute girl "to go play to herself *or among the women inside*" (*Symp.* 176E). During the centuries this book traces, women practiced a musical culture of their own in places now mostly hidden from the historian. As ladies and their maids worked over looms and as peasant women worked in fields or at washing places, they sang and talked of the songs they had learned from each other and from the poets who composed for women's choruses. What Circe sang at her loom is not beyond all conjecture, but it was public, civic, and male discourses that issued in formal literary criticism.[14]

Before leaving this scene, it is worth considering its place within Telemachus' coming-of-age story that opens the *Odyssey*. His speech, which amazes his mother (1.360), is but the first of a number of bold actions undertaken by the newly confident young man: it is immediately followed by his "high speaking and bold address" (1.385) to the suitors, and the next day he takes it upon himself to summon the Ithacans to assembly and air his grievances. Book 1 traces these developments to the arrival of the family's patron goddess Athena. Taking human form as an old family friend aptly named Mentes ("mentor"), Athena tutors the courteous but disconsolate young prince by taking him aside and "inspiring" (1.320–22) him: Mentes chides the boy (1.252), gives him fatherly advice about his rights and duties (1.308), and exhorts him in a tone similar to that of Greek gnomic poetry.[15] Upon Athena's departure, Telemachus, now described as wise and prudent (1.345, cf. 306), takes control of the situation by speaking up at the feast. It may be inferred that his attentive sitting at table beside a good man, which was the standard archaic setting for a nobleman's musical education, has played a part in preparing him to take an active role as speaker in his house and in the city.

Homer shows pronouncing about poetry as part of a male citizen's repertoire of public performances, and he suggests that it was something

---

[13] With *Od.* 1.358–59, cf. *Iliad* 6.492–93, *Od.* 11.352–53 (and 21.352–53, where Telemachus reprises the verse but speaking of weapons). S. West on *od.* 1.356–59 finds Telemachus rude to his mother, noting that Helen (4.121 ff.) and Arete (7.141 ff.) take part in after-dinner conversation. But these queens do not presume to call the tune.

[14] An excellent recent study is Stehle 1997, with generous bibliography.

[15] Note esp. the gnomological phrases: "Be sensible and take my words to heart" (1.271, cf. 305); "I will propose (*hupothēsomai*) wise counsels to you if you will only listen" (1.279); Mentes' values are those of a "sound and trusty" man (*pinutos*, 1.228–29).

they learned from well-disposed elders and kin. As the roles open to citizens and singers will change in the coming centuries, new mentors and new views of song will also appear. In the following chapters, I trace these changes through a succession of critical scenes in which song is praised or blamed. Reading these scenes with attention to their social and cultural backgrounds reveals not a progressive series of "discoveries" in which the philosophical and rhetorical nature of poetry comes to light, but instead a fundamental and broad shift from early responses to singing as a form of behavior regulated by social, political, and religious values to a conception of poetry as a verbal artifact, an arrangement of language subject to grammatical analysis, formal classification, and technical evaluation. This shift was completed in the fourth century, and the *Poetics* is its most conspicuous monument.

This opposition between early "functional" criticism and later concern with "inner" form develops perspectives from some recent histories of Greek literature, such as Bruno Gentili's *Poetry and Its Public in Ancient Greece* (1988), that valuably stress the embeddedness of archaic song in performative context.[16] The focus on song as an exchange between performer and audience rather than text and reader owes much in turn to Eric Havelock, who argued that literacy was quite restricted in Athens until late in the fifth century, when a "literate revolution" began to transform a musical culture centered on oral performance to one increasingly confronted with written texts.[17] Havelock's *Preface to Plato* (1963) is also a history of criticism, holding that this cultural upheaval is the subtext of Plato's notorious rejection of (orally performed) poetry in his (written) *Republic*. Some of Havelock's claims for the intellectual powers unleashed by alphabetic writing were over-broad and took too little account of the fact that the significance of any writing system will depend on the uses to which it is put in particular contexts.[18] There is, furthermore, de-

---

[16] See Gentili 1988: 36–37; Gentili and Cerri 1988: 97–102; and the history of Greek literature by Cambiano, Canfora, and Lanza (1992). Käppel 1992: 19–21, 33–43 gives a similar outline derived from the *Rezeptionsaesthetik* of H. R. Jauss (discussed in Käppel's theoretical introduction, 3–31), but see the review of D'Alessio in *Classical Review*, n.s. 44 (1994): 63, and D'Alessio 1997; and Schröder (1999: 101–9), who stresses the implicit formalism of cult practice. The works of Rösler have also made important contributions on these lines. By contrast, Cairns (1972: esp. 34–36, 70) shows how genres and "set pieces" were *made out of* early Greek poetic texts, but not that classical literary "genres" can be assumed to operate in Homer and early lyric. Cf. Russell and Wilson 1981: 31–35.

[17] Recent treatments of early Greek writing include Woodard 1997, Powell 1991, and, on Semitic letter forms, Burkert 1992: 25–30.

[18] Bowman and Woolf 1994, Thomas 1992. A recent critique of the more extreme claims of Havelock and of Goody and Watt (1968) is Nails 1995: 179–91. For balanced discussions of the influence of writing on intellectual activity, though without making it a sole cause, see Lloyd 1987: 70–78, 1979: 239–40; and Finley 1975. It is surprising that so subtle a

bate about how early writing was introduced into Greece and how rapidly and widely it spread. But any attempt to situate criticism in its contexts must consider that notions about the composition and transmission of song will at least reflect and may in part be determined by modes of performance and technologies of communication.[19] The following chapters will trace the role of written texts in the rise of approaches to songs as stable, structured objects rather than as time-bound performances tied to communal contexts. I hope to show why, for criticism to take the form it did in the fourth century, orally performed songs had to become "poems," texts rather than events, and "singing" became "poetry," rule-governed composition rather than an activity within the communal and cultic life of the city. Only when singers became "poets," craftsmen of words rather than performers, could a properly "poetic" literary criticism emerge as the special knowledge that discerns the excellence of poetry so understood.

Gentili says that the early, functional criteria became "increasingly irrelevant" in the fourth century and were replaced by "internal, rhetorical ones."[20] We shall see that this is too hasty, for the older criteria were flexible enough to continue to be invoked throughout antiquity. But Gentili is right that, for criticism to become "literary"—to become a properly technical approach based not on poetry's social and moral uses but on its constitutive linguistic and musical media—analysis could no longer be based on the varied and shifting demands of local occasions of performance. Criticism became technical by basing itself instead on a system that prescribed the correct aim (telos in the sense of function, rather than occasion) of each type of song, and this—not occasion or other context-derived obligations—in turn determined the correct form of any song.

A consequence of this development is that the most basic difference between archaic musical culture and classical literary criticism is centered on notions of genre. To highlight the change between my historical endpoints, and also to illustrate my method for reading preclassical criticism, I devote the rest of this introduction to considering how "genres" or kinds of singing were defined in the archaic age. This involves collecting archaic texts in which specific kinds of song are identified and interpreting them

---

historian as Oswyn Murray (1980: 96–97) can speak of archaic Greece as literate in our terms: see Anderson 1989.

[19] I differ with Svenbro's (1984a) Marxian emphasis on the "means of production" of poetry and the progressive "alienation" of the poet from his "product" (poiēma), but remain indebted to his pioneering approach. In this connection, the work of Detienne is also valuable, especially his (1967) survey of the many social forms of the archaic "master of truth." Havelock also influences Cole's (1991) convincing and important revisionist account of early rhetorical study.

[20] Gentili 1988: 169, underestimating the strength, on current accounts, of the restored democracy.

with Plato and Aristotle on a short leash. To bring out the contrast with classical analysis, I conclude with some texts on the same theme from the fourth century.

Archaic Genres

A basic reason that it is misguided to seek specifically literary criticism in the archaic age is that there was, as far as the evidence permits us to see, no unitary notion of poetry or literature. The many forms of song that were sung on various occasions were not referred to as instances of a single art or activity called "poetry" (*poiēsis*), or even "song." Instead, there were many different names for songs, most of them derived from the social contexts in which they were performed. What archaic Greece lacked, and what was not developed until the fourth century, was a literary system, a conceptual unification of songs as distinctive forms of speech to be understood in their formal relations to each other. Of course, long before Homer, Greek audiences had developed expectations about what kind of song was appropriate at what kind of occasion, and Greek singers created new songs in the knowledge that they would be praised or blamed accordingly. From this collaboration, distinct "genres" of song can be said to have been defined, if we bear in mind Dover's very important remark that in the archaic period, different genres amount to different occasions of performance.[21] Archaic song was made, received, and assessed in relation to its context rather than its conformity to some formal paradigm.

Accordingly, the oldest Greek song names usually express an aspect of the occasion: some are simply terms for social actions, such as the "lament" (*thrēnos*) for funerals or the *iambos* for occasions of ritualized "abuse."[22] Others are derived metonymically from the context, such as the "paean" and "dithyramb," which evolved from ritual refrains into names for kinds of song. The generic meaning of paean as "a song of praise or joy" derives from earlier, more context-based senses—a song for Apollo in his aspect as saving god, and behind this, it appears, a song invoking *Paiawōn*, a pre-Greek healing divinity.[23] Similarly, the songs called dithyrambs were properly connected with the cult of Dionysus

[21] Dover 1964: 189, with the pioneering work of Harvey 1955, on which see also Russell 1981: 148–58; Rosenmeyer 1985; Käppel 1992: 1–7; and Calame 1998: 102–4 and 1974, which critiques Rossi's (1971) "unwritten laws of genre" in the archaic period.

[22] For song types in Homer, see Diehl 1940; and cf. Ford 1997b: 400–401. Fowler 1987: 89–100 is a good survey of archaic kinds of song.

[23] See Burkert 1985: 43, 145; Heubeck on *Od.* 4.231 ff. On the etymology of *paian* in the fifth century, see Barrett (1964) on Euripides *Hippolytus* 1371–73.

dithurambos, an ancient epithet of the god that became as opaque to the Greeks as it is to us. This way of naming kinds of song persisted through the archaic period, yielding at its end such new names as "tragedy" (*tragōidia*, "goat-song," probably to be associated with a processional song leading a goat to sacrifice) and "comedy" (*kōmōidia* taking its name from *kōmos*, a kind of village revel-song).

A number of these old names were preserved through the classical age and entered Hellenistic scholarship as genre terms, whence the vocabulary of modern literary studies includes such a term as "goat-song." In this process, the archaic contextual meanings were typically replaced by rhetorical ones that defined song types according to content and form. The paean affords an example of this reduction. For the Hellenistic critic, the paean could be defined formally as a choral song and thematically as devoted to Apollo (or his sister Artemis). In this way, formal distinctions between choral, solo, and antiphonal singing overwrote earlier social conceptions about how performing roles should be distributed at a given occasion. In a similar way, scholarly conventions regarding which rhythms, melodies, and language—the key discriminants in formalist definitions of genre—suited songs of a particular kind depended originally on the actions (such as dancing, processing, or pantomime) that the song accompanied and on the effects it was hoped to have on the audience and the gods. What archaic paeans seem especially to have in common is that they are group songs to a god that reinforced the solidarity of the men participating in them.[24] To sing a paean was in the simplest terms to shout *iē paiōn* in unison. In early Greek texts, soldiers sing paeans as pleas for deliverance from some evil or threat (*Iliad*. 1.472–73), but also in triumph (22.391–94) and at a feast (*Homeric Hymn to Apollo* 517–18). Thus Hellenistic scholars had to include among paeans songs that invoked gods other than Apollo as well as songs that did invoke him but without the refrain.[25] The whole class was furthermore hard to distinguish from the broader category of group processional songs (*prosōidia*).[26]

Beginning in the fifth century, rhetorical criticism created new abstract "genres" that answered less to archaic practice than to the needs of formal

---

[24] Euripides represents girls singing paeans (e.g., *Hercules Furens* 689, on Delos), but normally women would at most add a ritual *ololugē* to the men's paean: Calame 1977, 1:78, 147ff.

[25] Käppel 1992: 65–70.

[26] Färber 1936: part 1, p. 32, and Ian Rutherford *ZPE* 96 (1992): 68, on the difficulties of distinguishing paeans from *prosōdia*; for paeans to other deities, Smyth 1906: xxxviii n. 1; and now D'Alessio 1997. On ancient debates on whether the refrain is obligatory, [Plut.] *De musica* 9–10; Athenaeus 696b–c, with Harvey 1955: 172–73, on the divergence of "literary" and "ritual" paean. Cf. Schröder (1999: 49–61), who goes some way toward vindicating Hellenistic scholars from characterizations as pure formalists: 110–26.

classification. Greek *humnos*, for example, at root meant simply "song": in the archaic and early classical period, the noun and verb have no particular connotation of "hymn" in the sense "song for a god."[27] The archaic vocabulary shows many names for songs to individual divinities, but no particular term for the class as a whole. Their various hymns were united in the yearly cycle of festivals, not in a library's pigeonholes. But the scholars, developing, as will be seen below, an idea of Plato's, used "hymn" as a genre term (based on "content") to embrace all songs to divinities. This was immensely useful in sorting the texts of archaic songs into classes.

Formalistic definitions downplay historical change and social nuance for gains in objective descriptiveness and classificatory power. But the needs of a literary taxonomist had little in common with the archaic culture that produced the songs. When we find statements in archaic Greek poetry about what is good or bad in singing, the predominant concern is whether the song is "appropriate" (*prepei*) to its context and occasion. There is no *literary* criticism in the archaic period because "the appropriate" and its congeners (*to prepon, metron, kairos*) always involved social and religious values. This is not to say that formal and aesthetic qualities were ignored: the gods were said to "take pleasure" in festival singing and dancing, and so the ritually or socially "right" way to perform a song had to look and sound right, too. Appropriateness to the occasion included qualities we could call aesthetic, but always as elements within a larger conception of the function of song: one of our oldest preserved choral songs, composed for a festival of Artemis in seventh-century Sparta, draws the audience's attention to the beauty of the dancers, their fine voices and nimble feet; but this comes after they have recounted a myth showing that gods avenge acts of hubris.[28]

This outline of the social nature of archaic genres can be tested by collecting passages of Greek lyric from the period 650 to 450 that mention distinct kinds of song and suggest why one kind is used on a given occasion and another is not. Reading such texts without the rhetorical prejudice of backward-looking intellectual history confirms the importance of

---

[27] See Calame 1995: esp. 2–4, with notes 4–6; and Càssola 1975: ix–xii, who gives as its fundamental meaning, "connessione, serie (di versi)." Examples of its broad use are, e.g., *Od.* 8.429 (of Demodocus' heroic songs, cf. Hesiod *Theogony* 99–101), Hesiod *Works and Days* 662 (of his own song), pseudo-Hesiod fr. 357 M–W (of Hesiod and Homer), *Homeric to Apollo* 161 (of a choral lyric, cf. Alcman 27 *PMG*, Sappho 44.34 V), Xenophanes 1.13–16 *IEG* (of sympotic song, cf. Anacreon 356b 5 *PMG*, Euripides *Medea* 192). The etymology of ὕμνος has long been debated; many associate it with roots meaning "to weave" or "to join," but the most recent analysis by Vine (1999: 575–76) is "sounding," connected with Latin *sonare*.

[28] Alcman 1 *PMG*. See Barker 1995: 262. On the gods' pleasure in song and festivity, cf., e.g., Homer *Iliad* 1.601–4, *Homeric Hymn to Apollo* 146–50.

the tendencies described above and the insignificance of "literary" approaches to song in the archaic period. Comparing archaic and classical instances of musical "decorum" can then make clear how "appropriateness" was redefined from describing a song's social and religious "propriety" to prescribing the "proper and fitting" relation between the formal and thematic elements within a text.

Archaic Appropriateness

The earliest example of the verb *prepei* ("it is fitting") applied to a song is from Alcman in the late seventh century: "At the banquets and feasts of the public messes it is fitting to strike up a paean among the diners" (98 *PMG*: θοίναις δὲ καὶ ἐν θιάσοισιν / ἀνδρείων παρὰ δαιτυμόνεσσι πρέπει παιᾶνα κατάρχην).[29] At the Spartan feasts for which Alcman composed, it was pious to acknowledge Apollo's festive aspect, and the men would at the same time form themselves into a group, even if simply by responding with the refrain. Here *prepei* joins what is religiously correct, customary in context, and conducive to the desired mood of the occasion; the paean "befits" the feast in the way that a grace may be "fitting" before meals.[30] This combination of ritual and social decorum is still in force in the late fifth century, when the chorus of *Frogs* calls for "songs, dance, and revels that befit this festival" (370–71: μολπὴν / καὶ παννυχίδας αἳ τῇδε πρέπουσιν ἑορτῇ). The festival in question is the feast of Dionysus, where the drama was staged, and the "befitting" genre is comedy itself, a customary way to honor this god.

A line from Sappho illustrates archaic genre-definition by speaking of a kind of song that is *not* fitting to sing. If around 600 B.C.E. one of the musically skilled women of Lesbos had asked the poet why she sang the kinds of song she did and not, for example, dirges (which traditionally accorded women a prominent role), Sappho could have replied in the words of one of her songs: "It is not right that there should be a dirge in the house of the Muses' ministers; this would not befit us" (οὐ γὰρ θέμις ἐν μοισοπόλων ⟨δόμωι⟩ / θρῆνον ἔμμεν' (. . .) οὔκ' ἄμμι πρέποι τάδε: 150 V). We need not credit the ancient biographical critic who took these words as Sappho's deathbed consolation to her daughter, but neither was she engaged in literary theory; as in Alcman, this comment functioned in its performative context as a speech act that simultaneously declared and enacted the "rightness" of the song. Nevertheless, the way the singer uses

---

[29] See Chantraine s.v. *prepon*; cf. Fraenkel on *Ag.* 242, and bibliography at Fowler 1987: 128 n. 17.

[30] Cf. Fraenkel on *Ag.* 245 ff.; and Aristophanes *Thesmophoriazousae* 310, *Peace* 453.

dirges as a foil to her own offering is revealing. Sappho says that laments are not *themis*—not customary, lawful, or even natural—for her group, which she represents as "ministers" or "temple attendants" of the Muses.[31] Although we cannot precisely reconstruct the nature of Sappho's group, its members clearly had a special status that derived from their closeness to the Muses, a status that was made concrete in their association with a special "house" or perhaps "temple" in the city.[32] Dirges were "unfitting" (*ou prepei*) for this group in the sense that they were not what the group performed when appearing (*prepei* in its root sense) in their customary social and religious contexts. This "generic" scruple expressed a social, religiously sanctioned bond among Sappho and her "companions" (160 V). In return for honoring them with "fitting" songs, the Muses made Sappho "blessed and enviable" (193 V), and perhaps even "honored" (τιμίαν, 32 V). Correspondingly, to be outside the group was to be banished from their songs, ceremonies, and distinctive ways, like the woman who "will have no share in the roses of Pieria when you descend to the house of Hades" (55.2–3 V).

The social basis of this generic distinction is clear, but Sappho's Muses also show that the social was bound up with the religious. An archaic musical "law" (Sappho's *themis*) of genre could be rooted in the association of different deities with different forms of cult, as comic drama "fitted" the cult of Dionysus. The idea is explicit in an early lyric by Stesichorus, whose (probably male) chorus also rejected dirges: "Sportive song and dance are dear to Apollo, while lamentations and groans are the lot of Hades" (παιγμοσύνας ⟨τε⟩ φιλεῖ μολπάς τ' Ἀπόλλων, / κήδεα δὲ στο ναχάς τ' Ἀίδας ἔλαχε).[33] Once again, the rejection of one kind of song is part of the song: Apollo will be pleased today by our singing in the ways that have pleased him before. But Stesichorus gives us a suggestion of *why* Apollo and Hades demand different songs: his use of the word "allotment" evokes the mythic division among Hades and his brothers of distinct spheres of influence (as in *Iliad*. 15.191) and suggests that different kinds of song and music were assigned to each god by the same sort of inscrutable but absolutely binding originary decision that fixed their other prerogatives.

---

[31] For bibliography on *themis*, see Heubeck on *Od.* 2.68; Snell 1953: 75 on Hesiod *Theogony* 886 ff.; and Pindar fr. 30 S-M. On *prepei* in 150 V, cf. Maehler 1963: 59, 93.

[32] Voigt prints Hartung's *domōi* for the unmetrical *oikia*: see references in B. MacLachlan in Gerber 1997: 160–61. On the nature of Sappho's *thiasos*, Calame 1977, 1:367–72 remains essential, and good recent accounts include Gentili 1988: chs. 6, 13; Seaford 1994: 257–62; Lardinois 1996; Stehle 1997: ch. 6. Morris (1996) notes that Sappho's house is also a cult of the East, the Olympian gods, and "elite" ideals of nobility and beauty.

[33] Stesichorus 232.2–3 *PMG*. Cf. Aeschylus 161 *TGrF* (μόνος θεῶν γὰρ Θάνατος οὐ δώρων ἐρᾷ οὐδὲ παιωνίζεται) and Euripides *Iphigeneia in Tauris* 181–85 ("Αιδας δίχα παιάνων). Inversions confirm the topos: Aeschylus fr. 255 *TGrF*, Euripides *Suppliants* 971–74.

For both Sappho and Stesichorus, the rules governing singing are indissociable from scruples about correct religious speech; to violate propriety is thus a far graver matter than mere artlessness or inelegance. This is to be expected when all musical occasions take place under the auspices of one divinity or another, making it hard to draw a sharp line between cult song and poetry among early Greek lyrics. But the dependence of archaic musical values on religious ideas could go much deeper. Ultimately, the musical activities of social groups could be defined not only by the predilections of the gods they honored, but also by the fact of human mortality in itself. The ethical and religious notions underwriting archaic generic distinctions are clear in a lyric fragment by Pindar from the fifth century (128c S-M). This poorly preserved text of what appears to be a dirge begins by listing a series of song types, first setting off paeans from dithyrambs:

> There are songs for the children of Leto of the golden distaff,
> paeans in due season, and there are other [songs] . . . from the garlands
>   of flourishing ivy
> that long for (?) . . . of Dionysus.

This text is used by Lutz Käppel in his valuable study of paeans to exemplify the pre-Alexandrian classification of genre by *Sitz im Leben*: paeans are songs that are "in season" (ὥριαι) at festivals for Apollo and Artemis, while Dionysus required dithyrambs (not named explicitly but clearly denoted by the metonymic reference to the ivy wreaths worn in his cult).[34] Käppel stops his analysis here, but Pindar immediately goes on to list a number of other songs:

> But [other songs] put to sleep three sons of Calliope, so that memorials
>   of the dead might be set up for her:
> one sang "alas Linus" (*ailinon*) for fair-haired Linus,
> another sang for Humenaios, whom the final song took when
> he first touched the skin of marriage,
> another was for Ialemos when his strength was stopped by
>   wasting disease.
> But the son of Oeagrus, Orpheus of the golden sword
>   [fragment breaks off].[35]

---

[34] Käppel 1992: 34–36. Pindar *Paean* 3.14 (cf. fr. 52c S-M) also speaks of the "seasonableness" (ὥριον ποτὶ χρόνον) of song. Further discussion with references in Calame 1998: 101–4, and commentary by Maria Cannata Fera, ed., *Threnorum fragmenta: Pindarus* (Rome, 1990), fr. 56.

[35] The text is too uncertain to be worth printing without an extensive *apparatus criticus*. For convenience, I follow the text of fr. 128c by Snell-Maehler (1989), which I translate following Race 1997, 2:360–63; for a different reconstruction by Bowra (fr. 126), see translation and comments by Barker (1984: 61).

This series of archetypal laments for mortal children of the Muse consti-
tutes a contrasting set, on the other side of a profound "generic" divide,
from songs for deathless gods. Human laments have specific, even tragic
moments of origin, while the paean and dithyramb recur in due season at
moments of "flourishing." The origins that Pindar imagines for laments
have both a mythological and an anthropological character. He implies
that the proper names of dying youths, repeated by their mothers in grief,
eventually came to be repeated by others until they became refrains marking genres of lamentation—lasting "memorials" to the figures named.
Such a story allows the singer to recognize the universality and antiquity
of lament songs while yet connecting his present offering with the origins
of the genre, and with divine sadness at human mortality. Beneath the
anthropological recognition of a kinship among all laments, the basic generic distinction is between the gods with their endless songs and mortals
with their *thrēnoi*. The issue was doubtless further explored at the end of
the fragment with the mention of Orpheus, who used music to cross this
fundamental divide in his quest for Eurydice.

This text bespeaks an age of anthropological interest in the varieties of
song types and points to new principles for synthesizing song traditions.
This approach, whose implications will be studied in chapter 6 below, was
developed in the fifth century without displacing older ways of thinking of
song. One final example of a song about genre from the fifth century
shows the persistence of religious notions even as various song-types were
being collocated in formal and functional classes. It was composed by
Bacchylides and is a "victory song" (*epinikion*), a genre whose social function has been well epitomized by Elroy Bundy as "the glorification, within
the considerations of ethical, religious, social and literary propriety of
[the] victor" at the Greek athletic games.[36] Bacchylides begins with conventional piety, warning that the happy winner is not thereby exempt
from the vicissitudes of fate; the speaker then declares that the best thing
for a mortal is to be lucky in the fortunes god sends, since sheer luck can
make a nobleman base, and vice versa (14.1–6).[37] From this he draws the
moral that the single best path to excellence is to preserve a sense of the
appropriate in the shifting situations of human life. This precious sense
has a name that was to have an important role in classical aesthetics, the
kairos (14.8–18 S-M):

μυρίαι δ' ἀνδρῶν ἀρεταί, μία δ' ἐκ
    πασᾶν πρόκειται,
ὃς τὰ πὰρ χειρὸς κυβέρνα-   10
    σεν δικαίαισι φρένεσσιν.

[36] Bundy 1986: 91.
[37] For the topos, ibid.: 15. Cf. Bacchylides 10.45–47 (followed by remarks at 49–50 on
money upsetting social distinctions), Solon 13.65–66 *IEG*.

οὔτ᾽ ἐν βαρυπενθέσιν ἁρμό-
  ζει μάχαις φόρμιγγος ὀμφὰ
  καὶ λιγυκλαγγεῖς χοροί,
οὔτ᾽ ἐν θαλίαις καναχά   15
χαλκόκτυπος ἀλλ᾽ ἐφ᾽ ἑκάστωι
καιρὸς ἀνδρῶν ἔργματι κάλ-
  λιστος εὖ ἔρδοντα δὲ καὶ θεός ὀρθοῖ.

Myriad are the forms of excellence for men, but one lies before all others—
that of the man who steers the thing at hand with justice in mind.
The voice of the lyre does not harmonize with grief-heavy battles,
  nor do clear-calling choruses;
nor in banquets is the clash
struck from bronze [harmonious]; but on every
work of men *kairos* is most fair. The one who succeeds is also raised
  up by god.

Kairos governs genres: choral odes do not "fit" or "harmonize" (*harmo-zei*) with the battlefield, just as war trumpets sound "out of tune" at festivals. But *kairos* is a universal power making any act or creation "most fair" (*kallistos*). For the poet, *kairos* is fundamentally a religious concept based on the idea that there are limits that mortals, qua mortals, must observe: no matter what the field of endeavor, the correct pursuit of excellence is mindful of the disposing power of the divine and keeps to things within human reach.[38] Piety rather than aesthetics or poetics enjoins observing the *kairos*, and enjoins it on all; hence the man who would "steer" (10) the ship of state may be reminded how much more desirable is peace than war. *Kairos* of course governs the poet's present singing as well; its most profound demands are not met simply by executing the formal expectations of epinician, but by including, in the context of exaltation, a reminder that success rests in god's hand. Bacchylides fulfills the "obligations of the moment" not as a matter of literary propriety or of rhetorical tact, but of speaking justly and appropriately as one mere mortal to another.

Classical Genres

I have noted that the classical period brought new perspectives on genres of song, such as the anthropology discernible behind Pindar's myth of threnodic origins or Bacchylides' use of conventional musical distinctions

---

[38] Cf. Theognis 401–2: "Pursue nothing to excess, for *kairos* is best in all human work" (μηδὲν ἄγαν σπεύδειν. καιρὸς δ᾽ ἐπὶ πᾶσιν ἄριστος / ἔργμασιν ἀνθρώπων). Ascribed to the Sage Chilon by Critias (7 *IEG*).

to illustrate the workings of *kairos*. At the time of their greatest success, sophists and other philosophers and teachers of eloquence increasingly focused attention on the formal, measurable properties of speech. The effect these new studies had on approaches to poetry is observable in the mid-fifth century, when we find attested for the first time names for types of poetry based on formal considerations, such as "iambic" and "elegiac" for songs in those kinds of meter. No archaic name for song is metrically based. The process went in the opposite direction: the archaic poetry of "abuse," *iambos*, generated the name "iambic" for its characteristic meter; similarly, the "elegiac" couplet seems to have been named because it was by that time prominent in the traditional family of songs long known as *elegoi*, "laments."[39]

Among the technical terms generated by these new studies was "meter" itself, a secondary meaning given to another important archaic word for appropriateness. The word *metron*, "measure," had an early ethical sense, "due measure": Hesiod preached observing "due measure" (*metra*) and "right degree" (*kairos*) in all things, even loading a wagon (*Works and Days* 694). Praise of the *metron* as mean underlies Solon's use of the word to describe the professional singer who "knows the measure of desirable wisdom because of the generous teaching of the Olympian Muses" (ἄλλος Ὀλυμπιάδων Μουσέων πάρα δῶρα διδαχθείς / ἱμερτῆς σοφίης μέτρον ἐπιστάμενος, 13.51–52 *IEG*). Here the word does not refer to a knowledge of metrics but to the singer's expert capacity of arousing pleasurable desire in the right way and to the right degree.[40] In context, Solon is not referring to his own elegiacs but is cataloging professions in the city and so estimates the worth of singers from a social and political perspective that values moderation. He allows singers their traditional claim to the Muses' "teaching," but expertise in singing is a gift bestowed unpredictably by divine condescension, hardly technical lessons in scansion. It is first in the fifth century that the word *metron* exhibits its formal meaning, the "measuring" of language that is meter. The novelty of such studies is indicated by a scene of higher education in Aristophanes' *Clouds* (first performed in 423), where understanding such matters as "dactyls" and "meters" (*metra*, 638) is beyond the ken of a yokel (655) who naturally takes *metra* as referring to bushels and pecks.[41]

[39] West 1974: chs. 1 and 2, and Steinruck 2000; the semantic history of *elegos* remains difficult: see Bowie 1986, Lambin 1988.

[40] *Contra*, e.g., Finkelberg (1998: 168), who interprets "the *metron* of delightful skill" as (Solon's) elegiac distichs. There is no passage in Greek to this time where *metron* must mean "meter" rather than "measure" in a broader sense. (See following note.) Cf. Theognis 873–76, which concludes: τίς ἄν σέ τε μωμήσαιτο, / τίς δ᾽ ἂν ἐπαινήσαι μέτρον ἔχων σοφίης.

[41] The metrical sense of *metron* may be inferred from Herodotus' reference to an iambic song (Archilochus 19 *IEG*) as a "three-measured *iambos*" at 1.12.2: ἐν ἰάμβῳ τριμέτρῳ.

The pattern in which evaluative terms that had had a moral and social force took on additional technical meanings in the fifth century was extensive. *Kairos*, for example, continued to be praised by poets as the ultimate, if elusive, standard for all forms of excellence, and this commonplace can be found among sophistically influenced writers who speak of the importance of *kairos* in speech.[42] The concept was secularized under the influence of fifth-century science, especially Hippocratic medicine, which adopted the term for the critical turning-point in the progress of a disease. As a critical "right place" or "right time" for action, *kairos* would be used by the end of the century among rhetoricians for the "opportune" or effective moment in which to deploy a certain style or topos in speech.[43] Fifth-century uses of *prepon* vary similarly: a Thucydidean orator uses the urbane litotes *ouk aprepes* for a theme "not unsuitable" to his present occasion (2.36.4), and Herodotus calls a certain Egyptian myth "most unseemly" for him to tell in public (2.47.2). These ethical or social scruples could also pertain to discussions of poetry: a scholiast preserves Democritus' critique (B 23 DK) that it was not "fitting" (*prepon*) for an exasperated Trojan herald (at *Iliad* 7.390) to exclaim, "I wish Paris had died!" *in the hearing of the enemy*. If *prepon* was Democritus' term, it accords with the socially inflected use of the word in Plato's *Ion*, where it means what is "appropriate" for a given kind of person (e.g., male or female, slave or free) to say before a given audience. But in Herodotus, *prepon* can describe what is appropriate in a given type of story, as when he says Homer discarded an old legend that Helen never went to Troy, "because it was not as appropriate to his epic composition as the one he used" (2.116.1).[44] The old meanings of *prepon*, *metron*, and *kairos*

For the meaning of the metrical terms in *Clouds* and their probable late fifth-century origins, see T. Cole, *Epiploke* (New Haven, 1988), 10–11, 220 n. 9. The only rhythmical term that comedy assumes its audience knows is *anapaestoi*, regularly used as a metonymy for the (typically anapestic) parabasis (e.g., *Acharnians* 627, *Knights* 504). On the metrics lesson in *Clouds*, see Ford 2001: 105–7.

[42] Cf. Pindar *Pythian* 4.286 ("For *mortals*, the *kairos* has but a small compass [*metron*]"), *Olympian.* 13.48, *Pythian* 9.78–79. The *Dissoi logoi* ("*Twofold Arguments*," 90 DK) quotes Aechylus on the moral centrality of *kairos* (3.12) and four trimeters to the effect that nothing is in all respects fine (*kalos*) or foul (*aiskhron*), but the *kairos* makes each what it is (2.19).

[43] E.g., Gorgias in *Palamedes* B 11a 32 pleads that "the present occasion" (i.e., his defense speech) allows an unusually high amount of self-praise. The idea was apparently much used by Gorgias (as Plato jokes: *Gorgias* 448A5): B 13, A 3 DK. On the history of the term *kairos*, particularly with reference to its use in medicine and in rhetoric, see Trédé 1993 and the works cited by Race 1981: 197 n. 1.

[44] More on this passage in chapter 6. Pohlenz (1933: 54–55) argued that an aesthetic sense of *prepon* and *prepei* arose near the end of the fifth century in Gorgias and Hippias; cf. Lanata 1963: 106, 211, 231, 263–64. But the evidence is questionable: (1) it cannot be assumed that Theagenes used the word; (2) Platonizing language is a concern in the testi-

continued alongside the new, and at the century's end, the discussion in *Frogs* of what makes a good song shows a blend of older notions of piety and social utility with newer interests in purely technical correctness and verbal skill.

Like its Latin translation, *decorum*, *prepei* never completely lost its connection with social value. In Aristotle's *Rhetoric*, it governs both the thoroughly linguistic propriety connecting diction to the subject under discussion and the "proper" relation between a speaker's language and his character: "just as a scarlet cloak suits a young man but not an old one."[45] As a practical art, rhetoric cannot flout an audience's moral and social assumptions; yet its technical treatment of language required a separation by which style could be regarded as the mere dress of thought. Rhetorical *kairos* (also expressed by *to prepon*) will refer to an indispensable but not rule-governed sense of when and how to put the tricks of speech to use. The elusiveness and indeterminacy of the "right" or "proper" preserves something of old religious caution, which indeed is an asset to its technical use. It enjoins flexibility in attempts to formalize the elements of effective speech and allows the validity of rhetorical studies to be maintained, even when the rules are followed but the speech does not work: one can say that the rules were not applied at the "right" moment. In the rhetorical system, the relationship between its many specific rules on the one hand and "success" on the other is always undefined and irreducibly "mysterious." The *prepon* or *kairos* names a central but unsystematizable value for which one must have a "nose."[46]

In the rhetorical criticism of the fourth century, *prepei* can express what "fits in" at a given point in a well-composed *text*, without reference to "external" appropriateness. The paradigmatic image for this new form of verbal appropriateness appears in Plato's *Gorgias*, when speakers are urged to follow painters, builders, shipwrights, and other craftsmen who construct self-standing objects by "compelling one part to suit and fit with another" (προσαναγκάζει τὸ ἕτερον τῷ ἑτέρῳ πρέπον τε εἶναι καὶ ἁρμόττειν, 503ε). In a famous passage from the *Phaedrus*, appropriateness is internalized to a well-composed text in Socrates' demand that every speech be constructed like a living body, with head, feet, and middle parts composed so as to "fit appropriately with each other and the whole"

---

mony about Hippias (A 10 DK = Plato *Hippias Minor* 364c, cf. 290b-d). Russell (1981: 88) concludes that "seemliness" in the fifth century can imply "moral and aesthetic" values; for *prepei* continuing to denote social seemliness, cf., e.g., Plato *Ion* 540a-b, Dichaearchus fr. 92 Wehrli (where the idea is expressed in *eutaktos*, "well-behaved").

[45] *Rhetoric* 3.2. 1405a13–14. See Halliwell 1986: 344–49. Key discussions of rhetorical *kairos* and *prepon* are in the third book of *Rhetoric* on style, esp. 3.2 and 3.7.

[46] The metaphor is ancient; cf. *muktēres* ("nostrils") in *Frogs* 893. Further in Most 1984, discussed in chapter 3 below.

(πρέποντα ἀλλήλοις καὶ τῷ ὅλῳ, 264c). Isocrates also uses *prepei* in this sense for the internal coherence of his written "speeches" that were designed to be read as texts. He informs readers of his fictional defense speech, the *Antidosis*, that it is composed of "some things that are fitting to be said in court and other things that do not harmonize with litigious contexts" (ἔνια μὲν ἐν δικαστηρίῳ πρέποντα ῥηθῆναι, τὰ δὲ πρὸς μὲν τοὺς τοιούτους ἀγῶνας οὐχ ἁρμόττοντα), but he avows that the various elements in the text cohere "not without reason nor without a sense of the context (*kairos*), but fitting together with the subject of discussion" (πολλὰ δὲ καὶ τῶν ὑπ' ἐμοῦ πάλαι γεγραμμένων ἐγκαταμεμιγμένα τοῖς νῦν λεγομένοις, οὐκ ἀλόγως οὐδ' ἀκαίρως, ἀλλὰ προσηκόντως τοῖς ὑποκειμένοις).[47]

This development coincided with the first systematic attempts, culminating in the *Poetics*, to analyze the entire range of song types into genres, classes of texts united not by a common social function or mythic origin but by shared formal and thematic properties. The preeminent example is the way Aristotle treats tragedy in his *Poetics*, defining its proper themes and diction in relation to those in other literary forms such as epic, dithyramb, and comedy; in no case does he refer significantly to the social and ritual occasions at which such works were performed. We shall see that Aristotle was very far from being a simplistic thinker, and he certainly recognized that generic conventions arose in the course of human history. But his teleological thinking tended to place less weight on the historical and contingent evolution of poetic forms than on generic form itself, as over time it achieved its true function and end (*telos*) with greater clarity and efficiency. For example, although the historian of poetry recognized that hexameter epic was the product of social evolution, the teleologist concluded that "trial and error" (*peira*) had selected the "heroic" meter as the only one that "fits" (*harmozei*) epic and that others were therefore "inappropriate" (*aprepes*).[48]

An important consequence of this view is that the excellence of poems can be assessed by examining their formal structure, above all by searching for a unity of all the elements the poet has deployed toward the end proper to his form. In this way, what I call a specifically "literary" criticism—in Aristotle's terms, a criticism based on principles specific to an

---

[47] *Antidosis* §§ 9–10. Cf. *Against the Sophists* § 16–17 (= *Antidosis* § 194), and see Vallozza 1985, Ford 1991. Race (1981: 198) notes that "in the period between Aristophanes and Menander, καιρός becomes increasingly temporal and gradually loses its normative meanings."

[48] *Poetics* 1459b31–34: τὸ δὲ μέτρον τὸ ἡρωικὸν ἀπὸ τῆς πείρας ἥρμοκεν. εἰ γάρ τις ἐν ἄλλῳ τινὶ μέτρῳ διηγηματικὴν μίμησιν ποιοῖτο ἢ ἐν πολλοῖς, ἀπρεπὲς ἂν φαίνοιτο. Only concordance work can make clear how fundamental *prepei* (*aprepēs*, *to prepon*, etc.), the "fitting" (*harmottein*), and "the proper" (*to oikeion*) are for the *Poetics*.

"art of poetry"—became an independent and distinct branch of knowledge. For those who were willing, in certain contexts, to dispense altogether with moral and ethical considerations in assessing artistic merit, the loss of these criteria was compensated for by making linguistic form expressive in itself. "Song" had become "poetry," and poetry was a special art of using language, the paradigmatic example of what we have called since the eighteenth century "literature."

For classical critics, a formalistic and technical approach to poetry could still be complemented by exploring how form "appropriately" matched its ethical and social implications. But as it moved from public acts of praising and blaming performances to school lectures or treatises on the optimal form of poetic texts, Greek criticism progressively effaced the social functions not only of song but of criticism as well. To recover these complex and sometimes conflicting roots of criticism, I begin with a closer look at how the social settings that shaped archaic Greek song shaped responses to it as well. For most of the archaic occasions for singing, we are unable to know in detail how the Greeks defined kinds of song and set criteria for their appraisal; but we have abundant evidence for one social institution that regularly included not only singing but discussions of songs and debates on their merits. I thus will turn to the Greek symposium and explore how this set of rituals and customs for drinking together forged a vocabulary and approach to song that, like the symposium itself, spread throughout Greece and had an immense impact on the language and practice of classical criticism.

PART I

ARCHAIC ROOTS OF CLASSICAL AESTHETICS

ONE

TABLE TALK AND SYMPOSIUM

O F THE many social contexts in which archaic Greece worked out its functionalist poetics, one of the oldest and arguably the most influential was the symposium, a form of drinking and singing together that evolved in the course of the archaic age. Thanks to a wave of renewed scholarly attention, the symposium is now well appreciated as a central institution of Greek musical culture.[1] Much of archaic elegy and iambus is thought to have been composed for symposia,[2] and the institution even contributed a name to the preclassical lexicon of song types: the *skolion*, or "crooked" song, may have been so called because of the way these short lyrics on wine, women, boys, and song were passed around the jar.[3] At least from the fifth century, symposia were also a setting for the reperformance of longer lyric songs that had been composed for public, often choral, performance.[4] Symposia deserve special attention in the history of criticism because, as songs were exchanged over wine, guests were expected to react to them, sometimes in responding songs of their own. The result is that we have a body of archaic song texts that discuss the symposium and the kinds of singing that suit it. This chapter will take an overview of such songs and describe the central values and

---

[1] See Slater 1991; and Murray 1990, with bibliography 332–35 and 342–43; to which add Stehle 1997: 213–61; Cameron 1995: 71–103; and Gera 1993: 132–91 (on Xenophon's *Cyropaideia*). On sympotic singing, Reitzenstein 1893: 1–86 and Vetta 1983 are indispensable. I have greatly profited from discussing this chapter with Marek Wecowski.

[2] Elegy: West 1974: ch. 1, with a warning against assigning all archaic poetry to the symposium; also, Bowie 1990, 1986; Tedeschi 1982. Iambic: West 1974: ch. 2; Bartol 1992. Lyrics: Trumpf 1973; Rösler 1980a; esp. ch. 2. More generally, Pavese 1972; Vetta 1977; Gentili 1988: esp, 89–104; Latacz 1990; and Pellizer 1990: 179–80 with references.

[3] Cf. Pindar fr. 122.11 S-M; for the custom of passing the myrtle branch, cf. Aristophanes *Banqueters* 235 PCG, *Clouds* 1364. On the Athenian practices illustrated by Aristophanes (cf. *Clouds* 1354–79, *Wasps* 1222–61, fr. 444 PCG), see Vetta 1977, Reitzenstein 1893: 24–43. By the later fourth century, the origin and meaning of *skolion* were obscure: Aristotle's students Dicaearchus (89 Wehrli) and Aristoxenus (125 Wehrli) give variant etymologies and debate which songs deserved to be so designated; cf. Reitzenstein 1893: 3–13, 16 n. 28; Färber 1936: pt. 1, 57–63; Harvey 1955: 162–63, 174. On the collection of Athenian lyric *skolia* preserved in Athenaeus 693f–694a, see Wilamowitz 1893, 2: 316–22; Bowra 1961: 373–97.

[4] E.g., Stesichorus and Simonides sung at symposia: schol. *Wasps* 1222, *Clouds* 1355–56; for Alcaeus and Anacreon, *Banqueters* 235 PCG; for Timocreon (731 PMG), schol. *Acharnians* 532. Cf. Herington 1985: 28, 49–50, 208; Nagy 1990: ch. 13, esp. 107–15.

terms of their criticism. Although symposia have been much studied of late, attention can still usefully be drawn to how they functioned as a context for the *evaluation* of singing.

The tradition of "table talk" is prominent in Western criticism, if less so in its histories. Already in Homer, as we have seen, princes would discuss songs they heard at feasts, and learned after-dinner discourse about poetry and everything else became a major literary theme in the fourth century, when Xenophon and Plato wrote prose accounts of symposia attended by Socrates. This tradition reached its belle-lettristic acme (though by no means its end) among learned writers of the Roman period such as Plutarch and Athenaeus, and it continues in many academic gatherings today that are sympotic in form, and often in name as well.[5] But sympotic songs figure little in histories of criticism because they seem to take songs at face value, asking if the sentiments expressed are socially and ethically salutary, with little interest in isolating distinctively formal or aesthetic qualities; when songs are praised as fair (*kalon, eu*), graceful (*kharieis*), or pleasing (*hēdus, terpein*), it is not specifically their musical or verbal form that is in view, but a complex whole in which sensuous, social, and moral fineness are mutually involved. As Athenaeus put it: "They would prevail upon each of the wise men to bring some song before the company (εἰς μέσον . . . προφέρειν). And the song they considered fine (καλήν) was the one that seemed to offer some advice or idea that was useful for life" (694b-c).

If sympotic songs, like Greek criticism generally, tended to keep *to kalon*, the "beautiful" or "fine," connected to the morally and socially good, this was not a failure of philosophical or rhetorical insight but an expression of the important role song played on such occasions. Symposiasts evaluated singing as a symbolic form of behavior in which the performer's observance of *to prepon*, *metron*, and *kairos* revealed his commitment to an order, *kosmos*, that was social and political as well as aesthetic. Though it did not go so far as to construct a formal rhetoric or poetics, the symposium may be said to have developed an "aesthetics" of singing aimed at reading off a performer's inner character from the "shape" of what he sang. Beginning in the early fifth century, table talk reflects new technical approaches to song, but the exchange was two-sided: academic criticism took over the symposium's social ethic to complement its focus on the elements of speech. Many of the key terms of sympotic criticism, richly resonant and usefully flexible, were retained in rhetoric and poetics as a way of rooting formal verbal analysis in the old values of "propriety," due "measure," and "right" behavior. Indeed,

[5] For an outline of literary symposia, see A. Hug in *RE* 8 (1932): 1273–82; J. Martin 1931; and, for an overview of early table talk, Bowie 1993a.

when one considers the antiquity and durability of the Greco-Roman tradition of table talk, it may appear that Greek rhetoric and philosophy added only methodological refinement and terminological precision to a deeply rooted aesthetics of singing in company.

To trace this process, it will be helpful to begin by considering some after-dinner speeches in epic poetry to show how speech and song at table were linked to ideas of civilized leisure and social harmony. This will prepare for examining representative samples of sympotic "criticism" from the sixth and fifth centuries. This combined concern of sympotic song with occasion and discourse—however idealized and fictionalized its picture of symposia may be—provides an invaluable point of entry into preclassical criticism.

Table Talk from Homer to Hippocleides

The origins of Greek symposia are not clear, but the reconstruction of Oswyn Murray usefully outlines two opposed types of ritual commensality in the ancient world. The first is the "feast of merit," designed to foster solidarity among a warrior class and to confirm their status as elite.[6] Murray points to the Iliadic banquets given by Agamemnon, where the king invites select chieftains to his tent and, amid much speechifying, distributes goods from the common store (notably, choice cuts of meat) as signs of honor and rewards for loyalty.[7] By the end of the seventh century, we find through most of Greece a second kind of male fellowship over alcohol, not warrior messes but leisured, sociable groups dedicated at once to pleasure and the conspicuous display of excellence (aretē, to agathon, to esthlon). The peacetime epic of the Odyssey has many scenes of feasts in which men gather in noble halls to feast, drink, and be entertained with music. But symposia were different in ceremoniously separating drinking from dining and in adding a number of new practices, such as reclining on couches.[8] Still, some aspects of Homer's idealized image of noble leisure will be relevant to the understanding of sympotic song.[9]

---

[6] On the social aspects of symposia, my account is greatly indebted to Murray 1980: ch. 12, 1983a, 1983b, 1991; and Von der Mühl 1976 (originally 1926). Van Wees (1995) importantly stresses continuities between epic banquets and symposia as forms of social-group formation.

[7] Murray 1983b: 196–98; for meat as a prize: Iliad 7.321–22, 9.69–75, 17.249–51.

[8] Allusions to specifically sympotic practices are first attested at the end of the seventh century (Alcman 93 PMGF), and the word sumposion in the sixth (Alcaeus 70.3 V, Phocylides 14 D, Theognis 298).

[9] It has been suggested, with great probability I think, that Homer knew of symposia but deliberately omitted them from his pictures of heroes of old: Slater 1990: 213; Murray 1991:

At Homeric banquets, guests ideally sit in silence while professional
singers (*aoidoi*) provide song and dance, the "ornaments of a feast" (*Od.*
1.152, etc.). Homeric princes know how to sing and dance, and even to
do so in their cups: "Foolish-making wine," Odysseus observes after a
meal, "can stir even a prudent man to singing and soft laughter, and even
dancing, and to throw out a word better left unspoken" (*Od.* 14.463–
66).[10] But, as this speech intimates, such indulgences could be regarded
with suspicion. In Homer, the cultivation of musical skill by nobles could
be a sign of an enviably peaceful and refined society, but being a good
dancer was also a taunt to the weak fighter.[11] Aristotle still had to
cope, not wholly without sympathy, with objections to citizens learning
to play the lyre instead of just having "others" provide their music: he
notes that Zeus as represented by the poets doesn't sing and play the harp,
and "we call those who do so servile, and think it an unmanly activity
unless one is drunk or playing" (βαναύσους καλοῦμεν τοὺς τοιούτους
καὶ τὸ πράττειν οὐκ ἀνδρὸς μὴ μεθύοντος ἢ παίζοντος, *Politics* 8.5.
1339b6–10).[12] The worry that singing is a step down from a citizen's
manly duties makes it worth noting that Homeric guests normally "perform" by conversing among themselves after or in the intervals of song.
The musician may have been an honored retainer, but he was not part of
the guests' conversation, or "taking pleasure in talk" (τέρπεσθαι μύθοις),
as it was called.[13]

Conversation was accounted a delightful pastime in itself (*Od.* 4.594–
98), but it was also a way to discover the inner qualities of one's associates. So suggests a fragment of Hesiod that could well have been sung at
table: sweet it is, someone declares, "to take pleasure in talk at a feast
and rich banquet once sated with dining"; to this the speaker, or perhaps
a fellow diner, adds, "This, too, is sweet among all that the gods have
ordained for mortals: to find out a clear sign to distinguish the base from

---

95. Bielohlawek 1940 suggestively collects epic and sympotic passages in praise of civilized
feasting; cf. Slater 1981; and West 1978a: 56 and his notes on *Works and Days* 582–96,
715–22. On women at symposia, see Van Wees 1995: 154–63.

[10] On musical entertainment at Homeric banquets, see Barker 1984: 24–30.

[11] See Janko on *Iliad* 15.508–12 and 16.617; and Veneri 1995 on the ambiguities of
singing for heroes.

[12] The Persians and Medes are examples enjoying music "others" perform (esp. *Pol.*
1339a26–b6; cf. Herodotus 1.155 (Croesus: learning play the kithara makes people woman-
ish and submissive) and Ion of Chios 392 F 13 *FGrH* (Themistocles could not sing or play
the lyre but knew how to make a city great), discussed in chapter 8.

[13] For the expression, cf. *Iliad* 11.642–43, Hesiod fr. 274.2 M-W (quoted below); for
muthos of talk and tales told at table, e.g., *Od.* 4.238–39, 21.291 (μύθων . . . καὶ ῥήσιος),
cf. Bielohlawek 1940: 19.

the brave."[14] In the very act of making such pronouncements, banqueters revealed their characters and invited responses that would test their quality. Homer's *Odyssey* shows us many such performances, the longest and most revealing being Odysseus' four-book speech before King Alcinous and the nobility of Phaeacia.[15] In the context of the Phaeacian episode (Books 6–13), this speech is the culminating display of Odysseus' true character, which had been in doubt since he washed up on the island, stripped of all signs of status and even of the clothes on his back. The Phaeacians have "tested" him "in many contests" (8.22–23), including athletics, to find out if he is a mere vagabond or a profit-hungry merchant (8.159–64, 11.363–66). But it is at table—after food, wine, and music—that the hero wins final confirmation as a true nobleman and worthy friend of the royal house.

Late in the festivities, Alcinous calls for the singer to stop and turns to Odysseus with the question any new guest could expect: "Who are you, and where do you come from?"[16] This was in effect a cue for Odysseus to present himself to the company in speech, and he begins tactfully (9.2–10):

> My lord Alcinous, how fine (*kalon*) it is to listen to the bard with his godlike voice. For I maintain that there is no occasion more gracious (*khariesteron*) than when festivity (*euphrosunē*) reigns among the people (*dēmon*), and in the halls diners sit in their proper places (*hexeiēs*) as they listen to the singer amidst plenteous food while a steward draws wine from the mixing bowl and serves it.

Praising the singer here is part of a subtle praise of his host's generosity. At the same time, Odysseus reveals his character in associating a fine banquet with social orderliness. This association, which will often be taken up in sympotic poetry, is epitomized in the word *euphrosunē*, which designates both an occasion of festivity and the *euphrōn*, "right-minded" or "sensible," comportment such feasts should embody.[17] So, too, *kharis*, "grace," implies not only elegance and refinement but good relations

---

[14] Hesiod frs. 274 and 273 M-W. The two quotations are obviously to be connected and suggest (even without Meineke's ἥδιστον δ' ἐν δαιτὶ beginning 274) the sympotic game of debating what is best or finest in life, on which see further Ford 1997a: 92–93.

[15] For a complementary analysis of the banquets in Book 8, see Slater 1990: esp. 216–19. Odysseus' prologue in Book 9 is further studied in Ford 1999c.

[16] *Od.* 8.536–86; cf., e.g., 1.170, 3.69–70, 16.57–59, and Hainsworth on 8.555. Arete had earlier posed this question (7.233) after Odysseus' first meal. The question is also posed by Xenophanes in a sympotic context (B 18 DK).

[17] On *euphrosunē* and feasting, see Bundy 1986: 2. On banquets associated with social orderliness, see Slater 1981: 205–14.

among the guests and between gods and men. Gracious festivity depends on all keeping to their assigned places and roles—the Phaeacians "sitting in order" (ἥμενοι ἐξείης; the expression is also used of men rowing together on ships), the performing singer, the busy servant. The opposite state of affairs prevails in Ithaca, where indeed Telemachus tried to calm down the raucous suitors with the same words as his father in praise of listening to a godlike singer (1.370b–71 = 9.3b–4).

Odysseus' own performance is in turn evaluated by his audience as a sign of his quality, and in the present circumstances this means deducing the "inner" man from the "shape" of his words. When he comes to a pause in his story, the queen asks the company: "Phaeacians, how does this man seem to you in his physical form (*eidos*) and stature and in his noble mind within (*phrenas endon*)?" (11.336–41). She answers her own question by declaring him her guest-friend and proposing a round of gifts. The king ratifies her judgment, "Shapeliness is on your words, and your mind is noble within" (σοὶ δ' ἔπι μὲν μορφὴ ἐπέων, ἔνι δὲ φρένες ἐσθλαί, 367). When Alcinous goes on to say Odysseus has recounted his tale as well as any bard, Homer's implicit self-praise should not go unnoticed.[18] But the king is after a reliable index to Odysseus' character, not artfulness of performance: the rhetorical potential of this opposition remains unexploited here and elsewhere in the epic. Alcinous' compliment is the inverse of a reproving speech Odysseus had made to an abusive prince: "The gods do not give everyone the same measure of grace in bodily form (*phuē*) or mind (*phrenas*) or speaking skill (*agorētun*); one man is exceptional in appearance (*eidos*), another's words are crowned by the gods with shape, and people look on him with pleasure."[19] We have to do here not with form matching content, but with inside matching outside, and both are gifts of the gods.

The king's verdict on Odysseus' speech confirms his status, and the castaway will end up laden with gifts and escorted to the port in regal pomp. This fictional, indeed highly idyllic story takes it for granted that dining halls were stages where speakers affirmed or established social identity through after-dinner performance.[20] Nothing shows this more

---

[18] In praising Odysseus' "enchanting" tales to Penelope, Eumaeus also compares him to a bard: *Od.* 17.514–21. See Goldhill 1991: 65–66, and 95–97, on Odysseus' "poetic" performance at Phaeacia.

[19] 8.170–77. Cf. Phocylides 3 D: "What is the advantage in noble descent if one lacks grace in conversation or in council?" (οὔτ' ἐν μύθοις . . . οὔτ' ἐν βουλῆι). On the relation of beauty to excellence, cf. *Iliad* 3.43–45 (Hector to Paris), Theognis 933–38, and Reitzenstein 1893: 64 n. 2.

[20] The drama of the disguised guest proving himself at dinner is replayed in a pastoral key in Odysseus' reception by the swineherd Eumaeus in Book 15, where they "take pleasure" (15.393) in listening to each other's stories.

clearly than Herodotus' well-known tale of how Cleisthenes, tyrant of Sicyon in the early sixth century, found a husband for his daughter.[21] In firm command of his city and with the resources to capture an Olympic victory, Cleisthenes determined to marry his daughter Agariste ("Nobility") to the "best man in Greece." He invited all marriageable Greek men to be his guests at Sicyon for a year so he might "make trial of their manliness, temper, education, and comportment."[22] In folktale fashion, the wise, the wealthy, the athletic, and the noble duly assembled to compete in a setting of lavish (*megaloprepeōs*) hospitality. For a full year, Cleisthenes "tested" the suitors in various ways, including "private and group discussions," but "the most important test was of their conviviality" (*sunestōs*, 6.128.5). At the culminating betrothal feast, the suitors competed "in music and in speaking before the company" (literally "speaking in the middle") after dinner (6.129.2). One of the candidates, a manly and wellborn Athenian named Hippocleides, had impressed everyone. But as the drinking went on, Hippocleides began to perform with rather too much enthusiasm, ending up literally dancing upside down on the tables. Cleisthenes was mortified and announced to Hippocleides, "You have danced your marriage away."

In some respects, we have not moved far from the palace of Alcinous, who also had a daughter of marriageable age, and Cleisthenes' magnificent hospitality doubtless was meant to recall old-style heroic feasting. But the influence of sympotic culture is reflected in the fact that the guests themselves perform musically. This will be the key to following song there.

Symposium: From Talk to Song

To participate fully at a symposium, a guest might sing throughout the evening. Sympotic practices were not strictly uniform, but a fairly standard composite would begin with the tables being cleared after the meal while guests washed, anointed themselves, and put on garlands; typically, libations and a paean sung in unison followed, thus uniting the group and showing it god-fearing.[23] After the paean and what Plato calls "the

---

[21] *Histories* 6.126–30. See O. Murray 1980: 202–3; Fehr 1990: 191–92; Seaford 1994: 53–54, with 31–38. On betrothal feasts, see Robertson in Slater 1991.

[22] *diepeirato . . . andragathiēs kai tēs orgēs kai paideusiou te kai tropou*, 6.128.4. On discerning a fellow drinker's temper (*orgē*) and character (*tropos*): Theognis 309–12, 963–70, 1059–62.

[23] On the opening sympotic rituals and paean, Xenophanes 1.1–17 *IEG*; Theognis 999–1002; Aeschylus *Agamemnon* 247; Xenophon *Symposium* 2.1, *Anabasis* 6.1.4–5; Plato Comicus fr. 71 *PCG*; Plato *Symposium* 176A. Cf. Athenaeus 149c and other texts cited by Mau in *RE* 6 (1900): 611–19. The paean is already standard at feasts in Alcman 98 *PMG*, discussed above in the Introduction. For the sympotic paean, Käppel 1992: 51–54.

other obligatory activities," a symposiarch was chosen as master of ceremonies, and rules were agreed upon about how much wine would be drunk and in what strength.[24] As the wine was served, guests reclined on couches and performed for each other in various ways, including singing songs. Even as the party ended, departing guests might sing a *kōmos* or "revel-song" through the streets. On the way they might knock at certain doors in hopes of being received, and, as in Plato's *Symposium*, they might interrupt a party still in progress so the singing could begin again.

In part, these rituals and games assured exclusivity: participants had to possess enough cultivation to demonstrate that they belonged, and this resource was most easily acquired by regularly attending such gatherings. Being able to join in the paean was doubtless no more demanding than participating in a grace before meals, but that first ritual only initiated a series of moments in which the guest's musical background would be on display. From this point of view, the heart of the evening was the guests' singing for each other, or speaking "in the middle" (εἰς τὸ μέσον) as it was called.[25] Depending on their abilities, participants performed songs they knew by heart or improvised new ones for the occasion.[26] To keep songs passing back and forth, there were toasts in verse (which invited responses in kind), and various singing games. As songs circulated, it was common to "take up" another guest's verse "smartly" (*dexiōs* or *kalōs*) and continue it, extemporize upon it, or switch to another song.

Singing games thus also served as a set of structures that allowed participants to "perform themselves" as they interacted with and competed against each other. As a form of speech "in the middle," sympotic song was simply a more formalized, stylized version of heroic "taking pleasure in talk" (τέρπεσθαι μύθοις). Murray suggests that it was by way of compensation for their declining martial preeminence that symposiasts constantly elaborated their rituals. Whatever the full story, the substitution of song for speech and the regulation of singing through games and other rituals may be seen as further ways in which sympotic conduct was refined. Sympotic songs do not support a distinction between song (poetry)

---

[24] Plato *Symposium* 176A (καὶ τἆλλα τὰ νομιζόμενα), on which see Reitzenstein 1893: 39–40.

[25] For "speaking in the middle," cf. in addition to Athenaeus 694b–c and Herodotus 6.129.2 quoted above, Theognis 493–95 (quoted on p. 38, esp. εἰς τὸ μέσον φωνεῦντες ὁμῶς ἑνὶ καὶ συνάπασιν), Xenophon *Symposium* 3.3; cf. 4.64.

[26] West 1974: 11–19; cf. Marcovich 1978: 10–11; Reitzenstein 1893: 43–44. Cameron (1995: 84–87) questions the assumption that improvisation played a significant role in these games, against Gentili (1988: 20) and Thomas (1992: 124).

and conversation (prose); they refer to themselves as the performer's "speech" (*epē*) or "sayings" (*rhēmata*) as frequently as "song" (*adoidē*).[27] Stylizing "speaking" by measured rhythms and pitch marked not a crossing from one genre to another but the special status of guest against professional musicians and other servants. The Homeric distinction between musician and guest was even sharper in symposia, where musical accompaniment was often provided by female *aulos* players with a status close to that of slaves.[28]

Like its heroic predecessor, then, the symposium was a setting for elite males to reinforce their solidarity and to demonstrate their distinction. Their enduring standards of judgment are summed up in an anonymous elegy from the late classical age:

> χαίρετε συμπόται ἄνδρες ὁ[μήλικες· ἐ]ξ ἀγαθοῦ γὰρ
>   ἀρξάμενος τελέω τὸν λόγον ἐς' ἀγαθόν.
> χρὴ δ', ὅταν εἰς τοιοῦτο συνέλθωμεν φίλοι ἄνδρες
>   πρᾶγμα, γελᾶν παίζειν χρησαμένους ἀρετῆι,
> ἥδεσθαί τε συνόντας, ἐς ἀλλήλους τε φλυάρεῖν   5
>   καὶ σκώπτειν τοιαῦθ' οἷα γέλωτα φέρειν.
> ἡ δὲ σπουδὴ ἐπέσθω, ἀκούωμέν τε λεγόντων
>   ἐν μέρει· ἥδ' ἀρετὴ συμποσίου πέλεται.
> τοῦ δὲ ποταρχοῦντος πειθώμεθα· ταῦτα γάρ ἐστιν
>   ἔργ' ἀνδρῶν ἀγαθῶν, εὐλογίαν τε φέρειν.   10

> Hail my fellow drinkers [and age-mates]; as I begin with the good
>   I will bring my speech to a close with the good.
> It behooves us, when we come together as friends on business
>   such as this, to laugh and sport with excellence,
> being happy in each other's company and teasing each other   5
>   with such jokes as can be borne with a laugh.
> Let serious pursuits follow, and let us listen to those who speak
>   in turns; this is excellence in a symposium.
> And let us obey the toastmaster; for this
>   is the work of good men, and to contribute fair speech.[29]   10

---

[27] One might infer from the anonymous elegist (27.7 *IEG*, in text below) that a distinction was drawn between (playful) singing and (serious) speech, as at Plutarch *Cimon* 9, where Cimon's agreeable "singing" at a banquet after the libations is "later" followed by conversation (in which he rehearses war stories).

[28] I only sketch the social distinctions at symposia: see Pellizer 1990, Fehr 1990, and Kurke 1999: ch. 5 for an ideological analysis of women at symposia.

[29] Anon. eleg. 27 *IEG*. See F. Ferrari 1988 for commentary. At line 10 I read with Ferrari (ibid.: 224) φέρειν instead of εὐλογίαν τε φέρει ("leads to good repute").

For the Greek soldier among whose effects this text was found, the song was a script for making a "speech" toward the beginning of a symposium. In an elaborate show of devotion to nobility, the speaker urges that the pleasure, laughter, and sport of drinking together be governed by a sense of admirable and excellent behavior (*aretē*, 4). If guests speak each in his proper turn (*en merei*, 8) and drink within limits, they will show themselves to be good men. Good form in this social sense is exemplified in the studied formality of the elegy itself: adapting hymnic style, the speaker places the good "first and last" in his speech (1, 10); the "fair speech" foretold at the end is already being realized in the scrupulous song itself.[30]

This song strikes a number of important themes that were sounded in the *Odyssey*, as in its wariness about throwing out words that were better left unspoken. The "excellence" defined in this sort of symposium (ἥδ᾽ ἀρετὴ συμποσίου πέλεται) has more to do with manners and morals than with martial and civic preeminence.[31] A contrast is provided by an archaic elegy for young soldiers in Sparta, which was one of the few parts of the Greek world to have retained a form of traditional soldier messes (*sussitia*). There, martial songs like the following lines by Tyrtaeus would have been in order:

> ἥδ᾽ ἀρετή, τόδ᾽ ἄεθλον ἐν ἀνθρώποισιν ἄριστον
> κάλλιστόν τε φέρειν γίνεται ἀνδρὶ νέωι.
> ξυνὸν δ᾽ ἐσθλὸν τοῦτο πόληί τε παντί τε δήμωι,
> ὅστις ἀνὴρ διαβὰς ἐν προμάχοισι μένηι. . . .

> This is excellence, this is the best and finest prize
>   of all that a young man can win.
> It is a noble thing in which the whole city and all the people can share:
>   to be a man who stands steadfastly in the front ranks of battle. . . .[32]

Whereas Tyrtaeus goes on to promise young warriors the admiration of the whole city and fame after death, the symposium of leisure offers only its own self-contained pleasures, where participants no longer functioned

---

[30] With the hymnic opening, cf. the beginning of Nestor's after-dinner praise of Agamemnon's feast at *Iliad* 9.96–97: Ἀτρείδη κύδιστε . . . ἐν σοὶ μὲν λήξω, σέο δ᾽ ἄρξομαι. With τελέω τὸν λόγον ἐς ἀγαθόν, cf. *Iliad* 9.102 (εἰπεῖν εἰς ἀγαθόν) and Dionysius Chalcis 6.1–2 *IEG*.

[31] Other definitions of sympotic "excellence," Theognis 971–72, Xenophanes 1.20 *IEG*. See the brilliant synthesis of Murray (1991), developing Bowie 1986 and 1990. The evidence from Lycurgus and Philochorus for contests in singing Tyrtaeus at Spartan symposia is discussed below.

[32] Tyrtaeus 12.13–16 *IEG*. There is a subtle change in the direction from *Männerbunde* to *salon* when these verses make their way into the sympotic Theognidea (1003–6) and νέωι is replaced by σοφῶι (1004).

as the front rank in war. But even the luxurious symposium required limits, and so the civic virtues of justice, respect (*aidōs*), and moderation were imported to link sympotic ethics to politics.[33]

Kosmos: Sympotic Order

The connection of symposia to "public" life was complex. Pauline Schmitt-Pantel is right to stress the symposium's relation to other civic forms of commensality, such as the sacrificial meal, and to insist that the dinner party of citizens remains a civic group, not a "private" one.[34] Murray is equally right to stress the homogenous and select nature of these groups, which typically met in rooms sized to accommodate anywhere from seven to thirty persons. In part, the tension between elite parties and the city at large was managed by an idea that orderliness in diners' comportment was a reflection of civic order. This ethic is implicit in Odysseus' image of festivity reigning among the people when diners "sit well in order" in the halls (*Od.* 9.8), and in his praise of song that is sung in an "exceptionally orderly" way.[35] Conversely, Hipponax speaks of a glutton and political nuisance eating in a "disorderly" way (οὐ κατὰ κόσμον, 128.2 *IEG*).

In what C. M. Bowra calls the "class of hortatory elegy which told men how they ought to behave once the drinking started," M. L. West has

---

[33] Sympotic prayers to be just: Ion of Chios 26.15–16 *IEG* (to Dionysus, "Hail, helper in deeds that are fair, grant us long life to drink, to play, and to think just thoughts"), Critias 6.14–21 *IEG*; cf. Phocylides 10 D, Anacreon 2 *IEG*. Concern for political, commercial, and sexual justice is pervasive in the Theognidea, e.g., Theognis 255 cited above, and 789–95: "Be just as you fill your mind with pleasure." Cf. Damon: "In singing and playing the lyre a boy ought properly to reveal not only courage and moderation but also justice" (B 4 DK).

[34] E.g., Schmitt-Pantel 1992: 112. One cannot insist rigidly on distinct, nonoverlapping categories of feasts, as Murray comments (1990: 5–6). I take the opposite view of Schmitt-Pantel (1990: 25), when she says, "Certainly, the *symposium* is not the *agora*, but poetic discourse does not have a different function when composed for one place rather than the other. *It has the same ideological effect*" (emphasis mine).

[35] *Od.* 8.489: λίην γὰρ κατὰ κόσμον ᾿Αχαιῶν οἶτον ἀείδεις. Usually taken as "well adorned," referring primarily to the artistic skills like "the *kosmos* of the [wooden] horse" in *Od.* 8.492: cf. Kannicht 1988: 10–13, *LfrgE* s.v. *kosmos* B 1b, 2. But this is not the kind of thing anyone else in epic says about a song, and Diller (1956: 48–51) argues for the relative unimportance of the sense "adornment" in archaic instances. In Ford 1992: 122–24 I stressed the sense "in conformity with social propriety," that is, as such a theme should be sung in such a context. Goldhill (1991: 57–59) takes it, as many do, to suggest "an accurate representation of reality, 'in order' . . . to sing according to how things are"; but to press the phrase further and make the hero vouch for the truth of poetry (i.e., "exactly the way it happened") runs into the problem that Odysseus at this point still pretends not to have been at Troy.

noted that "from the later sixth century throughout the fifth we find a tradition of elegy containing advice on the conduct of the symposium itself, with the emphasis being moderation and orderliness."[36] A classic statement of the close connection between orderly drinking, sympotic *euphrosunē*, and the city's "good government" or "good customs" (*eunomiē*) is Solon's description of social disorder (4.7–10 *IEG*):[37]

δήμου θ᾽ ἡγεμόνων ἄδικος νόος, οἷσιν ἑτοῖμον
   ὕβριος ἐκ μεγάλης ἄλγεα πολλὰ παθεῖν·
οὐ γὰρ ἐπίστανται κατέχειν κόρον οὐδὲ παρούσας
   εὐφροσύνας κοσμεῖν δαιτὸς ἐν ἡσυχίηι.

And unjust is the mind of the people's rulers, and for their great hubris
   much suffering is in store.
For they do not understand how to keep down excess, nor how to order
   the delights that are present before them in a peaceable feast.

This notion of order in *kosmeō*, which can denote a neat, effective arrangement and also an elegant, decorative one, reflects the characteristic archaic link between aesthetics, manners, and politics. Elsewhere, Solon says that "good customs" make everything "well ordered" and harmonious, or "well fitted-together" (4.32 *IEG*: Εὐνομίη δ᾽ εὔκοσμα καὶ ἄρτια πάντ᾽ ἀποφαίνει).[38] Wealth acquired by hubris, for example, does not come in a "just" or "orderly" way (13.11–12 *IEG*: ὃν δ᾽ ἄνδρες τιμῶσιν ὑφ᾽ ὕβριος, οὐ κατὰ κόσμον / ἔρχεται, ἀλλ᾽ ἀδίκοις ἔργμασι πειθόμενος). Hence the people's leaders, like good symposiasts, should make their minds observe "due measure" (4c.3–4 *IEG*: ἐν μετρίοισι τίθεσθε μέγαν νόον· οὔτε γὰρ ἡμεῖς / πεισόμεθ᾽, οὔθ᾽ ὑμῖν ἄρτια ταῦτ᾽ ἔσεται). *Kosmos* applies equally to the proper adornment of diners, their orderly behavior, and their speech. When Theognis predicts that handsome young men will sing his songs "in good order" (*eukosmōs*, 242) and "fair and clear" at banquets,[39] the performances will no doubt be elegant, but they will also

---

[36] Bowra 1953: 2, and ultimately Reitzenstein 1893: 50. West 1974: 15. Citing, in addition to Xenophanes 1, Anacreon 2 *IEG*, Theognis 467–96, 971, Euvenus 2, Critias 6 *IEG*.

[37] Solon's "leaders" of the city enjoying *euphrosunē* are to be compared with the sympotic "men at feast" (*euphrōnas andres*) in Xenophanes 1.13 *IEG*, discussed in the next chapter. As Slater (1981) has shown that Solon saw banqueting as a microcosm of the political world, we can understand why, as Schmitt-Pantel (1990: 21) notes, images of public sacrificial distribution may also be used to characterize sympotic equality. Plato uses metaphors from this tradition when he speaks of radical democracy as a spoiled drinking party where the demagogues "serve up" the "unmixed" wine of liberty to the people: *Republic* 562D.

[38] For *kosmos* as "constitution," cf. Nagy 1989: 57. On the philosophical sense of *kosmos* as "cosmos," attested from Heraclitus on, see Kahn 1960: 219–30 and Kranz 1955.

[39] 241–43: καί σε σὺν αὐλίσκοισι λιγυφθόγγοις νέοι ἄνδρες / εὐκόσμως ἐρατοὶ καλά τε καὶ λιγέα / ἄισονται.

reinstantiate the essential moral orderliness of the singer, who elsewhere proposed to "adorn" (*kosmein*) his city by moderation and justice.[40] When the cup was passed together with a challenge to sing, one "adorned" or "ordered" the feast (συμπόσιον κοσμῶν, Dionysius Chalcus 105 *IEG*) by "mixing in the Graces," spirits of elegance and reciprocal exchange.[41]

Because civic disharmony is tied to corrupt feasting, decadence in manners can lead to hubris and the destruction of the city. The wisdom poet Phocylides preached that a small city that was managed "in good order" (κατὰ κόσμον οἰκεῦσα) was better than once-mighty but fallen Nineveh, and he criticized the false show of those who "suppose that they are sound-thinking men (σαόφρονες) because their gait is orderly (σὺν κόσμῳ στείχοντες) though they are light-witted."[42] Xenophanes (3 *IEG*) blamed the fall of Colophon on the elite having learned useless ways of luxury from the Lydians. In the six-line extract quoted by Athenaeus (526a), he mentions their elegant clothes, distinguished (*euprepei*) hairstyles, and fine perfumes. And it is likely that he went on to allude to their undisciplined drinking habits, if Athenaeus is paraphrasing the poet when he adds that they lost their freedom on account of "untimely" or "inappropriate drinking" (ἄκαιρον μέθην).[43] The *kairos* here is at once good sympotic form, social decorum, and a mainstay of civilization.

At the same time, a certain amount of aggression was traditional in "the sweet compulsion of cups going round while the heart gets warm."[44] The specter of strife, especially about petty things, haunts Greek feasts.[45] There is always the danger of going too far in "the strife of cups" (Diony-

---

[40] Theognis 947; cf. 677–78: χρήματα δ᾽ ἁρπάζουσι βίηι, κόσμος δ᾽ ἀπόλωλεν, / δασμὸς δ᾽ οὐκέτ᾽ ἴσος γίνεται ἐς τὸ μέσον. Cf. Pindar *Pythian* 3.82 for *kosmōi pherein* as social and ethical decorum.

[41] On this custom, Reitzenstein 1893: 31, 51; West 1974: 16, citing Dionysius Chalcus 1 and 4 *IEG*; and Plato *Symposium* 214c ff., 222e.

[42] Phocylides 4, 11 D. West 1978b: 166 compares Theognis 965–67. Dodds (1959: 333, on *Gorgias* 506c ff.) traces the association of *kosmiotēs* with *sōphrosunē* to a Pythagorean notion of a just and orderly world-*kosmos* (cf. *Gorgias* 507e–508a): though Burkert (1972a: 78) reminds us that the idea is also to be found in Empedocles and Euripides.

[43] As noted by Lesher 1992: ad loc.

[44] Bacchylides fr. 20C.6–7. On *Homeric Hymn to Hermes* 55–56 and the young men at feasts who "exchange sly mockery in impromptu song" (ἐξ αὐτοσχεδίης . . . παραιβόλα κερτομέουσιν), see Reitzenstein (1893: 26 n. 2), who compares Isocrates, *To Nicocles* §47, Alexis 160 *PCG*. West (1974: 16) adds Theognis 453–56 and 1207–8.

[45] Quarreling over "mere mortals" threatens to spoil the gods' feast in Homer (*Iliad* 1.573–76); at *Od.* 18.403–4, the beggars' skirmish is a parodical counterpart of strife among the aristocrats. Sophocles employs the motif in his *Oedipus the King* when he puts the rankling insinuation that Oedipus is a bastard in the mouth of a drunk: "For a man at a banquet (*en deipnois*) over-full (*huperplēstheis*) with drink called me out beside the wine (*par oinōi*), saying that I was fake (*plastos*) in my father" (*Oedipus the King* 779–80).

sius Chalcus 2.2 *IEG*: κυλίκων ἔριδας), and an overcompetitive player can stir up contentiousness or awaken political quarrels among the group. It happened often enough that there was a word for the one who went too far in jesting, the buffoon (*bōmolokhos*).[46] The type is recognizable in Euripides' denunciation of clowns who practice sly mockery (χάριτας κερτόμους)[47] and, bereft of true wit, have unbridled mouths (fr. 492 Nauck). Aristotle used a telling expression when he said that the "well-tempered" dinner party (ὁμιλία τις ἐμμελής) depended on knowing just how much to say and avoiding aggressive boasting (*bōmolokhia*).[48]

On the other hand, silence and unrelieved gravity were also offensive: a guest was expected to "play," to assert himself and be able to respond in kind when addressed. Right behavior was a mean between overaggressiveness and a refusal to engage, just as the mean in conviviality lay between drunkenness and austere sobriety.[49] The ideal was jesting that was "easy to take," in the words of the anonymous elegist (οἷα γέλωτα φέρειν). Thus the symposium encouraged self-assertion and striving after "excellence," all the while enjoining moderation and justice, and these values were carried over into praising song. A passage in Theognis spells out what the stakes were when singing took the form of a formal competition (491–96):[50]

αἰνεῖσθαι δ᾽ οὐκ οἶδας. ἀνίκητος δέ τοι οὗτος,
ὃς πολλὰς πίνων μή τι μάταιον ἐρεῖ·
ὑμεῖς δ᾽ εὖ μυθεῖσθε παρὰ κρητῆρι μένοντες,
ἀλλήλων ἔριδας δὴν ἀπερυκόμενοι,
εἰς τὸ μέσον φωνεῦντες ὁμῶς ἑνὶ καὶ συνάπασιν·
χοὔτως συμπόσιον γίνεται οὐκ ἄχαρι.

---

[46] Cf. Aristophanes *Frogs* 358, discussed in the following chapter; *Peace* 748; Xenophon *Cyropedia* 5.2.18, with which Gera (1993: 172) compares Xenophon's favorable picture of the Persians at dinner. Hesiod *Works and Days* 704 has the expression *deipnolokhēs* for a "greedy" wife who eats too much.

[47] Cf. *Homeric Hymn to Hermes* 55–56, quoted above, note 44.

[48] For *bōmolokhia*, cf. *Politics* 1336b10, and Halliwell 1986: 272 n. 31 and 196 n. 39. For *eumelēs*, see Aristotle *Nicomachean Ethics* 1128a, and cf. the "well-tempered jesting" of the Spartans (*emmelōs skōptein kai skōptesthai*: fr. 611.13 Rose). In Plato *Sophist* 259E, "not *emmelēs*" is equivalent to "uncultured" (*amousos*) and "un-philosophical." The locution explains Plato's admiring reference to a kind of dance called *emmeleia* at *Laws* 816B.

[49] Theognis 479–80, 837–40. A portrait of the ill-humored symposiast is Xenophon's Hermogenes at *Symposium* 6.1–5 (cf. 4.50, 8.3), with which Gera (1993: 162) compares Aglaitadas in *Cyropedia* 2.2.11–16.

[50] Following Young on 491 rather than West who prints ἀρνεῖσθαι; for other elegiacs on contests: Theognis 993–96; Xenophanes 1.19–20 *IEG*. Xenophanes 6 *IEG* may well be an example of a challenge poem, according to Havelock 1982: 235; cf. *Od.* 8.477–81.

You do not know how to win praise; that man will emerge unvanquished
   who, though he has drunk much, lets no reckless word fall;
but speak well as you abide by the mixing bowl,
      keeping strife far away from each other
as you speak in the middle to one and all alike;
      in this way a symposium is not without grace.

Songs at a "graceful" symposium are not simply elegant (though they are
that) but also avoid excess (the litotes in οὐκ ἄχαρι avoids overstatement)
and create that mutuality and reciprocity expressed in the word *kharis*.

Metron: Sympotic Aesthetics

The highly prized order of the symposium was an imitation of larger public order: the symposiarch, sometimes styled the "king" (*basileus*) or
"master" (*despotēs*) or "magistrate" (*arkhōn*) exercised by consent a temporary authority over others who were in principle his equals.[51] So, too,
singing to display one's character (*gnōmēn anaphainesthai*) for the assembled company (*eis to meson*) was a playful imitation of proffering one's
views publicly (*gnōmēn pherein is meson*, Herodotus 4.97.5), for the public space for exchange of ideas and for confrontations in the city was also
called the *meson*.[52] As a ritualized imitation of behavior in the "outside"
world, singing was called "play" not in the sense of feigning or imitating,
but as sport that imitated more "serious action" (what is called the *spou-
daion pragma* in the Megarian collection of sympotic songs under the
name Theognis).[53] Just as athletic games could be symbolic substitutes for
warfare, songs at symposia were bracketed and stylized forms of what in
other contexts could be serious speech acts: sympotic jesting had to stop
short of being real abuse, and the encomia common at symposia tended
to focus on the laudandus' beauty more than his political power (and even
so were often mingled with slight deprecation to disarm resentment).[54]
The speeches were made into imitation speeches by the "playful" environment in which guests acted out roles of praise and blame, challenge and
response, seduction and rejection.

[51] Cf. Murray 1983a: 260. For symposiarch "titles," see Mau *RE* IV 1900: 612–13.
[52] On *to meson* as the city's space for oral "publication," cf. Detienne 1967: 60–74 and
Svenbro 1984a: 83. According to Svenbro (ibid.: 191 n. 36), the post-Homeric, civic "middle" implies equal discussion (*isēgoria*) as opposed to the hierarchical transmission of oral
tradition (as in *Od.* 8.66, where Demodocus sings *messōi daitumonōn*; cf. 8.262: *es meson*
of the agora).
[53] Theognis 115–16, 641–44; cf. *thurēphi* at 311 and Donlon 1985.
[54] Encomia were a class of *skolia* for the Alexandrians: cf. van Groningen 1960: 16–17.

Hence, "graceful speaking" in the symposium could be represented as a kind of rehearsal for graceful concourse with citizens in the agora, and the ideal symposiast could be represented as, at least potentially, the ideal citizen. In a song for the tyrant of Cyrene in 462, Pindar pleads for an exiled young man and promises that, if allowed to return, he will "tend to symposia beside Apollo's spring and often give his heart over to youthful sport, and among wise (*sophoi*) citizens, wielding the cunningly made lyre, he shall touch on peace (*hesukhia*), causing harm (*pēma*) to no man there and suffering none from the citizens."[55] Sympotic ethics, however, tended toward aesthetics to the extent that musical performance was interpreted as a sign of hidden qualities. At Cleisthenes' wedding, after all, a dynasty depended on a sense of decorum.

Symposiasts listened to songs to discover the singer who would show himself a "trusty and faithful comrade" when need arose.[56] The wish expressed in the Hesiodic passage for some clear sign of inner character is reprised in a skolion wishing for the power to open men's breasts and look at the mind (*nous*) within to discern the friend of "guileless heart" (889 *PMG*). The opposition of "inner" and "outer" is pervasive, for true intentions are difficult to discern from the outside: people can deceive with a false show of friendliness, and the tongue is no sure indicator of the mind.[57] Symposia were thus occasions to, in a key metaphor of the time, "assay" a man's character, applying a "touchstone" to find who is "counterfeit" beneath an agreeable exterior. The preeminent touchstone was, of course, wine, which "reveals the mind of a man."[58] Conventional wisdom urged guardedness in speech, husbanding one's words as a steward watches over household provisions;[59] but wine could act as a "mirror of the man" (Alcaeus 333 V) because it loosened the doors of speech. One who "exceeds the measure of drink" (ὑπερβάλληι πόσιος μέτρον) was no longer "master of his own tongue and wits" and could "speak lawless words that are disgraceful to sober minds" and "stop at no shameful act" (Theognis 479–83).[60] In the words of a fourth-century cultural historian,

---

[55] Pindar *Pythian* 4.294–97; cf. 1.70, where the ideal king fosters "harmonious peace" among his people (δᾶμον γεραίρων τράποι σύμφωνον ἐς ἡσυχίαν), with Demont in Murray 1990.

[56] A *pistos hetairos* (Theognis 529, etc.). See Donlon 1985: 229–30.

[57] Theognis 91–92, 851–52, 1219–20. Cf. Levine 1985: 186–89.

[58] Theognis 499–503. For the touchstone metaphor, cf. esp. Theognis 119–28, 415–18, 447–52, 965, 1164e–h; and Donlon 1985: 230–31. On the theme *in vino veritas* (Alcaeus 366 V, cf. Aeschylus fr. 393 *TrGF*), see Rösler 1995.

[59] "Stewarding": Hesiod *Works and Days* 719, Theognis 421–24, 504, 1185–86. Theognis both recommends dissimulation as self-defense (e.g., 59–68, 363–64) and deplores it (e.g., 87–90).

[60] Wine destabilizes wits: *Od.* 18.389–92; leads to disaster in the case of the Centaurs: 21.293–304. An ancient proverb ran, "Wine draws the sword like a magnet": *Od.* 19.13 (cf. 16.294), with Russo's comments.

"People drinking wine not only reveal what sorts of people they are themselves, but also uncover the natures of everyone else as they indulge in
unrestrained speech (*parrhēsian*)" (Philochorus 328 *FGrH* F 170).
The tropes here harmonize with the opposition in epic between the
"mind within" and the "shape" of words, but again, the rhetorical possibilities of this view are not developed. Because the purpose of singing
was to "display" ethical wisdom, sympotic criticism was fundamentally
performative rather than rhetorical. Seen as a revelation of what is hidden
in the heart, song was evaluated as drama more than composition. Aristotle is continuing this tradition when he begins both of his major ethical
treatises by quoting and critiquing a short verse ("Finest is the most just;
most desirable is health; but the sweetest of all is to get what one desires"),
which both was a skolion and was inscribed on a temple on Delos.[61] He
takes its author as "giving a demonstration of his judgment" (γνώμην
ἀποφηνάμενος).[62] Another skolion serves him as an example in his *Rhetoric* of how orators should quote general propositions (*gnōmai*) to indicate
their ethical views.[63] As in democratic lawcourts, at archaic dinner parties,
what one sang revealed one's values.

Symposia thus tend to idealize themselves as fora for ethical discussion
and debating wisdom (*sophia*): the Seven Sages were said to have partici-
pated in sympotic "conversations" (ὁμιλίας) at the palaces of the great,[64]
and a number of sympotic songs quote sayings of the Sages and other old
authorities for discussion:[65] a short lyric by Simonides takes issue with
Kleoboulos on the subject of fame (581 *PMG*), and another of his songs,
possibly an encomium performed in a sympotic context, quotes and dis-

---

[61] For the Delian epigram: Aristotle *Eudemian Ethics* 1.1.1214a5 (cf. *Nicomachean Ethics* 1.8.14.1099a27): Κάλλιστον τὸ δικαιότατον· λῶιστον δ' ὑγιαίνειν· / πάντων ἥδιστον δ'
οὗ τις ἐρᾶι, τὸ τυχεῖν.

[62] *Eudemian Ethics* 1214a5. This was a quasi-technical language for sympotic performance: see Plato *Critias* 108c. Symposia thus called for a "dramatic" presentation of one's
character, as can be seen by comparing the language of Aristotle's *Poetics*, where characters
reveal their "thought" (*dianoia*) to the audience in part through the general statements of
value they pronounce (ἀποφαίνονται γνώμην: *Poetics* 1450a7; cf. καθόλου τι ἀποφαίνονται
at 1450b12 and *Rhetoric* 1394a21. Cf. *phainesthai* in Damon B 4 DK, note 33 above.

[63] *Rhetoric* 1394b13 ("For man, health is best, as we at least believe"). The verse is
printed as Simonides (*dubia*) 651 *PMG*. Dover (1974: 123–24) notes *gnōmē* could be applied "to states or attitudes of mind we should regard as affirmation of a general moral
principle or sustained orientation of the will."

[64] DL 1.40–42; Athenaeus 463a. Cf. Plato *Protagoras* 343A, Ephorus 70 F 181–82 *FGrH*.
Cf. West 1974: 15; Rösler (1990), though his "intellectual dialogue with authorities of the
past" (233) may be too academic a description; and Gera 1993: 148.

[65] Alcaeus quotes and approves Aristodemos' saying "Money is the man" (360 V); see
Page 1955: 315; Critias the Lacedaimonian Chilon's " 'Nothing too much.' All fine things
are near the *kairos*" (7 *IEG*). Ion of Chios (30 *IEG*) referred to the wisdom of Pythagoras
(the object of mockery in Xenophanes 7a *IEG*).

putes the sage Pittacus on the perfectability of human nature (542 PMG).[66] Esteemed songs from the past also came in for evaluation: an elegy by Solon (20 IEG) quotes and criticizes an elegy by Mimnermus (6 IEG) on the optimal length of human life; an elegy by Simonides quotes a line of Homer on the ephemerality of human existence and pronounces it "very fine," and one of his short lyrics recalls a Hesiodic saying about the difficulty of virtue.[67]

Sympotic ethics and politics most closely approached aesthetics when certain kinds of singing were proscribed from the ideal feast. Discoursing on good singing around the jar, Anacreon manages to elevate his own light, erotic verse into a paradigmatic genre (fr. Eleg. 2 IEG):

οὐ φιλέω, ὃς κρητῆρι παρὰ πλέωι οἰνοποτάζων
    νείκεα καὶ πόλεμον δακρυόεντα λέγει,
ἀλλ᾽ ὅστις Μουσέων τε καὶ ἀγλαὰ δῶρ᾽ Ἀφροδίτης
    συμμίσγων ἐρατῆς μνήσκεται εὐφροσύνης.

I have no love for the man who, drinking beside the full mixing bowl,
    speaks of quarrels and tearful war,
but for the one who takes the gifts of the Muses and those of Aphrodite
    and blends them with his mind on charming festivity.

The poet rejects "speaking" about war and quarrels in symposia. The guest one wants to befriend "blends" (as civilized drinkers blended wine with water) song with eros, producing the kind of graceful pederastic ditties Anacreon composed. The opposition between songs that arouse contention and songs of peaceful festivity was widely invoked by the poets, as shall be seen in the next chapter. Along with the opposition between songs to gods and songs to mortals, it was one of the most basic and widespread "generic" distinctions among archaic songs.[68] Here the distinction is less theological than what is appropriate to the mood of the occasion and to social well-being, the complex of values summed up in Solon's εὐφροσύνας κοσμεῖν. Legible as a thematic distinction, its social and ethical bases are clear, as when Anacreon treats this theme in another skolion: rejecting the "din and clatter" of barbaric drinking in favor of "fair songs" such as his own, he adds to his plea for fair rather than harsh

---

[66] Among other possible examples of singing debates of which our sources preserve only one side of the exchange, cf. Theognis 153–54, which reads well as a revision of Solon 6.3–4 IEG, just as Clement says it is (Stromateis 6.8.8).

[67] Simonides 19 IEG (referring to Homer Iliad 6.146) and 579 PMG (cf. Works and Days 287–92), discussed in Ford 1997a: 91–92.

[68] Cf. Theognis 493–94, Xenophanes 1.15, Stesichorus 210 PMGF, Phocylides 14 D, Dionyius Chalcus 2 IEG, Cratinus Min. fr. 4 PCG. Cf. Od. 20.392, Hesiod Works and Days 723. Noted by Reitzenstein 1893: 50; Reinhardt 1916: 133; Bowra 1953: 3.

sounds a call for moderation—wine well mixed with water—"so I may play the Bacchant without hubris."[69]

In the long term, this broad notion of decorum and the words in which it was expressed will come to describe formal relations among the elements of an artfully composed speech. As notions of *to prepon* were extended from behavior that was fitting to well-fitting verbal construction, so *kosmos* was loosened from political and social order to signify ornamental arrangement, decoration.[70] This evolution can be recapitulated in the term *metron*. The ethical sense of the word noted previously applies easily to symposia, where wine was "measured" out and drinking "beyond due measure" (*huper metron*) was equatable with behavior that went too far (*hubris*).[71] In such contexts, the "man of due measure" (*metrios*) was he who followed the *metron* and *kairos*. In the later fifth century, a new technical meaning of *metron* as "meter" joined its older senses, as can be seen in a clever little poem by the Athenian Critias, Plato's uncle. In his elegiacs, Critias declared an admiration for restrained drinking parties where laughter is "measured" (*metrion gelota*, 6.16 *IEG*) and drinking is not "unmeasured" (*ametroisi potois*, 6.27). But observing due "measures" in singing coalesced with observing the rules of meter in a short elegiac encomium the sophisticated singer composed for Alcibiades. Because Alcibiades' name could not fit into the dactylic rhythms of the elegiac couplet, Critias substituted an iambic line in the second verse for the expected pentameter (4 *IEG*):

> καὶ νῦν Κλεινίου υἱὸν Ἀθηναῖον στεφανώσω
>   Ἀλκιβιάδην νέοισιν ὑμνήσας τρόποις;
> οὐ γάρ πως ἦν τοὔνομ' ἐφαρμόζειν ἐλεγείωι,
>   νῦν δ' ἐν ἰαμβείωι κείσεται οὐκ ἀμέτρως.

> And now I give a crown to the Athenian, son of Cleinias,
>   Alcibiades, in a song of novel character:
> For it was not possible to fit his name into the elegiac,
>   but now he reposes in an iambic not without measure.

---

[69] 356 *PMG*. Anacreon's *kaloi humnoi* should not be confined to "hymns."

[70] Linguistic ornament is an add-on to the essential plot in *Poetics* 1457b2, etc. See Halliwell 1986: 339 n. 9. The first clear example seems to be Thucydides 3.67.6, λόγοι ἔπεσι κοσμηθέντες; cf. *kosmein* of poets' "adornments" at 1.10.3, 1.21.1. *Pace* Diller (1956: 57), it is anachronistic to gloss Solon's κόσμος ἐπέων (1 *IEG*) as "poetry" versus "prose"; cf. above, Introduction, note 39. So, too, in Parmenides B 8.52 DK (cf. *Homeric Hymn to Dionysus* 7.59, "Orpheus" B 1 DK); Democritus B 21 DK is discussed in chapter 7 below.

[71] For sympotic praise of "the middle way" and "nothing in excess," Theognis 335–36, 401–6, 497–98; Phocylides 12 D; Critias 6, 7 *IEG*. On drinking "according to" or "in excess of" due measure (*kata/huper metron*), Bielohlawek 1940: 22–25 and Levine 1985: 180–84.

Though this broke the elegiac meter (*metron*), Critias is quick to claim that "new ways" (the phrase can refer as easily to wayward, even revolutionary character as to novel techniques) conform to the old: for Alcibiades' name "reposes" (*keimai*) in the iambic line "not without measure," just as a symposiast was expected to "repose" (*keimai*) decorously on his couch.[72] Toying with sympotic genre, Critias yet evokes its basic preference for *euphrosunē*: this little *jeu d' ésprit*, composed to welcome Alcibiades on his return from political exile, presents him as one who will sing of peace and not of war.

The terms evolved to praise and blame sympotic singing persisted in rhetorical and philosophical theories of poetry of the fourth century, when talking about what made a song good migrated from the dining hall to lecture hall, from speech "in the middle" to the academic lecture or treatise. The connection between musical and social form is expressed in the classical term of praise "cutting a good figure" (*eu-skhēmōn*), which was applied to a person's posture, attitudes, or behavior before *skhēmata* became "figures" of speech.[73] The social and moral values that Greek poetic theory could not, *qua* poetic theory, derive from its own formalist principles were rooted in the high leisure culture of archaic Greece. Certainly, the critical theory of literature owed much to the artificial behavior by which archaic elites confirmed their excellence.

Within the long tradition of Greek table talk, I have emphasized sympotic song as a stylized form of conversation. Whereas Homeric nobles exhibited their distinction by being served song, as they were served with other fine things, by professional musicians, the symposium turned noble conversation into song, one more way of making external, within a set of forms, one's "inner" judgment and wisdom. Symposiasts aspired to show themselves moderate and just, as well as gracious and noble. So they praised songs that showed admirable sense and were good for the community. The usefulness of sympotic terms for formalist criticism was already prepared, however, by their association of the old "right and fitting" with the new graceful and ornamental.

The wedding feast held by Cleisthenes of Sicyon proved to be a watershed in the old-style aristocracy, for the offspring of the bride and the eventual winner was a son named after his maternal grandfather, Cleisthenes of Athens. He ended up playing a major role in the overthrow of

---

[72] Similarly, when Sophocles was faced with the equally recalcitrant name of Archelaus, he took some liberties in its scansion, all the while insisting that the pronunciation was "in accordance with due measure/meter" ('Αρχέλεως; ἦν γὰρ σύμμετρον ὧδε λέγειν, 1 *IEG*).

[73] See Aristophanes *Wasps* 1212–17. Cf. Plato *Gorgias* 511E (*en metriōi skhēmati*), and *Republic* 365c (the "trappings" of virtue). Cf. Goldhill in Goldhill and Osborne 1999: 4–5.

the Peisistratid tyrants at Athens at the end of the sixth century, a fair enough marker of the beginning of the end of elite cultural dominance in the archaic age. Around the time of Cleisthenes' feast, Xenophanes of Colophon was born in wealthy and sophisticated Ionia. Sometime in the middle of the century, this man of more than ordinary intellectual curiosity and musical skill was forced to leave Asia Minor and undertake a career as an itinerant sage that would last into the early fifth century. On the way, he must have found accommodation at the tables of patrons eager for culture, and edified and entertained them by his "speaking." In the next chapter we shall study one of his songs, which presaged a crisis for sympotic culture and criticism.

TWO

XENOPHANES AND THE "ANCIENT QUARREL"

A CAPSULE history of Greek criticism before Plato is given to us by
Plato himself when he apologizes for dismissing poets from his
ideal city by referring to an "ancient quarrel between poetry and
philosophy" (*Republic* 607B). Plato may not be altogether serious: he
documents the poets' side of the quarrel with snatches of lyric and comic
verse that have nothing to do with philosophy but that do speak of pomp-
ous and arrogant types who may win a reputation among the undiscern-
ing. And whether he is joking or not, we should be wary of Platonic constructions of literary history that make it culminate in his own
philosophical positions.[1] Yet most histories of Greek criticism have taken
him at his word and traced this war to the later sixth century, when Xenophanes and his younger contemporary Heraclitus criticized the songs
of Homer and Hesiod.[2] A turning point—the beginning of the end of
traditional reverence for poets—is recognized when Xenophanes said,
"Homer and Hesiod have attributed to the gods every kind of behavior
that among men is the object of reproach: stealing, adultery, and cheating
each other."[3] Although Hesiod and Solon, and no doubt popular wisdom,
already knew that singers (*aoidoi*) often lie,[4] with Xenophanes the rational Greek critical spirit is supposed to awaken.

In this chapter I focus on one of the key documents in the standard
account: an elegiac song in which Xenophanes (fr. 1 *IEG*) rejects from a
well-ordered drinking party songs about "battling Titans, Giants, and
Centaurs—fabrications (*plasmata*) of men of old in which there is nothing
of use" (1.22–23). The phrase is usually interpreted as referring to epic,
and Xenophanes' condemnation of its outmoded mythological traditions
is seen as the ultimate precedent for Plato's rejection of poetry's harmful

---

[1] Cf. O. Murray 1995b: 231; Croally 1994: 18; Nightingale 1995: 60–67. As Goldhill
(1991: 168 n. 2) remarks, it is a "typical strategy of both myth and rhetoric—to construct
a teleological narrative to explain a present structure." Plato's quotations are printed at
987a–d *PMG*; see Halliwell 1988: 155.

[2] Esp. Xenophanes A 11, 19, B 10–12 DK; Heraclitus B 40, 42, 56, 57, 104, 106, and cf.
105 DK.

[3] Fr. B 11 DK: πάντα θεοῖσ᾽ ἀνέθηκαν Ὅμηρός θ᾽ Ἡσίοδός τε, / ὅσσα παρ᾽ ἀνθρώποισιν
ὀνείδεα καὶ ψόγος ἐστίν, / κλέπτειν μοιχεύειν τε καὶ ἀλλήλους ἀπατεύειν.

[4] Hesiod *Theogony* 27, where falsehood is an occasional and arbitrary fault in poetry;
see Katz and Volk 2000 on this much-discussed passage. Solon 29 *IEG* (πολλὰ ψεύδονται
ἀοιδοί), virtually a proverb: cf. West's testimonia ad loc; Burkert 1985: 246.

lies.[5] Following lines drawn in the preceding chapter, I read Xenophanes fr. 1 within its sympotic context rather than in the metaphysical and theological terms of the *Republic*.[6] In such a perspective, the categories of "epic" and "poetry" will turn out to have little significance in comparison with the symposium's traditional concern with justice and graciousness in speech. Although Xenophanes was truly an innovative religious thinker, his critique of song in fr. 1 remains within well-established sympotic forms: the values it advances conform to sympotic standards of excellence, and even in formulating these values in a new and profoundly suggestive way, he is faithful to the symposium's imperative to seek out ever more refined and graceful speech.

Reading Xenophanes fr. 1 as a battle between "philosophy" and "poetry" imposes Platonic categories on a very different milieu, when the exercise of wisdom was not yet a purely philosophic activity.[7] Neither in fr. 1 nor in his other surviving texts is Xenophanes concerned to set "philosophy" (a word that had no more specialized meaning at this time than "devoted to learning")[8] against "poetry" (a word that is not found in his or any other song until the late fifth century). He attacks Homer and Hesiod and the singers (*aoidoi*) who continue their tales, but not singing or "poetry" per se, for he himself was a "singer" (*aoidos*) as much as anything else. In the sixth century, the role and status of the intellectual were not yet clearly defined; nor were intellectuals clearly marked off from singers, who had been claiming to be "wise" at least since Hesiod.[9] Heraclitus grouped together in a single sentence Hesiod, the mystical philoso-

[5] E.g., Egger 1886: 93–100; Sikes 1931: 11–18; Atkins 1934: 11–15; Fränkel 1975: 328; Lanata 1963: 113–14; Grube 1965: 8; Pfeiffer 1968: 9; Detienne 1981: ch. 4, esp. 124–29; Russell 1981: 19, 87–88; Kannicht 1988: 16–21; Ferrari 1989: 110; Schäfer 1996: 249–57.

[6] This is not to deny that Plato was influenced by Xenophanes in the *Republic*, for fr. 1 seems to lie behind the discussion of battles of gods and heroes "against their kin" at *Republic* 378C. But Plato's reading expands on Xenophanes: note that he censors these tales "whether in stories or embroideries," here adding the visual arts (as he had in the *Euthyphro* 6B–C). Xenophanes' striking metaphor, "fabrications" (*plasmata*), may echo in Plato's *Timaeus* 26E, where Critias' aetiological story is praised as not a "fabricated story" (*plasthenta muthon*) but a "true account" (*alēthinon logon*).

[7] An important study of "prephilosophic" Greek wisdom is Detienne and Vernant 1974, on which see Nussbaum 1986: esp. 19–20, 307–11.

[8] See Ford 1993b: 39–41, with references.

[9] See Humphreys 1975 on intellectuals. The singer "exercises wisdom" (*sophizomai*) in Hesiod *Works and Days* 649; cf. Ibycus 282.23 *PMG*; *Homeric Hymn to Hermes* 483, 511; Theognis 19, 770, 995; for "wise" (*sophos*) poets, Hesiod fr. 306 M-W (of Linus); [Homer] *Margites* 1; Pindar *Ol.* 2.86; Aristophanes *Clouds* 547; etc. See Lanata 1963: 83–85. In this light, too much weight should not be placed on the fact that Solon 13.52 *IEG* is our first attested instance of *sophia* claimed for poetry, as in the developmental thesis of Snell (1973) that the "wisdom" of the poet evolves from a craftsmanlike skill to a spiritual activity. See pp. 58–60 below on Xenophanes as "spiritual revolutionary."

pher Pythagoras, the geographer-historian Hecataeus, and Xenophanes himself as all lacking intelligence despite their many studies (*poluma-thiē*).[10] The late archaic age was a time in which those who were ambitious to be thought "wise" (*sophos*) had to find a place within a wide range of discursive modes and a broad variety of authoritative styles.[11] Among these discourses, inspired song had to be confronted by anyone who would lay claim to the title for himself.[12] Xenophanes' attack on Homer was apparently quite sustained in his work: it is to Xenophanes (whom he styled "Homer-attacker") that Aristotle refers when he speaks of people who criticize poetic accounts of the gods for being neither edifying nor true.[13] But in the sixth century, the singer was one among many claimants to the title *sophos*, and in other fragments Xenophanes considered and sometimes disputed the views of nonsingers such as Thales, Pythagoras, and Epimenides of Crete, and he attacked Simonides for greediness.[14] In understanding these battles, Plato's distinction between poet and philosopher is of little use.

If we look at Xenophanes' songs as bids for authority by a late archaic wise man rather than as Platonic attacks on "poetry," we can answer the puzzling but finally unreal question of why Xenophanes attacks singers in "song" (i.e., elegiac couplets and hexameters) of his own. When this question is not avoided, the answers suggested have been weak, such as the argument that Xenophanes fell victim to force of habit, or oversubtle, as in the conclusion that he objected to the content of poetry rather than its form, a rhetorical distinction based in fifth-century metrical studies that cannot be supported from his texts.[15] Evidently, Xenophanes did not think that the fact that he sang put his discourse in the same category with that of his opponents. The reasons for his choice of "form" must be

[10] Heraclitus B 40 DK. On the groupings, Burkert 1972a: 208; cf. Nussbaum 1986: 123.

[11] Cf. Lloyd 1987: ch. 2, esp. 83–88 and Martin 1993.

[12] Lesher 1978 shows how deeply Xenophanes' epistemology and critical thought would have countered those professing a kind of knowledge descended from the gods.

[13] For "Homer-attacker," Aristotle fr. 75 Rose. *Poetics* 1460b35–61a1: I read Kassel's text, on which see Lucas 1968: 238–39 and, with a slightly different text, Janko 1987: 147.

[14] Xenophanes on Thales: B 19 DK; on Pythagoras: B 7 DK; on Epimenides: B 20 DK; on Simonides: B 21 DK.

[15] Force of habit: Havelock 1963: 51; Lanata 1963: 116: Xenophanes criticizes not poetry per se but only traditional epic; Nagy 1989: 34–35: he rejects the content not the *form* of poetry. This is to speak with Platonic distinctions (e.g., *Republic* 398B); cf. Ferrarri 1989: 110. Kannicht (1988: 2–3) suggests that prose was undeveloped as yet; but oral eloquence was not, and that was the prime path to publicity. Burkert (1985: 305, 307, 309) notes that Xenophanes' choice had to do with publicizing his ideas, though he still regards with dismay his "recourse to poetic form" (307) instead of matter-of-fact prose; but prose did nothing to make a Pherecydes philosophical. Burkert fruitfully adds that, by singing, Xenophanes cast his dispute with Homer and Hesiod in the legendary form of internal squabbles between wise men: hence "Xenophanes found hearers but no disciples" (309).

sought in the contexts where he hoped to publicize his wisdom. Xenophanes is recorded to have composed a "Colonization of Elea" in 2,000 hexameters: such a song would have been of a length (about equivalent to four books of the *Odyssey*) and theme quite suitable to rhapsodic performance at a festival.[16] Less solemn moments may have welcomed the hexameters later classified as "lampoons" (*silloi* or *parōidiai*), some of which contained his ridicule of the old poets. But singing skill would also have been useful in noble houses, and an apothegm attributed to Xenophanes says that one should associate with tyrants "either as little as possible or as comfortably as possible."[17] The most comfortable way of associating with tyrants was at their feasts, and almost all of Xenophanes' elegiacs strike themes and attitudes that were often sounded after dinner.[18] Noble halls were also, of course, places to compete for and display wisdom. What Xenophanes hoped to offer such companies can be seen by looking first at another song in praise of wisdom.

Fr. 2: "Our Wisdom"

At the age of 92, Xenophanes had lived as an itinerant wise man for sixty-seven years, "hustling my wits," as he put it, throughout Greece from the time he had been 25 (8.2 *IEG*; cf. 45 *IEG*). It is likely that threats from the East drove him to leave Asia Minor and his native Colophon, which fell to the Medes in 545–540.[19] Xenophanes joined a stream of wise men on the same westward path: not long after his emigration, another Ionian sage, Pythagoras, made his way to southern Italy from Samos, and Arion, a professional lyre-singer from Lesbos, first found welcome with Polycrates, tyrant of Samos, then undertook a western trip that made him quite wealthy.[20] Herodotus would later follow a similar westward path to fame as a lecturer. The western colonies had considerable local musical talent, but the leading men of the great cities in Sicily and southern Italy also patronized poets from abroad such as Simonides, Pindar, and Bacchylides. Hiero, who became tyrant of Syracuse in 478, near the end of Xenophanes' life, even attracted Aeschylus there from Athens to compose a play to celebrate a city he had founded.[21]

[16] So another attested work on the "Foundation of Colophon": for these works, A 1.20 DK.

[17] DL 9.19 (= 21 A 1.19 DK).

[18] Some of his hexameters refer to sympotic scenes (e.g., B 22 DK).

[19] Some put his departure earlier: see recent discussion in Schäfer 1996: 95–104.

[20] Pythagoras: 14 A 8 DK. Arion: Herodotus 1.23–24.

[21] Anecdotes associating Xenophanes with Hieron (A 11 DK) and Elea (A 1, 13 DK) may be influenced by doxographical readings of the poet in relation to the Eleatic philosophy of Parmenides (A 8 DK): Jaeger 1947: 215 n. 65.

When Xenophanes arrived in western Greece, he could present himself as a man of some accomplishments: he was quite familiar with Homeric poetry, which had had a strong presence in Colophon,[22] and he had a facility for composing in its popular panhellenic idioms; he also brought a knowledge of Colophonian history and its lessons for statesmen; finally, he brought from Ionia a familiarity with the new Milesian discourse on nature that dispensed with the traditional role of the gods. Xenophanes propounded this remarkable new vision of divinity in elegiac and hexameter songs. Declaring that "there is one god greatest among gods and men, / resembling mortals neither in bodily form nor in thought," who "effortlessly sways all things with his mind" (B 23, 25 DK), he issued biting critiques of Greek anthropomorphism: if animals could paint and sculpt, then horses would fashion gods that looked like horses and cows like cows (B 15 DK).

There is no disputing Xenophanes' radical intellectual disagreement with traditional song concerning the gods. But a man in search of accommodation needs a title. The *Odyssey* listed prophets, healers, carpenters, and singers as "public workers" (*dēmiourgoi*) worth inviting into a community (17.383–85). These four types recur around 600 when Solon listed the occupations of cities (13.43–62 *IEG*); he added merchants (for whom the *Odyssey*'s aristocrats have little love) and agricultural laborers, but not yet philosophers. Xenophanes was not a prophet, for he claimed no divine revelation; and he was not a healer, though, as we shall see, other philosophers and singers took up that line. Nor was he a professional singer (*aoidos*) or a specialist in epic poetry, like the sixth-century Homeridae on Chios.[23] Xenophanes could have been called a "rhapsode"[24] whenever he gave recitations of his songs, but his best hope was to be taken for a wandering *sophos*, a man of insight and intellect, worth entertaining and perhaps retaining for a time. Indeed, the kind of position he desired is described in his second-longest surviving text, a complaint about the privileges accorded prize athletes in the city (2 *IEG*). This song, which would have served well as an advertisement for his services, complains that an athlete, especially a victor in the Panhellenic games, reaps great civic rewards—he is the cynosure of all, has a prime seat reserved at public gatherings, eats at public expense, and gets gifts to lay up as his own possessions (7–9)—and yet "such a one is not so worthy as I: for greater

---

[22] A century after Xenophanes, Antimachus of Colophon made a name for himself in epic, and local tradition had Homer spending time at Colophon and composing the *Margites* there: see Bernabé 1988: 12 and 386; Huxley 1969: 174 ff.

[23] Burkert 1980: 7–8, 1992: 25, 43–46.

[24] So Reinhardt 1916: 133, following Diogenes Laertius 9.18. The testimony is often dismissed (e.g., Jaeger, 1947: 41–43), but Diogenes is using "rhapsode" in its classical sense of "performer of non-lyric poetry": see Ford 1988: 305.

than the strength / of men or horses is our wisdom (*sophia*)" (11–12). In contrast to the unsystematic (*eikēi*, 13) and unjust suppositions of men, strength is not to be preferred to "good wisdom" (14), for athletes do not ensure good government in the city (*eunomiē*, 19), add little graceful pleasure (*kharma*), 20 to civic life, and do nothing to "fatten the city's coffers" (22).[25]

A good deal of discussion has gone into how far "our wisdom" is compounded of technical poetic skill, practical advice, and some deeper philosophical insight.[26] The debate has tended unfortunately to fit the passage into a dubious Hegelian history in which Xenophon stands midway in a presumed evolution from wisdom as a craftlike skill to a purely intellectual and spiritual quality. But a stress on Xenophanes' "philosophical" side should not neglect the "charismatics and magicians" whom Walter Burkert has characterized as the "mobile intellectuals of their epoch."[27] Archaic wise men did not look like academics, nor did they all speak plain prose: with his golden crown and splendid robes, Pythagoras could appear as a hierophant or even as a living god on earth.[28] It is impossible to separate science from religion in the philosophy of this shamanlike figure. Empedocles (born ca. 496) adopted not only Pythagoras' noble manner (*semnotēs biou*), but also his general comportment (*skhēma*) and style of dress; he propounded his philosophy of nature in hexameters that came straight from the god (θεοῦ πάρα μῦθος, B 23.11 DK).[29] Even the epoch-making metaphysical arguments of Parmenides, his "reasoning and refutation" (B 7.5 DK), were sung by a wanderer from Elea who claimed to be divinely inspired (B 1.22); he, too, gave his philosophy as a revelation of the hidden nature of being, a *muthos* delivered by a goddess (B 2.1 DK).[30]

Burkert notes that the strong need in the archaic age for purification led to the success of shamanlike figures such as Epimenides of Crete, who

[25] Kannicht (1988: 18–19) well compares Solon 13 *IEG*, a prayer to the Muses to be both wealthy and a man of account.

[26] Lanata 1963: 114 reviews opinions and opts for Bowra (1953: 18): "He meant philosophical and critical poetry which he himself wrote." Similarly, Havelock 1963: 287 and 162–63 nn. 27, 28. Marcovich (1978: 21–22) interprets (Platonically) "practical, effective" wisdom, "the content of the poetry," rather than "poetic skill and art."

[27] Burkert 1992: 63; cf. 1979b: 24.

[28] On Pythagoras' dress, West 1971: 214; Burkert 1969: 26–27. Fifth-century sophists and rhapsodes were also splendidly arrayed. For rhapsodes, Plato *Ion* 530B, 535D; sophists, Gorgias A 9 DK, Plato *Hippias major* 291A, *Hippias minor* 368C; Aelian *Varia historia* 12.32.

[29] Empedocles *apud* DL 8.56; cf. 8.66 (= 12 A 8, DK), B 112.6 DK. Xenophanes caps a remark by Empedocles at A 1.20 DK.

[30] See Lesher 1994, and cf. Burkert 1969: 13, 28.

was summoned to Athens around 600 to free the city of pollution.[31]
Others whom we classify as poets also took up the trade in magical
healing: a legend attested in the fifth century recalled another Cretan purifier, Thaletas from Gortyn, who was brought to Sparta in accordance
with an oracle and cured a plague with his lyre-songs (*kitharōidia*).[32]
The kitharodic music of Terpander was said to have been introduced
into the city when the Spartans summoned him at a time of civic tur-
moil and were "restored to calm" by listening to his songs in their messes
(*sussitia*).[33]

For the traveling sage Xenophanes as well, the lines between philosophical, musical, and religious expertise were not sharp. Though his rejection
of Homeric myth is obviously rooted in a novel conception of divinity, he
was also a wandering singer who could critique local customs on the basis
of his experience about how such things were done elsewhere. In a story
preserved by Aristotle, Xenophanes was consulted on a religious question
that was also a generic one: when the Eleans asked him if they should
offer laments (*thrēnoi*) and sacrifices to Ino Leucothea, he told them to
sing *thrēnoi* if they took Ino to be a mortal and to sacrifice if they took
her to be a god.[34] In archaic musical criticism, critiquing a form of song
easily extended to commenting on religious practice and belief: Heraclitus
observed that if phallic hymns were considered apart from their traditional Dionysiac context, it would be thought shameful to sing them; in
holding that Dionysus was the same god as Hades, he implicitly undermined a generic distinction (what rites and songs suit each) along with a
theological one.[35] Expertise in cult song was an avenue to political influence for Lasus of Hermione at Athens: he composed dithyrambs for the
Athenians and advised the Peisistratids on the administration of Dionysiac cult.[36] Tradition linked Lasus with Xenophanes. In fact, this story (A
16 DK), in which Xenophanes finds a high-minded way of declining the
other's challenge to gamble at dice, could well have taken place at a feast.
But happily, we do not need to speculate further to see how Xenophanes
comported himself on such occasions.

---

[31] Burkert 1972a: 149–50, and Dodds 1957: ch. 5.

[32] On Thaletas, see [Plutarch] *De Musica* 1146b–c (= Pratinas *TrGF* 4 F 9); Campbell
1982–93: vol. 2, Thaletas testimonium 4, and cf. testimonia 5–7, 9.

[33] *Suda* M 701 = Terpander testimonium 9, Campbell 1982–93, 2: 301, with n. 1.

[34] Aristotle *Rhetoric* 1400b5; cf. the "floating" anecdotes from Plutarch collected at A
13 DK and Heraclitus B 127 DK. The story (A 1.20) that Xenophanes buried his son with
his own hands may express a rejection of traditional funeral rites.

[35] Heraclitus B 5, 15 DK; cf. Burkert 1985: 339; Sider in Laks and Most 1997: 145–46.
Xenophanes also referred to Bacchic cult in his lampoons (B 17 DK).

[36] On Lasus, see D'Angour 1997; and on his dithyrambs, Seaford 1977–78: 83 n. 1;
Barker 1984: 59 n. 20. On Peisistratid ministers of culture, see Shapiro 1990: 341–42.

Fr. 1: Xenophanes at the Feast

The twenty-four elegiac verses labeled Xenophanes fr. 1[37] may be regarded as a complete poem in the sense that they represent a coherent and nicely balanced "speech" that could be performed after dinner.[38] The first half describes the setting, as the speaker rises at the moment when the dinner has been cleared away and the music that had accompanied it still rings in the hall:[39]

νῦν γὰρ δὴ ζάπεδον καθαρὸν καὶ χεῖρες ἁπάντων
    καὶ κύλικες· πλεκτοὺς δ' ἀμφιτιθεῖ στεφάνους,
ἄλλος δ' εὐῶδες μύρον ἐν φιάληι παρατείνει·
    κρητὴρ δ' ἕστηκεν μεστὸς ἐυφροσύνης,
ἄλλος δ' οἶνος ἑτοῖμος, ὃς οὔποτέ φησι προδώσειν,   5
    μείλιχος ἐν κεράμοισ' ἄνθεος ὀζόμενος·
ἐν δὲ μέσοις ἁγνὴν ὀδμὴν λιβανωτὸς ἵησι·
    ψυχρὸν δ' ἔστιν ὕδωρ καὶ γλυκὺ καὶ καθαρόν·
παρκέαται δ' ἄρτοι ξανθοὶ γεραρή τε τράπεζα
    τυροῦ καὶ μέλιτος πίονος ἀχθομένη·   10
βωμὸς δ' ἄνθεσιν ἀν τὸ μέσον πάντηι πεπύκασται,
    μολπὴ δ' ἀμφὶς ἔχει δώματα καὶ θαλίη.

For now the floor is clean, as are the hands of all,
    and the cups; one [servant] places plaited garlands on us,
while another proffers fragrant myrrh in a dish;
    the mixing bowl is in place, brimming with festivity,
and other wine stands ready, promising never to run out on us,   5
    mild in its jars, giving out its bouquet.
In our midst, frankincense wafts its holy scent;
    and there is water, cool, sweet, and clean;
at hand are golden loaves and a lordly table,
    groaning with cheese and thick honey;   10
the altar in the middle has been decked on all sides with flowers,
    and song and celebration fill the hall.

[37] I have followed the text of West's *IEG*; bibliography on the poem: Marcovich 1978: 2 n. 2, to which add Adkins 1985, Lesher 1992, and Rösler 1980a: 33 ff.

[38] Bowra (1953: 1) found it "almost complete," pointing to the transitional flavor of the initial νῦν γὰρ δή; so, too, Ziegler 1965: 292 n. 1. But Rösler (1980a: 81 n. 126) argues that the opening is designed to give these generalities a connection to the particular occasion; for γὰρ δή as an arresting opening, see Denniston 1934: 243. The ending is discussed below.

[39] So I take *molpē* in 12, as often in the *Odyssey*, e.g., 1. 152; cf. 9.6–7. For the difficulties, see Herter 1956: 36, and for other interpretations, Marcovich 1978: 9–10.

In setting the scene, Xenophanes gives something more than a snapshot of a dining hall.[40] The details speak a great deal about the people in attendance. The rare myrrh and frankincense (not found in epic but to be met in the lyrics of Archilochus of Paros and Sappho of Lesbos) show that Eastern styles of luxury have reached this party.[41] But touches of epic-style language depict this symposium as a legitimate descendant of the heroic banquets in epic. The "lordly" (γεραρή) table suggests the heroic "prize of honor" (γέρας), the war booty awarded to a chief or great fighter.[42] The speaker thereby connects his host's munificence with heroic magnificence, as if the elegant furnishings of the dining hall were glorious treasures won at war.[43] The party is clearly deluxe, yet still in the good Greek tradition, and Xenophanes evokes the archaic standard of nobility as joining wealth, unstinting generosity, and scrupulous observance of form. It need hardly be added that such an opening also demonstrates the worthiness of the speaker for the role of honored guest. From this point of view, the poem is a companion piece to 2 IEG, though here Xenophanes will deploy "our wisdom" on the microcosmic level of describing the ideal drinking party.

In the second half the speaker offers suggestions for organizing the party, outlining the kinds of prayer and song to be performed:[44]

χρὴ δὲ πρῶτον μὲν θεὸν ὑμνεῖν εὔφρονας ἄνδρας
εὐφήμοις μύθοις καὶ καθαροῖσι λόγοις·
σπείσαντάς τε καὶ εὐξαμένους τὰ δίκαια δύνασθαι   15
πρήσσειν· ταῦτα γὰρ ὦν ἐστι προχειρότερον,
οὐχ ὕβρεις· πίνειν δ᾽ ὁπόσον κεν ἔχων ἀφίκοιο
οἴκαδ᾽ ἄνευ προπόλου μὴ πάνυ γηραλέος.

[40] Cf. Lissarague 1987: esp. 31 ff.

[41] Cf. Theognis 474: οὐ πάσας νύκτας γίνεται ἁβρὰ παθεῖν ("Not every night do we get to revel in luxury"). On habrosunē, see Bowra 1941: 123–24, and, more fully, Kurke 1992. Cf. Xenophanes against Colophonian luxury (3 IEG, discussed in chapter 1), and Critias (6 IEG) in praise of the restrained drinking practices of Lacedaimonia over those of Lydia.

[42] The line-ending γεραρή τε τράπεζα may be deliberate heroizing of an epic line-ending calling a banquet table "fine" or "elegant" (e.g., Od. 8.69: πὰρ δ᾽ ἐτίθει κάνεον καλήν τε τράπεζαν; cf. Iliad 11.628–29). Gentili and Prato (1979: ad loc.) compare Xenophanes 1.1 with Iliad 10.173, and Xenophanes 1.15 with Iliad 16.253; cf., too, παρκέαται in Xenophanes 1.9 with Homer's προκείμενα of the foodstuffs lying at hand in Od. 8.71.

[43] It may be that the compliment is leavened with humor: as Homer applies the adjective gerarēs only to persons, Xenophanes' phrase personifies the loaded table, a hero staggering from the assembly laden with plunder. It is good form to praise a host's "plate" (χαλκώματα) at Aristophanes Wasps 1214.

[44] The transition after line 12 is noted by all except Herter (1956: 37), who offers a tripartite division unconvincingly dependent on a change of time after line 7; Marcovich (1978: 1–3) subdivides further into elaborately parallel quatrains.

ἀνδρῶν δ' αἰνεῖν τοῦτον ὃς ἐσθλὰ πιὼν ἀναφαίνει,
   ὡς ἦι μνημοσύνη καὶ τόνος ἀμφ' ἀρετῆς,   20
οὔ τι μάχας διέπειν Τιτήνων οὐδὲ Γιγάντων
   οὐδέ ⟨τι⟩ Κενταύρων, πλάσματα τῶν προτέρων,
ἢ στάσιας σφεδανάς· τοῖσ' οὐδὲν χρηστὸν ἔνεστι·
   θεῶν ⟨δὲ⟩ προμηθείην αἰὲν ἔχειν ἀγαθήν.

Now it behooves men at feast first to hymn the god
   with reverent speech and purified tales
after they have made libations and prayed to be able to achieve   15
   what is just; for this in truth is our task at hand—
not acts of violence. And each must drink only so much as to get back
   home without a servant guiding the way, except if he be very old.
As for the guests, applaud him who gives a show of nobility when drinking
   so there may be recollection of and striving after excellence,   20
one who does not summon up battles of Titans, Giants,
   or Centaurs—fabrications of men of old—
or violent civil strife; in such things there is no profit.
But always keep a good consideration for the gods.[45]

Purity now emerges as the keynote of the speech: the room, the utensils,
and the participants have all been "cleansed" or "purified" (*katharos*, 1),
and "pure" water (8) waits to be mixed with the wine to transform "raw"
drinking into an act of culture, civilized and ritually correct.[46] So, too,
the speech to come must be "pure" and "reverent," or "of good omen"
(*euphēmos*, 14).[47] Xenophanes divides this second half into two equal and
balanced parts, so that the songs and prayers addressed to the gods (*men*,
13) are set beside the round of singing by the guests (*de*, 19). This suggests
that, at this occasion under the gods, one should purify one's drinking

[45] My translation of line 20 follows West 1974: 189. On the text at the end, see Heitsch
1994: 98–99.

[46] A paradigm of "raw" drinking is the *Odyssey*'s lawless Cyclops, who takes his wine
neat. Xenophanes discusses how to mix wine at B 5 DK.

[47] I take the pairing of εὐφήμοις μύθοις and καθαροῖσι λόγοις in line 14 as pleonastic,
since *muthos* does not yet mean "false story." Parmenides (B 2.1 DK) and Empedocles (B
23.11 DK) offer *muthoi* from a god, and Pindar has to specify when *muthoi* are "decked
out in fancy lies" (δεδαιδαλμένοι ψεύδεσι ποικίλοις ἐξαπατῶντι μῦθοι, *Olympian* 1.28–29;
cf. *Nemean*. 7.23, 8.33). Bowra (1953: 4 n. 4 and 6 n. 1) rightly noted that the Platonic
opposition between false *muthoi* and true *logoi* (as in *Protagoras* 320c, *Gorgias* 535a, *Timaeus* 26e, *Phaedo* 61b) need not apply at this time, but I do not see much point in his
proposed distinction between *logoi*, the "themes, subjects" of song, and *muthoi*, "tales,"
possibly true or untrue. Marcovich (1978: 9) imports a rhetorical distinction when he takes
logoi as "form" and *muthoi* as "content." Gentili and Prato (1979: ad loc.) assign the *muthoi* to prayers and *logoi* to narratives, but *muthos* is frequently used of talk at table: e.g.,
Od. 4.238–39, 597–98, 21.291; Hesiod fr. 274 M-W.

songs in the same way, and perhaps for the same reasons, as one avoids ill-omened speech in prayers, paeans, and libations.

But purification becomes literary criticism for commentators who connect Xenophanes' rejection of songs about Titans, Giants, and Centaurs with his theological views: fr. 1 thereby becomes a practical recommendation to banish from symposia the adulterous and thieving gods in Homer's and Hesiod's tales.[48] This goes too far too fast. These monstrous creatures hardly point specifically to the poetry of Homer, in whom they are little present, or to Hesiod.[49] One might think of sixth-century "cyclic" epic, which did expand on stories of Titanomachy and Gigantomachy (apparently with some relish), but even so, Xenophanes' target is wider and includes songs that awaken contemporary "civic strife" (stasias). This kind of song can be exemplified in Alcaeus' skolia against Pittacus, his peer and rival in the city, whom he abuses for his barbaric ("Scythian") drunkenness.[50] The fact that Xenophanes' proscriptions are broader than epic suggests that we should think of the Titans and Giants not as tokens of any particular poetic genre, but as stories of superhuman strife that provided a mythic paradigm for destructive aristocratic infighting.[51] So, too, the Centaurs (who did battle with Heracles in the Cycle) seem particularly relevant here as symbols of violent incivility at a feast,[52] a paradigmatic role they already fill in the Odyssey: with a great deal of irony, the story of their drunk and disorderly conduct at Perithous' wedding

---

[48] Lanata 1963: 113–14 gives crude equivalences: Giants and Titans = Theogony; Centaurs and Lapiths = Shield of Heracles 178–90. Fränkel (1975: 328) says Xenophanes "reminds us of Homer—and consigns the rhapsodes' tradition to the rubbish heap." Reinhardt (1916: 132 ff.) views the poem in terms of Xenophanes' competition with rhapsodes.

[49] The Titans are mentioned once in Homer (Iliad. 14.279); for Titanomachy, cf. Hesiod Theogony 629, and 209 for the play on τιταίνοντες. The Giants are referred to at Od. 7.59, and the Centaurs in Iliad. 1.267–68, 2.743–44; at 11.832; Cheiron is called "the most just among the Centaurs."

[50] On stasias, I follow Kranz (in app. to 21 B 1.23 DK); Herter 1956: 45–47; and Bowra 1941: 126. Contra Gentili and Prato (1979: ad loc.), who approve Havelock's interpretation of the word as alluding to the erin theōn in Hesiod's Theogony (705, 710, cf. 637). Russell (1981: 88) suggests a reference to the strife and wrath of the Iliad. But for sympotic and political stasis poetry, cf. Solon 4.17–22; Alcaeus 70 V; Theognis 39–52, 1081–82b, and the first Attic skolion (884.3 PMG) in which Athena is invoked in part to ward off "griefs and staseis."

[51] Cf. Bowra 1953: 10, 13; Herter 1956: 46–47; Svenbro 1984a: 98. If struggles in heaven were paradigmatic for political struggles, Marcovich (1978: 11–13) need not distinguish between political and theological reasons for the ban. Kannicht (1989: 38) is anachronistic, taking staseis as newly created, as opposed to "transmitted," strife songs.

[52] As noted by Babut 1974: 102–3. Many compare the Centaurs' battles against Heracles (Bowra 1953: 10; Herter 1956: 46–47; Ziegler 1965: 294), but their fight with the Lapiths (Iliad 1.267–68, 2.743–44; Od. 21.295–304) is at least as relevant to a feast.

feast is recounted at table by the criminal suitor Antinous.[53] Xenophanes' songs of war are not allusions to epic but symbols of the intragroup aggressiveness that the ceremony is designed to control.

It follows that Xenophanes is objecting to the *fighting* involved in Gigantomachies and the like rather than to blasphemy per se. This is confirmed by his summary judgment in 23 that songs of violence, whether human or divine, are "useless" or "unprofitable" (not *khrēston*).[54] Like any symposiast, Xenophanes wants singing that is conducive to social harmony. The value of solidarity was playfully introduced in verse 5, where the wine waiting to be mixed is called "trusty" (ἕτοιμος) and promises it will never "run out" on the company (ὃς οὔποτέ φησι προδώσειν).[55]

Xenophanes fr. 1, then, like fr. 2, is interested in promoting "good civil order" (*eunomiē*) and spreading the right kind of joy (*kharma*), with prosperity as the end result. Like other sympotic poets, Xenophanes proscribes themes that break the orderly, festive, and prudent mood that should prevail in the houses and the city. As such, his songs offered truly useful advice as he wandered through the cities of south Italy and Sicily, where nobles vied with each other for eminence, even as they kept an eye on the native populations inland and on the Carthaginians to the west and south. His view of a "purified" symposium instructs elites in strengthening their exclusivity and solidarity while maintaining a facade of piety and restraint. His rejection of bellicose myths of old along with contemporary songs of a revolutionary flavor stems from social and political as well as theological scruples.[56]

Xenophanes' theology and its radical anti-anthropomorphism come into play in this song in a single but significant word: in an unprecedented metaphor, he calls stories of Titans and the like "fashionings" of men of

---

[53] There is further irony in that Alcinous' speech is appropriate to the situation as he sees it: he uses the exemplum to dissuade the beggar-Odysseus, whom he supposes has drunk too much, from picking up the bow (*Od.* 21.305–10).

[54] *khrēston* is perhaps first used here, which led Bowra (1953: 10–11) to suggest that Xenophanes is revising aristocratic values. Gentili and Prato (1979): gloss "*utilis civitati,*" comparing Xenophanes 2.14–22 and Simonides' "justice that benefits a city" (ὀνησίπολον δίκαν, 542.35 *PMG*. On *khrēstos*, see Dover 1993: 212, 1987–88, 2:10–11, and 1974: 296–99; cf. "useful advice" in Aristophanes: *Birds* 1449, *Knights* 86, *Lysistrata* 648, *Frogs* 686–87, 1035, and 1057, advice to the city concerning the aristocratic party-goer Alcibiades. Marcovich (1978: 12) compares the "useless" (ἀνωφελεάς) ways of luxury that Colophon learned from the Lydians (3.1 *IEG*).

[55] The pun has been questioned, but cf. the Attic scholia 908 *PMG* (*mē prodidōsin*) and 907 *PMG* (*Leipsudrion prodōsetairon*); for *hetoimos* as "trusty," "reliable," cf. Aeschylus *Agamemnon* 842, LSJ s.v. II.

[56] Babut (1974) takes Xenophanes' critiques of singers in frs. 10–12 as essentially social, for epic gods are *lawless* (cf. *athemistia erga*, B 12 DK; B 11 DK: ὀνείδεα καὶ ψόγος).

old (πλάσματα τῶν προτέρων). The phrase invidiously adapts a traditional epic expression for oral traditions about the glorious deeds of heroes, "fames of men of long ago" (κλεῖα προτέρων ἀνθρώπων).[57] Xenophanes redescribes these oral traditions (*klea* is literally "what one hears") as *plasmata*, "fabrications," or "fashionings": the metaphor suggestively connects singers' false tales with the false, anthropomorphic images of divinity that are sculpted and painted by men.[58] The heroic "men of old," doers of famed deeds, are replaced by the "old-fashioned" singers who produced such songs, unenlightened types, if not primitive and gullible. A taste for such poetry is crude and outdated, more suited to men of the ancient bronze age described by Hesiod, "who concerned themselves with the groanful works of Ares and with hubris."[59] Xenophanes 1 offers symposiasts a new standard for refinement in singing rather than a lecture in theology.[60] It is a song to sustain the threatened elite culture of the late archaic age by urging them to modernize—with all due wisdom and piety—their traditions of peaceful leisure.

To Purify the Language of the Tribe

We saw in the previous chapter that Xenophanes' theme—the well-ordered feast—can be traced back as far as Homer. He was not the first to reject riotous sympotic song, and the "mindfulness" of excellence (*mnēmosune*, 1.20) he enjoins is *euphrosunē*. The whole is not far from Anacreon's recommendation to "keep one's mind on charming festivity" (ἐρατῆς μνήσκεται εὐφροσύνης, fr. Eleg. 2.4 *IEG*)[61] as he shuns the man who sings of quarrels and war. To refer Xenophanes 1 to sympotic traditions is not, however, to deprive it of significance. Its insistence on piety, even if traditional, is sustained, as is usefully underscored by a now-discarded interpretation of the poem. Hans Herter drew attention to the Pythagorean flavor of the final line: Xenophanes' closing injunction to

---

[57] Hesiod *Theogony* 100; cf. *Iliad* 9. 189, *Homeric Hymn to Apollo* 160.

[58] Cf. again B 15, further discussed in chapter 5. For "fabricating" and falsehood, e.g., Herodotus 1.68.5, [Aeschylus] *Prometheus Bound* 1030.

[59] *Works and Days* 145–46: οἷσιν Ἄρεος / ἔργ' ἔμελε στονόεντα καὶ ὕβριες, cited on Xenophanes 1.17 by West.

[60] It is at a banquet that Telemachus says the "newest" songs are preferred: *Od.* 1.351–52. Cf. Pindar *Olympian* 9.48–49: "Praise wine that is old but flowers of song that are new."

[61] Cf. Theognis 1055 ("Let that *logos* go as you pipe to me and let us remember the Muses together"), and for examples of "forgetting" one's manners, Panyassis 16 *PEG* (12 Ki), Critias 6.11 *IEG*; Rösler 1990: 230–31.

"keep a good consideration for the gods" resembles the (late reported) prayer at the end of Pythagorean banquets that all "keep a reverent and good consideration for the God, the Divine Power, and the heroes."[62] On this basis, fr. 1 has been read as describing an unusual kind of drinking party, a meeting of sages with a very highly developed sense of purity.[63] Other details fall into line: the table is "lordly" because it contains offerings to the gods,[64] the "sacred" frankincense is a bloodless sacrifice, the *euphronas andres* are the pious, and their prayer "to be *able to be* just" reflects advanced theological ideals.[65] As for Xenophanes' view of song, tradition held that between reincarnations, Pythagoras saw Homer and Hesiod on the rack in Hades for telling lies about the gods.[66]

This interpretation also goes too far: any drinking party was a ritual that, when well carried out, merited the epithet "pure," and elsewhere (7a *IEG*) Xenophanes poked fun at Pythagorean ideas of reincarnation. Yet I think Herter is right that Xenophanes has borrowed Pythagorean language at the end of his song.[67] The phrase is also adapted, for another context, in the pseudo-Platonic *Minos*: discussing praising and blaming in general, Socrates warns that ignorant poets cannot be trusted on the all-important question of whom to praise: "You must exercise a great deal of forethought always, whenever you set out to praise or blame a man, lest

[62] Iamblichus *Life of Pythagoras* 100: περὶ τοῦ θεοῦ καὶ περὶ τοῦ δαιμονίου καὶ περὶ τοῦ ἡρωικοῦ γέους εὔφημόν τε καὶ ἀγαθὴν ἔχειν διάνοιαν. Noted by Herter (1956: 37). The hierarchized triad here seems to reflect the triple sympotic libations to Zeus, the Olympians, and the heroes. Marcovich (1978: 15–16) objects that the phrase may have been circulating more widely, and Schäfer (1996: 200–201) judges the reference uncertain. Still, Xenophanes certainly knew of Pythagoras (7a *IEG*).

[63] Herter (1956), for whom (47) Xenophanes was the central figure or founder of the group addressed in fr. 1; a thesis much expanded by Defradas (1962), and cf. Schäfer 1996: 193–97. Vetta (1983: xlix) agrees with Defradas on the solemn tone, but suggests the song may have been intended for the ears of a figure like Simonides' apparently open-minded patron, Scopas. Bowra (1953: 13–14) puts Xenophanes in a society of nobles liberal enough to hear out his unusual doctrines; Reinhardt (1916: 126–27) takes Xenophanes as the "Gast eines grossen Herrn" and Svenbro (1984a) posits a Rhegine oligarch; this seems to me to fit his oeuvre better than Morris' (1996) view of Xenophanes as a "middling" poet not affiliated with the Orientalizing aristocracy.

[64] Defradas' "une table d'offrandes" (1962): 348, 355) is rejected by Marcovich (1978: 5), who suggests the epithet is used because the table holds bread, "the holy γέρας of Demeter."

[65] On Xenophanes' prayer (1.15–17), Marcovich (1978: 8) thinks Xenophanes "radically differs from the authors of traditional prayers" in asking for an *intellectual* capacity, citing Ziegler 1965: 293: "die innere Kraft zum sittlchen Handeln." Fränkel (1975: 327 n. 5) joins material and moral purification; Defradas (1962: 358–59) a prayer for efficacious "grace."

[66] Hieronymus of Rhodes 42 Wehrli (DL 8.21).

[67] *Pace* Fränkel (1975: 328), the Pythagorean phrase makes a nice close and produces a ring-structure: Marcovich 1978: 4.

you get this wrong."[68] Like Xenophanes, Socrates introduces a "respectful regard" for the superhuman as crucial in correctly attaching praise and blame, and Socrates suggestively denies such wisdom to poets. What is wrong with the broader interpretation is that Xenophanes' song is precisely not a song for a close circle of fellow believers of the Pythagorean type; it is a broadly applicable model of high-minded feasting.[69] Xenophanes' determination to be moderate, just, and scrupulous in dealing with the gods as well as with his fellows conforms to conventional aristocratic piety. His prayer "to be able to be just" and avoid hubris is fully consonant with the motto in a *skolion*, "loving the fair and having the power to get it."[70] One does not have to abandon the panhellenic culture of civilized feasting to have a refined symposium. Xenophanes speaks as a god-fearing man, without insisting on his own specific version of divinity.

The "purity" or refinement Xenophanes exhibits in this variation on a theme can be clarified from parallels in other forms of song. Bowra suggested that public festivals were the source of sympotic poetry's stigmatization of bellicose songs.[71] Peace is, after all, the first requirement for a festival, and it was apparently at a festival that Stesichorus, who was capable of setting heroic battles to music, asked his Muses to "thrust aside wars" in favor of celebrating "the marriages of gods, the banquets of

---

[68] [Plato] *Minos* 318E–319A: ἀλλὰ πάνυ πολλὴν χρὴ προμήθειαν ποιεῖσθαι ἀεὶ, ταν μέλλῃς ἄνδρα ψέγειν ἢ ἐπαινέσθαι, μὴ οὐκ ὀρθῶς εἴπῃς. For earlier uses of the word, cf. *Iliad* 16.388, Herodotus 9.76.2, and Pindar *Olympian* 7.44 (note the sympotic opening of the song): "*Aidōs*, born of forethought (*promatheos*), brings *kharmata* to men," with Xenophanes' *kharma* in 2.20 *IEG*. On *Isthmian* 1.40b, where forethought comes in the wake of such reversals in life as shipwrecks (ὁ πονήσας δὲ νόῳ καὶ προμάθειαν φέρει), see Bundy 1986: 52 n. 44.

[69] Bowra (1953: 13) is misleading in saying that fr. 1 was "sung at some serious dinner party at which the poet was in charge": such prescriptions need not come only from a symposiarch, as is indicated by the anonymous elegist 27.9 *IEG*. In Plato's *Symposium*, where Agathon is the host, Pausanias "begins the conversation" (*logou . . . katarkhein*) by asking the company how they would like to conduct the drinking (176A); as Dover (1980: 11) notes, Eryximachus more or less elects himself symposiarch, and reasserts himself after Alcibiades' intrusive "I elect myself *archōn* of the drinking" (213E).

[70] χαίρειν τε καλοῖσι καὶ δύνασθαι, 986 *PMG*. Cited by Reinhardt (1916: 126–27). Bowra (1953: 7–8) seems right to interpret Xenophanes' *ta dikaia* as "to do what is accepted by aristocrats as excellent." Cf. Fränkel 1975: 418 with n. 40 and 474; and Gerber 1982: 157: "Mere knowledge, however, of what is *kalon* is not enough; one must also have the *dunamis* to put this knowledge into practice." With Xenophanes' προχειρότερον (1.15–17), cf. Bacchylides 14.8–17 S-M (esp. 10, τὰ] πὰρ χειρὸς κυβέρνασεν δι]καίαισι φρένεσσιν) and Pindar *Pythian* 3.20–23 (esp. 59–60 for "before our feet") and *Isthmian*. 8.12, with Slater 1976–77.

[71] Bowra 1953: 12, citing *Od.* 21.258–60. Cf. Reitzenstein 1893: 49 ff. (citing *Od.* 4.193–94); so, too, in Archilochus' poem to Pericles (13 *IEG*): no citizen will blame κήδεα στονόεντα (as in *Od.* 9.12).

men, and the feasts of the blessed."[72] Xenophanes' insistence on pious (*euphēmos*) speech may then be viewed as importing into the symposium the city's need for auspicious rituals. But already by this time, metaphors are likely to have been flowing between the two contexts, and the basic posture of the speaker we find in fr. 1 was widely adapted thereafter. In the Athenian theater, Aeschylus prayed for the city's prosperity: "May singers lay songs of good omen upon the altars, and let the voice that loves the lyre be borne from holy mouths" (εὔφημον δ' ἐπὶ βωμοῖς / μοῦσαν θείατ' ἀοιδοί / ἁγνῶν τ' ἐκ στομάτων φερ- / έσθω φάμα φιλοφόρμιγξ, *Suppliants*, 694–97). Purified speech was also offered by Empedocles, praying that the gods would "turn madness away from our lips" and "pour out the pure stream from holy mouths" as he discoursed on nature and the gods.[73] He ended an invocation to his Muse, "Be with me once again as I pray, Calliope, and bring to light a good account of the blessed gods."[74]

A passage in the Theognidea goes so far as to suggest that to purify the language of the symposium is to save the city. The song seems to have been composed around the end of Xenophanes' life, when the East was encroaching yet again:

> Ζεὺς μὲν τῆσδε πόληος ὑπειρέχοι αἰθέρι ναίων
>   αἰεὶ δεξιτερὴν χεῖρ' ἐπ' ἀπημοσύνηι,
> ἄλλοι τ' ἀθάνατοι μάκαρες θεοί· αὐτὰρ Ἀπόλλων
>   ὀρθώσαι γλῶσσαν καὶ νόον ἡμέτερον.
> φόρμιγξ δ' αὖ φθέγγοιθ' ἱερὸν μέλος ἠδὲ καὶ αὐλός·
>   ἡμεῖς δὲ σπονδὰς θεοῖσιν ἀρεσσάμενοι
> πίνωμεν, χαρίεντα μετ' ἀλλήλοισι λέγοντες,
>   μηδὲν τὸν Μήδων δειδιότες πόλεμον.

> May Zeus, ever on high, hold his right hand over this city
>   as a guarantee of its safety,
> together with the other immortals; but may Apollo
>   make straight our tongue and thoughts.
> Let the lyre send out its sacred music, and the *aulos*;
>   as for us, when we have made libations to the gods,
> let us drink, speaking gracefully among each other
>   without fear of war from the Medes.[75]

---

[72] 210 *PMG*: Μοῖσα σὺ μὲν πολέμους ἀπωσαμένα πεδ' ἐμοῦ / κλείοισα θεῶν τε γάμους ἀνδρῶν τε δαίτας / καὶ θαλίας μακάρων.

[73] B 3.1–2 DK: ἀλλὰ θεοὶ τῶν μὲν μανίην ἀποτρέψατε γλώσσης, / ἐκ δ' ὁσίων στομάτων καθαρὴν ὀχετεύσατε πηγήν.

[74] B 131.3–4 DK: εὐχομένωι νῦν αὖτε παρίστασο, Καλλιόπεια, / ἀμφὶ θεῶν μακάρων ἀγαθὸν λόγον ἐμφαίνοντι. Cf. Burkert 1987b: 70 n. 15.

[75] Theognis 757–64. Fear of the Medes in a Megarian song is usually thought to be more appropriate to the time of Darius or Xerxes than to the mid-sixth century.

Like Xenophanes 1, this speech is set amid the preliminary sympotic rites, and indeed would have been quite appropriate as one of the opening prayers. The Olympians and their chief, Zeus, are invoked to preserve the city, and Apollo—as god of the paean and of bands of young men, and as purifier—is asked to "make straight" their tongues and minds, to purify their speech and thought. This call for ritual correctness suggests that "speaking gracefully among each other" may somehow help keep the Medes at bay.

Against such impending evils, symposia may be, at any rate, the best mortals may do. The lines that follow in the collection recommend the same strategy for coping with other pressing ills:[76]

> ὧδ᾿ εἶναι καὶ ἄμεινον εὔφρονα θυμὸν ἔχοντας
> νόσφι μεριμνάων εὐφροσύνως διάγειν
> τερπομένους, τηλοῦ δὲ κακὰς ἀπὸ κῆρας ἀμῦναι
> γῆράς τ᾿ οὐλόμενον καὶ θανάτοιο τέλος.

> So it is better, keeping a festive heart
>   with cares removed to pass the time in feasting
> with pleasure, keeping evil fates far at bay,
>   accursed old age and the end of death.

The singers may be optimistic about song, but are undoubtedly pious. For mortals who recognize their limits, pleasure can be the wise choice: "Now as we drink, let us take pleasure in speaking fair / as for what will come hereafter, that concerns the gods" (νῦν μὲν πίνοντες τερπώμεθα, καλὰ λέγοντες· / ἄσσα δ᾿ ἔπειτ᾿ ἔσται, ταῦτα θεοῖσι μέλει, Theognis 1047–48).

Like these singers, Xenophanes associates "fair speaking" with recognizing the divine. His closing Pythagorean watchword, then, borrowed from cults and sects their allure as mysterious, exclusive societies. His adoption of a religiously scrupulous tone in recommending refined and up-to-date song can be seen in exaggerated form in Aristophanes, who frequently toyed with mystery formulas.[77] A revealing comparison may be taken from *Frogs*, where the chorus of Dionysiac initiates addresses the audience in a parody of ritual proclamations (*Frogs* 354–60):

> εὐφημεῖν χρὴ κἀξίστασθαι τοῖς ἡμετέροισι χοροῖσιν,
> ὅστις ἄπειρος τοιῶνδε λόγων ἢ γνώμην μὴ καθαρεύει,   355
> ἢ γενναίων ὄργια Μουσῶν μήτ᾿ εἶδεν μήτ᾿ ἐχόρευσεν,
> μηδὲ Κρατίνου τοῦ ταυροφάγου γλώττης Βακχεῖ᾿ ἐτελέσθη,

---

[76] Theognis 765–68, taken as continuous with the preceding by Young (1961), who punctuates after ὧδ᾿ εἶναι.

[77] E.g., *Acharnians* 237–44; *Thesmophoriazusae* 39–44, 295–311; *Clouds* 263; *Wasps* 860–74; *Peace* 96–101, 1316–57. See Hubbard 1991: 118, 203–5.

ἢ βωμολόχοις ἔπεσιν χαίρει μὴ 'ν καιρῷ τοῦτο ποιοῦσιν,
ἢ στάσιν ἐχθρὰν μὴ καταλύει μηδ᾽ εὔκολός ἐστι πολίταις,
ἀλλ᾽ ἀνεγείρει καὶ ῥιπίζει κερδῶν ἰδίων ἐπιθυμῶν . . .   360

Avoid ill-omened talk and stand back from our choruses,
whoever is without experience of such speech, who has not been purified
   in mind,
who has neither looked upon nor danced the rites of the noble Muses,
nor been initiated into the Bacchic rites of Cratinus' bull-devouring tongue;
or whoever takes pleasure in buffoonish language with no regard for
   the occasion,
or does not break down hated civic strife and is not gentle to his
   fellow citizens,
but awakens and stirs up strife in his lust after his own advantage. . . .

The conceit running through this speech is to portray the *Frogs* as a secret
rite. Like Xenophanes, the chorus uses charged language in their demand
(354: *khrē*, as in Xenophanes 1.13; Euripides fr. 282.23 Nauck; Eleg.
anon. 27.3 *IEG*) for pious speech (354: *euphēmein*, cf. Xenophanes 1.14)
and purity of mind (355: *katharos*, cf. Xenophanes 1.1, 8, 14). Having
his cake and eating it, Aristophanes plays upon the bombastic rhetoric of
old comic poets like Cratinus (357) to connect comedy with the mumbo-
jumbo of mystery language. For the democratic poet, being "initiated"
(357) requires nothing more than attending the city's annual performances of comedy at Dionysiac festivals. Democratic and comic as well
are the profane catalogued in the lines following this extract, corrupt politicians and rival poets. Like bad symposiasts, they spoil rites with buffoonish talk (*bōmolokhia*, 358) and have no regard for the *kairos*. Aristophanes, like Xenophanes, banishes these inept performers on the
grounds that they encourage civic strife (359: *stasis*; cf. Xenophanes 1.23)
and are not gentle to fellow citizens. Allowing for Aristophanes' humor,
much the same is going on in Xenophanes 1: both singers evoke the air
of the mysteries to call for purified song in the name of communal good.

This prescriptive pose, including its right to weigh in on matters of
speechifying, remained recognizable and potent. Euripides stressed the
benefits of fair speech in a passage that is close to a parody of Xenophanes
1 (fr. 282.23–28 Nauck):

> ἄνδρας χρὴ σοφούς τε κἀγαθοὺς
> φύλλοις στέφεσθαι, χὥστις ἡγεῖται πόλει
> κάλλιστα σώφρων καὶ δίκαιος ὢν ἀνήρ,
> ὅστις τε μύθοις ἔργ᾽ ἀπαλλάσσει κακὰ
> μάχας τ᾽ ἀφαιρῶν καὶ στάσεις· τοιαῦτα γὰρ
> πόλει τε πάσῃ πᾶσί θ᾽ Ἕλλησιν καλά.

It behooves men who are wise and good
to deck themselves out with leaves, whoever thinks
thoughts that are best for the city, and whoever, prudent and just,
removes ill deeds with his speech
and takes away battles and *staseis*; such things
are fine for the whole city, and for the whole of Greece.

These are but a sample of passages that reaffirm the basic archaic distinction between bellicose and festive singing. In the *Contest of Homer and Hesiod*, Hesiod wins an epic contest with Homer because he "calls us to farming and peace," while Homer recounts "tales of war and slaughter" (τὸν πόλεμον καὶ σφαγὰς, Allen V 233.205–9). The same terms lead to an opposite outcome in Aristophanes' *Frogs*, when Aeschylus is chosen over Euripides because the former's bombastic, militaristic poetry prepares the kind of citizen a beleaguered Athens needs. So, too, Pindar, who in the generation after Xenophanes used the Giants as a foil for his own pious song, advised princes that the most scrupulous deportment avoids reckless slander against the gods no less than against other men.[78] Like Xenophanes, Pindar honors powerful men for their piety and "pure" minds.[79]

The quest for more purified manners continued in late fifth- and early fourth-century representations of sophisticated drinking parties: Xenophanes' mannerly tone in fr. 1 (and in fr. 2 as well) is reprised in Xenophon's *Symposium*, representing a banquet given by the wealthy Athenian Callias. Toward the beginning of the work, Callias is eager that Socrates and his circle attend his banquet because "I am of the belief that the provisions I have made will shine the more brilliantly in the company of men who have purified their souls with philosophy than it would among generals and captains."[80] In classical Athens, the powerfully influential board of generals has replaced the athlete on the A-list of guests, but some of those with social ambition have been persuaded to prefer the "thoroughly refined, spiritual" (ἐκκεκαθαρμένοις τὰς ψυχὰς) company of wise men.[81] Of

[78] E.g., *Pythian* 1–20, 8.12; *Olympian* 9.40–41; see Slater 1990: esp. 215, and 1981. Cf. Ibycus 310 *PMG*: δέδοικα μή τι πὰρ θεοῖς ἀμβλακὼν τιμὰν πρὸς ἀνθρώπων ἀμείψω.

[79] E.g., *Olympian* 4.14–16, where his hospitable patron is both a horseman and one who has "turned with a pure mind (*katharai gnomai*) toward Peace, friend of cities"; *Olympian* 3.41 (*eusebei gnōmēi*). Cf. Attic *skolion* 901 *PMG*: "Would I were an unfired golden vessel and a virgin carried me with a *katharos noos*."

[80] *Symposium* 1.1.4 : οἶμαι οὖν πολὺ ἄν τὴν κατασκευήν μοι λαμπροτέραν φανῆναι εἰ ἀνδράσιν ἐκκεκαθαρμένοις τὰς ψυχὰς ὥσπερ ὑμῖν ὁ ἀνδὼν κεκοσμημένος εἴη μᾶλλον ἤ εἰ στρατηγοῖς καὶ ἱππάρχοις καὶ σπουδαρχίας.

[81] Socrates is also a reformer of sympotic speech in Xenophon's *Symposium* (3.1–2). In Plato's *Symposium* 176A–177D, after the flute girl is sent away, philosophical, and overtly pious, speeches begin. Cf., too, *Protagoras* 347C–348A. Plato gives the locution a rich Pytha-

course, Callias expects these men to make his possessions shine (λαμπρο-τέραν), even as the "feast of fragrant myrrh" (εὐωδία, 2.3) with which he proposes to regale his guests reminds us of Xenophanes' "fragrant myrrh."[82] Xenophanes' rejection of war songs also finds an echo in fifth-century sympotic etiquette: Aristophanes' *Wasps* presents a scene in which a boor is being primed to make "impressive speeches" before a company of "learned and clever men."[83] His first idea of speaking of Lamia, a folktale ogress, is rejected by his teacher: "Don't tell me stories (*muthous*), but speak about human affairs, the sort of thing we talk about around the hearth."[84] The "myths" are rejected on social rather than theo-logical grounds as men at feast show themselves to be learned and clever.

Xenophanes 1 thus modernizes a tradition—early seen in festival as well as sympotic verse—of pleas for *stasis*-avoiding song. In this context, Plato's metaphysical condemnation of theologically and metaphysically incorrect poetry is yet a further variation, a refinement, on a traditional "generic" opposition, a need to discriminate against songs that harm the city's well-being. As an elegant, wise, and ethical performer, the sage's truest progeny are the gentlemen in Plato's *Symposium*: like Pausanias, Xenophanes intervenes at the moment after libations and paean to discuss the best way of drinking for the night (176A); like the following speakers, he blends a concern for wisdom with piety, and the Platonic: Agathon in fact alludes to (and updates) Xenophanes when he dismisses myths of gods being castrated and imprisoned and "those old stories that Hesiod and Parmenides(!) tell about the gods" (195C).

Xenophanes, then, marks not a point leading directly to Plato, but one moment in the constant refinement of singing styles that went on in elite symposia. In the sixth century, fr. 1 would have enticed its audience as a model of truly refined sympotic speech more than as a serious proposal for literary criticism. His songs about song reminded gracious symposiasts of the need for piety and the dangers of unshared wealth. As I noted above, Xenophanes had to present his ideas in competition with many wise men, and the value he puts on wisdom linked with elegance and propriety was

---

gorean turn in *Phaedo* when he speaks of "those who have been purified by philosophy" (114C); see Halliwell 1986: 187–88.

[82] See Lewis 1995 on perfumes and symposia. The suggestion, topping off flute girls and acrobatics, is of course turned down by the ever-sober Socrates.

[83] *Wasps* 1174–75: ἄγε νυν, ἐπιστήσει λόγους σεμνοὺς λέγειν / ἀνδρῶν παρόντων πολυ-μαθῶν καὶ δεξιῶν.

[84] *Wasps* 1179–80: μὴ 'μοιγε μύθους, ἀλλὰ τῶν ἀνθρωπίνων, / οἵους λέγομεν μάλιστα, τοὺς κατ' οἰκίαν. MacDowell (1982: ad loc.) glosses the last phrase (which Philokleon imme-diately goes on to misconstrue) "fireside stories." *Frogs* draws a similar contrast between Aeschylus' obscure, "bogey-faced" (*mormorōpa*, 925) language and Euripides' clear (*saphes*, 927) and "human" (*anthrōpeiōs*, 1058) speech.

condemned in a suggestive saying of Heraclitus. Heraclitus included Xenophanes among those who lacked true intelligence despite their learning (B 40 DK). Heraclitus offered his own vision of the world "to those who know" in pithy prose aphorisms, which he reportedly deposited in the temple of Artemis at Ephesus. Certainly, his own oracular style of philosophizing had much in common with that of Artemis' brother: "Lord Apollo, whose oracle at Delphi neither speaks nor conceals, but gives signs."[85] Disdaining public show, Heraclitus seems to contrast the true expression of wisdom with philosophizing in elegant table songs in a passage excerpted by Plutarch: "The Sibyl from her raving mouth utters things that are unamusing, unadorned, and unperfumed"; and yet "because of the god," her speaking lasts a thousand years.[86] Without claiming that this passage (which Plutarch adduces to describe the charm of Sappho's poetry) was aimed at Xenophanes, we can say that it takes a swipe at a form of discourse we know, one that dresses itself up, anoints itself with myrrh, and is spoken in a spirit of comity.

When innovative thinkers in the archaic period had something to say about song, a prime place to "publish" their ideas was the symposium, and Xenophanes 1 shows symposia as places to formulate and debate "literary" categories. His proscription of war songs from these events is inseparable from his regulations for ritually correct prayer, pious speech, moderate drink, and correct deportment on the way home. The categories involved are not prose against poetry or elegy against epic, but peace against war, justice against hubris, the new and refined against the old-fashioned and crude. In adding his new new wisdom to a standard sympotic theme, Xenophanes helped symposiasts distinguish themselves not only in their furnishings and decorous comportment, but also in the songs they chose to sing (including songs that gave advice about singing). As we shall see from considering Xenophanes' peers and successors in the next chapter, he was not the last to borrow religious language to portray his musical ideals as valuable, admirable, and not widely known.

---

[85] B 93 DK: ὁ ἄναξ, οὗ τὸ μαντεῖόν ἐστι τὸ ἐν Δελφοῖς, οὔτε λέγει οὔτε κρύπτει ἀλλὰ σημαίνει.

[86] Plutarch *On the Pythian Oracle* 397a (= B 92 DK): Οὐχ ὁρᾶις . . . ὅσην χάριν ἔχει τὰ Σαπφικὰ μέλη, κηλοῦντα καὶ καταθέλγοντα τοὺς ἀκροωμένους; "Σίβυλλα δὲ μαινομένωι στόματι" καθ᾽ Ἡράκλειτον "ἀγέλαστα καὶ ἀκαλλώπιστα καὶ ἀμύριστα φθεγγομένη" χιλίων ἐτῶν ἐξικνεῖται τῆι φωνῆι "διὰ τὸν θεόν."

THREE

ALLEGORY AND THE TRADITIONS OF
EPIC INTERPRETATION

SYMPOTIC and cult songs have been the focus of this study so far because they make the goodness of song an explicit theme. The concern they show for context and occasion and their limited interest in formal aesthetics owed something to the fact that a sympotic verse was often as ephemeral as the party at which it was sung, and the cult hymns brought forth each season were typically composed for that particular occasion and so presented themselves as unique speech acts. In both cases, the enduring verbal artifact behind the performance was hard to extract and appreciate without reference to the felicity of the entire event. But epic was different: in principle repeated exactly from one performance to the next (and indeed, from the performances of Homer himself to the present), these old hexameter tales had a status something like "texts." To be sure, epic was still most widely "published" in oral performance; quite apart from the small demand for epic texts at the time, public, especially festive, performance allowed singers who specialized in epic to bathe their songs in *euphrosunē*, all the while retaining possession of them in some sense, for rhapsodes claimed to have specially authorized versions of the songs that they passed down as sacred possessions, figured as father-to-son inheritances (the Chian rhapsodes called themselves "the Sons of Homer"). Still, at least pieces of the epics were passing out of their hands by the time of Xenophanes and came to be taught in elementary schools, discussed at dinner parties, and debated among those conspicuous experts on language known as sophists. With epic, then, we have a chance to consider a shared archaic song text as it passes through different social contexts.

Epic and its reception in the time of Xenophanes is also a good topic with which to conclude my survey of archaic critical scenes. For Xenophanes fr. 1 is also said to have revolutionized the interpretation of Homer by provoking allegorical defenses from his admirers. To cast light on this obscure moment of literary history, I shall situate epic allegoresis (allegorizing as an interpretative mode) in relation to other forms of exegesis in the late sixth century. Considering them as social practices as well as hermeneutic positions, I hope to make the methods and motives of early allegorists clearer, and also to turn our focus from evaluative to interpreta-

tive criticism. For allegoresis is the first approach we encounter to make
the problem of a text's meaning central—indeed, to make meaning problematic. Finally, as a way of moving from archaic to classical literary cultures, it will be worth following the fortunes of allegory as it interacts in
complex ways with fifth-century sophistry and oracular interpretation,
and as it is ultimately rejected from the techniques of criticism by Plato
and Aristotle in the fourth.

Theagenes and the Rhapsodes

In the last quarter of the sixth century B.C.E., in Rhegium, an old Greek
colony in south Italy, Theagenes wrote a work on Homer, the oldest
known Greek treatise on poetry.[1] Not one word survives from this work,
but it is clear that Theagenes interpreted Homer allegorically. The information comes from a Homeric commentary by Porphyry, a third-century
C.E. Neoplatonist philosopher. When the *Iliad* recounts how the Olympians descended to the Trojan plain to fight one another (20.67 ff.), Porphyry observes that Homer's "unsuitable" stories about the gods could
be defended by appealing to his "mode of expression (*lexis*), holding that
everything is spoken by way of allegory (*allēgoria*)." In the passage at
hand, the battling divinities could be taken to expresses the cosmological
truth that the dry opposes the wet, the hot the cold, and so on.[2] Porphyry
adds: "This kind of apology is very old and goes back to Theagenes of
Rhegium, who first wrote about Homer."[3] As Tatian (second century C.E.)
places Theagenes in the last quarter of the sixth century, and as Rhegium
was near the center of Xenophanes' activity,[4] Theagenes is usually taken
to have been responding to rationalizing attacks on epic myth like those
of Xenophanes.[5]

---

[1] That Theagenes *wrote* about Homer is specified in Porphyry (8.2 DK) and the *Suda*
(8.4 DK). Some of the evidence presented in this section is discussed more fully in Ford
1999a.

[2] Porphyry's account incorporates Stoic and perhaps Neopythagorean sources: Wehrli
1928: 89–91, and Cantarella 1967: 19–24.

[3] Porphyry *apud* schol. B *Iliad* 20.67. My translations are from Schraeder 1880: 240.14–
241.12, reprinted at 8.2 DK.

[4] Tatian *Oration to the Greeks* 31 (= 8.1a DK): "Those responsible for the most ancient
researches into Homer's poetry, birth, and time are Theagenes of Rhegium, at the time of
Cambysses [529–522], Stesimbrotus the Thasian, Antimachus the Colophonian, Herodotus
of Halicarnassus. . . ."

[5] For Theagenes as inventor of allegoresis, Lanata 1963: 104–12; Buffière 1956: 103–4;
cf. Wehrli 1928: 88–91: Feeney 1991: 8–14; Rispoli 1980. The fullest recent account is
Svenbro 1984a: 101–21, material collected by Sengesbusch 1855–56, 1: 210–14.

The rise of epic allegoresis is usually explained as a defensive attempt to recoup the authority of narrative traditions whose literal interpretation was becoming inadequate to new ways of thinking. But to take Theagenes as responding to Xenophanes fails to explain why allegoresis was the method he chose. It was, after all, a rather bold move for an expounder of Homer to say that the poems spoke about things quite other than Achilles at Troy or Odysseus on his way home to Ithaca. In his *Poetics*, Aristotle surveys methods for defending poets from spurious criticism without mentioning allegoresis; charges of the sort that Xenophanes made are to be answered simply by saying, "That's the way people tell the story" (*Poetics* 1460b36–61a1). In addition, to think that Theagenes concocted epic allegoresis on his own clearly oversimplifies the situation. Some two decades before Theagenes, Pherecydes of Syros had written a prose theogony and cosmogony with easily allegorizable passages.[6] The epic poets themselves offer extended personifications of abstract concepts that it seems hairsplitting not to call allegories, and even their characters can, like Porphyry, reduce mythical names to natural elements: Homer's Patroclus allegorizes when he upbraids Achilles for his inhuman anger by saying he must have been born from rock (his father Peleus suggesting Mount Pelion) and sea (the sea-nymph Thetis).[7] In addition, the predilection of epic poets to play upon the names of gods and heroes provided a methodological model if we realize, in Walter Burkert's phrase, that allegory is an etymologized narrative and etymology the allegoresis of an individual word.[8] For example, the popular allegorization of Hera as Air could be supported by a suggestively phrased line from Homer's theomachy—"A deep mist of *air Hera* / spread before the Trojans to check their flight" (*Iliad* 21.6–7: ἠέρα δ᾽ Ἥρα / πίτνα). This sort of magical etymology was exploited to interpret the sacred hexameter songs attributed to Orpheus and is applied to a cosmological song in the Derveni papyrus, discussed below.[9] In sixth-century south Italy, such etymologies were also used by Pythagoreans to bolster their esoteric teachings: the similar-sounding words for "body" (*sōma*) and "tomb" (*sēma*), for example,

---

[6] E.g., B1, 1a, 2, 3, 5 DK. For allegoresis as a positive exegetical technique that only became defensive with Theagenes: Tate 1934: 105–14, 1927: 214–15; and Jaeger 1947: esp. 67. More cautious about ascribing allegory to Pherecydes are Pfeiffer (1968) and his most recent editor, Schibli (1990: 99–100 with n. 54). See Schibli 1990: 1–2 for Pherecydes' floruit in 544.

[7] As pointed out by Most (1994a). For paronomasia of divine names among the early poets: Pfeiffer 1968: 4–5; Lamberton 1986: 38. Among allegorical personifications, verbal ones are the *Litai* ("Apologies") in *Iliad* 9.502–12 and *Phēmē* ("Rumor") in Hesiod *Works and Days* 760–64.

[8] Burkert 1970: 450.

[9] Orphics were already suggested in this connection by Nestle (1942: 129–30); cf. Apicella 1980.

were held to intimate the immortal soul's imprisonment in a perishable body.[10] At least at a later period, Pythagoreans also had a tradition of allegorizing passages of Homer with a moralizing slant.[11]

Porphyry places allegoresis in the class of defenses of poetry that appeal to its special use of language (*lusis ex lexeōs*);[12] in this vein, ancient as well as modern scholars have understood Theagenes primarily as a grammarian and proto-philologist.[13] But to focus on the linguistic aspects of allegoresis may reflect the bias of philological historians; others have more plausibly associated Theagenes with rhapsodes.[14] It is certain that in his own day, Theagenes would have been defined in relation to other experts in Homeric song, and so it is worth considering traditions of epic exegesis in the late archaic age.

The first experts in epic were the singers themselves: they could not compose or perform in the heroic style without some understanding of its traditional and often archaic language (the *glōssai*). In this sense, singers and rhapsodes have been credited with "a kind of Homeric philology"; but such (often fantastical) lore was only part of their professional expertise, for rhapsodes also commented on the songs they performed.[15] The rhapsode portrayed in Plato's *Ion* can recite passages from Homer on cue, but also can "embellish" (*kosmein*) the poet by discoursing on his "many fine thoughts" (*pollai kai kalai dianoiai, Ion* 530D). This extratextual commentary must have been substantial: Ion says that acquiring his stock of observations on the poems has cost him more effort than mastering the

[10] First cited in Plato *Gorgias* 493A: see Dodds 1959: ad loc. and 296–99; Burkert 1970: 450; and cf. Philolaus (?) 44 B 14 DK.

[11] E.g., Iamblichus *Life of Pythagoras* 64, 110, 164. On the tradition, see Delatte 1915: 110, 114–15; Buffière 1956: 520; Detienne 1962: esp. 14–16, 32. Wehrli (1928: 90) compares the fifth-century philosopher Alcmaeon of nearby Croton (B 4 DK), who was associated with Pythagoreanism. Reservations in Burkert 1972a: 291 n. 67; Pfeiffer 1968: 9, 258; Rispoli 1980: 253–55; cautious acceptance in Laqueur *RESA* (1934) s.v. "Theagenes (9)"; Lanata 1963: 107: Lamberton 1986: 31–40; and Richardson 1975: 74–76. The report (Heraclides Ponticus 89 Wehrli) that Pythagoras claimed to have been a minor Trojan hero, Euphorbus, in one of his previous incarnations may be connected with the text of Homer (*Iliad* 16.849–50): see Burkert 1972a: 138–41.

[12] On the *lusis ex lexeōs*, see Commellback 1987, *pace* Detienne (1962: 27 and n. 4), interpreting as an argument based on selected lines (= *lexis*).

[13] A scholiast on the *Grammar* of Dionysius Thrax credits Theagenes with initiating the study of correct Greek usage (*hellenismos*, 8 1a DK): cf. Praxiphanes fr. 8 Wehrli with Wehrli's comments (1967–78, 9:108), and Pfeiffer 1968: 11, 35. For Theagenes as a proto-philologist, downplaying his interest in allegory, see Svenbro 1984a: 111; Detienne 1962: 65–67.

[14] For Theagenes as rhapsode, see Wilamowitz-Moellendorff (1931–32: 219 n. 2; Pfeiffer 1968: 10–11; Svenbro 1984a: 103. Against, Rispoli 1980: 249–50; cf. Wehrli 1928: 91.

[15] Cf. Rzach, "Homeridae," in *RE* 8 (1913): 2147–48; Latte 1925: 147–49. On Homer and Hesiod glossing their own phrases (e.g., *polutropos* in *Od*. 1.1–2), Verdenius 1970: 23.

poems themselves (530C). It was also a traditional practice, for he claims to interpret Homer better than a host of contemporaries and "anyone who ever lived." Ion's "fine thoughts" suggest that his interpretations consisted in improving observations on the wisdom to be found in Homer's poetry.[16] How stable such traditions could be is suggested by Isocrates' criticism of certain "vulgar sophists" (i.e., experts in literature) who discuss Homer and Hesiod "all over the place" and have nothing original to say, but only repeat old bits of the poems with hackneyed commentary (*Panathenaicus* §18–19.).

Archaic rhapsodes also preserved other lore connected with the poems they performed, especially accounts of the poets' births and deaths and stories of their travels. This sort of material is at the root of the romantic fictions recorded in many later *Lives of Homer* and in the work known as the *Contest of Homer and Hesiod*.[17] In its present form, this antiquarian compilation is not earlier than the second century C.E., but it is manifestly reliant on a work by Alcidamas of Elaea, a conspicuous rhetorician and man of letters of fourth-century Athens. Alcidamas in turn drew on yet earlier traditions about the two poets, including a story of Homer's death that is attested in Heraclitus.[18] The *Contest* begins with accounts of the births of the two poets and ends with their deaths, filling in the middle with a pastiche of epic-style lines and quotations from them. Many archaic rhapsodes must have been capable of entertaining their audiences with a similar mixture of material; the traditions about Homer's wanderings in search of hospitality were so rich that a traveling rhapsode might draw the poet into connection with many a festive city.

Theagenes had important things in common with rhapsodes so understood. In Tatian he heads a list of those who have studied "Homer's poetry, birth, and time" (8.1a DK). His allegoresis (which it is difficult to imagine being sustained throughout the poem) could have been exhibited in the course of embellishing a passage of Homer just performed.[19] Unlike Theagenes, most rhapsodes did not write up this lore since it was their stock in trade. Theagenes' fame may spring from the fact that either he

---

[16] Cf. Aristophanes *Peace* 750, where the poet boasts of his fine language (*epea*), thoughts (*dianoiais*), and jokes (*skomasi*).

[17] For legends about Homer among the Homeridae: Isocrates *Helen* §65; for their preservation of special verses: Plato *Phaedrus* 252B. See Pfeiffer 1968: 72; Lasserre 1976: 127–30; and Burkert 1972b, a brilliant case study. See the forthcoming study of early epic reception by Graziosi (2002).

[18] On Alcidamas and Mich. 2754, see Dodds 1952. On the contributions of Alcidamas: West 1967: 433; Richardson 1981: 1–3; Janko 1982: 259 n. 80; Stehle 1997: 176; O'Sullivan 1992: ch. 3. On Homer's death (Heraclitus B 56 DK), Pfeiffer 1968: 11; Janko 1982: 259–60; O'Sullivan 1992: 63–66, 85. Local tradition about Hesiod's death: Thucydides 3.96.

[19] Feeney 1991: 9. So, too, Tate 1927: 215 n. 5.

was the first to do so or he did it so well that no earlier work on Homer reached later antiquity. Our sources thus leave open the possibility that Theagenes was a revolutionary less in critical method than in publicizing his skill. It is at least clear that the Homeric poems were being regarded from a number of new angles in the later sixth century, and that some Homerists were applying to their heroic narratives a kind of esoteric exegesis already developed for cosmic songs among certain groups. Why the Homerists did so may be suggested by considering the history of Greek terms for "allegory."

Ainos and Allegory

The word *allēgoria*, literally "saying other," in itself implies a rhetorical approach to song in terms of diction. I have suggested that proto-rhetorical theory is not the most important context in which to understand Theagenes, and it should be noted that the word *allēgoria* is postclassical: first attested among rhetoricians of the late Hellenistic age, it is used to designate a broad range of nonliteral expression—from extended metaphors to maxims (*gnōmai*) to riddles (*ainigmata*).[20] Writing around 100 C.E., Plutarch observed that what was called *allēgoria* in his day had formerly been called *huponoia*, "under-meaning" (*Moralia* 19E). This word can help us recover something of allegorical exegesis in the classical period.

In the fifth century, *huponoia* can refer to any thought that lies underneath (*hupo*) the surface of a text, whether or not that meaning is strictly allegorical.[21] Thucydides' Pericles declaims that Athens has no need of a Homer to praise her, nor of any poet "whose fine phrases (*epē*) may please, but whose under-meaning (*huponoia*) is opposed by the truth of things" (2.41.4). *Huponoia* is attested for specifically allegorical "under-meanings" in two texts of the fourth century B.C.E. describing exegetical practices of the fifth. In the first, Plato's Socrates rejects allegorical defenses of Homer's stories about the gods because the young are credulous: teachers are not to recount "the binding of Hera by her son, the casting out of Hephaestus from Olympus when he went to defend his mother from his father, and all the battles among gods Homer has composed, regardless of whether they are composed with or without under-mean-

[20] Richardson 1975: 67. Cf. Buffière 1956: 47, Pépin 1958: 85–88; Feeney 1991: 10. The history of terms for allegory is surveyed with bibliography in Whitman 1987: app I; cf. Pépin 1958: 87–92; Lanata 1963: 107; all without benefit of the Derveni papyrus.

[21] LSJ s.v. Cf. Pépin 1958: 85–88.

ings" (*en huponoiais, aneu hupnoiōn, Republic* 378D). We shall come back to this text, but now note that it shows the sorts of tale Xenophanes condemned being redeemed by positing "under-meanings" for them. In the second passage, Xenophon's *Symposium*, Socrates and some sophisticates are discussing the value of Homeric poetry in education; when one guest, Niceratus, boasts of knowing the *Iliad* and *Odyssey* by heart, the response is that this is no worthy accomplishment in itself: rhapsodes, after all, can do as much, and this company is unanimous in viewing them as the most stupid of men because they "do not know the *huponoiai*." Yet Niceratus is to be congratulated because he has "paid a good deal of money to Stesimbrotus and Anaximander and many others so that nothing of their valuable learning will escape you" (3.6).[22] In the classical period, then, allegorical readings of epic could be offered as an intellectual commodity under the term *huponoia*. If a rhapsode expounded on the "fine thoughts" (*kalai dianoiai*) of Homer, an education in poetry could still be called incomplete without an acquaintance with the "under-meanings" (*huponoiai*) available from a different class of experts. But we can recover a yet earlier stratum in the vocabulary by considering our oldest specimen of extended allegorical interpretation.

The Derveni papyrus, discovered in 1962 and still not yet fully published, is a half-rationalistic, half-mystical exegesis of an Orphic hexameter cosmogony.[23] The papyrus itself is dated archaeologically to the fourth century B.C.E. but its text clearly reflects pre-Platonic thought.[24] The author frequently resorts to allegoresis to explain the Orphic text, holding that the "entire poem is spoken in the way of a riddle (*ainigma*)" (7.3–4 L-M).[25] At times allegoresis is used defensively to reveal a cosmological truth beneath apparently scandalous utterances. In the best-preserved example, the author puzzles over the words, "Zeus swallowed the reverent one" (αἰδοῖον κα[τ]έπινεν), which are ambiguous enough to be construed as "Zeus ate the god's pudenda"; he voids this suggestion by saying, "since through the whole poem [Orpheus] is speaking allegorically (*ai-*

---

[22] Stesimbrotus is mentioned after Theagenes by Tatian; Anaximander is probably the younger from Miletus: Lanata 1963: 107.

[23] My Greek quotations and line numbers are taken from *ZPE* 47 (1982), but I cite the column numbers (generally higher by four than those used in earlier studies) from the fuller English version in Laks and Most 1997: 10–22, with contributions from K. Tsantsanoglou. I am indebted to André Laks for allowing me to see this indispensable work in advance of publication.

[24] For general accounts of the Derveni papyrus and its contexts, see Burkert 1970; West 1983: 75 ff.; Most 1997; Janko 1997. On the author's critical methods, Henry 1986; M. J. Edwards 1991.

[25] Cf. West 1983: 78; Laks 1997: 123.

nizetai) about things in the world, it is necessary to consider each word individually."[26] He then allegorizes "genitals" as the sun, the source of life, and concludes that Orpheus meant that the governing power of the universe also controls generation.[27]

Throughout the text, the proper term for allegorical writing is *ainittesthai*, "to speak in hints," or "to riddle," and the word for "allegorical" is *ainigmatōdēs*, "in the mode of an *ainos* or *ainigma*."[28] No form of *huponoia* or *allēgoria* is used. The Derveni papyrus thus suggests that, outside the philosophical-rhetorical tradition of the later fifth century, which sought the *huponoia* of poets, *ainittesthai* and its cognates supplied the standard set of terms in which to discuss what was eventually called allegory.[29] We may further venture that this usage goes back to the time of Theagenes if we compare a passage from Theognis that concludes an extended allegory of "the ship of state" by saying, "Let these things be riddling utterances (*ēinikhthō*) hidden by me for the noble. / One can be aware even of future misfortune if one is skilled."[30]

These texts indicate that in the sixth century, allegorical meaning was understood as a particular kind of riddling speech the Greeks called *ainos*. The *ainos* was a well-established mode of veiled expression.[31] One of its common forms was the animal fable such as Archilochus sang (called *ainos* in frs. 174, 185 *IEG*); Hesiod tells a story about a nightingale in the clutches of a hawk as an *"ainos* that kings will understand" (*Works and Days* 202). But *ainoi* included other ways of getting one's meaning across indirectly: in need of covering for the night, the beggar-Odysseus tells his swineherd about a ruse the "real" Odysseus had once used to

---

[26] 13.6–7 L-M: ὅτι μὲμ πᾶσαν τὴμ πόησιν περὶ τῶμ πραγμάτων <u>αἰνίζεται</u> κ[α]θ᾽ ἔπος ἕκαστον ἀνάγκη λέγειν. For a discussion of this ambiguous sentence, see Rusten 1985: 133–34, and for the interpreter's error, West 1983: 85, and, somewhat differently, Rusten 1985: 125, M. J. Edwards 1991: 207–8.

[27] In the same way, the poet "was riddling" when he used the anthropomorphic expression "he [i.e., Zeus] took in his hands": 9.10–11 L-M: ὅτι ἐγ χείρ[εσσιν ἔλαβ]εν ἠνίζετο ὥσπε[ρ τ]ἆλλα. Cf. Rusten 1985: 128–30 and 17.13 L-M, where Zeus as "head" (= fr. 21a.2 Kern) is taken as "allegorically expressing" (*ainizetai*) something else, probably "rule."

[28] As restored at 7.3–4 L-M: πόησις [αἰνιγμ]ατώδης, and 7.5 L-M: θεὰς λέγειν [. . . αἰ-ν]ιγματωδῶ[ς. West (1983: 78 n.14) and Feeney (1991: 22) note in passing that *ainittesthai* bears the sense "allegorize" for this author. See n. 37 below.

[29] Porphyry uses *ainittesthai* of Pherecydes in introducing fr. B 6 DK, though this is discounted by Schibli (1990: 99 n. 54 and 117 n. 30).

[30] Theognis 681–82: ταῦτά μοι ἠινίχθω κεκρυμμένα τοῖσ᾽ ἀγαθοῖσιν · / γινώσκοι δ᾽ ἄν τις καὶ κακόν, ἂν σοφὸς ἦι. For text and discussion, see Nagy 1985a: 22–26, and 1990: 149, 183–84, 269.

[31] The relation to epic's use of *ainos* as "complimentary speech" is unclear: see Richardson on *Iliad* 23.651–52.

secure a cloak on a cold night watch. Eumaeus is quick to perceive the point of the story and, commending the *ainos*, offers his guest a cloak.[32]

The significance of this lexical evidence for epic allegoresis depends on the important point, stressed by Nagy, that Greek epic does *not* present itself as *ainos*: though epic may incorporate *ainoi*, and though it may give us a portrait of a master of *ainoi* in "Odysseus *poluainos*" ("of many clever speeches"), it does not call itself *ainos*, nor does it suggest that its Muse-sent vision of the heroic age has a hidden meaning for the cognoscenti.[33] As subtle as Homeric poetry may appear to modern readers, it was not generally taken by the ancients as a cryptic text. Xenophanes, for example, objects not to any hidden implications in Homeric poetry but to the literal content of its stories. In this case, for an allegorizing critic to say that the epic poet "riddles" (*ainittetai*) this or that was to reposition narrative epic and assign it to another form of discourse. Early epic allegorists did not concoct a new method for reading Homer but rather transferred epic to an already established class of speech with its own special rules for speaking and decoding.

Among the reasons for taking this step was doubtless that it allowed some Homerists to present the poet as more pious and up-to-date than he appeared; Porphyry takes Theagenes as an apologist, and the Derveni commentator uses allegoresis to defend Orpheus. But the marked emphasis on esoterism in that text suggests that allegoresis had an additional use in creating a select community of those who "rightly" understood a text. The Derveni commentator repeatedly sets his allegorical interpretations against the ways of "the many," "those who do not understand."[34] He holds that Orpheus "speaks in signs" like an oracle (*sēmainein*)[35] and departs from language as it is commonly used because he "does not wish all to understand" (25.13 L-M).[36] The commentator justifies his esoteric approach by quoting the beginning of the poem, which bade the profane, "Put doors on your ears!" Quite aptly, he takes this ritual phrase of exclu-

---

[32] *Od.* 14.508: see the brilliant analysis of the scene by Von Reden (1995: 39–40), and Nagy 1979: 234–37 on *ainos* here. The scene is parodied in *Birds* 938–45: the beggar-dithyrambist utters "a Pindaric phrase" (*epos*) and bids his hearer "perceive" its meaning (ξύνες τί λέγω), to which the reply is: "I perceive you want a cloak."

[33] Nagy 1990: 148, 192–94, 196–200. *Pace* Svenbro (1984a: 40–41), Homeric epic is not shown to be *ainos* simply because quotations from epic could later be reused by others with ainetic force.

[34] 9.2–4 L-M; a similar distinction is at 23.2 L-M between what is "unclear to the many" but not "to those who rightly understand." See Laks 1997: 139–40.

[35] The word *sēmainein*, "to indicate by signs" (as in Delphic oracles), is used for what the poet means by his obscure expression in 23.7 and 25.13 L-M. Heraclitus also used the word as a model for his esoteric wisdom: B 92, cf. B 93 DK.

[36] 18.7–9; 23.7, 8 L-M.

sion as proof that the teaching was not intended for "the many."[37] Orphic exegesis thus replicated the esoterism of the songs themselves, one of which began, "I sing for the knowing" (*sunetois*).[38] This secretive posture, dismissive of the masses, finds a parallel in the oracular elitism of Heraclitus, but epic singers did not present themselves as purveyors of *ainoi*. In "inventing" epic allegoresis, Theagenes and other Homerists to come after him converted panhellenic epic into an esoteric text.

The Uses of Hidden Meanings

Nagy stresses that *ainoi* are made within and for "a marked social group"; the polysemy of *ainos* is decoded by those the speaker considers "wise" or "good" or "akin" to himself (the *sophoi*, *agathoi*, or *philoi* commonly referred to in ainetic poetry).[39] Its use in situations of social inequality is brought out by Thomas Cole, who notes that the form was said to have been invented by the slave and animal fabulist Aesop, and that Aristotle's *Rhetoric* associates *ainos* with the "slavish" habit of talking around a point when addressing a superior.[40] In the *ainos* Hesiod addressed to kings, the nightingale (*aēdōn*) in the clutches of a hawk seems to refer in some way to the power the king has over the singer (*aoidos*);[41] Odysseus tells Eumaeus the cloak *ainos* because a suppliant castaway must be cautious in making demands on his host. Encoding songs for their aristocratic coteries allowed Archilochus, Alcaeus, and Theognis discretion in times of political change and reinforced solidarity among those who "rightly understood" these issues.[42] *Ainoi* were doubtless also useful in wider contexts, as in stories of Stesichorus' using animal fables to dissuade the citi-

---

[37] Following the version of Laks and Most (1997: 12), who take 7.3–4 to refer to the poem at hand. West (1983: 78 n. 14), reading ἔστι δὲ α[ὑτοῦ πᾶσα ἡ] ποίησις [αἰνιγμ]ατώδης, compares [Plato] *Alcibiades II* 147b–c: "All poetry is by nature *ainigmatōdēs*, and is not such as to be understood by anyone happening along."

[38] ἀείσω ξυνετοῖσι (fr. 334 Kern), with which West (1983: 110 n. 82) compares Heraclitus B1 DK: ἀξύνετοι γίγνονται; cf. B 34 DK: ἀξύνετοι ἀκούσαντες κωφοῖσιν ἐοίκασι.

[39] Nagy 1990: 147; cf. index s.v. *ainos* and Nagy 1979: 222–41, esp. 235–38.

[40] Aesop a slave: Herodotus 2.134; slavish speech: Aristotle *Rhetoris* 1415b23–24; Cole 1991: 48–49, cf. 55–68. In Aristophanes, Agathon's house-slave speaks the esoteric language of mystery-cults (*Thesmophoriazousae* 39–45) and Euripides' utters sophisms: *Acharnians* 395–402; cf. Panarces (a) *IEG*, and Plato *Republic* 479b–c.

[41] Nagy 1979: 302; cf. perhaps Archilochus 223 *IEG* ("You have a tettix by the wing") and the Ptolemaic ostracon inscribed with an address to a king and then a hawk (*hierax*), with West 1978c.

[42] On *ainoi* in Theognis, Nagy 1985a: 22–30; Edmunds 1985: 105–6; more generally, Gentili 1988: 43–44, 197–213, and ch. 11, which draws detailed correspondences between Alcaeus' ship-of-state allegory (fr. 6 V) and Lesbian political history.

zens of Himera from giving Phalaris a bodyguard; in predicting a tyranny (and an extremely savage one, as it turned out), one doesn't dare be too offensive to a powerful man.[43] In this respect, the situation at the Sicilian courts had changed little when Plato was trying to advise the tyrant Dionysius: the Seventh Letter says that he and his friends thought it best to communicate their doctrines about just governing "not by expressing them straight out—which was not safe—but through riddles (*ainittomenoi*)" (332D).

In a world where political speech can take this coded form, and where oracles speak in the same mode, there was a need for interpretative expertise. For a dynast to sustain his position required not only force of arms but also the ability to read signs aright, to steer the "ship of state" through the tempestuous waters of politics in the classic allegory of the age. That the discernment needed to rule extended to the decipherment of peculiar messages can be illustrated from tales told by Herodotus: the Athenian tyrant Hipparchus had a dream in which a young man spoke a two-line hexameter riddle (*ainissomenos*) addressing him as a lion; in the morning, his interpreters could make nothing out of it, and he went out to be assassinated that day.[44] Because Croesus could not decipher an animal oracle predicting a mule sitting on the Median throne, he was unprepared for Cyrus, half-Median and half-Persian (Herodotus 1.55–56, 91). The ruling Peisistratids at Athens first patronized and then banished Onomacritus, a collector and interpreter of the oracles of Musaeus.[45] Nor were oracles the only pregnant speeches: the Persian court of the late fifth century remembered an old allegorical song that had been sung at a banquet to Astyages, ruler of the Medes; but its warning of a beast about to attack did not save him from Cyrus.[46] Thus the Greek king or prince striving to catch the political import of every shifting wind was well advised to cultivate courtiers of equal discernment. As Theognis said in capping his own *ainos*, "One can be aware even of future misfortune if one is skilled."

The kinds of epic story that preoccupied Xenophanes—scenes of theomachy and strife among gods—were the same ones that allegorists fo-

---

[43] Aristotle *Rhetoric* 1393b8–22; cf. 1394b34–95a2, 1412a22–26; and Nagy 1990: 427. Some passages from Solon bore similar messages, at least to later readers: he was said to be predicting the tyranny of Peisistratus when he sang, "Just as the force of snow and hail comes from a cloud, thunder comes from bright lightning," so the city should recognize in advance the destruction that threatens when some men become too great (9 *IEG*). Cf., e.g., DL 1.49–50 and others cited by West (1992a) on Solon 9–12 *IEG*.

[44] Herodotus 5.56. See Shapiro 1990 for other episodes.

[45] Herodotus 7.6. Euripides (*Heracleidae* 402–7) presents Theseus as such a king: before going into battle, he gathers oracle-singers (*khrēsmōn aoidous*) and consults the "ancient sayings" (*logia palaia*), both the commonly known (*bebēla*) and the "hidden" (*kekrummena*).

[46] Ctesias 90 F 66 *FGrH*; see Gera 1993: 159 and her ch. 1.2 in general.

cused on, and I suggest that this was for the same reasons.[47] For both critics and Homerists, talk of theomachy raised the issue of solidarity among the nobility.[48] At the same time, making Homer ainetic allowed allegorists to constitute a select audience who could distinguish themselves by their subtle understanding of panhellenic song. This was a time when rhapsodes were crossing the entire length of the Aegean performing Homeric epic and competing with each other at major festivals from Delos to Athens to Syracuse. Many of the references to Homer, which begin to crop up at this time, note his broad appeal. When Simonides says, "Homer and Stesichorus sang to the people" (564.4 *PMG*), he implies a wide and perhaps undiscriminating diffusion of the poetry by using for "people" an epic term (*laos*) for the army or citizen body as distinct from its leaders. Heraclitus calls Hesiod "most people's teacher" (B 57 DK) but has contempt for the "singers of the people" (*dēmos*) who use poets as teachers. Their popularity is dismissed with a saying by the tyrant-sage Bias of Pirene: "What discernment or intelligence do they possess? They place their trust in popular bards and take the throng for their teacher, not knowing that 'the many are bad and the few good.'"[49]

In this context, Theagenes may have offered some of the leading "1,000" who constituted Rhegium's aristocracy a deeper understanding of the poems than others who attended epic recitals at Syracuse.[50] With allegoresis, the authoritative and venerable ancient history presented by Homer to all of Greece became a riddle to be deciphered by the wise. Of course, other appropriations of Homeric poetry continued. To judge from the passage in Xenophon, rhapsodes do not appear to have typically included allegories in their commentaries; nor does Homer appear as a cryptic cosmologist among the non-epic poets who served the elite of western Greece in the generation after Theagenes. Singers like Pindar or Bacchylides

---

[47] Buffière (1956: 102–5) identifies four epic myths in particular: (1) the battle of gods; (2) the partition of spheres of divine influence among Zeus and his brothers; (3) Hera's seduction of Zeus; (4) the chaining of Hera. This squares with Xenophanes' "thieving, adultery, deception" (B 11.3 DK = B 12.2), and Sextus on B 12 DK may be paraphrasing Xenophanes when he mentions Kronos' mutilation of his father and eating of his children along with Zeus' imprisonment of Kronos. Such tales underlie objections to poetic and popular traditions in Euripides *Heracles* 1314–19, 1341–44; Plato *Euthyphro* 5E–7C, *Republic* 377E–378C; Isocrates *Busiris* 38. Cf. Longinus *On the Sublime* 9.6,7.

[48] Plato explicitly says that stories of theomachy encourage internecine strife in the city, *Republic* 378C.

[49] B 104 DK: τίς γὰρ αὐτῶν νόος ἢ φρήν; δήμων ἀοιδοῖσι πείθονται καὶ διδασκάλωι χρείωνται ὁμίλωι οὐκ εἰδότες ὅτι' πολλοὶ κακοί, ὀλίγοι δὲ ἀγαθοί.' For Heraclitus' attacks on *hoi polloi* (B 17, B 29 DK), see Kirk 1954: 203. On evidence of the visual arts for the spread of Homeric poetry at this time, see most recently Snodgrass 1998.

[50] On the Rhegine "1,000," cf. Rispoli 1980: 256 with references.

characterize their own songs as *ainoi* with a valuable moral to be divined by "the discerning" (*sunetoi*).[51] This not only enhances their value as wise associates but also idealizes the ruler as pious, powerful, and "wise" (*sophos*) or "discerning" (*sunetos*), and so skilled in interpreting *ainoi*.[52] In these singers, Homer and Hesiod are ainetic only as sources of moral adages; their songs are mines for wise sayings that are appreciated by an elite with an affinity for the Muses.[53] For them, Homer's quotable bits of wisdom are not enigmatic texts. In the only place Pindar quotes Homer by name, he urges his patron: "Of the sayings of Homer, take this one to heart as well"; he thus presents his patron as an epic connoisseur and a devotee of ethical verse.[54] In another text he discusses with Hiero of Syracuse "a choice part" (κορυφάν) of wisdom to be found in Homer (the great allegory of the jars of Zeus: *Pythian* 3.80–82). Pressing a select line of Homer for its ethical message was one way to display wisdom for Simonides, who (probably at a symposium) singled out a moralizing hexameter from *Iliad* 6 (146: "As the generation of leaves, such is the generation of man") and pronounced it "one very fine thing the Chian man said" (19 *IEG*). This way of "interpreting" epic harmonizes with the high aspirations of the symposium and seems close to what rhapsodes must have been doing in discoursing on the *kalai dianoiai* of the poet.

Hesiod also afforded quotable and admirable sayings, such as this half-line from *Works and Days* 412: μελέτη δέ τοι ἔργον ὀφέλλει ("Devotion furthers the work"). This line was apparently a motto for Lampon of Aegina, who was so devoted to the benefits of athletic practice that he engaged the sought-after Athenian trainer Menander and set him to work with his boys. Hesiod's line is introduced into a song Pindar composed to celebrate a pancratic victory of one of Lampon's sons (*Isthmian* 6.66–68 S-M):

> Λάμπων δὲ μελέταν
> ἔργοις ὀπάζων Ἡσιόδου μάλα τιμᾷ τοῦτ᾽ ἔπος
> υἱοῖσί τε φράζων παραίνει.

---

[51] E.g., Bacchylides 3.85: φρονέοντι συνετὰ γαρύω; Pindar *Olympian* 2.85: φωναέοντα συνετοῖσιν (amid an excursus into Orphic eschatology). On *sunetos*, cf. Battisti 1990.

[52] See discussion in Cole 1991: 49–54, citing (164 n. 7) Pindar *Olympian* 2.82–86 and 11.10, *Nemean* 7.12–19, *Pythian* 2.72 and 3.80–84 (where it is a question of the addressee being wise enough to appreciate the import of *Iliad* 24.527–30). Cf. *Isthmian* 2.11–12.

[53] Cf. Bundy 1986: 25–26, and Maehler 1982, on Bacchylides 5.3–6; e.g., Pindar *Olympian* 10.13–15, 11.17–18, 13.22–23, *Pythian* 5.114, 6.47–49, 10.37–39, *Nemean* 7.9–23; Bacchylides 3.63–71. Hiero of Sicily was particularly certain to be praised for his discernment in song: Bacchylides 5.3–6, Pindar *Olympian* 1.103–5.

[54] *Pythian* 4.277–78: τῶν δὲ Ὁμήρου καὶ τόδε συνθέμενος ῥῆμα πόρσυν᾽. See further Ford 1997a: 96–98.

In his lavish "*devotion to work*" Lampon truly honors that saying of Hesiod, which he quotes when exhorting his sons.

Bacchylides also composed an ode on this victory, in which he significantly described the boys' trainer: "Menander, whose devotion benefits mortals" (μελέταν τε βροτωφελέα Μενάνδρου).[55] Maehler makes the brilliant suggestion that both poets allude to Lampon's favorite line of Hesiod.

Early allegorical readings of epic would have provided those with pretensions to cultural leadership an elite purchase on a kind of poetry that was increasingly becoming the possession of all Greece. It did for those wishing to be distinguished in the city what the recherché interpretations of Orphic texts or Pythagorean secret sayings (*sumbola*) did for those desiring to form their own communities at the city's margins, uniting them and their common beliefs by a shared interpretation of cherished texts.[56] The reappropriation of epic as *ainos* continued in the fifth century, but it confronted a new range of alternative approaches.

Allegory in the Fifth Century

Although allegory as an interpretive mode never died out in Greece, it did not find its way into Aristotle's *Poetics*. The reason has been thought to be the sophists and other fifth-century pioneers in the grammatical and formal study of language. The more rational and objective approaches to language developed among these professors of speech are held to have made the extravagances of allegoresis so apparent that it was rejected by Plato and Aristotle. The story appears to be a little more complicated: the use of allegoresis to create distinguished audiences continued through the fifth century, when certain Homerists could sell "under-meanings" (*huponoiai*) that were not available from the rhapsodes.[57] Then, as I think already in the sixth century, traveling experts in literature who were not affiliated with rhapsodic guilds had an interest in presenting themselves as possessing a hidden knowledge of poetry, one that was not so public as the declamation of a rhapsode and was not controlled by guilds on

[55] Maehler 1982: 284, on 13.191–92. Note that Hesiod goes on to say that the poor worker is always "wrestling" with difficulties (413: αἰεὶ δ' ἀμβολιεργὸς ἀνὴρ ἄτῃσι παλαίει).

[56] At the end of the fifth century, the "Exegesis of Pythagorean *Symbola*" of Anaximander of Miletus (58 C 6 DK = *FGrH* 9 T 1; cf. 59 A 1.11 DK) appears to have applied to Pythagorean sayings the kind of allegorical explanation that had been used on Homer: cf. Burkert 1972a: 166–75.

[57] See Whitman 1987 and, for a concise overview of epic's long-standing affinity for allegoresis, Whitman 1994: 31–36.

Chios or Samos or by the Athenian state. In addition, the evidence of the fifth century suggests that sophists had no principled objection to allegoresis, and that Plato objected more to the wide dissemination of such readings than to the readings themselves.

The standard account of the decline of allegoresis owes much (as does the present book) to Rudolf Pfeiffer's great *History of Classical Scholarship* (1968). It is part of Pfeiffer's broader argument that the "true interpretation of the poets" (*hermeneia tōn poiētōn*, 37), the "art of understanding, explaining and restoring the literary tradition," only came into its own in the postclassical age.[58] Pfeiffer recognized that "attempts at studying the language [of the Greek literary tradition], collecting learned material and applying some form of literary criticism" can be found among sixth-century poets, historians, and other wise men; and he allowed that the fifth-century sophists signaled a new level of scientific interest in language. But for Pfeiffer, sophistic discussions of poetry at most "foreshadowed" literary hermeneutics; it was only later in Hellenistic academies that these "formerly disconnected activities" were united into one "self-conscious discipline." As a historian of classical philology, Pfeiffer has a rather specific conception of what counts as criticism, but his perspective usefully focuses on how rare it is to find in Greek criticism a systematic theory or even a controlled method for determining the meaning of texts. Pfeiffer's view is carried further by Glenn Most, who locates the basic difference between ancient and modern literary culture in the fact that the ancients (not excluding the Alexandrians, for Most) never developed a true hermeneutics.[59] Fruitfully developing an analysis of Hans Georg Gadamer, Most opposes ancient rhetoric to modern hermeneutics: hermeneutics arises in heavily literate cultures that need to understand texts whose author is absent; classical rhetoric was an art of performed eloquence and was aimed at the needs of prospective speakers rather than of readers and interpreters.[60] Where author and receiver were present to each other and able to interact, whether in the assembly, the courts, the agora, or the *salon*, there was less need for an impersonal method for understanding texts from the texts themselves.[61]

I think both scholars are right to point out that in the fifth century there was no discipline, no single art or science (*tekhnē*) dedicated to literary

[58] Pfeiffer 1968, quotations from 37, 1.

[59] Most 1984: esp. 76. Cole (1991: ch. 4) similarly cites the lack of evidence for theoretical discussions of interpretive strategies before the fourth century.

[60] Most 1984: 68–69, noting that Dionysius of Halicarnassus on Pindar and Longinus on Sappho take the "message" as transparent and ask how far the poets have achieved their goals; on which compare Russell's remarks (1981: 7–12).

[61] Similarly Vernant 1991: 315. Here Most differs from Gadamer (1976: 22), who begins the history of hermeneutics with Odysseus and Nestor.

interpretation. For teachers of rhetoric, purely linguistic matters occupied only a part of their teaching, and were useless without mastering techniques of performance (memory, delivery) and adapting all this to the context of delivery. This includes sophistic discussions of poetry, for in Aristophanic and fourth-century representations of sophists debating the meaning of songs with their students, the primary concern is not to arrive at the correct meaning of the text but to prepare the student to make a speech or text of his own on the topic.[62] Of course, the Greeks practiced interpretation daily, and we should not neglect instances of undoubted hermeneutic activity practiced on other texts, most notably attempts to comprehend the traditionally enigmatic messages of oracles.

The difficulty of interpreting divine messages is a theme already in the *Iliad* (e.g. 12.211–50). In Homer, however, understanding natural signs—omens and portents—is at least as important as recalling and reperforming oracles (usually unproblematic in their purport if not in their fulfillment); but fifth-century examples of oracular interpretation require hermeneutics as a matter of textual interpretation. The Derveni commentator, for example, clearly qualifies as a hermeneutician in his aim of deciphering the text of an absent author through a methodical "word-by-word" study of the poem. Closely related to this reading of "Orpheus" is the way that Herodotus, Thucydides, and Aristophanes show prophecies being subjected to a most self-conscious verbal analysis that fully deserves to be called hermenutics.[63] Most offers four criteria for hermeneutics. First, the author—whether the god or Orpheus—is crucially absent from the scene of interpretation. Second, while oracles were often recited and transmitted orally, their interpretation is decidedly a matter of interpreting a text—a set of words in principle immutable—and not a speech; every attempt is made to guard against corruption in transmission and to secure from the words themselves the key to their meaning. Third, the primary goal is arriving at a correct understanding; though this is usually with a view to future action, the determination of the meaning of the oracular text is separate from the debate about what policy should be followed in consequence of the meaning. And fourth, the understanding of the oracular text is not aimed at producing more oracles—they are already there, and only the god can produce new ones; it is a receptive rather than a rhetorical aesthetic.

Two examples show that the analysis of oracles could meet Most's criteria. The most famous story is the oracle the Athenians received when Xerxes' Persian armies were pressing into Greece (Herodotus 7.140–45).

---

[62] Cf. Ford 2001, which takes the evidence for Protagoras as a case study.
[63] Kennedy in Kennedy 1989: 78–80. Cf. Vernant 1991: 311, 313–14, on the distinctive "dialogism" of oracular interpretation.

Delphi's hexameters included the apparently discouraging advice that the Athenians take refuge behind "wooden walls." This phrase was much debated in the city, with notable men offering their interpretations (*gnōmai*, 7.147.3) to the people at large, "in the middle" as Herodotus puts it. Some older men remembered that the Acropolis had once been surrounded by a thorn hedge and advised taking refuge there. Others took the god to have used "wooden walls" as a virtual allegory for ships and urged arming the fleet (7.142.2). The latter party had their interpretation "tripped up" by the last two verses of the oracle, which began, "O divine Salamis, you shall destroy the children of women."[64] The oracle experts said this presaged a disastrous battle by that island off the Athenian coast. At this point, Themistocles rose up and supported the naval program. Already remarked for service to the state, he might have expected a favorable hearing; but he apparently made a case that the other side had not "taken" the oracle "rightly."[65] Seizing on the phrase, "O divine Salamis," Themistocles reasoned that it predicted disaster for the Persians, since the god, if predicting destruction for the Greeks, would have more likely said, "O wretched Salamis." With this plausible suggestion from an inspiring young military leader, and one with the culture to improvise hexameters ("wretched" and "divine" scan equally well), the Athenians judged Themistocles' reading preferable and followed his advice to spectacular success against the Persians.

Even if much of the Themistocles story is folktale congregating about a fondly remembered hero, the keen attention to textual interpretation is notable. A second example of public oracular criticism (Thucydides 2.54) even involves emending the text. During the plague at Athens, people looked about for its causes; if doctors had one view, certain old men remembered a phrase "sung long ago" that "Dorian war will come and with it plague" (λοιμός). A dispute (*eris*) arose because others remembered the line as predicting famine (λίμος).[66] Thucydides observes that "men's memory conforms to their experiences" (2.54.3),[67] but he does not dismiss the effort at interpretation: he notes some Athenians knew of an oracle the Spartans had received three years earlier in which Apollo promised to assist them in the war (cf. 1.118). They put this together with the plague

---

[64] As oracles were written down by the *theōroi* but then read out to the assembly, the closing tag (*akroteleution*) of orally performed verse had special interest: cf. Herodotus 2.17.

[65] 7.143.1: *orthōs, hupolambanein.* Cf. *(sul)lambanō* for "taking" an oracle to mean something in 1.63, 68, 91, 142.3.

[66] On the antithesis *limos/loimos*, cf. Hesiod *Works and Days* 240–43, *Iliad* 1.408–10, etc. With Thucydides' rhetorical view on oracle experts, cf. Aristotle *Rhetoric* 1407a31–39.

[67] Cf. 2.21.3 for interpretations of an oracle according to people's "inclinations"; on Thucydides' complex attitude to oracles, see Dover 1987–88, 2:65–73.

oracle and could well conclude that Apollo was helping his side, as he had in the *Iliad*, by visiting a plague on its enemies. They reasoned from similarities (ἤκαζον τὰ γενόμενα ὁμοῖα εἶναι) with the present events (2.54.5). Thucydides has little faith in men's memory, but is interested, as were many others, in the reasons given to justify an interpretation.[68]

Such debates may be thought methodologically naive, but they exhibit a concern for establishing the text and teasing out its meanings that approaches hermeneutics. It is quite true, as Most argues, that interpretation remains eclectic and rather ad hoc, but method depended on context, and critical scenes played out in the assembly were democratic in refusing to recognize a class of expert interpreters.[69] All forms of explanation were considered, some traditional, emanating from chresmologues or those possessing secret oracular texts, and some from acutely perceptive men or old men with long memories.

On the views of Pfeiffer and Most, this suggests that we may say that fifth-century Greeks were quite capable of closely reasoning about the meaning of texts, but that such attentiveness was not normally felt to be demanded by the texts we call literary. Greek prophecies and sacred songs could serve as "texts" in the sense of fixed structures of words that required the most scrupulous analysis, a true hermeneutic by which the intentions of the absent speaker could be derived from the words. What seems to be the case is that such texts were traditionally treated in a different, more searching way than heroic songs. The rise of epic allegoresis thus appears to have been an early breach in the wall between esoteric and panhellenic verse, and traffic followed in both directions: just as old epic poems, and Homer especially, could be treated not as common culture but as venerable old texts whose true and valuable insights had to be teased out by special forms of critical attention, so, too, mystical and revelatory songs came to be regarded as just another species of ancient hexameter poetry. We have seen Homer and Hesiod paired by Xenophanes, Heraclitus, and Herodotus; we will see Orpheus and Musaeus brought in beside them by the time of Aristophanes.

To postulate hidden meanings in a text defined a social as well as a hermeneutic position, and so inhibitions on the spread of allegoresis into rhetorical and philosophical education were owed less to an intellectual defeat than to its cultlike modes of dissemination among individual entrepreneurs or sects. Indeed, Pfeiffer seems to have made the sophists out to

---

[68] Plagues, oracles, and arts of interpretation are discussed throughout Sophocles' *Oedipus the King*: the chorus reasons that if Oedipus is as good at "riddles" as Teiresias, there is "no certain way of judging among interpretations" (κρίσις οὐκ ἔστιν ἀληθής, 501). To Jocasta, the "fact" that the oracle that Laius would be killed by his son went unfulfilled shows that we have no true "seer's art" (709).

[69] Kennedy in Kennedy 1989: 78–80.

be more rational and systematic than they actually were, for his attempt to argue that they shunned allegoresis overstates the case. N. J. Richardson has persuasively argued that methodological purity was not vitally important to these pioneers and that we are wrong to draw too sharp a line between sophistic close verbal analysis and allegorical reinterpretation: "In Plato's day, both might be said to be discovering the poet's *huponoia*, what he *ainittetai*."[70] Plato not only is a valuable witness for this but also illustrates a wide range of attitudes toward allegoresis in the later classical period.

Allegoresis and Rhetoric in Plato

The rhetorical mode of interpretation posited a *dianoia*, a thought or intention in the mind of the poet, which he expressed in words. In the *Protagoras*, a clearly involuted construction of a song by Simonidean is offered as what "Simonides intended (*dianooumenos*) when he composed the ode."[71] In the close verbal analysis of his poetic text, the search is for the author's *dianoia*, the "thought" contained in his "expression" (*lexis*).[72] But, as the extended discussion of another Simonidean text in the *Republic* shows, the rhetorical approach came close to allegory when the poet was granted license to use another word for the literal one. Evaluating the ethical content of Simonides' advice to "give to each what is *owed*" (*opheilomenon*), Socrates finds the saying too simplistic and argues that the poet should have said give to each "what is *fitting*" (*prosēkon*). He ironically defends Simonides' reputation as a wise man (and so enlists the admired poet in his own camp) by assuming that the expression was spoken "in riddling fashion as is the way of poets" (ἠνίξατο ἄρα . . . ποιητικῶς, *Republic* 332B).[73] Once the poet is allowed to "riddle," interpretation is effectively allegorical, since the word Simonides used (ὠνόμασε, i.e., "owed") may be completely different from what he "intended" (διενοεῖτο, i.e., "fitting": 332C).

The vocabulary for riddling discussed above shows allegoresis penetrating other modes of interpretation, as sophists and allegorists alike found

---

[70] Richardson 1975: 67.

[71] *Protagoras* 347A: ταῦτά μοι δοκεῖ . . . Σιμωνίδης διανοούμενος πεποιηκέναι τοῦτο τὸ ᾆσμα.

[72] Cf. *noei* for what Simonides "meant" by "giving to each what is owed" (Plato *Republic* 335E), and *Hippias minor* 365D: "Let's dismiss Homer since it is impossible to ask him what he meant (*noōn*) when he composed these *epē*" (i.e., the lines quoted at 365A–B.). Cf. Aristophanes *Wealth* 55 (*noei*, of an oracle).

[73] Cf. *Charmides.* 162A (ἰνίττετο ἄρα, ὡς ἔοικεν . . . ὁ λέγων τὸ τὰ αὑτοῦ πράττειν σωφροσύνην εἶναι). For Homer substituting words, cf. *Theaetetus* 194C.

a space for their own expertise by granting poets the license to "riddle."
Allegoresis is viewed by Plato as an uncertain method and dangerous
where children are concerned, but he never denies outright the possibility
of its being used in a more philosophical way. In the passage rejecting
allegory from the *Republic* discussed above (378D), the reasons are primarily pedagogical and social rather than theological or methodological.
A different critique of allegoresis is offered to a young man past primary
schooling when Socrates faults allegoresis because it does not result in
certain interpretations (*Phaedrus* 229E–230A). However, this is not a
problem with allegoresis in particular: Plato's Socrates argues on several
occasions that no form of poetic exegesis can get around the fact that
the texts of old poets can be construed in various ways and, unless one
has the poets at hand to cross-question, one cannot be certain that the
meaning construed from a text is what the poet "meant."[74] The Socrates
of the *Phaedrus* shows himself able to use allegoresis to reinterpret a story
about divine impropriety but in the end turns away from the method for
a different, social reason. In answer to Phaedrus' question whether he
truly believes the story (*muthologēma*) about Boreas' rape of Oreithyia,
Socrates is prepared to give a rationalizing (*sophizomenoi*) account of it
in naturalistic terms. Like any sophisticated reasoner (*sophizomenos*), he
is willing to dispense with a literal meaning of a myth (*Phaedrus* 229c–
E) and suggest that a blast of wind pushed a girl off a cliff, but people
ended up saying that she was "snatched up" or "raped" (*anarpaston*) by
Boreas.[75] Socrates then delivers a verdict on such wisdom: "I consider
such things elegant and amusing (*kharienta*), but an occupation suited for
someone who is formidably clever (*deinos*) and painstaking (*epiponos*)
and not altogether enviable" (229D). Socrates finally objects to the pro-
fessionalization of the practice and to its use as a source of amusement
and show of brilliance rather than as part of a philosophical search for
ethical truth.

A more revealing indication of Plato's views is hinted at in a passage
just preceding the dismissal of allegoresis in the *Republic*: Socrates is
discussing the evil influence that Hesiod's account of the castration of
Ouranos by Kronos may exert; without denying the possibility that an
edifying truth may lie beneath the surface of the story, he insists that such
an "unspeakable" (i.e., harmful even to repeat) tale should never be told,

[74] E.g., *Protagoras* 347c–348A, esp. 347E, *Hippias minor* 365c–D. The problem applies
to philosophical texts as well, e.g., Gorgias in *Meno* 70c–D. Cf. the allegoresis of
Protagoras' saying in *Theaetetus* 152c, with Ford 1994: 207, 212.

[75] Cf. Richardson 1975: 68 n. 5. This form of rationalizing apology is already in Pindar
Olympian, 1. where the tale of Pelops' being "snatched up" by Poseidon (40) is attributed
to the malicious gossip of neighbors (47).

or at best should be kept to a "very small audience, bound by pledges of secrecy and requiring extraordinary sacrifices, not of a pig but of some great offering that's hard to come by" (378A). The pig refers to the Eleusinian mysteries, which, for this relatively affordable sacrifice, communicated to initiates its arcane eschatological myths (*ta legomena*) of salvation through Demeter and Persephone.[76] Plato's Socrates would have been the last to reject the possibility of a mystical knowledge that can transform even the most horrific tale into a saving story, but he does object to disseminating such lore indiscriminately, as the Eleusinia promulgated its "unspeakable" (i.e., secret) myths and meanings to Greeks and foreigners alike, slave and free.

Plato's disquiet is focused on popularizers of subtle interpretation, not on the method itself nor on the project of redeeming traditional accounts of the gods. This antidemocratic desire to restrict the circulation of epic allegories appears in *Theaetetus* (180D) when Socrates alludes to Homer's description of Ocean and Tethys (a sea-nymph) as parents of the gods (cf. *Iliad*. 14.201, 302): this bit of Near Eastern cosmogony was allegorized as expressing a Heraclitean cosmology in which all things are in flux.[77] Socrates rejects the Heraclitean worldview, but allows that poets of the good old days used allegory to hide cosmic truths from the masses: "The ancients concealed their meaning from the many (*polloi*) with poetry, but the moderns, being 'wiser,' spell out everything in their public performances (ἀναφαδνὸν ἀποδεικνυμένων) so that even cobblers can hear and become wise and lose cease from their beliefs." The opposite view of hidden meanings, democratic and philanthropic, is held by the hero of the sophistically inspired *Prometheus Bound*: when asked to identify himself, he replies openly, "I will say clearly (*toros*) everything that you desire / without weaving in *ainigmata*, but with a simple (*haplos*) speech / as is right to speak to friends."[78] "Riddling" (*ainigmata*) in this piece is associated with antidemocratic sentiments and repudiated in favor of "simple speech." Allegorists are never democrats. They thrive by detaching their pupils from mass audiences.

In the classical period, then, allegorical interpretation remained one among a number of modes of seeking hidden meanings beneath the ostensibly literal purport of a text. Within this methodological melting pot, the promise of a recherché knowledge of Homer continued to hold out an

---

[76] Cf. Aristophanes *Acharnians* 764.

[77] Burkert 1992: 91–93.

[78] [Aeschylus] *Prometheus Bound* 609–11: for other references to the good teacher's simple speech (cf. *haplos logos*, 641), see Griffith 1983b: ad loc. (who takes the passage as sophistic) and Detienne 1967: 141 n. 131.

appeal, as allegorists and other up-to-date explicators of old poetry sought students among the educated young men of the democracy. Methodological quarrels doubtless arose in the ongoing contest to be truly *sophos*, but the appeal of possessing recherché knowledge of Homer united sophists, allegorists, and those Plato refers to as "the ones who are so clever (*deinos*) about Homer today": when they "explained" (*exhēgoumenoi*) that Homer "intended" (*dianoeisthai*) the name "Athena" to signify "divine intelligence" (*ha theonoa, Cratylus* 407A–C), there was little difference between allegorizing a divine figure in the tradition of Theagenes or etymologizing an apparently opaque word in the tradition of the sophists and grammarians. Less important than method was the result: a belief in godlike intelligence was compatible with traditional piety, and especially attractive to those endowed with enough intelligence to recognize it beneath the name of Homer's Athena.

In taking leave of Theagenes and his successors, it is necessary to repeat that allegoresis was only one strand in the archaic reception of Homer. Whatever debts Theagenes may have had to early Orphics or Pythagoreans, his allegoresis of Homer was a strategic reappropriation of epic as a kind of *ainos*. The later sixth century was a time when Homeric song was widely admired, but roundly criticized in some circles, and also a time when language itself was being plumbed for cues about ultimate reality. As certain religious fraternities were organized around their esoteric texts, Homer was made to speak in a new way, and at the same time a new class of experts in Homer was constituted. Epic allegorists found a place somewhere between the secret brotherhoods and the circles of wise men that archaic tyrants collected to advise on the meaning of dreams and oracles and to assist in managing the musical life of the state. Whether these allegorists' motives were to answer attacks on Homer or to sustain his authority in changing times, their novel way of interpreting these old songs provided a new way to possess them. These and other interpreters crowded into the assembly of democratic Athens and offered their skills when foreign armies were threatening; in peacetime, allegoresis continued to create a secret knowledge binding its believers in select fraternities within this most sophisticated and cosmopolitan city.

For all its willingness to outrage "common sense," allegoresis may be said to persist today in any literary study that postulates an "other" meaning, whether a "deeper" or "hidden" one, for a story or song. And yet it did not enter the *Poetics*. The reason was not simply the rise of the sophists or the powers of rhetorical modes of analysis. Nor could Plato's qualified objections to the form have ruled it out of bounds for the independent-minded Aristotle. In part, its lack of official sanction in the science of poetry was a success in its own terms, for in its roots, allegoresis was an esoteric activity. But the *Poetics* could neglect it because an alternative way of thinking about songs had been prepared in the fifth century. It was not simply the proto-discipline of rhetoric, but a wider movement that radically transformed archaic modes of evaluating and interpreting song. The following section describes this new development, an essential prelude to the development of poetics, which can best be called the invention of poetry.

PART II

THE INVENTION OF POETRY

FOUR

SONG AND ARTIFACT

SIMONIDEAN MONUMENTS

THIS AND the following two chapters locate the major difference between archaic and early classical criticism in the development, during the early fifth century, of an approach to song as verbal craftsmanship. I call this change the invention of poetry because it was signaled by the popularization of a new vocabulary to describe singers as "makers" or "poets" (*poiētai*) and songs as "made things" or "poems" (*poiēmata*). Viewing songs as objects produced by a craftsmanly kind of "making" (*poiēsis*) supported fifth-century rhetorical analyses based on language and structure, and paved the way for the fourth-century study of poetics, "the art of (verbal) making." The rise of this vocabulary will be documented in chapter 6, but it would be obviously fallacious to assume that the absence of such terminology earlier in the record proves that the corresponding concepts were also absent; it is therefore necessary first to trace early Greek conceptions of artistic making and their relation to conceptions of song. The present chapter considers the first attested comparisons between the two in Simonides of Ceos, who seems to have been professionally active from the later sixth century through the first quarter of the fifth. Although he is often invoked as the one who discovered the mimetic nature of poetry and thus the unity of the arts, his references to painting, sculpture, and monument-making will be seen rather to discriminate song from other means of celebration and to stress its unique power to praise and commemorate. This reading will prepare us to take up in chapter 5 the many metaphors for composing poetry as an artisanal activity presented by Simonides' poetic successors, Pindar and Bacchylides. These will show that, if the craftsmanly view facilitated technical analyses of poetry, it also implied a narrow view of song that encountered opposition from the singers themselves.

To appreciate the issues involved in interpreting Simonides, it is helpful to recall in outline the central role of *mimēsis* in the development of classical literary theory. The great influence of Plato and Aristotle may make it hard to realize that "art" had no capital "a" in early Greece: the word *tekhnē* referred to any "craft" or specialized "skill" in acting or making, and the artisans represented in epic are valued less as creators than as servants executing the commissions of others.[1] Among the wide range of *tekhnai*, special skill in singing, music, and dance had long been closely associated in practice, and in the fifth century bore a distinct name as the "Muses' arts"–*mousikē*.[2] The word means skill (the suffix *-ikē* implying *tekhnē*) in the activities associated with Muses, but there is no implication that *mousikē* produces *objets d' art* comparable to paintings and sculptures. For this conception to come into focus, the "Muses' arts" had to be combined with certain artisanal activities under the term "imitative arts" (*mimētikai tekhnai*). It seems to have been Plato's achievement to define this special new class of arts, one that included poetry, music, and dance, along with a select group of the crafts (painting, sculpture, sometimes architecture), as performing an essentially similar task.

To name this task, Plato seized on a derivative, probably fifth-century meaning of a word for "mimicking" or "imitating." The earliest uses of *mimēsis* and its cognates are for "miming," using the body and voice to copy human or animal behavior. Its first attestation, in the sixth-century *Homeric Hymn to Apollo* (163), refers to a panhellenic chorus "mimicking" (*mimeisthai*) various dialects in a ritual musical performance, and the sense "impersonate" or "reenact" is predominant in pre-Platonic occurrences.[3] It appears to be a secondary development when these words are used in the later fifth century to express the reproduction of appearances by artifacts: when Herodotus calls a carved wooden figurine an "imitation" corpse (*memimēmenon*, 2.78; cf. 3.37), he must mean it copies its form, even if the statuette in question serves as a *memento mori* rather than a piece of fine art. At this time as well is attested a new word for "likeness": *eikōn*, from a root meaning "to resemble," is used both for crafted "likenesses" and for verbal "images."[4] From this it has been inferred that, at least in certain circles, songs were being compared with works of visual art as forms of "representation" in the later fifth century.[5] But *mimēsis* plays no significant part in discussions of art before Plato: it is not used by Gorgias of Leontini when he discusses the illusive power

---

[1] On the relatively low status of the artisan in Homer's day: Schweitzer 1963: 1–40; Finley 1965: 71–72; Lloyd 1966: 208–9, 272 ff., 292 ff.; Schibli 1990: 54.

[2] First in Pindar *Olympian* 1.15 (Hiero "is glorified in the flower [finest form] of *mousikē*"), frs. 32; cf. 52k.39 S-M, and *Nemean* 1.25; on the suffix, Chantraine 1956: 15, 97 ff. On *tekhnē*, see Pollitt 1974: 32–37; Kube 1969: ch. 1.

[3] The connections with cult drama were overstated by Koller (1954); see Else 1958: 79, Nagy 1990: 42–45; Halliwell 1986: 110–16. Burkert (1985: 110) takes the "mimicking" of the *Homeric Hymn to Apollo* as a kind of speaking in tongues.

[4] On *eikōn*, used together with *mimēma* in Euripides *Helen* 72–74, see Webster 1939: 166.

[5] Harriott 1969: 142–44, citing Socrates' conversations with sculptors and painters on how they "represent" or "portray" inner character (Xenophon *Memorabilia* 3.10). Cf. Philipp 1968: 58–59.

of poems and paintings, nor is it prominent in comedy's many references to drama except in its basic sense of dressing up and disguising oneself.[6]

Whatever Plato may have owed to this generation, he significantly combined the term "imitation" with the notion of "art" to collocate a class of objects that is the closest ancient approximation to the enlightenment notion of Beaux Arts, arts that give a particular kind of pleasure without necessarily embodying or expressing philosophical truth.[7] Of course, "imitation" was a negative term in Platonic ontology, and, in principle, the imitative "arts" included such tricks as mimicry and vocal sound effects.[8] But with a further revision of the concept, Aristotle installed *mimēsis* at the center of his theory of poetry as "representation." The *Poetics* begins by pointing out that poetry, like painting, sculpture, instrumental music, and dance, is an art of "representing" human characters and actions. Aristotle's conception of the imitative arts embraces roughly the same range as Plato's, but against Plato's tendency to reduce artistic imitation to the copying of phenomenal appearance, he defines the mimetic arts as those that represent human characters and actions, and he permits scope to painters and poets to make representations better or worse as well as like their originals (1448a1–18, 1454b8–11, 1460b8–11: 33–35).

What makes Aristotle's theory of *mimēsis* a "literary" theory is his observation that audiences respond to *representations* in ways that are different from how they would respond in encountering the originals: in the famous case of tragedy, for example, *imitations* of events that would cause pain to an onlooker in real life can be contemplated (*theorein*) with pleasure (*Poetics* ch. 4). Many interpreters of the *Poetics* hold in addition that Aristotle thought poetic representations should communicate deeper truths about human life, a thesis that will need separate discussion in my

---

[6] Halliwell (1986: 114) is inclined to accept the existence of a mimetic theory of drama in the late fifth century, as in Zeigler *RE* 6A (1937): 2018–19; he cites as the first attested use of the word for artistic *mimēsis* Aristophanes' *Thesmophoriazousae* of 411, but it is applied there to the composing poet rather than to his product: Agathon says what the poet "does not possess by nature he must hunt up by *mimēsis*" (ἃ δ' οὐ κεκτήμεθα, / μίμησις ἤδη ταῦτα συνθηρεύεται, 154–55). See Muecke 1982: 54, for a convincing interpretation of the word as "disguising oneself, as a mime actor does," its usual sense in drama (e.g., Aeschylus *Choephoral* 560–64, Aristophanes *Frogs* 109). Cf. Else 1958: 73 ff., esp. 81.

[7] Plato's role in this change is stressed by Havelock (1963: 57–60, 212–13). To his survey of scholarship, add Sörbom 1966: esp. 78; Nehemas 1982: 56–58; Finkelberg 1998: 5–7, with references. Reservations in Halliwell 1986: 110. For Plato's complex uses of the analogy between poetry and the arts, see Janaway 1995: esp. chs. 1–2. I cannot discuss the attempts of Koller (1954: 125 ff.) and Rostagni 1922 to make Pythagoras a key influence on Plato; cf. Gentili 1988: 249 n. 9, tracing *biou mimēmata* at *Republic* 400A–B to Damon. Stimulating as they are, such theories must build very much on very little: cf. Burkert 1972a: 291 n. 65.

[8] Esp. *Gorgias* 463–65, *Republic* 597–601, *Sophist* 265–66; cf. *Phaedrus* 248D.

penultimate chapter. At present it is worth stressing that the basis for the idea of imitative arts lies in analogizing songs to sculptures, paintings, and other concrete products of the crafts; indeed, both Plato and Aristotle introduce their discussions of poetry as imitation with such comparisons.[9]

In tracing possible antecedents to the Platonic and Aristotelian theory of mimetic arts, it is worth remarking that explicit comparisons between poetry and the visual arts cannot be traced back further in Greece than Simonides.[10] Beginning with a much-quoted remark of his that compares poetry and paintings, I argue that passages from his songs that may appear to be early adumbrations of Aristotle engage with quite a different set of issues, both social and philosophical. In fact, his concern to present song as the truest embodiment of fame precluded any assertion of purely aesthetic values. In addition, I propose that such comparisons appear to have been prompted not by a dawning aesthetic consciousness, but by a change in the relations between song and writing in Simonides' time; in particular, the songs of Simonides will be shown to respond to memorial inscriptions from the later sixth century that presented themselves as the best way to preserve fame.

Singing, Painting, and Speaking

A very large house of cards has been build on a one-line apothegm Plutarch attributes to Simonides: "Painting is silent poetry, and poetry painting that talks."[11] Plutarch is paraphrasing here, and he clearly imposes a Peripatetic interpretation on the poet when he takes Simonides to say that the two arts have the same objects but different media (cf. *Poetics* 1447a18–22).[12] Since then, these words have often been invoked to credit Simonides with having discovered the kinship of poetry and the represen-

---

[9] E.g., Plato *Republic* 605A, already in *Ion* 532E–533C; Aristotle *Poetics* 1447a 17–23. Cf. Horace *Ars poetica* 1–9 (his *ut pictura poiesis*, 361, is making quite different points). See Halliwell 1986: 53, 116–22 on Plato, and esp. 128 on Aristotle.

[10] This important point is not always noted, but see Lucas 1968: 269–70; Halliwell 1986: 53 n. 11; and Segal 1989: 333.

[11] Plutarch *De Gloria Atheniensium* 346F: ὁ Σιμωνίδης τὴν μὲν ζωγραφίαν ποίησιν σιωπῶσαν προσαγορεύει, τὴν δὲ ποίησιν ζωγραφίαν λαλοῦσαν. For other versions, Schmid-Stählin *GGL* I.1.516 n. 6. I find myself much in agreement with Benediktson (2000: 12–18).

[12] Lanata (1963: 68) notes that Plutarch's use of *poiēsis* for "poetry" in general is otherwise not attested before Herodotus. A stronger objection, in my view, is that this word is not found at all in fifth-century high lyric. As Lucas (1968: 269 n. 2) notes, Plutarch's use of λαλεῖν as a synonym for λέγειν sounds post-Simonidean. But perhaps diction was freer in the collections of Simonidean *apothegmata* circulating by the time of Plato: Wilamowitz 1913: 148–50.

tative arts, and even with a theory of poetry as verbal *mimēsis*.[13] Two other brief Simonidean texts are usually adduced to represent him as responsible for "the birth of the image."[14] The first is another apothegm, "Speech is an *eikōn* [an image, picture, statue] of things" or "of actions" (ὁ λόγος τῶν πραγμάτων εἰκών ἐστιν; 190b Bergk), but it is attested very late and may be a derivative of the aphorism on poetry and painting.[15] The second is a fragment from one of his songs, "seeming overmasters even truth" (598 *PMG*), which is taken as the self-description of an "illusionist of speech." But to take Simonides as glorifying "opinion" (*dokein*) over truth is to read rather Platonically, which is in fact precisely the way one of Plato's character's interprets the phrase (quoted without attribution) in the *Republic* (365c). In an epinician poet, τὸ δοκεῖν καὶ τὰν ἀλάθειαν βιᾶται could simply mean that false stories or reputations (*dokein*) can prevail over the truth, as when Pindar warns that envious speech can "overmaster" the glory of the deserving (*Nemean* 8.32–34: πάρφασις ἦν καὶ πάλαι . . . ἃ τὸ μὲν λαμπρὸν βιᾶται).[16] Pindar goes on to say that a good singer helps prevent such misfortune, a sentiment a professional singer like Simonides might have endorsed in the now-lost context of his line.

This is not overabundant evidence for attributing to Simonides aesthetic theories that are only explicitly articulated in the fourth century.[17] It is worth mentioning that Simonides never uses *mimeisthai* or related

[13] E.g., Schmid-Stählin *GGL* I.1. 516 ("der Keim der platonisch-aristotelischen Theorie") and Thayer 1975: 14. Cf. Webster 1939: 169; Nestle 1942: 319–24; Treu 1968: 297; Lanata 1963: 68–69, with further discussion.

[14] Detienne 1967: 105–19; Vernant 1991: 172; similarly, Maehler 1963: 78–79; Harriott 1969: 143–44. Sometimes such ideas are supported by question-begging characterizations of Simonides' style as "plastic" or vivid so that his comments on icons become the program for his visualizing imagery: Bowra 1961: 363; Treu 1968: 295–305; Carson 1992. The idea of a "plastic" style derives from a late rhetorical tradition (as in Longinus *On the Sublime* 15.7) whose relevance to fifth-century aesthetic experience cannot be taken for granted.

[15] So Schmid-Stählin *GGL* I.1.516 n. 6. It is first in Michael Psellus 821B Minge. If genuine, the point may have been ethical rather than aesthetic, as in the similar expression attributed to Solon, "Speech is an *eidolon* of deeds (*erga*)," DL 1.58; cf. Democritus, "speech is the shadow of a deed" (λόγος γὰρ ἔργου σκιή, B 145 DK), with Gentili 1988: 250 n. 21. Contrast Plato *Cratylus* 431D, 439A.

[16] For "doing violence" to truth with lies, cf. *Iliad* 23.576 (ψεύδεσσιν βιησόμενος) and Bacchylides 13.200. The paradigmatic case of the epinician poet correcting slander that has gained a foothold is Pindar *Olympian* 1, esp. 28b–29, 47.

[17] Webster 1939: 169: "The origin of the *mimēsis* theory lies in the third quarter of the sixth century but it does not become dominant for a hundred years. Before that artist and poet must reach technical perfection in the realm of realistic representation, in the art of producing an illusion of reality." Similarly, Durante (1976: 171–72) posits progress in the visual arts leading to "what sounds like a discovery in Simonides—the equation of poetry and the plastic arts," subsequently developed in the sophistic milieu.

words, which, as used in the *Homeric Hymn to Apollo*, a work compiled during his lifetime, meant copying behavior, not representing. It remains noteworthy, of course, that Simonides did compare the two arts, and it may be possible to parallel the idea in his time. We should probably ascribe to Xenophanes a sense that both singers and painters or sculptors provided images, at least where the gods were concerned. His objections to the stories about the gods in Homer and Hesiod are complementary to his criticisms of divine images "drawn" and "carved" by painters and sculptors.[18] It is tempting to put such passages beside his reference to songs about battling demigods as *plasmata* (1.22 *IEG*), for *plasmata* can neatly cover both verbal "fabrications" and artistic "shapings." But there is no reason to infer that Xenophanes thought the ability of language to picture reality was particularly confined to song, and the primary force of *plasmata* in its philosophizing context is that such "fabrications" are false.

Rather than search for the roots of some transcendental notion of the aesthetic—an idea that was never very clearly articulated in antiquity—we should consider Simonides' statements about the arts in the light of the fact that archaic tyrants and aristocrats called on the talents of sculptors, painters, and architects as well as musicians for their civic displays. The way is pointed by Gentili, who notes that song and sculpture were most obviously linked at this time as two skills for memorializing outstanding human achievement. Hence singers sometimes point to a "gap between poetry and the figurative arts" that was "communicational, not technical or intellectual."[19] In this context, for a professional singer to speak of painting's silence is to point to a lack, for the very word glory—*kleos*—means literally "what is heard" (*klu-*).[20] This point of view favors interpretations of Simonides' apothegm as a polemic against paintings, as Pindar in the next generation would insist that his poems are *not* like statues, which he castigates for their silence (*Nemean.* 5.1–3; *Isthmian* 2.44–48).[21]

However this apothegm be taken, a demonstrably more significant set of Simonidean texts for the subsequent history of criticism treats another

---

[18] B 15.1–2, 4 DK distinguishes between γράψαι χείρεσσι and ἔργα τελεῖν, and θεῶν ἰδέας ἔγραφον and σώματ' ἐποίουν; cf. *demas* in B 14.2 DK. A similar pairing of painted and sculpted images seems to have occurred in B 16 DK, to judge from the opposition of διαζωγράφουσιν and ἀναπλάττουσιν in Clement's paraphrase (*Stromateis* 7.22, printed at Xenophanes 18, Gentili-Prato 1979: 175).

[19] Cf. Gentili 1988: 163 ff. and Nisetich 1977: 147. The Epicurean Philodemus of Gadara remains the closest ancient approximation to an aesthetic position.

[20] See Svenbro 1993: esp. 14–15.

[21] Christ 1941: 40–45; Karuzos 1972: 141–42 (first published 1941). *Contra* Philipp 1968: 58–59. Particularly acute is Svenbro 1984a: 127–36.

kind of craftsmanship as a foil to his own song: these are memorials, especially inscribed monuments that promise fame. These other references to works of sculpture and the arts, whenever we can judge from context, suggest that it is anachronistic to read Simonides as the first of the *mimēsis* theorists rather than as one of the last of the *kleos* theorists. As a poet of civic celebration and commemoration, his interest in artifacts was less the aesthetic one of how to marry truth to representation than the traditional singer's concern to confer wide and enduring praise on notable exploits. Simonides will be seen to argue that no physical object—even stones on which songs may be inscribed—can broadcast fame so widely as or so long as performance.

Tracing this theme in Simonides will suggest that one factor that provoked him to compare songs with artifacts was the great expansion within his lifetime of verse inscriptions on funeral memorials. From the beginning of the seventh century, we find writing used as a means of recording fame, as in dedications that are inscribed with the name of the dedicator. Such inscriptions expand in both number and complexity through the sixth century, and by the century's end it was increasingly common to add a few hexametric or elegiac lines, especially to grave markers. It is hardly surprising that some of these inscriptions borrow commemorative tropes from epic: when they promise a "fame that is unfailing always" (κλέϝος ἄπθιτον αἰϝεί, 44 Friedländer-Hoffleit [1948]) or a "memorial for many men, even for those to come" (πολλοῖς μνᾶμα καὶ ἐσομένοισι, 136 CEG), they assume song's ancient office of preserving unperishing fame "even for those to come to find out" (καὶ ἐσομένοισι πυθέσθαι, *Iliad* 22.305).[22] But in the world represented by Homer, heroes know about their past only through oral traditions, the "sayings that have been heard before" (πρόκλυτ' ἔπεα). They hope to leave behind a conspicuous monument if they fall, but envision it as an uninscribed stone marker that can only provoke oral tradition: its task is simply to stay fixed in the landscape (*empedos*) until a passerby may prompt a local exegete to utter again the name and the fame of the one beneath it.[23] Naturally enough, singers like Homer suggest that those ambitious for a fame that is "unfailing" or that "never withers away" (κλέος ἄφθιτον) must win their way into the traditions of heroic song, the "fames of men" (κλέα ἀνδρῶν).[24]

Because the sense of fame as *kleos*, as repeated oral performance, persisted through the archaic period, the mere fact of a song's being inscribed on durable matter might give a powerful new image of lasting fame. Now

[22] Cf. *Iliad* 7.87; *Od.* 1.302, 8.580, 11.76 (of a grave marker), and 64, 134, 356 CEG.

[23] E.g., *Iliad* 6.357–58, 7.81–91, 9.413; *Od.* 24.196–97. Ford 1992: ch. 5; Svenbro 1993: 16.

[24] See Nagy 1979: 229–61.

Simonides on at least one occasion was content to compose an elegiac couplet to be inscribed on a friend's memorial, and it seems to me quite possible that he wrote down at least some of his songs, and indeed, that lyric texts go back to the time of the earliest poets whose words have come down to us. When and whether Homer wrote is notoriously unclear, but texts of Alcman must have already been produced in seventh-century Sparta, for it is hard to imagine how Hellenistic scholars came to possess such an abundance of his archaic and often obscure songs if there were not some copies from a very early time.[25] Still, fame was hardly spread through wide readership in the archaic period: few copies of lyrics were circulated apart from presentation copies or archived manuscripts,[26] and the transcript of an archaic ode might have helped one who had heard the song remember its words, but it is difficult to imagine outsiders getting much out of texts that lacked not only an indication of the music and dance steps, but even a standard orthography and a way of distinguishing the length of certain vowels. It was surely far easier for Alcman or Simonides to teach a song to nine or fifty choristers by repeating it stanza by stanza than by passing out laboriously duplicated copies.

Against this background, Simonides' sayings may be read as reassertions, provoked by the increasing number and ambitions of epitaphs, of the traditional understanding of fame as secured through repeated oral performance. Simonides had a point: a short piece of inscribed poetry may be enduring, but it could be inconveniently out of the way—gravestones were usually situated along roads outside of towns, and victory dedications, though a signal honor, were left in temple precincts at the place of competition. Recent estimates suggest that their inscriptions would have been mute to the vast majority of even an urban population.[27] But a clamorous dancing chorus could bring a memorial back into the house and transport a statue dedicated at an overseas shrine back to the victor's city.[28]

To follow this theme, my discussion focuses on three related texts. I begin with an archaic sepulchral epigram that boasts that it will commemorate a certain Midas forever. I then take up a song in which Simonides (581 *PMG*) alludes to the Midas epigram and criticizes its presumption

---

[25] Davison 1968: 101; Pöhlmann (1990) makes the point, though the size and scope of Alexandrian editions of archaic authors is not a direct reflection of the conditions of production at the time.

[26] As Maehler notes in another connection (1997: 199). Cf. Rösler 1980a: 103–4.

[27] Harris 1989: 114–15; cf. Thomas 1989: 35.

[28] Song was even more portable if, as has been argued, epinician was performed by a solo singer with a symbolic or dancing chorus: for the thesis and a review of recent discussion, see Lefkowitz 1995 and Heath 1988. I keep this important possibility in mind, though I still take the poets' personae as at least imitating the voices of public, collective recognition.

of enduringness. Finally, I compare how Simonides describes his most ambitious commemorative song, that for the Greeks fallen at Thermopulae (531 PMG). In these songs, we shall observe a significant argument through imagery that prepares us to see why Pindar and Bacchylides dwell so significantly on the unique ability of song to "move" and "speak."

The Midas Epigram

Some said it was Kleoboulos, others Homer who composed the hexameters on the tomb of Phrygian Midas (not the legendary king of that name). They are first quoted in Plato (*Phaedrus* 264D) in the form of a four-line "cyclic poem" whose verses may be read in any order. Cyclic and noncyclic versions of the poem are found in many places thereafter. Because the poem circulated widely in oral tradition, as the many minor variations in its transmission indicate, we cannot reconstruct with certainty the version Simonides had in mind.[29] I cite the version given by Diogenes Laertius, who is also our source for Simonides' response (1.89–90):

> χαλκῆ παρθένος εἰμί, Μίδα δ᾽ ἐπὶ σήματι κεῖμαι.
> ἔστ᾽ ἂν ὕδωρ τε νάῃ καὶ δένδρεα μακρὰ τεθήλῃ,
> ἠέλιός τ᾽ ἀνιὼν λάμπῃ, λαμπρά τε σελήνη,
> [καὶ ποταμοί γε ῥέωσιν, ἀνακλύζῃ δὲ θάλασσα,]
> αὐτοῦ τῇδε μένουσα πολυκλαύτῳ ἐπὶ τύμβῳ,
> ἀγγελέω παριοῦσι, Μίδας ὅτι τῇδε τέθαπται.

> I am a maiden of bronze, and I rest upon Midas' tomb.
> So long as water shall flow and tall trees bloom,
> and the sun rise shining, and the shining moon,
> [and rivers flow and the sea toss up its waves,]
> remaining on this very spot, over this much-lamented tomb,
> I will announce to those who pass that Midas is buried here.[30]

[29] The relation of Simonides' model to the cyclic version quoted by Plato is much discussed, but we must reject the thesis that the poem was actually composed by Plato and that Simonides had another poem entirely in mind. For Critias clearly knew something like our poem (B 1 DK, see p. 107 below). The fullest treatment of variants is Markwald 1986: 34–83, though his purpose is to ascertain what might actually have been written on a seventh-century gravestone.

[30] For reasons given more fully below, I see no reason to jettison the first line and its mention of bronze: if it is post-Homeric, as Markwald (1986: 44) argues on linguistic grounds, it need not be post-Simonidean. In the second line, I have printed, chiefly to draw attention to it, a variant for "flow" (νάῃ for ῥέῃ) in the ms. of Diogenes Laertius, Plato, and other citations: see Markwald (ibid.: 46 n. 35). My discussion will not rely on the fourth line: absent from Plato and several other witnesses, it has what seems to be a late form in ἀνακλύζῃ; but what especially gives pause is the possibility that the line has been interpo-

The verse describes a top-of-the-line memorial of the late seventh century, when casting bronze was still a novel technique and epitaphs of more than a verse or two were beginning to become common.[31] The "bronze maiden" is likely to have been a Siren or a Sphinx, and the *sēma* on which she sits a stone pillar or column. The verses could have been inscribed on the stone column or on the statue itself.

Equally impressive, and innovative, is the promise the memorial makes. The fiction of an inscribed object "speaking" its text is as old as the alphabet in Greek, but the verse adds a heavy stress on its material durability and exact repeatability.[32] Its implication is that, though men may come and go with the seasons, the fame of Midas has found a solid, permanent form. What makes the boast possible is that fame–Midas' name–has been written down. One can contrast a well-known passage from the sympotic Theognidea (237–54) in which Theognis predicts that his songs will be sung in the future, "even among those to come, as long as there is sun and earth" (καὶ ἐσσομένοισιν ἀοιδή / ἔσσηι ὁμῶς, ὄφρ' ἂν γῆ τε καὶ ἠέλιος, 251–52). But Theognis envisions such fame residing "on the lips" of fair boys who will "sing with clear voices" at symposia (240–42) and so is consonant with the oral view of transmission in the epic mode (cf. *Od.* 24.93–94).[33] Unlike the generations of fair boys, Midas' bronze maiden will herself outlast the cycles of nature, and her speaking balloon will allow her to repeat her message forever. Thus she stands above and apart from the mournful and confused ritual cries that will be rehearsed on the spot ("this *much-lamented* tomb"). A kind of eternal attendant for his cult, the indestructible speaking machine represents an advance on the oral tradition's age-old techniques for preserving fame. Under this remarkable sign (*sēma*), Midas need have no fear that those to come will fail to recognize his tomb (*sēma*) or call his name when they pour libations on the spot.

The implication that writing allows monuments to surpass oral commemoration is made explicit in a remarkable inscription from the middle of the fifth century, which may well have been influenced by a version of

---

lated from Simonides' riposte, possibly during the second sophistic when the two poems were often cited together: so Markwald 1986: 63. Finally, there is no good reason to excise verses 3–4 from Simonides' model simply because they break up Plato's cycle: it is problematic to put too much weight on the version quoted by Plato, since for the poem to fit the cyclic game, inconvenient verses may have had to be "forgotten."

[31] See Raubitscheck 1968: esp. 13–15; Weber 1917: 543.

[32] Cf. Burzachechi (1962), who argues that in earlier inscriptions the statue (usually a divinity) "speaks" because it is viewed animistically, but from around 550 the "speaking" statue begins to be seen rationally and "loses its ancient halo of magic" (p. 53).

[33] In a similar vein I would interpret the much-discussed Ibycus 282.46–48 *PMG*. On the importance of song for immortality in the world of oral communications, see Thomas 1992: 114–15; Anderson 1987: 39–40.

the Midas epigram. It begins by bidding passersby to *"read* who is buried here" (108.1–2 *CEG*: χαίρετε τοὶ παριόντες, ἐγὸ δὲ θανὸν κατάκειμαι / δεῦρο ἰὸν <u>ἀνάνειμαι</u>, ἀνὲρ τίς τᾶδε τέθαπται). After providing the name and essential information about the deceased, the inscription concludes with a boast of permanence (108.4–8):

> καὶ μοι μνῆμ᾽ ἐπέθεκε φίλε μέτερ Τιμαρέτε
>   τύμοι ἐπ᾽ ἀκροτάτοι στέλεν ἀκάματον,
> hάτις ἐρεῖ παρίοσι διαμερὲς ἄματα πάντα·
> Τιμαρέτε μ᾽ ἔσστεσε φίλοι ἐπὶ παιδὶ θανόντι.

And my dear mother Timarete placed a memorial for me
    atop my tomb, an unwearying stele,
which[34] will say to passersby through all days constantly:
Timarete set me over her dear child, dead.

An epic pleonasm, "through all days constantly,"[35] stresses the lastingness of this message, as does the epithet "unwearying" (*akamatos*, 5). Epic *akamatos* usually describes dynamic forces and objects, often of a divine and destructive power.[36] In the epigram, this "epic word in unepic use" transfers to the stele the sort of force that would be needed to uproot it.[37]

The new "machines for fame," in Svenbro's apt phrase, are given a special name in an inscription on the base of a bronze statue from around 475 (429 *CEG*):

> αὐδὲ τεχνέεσσα λίθο, λέγε τίς τόδ᾽ ἀ[γαλμα]
> στῆσεν Ἀπόλλωνος βωμὸν ἐπαγλαΐ[σας]
> Παναμύης υἱὸς Κασβώλλιος, εἴ μ᾽ ἐπ[οτρύνεις]
> ἐξειπεῖν, δεκάτην τήνδ᾽ ἀνέθηκε θε[ῶι].

---

[34] Svenbro (1993: 49–50) may be right to read οὖ τις, "where someone will say," but I find his interpretation of the text strained.

[35] With its metrical position in the epigram, cf. *Od.* 4.209. Note that in *Iliad* 16.499 the phrase describes persistent *oral* report: reproach will follow the unvaliant "through all days constantly."

[36] Friedländer-Hoffleit 1948: 131. In Homer, *akamatos* is applied only to fire, especially god-kindled conflagrations, and in Hesiod to Atlas' hands and Typho's feet: see *LfgrE* s.v. Pindar uses *akamatos* for Pelops' god-given horses (*Olympian* 1.87) and the sea (*Nemean* 6.39); Bacchylides for the sea (5.25), the "untiring stream" of the Alpheus (ἀκαμαντορόαν, 5.180), and the ever-watchful eyes of Argus (19.20). Empedocles applies it to the wind (B 111.3 DK), and Aeschylus to the "unwearying strength" (*sthenos*) of Darius' armies (*Persians* 901).

[37] For fifth-century reminiscences of "unwearying" poetic fame, cf. Bacchylides' praise of the Greeks fallen at Troy: "All-shining Virtue is not diminished, hidden in dark night, but flourishes steadfastly with unwearying reputation" (ἀλλ᾽ ἔμπεδον ἀκ[αμάτᾳ] βρύουσα δόξᾳ), and is "spread over land and sea" (13.175–81, following Blass). Sophocles combined "unwearying" with the Homeric epithet for "unfailing" fame to name the most enduring of the gods, Earth: Γᾶν / ἄφθιτον ἀκαμάταν (*Antigone* 339).

Voice contrived of stone, tell who set up this delightful work
 enhancing the altar of Apollo;
Panamye's son Casbollius—if you urge [?] me
 to speak out—dedicated it as a tithe to the god.

"Voice of stone" is as strong an oxymoron in Greek as in English, since *audē* was typically the voice of living, especially human, beings; the phrase encapsulates the paradoxical achievement of the inscriber's art, which can fix oral tradition as fast as the statue above has captured a body in bronze.[38]

The Midas song also uses paradoxical language as it fixes oral report ("I will announce") in bronze. Its seasonal images hardly bear too much analysis, but set the untouchable maiden amid a world of constant change and even ephemerality. In Homer, the simile of "leaves, which the wood brings forth in bloom" (ἄλλα δὲ θ' ὕλη / τηλεθόσα φύει, *Iliad* 6.144–51), expresses the transitory nature of human generations.[39] The maiden will always "lie" atop Midas' tomb (v. 1), but to "lie" in epitaphs is normally to be dead.[40] The tensions between statue and nature are summed up in its opening phrase: "bronze maiden" is an oxymoron if "maiden" is given its force as a transitional stage in life, the verge before the change into marriage. Much stronger than an expression like Homer's "golden Aphrodite" (χρυσῆ 'Αφροδίτη, *Iliad* 22.470), χαλκῆ παρθένος suggests that the price of durability is arrested development, as in the famous Phrasikleia inscription from the second half of the sixth century (24 CEG):

> σῆμα Φρασικλείας. κόρε κεκλέσομαι αἰεί,
> ἀντὶ γάμο παρὰ θεὸν τοῦτο λαχοσ' ὄνομα.

> I am the tomb of Phrasikleia. Maid I will be called always,
> in place of marriage the gods allotted me this name.

This *sēma* for a woman whose name means "speak the fame" fulfills its function by making that name resound anytime it is read.[41] But it also fastens another name on Phrasikleia, "maid," which encapsulates her early death. Just as the writing will never change, Phrasikleia will never take on any other title—"mother," for example; immortalized in one

---

[38] Cf. Theognis' remark that once our soul leaves us, we become "like a stone without a voice" (λίθος ἄφθογγος, 568–69). My interpretation is, again, *pace* Svenbro (1993: 56 ff).

[39] Apollo gives voice to a similar perspective on the human condition in *Iliad* 21.463–66; Nagy 1979: 178–79. Cf. also Mimnermus 2 *IEG* and Griffith 1975.

[40] This play on the word may be clearly seen in Theognis 240.

[41] Svenbro (1993: 24–25) interprets the flower Phrasikleia holds as the ever-renewed "blooming" of her fame in sound.

sense, she yet will not ripen and grow into a bearer of children who would write a different epitaph.

To a writer on stone, the marriage of sculpture and song seemed to be a permanent union with an immortal progeny of fame. That is why, I suggest, the union was rent asunder along with the monument by Simonides.

Simonides on the Midas Epigram (581 *PMG*)

The same passage of Diogenes asserts that the Midas inscription was answered by the following lines of Simonides:

τίς κεν αἰνήσειε νόῳ πίσυνος Λίνδου ναέταν Κλεόβουλον
ἀενάοις ποταμοῖς ἄνθεσί τ' εἰαρινοῖς
ἀελίου τε φλογὶ χρυσέας τε σελάνας
καὶ θαλασσαίαισι δίνης ἀντιθέντα μένος στάλας;
ἅπαντα γάρ ἐστι θεῶν ἥσσω· λίθον δὲ
καὶ βρότεοι παλάμαι θραύοντι· μωροῦ φωτὸς ἅδε βουλά.

Who if he trusts his wits would praise Kleoboulos who dwells in Lindus
for setting beside ever-flowing rivers and the flowers of spring
and the flame of the sun and the golden moon
and the eddies of the sea, the force of a stele?
For all things are weaker than the gods; and stone
even mortal hands can shatter; this is the devising of a fool.

Campbell pronounced Simonides' song complete because it is the same length as Kleoboulos' epitaph.[42] This may be disputed, since the "original" circulated in versions of different lengths, but I am inclined to agree: Simonides seems to seek closure in ring-composition—the name of Kleoboulos, which ends the first line, is recalled with a pun in the last phrase, where the one "famed for advice" turns out to have offered "a fool's advice" (μωροῦ φωτὸς 'δε βουλά).[43] If this is so, we cannot base interpretation on speculations about what the singer might have gone on to say in some following verses.

This rejoinder to Kleoboulos resembles Simonides' song on Pittacus (541 *PMG*), excerpted in Plato's *Protagoras*, for both are polemics against Sages. The Kleoboulos verse seems less formal, even playful: its rhythms—dactylo-epitrites—are appropriate to praise, as in epinicia, but praise is explicitly ruled out in the first line; a number of epicisms give the

---

[42] Campbell 1967: 393.

[43] Cf. the play on the names Thrasyboulus and Thrasymachus recorded in Aristotle *Rhet.* 2.23, 29.

language[44] a solemn air, as if Simonides were engaging Kleoboulos in a heroic debate. This light, bantering ditty would have been appropriate at a symposium where, we have noted, the Seven Sages were often a topic of discussion.[45] Simonides' song would have been quite effective if recited after someone had performed Kleoboulos' epitaph.

Simonides' argument is rooted in traditional Greek piety even as he articulates one of his characteristic themes—the transience of all things beneath the sun. In line with popular notions of divinity, Simonides denies that anything humans might make can remain fixed in a nature that is constantly changing.[46] His point emerges into sharper focus if we consider two earlier songs that expressed related themes in similar words. The ultimate paradigm for the lesson that Simonides reads Kleoboulos may be Homer's famous passage on the storms sent by Zeus against hubristic men: there, the "works of men" are diminished (μινύθει δέ τε ἔργ' ἀνθρώπων) when "swollen rivers flow" (πάντες μὲν ποταμοὶ πλήθουσι ῥέοντες).[47] Even closer is Solon's hymn to his Muses (13 *IEG*), which shows that "works of hubris do not long endure" (οὐ γὰρ δὴν θνητοῖς ὕβριος ἔργα πέλει, 16) by conjuring up a storm that "shakes the foundations of the sea and lays waste the fair works of men" (πυθμένα κινήσας, γῆν κάτα πυροφόρον / δηιώσας καλὰ ἔργα, 19–20). When the storm subsides, the "force of the sun" shines clear again (λάμπει δ' ἠελίοιο μένος, 23); such is the vengeance of Zeus, the truly "constant" (διαμπερές, 27) watcher. Solon's topic is wealth, and his theme is that only justly acquired "possessions" (χρήματα, 7) stay "fixed fast in the ground" (ἔμπεδος, 10).[48] But both singers deny lastingness to merely human "works" beneath the sun, and both invoke the dynamic power of nature, *menos*, as the destroyer of unjust makings.

What is distinctive in Simonides' use of the topos is that he applies it to a human artifact: Hermann Fränkel and Bowra note that whereas in Solon and Homer, the "works" destroyed were works of agriculture, Simonides' target is a stele.[49] Some have gone further along these lines and taken Simonides to hint at the superiority of song over monuments in

[44] See Campbell's commentary for details.

[45] In the *Protagoras*, Socrates condemns the sympotic practice of bringing in flute girls (Simonides' lyric is of the sort that was sung to the flute) and carrying on conversations via poetry rather than discussing more important topics (347c–d).

[46] Cf. Wilamowitz 1907: 459.

[47] *Iliad* 16.392, 389. This passage appears to have affected one version of the Midas epigram (*Certamen* 235.267 Allen [1946]) boasting it will last "as long as rivers swell" (καὶ ποταμοὶ πλήθωσι). Cf. Markwald 1986: 53.

[48] Simonides also praised "wealth won without trickery" (πλουτεῖν ἀδόλως, 651 *PMG*).

[49] Fränkel 1975: 305–6; Bowra 1961: 370–71: Simonides "knew that he must not claim too much for [art]." Note that Apollo and Poseidon unleash rivers to destroy a great wall in *Iliad* 12.13–33. See note 36 above.

providing truly immortal fame.[50] But Fränkel seems right that Simonides was no less pious with regard to his own art: even song sinks at last into the ground (594 *PMG*); hence, Simonides says at most that song will last *as long as* rivers flow.[51]

Whether or not we read a qualified praise of song in Simonides, Fränkel is right to stress that he "directs heavy fire against the presumptuous claim made by an inscription ascribing immortality to the grave-monument of which it formed a part." But every stone marker ever erected had been by its very purpose an equal affront to time and the gods. I suggest that this particular monument provoked Simonides because it was inscribed: it not only opposed a brazen face to the ravages of divine nature, but it presumed to speak Midas' fame forever. Simonides is clearly interested in the epigram for its promise of *fame*: Kleoboulos, the one of "famous devising," is also, as the epigram's author, one who has devised a plan for fame. In fact, a parody by Critias (B 1 DK) exploits the Midas song for just such a claim of poetic endurance. In epic hexameters, Critias says that Anacreon's songs will never grow old or die, "as long as water is mixed with wine" at symposia. In this *jeu d' esprit*, Critias reappropriates for poetry the perpetual flux that Simonides had denied to the stele by playfully converting it to the flow of drinks at symposia.[52] Critias also alludes to the epigram in his concluding image, saying that Anacreon's songs will be sung as long as the "scale-pan, daughter of bronze, sits a top the cottabus" (B 1.16 DK). As with the "bronze maiden," the durability of an artifact is expressed with the trope of its being a maiden in metal; for specially enduring objects, a special "generation" is required.[53]

What Simonides opposes is transferring the imperishability of fame from the unceasing oral tradition to the stone itself. His attack culminates with breaking *stone* (line 5), which has puzzled scholars who expected him to say "mortal hands can break *bronze*." Some have concluded that, since Simonides says nothing about a bronze figure, he did not know the song in the form given by Diogenes Laertius.[54] But stone is the ultimate

---

[50] For a "polemic" against statuaries here, Christ 1941: 40–45, following Snell (1938: 175), who supposed a continuation of the poem; more tentatively, Segal 1998: 134.

[51] Fränkel 1975: 430.

[52] Cf. Wilamowitz 1913: 109. The allusion is quite hearable: Critias' fifth line begins ἔστ' ἂν ὕδωρ, as does line 2 of the Midas epigram.

[53] For a similar troping, cf. Critias 2.12–14 *IEG*, where he caps a list of useful inventions from various cities with Athenian pottery; this is named in the witty and pregnant kenning "the offspring of earth and the furnace, invented by the people who set up the fair trophy at Marathon."

[54] So Bergk (on fr. 57 B) and Bowra (1961: 370–71). Alternatively, Snell (1938) suggested that the text Simonides knew began παρθένος εἰμὶ λίθοιο. Fränkel (1975: 306 n. 6) imagines that Simonides missed the epigram's point, as the poem probably dates from the time when bronze casting was a recent advance, an idea seconded by Philipp (1968: 136 n. 194). These

target because that is where Simonides imagines the inscription to be (cf. αὐδὲ τεχνέεσσα λίθο above, also on the base of a bronze statue). Simonides is objecting to the idea that inscribing a song on durable material will make fame last; his point is that only a fool would trust an inscription to guarantee immortal fame. A statue, a burial mound, or any uninscribed artifact had been the silent partner rather than the rival of oral tradition; but once such objects make much of their engraved messages, Simonides attacks their hubristic guarantees of fame.

In Simonides' hands, Kleoboulos' symbols of eternal endurance become images of a relentlessly corrosive nature. His attack is summed up in the pair of terms that begin and end its main sentence, opposing "ever-flowing" (*aenaos*) nature to the "force of a stele" (*menos stalas*). To speak of the "force" of a stele is catachrestic, for *menos* in Homer is vital energy, whether in the willful strength of men or in the forces of nature—the sun, winds, rivers.[55] In Simonides, *menos* may play ironically on the epigram's μενοῦσα, undermining its staying power with Homer's "force of fire" (e.g., πυρὸς μένος, *Iliad* 6.182) or Solon's "force of the sun" (ἠελίοιο μένος, 13.23 *IEG*).[56]

With the other key term, "ever-flowing" (ἀενάοις), eternity (ἀεί) is granted to Kleoboulos' "flowing" (νάῃ or ῥέῃ) waters but implicitly denied to the stele. Though never departing from its literal meaning, "ever-flowing" was a very evocative word throughout Greek literature:[57] Simonides' younger contemporary, Pindar, used it only in connection with the gods, and he glorified music by saying that the phorminx quenches even the "ever-flowing fire" of Zeus' thunderbolt (ἀενάου πυρός, *Pythian* 1.6).[58] Pindar's use of the term has in turn been connected with the Pytha-

---

objections are weakened if we believe that the epigram, if not fictional, at least circulated orally (perhaps in connection with Seven Sages traditions). Yet my reading can accommodate such speculations as that Midas' tomb must have had the bronze figure on a base of stone (Campbell 1967); or that "stone" means to include statue and base: Gerber 1970: 328.

[55] Redfield 1975: 172. Fränkel (1975: 306–7) puts it that the epigram's mistake "lay in assigning to mere human handiwork the same vital energy (*menos*) as that which dwells in the infinite power of the gods."

[56] Cf. μένος ἠελίοιο, *Od.* 10.160, *Homeric Hymn to Apollo* 371, where "the holy strength of Helius" makes Pytho rot; cf. *Iliad* 12.18 (of rivers), Solon 9.1 *IEG* (of snow), Pindar fr. 129.1 S-M, and Bremer 1983: 57–60.

[57] Its sole use in Homer characterizes the water in the cave of the Nymphs (*Od.* 13.109), and the sense of a quasi-magical, abundant, and fecund flowing remained within the ambit of the word: Hesiod *Works and Days* 550, 595; Aeschylus *Suppliants* 553; Euripides *Ion* 1083. *LfrgE* s.v. ἀενάοντα.

[58] *Olympian* 14.12: αἰέναον . . . τίμαν of Zeus. Cf. *Nemean* 11.8: perennial feasts held in the Hall of Hestia at Tenedos are "ever-flowing," presumably with libations to her. Fr. 119.4: the "cloud of ever-flowing wealth" sent by the gods to the Rhodians.

gorean concept of divinity as manifesting itself in "ever-flowing" flux.[59] It is suggestive that Pythagorean texts speak of the tetractys as "the spring of ever-flowing nature" (παγὰν ἀενάου φύσεως), and that in one of his rare descriptions of his own song as immortal, Pindar calls it a "spring of ambrosial words" (παγὰν ἀμβροσίων ἐπέων, *Pythian* 4.299).[60]

While Pythagoras was speaking of an ever-flowing divinity, Heraclitus saw nature as a flowing, fiery river, constantly exchanging life and death. For Heraclitus, not even this eternal and ever-changing cosmos could ever be "made," but "always was, is, and will be an ever-living fire" (πῦρ ἀείζωον).[61] In such a cosmos, true fame could only subsist in flux, not "fame that does not fail" but "ever-flowing": "The best choose one thing above all—ever-flowing fame from mortals; but the many are satisfied glutting themselves like beasts."[62] Tinged with esoterism, "ever-flowing" remained a powerful term in poetry: it is the first word in the parabasis of the *Clouds* to signal the flexibility, insubstantiality and omnipotence of sophistic thought.[63]

In Simonides, *aenaos* sums up both the endless change of nature and its perpetual renewal through generations. For fame to last, it must itself "flow" rather than just stand still. If song would hope to continue through a time that may erode monuments, it must become somehow attuned to time as Critias later described it, "unwearying" and "full of an ever-flowing stream."[64] In Simonides' vision of song, enduring fame is not achieved by writing on rocks or metal; the only possible fame for mortals comes from ever-flowing oral traditions, as songs are taken up and performed to make the names of the dead sound again in time.

---

[59] Duchemin 1955: 73–74, cf. 260–61. For mystery elements in Pindar's poetry, see Lloyd-Jones 1990: 80–109.

[60] Cf. 58 B 15 DK, with Delatte 1915: 249 ff. and Burkert 1972a: 72, 186–87.

[61] Heraclitus B 30 DK: κόσμον τόνδε, τὸν αὐτὸν ἀπάντων, οὔτε τις θεῶν οὔτε ἀνθρώπων ἐποίησεν, ἀλλ᾽ ἦν ἀεὶ καὶ ἔστιν καὶ ἔσται πῦρ ἀείζωον, ἁπτόμενον μέτρα καὶ ἀποσβεννύμενον μέτρα. Cf. the Orphic-sounding beatitude in Euripides: happy the one who gazes on "the ageless order of deathless nature" (ἀθανάτου καθορῶν φύσεως κόσμον ἀγήρων, fr. 910.5–6 Nauck), on which see West 1983: 192. Snell (1953: 81–82) compares with Pindar Heraclitus' "energetic tensions," which required that any individual thing be completed, as victory, by "indestructible song." Hubbard 1985 is devoted to these tensions.

[62] B 29 DK: αἱρεῦνται γὰρ ἓν ἀντὶ ἁπάντων οἱ ἄριστοι, κλέος ἀέναον θνητῶν· οἱ δὲ πολλοὶ κεκόρηνται ὅκωσπερ κτήνεα. Cf. Anon. Iamblichus 5.2 c. 88, 5g E (II.402.20 DK): "Since we are mortal, we should not spare our lives but seek ever-flowing good report, ever alive" (εὐλογίαν ἀέναον καὶ ἀεὶ ζῶσαν). A similar theme is found in plainer language in Isocrates *Archidamus* 109.

[63] *Clouds* 275. This usage is close to Hesiod's mists arising from "ever-flowing rivers" (*Works and Days* 550).

[64] Critias B 18.1–2 DK (printed as Euripides fr. 594 Nauck): ἀκάμας τε χρόνος περί τ᾽ ἀενάωι ῥεύματι πλήρης.

"Ever-Flowing" Fame and Thermopulae:
Simonides 531 *PMG*

A final Simonidean lyric on death and remembrance promises precisely to build an ever-flowing monument in song to Leonidas and his 300 Spartans. In an extraordinary and crucially important show of valor, this hopelessly outnumbered band of soldiers died to a man holding off the Persians at Thermopulae. They gained a lasting renown in the old style: a generation later, Herodotus found out the names of each Spartan who died there and committed them to memory "as names of men that deserve to be remembered" (7.224). Equally memorable was the fate of Leonidas' body: when he fell, Xerxes ordered his head cut off and impaled on a stake (7.238), an impious indignity that rankled in Greek memory for decades. Eventually the Spartans retrieved what were said to be Leonidas' remains and enshrined them in their city, where they became the focus of a hero cult (9.78–80). But it was in the wake of the battle, with Leonidas still unburied, that Simonides composed the following song (531 *PMG*):

[τῶν ἐν Θερμοπύλαις θανόντων]
εὐκλεὴς μὲν ἁ τύχα, καλὸς δ' ὁ πότμος,
βωμὸς δ' ὁ τάφος, πρὸ γόων δὲ μνᾶστις, ὁ δ' οἶ[κ]τος ἔπαινος·
ἐντάφιον δὲ τοιοῦτον οὔτ' εὐρὼς
οὔθ' ὁ πανδαμάτωρ ἀμαυρώσει χρόνος.   5
ἀνδρῶν ἀγαθῶν ὅδε σηκὸς οἰκέταν εὐδοξίαν
Ἑλλάδος εἵλετο· μαρτυρεῖ δὲ καὶ Λεωνίδας,
Σπάρτας βασιλεύς, ἀρετᾶς μέγαν λελοιπὼς
κόσμον ἀέναόν τε κλέος.

[Of those who died at Thermopulae,]
well-famed is their fate, and fine their fall.
Their tomb is an altar; instead of lamentations they have remembrance,
    groaning for them is praise;
they are wrapped in such a shroud as neither stain
nor all-subduing time will darken.   5
This shrine for worthy men has as its attendant the esteem
of Greece. Leonidas, too, bears witness,
the Spartan king, who has left behind a great ornament of his excellence
and an ever-flowing fame.

Scholars have been unsure whether this song was simply a literary encomium or was an actual ceremonial hymn to be performed either at Thermopulae where the dead were buried (Herodotus 7.228), or back in

Sparta.[65] The reason for our uncertainty is not simply a lack of external evidence, but the song's own insistence that these heroes' commemoration is not to be associated with any monument or ritual. Because their immortal fame has made them like ever-living gods, the usual ceremonies and lamentation are replaced by memory and praise; instead of a tomb, they have an altar; the flimsy shroud in which a corpse was wrapped becomes for them an eternal artifact that cannot be impaired by "all-subduing" time.[66] The glory of these soldiers is "enshrined" in words of praise (6–7). It is not inscribed on stelae left behind in far-off Thermopulae (one of which bore verses by Simonides: Herodotus 7.228 = 28 Page [1981]), nor in a heroic precinct in Sparta. The memorial that will never be defeated by time (4–5) is no physical construct but the memory, praise, and glory (*doxa*) of their deeds. This is summed up at the end as the "great ornament to virtue and a fame that is ever-flowing" (9). Once again, the epithet ἀέναος assures that praise will escape the predations of "all-subduing time." Such deeds merit not a tangible "ornament" (*kosmos*),[67] but a glory (*kosmos*) matching the "great" order (*kosmos*), of nature. As in the other Simonidean texts considered, religious values and social usages far outweigh any theory about song's representational status.

I have argued that to credit Simonides with "discovering" the mimetic basis of the arts is an anachronistic, Platonizing interpretation poorly attested in his corpus. As a professional singer, he was rather interested in artifacts that promised lasting fame. The Kleoboulos epigram implied that inscription, not singing, was the true means to immortality, an implication that other new machines for fame also advanced. In a culture in which "fame" continued to mean "what is heard," such ambitions were somewhat paradoxical and disturbing to professional singers and other wise

---

[65] Cf. most recently Palmisciano 1996. Bowra (1961: 345–49), positing cult performance at Sparta, puts weight on the first line, but it is strongly suspected by West (*CR* 17 [1967]: 133; *CQ* 20 [1970]: 210). Wilamowitz (1913: 176 n. 3) sees in "good men" an indication of cult at Thermopulae; Podlecki (1968: 257–62) an informal encomium or threnos, perhaps sung at messes in Sparta; Gerber (1970: 315–17) takes our source Diodorus (11.11.6) at his word in calling it an encomium.

[66] The word *epitaphion* usually means a shroud and is likely figurative here, an unexpected word either for "monument" (as Fränkel [1975: 320] takes it), "fame" (Maehler 1963: 84 n. 1), or commemorative ritual (Bowra 1961: 346). Goldhill (1991: 124–25) sees the significance of the poem in its advertising the virtues of the fine heroic death to the citizens of the collective polis.

[67] Cf. Pindar *Olympian* 8.82–83 (of 460), the "gleaming adornment" (*liparon kosmon*) that is both the victory and the song commemorating it; Segal 1998: 142 compares Pindar fr. 194.2–3, discussed in chapter 5. *Kosmeō* in Aristophanes *Frogs* 1027 (cf. *Knights* 568) shows that in such contexts, *kosmos* should not be glossed as poetic "structure," *pace* Verdenius (1987 on *Olympian* 11.13, with literature).

men of the age. Philosophers and moralists undermined the solidity of the phenomenal world and stressed the inevitability of change. Simonides repeated their charges and, so to speak, dematerialized the fame he offered. From the Midas song to Thermopulae, Simonides portrays monuments in images that establish an opposition between flux and stability, with flux favored as the only form of continuing life. Insisting on the unique value of living, moving, and sounding song reasserted its connection to the life of a just and happy city.

In this context, it seems relevant that Simonides lived during the flowering of the epigraphic habit of inscribing commemorative verses on monuments, and that when he refers to such inscribed memorials, he stresses song's superior ability to capture fame and preserve it. Because they arose from a confrontation between singing and making, between performance and writing, Simonides' themes and images proved useful into the fourth century and beyond. The next chapter will show that the two Simonidean charges against works of art—silence and fixity—generated in Pindar and Bacchylides the complementary trope that well-made texts of celebration and commemoration have a unique sort of *voice* and *motion* of their own. With these terms, singers began to transform the "ever-flowing" nature of song from a quasi-religious or cosmological value into a special property of poetic language, a power to capture and communicate an essential aspect of life that came to be thought characteristic of works of art in words. The definition of literature in the fourth century required not only that songs be viewed as valuable even when extracted from their contexts, but also that songs and all writing worth preserving share some special property not to be found in ordinary speech. The culminating text in this discussion, as we shall later see, was when Plato took up the Midas epigram yet again and argued that writing should have an organic, living, dialogic form. The next chapter studies the intervening career of these analogies, still in their social and ethical contexts. For the conflict between dynamic song and static monument was taken up by Pindar and Bacchylides in their numerous and complex self-presentations.

FIVE

SINGER AND CRAFTSMAN IN PINDAR
AND BACCHYLIDES

T HE PREVIOUS chapter argued that in archaic Greece, where song was overwhelmingly more present as sounds on the air than as brief inscriptions or rare book rolls, there was little incentive to connect singing with the production of tangible, solid objects. Yet the fact that we cannot find explicit comparisons between songs and works of art before Simonides may be regarded as merely accidental. Even in the absence of a developed theory of verbal imitation, it is quite possible to find resemblances between composing songs and painting, sculpting, or embroidering. Indeed, comparative linguistics has assembled an array of Greek metaphors for composing song taken from such crafts as building and weaving that go back to the Indo-European ancestors of the Greeks.[1] Certainly our evidence is too lacunose to rule out the possibility of such thinking before our first choral poetry in Alcman, and indeed, in the sketchily attested period between Alcman and Simonides. But within this *longue durée*, the craftsmanly conception of poetic making may be more or less central to conceptions of song, and there is little evidence of such language or of such an emphasis in early Greece: archaic epic and lyric singers describe themselves with verbs of performing rather than of making: they "sing," "celebrate," "hymn," or "provide festive music" (ἀείδειν, κλείειν, ὑμνεῖν, μέλπεσθαι).[2] Epithets for singers in Homer and Hesiod (especially θεῖος and θέσπις, "godlike") stress the divine sponsorship of song rather than the singer's skill in language, and when songs are praised, it is not for being well "made" or artfully constructed.[3] The singer is classed in Homer among the itinerant specialized workers (*dēmiourgoi*) along with healers, seers, and carpenters,[4] but Jesper Svenbro

---

[1] Schmitt 1967: esp. 296–301, though not, it should be noted, "making" (*poiein*). Durante 1976: esp. 167–84.

[2] For epic, see *LfrgE* s.v. ἀείδω, and for archaic lyric, cf. Archilochus 117 *IEG*; Alcman 14a, 28, 29 *PMG*; Sappho 160 V; Simonides 564 *PMG*; Corinna 655 I.1.2 *PMG*. For *melpesthai* ("singing accompanied by dance"), see Bielohlawek 1924–27.

[3] See in general Walsh 1984: ch. 1, and Ford 1992: 35–39, 168–70, 193.

[4] *Od.* 19.135. See Nagy 1990: 56–57. The name "Homer" (first attested in the sixth century) has been etymologized as the one who "fits" (*ar-*) song together: Nagy 1979: 296–300; differently, Durante 1976: 185–204; a Semitic derivation is now proposed by West 1995; cf. 1966 on Hesiod *Theogony* 39.

seems right to stress that Homer never speaks of the poet's activity in terms of "skill" or "craft."[5] In epic, "crafting" speech is associated with cunning deception.

It is therefore remarkable that we find an explosion of craft metaphors for song in Pindar and Bacchylides, composing in the wake of Simonides in the first half of the fifth century. Moreover, this language is used to illustrate the *composition* of songs and not only, as in Simonides, their modes of communicating. Pindar's numerous references to the power and value of his song have many times been synthesized into a theory of art. In such reconstructions, his comparisons with works of plastic art are usually taken as proclamations of his technical skill as he weaves words and embroiders language to produce valuable and enduring artifacts—in short, poems. Bruno Snell and Herwig Maehler have gone further and discerned in Pindar's insistence on the mobility as well as the fineness of his works the discovery that poetry can be literature, a precious artifact no longer tied to any occasion of performance.[6] Maehler adds that the choral lyric poets are the first to say that a mortal's song can be immortal, whereas earlier poets had spoken at most of *the Muses'* "immortal song and dance."[7]

It is a complication for such views that Pindar never refers to his own poetic "wisdom" (*sophia*) as a *tekhnē*, and that he values god-sent wisdom over merely learnable skill.[8] Pindar's preference for being wellborn to being well-trained can be fit back into his alleged role as verbal artist by claiming, in neoclassical fashion, that the poet's innate "genius" must be complemented by technical skill to produce a finished work of art.[9] Still, a singer's premeditation and cunning ways with words did not in

---

[5] Svenbro 1984a: 156–79; cf. Scheid and Svenbro 1996: 11–21; Finkelberg 1998: 101–5. The only exception in pre-Simonidean literature may be pseudo-Hesiod fr. 357 M-W, in which singers "stitch" (*rhapsantes*) songs. Durante 1976: 170–71 points to Homeric *aoidē* being governed by the verb *entunein*, "prepare" (*Od.* 12.183; also used of horses, beds, a drinking cup), and *teukhein*, "fashion" (*Od.* 24.197, Homeric Hymn 6.20, also of houses, chambers, tripods). In both cases the fashioner is a divinity rather than a poet: see Ford 1992: 37–38.

[6] Snell 1961: ch. 4, esp. 61–62; Maehler 1963: 89–90.

[7] Maehler (1963: 25), pointing to Pindar's "spring of ambrosial words" (παγὰν ἀμβροσίων ἐπέων, *Pythian* 4.299); cf. Braswell 1992: ad loc. For Bacchylides, cf. Maehler 1997: ad 19.2 (*ambrosiōn meleōn*) and 10.11 (the *athanaton agalma Mousan*). Contrast, e.g., the Muses' *ambrosiē molpē*: Hesiod *Theogony* 69; cf. Theognis 18; Aristophanes *Birds* 220–22.

[8] Esp. *Olympian* 2.86–87, *Nemean* 1.25, and the other passages cited by Lanata (1963: 83–84). Pindar speaks of making a dedication to the "Muses' *tekhnai*" in *Paean* 52k.29 S-M, but the suite is unclear.

[9] See, e.g., Bernadini 1967; Gianotti 1975: 65 and 99–109, esp. 107; Steiner 1986: 41–52, 65. Maehler (1963: 94 n. 2) falls back on a developmental hypothesis in which Pindar at first thought of himself as a poet-technician and later became aware of his artistic uniqueness.

themselves cast glory upon a patron, and it is hard to gainsay Bowra's conclusion: "Though [Pindar] uses imagery drawn from handicrafts to illustrate certain aspects or features of his art, he does not regard this art itself as a handicraft."[10] The present chapter will attempt to understand why.

At this point, a methodological note is in order. The attempt to extract an implicit theory of poetry from archaic songs seems to me a more difficult task than is often realized. So much archaic song is speechifying, and so its declarations project a persona appropriate to the occasion rather than the poet's individual views. In songs for ceremonies of praise, references to the singer and the performance are part of the rhetoric generated by the occasion. One indication of this is that most of what Pindar says about song in his epinicia finds parallels in Bacchylides' songs of the same type. Their personae shift within songs and from song to song, and there is no reason to give priority to a singer's self-description as artisan over, for example, those as athlete or fellow reveler or close friend of the victor.

At the same time, the images, metaphors, and topoi repeatedly used in connection with song can tell us something about the ideas that patrons, audiences, and singers had about what was transpiring, and can perhaps indicate some of the terms that governed their discussions. A review of such passages will show that to take Pindar as a verbal artisan grossly oversimplifies his self-presentation. After considering the epic background to epinician images of songs as works of art (*agalmata*), I shall argue that Pindar and Bacchylides do not present themselves primarily as "makers" of song, and in many cases they significantly qualify such comparisons in the same way, and for similar reasons, as Simonides. The risk of turning eloquent praise into literary theory remains, but at the chapte's end I shall supply some confirmation of the importance of these themes as their complicated stance toward praise was taken up by public orators of the following generation.

Song as *Agalma*: From Epic to Epinician

Artisanal metaphors figure little in the songs studied so far because the value of sympotic and festive singing was indissociable from context and occasion, and even epic, in principle repeated exactly from one perfor-

---

[10] Bowra 1964: 4. Cf. Dornseiff 1921: 57–60: "Sein Kunst ist ihm φυᾷ, nichts Gemachtes, sondern Schöpfung, geweachsen wie ein Ölbaum . . . . Kein Kunstprodukt" (60). Similarly, Gundert (1935): 46–47, cf. 61–62. The praise value of the posture is brought out by Bundy (1986): 32): "Disdaining all device, [Pindar] makes his straightforward enthusiasm and confidence the measure of the *laudandus*'s worth" (though *Olympian* 11.19–20 is surely not an example). Dickson (1990) well connects these attitudes with the oral performance of epinician.

mance to the next, presented itself as song rather than work of art. Yet it
often has been claimed that an implicit idea of poetry as verbal crafting
is present right from the start in Greek literature, notably in ekphrastic
passages of archaic epic. Homer's account of how Hephaestus made
Achilles' shield in *Iliad* 18 has often been interpreted as a symbol for the
poem itself, each being the product of shaping skill.[11] The idea goes back
to Lessing's *Laokoon*, which countered neoclassical objections to this apparent digression by reading it as a statement about the differences between verbal art and visual representation. The reading is, however, based
on no explicit cue in the passage, and other considerations tell against
making the equivalence at the time. Neither Homer nor Hesiod compares
song to artifacts, for reasons Charles Segal has well expressed: "Because
he is immersed in the oral tradition, where 'fame,' *kleos*, is what men
'hear,' Homer does not draw explicit analogies (positive or negative) between the monumentalizing of poetry and the tangible monument of stone
or bronze."[12] To read the shield as a symbol for the poem, then, may be
to allegorize a passage that offends modern critical standards by making
it speak about something more up-to-date. It will at least be allowed that
the meanings of this magic talisman are multiple,[13] and perhaps the nature
of art objects in Homer can be more clearly seen in a smaller example of
artistic production.

When Menelaus' thigh is pierced by an arrow, the streaming blood elic-
its a simile describing an ivory cheek-piece for horses (*Iliad* 4.140–47):

> . . . And straight away darkening blood flowed from the wound—
> as when a woman in Maeonia or Caria takes ivory
> and stains it purple to be a cheek-piece for horses;
> and it lies stored up in a chamber; though many knights
> long to bear it on their horses, it remains a treasure (*agalma*) of the king,
> an adornment (*kosmos*) for his horse, an ornament (*kudos*) for its driver—
> so your thighs, Menelaus, were stained with blood
> and your noble (*euphuees*) legs beneath, with the fair (*kala*) ankles below.

The skill in combining these (rare and socially significant) materials is
undoubtedly artistic, but craftsmanship is only a small part of what gives
this object its value.[14] The nameless Maeonian or Carian woman, who

---

[11] Marg [1957] 1968: 33–71; most recently Becker 1995, with discussion of earlier literature, including Lessing.

[12] Segal 1989: 334; see his entire discussion (333–39), and Ford 1992: 168–71.

[13] See Taplin 1980.

[14] Philipp (1968: 4–5, 13) notes that artifacts are typically praised not for their propor-
tions or beauty but for the rareness of the materials (ivory was always exotic for Greeks,
and purple the quintessentially royal hue from the wealthy East) and for the craftsman's
skill in deploying them.

could well have been a slave or a palace domestic, makes the object, princes aspire to it, the king has it and disposes of it as he wishes.[15] When put to "use," the cheek-piece radiates the authority (*kudos*) of its noble possessor, and his treasure room serves, as did sanctuaries and as museums later would, to confer a special aura on the object, transforming it into an *agalma*, an "object of delight" such as would be dedicated in temple precincts to please, honor, and adorn a divinity.[16]

This passage shows in miniature the social complexity surrounding an artifact's value. Adorning (*kosmos*) a horse, putting raw materials in order (also called *kosmos*), is inseparable from the organization (*kosmos* again) of social life. As the simile breaks off, the aristocratic provenience of beauty is restated: the poet returns to the blood streaming down Menelaus' legs and calls those legs *euphuees*: literally "well-grown," *euphuees* implies wellmade by nature and so, in effect, well-born. The prince's body is itself "fine" or "elegant" (Menelaus' *kalos* ankle would be best shown off in the dance) according to the heroic norm in which nobles, not excepting Paris, are fine or fair, while the commoner Thersites is foul in appearance as well as shameful in behavior.[17] Good stock will produce good men; good men will have what is fair from nature and will command what is fine in art.

Although Homer's cheek-piece still reposes in its chamber when we last see it, such treasures were commonly exchanged among elites as "gifts" in a display of wealth and generosity.[18] In this logic of exchange and display, we should understand Pindar and Bacchylides when they offer their songs to powerful and successful men as *agalmata*. Such passages present songs as signs of rank and mutuality rather than as products of craft. When Bacchylides calls his song for Hiero of Syracuse "an *agalma*, a sweet gift of the Muses" (Μοισᾶν γλυκύδωρον ἄγαλμα, 5.3–6), he does not stress the materiality of the work (which indeed is confounded by calling it "sweet"); he rather features it as a gift that a god has bestowed on him and that he passes along to his patron in a network of mutual friendships governed by pleasure. The same applies to Pindar's often-re-

[15] Exclusive use is a way of glorifying objects: Achilles is the only one who can wield or even bear to look upon his shield (*Iliad* 19.14–22), and he has a drinking cup used by himself alone (16.225–28). Comparable is Nestor's splendidly worked cup, which he alone could lift (*Iliad* 11.636–37); in the fifth century, this passage was interpreted as a lesson on temperance by Stesimbrotos (107 F 23 *FGrH*).

[16] E.g., *Od.* 3.273–74, 438, 4.602, 8.509, 12.342–45. My analysis is much indebted to the ground-breaking study of Gernet (1981: ch. 4), well deployed by Kurke (1991: 163–94).

[17] On the noble bodies of heroes, see especially Vernant 1982. On Thersites, Ford 1992: 86–87.

[18] E.g., Agamemnon's chest-piece as described at *Iliad* 11.19–28. Finley 1965: 73–75, 111–13, 140–43.

marked image of his song as a "tinkling embroidered Lydian headband" (Λυδίαν μίτραν καναχηδὰ πεποικιλμέναν), which he offers to a victor as an *agalma* (*Nemean* 8.15). The "embroidery" is usually stressed as an allusion to the fineness and complexity of Pindar's style;[19] but again, artful design is only one aspect of the symbol's relevance. Leslie Kurke has well argued that to take such comparisons as exalting poets as artists anachronistically makes them competitors with sculptors in a market economy.[20] She regards an artifact like the headband (and others like it, as at *Olympian* 11.13–14) as gestures toward the tradition of elites exchanging "top-rank" objects, especially luxuries from the East. This elaborate artifact, surpassing the ephemeral wreath offered on the occasion of victory (the *tainia*), shows the victor how to convert his wealth and momentary success into the lasting esteem of his city.[21]

A different contextualizing approach attributes Pindar's many allusions to artifacts to the fact that he flourished at a time when singers began to use writing not only to preserve songs but also to compose them. The length and complexity of certain Pindaric odes has been taken as an indication that he wrote down at least some of them in advance.[22] There is, in addition, a "sudden appearance" of references to writing and reading in poetry and art from the 470's.[23] Charles Segal discovers a tension in Pindar between singer and craftsman, and takes this as the result of the recent incursion of writing into a traditionally oral practice: "No longer a purely oral poet whose work is exhausted in moment of performance," Pindar "perhaps even thinks of a literate as well as oral/aural reception."[24] However Pindar may have conceived his creative activity, Segal argues in detail that both he and Bacchylides present song as normally received through performance or re-performance and not reading and re-reading.

Like other singers of his time, Pindar uses writing as a metaphor for memory, one of its most frequently mentioned powers, but without dero-

---

[19] Maehler 1963: 91–93, though he qualifies his picture of Pindar as verbal artisan by speaking of an "ideelen, nicht einen materiellen Auftrag" (88); cf. Lanata 1963: 90. On the complex notion of *poikilia*, cf. Detienne and Vernant 1974: 27–28.

[20] Kurke 1991: 250–52 and ch. 7, esp. 187–94. See, too, Kurke 1999: ch. 4, and, differently, Von Reden 1995. In a similar vein, Pindar opens *Olympian* 7 by comparing his song to a wine bowl, termed "chief of possessions" (4).

[21] Kurke 1992: 113–14; cf. Nisetich 1975, 1977.

[22] Pöhlmann 1990. That Pindar need not have used writing is argued by Havelock (1982: 16).

[23] Pfeiffer 1968: 24–25, citing Aeschylus *Suppliants* 179 (cf. [Aeschylus] *Prometheus* 460–61, 788–89), Pindar *Olympian* 10.1–6, Sophocles *Triptolemus* (ca. 466 B.C.E.) fr. 597 *TGrF*.

[24] Segal 1986: 9–11, 153–61, arguing partly from the extraordinary length and complexity of *Pythian* 4, and partly from Pindar's references to writing (discussed in the note below)

gating the importance of performance: memory as a "writing on the heart" does not intrude upon the prerogatives of oral tradition, in which vision and presence remain the primary sources of truth and oral performance the indispensable condition of their appearing on earth.[25] A song that speaks to the wise may be referred to as "the Muses' *skutalē*," a kind of coded message scroll; but as he hands over this device to a certain Aeneas, Pindar bids him to "stir up" the song among companions around the "mixing bowl of loud-ringing songs" (*Olympian* 6.90–91: κρατὴρ ἀγαφθέκτων ἀοιδᾶν).[26] Hence, as Segal well observes, epinician does not present itself as an artifact, because "songs, not statues, are the appropriate medium to catch the energies, the flowering ripeness and the passions of mortal life."[27] This view agrees with the reading of Simonides given above, and Simonidean themes will be seen clinging to epinician representations of statues and other memorials.

Singer and Sculptor in Pindar

On two occasions, Pindar explicitly rejects the role of artisan in the form of sculptor of words. Pindar's fifth *Nemean* ode was for a family of Aegina, which was renowned at that time for its bronze work.[28] Hence it is striking that the singer begins by pitting song against statuary (1–3):

> Οὐκ ἀνδριαντοποιός εἰμ᾽, ὥστ᾽ ἐλινύσοντα ἐργάζεσθαι ἀγάλματ᾽ ἐπ᾽
> αὐτᾶς βαθμίδος
> ἑσταότ᾽· ἀλλ᾽ ἐπὶ πάσας ὁλκάδος ἔν τ᾽ ἀκάτῳ, γλυκεῖ᾽ ἀοιδά,
> στεῖχ᾽ ἀπ᾽ Αἰγίνας διαγγέλλοισ᾽, ὅτι. . . .

> I am no statue maker, to fashion delightful objects (*agalmata*) that
> stand idle on their bases;
> but on every merchant ship and every skiff, sweet song,
> go forth, spreading the news from Aegina that. . . .

---

and the phrase "rows of words" (ἐπέων στίχες) at *Pythian* 4.57; but this trope for Medea's prophecy may be martial ("ranks"), as is *kosmos epeōn* in Solon 1 *IEG*.

[25] *Olmpian* 10 begins by invoking the Muses to "read off" the names of the victors at Olympia written in the poet's heart. I suggest that the names were "written" there by Pindar's eyes when he *saw* the games himself, a point he emphasizes near the poem's end (10.100). Further on this ode's writing, Mullen 1982: 187.

[26] *Isthmian* 2 is similarly entrusted to a certain Nicasippus; whether we understand him as a substitute musical director or as a fictional choral persona, his mission is to travel to the site of performance and "read out" the song (46–48, quoted on p. 120).

[27] Segal 1998: 179.

[28] For Aeginetan bronze work, cf. Pliny *Natural History* 34.10; and for the suggestion of specifically bronze statuary here, see Müller 1974: 165. Cf. Cole 1992: 61–63 for possible historical contexts.

The charge that statues are "idle" and just stand in one spot seems to contrast with the motion of song as it travels (στεῖχε) and "proclaims" its message.[29] The conclusion to *Isthmian* 2 also disparages the "idle" work of art and adds the Simonidean charge of silence (44–48):

> μήτ' ἀρετάν ποτε σιγάτω πατρῴαν,
> μηδὲ τούσδ' ὕμνους· ἐπεί τοι
> οὐκ ἐλινύσοντας αὐτοὺς ἐργασάμαν.
> ταῦτα, Νικάσιππ', ἀπόνειμον, ὅταν
> ξεῖνον ἐμὸν ἠθαῖον ἔλθῃς.

> May [the victor] never let his father's excellence fall silent,
> nor these hymns, for I surely
> did not fashion them to be idle.
> This is what you are to read out, Nicasippus, once
> you have reached my trusty friend.

The fact that these passages respectively open and close their poems may encourage us to take seriously their Simonidean critiques of monumental silence and stillness.

Fame for Pindar, as for Homer, was a matter of making names re-*sound* throughout time: a king wants "always to hear sweet report" (ἀκοὰν ἀδεῖαν αἰεὶ κλύειν, *Pythian* 1.91). Cinyras, a mythical early king of Cyprus, has won "resounding song" (εὐαχέα . . . ὕμνον) because the *voices* of his people make his name continue to sound (κελαδέοντι μὲν ἀμφὶ Κινύραν πολλάκις φᾶμαι Κυπρίων, *Pythian* 2.14–16). Pindar once, suggestively for *mimēsis* theorists, speaks of fame as a "mirror," but adds that the only way to "mirror" noble deeds is through "songs made of words repeatedly heard" (κλύταις ἐπέων ἀοιδαῖς, *Nemean* 7.16).[30] Even when epic is regarded as a text constructed long ago, as when *Pythian* 3.112–15 speaks of "the report among men" of epic heroes that "wise craftsmen have fitted together," he adds that these are composed "from sounding words" (ἀνθρώπων φάτις / ἐξ ἐπέων κελαδεννῶν, τέκτονες οἷα σοφοί / ἅρμοσαν).[31]

In fact, a word for "loud" or "sounding" almost invariably qualifies epinician comparisons between songs and works of art. The Lydian head-

---

[29] Pindar's διαγγέλοισα goes Midas' ἀγγελλέω one better. Cf. *Pythian* 11.59–61: ἅ [sc. χάρις] τε τὸν Ἰφικλείαν διαφέρει Ἰόλαον ὑμνητὸν ἐόντα.

[30] For the enallage, cf. κλύταισι . . . ὕμνων πτύχαις, *Olympian* 1.105; for activating the "hearing" in *klu-*, cf. *Pythian* 10.6: ἐγκωμίαν ἀνδρῶν κλύταν ὄπα, and *Isthmian* 7.19: κλυταῖς ἐπέων ῥοαῖσιν, which Sandys well translates, "sounding streams of song." Cf. Segal 1985: 204 n. 21.

[31] For a compressed version, cf. *Nemean* 3.4–5: μελιγαρύων τέκτονες ὕμνων ("builders of honey-voiced songs"), of a performing chorus.

band mentioned above is not only embroidered but "tinkling" (κανα-χηδά). Such details are significant, since epinician relied heavily on the traditional trope of oblivion as silence.[32] Deborah Steiner observes that "each [of Pindar's *agalmata*] comes complete with some expression indicative of its capacity for speech and song"; they are "clamorous things."[33] If Pindar's songs may be "laid up" for victors like dedicatory objects (*Olympian* 11.8, 13.36), his monuments are constructed not from stone but from "powerful words" (λόγων φερτάτων μναμήι', *Pythian* 5.48–49).[34] A commemorative song is like a monument, but it is a "loud stone of the Muses" (*Nemean* 8.46–48).[35] This is because speech "lives" longer than doings or makings (ῥῆμα δ' ἐργμάτων χρονιώτερον βιοτεύει, *Nemean* 4.6, cf. *Olympian* 4.10). The metaphor of song as a "chariot" can be traced back to Indo-European poetics, but Pindar's chariot of the Muses is not simply an object of craft, but one that "speeds" to make a memorial "resound" (ἔσσυταί τε / Μοισαῖον ἅρμα Νικοκλέος μνᾶμα πυγμάχου κελαδῆσαι, *Isthmian* 8.61–62).[36]

The speeding chariot reminds us that Simonides' other charge against statues was their presumptuous stability, and we find immortal fame in Pindar always in motion: the deathless speech of praise "creeps along forever" (τοῦτο γὰρ ἀθάνατον φωνᾶεν ἕρπει / εἴ τις εὖ εἴπει, *Isthmian* 3/4 58–59 S-M), for song is associated with festivity and movement. Thus when Pindar spreads a victor's name over land and sea (*Nemean* 6.48–49), gives "wings" to victory (*Pythian* 8.34), and makes glory "shine inexhaustibly over earth and sea" (*Isthmian* 3/4 59–60) or circulate "faster than horses or ships (*Olympian* 9.21–25), I take these images as referring

[32] E.g., Pindar *Pythian* 9.92, *Nemean* 9.7, fr. 121.4 S-M (θαάσκει δὲ σιγαθὲν καλὸν ἔργον). Cf. Simonides 582 *PMG* (ἔστι καὶ σιγῇ ἀκίνδυνον γέρας), Bacchylides 3.94–98. Adapted to drama by Euripides (*Hippolytus* 1428–30, where annual maiden choruses will ensure that Hippolytus "will not have died nameless" and that "Phaedra's love will not be silenced."

[33] Steiner 1993: 176.

[34] For epinician passages on song as monument: Maehler 1963: 87 n. 9, and 1982: 87, on Bacchylides 5.4. On Pindar's funerary imagery, Segal 1998: 135: "The aural dimension of this communication receives particular stress."

[35] *Nemean* 8.46–47: σεῦ δὲ πάτρᾳ Χαριάδας τε λάβρον ὑπερεῖσαι λίθον Μοισαῖον. Sandys' τ' ἐλαφρόν, accepted by Snell-Maehler, is smoother syntax and has a parallel in *Nemean* 7.77. But the "loud" (i.e., "speaking") stone of the ms. (glossed by the scholia) may be contrasted with the κρυφίαισι . . . ἐν ψάφοις in line 26; it is defended by Bury (1965: 157–58) and read by Race (1997).

[36] On songs spreading fame: Maehler 1963: 89, citing Pindar's "Letter of the Muses" (*Olympian* 6.9, cf. *Nemean* 3.29, *Olympian* 9.21–28) and song as "ship" (*Nemean* 5.2, Bacchylides 16.2). A connection between shipbuilding and fame is embodied in the name *Phereklos Harmonidēs* ("Fame-bearer, the son of MacFitter"), who built Paris' ships, the origin of all the *Iliad*'s woe: *Iliad* 5.59–64; Phereklos is Theseus' helmsman in Simonides 550 *PMG*; cf. 535 *PMG*.

not to publishing but to performance—"speech wafted on the air," spreading and echoing glory.[37]

Comparing such passages with the opening of *Nemean 5*, Segal has brought out "a continuous dialogue within Pindar's work between song (poetry) on the one hand and monumentalization in statuary."[38] A tension arises in this dialogue, because epinician presents itself as song and festival celebration (ἀοιδή, ὕμνος, κῶμος) rather than as artifact (ποίημα).[39] One form in which this tension is expressed is through images of fame as growth and flowering: virtue "blooms" through time in "famed" song, that is, in song that is heard (*klu-*) in performance (*Pythian* 3.115: ἀρετὰ κλειναῖς ἀοιδαῖς χρονία τελέθε). The sense of "unwithering" in Homer's κλέος ἄφθιτον is unpacked in Pindar's "fruit of words that does not wither" (*Isthmian* 8.46: ἐπέων καρπὸς οὐ κατέφθινε).[40] Vegetal imagery presents fame not as uneroding solidity but as perpetually recurrent flowering; it places song's "force" in "its movement, its liveliness."[41] Such metaphors are often complemented with images of fame as liquid and flowing. As in Simonides, "the vital energies that poetic fame confers" are associated with "life-giving 'streams of song.'"[42]

A final example of Pindar's complex imagery is his most striking musical artifact, a tiara welded by the Muses: "It is easy to weave garlands (*stephanous*). Strike up the tune: the Muse you know welds a crown from gold, ivory, and the lily-flower [coral] taken out of the dewy sea in which it grows" (*Nemean* 7.77–79). This gorgeous object has often been paired with the Lydian headband as a symbol for the poem as artful construct.[43]

---

[37] *Isthmian* 3/4.27–29: ὅσσα δ᾽ ἐπ᾽ ἀνθρώπους ἄηται / μαρτύρια φθιμένων ζωῶν τε φωτῶν / ἀπλέτου δόξας. Cf. *Pythian* 4.3: οὖρον ὕμνων; *Nemean* 6.28–29: οὖρον ἐπέων εὐκλέα; *Isthmian* 1.64–65; and Simonides 595 *PMG*, with Maehler's discussion (1963: 79).

[38] Segal 1986: 156; cf. 154 on Pindar's "vacillation between the poet as craftsman and poet as inspired, untaught prophet." Cf. Lefkowitz 1963: 199–201, and see Benediktson 2000: 18–25.

[39] Segal 1998: 178.

[40] Cf. *Nemean* 8.40–42. Such images in Pindar *Parthenaion* (fr. 2.11–12) suggest that song is like a maiden whose fruit or bloom never withers; the opposite imagery is in Archilochean *iambos* 188.1, 196a.27, 42–43 *IEG*.

[41] Bowra 1964: 20. Cf. Duchemin 1955: 74: "Pindare a emprunté de metaphores à la vie de la nature, à la puissance de ses forces fecondantes, et tout ce qu᾽ il a exprimé à l᾽ aide des symboles que ces images lui fournissent, à chaque moment d᾽ une création sans cesse renouvelée" (cf. 259–61). Cf. Steiner 1986: ch. 3. The word for "feast" or festival (*thalia*) is connected with blooming and fertility: see Kannicht 1989: 31–32.

[42] Segal 1998: 202–8, cf. 110. For the many metaphors in Pindar in which song or fame is a liquid, see Steiner 1986: 44–46.

[43] E.g., Bowra 1964: 16–17; Maehler 1963: 90–91; and Steiner 1993: 164. Cf. Snell 1953: 85–87; also Lanata 1963: 81; Fränkel 1975: 423–28; Verdenius 1983: 23–24. Segal 1989: 333: Pindar is "signaling that he like Simonides conceived of his poetry as text, as tangible artifact."

But just as the headband is made to "tinkle," so the Muses' "welding" is set amid images of liquidity, flowers, and growth. More than a splendid object wrought from precious materials, this is a magical *agalma* from the sea.[44]

I have perhaps gone too far out on the slender limb of reconstructing poetics from poets' images, and it is worth repeating that images of song within songs have other things to do than encode a rhetorical theory of poetry. As the elaborate paraphrase of coral as a "lily from the sea" indicates, Pindar's tiara is finally an *ainos*. As a form of kenning, it involves indeed verbal cunning, and the metaphors of craft should not be ignored; but it is also a form of knowing, a mode of addressing the *sophoi*. Those in Pindar's audience who could catch and decipher the words wafted on the air were not being encouraged to see him or themselves simply as craftsmen. *Sophia*, not *tekhnē*, was on display.

Songs and Buildings

Vitality and vociferousness were satisfyingly concrete manifestations of public esteem, but Pindar's patrons also wanted a glory that lasted through time. Anne Burnett points out that epic set a standard for enduring fame that was beyond the reach of the epinician poet.[45]

> The point about an epic, after all, was that it could be repeated. . . . Epic would literally keep a man's deeds alive in the mouth of posterity. A victory ode, on the other hand, was sounded out only in its one costly performance and was never produced again. . . . It could not be said with accuracy that Pindar and Bacchylides kept a victor's name physically on men's tongues, as Homer had the name of Agamemnon.

As a matter of literary history, it is now thought possible that epinicians could be reperformed after their premieres, even taken up as monody.[46] Yet it remains true that epinician singers, bound as they were to refer to a particular victory and often the occasion of performance, had to negotiate with the timeless and universal fame that epic offered. They had to

---

[44] Cf. Kurke 1991: 104–5 for *agalmata* associated with divine origins and retrieved from the sea.

[45] Burnett 1985: 76.

[46] As is suggested by *Nemean* 4.13–16, where Pindar says that if Timasarchos' father were alive, he would take up the lyre and, "leaning on this song, make the καλλίνικος of his son resound (κελάδησε) on many an occasion (θαμά)." But see Cole 1992: 99 n. 20 for a different view. For other evidence (including *Clouds* 1353–73), see Nagy 1990: ch. 13, esp. 107–8, 113–15; and Herington 1985: 28, 48–50, who asks, "What would be the point [scil. without subsequent reperformance] of the poets' universal claim, from Homer to

connect victories with fame that lasts beyond passing celebration.[47] In part, as Burnett says, the ritualized context of choral singing and dancing "liberated [epinician performance] from the confinement of the unique," and Nagy has shown in detail how this dimension of choral poetry makes epinician a ritual speech act linking the exertions of poets and athletes in the present to the travails of founding heroes.[48]

Accordingly, when Pindar depicts his own songs as enduring, monumental constructs, these are, as in Simonides' Thermopulae poem, memorials that transcend material makings—"a stele whiter than Parian marble" (*Nemean* 4.81).[49] In his best-known comparison of an ode to a building, Pindar begins *Olympian* 6 by depicting his proem as "columns of gold" set up before his house of song (1–4):

Χρυσέας ὑποστάσαντες εὐ-
   τειχεῖ προθύρῳ θαλάμου
κίονας ὡς ὅτε θαητὸν μέγαρον
πάξομεν· ἀρχομένου δ᾽ ἔργου πρόσωπον
χρὴ θέμεν τηλαυγές.

Let us erect golden columns
for the well-built forecourt to our edifice, as if
we were building a palace to be looked at in awe.
When a work is beginning, one must lay down a far-gleaming facade.

The elaborate *adunaton* dematerializes this temple of song. As Fränkel comments, song "transcends material, visible constructions and provides a more secure house for the fame of those whom it celebrates than the treasury of Delphi does for the statues of victors."[50] It is precisely not the song as text that will be "gazed at" and "far-gleaming," but the performance and the fame it creates.[51]

Pindar adds vociferousness to another building of song (fr. 194 S-M):

Pindar, that they conferred lasting and widespread glory, *kleos*, on the subjects of their songs?" (p. 50).

[47] For the epinician thematic of present joy and immortal fame, Bundy 1986: 11, cf. 87–88.

[48] Burnett 1985: 77; Nagy 1990: ch. 5, esp. 142, following Calame 1977.

[49] Müller (1974: 97) points out the passage is an *adunaton*.

[50] Fränkel 1975: 430 n. 9. Cf. Kurke 1991: 189–90; Steiner 1993: 169–70. Note, too, that Pindar's prayer toward the end of the poem—μὴ θραῦσαι χρόνος ὄλβον ἐφέπων (6.97)—averts a threat to his patron's permanent happiness that is reminiscent of the end of Simonides 581 *PMG*: λίθον δὲ / καὶ βρότεοι παλάμαι θραύοντι.

[51] For Pindar's use of gold as a symbol of divine incorruptibility, see Duchemin 1970. "Far-gleaming" is a concretized image from Homer for fame: see Ford 1992: 159–60, on *Od*. 24.83, and Hubbard 1985: 22 n. 34, on "gazed at."

κεκρότηται χρυσέα κρηπὶς ἱεραῖσιν ἀοιδαῖς·
εἶα τειχίζωμεν ἤδη ποικίλον
κόσμον αὐδάεντα λόγων

A foundation of gold has been clapped together for holy songs:
come now, let us construct an embroidered
adornment that can give voice to words.

Clashing metaphors complicate taking this simply as a solid building: the
foundation has been "hammered" for the present occasion, and the performers take over that sound and erect upon it a decorative object;[52] but
this adornment, *kosmos*, "speaks" and is composed of words.[53] Working
once again in gold and embroidery (*poikilos*), Pindar's "ornament voicing
words" (κόσμον αὐδάεντα λόγων) is a singer's response to the inscriber's
"voice contrived from stone" (αὐδὲ τεχνέεσσα λίθο).

These Simonidean themes can also be found in Pindar's fellow epinician
poet Bacchylides.[54] For Bacchylides, the most valuable artifact the dead can
leave behind is the "much sought-after *agalma* of good report" (πολυζήλω-
τον εὐκλείας ἄγαλμα, 1.184).[55] The truly deathless *agalma* combines motion, sound, activity, presence, joyful festivity, and glory (10.10–14 S-M):

ἐκίνησεν λιγύφθογγον μέλισσαν,
ἐγχειρὲς ἵν᾽ ἀθάνατον Μουσᾶν ἄγαλμα
ξυνὸν ἀνθρώποισιν εἴη
χάρμα, τεάν ἀρετάν
μανῦον ἐπιχθονίοισιν.

He has stirred the clear-voiced bee into motion so as to make present[56]
an immortal *agalma* of the Muses, a joy to be shared among men as
it proclaims your excellence to men on earth.

---

[52] κροτέω can mean "hammering" or "clapping": see LSJ s.v. II. 2.

[53] *Kosmos* is given a similarly abstract and "sounding" sense in *Olympian* 11.13–14,
where the poet "will make resound a sweet-tuned adornment for the wreath of golden olive"
(κόσμον ἐπὶ στεφάνῳ χρυσέας ἐλαίας ἀδυμελῆ κελαδήσω). Cf. *Nemean* 3.31–32: "You have
been allotted a fitting adornment to make sweet speech" (ποτίφορον δὲ κόσμον ἔλαχες γλυκύ
τι γαρυέμεν), and Kurke 1991: 190. Plato uses the same phrase in his mock encomium,
Menexenus 236ε.

[54] See Maehler 1982 on 1.183 for a general discussion of fame in Bacchylides.

[55] Cf. Pindar *Pythian* 11.57–58, where the good reputation left behind by a just man is
"the best of all possessions for his sweetest offspring" (γλυκυτάτᾳ γενεᾷ / εὐώνυμον κτεάνων
κρατίσταν χάριν πορών). Similarly vitalist is Sophocles' Haemon (*Antigone* 703–4): "What
better monument can children have than the good reputation of a still-flourishing father?"
(τί γὰρ πατρὸς θάλλοντος εὐκλείας τέκνοις / ἄγαλμα μεῖζον;).

[56] So Maehler (1982: 182) interprets Snell's ἐγχειρές, a word not otherwise attested. Snell
pronounces Jebb's ἀγχειρές impossible ("certe non A"), but the sense would be apt: the
immortal statue is "one such as is not made by (mortal) hands."

In his quest to define poetic expertise, Plato's Socrates glossed the poets' bees as "light, winged, and holy," and so irrational; but Bacchylides shows a bee that flits everywhere and keeps buzzing.[57] The moving susurrus somehow makes a deathless, divine *agalma* present on earth and unites the community as it heralds (*manuon*) the excellence of the victor.

In his song for the same occasion as Pindar's *Nemean 5*, Bacchylides also makes a point of the vulnerabilities of monuments. Allowing that the "wise" or "skilled man" deserves praise, Bacchylides yet adds that, sooner or later, "blame fastens on all the works of men" (13.199–207):[58]

> εἰ μή τινα θερσιεπὴς
>   φθόνος βιᾶται,
> αἰνείτω σοφὸν ἄνδρα
> σὺν δίκᾳ. βροτῶν δὲ μῶμος
> πάντεσσι μέν ἐστιν ἐπ' ἔργοις·
> ἁ δ' ἀλαθεία φιλεῖ
>   νικᾶν, ὅ τε πανδαμάτωρ
>   χρόνος τὸ καλῶς
> ἐργμένον αἰὲν ἀ[έξει·

If there is anyone whom bold-speaking envy does not overmaster, let him in all justice praise the *sophos* man. Blame fastens on all works of men; but Truth loves conquering, and all-subduing Time makes that which has been well done continue [to grow] forever.

In the epithet "all-subduing," Bacchylides actually anticipates Simonides by a few years (cf. 531.5 *PMG*), but his thought is slightly different: time, which destroys everything else, will actively preserve true excellence against the misrecognition of contemporaries.[59] If Bacchylides implies here that his song is also a "product" (*ergon*) of wisdom, he remains a pious artisan in appealing to Time and Truth to let "what has been well done" or "made" (e.g., by poet, artisan, or athlete) continue to live, to flourish.[60]

---

[57] Plato *Ion* 534в. For the poet as a flitting bee, going everywhere, cf. Simonides (?) 46 B; Pindar *Pythian* 10.53–54.

[58] Maehler (1982) construes 201–2 as "*blame of men* fastens on all works." Cf. Simonides 542 *PMG* on the difficulty of being a man "fashioned" (*tetugmenos*) "four-square" and "without fault" (*aneu psogou*), with the remarks of Svenbro 1984a: 135: "Like Pindar, Simonides considered poetry superior to marble; the perfection of the four-square man resides thus, rather than in his marmoreal virtue, in the perenniality suggested, but not realized, in sculpture. Only in the atemporal dimension of poetry does man join eternal perfection."

[59] Commentary is provided by Segal 1998: 134–35, see also 144 n. 8.

[60] Reading Kenyon's ἀ[έξει at 13.207. (Cf. *Od.* 15.372, where the gods "make prosper" the agricultural *ergon* of Eumaeus). Maehler objects to the metaphor ("Bacchylides kann

Finally, Bacchylides also produces musical monuments of a transcendent sort. He winds down his fifth epinician by bidding his Muse to "bring the well-made chariot to a stop" (177–78: στῆσον εὐποίητον ἅρμα αὐτοῦ) and celebrate unending things: the king of the gods, the river Alpheus "flowing unwearyingly," and the ever-potent Pelops (179–82). After a signature and a reference to his song as the "tongue of good fame" (196), his final image seeks to implant endurance in a nature (198–200):

> πυθμένες θάλλουσιν ἐσθλῶν
> τοὺς ὁ μεγιστόπατωρ
> Ζεὺς ἀκινήτους ἐν εἰρηνῇ φυλάσσει

> The foundations of the noble flourish,
> which Zeus, greatest of fathers, preserves in peace.

Bacchylides shares Pindar's respect for birth and generation and Solon's piety (13.19 *IEG*) that only god can preserve the foundations of things. Only under Zeus, "greatest of fathers," can noble houses remain undisturbed. The lineages of the great are a kind of "foundation" of their house that lasts, "flourishes," so long as they maintain peace.

The comparisons of songs to artifacts in these two poets are insistent that truly immortal fame is embodied in no mere material construct. The excellence of outstanding families is made manifest in lively and loud celebrations, and these will recur in due season if rooted in the cycle of a just nature. Fame, insofar as human fame may be permanent, remains a gift of the Muses repeated through the generations. If the best craftsmen were acknowledged as producing delightful and durable things, Simonides and his fellows wished to make it quite clear that poets offered a distinctive contribution to excellence: the old oral ways of preserving traditions were by no means dead, and prime among those means was song.

The frequency of such sonorous artifacts and their connection to the poet's persona as celebrant suggest that Simonides' remark on poetry as speaking painting may derive from an analogous figure of speech, an early variation of the epinician "voiced" artifact. What Plutarch interpreted as an aesthetic apothegm seems likely to have been yet another insistence that "voice" gives poetry a monumentalizing power as great as any other attempt to capture human life.[61]

---

aber kaum gemeint haben, dass die Zeit den Sieg 'fordert' oder gar 'vergrössert,' sondern nur dass sie ihn 'bewahrt')," but the expression is in line with vegetal imagery elsewhere in the song: *trephei* (63; cf. 3.90–92; Pindar *Nemean* 7.32–33) and *bruousa* (179).

[61] Cf. the fifth-century interest in Daedalus whose lifelike sculptures can move and "lack only a voice": Aeschylus fr. 78a.6–7 *TGrF*; Euripides fr. 372 Nauck; cf. Plato *Meno* 97D. Pindar refers to such legends apropos of the Rhodian Heliadae, *Olympian* 7. 50–52. See Frontisi-Ducroux 1975: esp. 95–117, on animated statues.

Aftermath of an Image

Like Simonides, Pindar and Bacchylides insisted that sound that was the substance of true fame. In restating the idea of immortal fame for the early classical age, they developed his oppositions between silent, static works of art and sounding, mobile choruses into a set of highly charged antithetical images: fame and celebration had to take the form of acclamation, motion, and activity, with the possibility of perpetual renewal; these were more valuable, and more humanly attainable, than solid but silent statues and enduring but motionless monuments that mimicked the silent unchangingness of death. Their artisanal metaphors present song as a dynamic and mobile artifact, composed of nothing more tangible than sound; rather than equating singer to maker, they dematerialize idea of poetic glory, linking epinician fame to the heroic tradition of immortal glory as "what is heard" (*kleos*).

I have highlighted these themes not to replace one epinician "poetics" with another. To be sure, I have identified strands of imagery that complicate their references to works of plastic art, but I take such language less as an expression of their philosophies of composition than as an appropriate element in the rhetoric of the occasion. Their public odes include representations of genuine praise as singers had traditionally described it and as patrons and audiences had come to expect. On such occasions, a theory of song as the production of verbal artifacts would have had little value for them. But the series of oppositions exploited by Pindar and Bacchylides would, when removed from its original contexts, prove influential in later discussions about the value of written works and the worth of preserving them, in short, in the theorization of literature. An important interim stage in this history was when the discourse that began in the courts of wealthy princes was adapted by fifth-century orators, who offered their services to a new patron, the democratic city.

The politicians and prominent men who gave eulogies at state-sponsored funerals for the Athenian war dead borrowed the poets' topics, including their opposition between the limited fame that is inscribed and that which is everywhere and always proclaimed. Although these speeches at first were not written down, their themes are epitomized in the funeral oration that Thucydides attributes to Pericles.[62] Pericles promises the fallen a "praise that does not grow old" and points out that this is not the fame that comes from any physical marker in the landscape. Simonidean

---

[62] See Loraux 1986: 42–55, 230–31, and the entire study on how these themes were adapted to the ideology of the democratic city. On Simonides' influence here, cf. Karuzos 1972: 139. On the rhetorical aspects of Thucydides' historiography, see Woodman 1988, and cf. Cole 1991: 104–11.

themes begin to cluster when Pericles speaks of their "eminently conspicuous tomb": it is "not the one in which they lie, but where their reputation remains always to be remembered, on every occasion of word or deed that may arise."[63] True commemoration persists in acts and words, and such fame will have no limits in time or space: "The whole world is their tomb," says Pericles as he goes on to reflect on the limitations of written epitaphs; "it is not only the inscriptions on steles in their own land that act as signs of this, but even in distant lands an unwritten memory persists in the thoughts of each person rather than in a physical work (ergon)."[64] Although Thucydides himself was an innovative and writerly author, his public speaker, like an epideictic poet, declares that fame in human speech counts more than what is written in stone.

Pericles' themes are not only high-quality boiler-plate, but a thoughtful response to the question singers posed: How can mortals leave behind signs that tell the story of their lives? In fact, the attitudes Pericles expresses are consonant with those of Thucydides the historian toward poetry and monuments, both of which he regards as unreliable signs (sēmeia) of greatness. Poetry chiefly interests Thucydides as a way to learn about the past. He takes it for granted that poets cannot be trusted in their accounts of old wars,[65] but the cautious historian can make guarded inferences: "if it is sound to take evidence (tekmērion) from Homer," Thucydides infers from the catalogue of ships that Agamemnon had the largest naval contingent (1.9: cf. Iliad 2.576, 612; cf. 101–9). But as a rule, one wishing to base conclusions "on the clearest signs" (ek tōn ekphanestatōn sēmeiōn) of the past should distrust both the accounts of poets who "adorn and magnify in their praise" (epi to meizon kosmountes) and any accounts by writers (logographoi) who have composed "to please the ear" (1.21.1). Poets may distort the truth, they may exaggerate to please their audiences, and oral tradition is no sure guide. Pericles, indeed, held that Athens' greatness was superior even to its reputation (akoē, 2.41.3).

Thucydides is equally skeptical about the reliability of physical monuments as signs (sēmeia) from the past: one could underestimate the power

[63] Thucydides 2.43.2: τάφον ἐπισημότατον, οὐκ ἐν ᾧ κεῖται μᾶλλον, ἀλλ᾽ ἐν ᾧ ἡ δόξα αὐτῶν παρὰ τῷ ἐντυχόντι αἰεὶ καὶ λόγου καὶ ἔργου καιρῷ αἰείμνηστος καταλείπεται. The conceit of a "living monument" was carried to a grotesque extreme in Gorgias' troping graves (taphoi) as "living vultures" (B 5a DK).

[64] Thucydides 2.43.3: καὶ οὐ στηλῶν μόνον ἐν τῇ οἰκείᾳ σημαίνει ἐπιγραφή, ἀλλὰ καὶ ἐν τῇ μὴ προσηκούσῃ ἄγραφος μνήμη παρ᾽ ἑκάστῳ τῆς γνώμης μᾶλλον τοῦ ἔργου ἐνδιαιτᾶται. The contrast between "work" (ergon) and "unwritten memory" seems to rule out such views as Immerwahr's (1960: 287), who would take ergon as the soldiers' "deeds" or the "outcome"; but his study remains valuable for highlighting the roles of monuments and oral report in Thucydides' conception of history. See Harris 1989: 90 and n. 121.

[65] E.g., the figures Homer gives in his "catalogue of ships" are unreliable "because, being a poet, he is likely to have embellished (kosmēsai) his account" (1.10.3).

of ancient Mycene or present-day Lacedaimonia if one judged solely from their temples and building foundations, just as Athens' spectacular buildings might give an exaggerated image of its true power (1.10). These archaeological themes are also present in Pericles' funeral oration, for in both cases we have to do with leaving signs of greatness. To prove that his praise of Athens is the truth of the matter (*ergōn alētheia*) and no mere boast (*logōn kompos*) for the present occasion, Pericles points to the true signs (*sēmainei*, 2.41.2) of its power: the colonies and outposts it has planted all over the Aegean and the graves of those fallen in foreign lands constitute its "everlasting memorials" (*mnēmeia aidia*, 2.41.4). There are so many witnesses to these "great signs" that there is no need for any additional praise to make Athens an object of wonder for the present and the future: "We have no need for a Homer or some eulogist to add his praises that may give a passing pleasure from the verses (*epea*) but whose underlying message (*huponoia*) cannot stand up to the truth of the matter" (*ergōn alētheia*, 2.41.4).

Like the poets, public orators did not present themselves as artful composers or monument-makers, but as performers who supplied the speech essential to praise and memory. We shall see that it was not singers or orators but *readers* who regarded oral performances as realizations of a task that was essentially artisanal composition in speech. This will emerge as we take up the final component of the invention of poetry: a new set of terms that brought singers and their songs firmly under a craftsmanly conception of making.

SIX

THE ORIGIN OF THE WORD "POET"

THE WORDS "poetry," "poet," and "poem" have entered English and many European languages from ancient Greek, but not from very old Greek. Before the fifth century, the general Greek term for what we call poets was *aoidoi*, "singers," which did not differentiate composers from performers. To speak of a "song" when no specific kind was in view, words like *humnos* or *melos* ("tune") served, or the more general *aoidē*, "singing" as an activity rather than an object, a "poem."[1] Apart from these words, capable of a more or less general usage, the archaic lexicon lacked a unitary term comprehending the many individual forms of singing that were attached to specific contexts. The recognized kinds of song were defined not as parts of a realm of discourse to be distinguished from something like "prose," but as familiar activities connected with particular social and religious occasions.

To change the terms by which song is designated may imply different definitions of the activity and its place in the social world, and so it is worth noting that it is first in texts of the fifth century that we find those who composed songs called "makers" or "poets" (*poiētai*) and clearly distinguished from the "singers" (*aoidoi*) who performed them; instead of "singing" (*aeidein, aoidē*), they are said to be engaged in "making" or "poetry" (*poiēsis*, from the verb *poiein*); finally, what they produce may be called a *poiēma* or "made thing." Allowing for the fact that this might be mere coincidence or a trick played on us by our very incomplete evidence, I yet argue that the sudden appearance of this vocabulary signaled a fundamentally new conception of verbal art in classical Greece. The dissemination of these terms coincided with new critical researches into ancient song traditions and supported a rhetorical approach to song that was indispensable to the establishment of poetics in the fourth century.

Any poetics depends, logically and etymologically, on a unitary term for poetry simply to circumscribe the field of study. But such a central term will also define, at least implicitly, what is specific to such works that demands poetics' special analyses. In the classical "making" vocabulary, the composition of a song was emphasized over its performance, and its "maker's" verbal skill was highlighted over other qualities, such as wis-

---

[1] See *LfrgE* s.vv. The rise of these terms is remarked in Nagy 1989: 23–24; Ford 1992: 13; Finkelberg 1998: 176.

dom, truthfulness, or tact, that were traditionally desired of a singer. Correspondingly, when singing (*aoidē*) or "song" (*humnos*) became an object, a *poiēma*, poems were more easily regarded not as utterances or events embedded in social life but as verbal *objets d' art*, the almost tangible products of an artisanal process. Language in turn was conceived in rhetorical terms as if it were inert raw materiel that the poet "put together" (commonly συν-τιθέναι, translated into Latin *com-positio*) and shaped by artistic skill. Because one of the most noticeable and easily demonstrable formal qualities of song was its organized rhythm, we find attached to the "make" words a fifth-century view that poetry is essentially speech (*logos*) in metrical form. This formalist perspective was extended to other quantifiable linguistic features of song, from diction to structure, and so the rise of "poetry" expressed a conception of song that was especially susceptible to rhetorical analysis. Expertise in "poetry" did not require knowing how to sing or compose; it could focus on breaking down a poem as a verbal construct, the product of intelligible design, rather than as a speech act by, within, and for members of a community.

This chapter is devoted to exploring the early career of *poiētēs* and its cognates to determine when and by whom the conception of singers as "craftsmen" of words was promulgated among the Greeks. Tracking the lexical evidence will suggest that the terms were neither the creation of the sophists, as is sometimes thought, nor an unremarkable surfacing of very ancient, even pre-Greek ideas. I shall rather place the rise of this vocabulary in the context of new historicizing and demystifying approaches to Greek traditions, explorations carried out by mythographers, historians, and doctors, as well as by a range of experts in language. My account will point out the advantages these terms brought in explanatory power, but will also make clear why the new perspectives were not altogether congenial to singers of the time.

The Origin of the Word "Poet"

Because we have virtually no prose and only a tiny sample of song before the fifth century, we cannot be sure how old the vocabulary of "making" songs may be. In what we do have, the verb *poiein* occurs once in reference to song: recalling some elegiacs in which Mimnermus prayed for a quiet death at 60 (6 *IEG*), Solon bids him "take out" that part of his song (ἔξελε τοῦτο) and "redo" it, "singing 'let me die at 80' ": καὶ μεταποίησον . . . ὧδε δ' ἄειδε, 20 *IEG*). This may be taken as preclassical evidence, albeit isolated, for a widespread connection of "making" song with a view of it as a construct one may "remake" by taking it apart and putting it together differently.² When we come to Herodotus, our first extended sample of prose, we find *poiētēs* and *poiēsis* well established along with *poiein* for "making poetry" in the sense of "composing" it.³ Herodotus uses but once, to designate not the undifferentiated singer-performer of archaic poetry but one who performs a song.⁴ Correspondingly, "singing" (*aeidein*) is now used for performing songs as distinct from composing them. For example, the kitharode Arion "makes" or composes a dithyramb, then names it and produces it (ποιήσαντα / ὀνομήσαντα / διδάξαντα); the song is then "sung" or performed by others (ἀειδόμενα).⁵

Lacunose as our evidence is, it suggests that the fifth century saw if not the origin, then at least the popularization of these words, for the period also witnessed a proliferation of an entire "-maker" vocabulary that used the suffix -ποιός to name specialized poets and other artisans: Herodotus uses ἐποποιός ("verse-maker" or "maker in speech") for epic poets, and has the abstract noun ἐποποιίη ("verse/speech-making") for epic poetry. This is a formal conception: lyric poets, by contrast, make "songs" or

² One other archaic use of *poiein* in connection with poetry may be Theognis, who usually employs the "singing" vocabulary (*aeidō*, e.g., 4, 16, 533; cf. *aoidē* in 251). But at 771–72 he seems to say a singer "thinks, displays, and makes" (ἀλλὰ τὰ μὲν μῶσθαι, τὰ δὲ δεικνύεν, ἄλλα δὲ ποιεῖν; but with West's text and punctuation, the verb means only "do" (τὰ δὲ δεικνύεν· ἄλλα δὲ ποιῶν . . .). *Poiein* appears in another passage from Theognis, where it means "fabricating" and replaces λέγειν ("speak") in a traditional description of deceptive eloquence as "*making* lies that are like the truth" (713–14: οὐδ' εἰ ψεύδεα μὲν <u>ποιοῖς</u> ἐτύμοισιν ὁμοῖα, / γλῶσσαν ἔχων ἀγαθὴν Νέστορος ἀντιθέου); the phrasing recalls Odysseus, who "dissembles, *speaking* many lies like the truth" (ἴσκε ψεύδεα πολλὰ <u>λέγων</u> ἐτύμοισιν ὁμοῖα, *Od.* 19.203), and Hesiod's Muses, who know how to "*speak* many lies like the truth" (ἴδμεν ψεύδεα πολλὰ <u>λέγειν</u> ἐτύμοισιν ὁμοῖα, *Theogony* 27).

³ Among these, *poiētēs* seems to have led the way, for it was early confined (almost) exclusively to the sense "maker of poetry," whereas *poiēma* and *poiēsis* sometimes retained a broader sense based on "making" in general: Braun 1938: esp. 265 ff. *Poiēma* kept its etymological sense ("thing made") most strongly: it is first attested for "poem" in Cratinus 198.5 *PCG*, Herodotus using it only for manufactured artifacts. It is perhaps significant that Plato's Diotima objects to restricting *poiēsis* and *poiētēs* to "poetic" making, but does not mention *poiēma* (*Symposium* 205C). Herodotus once calls a lyric a "sung thing" (ἄεισμα; 2.79). This word (also in Heraclitus B 15 DK of a phallic hymn, and of a Simonidean lyric in Plato *Protagoras* 343C) did not catch on, perhaps because it sounded pretentious; cf. the comic coinages "song-wright" (ἀσματοκάμπτης; Aristophanes *Clouds* 333) and "songlet" (ἀσμάτιον, Plato Comicus fr. 263 *PCG*).

⁴ Herodotus 1.24.5 (of Arion). So *aoidē* means "singing" as the performance of melodic poetry, not its composition: 1.202.2 (of the drug-induced singing of the Massegetae), 2.79.3 (of the traditional Egyptian dirge for Linus). Both cases also differ from epic usage in that they are not associated with professional *aoidoi*.

⁵ Herodotus 1.23. Phrynichus "makes" and "produces" a play (6.21.2, cf. 2.48.2, 60.1), and Olen "makes" hymns that are "sung" or performed by others (4.35.3: ἐποίησε ὕμνους . . . ἀειδομένους).

"tunes" (μέλη).[6] In Aristophanes we find μελοποιός ("tune-maker") for lyric composers and generic names such as τραγῳδοποιός ("tragedy-maker"); Euripides gives ὑμνοποιός ("song-maker"). The suffix was so productive of literary terminology that Aristophanes mocked it with his own coinages—"beggar-maker" (πτωκοποιός, χωλοποιός) for Euripides and "savage-maker" (ἀγριοποιός) for Aeschylus (*Frogs* 842, 837). By the fourth century, writers on poetry enjoyed a range of generic terms formed from this suffix to name composers of dithyrambs, elegies, iambics, comedies, and fables or stories (διθυραμβοποιός, ἐλεγειοποιός, ἰαμβοποιός, κωμῳδοποιός, and μυθοποιός).

The "making" in all these words suggests the production of something material, especially in an artisanal context. There is no suggestion of creation *ex nihilo*:[7] Hesiod's Zeus "made" (ποιεῖν) the races of men by "working" (ἐργάζεσθαι) them out of various metals (*Works and Days* 110, 128, 144, 158); when Semonides describes how different kinds of women were created, he alternates between saying they were "made" (ποιεῖν) and they were "fashioned, shaped" (πλάσσειν).[8] *Poiein* is the standard verb in early inscriptions to declare who "made" the artifact,[9] and one such object from around 525–500 was designated by its maker as a "made thing" or ποίημα.[10] Distinguishing a song's "maker" from its performers seems to fit with a wider trend to identify specialists in the arts: L. H. Jeffery reconstructs an increasingly specialized vocabulary for artisanal production beginning in the sixth century, when signatures distinguished those who painted pots (γράφειν) from those who "made" them (*poiein*).[11]

---

[6] ἐποποιίη, 2.116.1; ἐποποιός; 2.120.3, 7.161.3. Herodotus frequently cites hexameter and elegiac (5.113.2: see note 63 below) poems as "verses" (ἔπεα). Contrast his reference to Alcaeus "composing in song" (ἐν μέλει ποίησις, 5.95.2). This may favor reading μουσοποιός and not μουσόπολος at 2.135.1 for Sappho (though Sappho referred to herself as among the "Muses' ministers," μοισοπόλων, at 150.1 V): see Svenbro 1984a: 208 n. 93.

[7] Weil (1900: 237) had to make this point in his time, though the notion persists in the "natural creation" that grounds the study by Lledo Íñigo (1961); cf. Curtius 1953: 145–46; Sperdutti 1950: 220–21; and Blumenberg 1957, on the fusion of Greek and Christian in early modern notions of artistic making.

[8] Semonides 7 *IEG*: *poiein* 1, 96, 115; *plassein* 21. Hesiod uses (*sum–*)*plassein* for Hephaestus' "fashioning" Pandora from earth like a potter (*Works and Days* 70, *Theogony* 571).

[9] Cf. Powell 1991: 127–28; and fig. 1 in Jeffery 1990. For other verbs (τελεῖν, ἐργάζεσθαι, πονεῖν, ἐκποιεῖν), see Philipp 1968: 140 n. 248.

[10] 413 *CEG*. Cf. the inscription on a pedestal made in the same period by Onatas, quoted by Pausanias (5.25.10): τῷ Διὶ τἀχαιοὶ τἀγάλματα ταῦτ᾽ ἀνέθηκεν .... πολλὰ μὲν ἄλλα σοφοῦ ποίηματα καὶ τόδ᾽ Ὀνάτα / [ἔργον] Αἰγινήτεω, τὸν γείνατο παῖδα Μίκων.

[11] Jeffery 1990: 61–63; cf. the complementary analysis by Philipp (1968: 67–68), tracing a diminishing role of divine patronage in the process. Cook (1971: 137–38) argues that at least for some pots, the "maker" is the one from whose workshop it came. Cf. *JHS* (1990).

In accordance with this background, Herodotus' uses of *poiēsis*, *poiētēs*, and *poiein* do not imply creativity so much as "making poetry" in the sense of "rendering stories in poetry," that is, putting them into verse.[12] This formal, metrical conception is why Herodotus needs another word, *logopoios*, for Aesop as composer of (prose) fables and quotes his predecessor Hecataeus from his "stories" or "accounts" (*logoi*, 6.137.1). The idea that all poetry was nothing more than speech with meter is flatly declared by Herodotus' contemporary, the sophist Gorgias (*Helen* §9). The tendency of this vocabulary to suggest that poetry was simply metrical composition became so widespread that both Plato and Aristotle had to argue against it to proffer their own more subtle conceptions of poetry. In Plato's *Symposium* (205c), Diotima complains that there is no good reason that popular usage has restricted the word *poiēsis* to "productions" (ἐργασίαι) in meter and music and *poiētēs* to their "makers"; she goes on to enunciate a higher conception of true "making" that involves creation. Early in the *Poetics* (1447b13–20), Aristotle finds it necessary to attack the common use of such terms as *epopoios* and *elegopoios* ("maker in elegiac meter") because of their implicit equation of the poet's task with versification; only then could he argue that versified philosophy or history was not poetry and that the heart of the poet's activity was representation or *mimēsis*.

The sources and significance of this vocabulary have been variously interpreted. One approach suggests that "singers" became "poets" when the arts of composing and performing became separated.[13] This would suppose, on no evidence, that the words go back to the seventh century and beyond, for poets had been handing over pre-composed songs for others to perform as long as there had been choral poetry in Greece. Other approaches hold that the appearance of the "make" words in our records reflects some later change in poets' circumstances. Svenbro, for example, argues that the word "poet" reflects a new economic position of the poet as seller of his goods in the late archaic city. On his view, "making" came to characterize the poetic process when choral poets began to function as economic "free agents," selling their songs to cities and patrons. This led to a "materialization of speech" that he finds in Simonides and Pindar, claiming that they view their songs as alienable *object*s of

---

[12] Cf. 4.16.1 (Aristeas ἐν τοῖς ἔπεσι ἔφησε), 3.38.4 (ὀρθῶς μοι δοκεῖ Πίνδαρος ποιῆσαι ... φήσας). The meaning "put into verse" is well illustrated in Plato *Phaedo* 61B, where μύθους ποιεῖν describes Socrates versifying Aesop's fables. On the lack of inventiveness, cf. Herodotus 2.156.6, where Aeschylus is said to have taken from the Egyptians the idea that Artemis was Demeter's daughter and "made" it into a play.

[13] Weil 1900, and already in Wolf 1985: ch. 12, esp. 72 (= 1795: 42).

art to be sold to the highest bidder.[14] On this view, *poiein* was the "*mot-clé* to designate transforming material by paid work."[15] Svenbro's market analysis has been criticized as anachronistic; a further difficulty for his thesis is that the supposedly alienated choral poets never use the "making" words of their (or others') song (and, as we have seen, heavily qualify artisanal analogies with song).[16] On compatible lines, the rise of the "make" vocabulary has been taken as symptomatic of a decline from an earlier view of poetry as divine.[17] It has been suggested that "poetry" arose when the enthusiastic concept of inspiration was waning in response to increased emphasis on the individual's technical contributions. But Penelope Murray has noted that the concept of the frenzied, ecstatic poet is in fact *not* archaic but is attested only in the fifth century, and the strong opposition of inspiration and technique seems to be a Platonic idea.[18] Democritus, the first Greek writer to mention poetic "enthusiasm" (*enthousiasmos*), uses "poet" in the very same sentence.[19] The concept of irrational inspiration is more easily understood as arising concomitantly with this new vocabulary: it accounted for aspects of poetry that could not be comprehended under the artisanal conception of poetic making.

Finally, many point to the sophists. In a valuable analysis, Marcello Durante argues that to focus on the "creative process" out of all of a singer's activities and to reduce to one term the various poetic forms "could not come about through observation of particulars. . . . A unitary term for poetry can only arise in a learned context, i.e. within a problematization of poetry. And this occurs, precisely in the fifth century, with the

---

[14] Svenbro 1984a: 155–79. In many respects this may be read as a Marxian account of a process that Detienne (1967: chs. 5–6, esp. 121–24) discusses in political terms, arguing for the desacralization or "laicization of speech" in the same time and among the same figures. Critique and discussion in Von Reden (1995), while yet accepting some major shift in the notion of poetry's value around the time of Simonides.

[15] Svenbro 1984a: 170. For a different view, Nagy 1989: 19–21.

[16] Another difficulty is that Herodotus already uses this putative "choral" metaphor for epic, Homer, which supposes a rather quick "generalization" from its original association with choral poetry. Svenbro's explanation (1984a: 170–72) involves oversubtle distinctions in the way Herodotus uses *poiein* to suggest that the verb refers to Homer's "fabrication" as opposed to his own "true" research; but Herodotus uses *poiein* of Sappho and Alcaeus while accepting the testimony in question (2.135, 5.95).

[17] So Gudeman 1934: 86 and Diehl 1940: 84, for whom "singer" was associated with "Wüten, Rasen," something "Seelisches, Geistiges," while the "maker" suggested "Herrichtens, Ordnens, Schreibens, Abfassens, also etwas mechanisches." Lanata 1963: 229–30, with a discussion of earlier views, presents an essentially similar, though positive, development.

[18] P. Murray 1981 and 1996: 6–12, building on Tigerstedt 1970.

[19] B 18 DK; cf B 21 DK, both discussed in chapter 7.

sophists, Antiphon and Gorgias in particular."[20] Durante acutely draws out the enlightened, empirical attitude toward singing implied in this vocabulary. But there is no reason to ascribe these words particularly to Antiphon and Gorgias as rhetorical teachers. It is likely that they already were used by the historians and scientific writers of late sixth-century Ionia since they are well installed among their successors in the fifth. Abstract nouns in -σις (like *poiēsis*) are a marked feature of Ionian abstract thought, and other words of same type were making their way into discussions of poetry through the fifth century.[21]

None of these explanations fully takes into account a fact that is rarely given its due: the word for "poet" and its fellows are consistently avoided by all the high poets of the fifth century. By contrast, the new words are at home in prose and in fifth-century comic or light (e.g., sympotic) verse.[22] When tragedy, epinician, and other forms of formal lyric mention poets and poetry, they speak of singers and songs rather than makers and poems.[23] The single, telling exception is Euripides, who in a much-quoted paradox said, "Love can teach anyone to be a poet, even the one who has never cultivated the Muses."[24] Euripides uses the word "poet" rather than, say, "singer" (*aoidos*) to stress the god's power in bestowing something thought to require extended and studious application. To make someone into a "singer" would be a less impressive feat. It has been suggested that tragedians avoided *poiētēs* merely as a nonheroic or "prosaic" word unsuited to their dramatic world.[25] But compound forms show that it is the very idea of "song-making" that is ruled out: -*poios* suffixes are

---

[20] Durante 1976: 170–71. Similarly, Lledo Íñigo 1961: ch. 3.

[21] E.g., ῥῆσις ("speaking" in Homer) is a technical term for recited dramatic speech in Aristophanes (*Clouds* 1371, *Frogs* 151). Handley (1953) notes that -σις abstracts are disproportionately concentrated in Aristophanes' *Clouds*, *Frogs*, and *Thesmophoriazousae* and ascribes this to their respective concerns with sophistry, poetic criticism, and parody of intellectual poets such as Euripides and Agathon. Cf., too, Browning 1958: 60–72 and Long 1968: 17, 27 ff. Object nouns in -μα, such as *poiēma*, often accompanied such coinages: Peppler 1916; cf. Chantraine 1979: 175–90. For -της agent suffixes connoting an expert in a specialized craft, cf. Chantraine 1979: 310 ff., and Dover 1968, on *Clouds* 94 and 1397.

[22] The fact is noted by Kuhlmann (1906: 5, 36–39). For light verse, Dionysius Chalcus 1.2 *IEG*; cf. *ōidēn teuxen*, Sophocles 5.1 *IEG*.

[23] E.g., *aoidos*: Aeschylus *Suppliants* 695, three times in Sophocles, over thirty times in Euripides.

[24] 663 Nauck: ποιητὴν δ' ἄρα / Ἔρως διδάσκει, κἂν ἄμουσος τὸ πρίν. Quoted by Aristophanes at *Wasps* 1074 and very often thereafter: see Nauck ad loc. For Love as a resourceful teacher even in desperate situations, cf. Euripides fr. 430 Nauck. A similar irony is implied by Euripides' juxtaposition of "song-makers" with the vocabulary of "giving birth" at *Suppliants* 180–81 (τόν θ' ὑμνοποιὸν αὐτὸς ἂν τίκτῃ μέλη / χαίροντα τίκτειν) and *Rhesus* 651 (τῆς ὑμνποιοῦ παῖδα . . . Μούσης).

[25] Bowra 1964: 2.

not objectionable per se in tragic diction, but for "song-makers," tragedy prefers compounds with *aoidos* as the second element.[26] Here again Euripides can be more up-to-date than the others. In *Trojan Women*, for example, Hecuba laments her son, asking, "What can a muse-maker write on your tomb?" (τί καί ποτε / γράψειεν ἄν σοι μουσοποιὸς ἐν τάφῳ;). The language of making together with the reference to writing sets her outburst of present grief against future memorials, carefully composed by poets; the untraditional language perhaps points the spectators at a heroic drama toward that future in which Euripides will write his commemorative play.[27] Similarly prospective is the reference in *Hippolytus* to a "muse-making mood of care" (μουσοποιός μέριμνα) that will produce songs about Hippolytus and Phaedra in the future (1428). Tragedy, with the exception of a few ironic passages in Euripides, avoids the language and idea of "making" song.[28]

Epinician also eschews the "making" vocabulary even at moments when the poet presents himself as an artisan of song. I have argued that the craftsmanship dear to a rhetorical critic was not the primary virtue such poets wished to project. Because it was more valuable to them to preserve their connection to civic life than to stress their personal skill, they have no use for the lexicon of "making." Comedy, of course, keeps its ear attuned to contemporary jargon, and Aristophanes not only uses the vocabulary of "poetry" freely, but mocks its popularity in hyperextended forms such as τραγῳδοποιός ("tragic-singer-maker"), κωμῳδοποιός, κωμῳοποιητής ("comedy-singer-poet"), and the punning τρυγῳδοποιομουσική for comedy.[29] Correspondingly, comedy frequently represents poetry as a *tekhnē* like any craft, reflecting the perspectives of poetry experts and other intellectuals.

The "making" vocabulary suited analytical and technical approaches to song that placed emphasis on its construction rather than its perfor-

[26] For -*poios* suffixes, cf. Aeschylus *Eumenides* 13 (κελευοποιοί), Sophocles *Philoctetes* 32. Contrast, e.g., θεσπιῳδός (Aeschylus *Agamemnon* 1134), θεσπιῳδήσειν (*Agamemnon* 1161, Sophocles fr. 456 *TGrF*, Euripides *Helen* 145), μελῳδός (Euripides *Hypsipyle*. i.2.14, *Iphigeneia at Aulis* 1045, *Iphigeneia in Tauris* 1104, *Electra* 1109, and *Rhesus* 351, 393; cf. μελῳδία, 923). Euripides seems to have been particularly fond of compounds in -*ōidos*, for many of his are not elsewhere attested in tragedy: ὑμνῳδός, ξυνῳδός, παρῳδός, ἐπῳδός as substantive.

[27] *Trojan Women* 1188–89. With γράψειεν μουσοποιός contrast the traditional vocabulary in *Alcestis* 445–46: πολλά σε [Alcestis] μουσοπόλοι μέλψονται.

[28] The one other Euripidean use of "poet" is unclear: ἄνθηρος ... ποιητής (*Photius* 139.14 Reitzenstein). Some have supplied "poet" at *TrGF* 646a.36: θεαί, τραγικῶν ὃ παρῶσι πο[. But at v. 32 the author speaks of the "great Salaminian singer" (*aoidos*), referring either to Homer or to Euripides. On μουσοποιεῖ in Sophocles fr. 245 *TGrF*, Radt (ad loc). doubts that this word belongs to the quotation.

[29] Cf. *poiētēs* in a satyr play of Astydamas II (*TrGF* 60 F 4.2), possibly from a parabasis.

mance and on its maker's artful designs rather than his moral wisdom or divine inspiration. In addition, its pattern of usage suggests that it was not singers who needed this new conception of and new name for doing what they had always done, but those outside that field, champions of new forms of knowledge and new ways of using traditional song. To define these outsiders, we must look beyond and somewhat before the notorious sophists of the early fifth century.

History and the History of Literature

Durante ascribes the new vocabulary to the sophists in view of their interest in language and rhetoric. But giving rhetoric pride of place in the invention of poetry fits neither chronology nor the evidence, since *poiēsis* and *poiētēs* are fully established already in Herodotus, who was born (around 484) not much later than the first great sophist Protagoras. We should rather ascribe the popularization, and perhaps the origin, of this vocabulary to the tradition in which Herodotus wrote, Ionian critical "inquiry" (*historia*) into past and present cultural forms. Active at the beginning of the fifth century, Hecataeus of Miletus was credited with a work known as "On Poetry" (Περὶ ποιήσεως); we cannot be sure that title is his own, but he certainly critiqued some of the same poetic stories and poets as Herodotus.[30] Most of Herodotus' contemporaries and immediate successors in mythography and ethnography took song into their purview. Hellanicus of Lesbos (ca. 480–395) examined records of musical performances preserved in connection with the Spartan festival of the Carnea; these allowed him to identify his fellow Lesbian Terpander as the first kitharodic victor there and the Lesbian Arion as the first to make cyclic choruses sing standing still.[31] The polymathic sophist Hippias composed an Olympian Chronicle in a similar spirit, and Damastes of Sigeum, a younger contemporary of Herodotus, wrote *On the Ancient Poets and Wise Men*, the first known and possibly first ever monograph specifically devoted to what we should call the literary history of Greece. Toward the century's end, Glaucus of Rhegium gave a history of music in a work known as *On Poets*, which, via the Plutarchan *On Music*, provided a still-

[30] It is possible that Hecataeus already used *poiein* in the sense "say in poetry" when he disputed Hesiod on the number of Danaids: ὡς μὲν Ἡσίοδος ἐποίησε, πεντήκοντα, ὡς ἐγὼ δὲ, οὐδὲ εἴκοσι, 1 F 19 *FGrH*). However, the fact that Hecataeus doesn't name his own activity with a contrasting verb leaves open the possibility that ἐποίησε is periphrastic for something like ἐγενεηλόγησε.

[31] Hellanicus: Kleingünther 1934: 131. Terpander: 4 F 85A, 86 *FGrH*. On the many traditions about Arion, cf. Kleingünther 1934: 23 n. 19; Barker 1984: 59 n. 18; Pickard-Cambridge 1962: 11 ff.

influential framework for reconstructing early Greek literary history.[32] By
the time of Isocrates, such works formed a conspicuous body of prose
writing that he referred to as "advanced research" or "philosophizing"
about the poets (*Antidosis* §45).

These writers shared a new, enlightened, and historical approach to
Greek song traditions for which Hippias may have coined the term
arkhaiologia. Arnaldo Momigliano associates the "new urge to collect
information about Greek literary antiquities" with the "intellectual atmo-
sphere in which history was born," one of "faith in collective organization and of trust in natural explanations."[33] Encouraging this inquiry was
the fact that musical styles and institutions were changing: sixth-century
tyrants had been wont to revise their cities' epic and dithyrambic festivals,
and the rise of new forms of choral singing after the Persian wars, such
as Attic *tragōidia*, made some of the older forms into curiosities.[34]
Hence the origins of dithyramb were to be a topic of interest to both
Pindar and Herodotus, and the origins of tragedy were hotly contested.[35]
In addition, a cross-cultural interest in musical practices was doubtless
encouraged by what Nagy has described as the panhellenization of lyric
poetry in this period—the flux of regional song types into and out of
cultural centers.[36]

From the early fifth century, then, such historical records as were available were collated with traditional legends about early inventors of song
to construct a history of human singing. Most of this material survives
only in fragmentary or digested form, but the general approach can be
indicated by considering Glaucus' history of music as reconstructed by

[32] Hippias: B 3 DK; cf. Huxley 1968: 47–54, and Jacoby 1941: 101 n. 1. Damastes:
Schwartz s.v. "Damastes (3)," *RE* 4 (1901). Glaucus: Hiller, *RE* 7 (1912). Jacoby, "Glaukos
(36)" *RE* 7 (1912): 1417–20.

[33] Momigliano 1971: 28; cf. 40.

[34] See Dover 1964: 211. Because the Delian festival had been reorganized several times
in the sixth century (by Polycrates and by the Athenians), Thucydides had to quote from
the *Homeric Hymn to Apollo* to prove that musical contests had been a part of the old
festival: see Wade-Gery 1952: 74 n. 57. At Sicyon, Cleisthenes revised a festival of Dionysus
by incorporating heroic laments (*tragikoi khoroi*, Herodotus 5.67), while Arion turned a
traditional processional dithyramb into a stationary chorus (possibly of satyrs) performance
at Corinth: Herodotus 1.23; Seaford 1984. Changing festival customs are likely to have
abetted Athenian confusion about when and by whom rhapsodic recitations of Homer were
joined to the Pantheneia: [Plato] *Hipparchus* 228B, Isocrates *Panegyricus* 159, Plutarch
Pericles 13.6, cf. Lycurgus *In Leocratem* 102, and DL 1.57, on which see Merkelbach 1952.

[35] Herodotus 5.67. Sicyonians maintained the Athenians took *tragōidia* from their own
tragikoi khoroi. Athenians opposed this with an old tradition reaching back in Corinth at
least to Arion. In a very late notice from John the Deacon, Solon (30a *IEG*) claimed that
Arion blended the dithyramb and the *tragikos tropos*: Pickard-Cambridge 1962: 72, 89,
294; West on 30a.

[36] Nagy 1990; see the review by K. Crotty in *Arion*, 3d ser. 1 (1991): 155–70.

Felix Jacoby.[37] Glaucus identified the oldest music as a mode for the *aulos*, which he probably ascribed to the mythical Marsyas, the one who was flayed when he lost a contest to Apollo on the instrument. Among Marsyas' successors, Glaucus named Olympus of Phrygia, who was popularly thought of as the inventor of one of the most ancient musical modes for the *aulos* (the *harmateios nomos*). Then Orpheus invented singing to the lyre (*kithara*), probably followed by Homer. After him came Terpander's lyre-singing (*kitharōdia*), and then singing to the *aulos* with Klonas of Thebes; from him derived the popular nonepic songs of Archilochus and Stesichorus, a virtual *Landsmann* of Glaucus.

This history gave substance to the unitary conception of Greek song implied in the "make" words. Discrete musical traditions from various locales were united into a comprehensive evolution in which each was "invented" by a figure whose name was current in the fifth century and who was known as one of the most ancient practitioners in the form. The main classificatory principles in this story as told by Glaucus are formal: it is based on musical modes, meters, and instruments rather than on social events like funerals or festivals. As is usually the case with histories, Glaucus' account also functioned as a story about the present. He ranked musical forms in an evolution toward increasing rationality and formal complexity as music moved westward. In beginning with Marsyas, Olympus, and the *aulos*, Glaucus placed the origins of Greek music in the East and in the kind of music classical Greeks found most passionately exciting. (Organologists tirelessly deplore the conventional mistranslation of the double-reeded *aulos* as "flute" rather than "oboe"; but in view of its exciting and often controversial repertoire, we should rather associate the *aulos* with the jazz saxophone.)[38] Glaucus thus associates the first music with human passion (and perhaps violence); it was only at a later stage with Orpheus and Homer that words and reason—*logos*—entered song, and did so on a different instrument: the lyre was felt to be conducive to "Doric" music—conservative, ethical, and Greek. Even within lyre songs, placing Orpheus' mystical and cosmogonic songs before Homer may have suggested that heroic epic was a humanization and secularization of magical singing. And whereas Hellanicus had named Terpander as the first kitharodic victor at the Carnea, Glaucus' placing him after Orpheus and Homer characterized his archaic songs in dactylic rhythms as a blend of the lyre's musical powers with Homer's heroic themes. Finally, with Klonas, the eastern *aulos* was at last subdued to the *logos*.

Glaucus' history also—and this may be the most fundamental new idea brought on by the invention of poetry—presents the evolution of song

---

[37] Jacoby, "Glaukos (36)," *RE* 7 (1912): 1418; further in Lanata 1963: 270–81.
[38] On the *aulos*, see Wilson 1999, 2000.

types as the work of human "first discoverers" (πρῶτοι εὑρηταί). If his mention of Marsyas left open the possibility of some divine origin of song, his history sees progress in that activity as a series of fully historical, fully human developments. Although the idea of the poet as maker was to suit rhetorical approaches to language, it also encapsulated a humanistic and rationalistic perspective on song that strongly distinguished fifth-century accounts of poetry from earlier traditions.

Singing had always had a mythic and legendary history, and some of these stories appear in choral lyric of the age.[39] For example, in a song for a Corinthian audience, Pindar says the dithyramb was invented in Corinth, but elsewhere he placed its origin in Thebes or Naxos.[40] Pindar is not simply an indifferent historian but a public celebrant connecting the performance to its mythical origins. He gives a history of epinician in an epinician for a Nemean victor: "The revel-song (epikōmios) existed long ago indeed, even before the strife of Adrastus and the Kadmeians" (Nemean 8.50–51). With these words, the present song, under one of its designations as kōmos or "revel," is given roots that lie deeper even than the games that occasioned it, for legend held that the Nemean games were founded by Adrastus while leading the Seven to Thebes. The antiquity of the form ennobles it, but Pindar's history also has an ethical point: in the terms of the archaic war/peace dichotomy, the revel-song is a desirably peaceful one that can claim social as well as chronological priority over cyclic epics about Thebes' strife (and a fortiori over Homer's Trojan epics as well). A singer's history of song enhanced the occasion by giving the ephemeral event an anchor in past greatness and positing future repetitions.

The festival poets' conception of sacred time renewable in reperformance was radically opposed to the historical approach, which, aspiring only to trace rather than to overcome time, viewed origins as unique and isolable human events. As singers qualified the craftsmanly image of their art, so they labored to reattach the merely human history of song to divine roots. Pindar usually presents the origin of song as a divine gift to early heroes. In a hymn for Thebes, he spoke of Theban Kadmos listening to Apollo as he "demonstrated correct musical art."[41] This first king of the Kadmeians was also privileged to hear the Muses themselves singing

---

[39] Kleingünther 1933: 21 ff., who cites especially Pratinas fr. 3 TGrF (708 PMG), on which see Lloyd-Jones 1990: 227–30, Barker 1984: 273 n. 61, 235–36; but this text may belong to the late fifth century: Seaford 1976.

[40] Pindar Olympian 13.17 for Xenophon of Corinth, in a passage (14–23) matching Corinthian athletic success with the inventiveness of the Corinthians (e.g., Sisyphus, Medea, and Bellerophon). For Naxos and Thebes, cf. schol. on Olympian 13.25c (= fr. 715, 71 S-M).

[41] Fr. 32, in context with other fragments of the Hymn to Thebes, frs. 29–35c S-M.

at his marriage to Harmonia ("Concord," with social as well as musical senses). Festive song naturally is traced to occasions when "the gods feasted [mortals] and gave them gifts" (*Pythian* 3.86–95). Weddings between divinity and mortal were an especially apt occasion for song to descend to earth. Kadmos' wedding is also cited near the beginning of the Theognidea, where the Muses first sing a verse that might be a motto for the collection (15–18).[42] At the wedding of Peleus and Thetis, the Muses "generously" sang for mortals under the direction of Apollo: like their brother singing to Kadmos, they showed correct music in first singing of Zeus before going on to a heroic tale concerning Peleus (*Nemean* 5.22–26).[43] A tantalizing one-sentence report says Pindar recounted the origin of all song: at his marriage or upon the occasion of his ultimate ascendancy over the heavens, Zeus asked the gods what else was needed, and they asked for Muses to provide music and words to serve as a *kosmos*, an adornment that is an original and final ordering, over all (fr. 31 S-M).[44]

As mortals are ephemeral, singers do not neglect change in time. Pindar can contrast his formal ode performed at the victor's local shrine with the spontaneous chant at the site of victory. This simple, thrice-shouted "Hail victor!" ("triple-refrained *kallinikos*") he calls the "Archilochean *melos*" and says it was already sung at Olympia in the time of Ajax (*Olympian* 9.1–10). The axiological implications of such histories may vary depending on whether one values progress or earliness, artfulness and sophistication or purity and closeness to origins. In a dithyramb (fr. 70b.1–3 S-M), Pindar can oppose his new "uninhibited" style to the overrefined mode of the past when "the Dithyramb crept along in a drawn-out line and the *sigma* came from the mouths of men as if it were base-born/counterfeit."[45] He presents his own way of honoring the god as sanctioned by the Olympians: "The Muse has set me up as the herald of wise words for Greece of fair choruses" (fr. 70b.23–25). Similarly, he contrasts spontaneous love poetry of the olden days with the present in which the "silver-faced Muse" has become a hired worker selling songs; we should take this not as a reflection of actual economic conditions of his time, but as providing an ethical and ideological frame for his song.[46] The view that

[42] Also at Euripides *Bacchae* 881, 901; cf. Plato *Lysis* 216c and schol. ad loc.

[43] Euripides *Iphigeneia at Aulis* 1040–45 describes the first *humenaios* sung by the Pierides at the marriage of Peleus and Thetis; cf. Euripides *Phoenicians* 822.

[44] Cf. Snell 1953: 94–95, and Pucci 1980.

[45] Discussion in Barker 1984: 59 n. 19, 252, and see now D'Angour 1997.

[46] For studies of *Isthmian* 2.1–11 and the Mercenary Muse, see Woodbury 1968; Barker 1984: 58–59, 240, Nagy 1989: 18–24; Kurke 1991: 32–33, ch. 10. For Svenbro (1984a): 155–60): Simonides' conception of the poem as a dense and durable object is related to his economic position as seller of alienable works of art; but see Von Reden 1995: 42–43.

earliness is good can suggest that the essential qualities of poetry are those that were present in its most primitive manifestation; this tends to put the emphasis on song's rhythm and music. Or the origin can be a sort of fall or wrong path taken: Euripides' *Medea* complains that it was useless wit to invent songs of festivity without also inventing songs that can heal (190–203).

The development of a scientific literary history is the leading instance in Kleingunther's classic study (1933) of the Greek penchant to name "first inventors" in the arts. The first extant example of an inventor catalogue occurs in the *Frogs* (1030–36), when Aristophanes' Aeschylus gives a historical proof of the thesis that poetry should teach useful things:

> Consider the matter from its beginning:
> how the noblest of the poets have been beneficial.
> For Orpheus revealed rites of initiation to us and to abstain from
>   illicit slaughter;[47]
> Musaeus healings of disease and oracles; Hesiod working the earth,
> the seasons of fruitfulness, and plowing; as for godlike Homer,
> whence come his honor and his fame but from teaching useful things:
> marshaling, acts of courage (*aretas*), and the arming of men?

Although this passage is often cited as a simple statement of Greek reverence for poetry, the comedian is offering a pastiche of the latest anthropological reinterpretation of poetic traditions. Familiar names of old poets serve to mark successive stages in an enlightened account of human progress from savagery to civilization.[48] The inclusion of Orpheus as Homer's predecessor (as in Glaucus of Rhegium) reveals the kind of historicizing synthesis at work. West has richly suggested that fifth-century representations of Orpheus as an epic singer reflect a rationalization of his shamanistic aspects, especially his magic songs.[49] For Aristophanes, Orpheus is seen as a religious reformer, and his taboos serve as the basis of (a decreasingly pious) social development: after him, the way is clear for the prophetic and healing arts, agriculture, and lastly warfare. In the same perspective, Aeschylus can be presented in the play as a founder in the arts, as the first (*prōtos*) to "build up" the style of tragedy "like a tower" (*purgoō*, *Frogs* 1004).

The fact that the singers Aristophanes lists all used hexameters shows that the historicizing, anthropological view was allied with fifth-century formalist studies of poetry, especially the study of metrics. Making Or-

---

[47] Usually taken to refer to vegetarianism, though Dover (1968 on 1032) understands laws on homicide; his grounds, however, are questionably preserving a consistent view of Aeschylus.

[48] See Kleingünther 1934: esp. 134–43, and Dover 1993, on *Frogs* 1032, comparing Democritus B 5.8, 1 DK; Hermippus (fl. 430's) PCG V 561 ff.; and Critias B 25.1–4, B 2 DK.

[49] West 1983: 6–8.

pheus presage the epic poets assimilated his spells and theogonic songs as one more variety of hexameter poetry. At first this science coped better with stichic meters than with stanzaic rhythms, so that the hexameter—instantly recognizable in the oldest songs—came to be regarded as the most ancient meter. Many candidates were proposed as its inventor: Democritus attributed the hexameter to Musaeus, Critias to Orpheus, and a Delphic tradition could cite Boeo, a poetess and speaker for Apollo, proclaiming Olen "the first to fashion song from ancient words."[50] Closely related was an interest in Homer's date and predecessors in hexameter poetry.[51] Gorgias traced Homer's genealogy back to Musaeus, as did Damastes, who added Orpheus as an intermediary; Orpheus was also made an ancestor of Homer by Pherecydes and Hellanicus.[52] Eventually a standard sequence was worked out in Athens: Orpheus-Musaeus-Hesiod-Homer.[53] (Musaeus was associated with the Eleusinian mysteries and the founding figure of the Eumolpidae, Athenian singers of theological and eschatological poetry).[54] The rational and measurable category of metrics allowed a conspicuous body of religious and metaphysical song, normally preserved in small sects or inherited within priestly clans, to be fit into the family of panhellenic song.

Rationalizing constructions of musical history were also stimulated by ethnographic inquiries into musical practices in various parts of Greece as well as among its neighbors. Men of curiosity were able to look at song performances not only as engaged members of a civic audience but with an eye to song's cross-cultural uses as a political and sociological activity. Even occasional lyric songs, whether the "personal" lyrics ascribed to historical individuals like Solon and Sappho or cult songs performed at annual Delian festivals, could be removed from their contexts and regarded as sources of historical information or evidence of practices.

One of the most productive thinkers along these lines appears to have been Democritus, who conceived a cultural anthropology that touched

[50] Democritus B 16 DK: cf. Lanata 1963: 254; Democritus perhaps relies on Orpheus fr. 356 Kern: West 1983: 40 n. 1, 232. Critias B 3 DK: Lanata (1963: 221) compares his elegy on Anacreon (B 1 DK), which might have mentioned Homer (cf. B 50 DK). "Boeo" (Pausanias 10.5.8): πρῶτος δ' ἀρχαίων ἐπέων τεκτάνατ' ἀοιδάν. Cf. Parke and Wormell 1956, 1: 34, and Parke: 66.

[51] On placing Homer in relation to early poets, see Allen 1924: 130–39.

[52] Gorgias B 25 DK. Damastes 5 F 11 *FGrH*. Pherecydes 3 F 167 *FGrH*. Hellanicus 4 F 5 *FGrH*.

[53] So Hippias (B 6 DK), Aristophanes (*Frogs* 1032–36ff.), Plato (*Apology* 41A), cited by West (1966: 47) as evidence of the actual priority of Hesiod to Homer. Cf. *Republic* 363A ("Hesiod and Homer"), 377D ("Hesiod and Homer and the others," i.e., Orpheus and Musaeus), 612B. Cf. Chrysippus *SVF* II.316.12 (cf. 316.16). Xenophanes said that Homer antedated Hesiod (B 13 DK), as did Heraclides Ponticus (177 Wehrli).

[54] West 1983: 23, 40, citing Graf, *Eleusis* (1974): 18–19. Cf. Kleingünther 1934: 108.

on the origins of singing, religion, and perhaps writing.[55] Democritus regarded poetry as a purely human contrivance to meet human needs, and
first articulated a very important distinction between arts that have their
origin in necessity (e.g., housebuilding) and those that, like music, arise
only when a condition of surplus has arisen.[56] This naturalistic, progressivist account significantly classed poetry as a pastime of leisure, thereby
severing it from any sacral or political function. Although this rupture is
not in evidence in Aristophanes, its implicit notion of "fine arts" was to
have a great influence on Plato and Aristotle.[57] Democritus took an
equally hard look at traditional religious beliefs, which he attributed to
the imposition of a small group of men who were simply good with language (*logioi*). As for poetry (his term), it may be that he saw the importance of written texts for reconstructing its early history. Cole has inferred
from his making Musaeus Homer's ancestor that Democritus put poetry
back to a time just before the Trojan War, probably along with the invention of writing (thus enabling the war to be "reported" by Homer?).[58]

In the fourth century, these new perspectives on song will be fundamental assumptions of the science of poetics; but they can already be seen
emerging in the witness with whom we began this chapter, the historian,
historian of poetry, and reader of texts, Herodotus. A look at some of his
uses of poetry in context helps fill in the sketch provided by the lexical
evidence. These passages also raise the important but difficult questions
of how far this new approach to song relied on examining them in textual
form, and what difference this might have made to their analyses.

Herodotus and Poetry

It is hardly surprising that the first Greek historians examined old epic
poems for information about the way things used to be.[59] The idea that
not everything poets say is trustworthy was traditional, and a certain mis-
trust of Homer surfaced in so conventional and high-minded a poet as

[55] Democritus B 16 DK. Kleingünther 1934: 108.

[56] B 144 DK; cf. Cole 1967: 43.

[57] B 154 DK, cf. Kleingünther 1934: 107–9. As noted by Cole (1967: 52–53, 97–130),
Plato and Aristotle share Democritus' belief in a progress from the useful to the fine arts,
but they degrade the technological phase in human history to a mere prelude to truly civilized human life: cf. Plato *Laws* 677A–D and *Republic* 372B, where poets and the tribe of
imitators arise late and out of people's desire for superfluous luxury, and esp. *Laws* 889C–
D, where the late-arising mimetic arts ("painting, *mousikē* and their kin") are discussed in
a context of Leucippan-Democritean atomic materialism. For Aristotle, see *Politics* 1341a
8–29, *Metaphysics* 981b13–20, and *Poetics* ch. 4; cf. Isocrates *Busiris* 15.

[58] Cole 1967: 57. On the *logioi*, see, too, Pfligersdorfer 1943–47.

[59] See Koster 1970: 13–15.

Pindar, who could blame Homer for exaggerating (*Nemean* 7.20–23). But Herodotus repairs to Homer and Hesiod for their testimony, often unwitting, to the beliefs and customs of their times. Similarly, he tends to regard lyric monodies as records "in song" of the poet's life. Alcaeus "rendered in song" (ἐν μέλεϊ ποιήσας) an experience in battle that he sent to a friend as if it were a letter, and Sappho "heaped abuse on her brother in a song" (ἐν μέλεϊ Σαπφὼ πολλὰ κατεκερτόμησέ μιν) for purchasing the freedom of the courtesan Rhodopis.[60] Such references may owe something to fifth-century lives of poets,[61] but they also appeal to an audience that was receiving much of its poetry in oral performative contexts. Herodotus expects at least a part of his audience to be familiar with certain short lyrics. He places Gyges of Lydia in time by saying that he is the one mentioned in the trimeter iambic (abuse) poem by Archilochus of Paros.[62] Aristotle (*Rhetoric* 1418b30) tells us that the poem (19 *IEG*) Herodotus seems to be thinking of was spoken in the persona of Charon the carpenter; but Herodotus knows, and expects his audience to know, it is by Archilochus. In speaking of a king who died in the revolt against Persia, Herodotus identifies him through his father, whom "Solon, on the occasion of his arrival in Cyprus, praised in recited verses more than any tyrant."[63]

The kinds of lyric Herodotus cites suggest a level of literary culture that could be picked up at symposia: on the subject of courtesans, he claims "all Greece has learned the name" of Rhodopis, but adds that Archidike, though not as much "talked of in every club" (LSJ s.v. *perileskhēneutos*), was "sung about" (*aoidimos*) throughout Greece in her time. A symposiast might know when Simonides praised a certain Eretrian (5.102.5). Herodotus knows Simonides' verses inscribed for the fallen at Thermopulae, and probably is paraphrasing closely when he add that the one for Megistias was composed "for friendship's sake" (7.228.4). In sympotic fashion, Herodotus will occasionally cite a poet for gnomic wisdom, as when he says Pindar "rightly composed" when he said *nomos* ("law" or "custom" in his interpretation) is the "king of all."[64] But epic is a different matter:

---

[60] *Histories*. 5.95.2 on Alcaeus; cf. 3.42.4, where Polycrates writes a *biblion* and sends it to Egypt. On Sappho's poem (*Histories* 2.135.6), cf. Page 1955: 48–51. A. B. Lloyd 1986: 86–87, citing Jeffery 1990: 102 and Athenaeus 596c.

[61] Lanata 1963: 227; Jacoby, "Herodotus" *RE, suppl.* 2 (1913): 285. In general, Lefkowitz 1981.

[62] *Histories* 1.12.2. On the passage, Diels 1910: 21 n. 5.

[63] Diels (1910: 23 n. 3) calls Herodotus *Ungenau*, as he should have said "taking leave of the island." Note Herodotus speaks of "recited verses" (*en epesi*, 5.113.2) for a poem cited as "elegiacs" (*en elegeiais*) by Plutarch (Plutarch *Solon* 26 = Solon 19 *IEG*). In Herodotus' lyric quotations, a phrase specifying "form" often comes first (5.95.2, 2.135.6).

[64] Herodotus 3.38.4 = Pindar fr. 169a S-M. The Pindaric tag is alluded to by Plato's Hippias (*Protagoras* 337D) and interpreted by Callicles (*Gorgias* 484B), a reading (justice

Herodotus has real expertise in such poetry that has come from carefully studying and comparing texts.

Herodotus exhibits a precise knowledge of the contents of individual epics, and his command of the text of the *Iliad* (he is the first Greek we know to use that title) is such that he can buttress an interpretation of Homer by saying, "Nowhere else does he contradict himself over this point."[65] This expertise allows him to question the authenticity of epics that were commonly regarded as "by Homer" in his day, such as the *Cypria*, because its account of Paris' voyage back to Troy does not square with that given in the *Iliad* (2.117). For similar reasons, he expresses doubts about the *Epigonoi* (4.32) and does not take the *Melampodia* to be Hesiod's (2.49). For his critical attitude toward sources, he has been hailed as the father of philology, and, in demanding logical consistency from poets, as a proto-sophist.[66] But close comparison of differing accounts of the past was the daily bread of the inquirer.[67] In fact, the key factor in Herodotus' approach to epic is his refusal, in the best modern way, to give poets any divine authority and his treatment of them as historically situated storytellers. As such, poets turn out to be not so different from himself: like the historian, they "find out" (*puthesthai*) things from various sources, select among them, and perform their accounts in public. This projection of the historian's habits onto the singer is observable in Herodotus' discussion of the *Arimaspeia* of Aristeas. It might be thought that a historian would dismiss this lost shamanistic poem whose author claimed "in his verses" (*poieōn epea*) that he was "snatched up by Phoebus and journeyed to the Issidones and then farther North." But, ever in search of information about the North, Herodotus has read it attentively for Aristeas' testimony. "No one has true knowledge of these regions," he concludes, "and Aristeas himself avers in a certain passage (*en tisi epesi poieōn*) that he got no farther than the Issidones; the things beyond that he recounts from hearsay (*akoē*), admitting that the Issidones are the ones who told him."[68] Similarly, he sometimes reads Homer for such traditions as the poet has found out (*puthesthai*). This is evident in an excursus on

---

is the interest of the stronger) reprised at *Laws* 714c–e. On the fragment, cf. Dodds 1959: 270; Lloyd-Jones 1990: 154–66.

[65] Cf. Ford 1997a: 102–3.

[66] Diels 1910: 25; the philological method (*Sachlichen und Sprachlichen Kritik*) is "unbestreitbar Herodots Entdeckung." Simonides is charged with logical contradiction (*enantia legei*) in Plato *Protagoras* 339D, and inconsistency figures among the charges against poetry in *Republic* 10. Cf. *Meno* 95c on inconsistent statements in the Theognidea about the teachability of virtue.

[67] Cf. 7.188.1, where, as Eusthathius notes, Homer's description of ships at *Iliad* 14.33–34 is closely interpreted by Herodotus.

[68] 4.13. Cf. his dismissal of Abaris (4.36, 3.116), and West 1983: 54 n. 62.

Trojan legends in his Egyptian Book 2, in which Herodotus exhibits such a sharp eye toward Homer's storytelling that the section sounds like a riposte to rhapsodes.

In Egypt, priests persuaded Herodotus that the true version of what happened at Troy was quite different from that recounted in the *Iliad*. In their version (which is probably a Greek story in origin), Helen and Paris were driven by a storm to Egypt, where she and her wealth remained while King Proteus sent Paris on to Troy (2.113).[69] When the Greeks took Troy, it was empty, and Menelaus went on to Egypt to recover his wife.

Herodotus may have been a little gullible before Egyptian priests, but he puts his usual historical tools to work on this tradition: he is clear that the Egyptians knew about what happened at Troy by hearsay (*historiēsi*) from Menelaus when he came there (2.118.1): "Some things they had by hearsay (*historiēsi*), but what happened in their own place they could tell accurately" (*atrekeōs*, 2.119.3). A close reader of Homer, he is able to quote from the epics to prove that the story as told by the Egyptians was current in the poet's day. In the *Iliad*, Homer "recounted in poetry" (*kat'-epoiēse*) Alexander's wandering with Helen to Phoenician Sidon when he mentions robes "woven by women whom Paris brought from Sidon when he sailed home with Helen" (quoting *Iliad* 6.289–92).[70] The geographer in Herodotus knows Sidon belongs to Phoenicians living in Syria, and Syria borders on Egypt; the traveler notes that Phoenician Tyrians live around the Egyptian precinct of Proteus, where a temple of "Athena the Stranger" can obviously be connected with Helen. Thus, Homer's reference to Paris with Sidonian goods turns out to be deeply significant.

Herodotus inclines to the Egyptian version of Helen's voyage (2.120.1) partly on grounds of historical verisimilitude, present remains, and references in old poetry, and partly, too, because it suits his moral view: he reasons that the Trojans would certainly have surrendered Helen if she had been there, and can only conclude that the war must have gone on so long either because they lied to the Greeks or were disbelieved "through the agency of providence to show by tremendous destruction how evil deeds meet great punishments."[71] With this phrase Herodotus derives a moral from the Trojan War as historical event: the complete destruction of the city shows how great are the punishments for great

---

[69] On the sources of this story and Hecataeus *FGrH* (1 F 307–8, cf. 309), see A. B. Lloyd 1986: 47–48. Neville (1977: 5) notes that Herodotus emphasizes (cf. 2.115.4–6, 118.3) Menelaus' loss of both Helen and money—as in Homer *Iliad* 7.362–64, 13.626.

[70] On this passage, see Farinelli 1995; Neville 1977: 10 n. 7. Alexander sacked Sidon on his way back to Troy in the *Cypria*.

[71] On verisimilitude as a principle of reading, esp. in Euripides, see Scodel 1990.

crimes. The moral is close to the old wisdom to be found in Hesiod that a whole city can perish from the wickedness of a single man.[72]

Here Homer is being pressed to the limit for tidbits about the past, even as Herodotus recognizes that he had no mission to be truthful. Herodotus concludes that Homer was aware of this story but rejected it, "for it was not so well suited to his epic as the one that he ended up using."[73] This passage is taken to be a sophistic moment in Herodotus, a concession to an aesthetic value of art;[74] but all enlightened thinkers of the fifth century take it for granted that Homer's stories are not reliable history.[75] Nor does this lead to a literary appreciation of Homer: Herodotus draws his moral not from the *Iliad* but from the Trojan War; providence is seen in the historical events at Troy, not in poems that in fact obscure the truth of what happened. Herodotus does not tell us why the version Homer used was more "suited" for his poetry: a Trojan War with no Helen inside the gates might be thought a less dramatic affair, but I suspect such a song would have been "unsuitable" because it shows the Greeks as dupes, and Herodotus assumes that epic poetry is praise poetry. When he refers to Cleisthenes banning Homeric epics from Sicyon because they "celebrate Argos and the Argives throughout" (*polla panta humneatai,* 5.67), he does not demur at Cleisthenes' interpretation. Indeed, that reading is close to his own view, since he himself (1.1.2) seems to infer the preeminence of Argos from such poetry as the *Iliad,* in which Agamemnon rules over Sicyon and "Argives" is used as a general term for Greeks.[76]

Herodotus, then, is a close reader of Homer and a proponent of the enlightened view of poetry, historical in its basic orientation, anthropological in its breadth of reference, and metrical in its recognition of what counts as poetry and kinds of poetry. His perspective can be epitomized in a final passage, an account he gives of the origin of the Linus song that is also the invention of poetry (2.79). Where possible, Herodotus traces poetic forms to human inventors: Olen of Lycia is identified as the real composer of certain ancient Delian and other hymns (4.35.3), and Arion

---

[72] Hesiod *Works and Days* 240–47. It is suggestive again for possible early Pythagorean interpretations of the *Iliad* that a late account (Iamblichus *Vita Pythogorae* 42) interprets the story as showing the disastrous consequences to a city of the intemperance (*akrasia*) of a single man, Paris; cf. Detienne 1962. The idea appears in the new fragments of Simonides, 11.10–13 *IEG,* esp. with West's supplements (1993: 6).

[73] Herodotus 2.116.1: Δοκέει δέ μοι καὶ ῞Ομηρος τὸν λόγον τοῦτον πυθέσθαι· ἀλλ᾽ οὐ γὰρ ὁμοίως ἐς τὴν ἐποποιίην εὐπρεπὴς ἦν τῷ ἑτέρῳ τῷ περ ἐχρήσατο, [ἐς ὃ] μετῆκε αὐτόν, δηλώσας ὡς καὶ τοῦτον ἐπίσταιτο τὸν λόγον.

[74] E.g., Lanata 1963: 211, following Pohlenz 1933: 54.

[75] Cf., e.g., Hecataeus 4 F 1 *FGrH,* Thucydides 1.1–22, 2.41.4.

[76] Herodotus possibly also has in mind the cyclic *Thebais* and *Epigonoi:* cf. Cingano 1985. On Homer's Argive references, see Jacoby on Philochorus 328 F 209 *FGrH,* and cf. *Contest of Homer and Hesiod* 378 (Allen).

from Lesbos is "the first of human kind as far as we know to have made
and named and taught the dithyramb when he was in Corinth" (1.23.1).
While he admits that poets preceded Homer, he is skeptical about the
repositioning of Orpheus and Musaeus: "Homer and Hesiod lived 400
years before my time, those poets said to be earlier are in fact later"
(2.53.8).[77] But this same historical empiricism posed a challenge in ac-
counting for the Linus song.

Linus was a legendary figure identified with, if not generated from, a
lament formula *ailinon*, interpreted as "alas Linus."[78] The refrain was
found in many contexts in early Greece: in *Iliad* 18.570, a boy sings a
Linus song at harvest for dancing boys and girls, and the song was also
connected with funerals. Hesiod had made Linus the son of the Muse
Urania, and said, "All singers and kitharists lament him in their banquets
and choruses, beginning and ending their song with Linus" (fr. 305
M-W). "Learned in all kinds of wisdom" (fr. 306 M-W), Linus was said
to have been killed by Apollo for claiming he could sing as well as the
god (Pausanius 9.29.6). Pindar, as we saw, mentions him as one of the
earliest subjects of lament (128c S-M), and a version of the Muses' lament
for Linus portrayed him as an inventor in lyric: "To you the gods gave a
melos for mortals to sing with piercing voice" (880 *PMG*).

Herodotus takes Linus as a prototypical but historical figure, and places
the earliest version of this song, as he does so much else, in Egypt. Synthesizing traditions, he allows that the song's name (i.e., the refrain) varies
from people to people as it is sung in Phoenicia and Cyprus and elsewhere.
But Herodotus (2.79) opines that the Egyptians invented, or at least never
imported, "what is called the Linus song" that is "so widely sung." He
accepts their etymology of Linus as Maneros ("Let us sing"), a typically
opaque archaic song-name. The Egyptians persuaded him that the word
originated as the name of the early-dying, only son of their first king: "His
dirge was their first and for a time their only *aoidē*."[79] A complete cultural
theory of song is implied in the account: a euhemerist, Herodotus is willing to find the original meaning of a Greek cult refrain in a foreign proper
name retranslated and then misunderstood. And this foreigner is no god
or son of god, but a prince whose early death may account for the one
universal feature of the song, a certain elegiac, "piercing" tone. The occasion in which it arose marked the song indelibly, even as the refrain was
changed from place to place, surviving intact only in traditionalist Egypt.

---

[77] Cf. 2.23: οὐ γάρ τινα ἔγωγε οἶδα ποταμὸν Ὠκεανὸν ἐόντα, Ὅμηρον δὲ ἤ τινα τῶν
πρότερον γενομένων ποιητέων δοκέω τοὔνομα εὑρόντα ἐς ποίησιν ἐσενείκασθαι.

[78] Chantraine s.v. λίνος. On the Linus song: Häussler 1974; Calame 1977, 1:154–55,
with bibliography at n. 217; on Linus: West 1983: 56–67.

[79] 2.79.3 Cf. West 1983: 56 n. 70.

In addition, the origin of this song, and it may as well be of all song, has a particular historical context: it arises in the first kingship of that very ancient kingdom, at the moment when succession fails. The point is not that Herodotus is a royalist or an Egyptomaniac, but that song arises in a social context, and follows upon the establishment of political order. Young Greece, of course, is filled with songs of all kinds that only the wide-ranging and critical eye of the historian can sort out.

Herodotus' terminology of "making" matches a view of song as the production of artifacts that may be left behind by their makers to become usable historical documents. In his historicizing approach, Herodotus regards epics fundamentally as texts, valuable for their antiquity but to be critically and closely collated with other traditions and other texts. So, too, archaic lyrics that may have been circulating orally were seen as historical records, and part of a decisively human history of song types. The historicization of poetry was abetted by the use of written texts not only as archival material but as documents perused outside the theater and away from the rhapsodic performance. We have seen that the inventors of poetry tended to be good readers, archivists, and critical readers of song texts. The role of writing in fostering this new approach is worth considering here.

Making and Writing

I have suggested, in this chapter and in my discussion of Simonides, that the rise of the notion of the poet was related to changes in the dissemination and reception of song in the early classical period. The evidence for literacy in the ancient world has many times been examined, but estimates are not firm.[80] Even with better evidence than we have, literacy is an especially hard thing to quantify because it admits of many levels and forms. The unlettered in a society may be surrounded by a wider literacy network, so generalizations about when "the production and circulation of books became common" or statements that "literacy had become general by the date of the *Frogs*" are incomplete.[81] I see no reason to dispute William V. Harris' thorough and unidealizing account, which estimates that in classical Athens only one or two people in twenty could read and

---

[80] For surveys on reading and books, Turner 1975, Anderson 1987, and Knox 1985.

[81] Cf. Gentili 1988: 19. Woodbury (1986: 242 and 1976) argued that there was common literacy at Athens before 440–430, against Havelock 1982: 27, 185–88; Burns (1981) is blithely optimistic. Harris (1989: ch. 3) hypothesizes a relatively rapid period of advance in the period 520–480, with rates remaining relatively low thereafter (5–10%) into the fourth century.

write with ease.[82] But even percentages do not tell much of a story. Writing makes its way into different cultural realms at different rates,[83] and means different things to tradesmen, teachers of ten-year-old boys, and professors of rhetoric. Tragedy has seemed to some to require a script.[84] But it is quite clear that performance and reperformance remained paramount in fifth-century Athens, where the theater, song hall (ōdeion), and other public spaces like the agora and gymnasia offered opportunities for musical exhibitions. Much has been made of Dionysus' solitary reading of Euripides' *Andromeda* in *Frogs* (52–54) of 405, but it is easy to see Dionysus as an eccentric in a world where books "did not yet fit easily into the general view of life."[85]

The point is made by Cole, who gives a memorable analogy of the place of tragic texts in the cultural life of late fifth- and early fourth-century Athens: "Anyone now who turns down an invitation to an opera or concert on the grounds that he would rather stay home and read the score of the work to be performed is likely to be dismissed as a genius, an eccentric, or a fraud"; for the Greeks as well, "An evening spent with the text of *Oedipus Rex* or the *Medea* would have been as unrewarding for all but a handful of them as an evening spent with the score of *Tristan und Isolde* would be for the nonmusical today."[86]

The picture of Dionysus reading Euripides also makes clear that a poetic text is a cultural construct and not a natural object. The question for

[82] Harris 1989: ch. 4, esp. 102–11.

[83] Though I disagree with Pfeiffer's (1968: 24–26) assumption of widespread literacy, he rightly identifies that "the important questions are how far first poetry and then philosophy were written down and at what time some form of commercial publication came into being" (24).

[84] For tragedians as producers of written texts, Segal 1982: 131–54, 1984: 44 ff. For oral composition of Greek tragedy, see Havelock 1982: 261–313; Herington (1985: 46–47) notes that in Aristophanes' depictions of tragic poets composing (*Acharnians* 393–479 and *Thesmophoriazusae* 25–265), no pen and paper are in evidence, discounted by Cameron 1995: 87. On the circulation of tragic texts, see Sedgwick 1948 and Griffith 1977: 347 n. 56, 357 n. 158, against Wilamowitz's assumption (1907: 121–30) that tragedy was the source of a flourishing book trade. The Athenian captives in 413 who knew (and could teach each other) Euripidean songs (*melē*) by heart (Plutarch *Nicias* 29.3) need not have learned them from texts.

[85] Woodbury 1986: 242. The implications of *Frogs* 1114 for Athenian literacy at this time are discussed by Woodbury (1976), concluding that it is a backhanded compliment that the Athenians are "bookish to the extent that they have been to school and have acquired the skill of reading" (353).

[86] Cole 1986: 186. On the evidence of literary allusions in Aristophanes, see Pickard-Cambridge 1988: 276, who estimates that not more than a tiny fraction possessed books. He also notes that, apart from a few recondite allusions, many of Aristophanes' literary parodies are from plays recently produced or imitate an author's style and manner rather than particular passages.

the history of criticism is whether and how the presence of written texts may have affected approaches to Greek song traditions. On this question, as always, one should not overdramatize the novelties of writing. It was quite possible in the archaic age to conceive of a song as a text in the sense of being a fixed structure of words: Solon could speak of "redoing" or "remaking" a verse when he recomposed a line of Mimnermus, and sixth-century symposiasts made use of Greek songs as quotable texts to be discussed.[87] The intellectuals who gather for discussion in Plato's *Protagoras* rely on their collective memory to quote large portions of a complicated Simonidean ode that they proceed to subject to extremely close verbal analysis (339A–347A): the song is broken down into its sentences, which in turn are divided into syntactical units (the technical term, *dialabein*, is used by Socrates, 346E); individual words, even descending to the particle *men* (343D), are isolated and examined for their meanings with reference to dialect, word order, and usage; grammatically related words that are separated in the phrasing are brought together through *hyperbaton*, a technical rhetorical term first found here.[88] Now this is sophistic criticism, and the bookishness of sophists like Prodicus was remarkable and evoked suspicion that it corrupted the young.[89] The sophists' colleagues and followers were the sort of people referred to by Euripides when he begins a story, "All those who have *writings* (*graphas*) from the ancients and are forever with the Muses, know the story about how Zeus fell in love with Semele and. . . ."[90] These savants are doubtless exceptional, and the scene in *Protagoras* come from one of the most literate of fourth-century authors, but nothing in principle prevents an orally circulating song from being carefully quoted and studied.

On the other hand, nothing makes stripping away a song's music and rhythm to focus on its diction and structure an inevitable way of appropriating it, and the evidence from the fifth to the fourth centuries suggests that a sense of songs as texts to be studied rather than performed arose only slowly. It is only at the end of the fifth century that we find a Greek

[87] In Ford 1985, I have argued that the seal of the late archaic Theognidea testifies to a tendency to codify and regularize sympotic song in the interests of political authority. Cf., too, Nagy 1990: ch. 6. Evidence for quotation in lyric poets is discussed in Davison 1968: 70–86 and Ford 1997a. See also the appendix to Powell 1991.

[88] *hyperbaton*: 343E, 345E, 346E: Pfeiffer (1968: 34) takes this passage as the source of the technical term. Recent studies of the literary criticism of the *Protagoras*: Dimas 1999, Most 1994b, Giuliano 1991, Scodel 1987.

[89] Cf. Aristophanes *Tagenistai* fr. 490 PCG, on a man being corrupted "by a book, or by Prodicus or some chatterer or other." The linguistic and bookish aspects of Prodicus are well epitomized by Dover (1968: liv–lv): cf. Segal 1970.

[90] *Hippolytus* 451–53. On *graphas* (not "paintings"), Barrett ad loc.; Pickard-Cambridge 1988: 276.

writer presenting his own work in this way: this is Thucydides' famous claim to have composed not a work to please contemporary audiences but a "possession for all time."[91] Thucydides "wrote" (*egrapse*, 1.1.1) an account of the Peloponnesian War that was meant to have permanent interest insofar as human nature remained constant. Unlike Herodotus' lectures (*apodeixis*, 1.1), Thucydides' text was composed not to be heard but to be read and re-read.[92] He shows contempt for the "competition pieces" (*agōnismata*) performed to win the temporary approbation of uncritical listeners (1.22). A conservative like Thucydides places his trust in such careful readers as existed in his day and would arise in the future rather than in the mass response of his contemporaries. The kind of audience he shuns is described by his Cleon, "mere spectators and listeners," in thrall to the "pleasures of the ear"; Thucydides' qualities will be judged not by such "badly run contests," but by Time, the final court of appeal for enlightened, progressive, written-down thought (3.38).

Turning back to song, I suggest that what might be called an increasing "textualization" of song through the fifth century abetted the formal study of its "inner" properties. This is not to say that songs were being written down with greater frequency during this period (it seems likely, but we cannot know), but that texts of songs began to come into the hands of more and more students and readers in addition to professional performers and archivists. That such a development might change ideas about song is supported by an observation of Albert Lord's on the interactions of epic singers with writing. Lord concluded that it is not writing per se that changes traditions of composition in performance, but that written copies of songs can lead to new ideas of their nature; he argued that as epics came to be written down, "the concept of a *fixed text* and of *the* text of a song became current. With that concept arose the need for memorization rather than recomposition as a means of transmission."[93] In the fifth century, the possibility of appealing to a definitive (or at least agreed-upon) text facilitated kinds of interpretation that exploited the precise observation of word usage and formal patterning. It was only by having examined a text scrupulously that Hippias of Elis could note that Homer never used a particular word, and Protagoras' comment on the battle of the gods in *Iliad* 21 was that the fight between Xanthos and Achilles was intended to provide a break (*dialabein*, cf. Plato *Protagoras*

---

[91] On this passage, see Edmunds 1994: esp. 847; Longo (1978) is extravagant.

[92] See Gentili 1988: 169, for the first literature *tout court* in Thucydides, Plato, Isocrates, and Aristotle. On Herodotus' "publication," see most recently Thomas 1993, and cf. Cobet 1977.

[93] Lord 1995: 102.

346E) in the battle, in order that the poet might make a transition (*meta-bēi*) to the battle of the gods (A 30 DK).[94]

By the late fifth century, the subtle formal beauties of poetry are associated with writing and with working over a text in a craftsmanly way. Aristophanes describes the highly refined and self-conscious composition of the poet and tragedian Agathon "the eloquent" (*kalliepēs*, *Thesmophoriazousae* 49) in the language of shipbuilding, carpentry, and metalwork. Agathon

δρυόχους τιθέναι δράματος ἀρχάς.
Κάμπτει δὲ νέας ἀψῖδας ἐπῶν,
τὰ δὲ τορνεύει, τὰ δὲ κολλομελεῖ,
καὶ γνωμοτυπεῖ κἀντονομάζει
καὶ κηροχυτεῖ καὶ γογγύλλει
καὶ χοανεύει. . . .

lays out the keel for his new drama, bends the young stock of words into shape, turns them on the lathe, glues the pieces together and stamps out new ideas along with new words, melts wax and smooths the whole and puts it in molds. . . .[95]

Uniting this pastiche is a craftsmanly perspective on language as raw material to be shaped and fitted together by the wordsmith. Among the metaphors, gluing (*kollomelei*) is noteworthy since it suggests "glued" papyrus paper (*kollēmata*) and embodies a transfer from the technology of writing to that of composing (something like our "cut and paste").[96] It has the same somewhat dubious flavor in Plato, who famously condemned reliance on written texts in his beautifully written *Phaedrus*. Allowing that texts may be useful as *aides-mémoire* or for achieving a certain finish in style, Plato deflates those who are mere "poets of speeches" without true philosophical knowledge: they have nothing more worthwhile to show than what they have written, "turning it back and forth, gluing it and taking things away" (278E).[97]

It is easy to see why singers were the targets of this new perspective and not its proponents. A transcript of the words of a performance was not

---

[94] Hippias B 9 DK; cf. Lanata 1963: 212–13. Protagoras A 30 DK is identified as a recognition of Homer's fictionality by Finkelberg (1998: 26); but Protagoras is more likely to be using Homer to exemplify a point in a discussion of rhetorical praise.

[95] *Thesmophoriazousae* 52–57. My translation reflects the discussions of Harriott (1969: 96) and Sommerstein (1994: ad loc.). See Taillardat 1965: §758 on this passage, esp. 443 n. 2.

[96] See Kassel-Austin on [ἐξεσ]μήχετο in Aristophanes fr. 656 *PCG* and Taillardat 1965: §418 on "gluing." In Empedocles B 96 DK, cosmic Harmonia "glues together" the parts of living forms: Wright 1981: 210.

[97] Cf. *sugkollōsa* in *Menexenus* 236B for the context.

only reductive in omitting musical pitch, tempo, and timbre, but in itself removed the song from the social and occasional context that would have shaped its meaning and emotional force. On the other hand, reductionism is a powerful first step for analytical study, and when a song was converted to letters on skin, papyrus, or stone, it became easier to regard it as an object in itself. As a fixed and stable structure of words, the written song was most easily analyzed in terms of its diction and patterns of language, the central technical elements of rhetorical criticism. As a written "work," a song existed palpably in space and remained unchanged through time; it was a complete, self-standing poem containing its meaning and unity in its form. Though as an authored work a song beckoned to an authority outside itself, that authority was no longer the transcendent Muses or Graces, but the designing poet as artist: by his creative and combinatory skill, he "wrought" the raw and inert matter of language into a work of art.

Nagy sets the influence of written texts on criticism far below the impulse to panhellenism,[98] but an increasing awareness of the lasting powers of texts supported the conception of song as a stable work rather than a performance, as an object produced by the skill of an artist rather than a time-bound event. If writing in itself cannot not produce literature, the conversion of the Greek heritage of song into fixed and tangible forms that could be studied, analyzed, and revised at leisure assisted the development of technical, structural criticism as the most adequate account of song. But the rhetorical approach, powerful as it evidently was, needed more to appeal to fifth-century devotees of song. As we shall see in part III, the idea of poetic "making" was deepened when it was brought into contact with the newer philosophies of nature.

[98] Nagy 1989: 10, 34, 44–45, also 1990: 56–57, 60, 84, 404.

PART III

TOWARD A THEORY OF POETRY

SEVEN

MATERIALIST POETICS

DEMOCRITUS AND GORGIAS

THE SHIFT from "song" to "poem" involved a double reduction: first a song was viewed primarily as language, and then language was analyzed primarily in formal terms. The first reduction has been studied in the preceding chapters; in this chapter I shall illustrate the second, which may be called the "materialization of speech." Here I adopt a phrase used by Svenbro, though I connect it with the philosophy of language in Democritus and Gorgias rather than with poets like Simonides and Pindar. Poetics exploited not only the historicization of poetry as a verbal craft but also a scientific reduction of speech to language as substance with inherent properties and powers. In my view, this materialist orientation to language became significant for literary culture when teachers of eloquence sought a theoretical basis for their expertise in the sciences, both the philosophy of nature and the scientific study of man in Hippocratic medicine.

Aristotle traced the origins of rhetoric to the expulsion of the tyrants in Sicily, when those who had been dispossessed had to reclaim their rights in legal processes.[1] The social *aition* must be right to the extent that fifth-century democracies encouraged new experts in persuasion who claimed that "speaking well" (*eu legein*) in public was neither a divine gift nor a natural capacity heritable from eloquent ancestors, but a useful and learnable skill. This orientation is reflected in the very name the enterprise eventually assumed: "rhetoric" (ἡ ῥητορικὴ [τέχνη]) means "the *art* of public speaking."[2] This was a new, and in some ways unsettling, view, and professors of rhetoric were challenged to validate the status of the language arts. One of the most important ways they did so was to draw parallels between their verbal procedures and those of artisans. Many metaphors used in rhetorical discourse present that skill as "crafting" or "shaping" language into a "work" designed to produce a given effect. To speak of "crafting" language not only implied the teachability of the

---

[1] Aristotle's history of rhetorical studies: V A 6, 9 AS. Plato depicts men whose property has been taken away being obliged to speak before the people (*Republic*. 8.565B) in a scenario like that of Telemachus in *Od*. 1–2.

[2] Schiappa (1990) and Cole (1991: 2, 12, 98–99), have argued (independently) that this use of *rhētorikē* was coined by Plato.

art but also concretized its products: the "finished" and "polished" speeches that teachers presented to patrons or distributed among students or performed as specimens of their skill were the tangible products of their craft.[3]

As rhetoric became an art, then, artistic speeches became valuable artifacts. But one problem was that the arts and crafts continued to have an ambiguous social status. Rhetoricians would not have wished to be placed among the banausic workmen in the agora exercising small crafts for small sums. A more appealing model for rhetoric as a *tekhnē* was medicine, especially as represented in such Hippocratic treatises as *Ancient Medicine* and *On the Art*. In these works, the prestige and power of the art was vindicated by presenting true medicine as a resolutely rational and progressive contribution to human happiness. As the preeminent example of a desirable, clearly teachable expertise, scientific medicine showed the most ambitious rhetoricians how to distinguish themselves from low-status rivals and present themselves as students of human nature, free from superstition, mystification, and quackery. Medicine offered the rhetorician a further advantage in that its authority could survive failure in individual cases: it was sometimes useful for the speech-teacher to maintain, like a doctor, that the operation had been a success even though the patient died or lost his case.[4]

Speech as Air

Rhetoricians thus had good reasons to model their self-presentation on that of doctors. But medical science also provided philosophers on language with a bridge to another field of advanced inquiry into human nature and the world, fifth-century natural philosophy.[5] Scientific doctors shared with many philosophers of nature a tendency to view the mind as a material object and to analyze mental phenomena in physical terms. Rhetoricians drew on materialist accounts of human perception and cognition in explaining the effects worked by their verbal arts. To illustrate this connection, I propose in this chapter to compare passages from the atomic physicist Democritus with passages from the great sophist Gorgias of Leontini. It will emerge that these strands of thought all have in common an enlightened "scientific materialism," a determination not to be

[3] See Ford 1993a: 38–41, 44–49.

[4] See Cole 1991: 3, 85–88, 146–47.

[5] On interrelations between doctors and physicists at the time, Longrigg 1963, 1983; Lloyd 1987: ch. 2, esp. 88–108, and 1979: 86–98, for interactions between rhetoric and the natural sciences.

deceived by myth and to confront nature (*phusis*) as a physical cosmos with inflexible laws of cause and effect. Such views enabled philosophers of *logos* to claim that the phenomenon of persuasion—venerated at an altar in the Athenian agora—could be understood on scientific grounds, and that the workings of language (*logos*) could be understood as a mechanical process abstracted from political and social variables. This demystified, wholly naturalistic view of a social phenomenon that was vital to democracy underpins of a famous line of Euripides (fr. 170 Nauck) that Aristophanes reprised in his *Frogs* (1391): "There is no other shrine to the goddess Persuasion than speech (*logos*), and her altar is found in the *nature* of man."

Materialist accounts of perception may be traced, like rhetoric, to western Greece, which was a leading center for medicine, natural philosophy, and eloquence in the later sixth and earlier fifth centuries. Parmenides of Elea seems to have held that thought or the mind (*noēma*) could be influenced by its physical environment, and Empedocles offered an account of perception as a physical process of effluxes and emanations.[6] In the fifth century, such approaches focused attention on the role of air both as a cosmic principle and as an exceptionally subtle and pervasive medium for hearing and seeing. For Diogenes of Apollonia, sensation was a matter of outer air affecting inner air;[7] viewing air as a cosmic element imbued with intelligence and constituent of human souls, Diogenes eulogized it as "steering all things and having power over all" (B 5 DK: καὶ ὑπὸ τούτου πάντας κυβερνᾶσθαι καὶ πάντων κρατεῖν) and commended Homer for having spoken about the gods "not in a mythical way but truly: for he says Homer considered air to be Zeus, since he says that Zeus knows all."[8] Such views appear in the Derveni commentator when he interprets Orpheus' *Moira* ("Fate") as air, for "all other things are in air, being breath" (18.1–2 L-M), and "air dominates all as far as it wishes" (19.1–4, cf. 23.3). In a similar way, the Hippocratic *Sacred Disease* rejects mythical explanations of epilepsy as due to divine interference in the mind in favor of a doctrine of some fine, motile substance like air affecting the seat of thought: the essay attributes the onset of epilepsy not to being "snatched up by a god," as the name "sacred" could imply, but to prevailing southerly winds interacting with moisture of the brain.[9] At Athens, the foremost

---

[6] Parmenides A 46, B 16 DK; Empedocles B 89, 109a DK; cf. A 57, 88–90, 92 DK.

[7] Diogenes called air λεπτομερέστατον ("composed of extremely fine/subtle particles") and the mind λεπτότατον ("extremely fine/subtle," A 20 DK). On Diogenes' theory of sensation (esp. A 19 §44 DK): KRS 442–43, and Guthrie 1965: 373 ff.

[8] A 8 DK, on which see Lanata 1963: 244–45.

[9] *Sacred Disease* 16.6–17.5, with further suggestive remarks on the brain as the physical seat of sensation, the organ of thought and of "discerning fair and foul." At times, for example, our judgments can be affected by our perceptions: an unhealthy brain, colder or

exponent of such views appears to have been Anaxagoras of Clazomenae, the first pre-Socratic to settle there. He defined "Mind" or "intelligence" (*nous*) as a very subtle but irreducibly corporeal physical element: the "finest and purest of things," Mind was an intellectual force controlling cosmic processes.[10] The wide impression that Anaxagoras' ideas and the ideas of his fellows created is perhaps most strikingly attested in Aristophanes' casting "Clouds" as the central chorus in his play about sophistry's airy fancies.[11] In that play, Socrates prays to "Inexhaustible Air, my lord and master" (ὦ δέσποτ' ἄναξ, ἀμέτρητ' 'Αήρ, 264), along with "fiery Aether." His method of studying "matters on high" (τὰ μετέωρα) is quite material—being suspended in a basket so as to mix his thought with the "subtle air that resembles it" (230–31: κρεμάσας τὸ νόημα καὶ τὴν φροντίδα, λεπτὴν καταμείξας εἰς τὸν ὅμοιον ἀέρα). Socrates, of course, also teaches tricky speaking, and Aristophanes will prove to have been an insightful cultural diagnostician when we focus on two major thinkers of the time.

Democritus and Gorgias are the culminating figures in the materialization of speech as it affected natural philosophy and rhetoric respectively. Neither doctors nor scientists took any particular interest in poetry, but Democritus was a polymath who wrote on cultural institutions as well as the atomic theory of matter. Enough of his fragments remain to suggest that he carried the implications of materialist accounts of perception into questions of poetry (and probably into other arts as well). A reading of some of Democritus' remarkable statements on poetry, following along lines suggested by Armand Delatte, though without going as far as he, will outline the scientific basis he offered for those who would treat composing poetry as a productive art: his materialist perspective could support a view of "making" poems as a process of selecting elementary substances (atomic sounds) and organizing them into a structure or "system" that, by virtue of its constituents and their organization, produced a specific effect on the auditor's psyche, itself having a physiological

---

moister than it should be or upset by humors, will create madness, fears, forgetting, and prevent steady sight or hearing: "Because of this, varying visual and acoustic sensations are produced, while the tongue can only describe things as they appear and sound." The latter point is reminiscent of Gorgias' third thesis in *On Not Being*.

[10] Anaxagoras B 12 DK, on which Furley (1956: 15) remarks: "Anaxagoras wished, apparently, to make the *nous* as little material as possible, and so he called it 'the finest' or 'the thinnest' of all things, but he could not altogether avoid making it material." Cf. KRS 364.

[11] Esp. *Clouds* 225–36, 264–65, 627. *Aithēr* is the first deity invoked by the sophistic Euripides in *Frogs* 892. Cf. Burkert 1970: 445, who compares Xenophon *Memorabilia* 1.4.8, 17. These connections are elaborated by Janko (1997), proposing Diagoras as the author of the Derveni papyrus.

substratum.[12] Democritus also in my view provides the best way to approach one of the most notable fifth-century texts about language, the praise of *logos* in Gorgias' *Helen*.

Poetic Inspiration and Atomic Poetics

Democritus, born around 460, wrote widely (A 33 DK) on topics we would assign to aesthetics, literary criticism, and art theory. Among these works are *On Rhythm and Harmony* (B 15c DK),[13] *On Song* (*aoidē*, B 25a DK), *On Poetry* (*poiēsis*, B 16a DK),[14] and *On Painting* (B 28a).[15] I have earlier discussed Democritus' account of poetry's historical and cultural origins; here I shall be interested particularly in his view of language, and specifically poetic language as treated in *On the Beauty of [Poetic?] Expressions* (*epea*, B 18 a), *On Pleasant- and Ill-Sounding Letters* (B 18b), and *On Homer*, alternately called *On the Proper Use of Words* (*orthoepeia*) *and Glosses*.[16] I do not claim that these works were written simply to illustrate atomism, but I do think that atomists, as thoroughgoing materialists, would have sought to offer a materialist account of how such things worked, and we may expect that the way Democritus discussed poetry was at least consonant with his materialist account of perception. Applying an atomistic frame to some of Democritus' explicit sayings on poetry in fact yields a coherent account of speech in all its workings. One can even speak of an "atomist poetics" underlying his approach that will prove to have much in common with that of Gorgias.

Greek atomic theory brought to a head the materialistic tendencies of earlier natural philosophy as it carried physical explanations of the universe into the field of human perception and sensation.[17] There are problems with reconstructing the Democritean doctrines of sight and sound in detail, but perception was clearly a physical affair: according to Aristotle, atomists developed the Empedoclean account of sight and sound as material effluxes and held that all sensation was a form of touch or contact of

---

[12] Delatte 1934: 28 ff., esp. 50–51.

[13] Also studied by Hippias (A 11).

[14] Examples of Democritus' interest in minute exegesis of epic are B 22, 23, 24 DK.

[15] *Peri Zōgraphias*, see Lanata 1963: 266, perhaps referred to a theory of colors, as in A 135 DK.

[16] B 20a DK. Latte (1925: 148–49) and Lanata (1963: 261) take *orthoepeia* anachronistically as the discrimination of literal (*kuria lexis*) from archaic or obscure usages, as in Aristotle. See Ford (2001: 100–103) and note 39 below.

[17] Cf. Guthrie 1965: 453–54. Note that Democritus wrote treatises on medical topics, such as *Prognostics, On Diet, On Fever and Coughing*.

atoms.[18] Democritean atoms have individual shapes (*morphai*), arrangements (*skhēmata*), and size (*megethos*); they are so small as to escape detection, but, when aggregated, are perceptible to sight and the other senses. In vision, for example, atoms from the object help create a visual image (*emphasis*) in the perceiver. The atomistic account of hearing is less clear, but Greek theories of sight and hearing tended to be analogous with each other, and atomists must have viewed hearing as a corporeal phenomenon, since "all alteration and being affected" comes about through atoms coming into contact and combining with each other (Leucippus A 7 DK). On one modern interpretation, "sound is transferred when the particles of voice or noise mingle with similar particles in the air"; the air is "broken up into particles of similar shape (*homoioskhē-mona . . . sōmata*) and is rolled along together with the fragments from the voice (*phōnē*)"; thus are formed acoustic "images" (*eidōla*) in the air that enter the hollow of the ear and from there impart certain sensations to the soul.[19]

According to Aristotle, atomists illustrated how the positioning of an atom could make a perceptible difference by referring to the difference between the letters Z and N, and they illustrated the effects of varying the arrangement by referring to the difference between the syllables AN and NA.[20] This suggests that for them, words were analyzable into their constituent syllables and single sounds (letters), and ultimately into the atoms whose shape, arrangement, and positioning created qualitative differences among them.[21] It is logically compatible with the atomistic account of sight that spoken words should be, like any perceptible object, nothing more than conglomerates of atoms perceived by the ear. As composite physical objects, words were arrays of invisible sound atoms that move through the air, create sonic impressions in the ear, and affect the psyche in turn.

The mechanistic account of perception entails a certain "necessity" in how we are affected by the impact of these atoms as they rebound against us and each other.[22] The physical compulsion at the root of sensation may be what Democritus means to indicate when he says that *logos* is often "mightier" (ἰσχυρότερος) in persuading than money (B 51 DK). Yet the existence of such words as synonyms and homonyms suggested that

---

[18] KRS 309–10, cf. 428 ff.

[19] KRS 429 n. 1, citing A 128 DK.

[20] Leucippus A 6 DK. The "grammatological" implications are profound: see Calame 1993: 791, on Aristotle *Metaphysics* 985b–20, with n. 14, referring to the work of Heinz Wismann.

[21] Cf. KRS, esp. 413–15.

[22] KRS 418–19.

words were only arbitrarily connected to the things they named (B 26 DK). The names for the gods are conventional, like cult images of them composed of sound (ἀγάλματα φωνήεντα, B 142 DK).[23] This may be connected with Democritus' account of the origins of religion in which a few men skilled in speech (logioi) induced others to believe in phantoms (B 30 DK).[24] Atomism does not necessarily entail either atheism or skepticism, but there is no doubt that Democritus thought many human conceptions and accounts of the world were false and that he called such accounts, and perhaps even the words they used, "made up" or "fabricated" (πλάσσειν). As a mechanical determinist, he reproached men who "fabricated" a false "image" of Chance (τύχης εἴδωλον ἐπλάσαντο) to excuse their own lack of prudence; the same trope was used for those who, in ignorance of his true account, falsely "story-fashion" (μυθοπλαστέοντες) what happens after death.[25]

What applies to logos applies to poetry as well. Though it may be even more complexly arranged and composed than other utterances, poetry, like any sound, is a shaping of atoms. Aristotle says atomists also illustrated the varying effects of atomic rearrangement by pointing out that comedies and tragedies are composed of the same letters (i.e., basic sounds), and yet have diametrically opposite effects (A 9 DK). Such concerns may have been explored in the lost On Rhythm and Harmony, On Song, or On Pleasant- and Ill-Sounding Letters. But two brief sentences by Democritus on poetic inspiration may be used to show how the art of poetry was approached by a thoroughgoing materialist.

Greek conceptions of poetic inspiration did not traditionally involve ecstasy or possession, ideas that are largely lacking from Homer, though madness could be seen as divine interference in the soul.[26] Prophetic delirium was mentioned by Heraclitus in reference to the Sibyl possessed by "the god" (Apollo), and the idea was to become common in the classical

[23] Democritus is often assumed from B 26 DK to have held a "thesis-theory" of the origin of language avant la lettre, e.g., Guthrie 1965: 475; Cole 1967: 67–68; cf. Fehling 1965: 218–29. On agalmata phōnēenta (B 142), see Cole 1967: 68 n. 17 and app. 4, and Guthrie 1965: 475 n. 1 for other suggestions.

[24] Kleingünther 1934: 109–14. On B 30 DK, see Cole 1967: 58 n. 34. Prodicus' (B 5 DK) account of the origin of men's belief in gods, which traces it to fear and awe, may be Democritean: Henrichs 1975: 96–106, cf. 1984. Both are subsumed in Critias' Sisyphus (B 25 DK, sometimes attributed to Euripides): the impious Sisyphus cynically accounts for the origin of religious thought as a political deception put over by politicians so they could control even unobserved behavior.

[25] Democritus B 119 DK: ἄνθρωποι τύχης εἴδωλον ἐπλάσαντο πρόφασιν ἰδίης ἀβουλίης. B 297 DK: φύσεως διάλυσιν οὐκ εἰδότες ἄνθρωποι . . . ψεύδεα περὶ τοῦ μετὰ τὴν τελευτὴν μυθοπλαστέοντες χρόνου.

[26] P. Murray 1981: 100. Cf. Dodds 1957: 67; Simon 1978: 65–71. Yet see now Katz and Volk 2000, with a thorough bibliographical discussion.

period.[27] In the later fifth century, we can discern in Athens an interest in the peculiar nature of the poet, especially in Aristophanes' portrait of Agathon in *Thesmophoriazousae* (of 411).[28] The first clear analysis of poetic inspiration as a passive, ecstatic possession by a god appears in the fifth century, and it is only in the fourth that inspiration is opposed to conscious artistry in what is perhaps a Platonic innovation.[29]

The first Greek writer we have to use the word "enthusiasm" (*enthousiasmos*) and apply it to poets is Democritus. Lack of context makes Democritus difficult to interpret, as in the following sentence, which can be given various meanings depending on where one puts the stress (B 18 DK):

ποιητὴς δὲ ἅσσα μὲν ἂν γράφηι μετ᾿ ἐνθουσιασμοῦ καὶ ἱεροῦ πνεύματος, καλὰ κάρτα ἐστίν.

Whatever a poet writes with *enthousiasmos* and divine breath is exceedingly beautiful.

Here attention has fallen on the final phrase and on Democritus' deriving a poem's beauty from inspiration rather than, as traditionally, its truth, and so Democritus is read as championing an aesthetic value in poetry.[30] But calling admired poetry *kalos* is perfectly usual, and attempts to find here a pure aesthetics run against the fact that for this considerably ethical philosopher, *kalos* has its usual moral and social connotations as well.[31] From the point of view of atomic physics, we might rather focus on the proximate causes of fine poetry, the inspired state of the soul (*enthousiasmos*) and the "divine breath" (*hieron pneuma*). The word *pneuma*

---

[27] Delatte (1934: 7–21) fleshes out a Heraclitean theory of divine inspiration having to do with the particular ability of dry, fiery souls to receive exhalations from the divine. For all Delatte's caution, the interpretation may be too Stoic.

[28] *Thesmophoriazousae* 167, on which see Muecke 1982: esp. 43–45. As *phusis* comes to be used in the fifth century not only of "nature" in general, but of individual human natures, the question is put as to how far poets' qualities depend on their particular natures: cf. Aristophanes *Frogs* 810; Plato *Apology* 22c, *Phaedrus* 269d, *Laws* 682a, 700d; Aristotle *Poetics* 1448b22–42, 1449a 2–6, and esp. 1455a32–34; cf. Halliwell 1986: 82–90.

[29] Tigerstedt (1970) argues that an explanation of poetry on the lines of Dionysiac possession did not appear until the fifth century, and was a philosophic refinement of the Homeric conception of the relation between the poet and the divine. The thesis remains significant, despite Finkelberg's dismissal (1998: 19–20). For images of inspiration making the poet simply the mouthpiece of divinity: *Ion* 533e, 534e–36d, *Phaedrus* 245a.

[30] Lanata 1963: 256–57, with references.

[31] E.g., B 194 and B 63 DK: εὐλογέειν ἐπὶ καλοῖς ἔργμασι καλόν· τὸ γὰρ ἐπὶ φλαύροισι κιβδήλου καὶ ἀπατεῶνος ἔργον ("Praise directed at fair deeds is fair; but at low deeds is the act of a counterfeit and deceptive man"). The image of the counterfeit man is traditional in sympotic verse, the general idea a commonplace adapted by Gorgias *Helen* §1 DK.

evokes epic images of divinity "breathing" qualities and ideas into heroes or the Muses "breathing" poetic voice into Hesiod (*Theogony* 31).[32] At the same time, since Anaxagoras had used *pneuma* for moving air that creates sound when it strikes stable air, we may suspect that the atomist is prepared to analyze this inspiring breath as a moving stream of atoms in the air.[33] This is supported by Democritus' word for "sacred," which may bear some of its root meaning "endowed with supernatural force": the ambiguity would account for inspiration physically as the effect of certain fiery atoms that could equally be called "sacred" or "divine," since inherently mobile particles were, by definition, the source of all motion and life.[34] Democritus' phrase conveniently sidesteps rudely pointing out that the traditional Muses are just mythoplasty; what is stressed is the influx of something airlike and volatile that puts the poet's soul in such a condition (*enthusiasmos* means "having the god within") that the poetry it produces will be correspondingly fine and powerful. The traditional account of inspiration is "saved" under the atomistic description of a "holy breath" inhaled by the poet and transferred to what he writes.

Another of Democritus' statements about inspiration presents similar ambiguity (B 21 DK): "Homer, chancing to get a divinely acting nature, constructed a universe of all sorts of words" (Ὅμηρος φύσεως λαχὼν θεαζούσης ἐπέων κόσμον ἐτεκτήνατο παντοίων). Here, too, Democritus has often been taken to be proclaiming the verbal artistry and unity of Homer's poems, since the verb *tektainomai* is used of carpenters and smiths, and *kosmos* may imply an "ordered structure" of words.[35] But the sentence takes on a different significance if we think of it, with Diels-Kranz, in connection with Democritus' work *On the Proper Use of Words and Glosses* (B 20a). For fifth-century readers, epic was so full of "glosses" as to constitute a veritable "universe" (*kosmos*) composed of

[32] Cf. Wehrli 1948: 11. On epic gods "breathing" feelings and thoughts into heroes (e.g., *Od.* 19.238, where a god *enepneuse* the weaving-ruse into Penelope), see Russo on *Od.* 18.406–7 and Heubeck on 22.347–49.

[33] On sensation in Anaxagoras, see Guthrie 1965: 318 with n. 3. Embedded in a quotation from Clement, Democritus' "sacred *pneuma*" sounded suspiciously Christian to Guthrie (ibid.: 477 n. 2) and Delatte (1934: 50–51 with n. 2), who found this element hard to justify in the theory since breath has no special role in Democritean physics and psychology (albeit Macrobius mentions *spiritus* in A 103, cf. A 140). But I take it not as "spirit" but as "moving air" that can be inhaled. For the soul as an "inhalation," see n. 43.

[34] Cf. Delatte 1934: 35–36, who goes further by adducing Heraclitus' notion of fiery souls getting inspired visions in sleep or waking visitations.

[35] See Lanata 1963: 261–62; Russell 1981: 72–73. The possibly Pythagorean idea of *kosmos* as the ordered ensemble that is the world is common in the fifth century: e.g., Empedocles B 134 DK, Anaxagoras B 8 DK, Diogenes of Apollonia B 2 DK; cf. Kahn 1960: 219–30.

"all sorts of expressions."[36] This sentence would make an appropriate attention-getting opening statement for a work on such words, and would account for its alternate title, *On Homer.*

Democritus' treatise may have explained a number of such expressions by breaking them into their constituent compounds, which were explained through etymology.[37] There are "all kinds" of such words, for their constituent elements, like atoms, permitted innumerable combinations and permutations. Democritus' "constructed" attributes to the poet the combinatory art of the builder, joining sounds into syllables and compound words to construct new and useful expressions. In this context, the emphasis would fall on the enlightened notion that early poets, and not gods, were responsible for enriching the language with words of their own creation.[38] This is praise of Homer as word-constructor, not poemmaker. Even a far-fetched defense of an epic epithet such as Democritus' explanation of *Tritogeneia* as referring to Athena's triple concerns with proper reason, speech, and action (B 2 DK) would have responded to charges that old Homer was a poor word-maker such as Protagoras appears to have publicized in his lectures on the "proper use of words (*orthoepeia*)."[39] Neither was it unprecedented to speak of poetry as a *kosmos*, especially the stichic verses of recited poetry that are already in the sixth century called a "marshaling" or "arrangement" of speech; with *kosmos*, Democritus need imply no more than that epic language is a coherent and intelligible, if no doubt ornamental, whole.[40]

Further, this sentence establishes Homer as a legitimate founder of words by attributing to him a *phusis* that chanced to be of a divine, productive sort.[41] Debating the relative contributions of "nature" and "art" (*phusis* and *tekhnē*) to fair speech had already been a concern in Pindar and among early sophists.[42] But Democritus' is a different kind of na-

---

[36] Aristotle *Poetics* 1459a9 associates *glōssai* particularly with epic; Aristophanes *Daitales* 235 *PCG* shows that instruction in recondite epic vocabulary (*glōttas*) was a regular part of Athenian education by the later fifth century.

[37] For Democritus etymologizing a Homeric phrase: A 101, and cf. B 2 DK.

[38] A view shared by Herodotus 2.23, the Hippocratic *On the Art* (2), confined by Aristotle to the "made-up" word (πεποιημένον, *Poetics* 1457b33).

[39] Cf. Fehling 1965: esp. 214–16, on Protagoras' *orthoepeia* (A 28, 29 DK), against such accounts of *orthoepeia* as Lanata 1963: 260–61, Classen 1959, and Pfeiffer 1968: 37–38.

[40] For *kosmos epeōn*, see Solon 1.2 *IEG*; Parmenides B 8.52 DK. Cf. Empedocles B 17.26 DK and Pindar *Pythian* 4.210 (*stikhoi epeōn*).

[41] With λαχών in B 21, Delatte (1934: 45) compares Democritus' prayer to "hit upon lucky *eidōla*" (εὐλόγχων τυχεῖν εἰδώλων, B 166) and Horace *Ars poetica* 295–97: "ingenium misera quia *fortunatius* arte / credit et excludit sanos Helicone poetas / Democritus. . . ."

[42] E.g., Pindar *Olympian* 2.86, *Nemean* 3.40–42; Protagoras B 3 DK. On *phusis* and teaching in the fifth century, see Woodbury 1976, 351–53, with references.

ture—not the poet's good birth or rearing that makes him a tactful speaker, but his physical constitution. As in the fragment on inspiration discussed above, poetic success is not simply a matter of craft but of broader material causes. A poet's extraordinary verbal creativity can be described as a nature favorably opened to helpful images and influences.[43] On a plausible reconstruction by W.C.K. Guthrie, "Democritus can well have supposed that certain more favorably constituted souls [Guthrie thinks of Homer's *phusis theazousa*] absorb a greater wealth of 'images' and are by them aroused to a more lively motion than others, and this is the basis of the poetic gift and temperament."[44] On the principle of like-to-like, individual genius is the possibility of receiving good images; such images flow onto the poet from the divine world and beings that surround him.

The passages can be combined to give a picture of the poet as a person of an exceptional nature suited to enter into contact with divine simulacra and name hidden things in a crisis of exaltation called divine. Passages from fifth-century drama reflect the ideas that a poet's nature and temperament affect what he writes and that a poet's "nature" should resemble what he proposes to represent.[45] The atomist account of speech and poetry was consonant with the rhetorical in that for both, affective language was analyzed into its constituent basic elements, which were to be selected, combined, and arranged to give specific effects. But the scientists' way of looking at speech added something to the artisanal idea of the eloquent speaker or poet: it placed more emphasis on the intrinsic powers of the complex, constructed object. The mechanistic view stressed the autonomy of the artful speech; it was a shape of words that imposed itself on the soul as a signet ring stamps wax or as a magnet compels another object to move.[46] According to Theophrastus, our main source for Democritus' theory of vision (A 135 DK), Democritus held that both ob-

---

[43] Probably the poet's soul was made, like any other, by inhalations: cf. B 21 DK with KRS 427 n. 1; and Guthrie 1965: 450, 477–78, 482, esp. for criticism of ascribing some "sixth sense" to poets and other sensitive souls.

[44] Guthrie 1965: 478 n. 1, following Zeller. But Burkert (1977) argues that the *eidōla* may be a post-Aristotelian addition to the doxography. I leave out of account the nature of Democritean gods.

[45] E.g. Euripides *Suppliants* 180–83 (esp. τόν θ' ὑμνοποιὸν αὐτὸς ἂν τίκτῃ μέλη / χαίροντα τίκτειν), Aristophanes *Thesmophoriazusae* 149–50, *Frogs* 1040, 1059–61 (Aeschylus' [n.b.] mind "gives birth to" words), 1451, and fr. 694 PCG. The use of *phusis* for a poet's "inclination of mind" is not in *Ion* or *Phaedrus*, but is in Plato *Apology* 22B: φύσει τινὶ καὶ ἐνθουσιά-ζοντες, cf. Lanata 1963: 261. Aristotle defines enthusiasm as an affect in the character of the soul (τοῦ περὶ τὴν ψυχὴν ἤθους πάθος, *Politics* 1340a11).

[46] On Democritus' use of the seal impress on wax, Burkert 1977: 98 with n. 6. Democritus wrote a treatise on magnets (B 11k DK); cf. Delatte 1934: 59–63. Plato's *Ion* of course uses it as an analogy for the irrational attraction of poetry (533D–E).

server and object generate effluences (*aporrhoai*), and "the air between eye and object is stamped (*tupousthai*) by the object and the seer," forming a solid impression (*entupōsis*). The mechanistic impact by which this physical *entupōsis* is produced will be connected with Gorgias' use of *tupoō* for persuasion as the irresistible "stamping" of a speech or image on the soul.

Gorgias: A Theory of Art?

There is reason to be cautious about the widely held view that "of all the sophists and teachers of rhetoric of his day, Gorgias has the most to do with the beginnings of critical theory."[47] The fact that we have far more of Gorgias' actual words than of any other fifth-century sophist may lend him an adventitious centrality to theories of poetry and language of the time. We can see from Greek comedy that figures like Protagoras and Prodicus impressed or shocked the Athenian public at least as much, and, whereas Gorgias' views of poetry and language were developed as incidental to other discussions, polymaths like Democritus and Hippias wrote treatises dealing with these topics specifically. Another troubling aspect of the usual view of Gorgias is that the long tradition that makes him a pioneer in rhetorical theory[48] owes much to Plato's representations, but what we have of the sophist's own words never offers to teach an art of persuasion. Indeed, Gorgias' assertion in *On Not Being* of the impossibility of using language to communicate reliably would seem to make it difficult for anyone to claim to have escaped from its domination and to have mastered it in an art of rhetoric.[49]

Still, there is no doubt that the great orator and teacher from Sicily (ca. 485–ca. 380) made an immense impact at Athens and said a number of extraordinary things about poetry and language. Most radical was the set of paradoxical theses put forward in *On Not Being* (B 1–5 DK) that nothing exists, and if it did, we could not know it, and if we could know it, we could not communicate it, because language is a fundamentally different thing from what it may be thought to convey. An additional statement,

[47] Russell 1981: 22. Caution is urged, e.g., by Dover (1993: 31–32).

[48] Especially Süss 1910: 46 ff. Pohlenz (1933: 54) makes rather much of Dionysius of Halicarnassus' statement that Gorgias was the first to write about the *kairos* (B 13 DK), since Dionysius goes on to complain that Gorgias had little of substance to say on the topic, and Isocrates (13.14–15) is following Gorgias when he insists that *kairos* is not reducible to an art. Cf. pp. 19–20 n. 44 on Pohlenz and the *prepon* among the sophists. See also Ford (2001: 94–95).

[49] Cf. Wardy 1996: 24.

short but highly suggestive, declared that in tragedy, "the deceiver is more just than the one who does not deceive, and the one who is deceived more wise than the one who is not deceived" (B 23 DK). Such provocative theses have been a springboard for attributing to Gorgias a theory of aesthetic illusion (*apatē*).[50] But "deception" and "cheating" were primarily social terms, and the purpose of the saying may have been to point out an ethical paradox, as in the sophistically inspired *Dissoi logoi* of a near date: "In tragedy and painting, the best [poet and painter] is whoever deceives most thoroughly in making [things] like the truth."[51] There is more substantial evidence than this apothegm and than *On Not Being*, which survives only in a paraphrase: we have the whole of the so-called *Encomium of Helen* (B 11 DK), including its extensive account of language or *logos* in Gorgias' own overwrought words. In the course of this speech, Gorgias compares the influence that speech (*logos*) has over the soul with the workings of drugs on the body and illustrates its power by adducing poetry and magic spells. The *Helen* also offers a parallel description of how visual sights (among which Gorgias includes paintings and statues) create "impressions" in the perceiver's soul. A reading of this text suggests a Gorgias much closer to the scientists and more interested in theories of perception than in theories of art.

The prevailing view of Gorgias makes him a teacher and theorist of rhetoric who sought to give a rationalized account of poetry's effects, effects that from Homer to Aeschylus had been described as a kind of enchantment (*thelgein*).[52] In the formulations of Jacqueline DeRomilly, Gorgias wished to methodize, on the analogy of medicine, the incantatory appeal of speech and subject it to formal art (*tekhnē*). His invocation of empirical medicine did away with the need for inspiration to achieve eloquence and opened up the high style to all: he was a "theoretician of the magic spell of words," and his *Helen* may be read as a "program for

---

[50] Finkelberg 1998: 177: "With Gorgias for the first time fiction is legitimized as an autonomous sphere which cannot be evaluated by using ordinary standards of truth and falsehood." Fundamental for Gorgias as aesthetic theoretician are Rosenmeyer 1955; Segal 1962; and DeRomilly 1973, 1975. Similar views: Untersteiner 1954; Harriott 1969; 143; Guthrie [1969] 1971: 269–74; Kerferd 1981: 78–82 ("the theory of literature and rhetorical art was largely a sophistic creation"); Barnes 1982: 463–66; Porter 1993; Wardy 1996: 35–37.

[51] ἐν γὰρ τραγῳδοποιίᾳ καὶ ζωγραφίᾳ ὅστις πλεῖστα ἐξαπατῇ ὅμοια τοῖς ἀληθινοῖς ποιέων, οὗτος ἄριστος (*Dissoi logoi* 90 3.10 DK; cf. 3.17, 2.28). Heath (1987: 40) makes the point that Gorgias is talking about spectators being absorbed in the dramatic illusion rather than any long-term educative effects; he opposes interpretations of the fragment by Taplin (1977: 167–69, cf. 1983) and Halliwell (1986: 16).

[52] See, e.g., P. Murray 1992; Segal 1962; Havelock 1963: 161 n. 75, 145–60; Walsh 1984: ch. 5.

rhetoric."[53] A radically different account has recently been proposed by Cole,[54] who points out that, apart from representations by Plato, Gorgias (along with other early sophists) never claims to be able to teach how to manipulate people, but only stresses the pervasive and irresistible power of speech over human thought. As Cole says: "Power, not artfulness, is the quality that makes [logos] similar to those tekhnai that operate by means of drugs."[55] Gorgias' works, including the Helen, at most "exhibit" the persuasive power of logos, but do not pretend to be able to control it: his psychological views must allow for the irrational in human response that makes any attempt to control these powers precarious.

It is at least clear that Gorgias was one of the most successful sophists of his generation and that he was a conspicuous representative of sophistic rhetoric for Plato, Isocrates, and Aristotle. We may get a better idea of his position in his own time if we situate his Helen in relation to other speculative thought of the time.[56] In Helen, this means considering the various tekhnai of logos, "arts of speech," that Gorgias acknowledges to have arisen in the course of time. But a close reading also shows that Gorgias distances himself from experts who write for courts and assemblies. He thus recognized the existence of skills in persuading, as in composing poetry; yet, as Cole says, the view he takes is that language in the end is man's master, not the reverse.

I shall try to show that in his discussion of language and poetry, Gorgias reflects both contemporary medical discourses about the nature of human emotions and accounts of sensation given by natural philosophers. The most direct influence is likely to have come from Empedocles, Gorgias' slightly older compatriot; but the Helen also speaks of poetic language in accents that reflect views to be found in Democritus and in Hippocratic treatises. It shares the atomist view of speech as an invisible but material

---

[53] De Romilly 1975: 16 ("theoretician of the magic spell of words"), 3 ("program for rhetoric"), and 19–21, differing with Wehrli (1948), for whom Gorgias was still a believer in inspired eloquence; also DeRomilly 1973 for tekhnē.

[54] Cole 1991: 146–52 for Gorgias, with reference to B 11.8–14, B 3.83–87 DK. Cf. Mourelatos 1985: esp. 624–30, for the "stimulus-response" theory of speech in Helen. In a deconstructive reading, Porter (1993) holds that "prima facie there are no grounds for doubting the accuracy of Plato's portrait" (269), and returns us part way to Gorgias as rhetorical theorist whose irreducibly self-contradictory views achieve persuasiveness (or "seduction") in their negative play.

[55] Cole 1991: 148. With reference to On Not Being, Striker (1996: ch. 1) characterizes sophists as neither philosophers nor rhetoricians (a distinction she places in the fourth century).

[56] Lanata 1963: 190–204 provides a valuable commentary on the discourse on logos, with references to earlier works, though her views tend toward the Crocean idealism of Untersteiner (1954).

substance, capable of directly shaping the psyches of those it encounters. Gorgias' *Helen* also develops the corollary that if *logos* is corporeal, it can as such be *worked* and *molded* into particular shapes with particular effects. This view gives a metaphysics for the rhetorical conception of language as style and content, even if Cole is right to say that the effects are seen as not always manageable and predictable. I would thus claim that *Helen* does document an important stage in the rise of the rhetorical art. Limited as Gorgias' claims for his own *tekhnē* (A 8) may have been, his drug analogy invoked a field of inquiry that some thinkers were re-trieving from traditional associations with magic and divine intervention (e.g., Helen in *Odyssey* 4.219–32), to put on a properly scientific basis. Gorgias expanded on and made popular an idea of persuasion as a process explicable in physicalist terms that laid the foundation for idealizations of verbal art as language worked into organic form.

Logos in the Helen

As a check against the preemptive assumption that the entire *Helen* is Gorgias' indirect praise of his own art, it is necessary to put the passage on *logos* in its context. The *Helen* is a *tour de force* exonerating the most notorious adulteress in Greek legend. Gorgias structures it by setting out four probable (§5) causes for Helen's abandoning her husband and sys-tematically going through them to argue that she was a victim of overmas-tering force in each case: Helen is blameless whether (1) she was con-strained by some superhuman force like Chance, the gods, or Necessity,[57] or (2) she was carried off bodily by Paris, or (3) she was persuaded by his speech, or (4) she was literally swept off her feet by his compelling physi-cal beauty (§4).

The first two causes, cosmic or human *force majeure*, clearly bring no reproach on the victim; it is in defending Helen for being seduced by words that Gorgias discourses on *logos* (§§8–14). His aim is to show that to be persuaded is to suffer compulsion no less than to be physically carried away (12), and he begins with an assertion about the nature of language:

[57] Gorgias' lumping together Chance, the gods, and Necessity as causes in §4 (cf. "Chance and the God," §6) suggests that he regards the "divine" in enlightened terms, like the author of *Sacred Disease*, who argues that because all diseases are caused by changes in the natural environment, and since cold and sun and wind are "divine," there is no reason to regard epilepsy as more divine than any other disease (§21). In this context, we may understand his explanation of the dramatic power of Aeschylus' *Seven against Thebes* as being "full of Ares" (B 24 DK; cf. Aristophanes *Frogs* 1021).

εἰ δὲ λόγος ὁ πείσας καὶ τὴν ψυχὴν ἀπατήσας, οὐδὲ πρὸς τοῦτο χαλεπὸν ἀπο-
λογήσασθαι καὶ τὴν αἰτίαν ἀπολύσασθαι ὧδε. λόγος δυνάστης μέγας ἐστίν,
ὃς σμικροτάτωι σώματι καὶ ἀφανεστάτωι θειότατα ἔργα ἀποτελεῖ· δύναται
γὰρ καὶ φόβον παῦσαι καὶ λύπην ἀφελεῖν καὶ χαρὰν ἐνεργάσασθαι καὶ ἔλεον
ἐπαυξῆσαι. (§8)

But if it was *logos* that persuaded and misled her soul, the charge is no
less easy to dismiss thus: speech is a great potentate that, with a minuscule,
altogether invisible body, accomplishes the most divine things. For it has
the power to put an end to fear and take away grief, and to create joy and
increase pity.

The mention of pity and fear has led some to insert this passage in a
Gorgianic theory of tragedy, but he is not yet talking about poetry, but
about language in general.[58] These two paradigmatic emotions illustrate
the sentence's main thesis, which concerns the power of all language: in
calling speech a lord and ruler, Gorgias implies that it works autocrati-
cally, with no need of truth or goodness to wield power.[59] Equally significant for the rest of the oration is the assertion that speech is an invisible
but material substance with inherent capacities (*dunatai*). In this, Gorgias
assumes the perspectives of the natural philosophers: Democritus' corporeal approach to language has been discussed as a particularly clear paradigm for this all-potent but invisible substance, but Gorgias' "very fine"
and powerful *logos* also recalls Anaxagoras' "Mind" as the "finest and
purest substance" dispersed through all things that have soul and exercising "the greatest power" (*iskhuei megiston*, B 12).[60] Among the doctors,
I have mentioned how *Sacred Disease* attributes the onset of epilepsy to

[58] The association of pity and fear was not original with Gorgias: Halliwell 1986: 170,
188–89. Nor was the theater the only place to invoke these emotions: using speech to banish
fear and keep men in line was a military necessity, and orators had encroached on the poetic
office of leading laments with their funeral orations, of which Gorgias himself offered
a specimen that mentioned the "immortal longing" felt for those dead in war (B 6 DK).
Thrasymachus of Chalcedon (85 DK, IX AS) dealt with laments at this time; early in the
fourth century, Antiphon "found an art to cure griefs analogous to that which among doctors served to treat diseases": see Gill 1985a.

[59] Immisch (1927: ad loc.) compares Euripides *Hecuba* 814–18, where Persuasion is
called a "tyrant" (*Peithō, turranos*), taken as an animadversion to Gorgias; the passage at
least gives a basis for Plato's elaborations on the theme in *Philebus* 58A ("I have often heard
Gorgias saying that the art of persuading is far superior to all the other arts. For it makes
them all its willing slaves . . .") and *Gorgias* 452E ("Even the doctor is my slave").

[60] Anaxagoras B 12 DK (esp. λεπτότατόν τε πάντων χρημάτων καὶ καθαρώτατον).
Jouanna (1988: 134 n. 2) compares the aretology of air in Diogenes of Apollonia (B 5
DK): καὶ ὑπὸ τούτωι [sc. "air"] πάντας κυβερνᾶσθαι καὶ πάντων κρατεῖν. The closeness of
Diogenes' outlook to that of the doctors is indicated by C 2 DK, which is from the Hippo-
cratic *On Winds*.

winds interacting with the brain (esp. §16), but the most striking parallel is provided by a writer on the border between natural philosophy and medicine, the author of the Hippocratic *On Winds* (*De ventibus*). This epideictic treatise, whose extensive similarities in rhetoric and ideas to Gorgias' *Helen* have been illuminated by Jacques Jouanna, praises air as a vital cosmic force essential for man and for all animals. In an early passage notable for its personification, the speaker calls air "the greatest potentate of all in all things" (3.2: οὗτος δὲ μέγιστος ἐν τοῖς πᾶσι τῶν πάντων δυάστης ἐστίν), and adds that it is "fine" and superhuman in being "ever-flowing" (3.3: ὁ ἀὴρ ἀέναος καὶ λεπτὸς ἐών).[61] Both speakers strike the tone of enlightened inquirers into nature and stress the influence of the physical environment on the human mind. In beginning his discourse about *logos*, Gorgias adopts the tone of a medical scientist, and the rest of his discussion will maintain this outlook. I shall pick up and follow the argument in such terms.

As specific instances of *logos* that produce powerful effects, Gorgias adduces poetry and magic spells. Poetry is introduced in the following terms:

τὴν ποίησιν ἅπασαν καὶ νομίζω καὶ ὀνομάζω λόγον ἔχοντα μέτρον· ἧς τοὺς ἀκούοντας εἰσῆλθε καὶ φρίκη περίφοβος καὶ ἔλεος πολύδακρυς καὶ πόθος φιλοπενθής, ἐπ' ἀλλοτρίων τε πραγμάτων καὶ σωμάτων εὐτυχίαις καὶ δυσπραγίαις ἴδιόν τι πάθημα διὰ τῶν λόγων ἔπαθεν ἡ ψυχή. (§9)

All poetry in my view and in my use of the word is simply speech that has meter. Over those that listen to it comes fearful shuddering and tearful pity and the welcome pain of longing,[62] and it is through language that the soul of the listener experiences a response of its own at the good and ill that befall other people and their affairs.

Again, this passage has been combined with the mention of pity and fear (§8) to make Gorgias Aristotle's forerunner not only in viewing art as purposive illusion but also in defining its end as a sort of catharsis.[63] Sup-

---

[61] On the similarities between *On Winds* and *Helen*: Jouanna 1988: 13–17; on the personification of air, ibid.: 25. Hence I drop the qualifiers of Segal (1962), who says (102) that the processes of the psyche have only a "quasi-physical" reality and (105) that *logoi* have an "almost physical impact" on the psyche. Segal greatly illuminates *Helen*'s concern with the psychology of speech, esp. pp. 101–5 on Gorgias' relation to natural science. As for going on to infer a Gorgianic theory of rhetoric as artful persuasion, see Segal's own qualification on p. 134.

[62] On this, cf. Aristotle *Rhetoric* 1.11.11 ff.

[63] E.g., Süss 1910: 85–86; Pohlenz 1920: 172–73. See Segal 1962: 132, 154 n. 123, for a discussion. Critique in Janaway 1995: 42–44. For a different conception of pity and fear in their more irrational, physiological aspects, see Schadewaldt 1970.

port may be found in the above-mentioned ethical paradox that a tragic poet is "just" to deceive and a spectator "wise" to be deceived (B 23 DK); but in *Helen* §9, poetry has its powerful effects not *qua* poetry but *qua* *logos*: Gorgias' point in defining poetry as speech with meter added is to identify it as a form of *logos* and so to ascribe its acknowledged emotional effects to the previously mentioned powers of language (note διὰ τῶν λόγων ἔπαθεν ἡ ψυχή).[64] The striking fact that the misfortunes of tragic characters are *not* those of the weeping audience testifies to the power of *logos* to instill these emotions of its own force.

Gorgias continues in the same vein when he goes on to speak of the effects of magic spells (§10):[65] incantations have a "divine" power to bring on pleasure or take away pain because of the *logoi* in them (αἱ γὰρ ἔνθεοι διὰ λόγων ἐπωιδαί).[66] Incantations are adduced as *verbal* formulas with an inherent capacity (δύναμις) to make contact with the apprehending part of the soul and change its constitution.[67] Gorgias closes the topic by referring, somewhat obscurely, to "two arts (*tekhnai*) of magic and sorcery" that have been "invented" or discovered to "trick the mind and deceive the soul."[68] What these two magic arts are is not clear, but nothing prevents "arts" of using speech from arising, as is seen by reading on.

---

[64] Russell (1981: 23) well sees that in saying all poetry is *logos* with *metron* added, Gorgias does not seek to define poetry but to appeal to a common view ("One must use *doxa* to show this to one's hearers" §9) that underlies, e.g., Herodotus' terms for and references to poetry. Cf. Feeney 1991: 25.

[65] A prototype for Gorgias' treatment of Helen's enchantment is provided by Pindar's account of how Jason seduced Medea (this time from the East to Greece) in *Pythian* 4.213–19: Aphrodite gave Jason a love charm ("the *iyunx* that drives one mad") and added instruction in prayers of supplication and incantations (*litas kai epaoidas*, 4.217) whereby he might take away (*apheloito*, 4.218) her respect for her parents; and Greece, "now become an object of longing to her (*potheina*, 4.218), might set her burning heart spinning with the whip of Persuasion."

[66] So Buchheim 1989: 166 n. 22. On these incantations, see further Burkert 1962: 42, arguing that Gorgias is indebted to a Greek version of shamanism (also detectable in Empedocles). For Plato, both mimetic poet and sophist are assimilated to the *goēs* as "shapeshifter" and marvel-worker: cf. *Gorgias* 483E–484A, *Meno* 80A, *Symposium* 203A, *Laws* 909b; cf. Pfister, "Epode," *RE* suppl. IV (1924): 324–43.

[67] For "contact" and "change the constitution": συγγινομένη γὰρ τῆι δόξηι τῆς ψυχῆς ἡ δύναμις τῆς ἐπωιδῆς ἔθελξε καὶ ἔπεισε καὶ μετέστησεν αὐτὴν γοητείαι (B 11 §10 DK). Cf. Gorgias' *omma psuchēs* ("eye of the soul") below, which seems to serve as a receptive faculty or organ for sight impressions. This seems to reflect the atomists' tendency to postulate intermediary organs for sensations that are not the result of a visible external impulsion.

[68] The run of sentences makes it difficult to take the terms as referring to the art of poetry and that of using incantations, though this interpretation is common: Segal 1962: 112; Lanata 1963: 201; Kennedy 1963: 52; DeRomilly 1975: ch. 1. There are no grounds for identi-

Having established the strong emotional effects speech can produce, Gorgias now turns to its power over belief. He considers in turn the discourses of natural scientists, courtroom speeches, and philosophical debates. In all these cases, some people can induce belief about matters not clearly known—the way things truly are, have been, or will be—by "fashioning" a false account (ψευδῆ λόγον πλάσσαντες, §11) which "stamps" or "impresses" (τυποῦν, §13) upon the mind any image the speaker may wish.[69] Xenophanes had used the word πλάσματα for the "fabrications" or falsehoods of old poetry (1.22 IEG), but the passages from Democritus discussed above provide closer parallels in the false "image" of Chance "fabricated" by foolish men and the "story-fashioning" to gratify men's ignorance about what happens after death.[70] In Gorgias, the correspondence of "fabricating" a speech with a mind's being "stamped" by it implies that a persuasively constructed account of things beyond perception imposes its shape directly on the mind.[71]

An irresistible, almost mechanical impact of *logos* on belief is present in each of Gorgias' three illustrations: natural scientists use speech to appeal to "the eyes of the intelligence"—evidently an organ[72] of the soul that translates verbal impressions into images—and they induce or change beliefs about what is beyond certain demonstration or clear knowledge (*apista kai adēla*, §11). In the courts, "a single speech written with art (*tekhnē*) rather than spoken with truth delights and persuades a mass audience" (§13). Here we have a reference to the art of the professional speechwriter, but the emphasis continues to be less on the skill of the artist who manipulates language than on the inherent power of *logos* itself: this power is expressed in the one-many paradox that a single speech can overmaster a large throng (juries amounting to 500 in some cases). The same logic was earlier used to praise Helen's "godlike beauty" (§4): the supremely compelling physical endowment (φύσει καὶ γένει, §3) she in-

---

fying the two arts as incantation and oratory: Verdenius 1981: 122 n. 37. Buchheim (1989: 168–69) sees little difference between the two arts.

[69] Segal 1962: 142 n. 44.

[70] Democritus B 119 DK, B 297 DK, quoted in note 25 above.

[71] In speculating about such matters, *doxa* (the conclusions we draw from our impressions) "surrounds those who exercise it with arbitrary but binding chanciness" (*eutukhia*, §11). Gorgias' stress on our human lack of *pronoia* (§11) and our inability to master the divine with "human forethought" (§6: θεοῦ γὰρ προθυμίαν ἀνθρωπίνηι προμηθίαι ἀδύνατον κωλύειν) is in line with traditional piety, as in Solon on the hubris and destruction that can follow from human lack of *pronoia* (esp. 13–67 IEG) and Xenophanes' urging an awareness of our limited foreknowledge in relation to the gods (1.24 IEG: θεῶν δὲ προμηθείην αἰὲν ἔχειν ἀγαθήν).

[72] Aristotle charged atomists with neglecting the distinction between perceptive organs and faculties: KRS 375.

herited from her mortal father, "mightiest of men," and from her divine father, "tyrant of all," effected (ἐνεργάσατο, §4)[73] such strong desire in her suitors that "her single body drew together" (as a magnet would, one may speculate) "the bodies of many suitors" (ἑνὶ δὲ σώματι πολλὰ σώματα συνήγαγεν ἀνδρῶν, §4). In the same way, the single artfully composed speech shows its power by moving a great crowd. It may indicate something about Gorgias' view of democratic oratory that he says the speaker "*pleases* and persuades" a mass audience, which is perhaps to say he persuades by pleasing rather than with truth. He moves on to a more strictly reasoned sphere of debate in his final example of the "philosophers": there, the disputants' "quickness of mind" in "heated contention" shows how easily "shifted" or even "metastasized" (εὐμετάβολον) is the mind's belief on their abstruse topics (§13).

Thus *logos* can stamp the mind with images of realities of which we have no direct experience; it can please and persuade large crowds without being true, and it can undermine a soul's reasoned reliance on such persuasion. Summing up these cases, Gorgias suggests that persuasion is a rather physical, automatic process by comparing it with drugs: the power of speech to affect the "arrangement" (*taxis*) of the soul is analogous to the way a selection or "arrangement" (*taxis*) of drugs affects the physical structures of the body (τὸν αὐτὸν δὲ λόγον ἔχει ἥ τε τοῦ λόγου δύναμις πρὸς τὴν τῆς ψυχῆς τάξιν ἥ τε τῶν φαρμάκων τάξις πρὸς τὴν τῶν σωμάτων φύσιν, §14.[74] The repetition of *taxis* ("drawing into formation, arrangement") in complementary senses in each half of the analogy implies that the ordering of the elements composing a speech will have a determining effect on the constitution of the soul. In such cases, the *taxis* or organization of elements is being impressed on the hearer, not truth. The general picture is of language as a corporeal, airlike impulsion that passes in through the ears and, through the mediation of naturally compatible organs, reshapes the psyche, itself a physical structure communicating with the physically constituted body. Such a materialist perspective again suggests Anaxagoras, for whom change was rearrangement, a matter of *taxis*, and the emotions were disturbances in the ordering of the soul.

This concludes the argument on *logos*; but it is set in a broader context by Gorgias' treatment of his fourth and final topic, the compelling visual impressions created by beautiful bodies. This discussion confirms and

---

[73] For a good example of this word for the effects attributed to physical processes, see Plato *Philebus* 47A.

[74] Empedocles, named by Aristotle as a founder of rhetoric (DL 8.57, p. 28 *AS* with notes), also boasted of lore about drugs and magic (B 111 DK).

clarifies his account of language and places it among an array of sensory impressions that "stamp" and command the soul. For Gorgias, physical desire is created by a visual emanation from the beloved's body: an efflux of an Empedoclean or atomistic sort passes into the eyes where the faculty of sight "engraves" or "paints" pictures of the object on the mind (εἰκόνας τῶν ὁρωμένων πραγμάτων ἡ ὄψις ἐνέγραψεν ἐν τῶι φρονήματι, §17). The doctrine lets him claim that Helen is guiltless because her moral character was imposed on, in all senses "impressed," by the appearance of Paris. It also suggests that, if we wish to construct a theory of dramatic illusion for Gorgias, *logos* takes its place beside spectacle as a component of what Froma Zeitlin has called drama's "somatic" poetics of representing the body.[75]

Gorgias describes the operations of visible objects on the soul in the same terms he used for the effects of speech:[76] the soul is "stamped" by vision, and this affects even its moral character (διὰ δὲ τῆς ὄξψεως ἡ ψυχὴ κἂν τοῖς τρόποις τυποῦται, §15). One illustrative example is the spectacle of an enemy army: the physical gleam of their bronze and iron is transmitted through sight and can "strike" a soldier and disturb his soul so that, though the danger is not immediately at hand, he forgets his duty and runs off (§16). Lovely sights can have equally strong effects: Paris' fair form demanded submission in the same way as a well-composed painting or sculpture makes viewers suffer pleasure:

ἀλλὰ μὴν οἱ γραφεῖς ὅταν ἐκ πολλῶν χρωμάτων καὶ σωμάτων ἓν σῶμα καὶ σχῆμα τελείως <u>ἀπεργάσωνται</u>, τέρπουσι τὴν ὄψιν· ἡ δὲ τῶν ἀνδριάντων ποίησις καὶ ἡ τῶν ἀγαλμάτων <u>ἐργασία</u> νόσον[77] ἡδεῖαν παρέσχετο τοῖς ὄμμασιν. οὕτω τὰ μὲν λυπεῖν τὰ δὲ ποθεῖν πέφυκε τὴν ὄψιν. (§18)

Whenever painters bring to completion from many colors and shapes a single finished body and form, they delight the sight. The making of statues and the crafting of images gives an agreeable pathology to the eyes. Thus vision is naturally suited to feel pain at some sights and pleasure at others.

Again, the mention of "one body" here should not distract us with Platonic notions of organic unity: Gorgias has in mind stories like that of Zeuxis painting a picture of Helen by combining the best features of five

---

[75] Zeitlin 1990: 71–75, 84–86.

[76] The passage and the relation of Gorgias to Empedocles is well analyzed by Buchheim 1985: esp. 426–27; cf. Buchheim 1989: 164–65, and Segal 1962: 101. With images passing διὰ δὲ τῆς ὄψεως, cf. διὰ τῶν ὤτων at Plato *Sophist* 234C in a discussion of the sophist's "magical power" to produce images in the mind (233C–234D: including an analogy with painters).

[77] Dobree's reading, printed by Buchheim and others; DK: θέαν.

beautiful women.[78] An object that manages to combine many beautiful impressions will be highly potent. The thought is (again, quite in line with Empedocles or atomism) that a selective use and combination of visible stimuli can impose on the sight and from there transmit an irresistible desire to the soul: so it was that "Helen's eye was pleased by the physical form of Paris and so communicated passionate desire to her soul" (τῶι τοῦ Ἀλεξάνδρου σώματι τὸ τῆς Ελένης ὄμμα ἡσθὲν προθυμίαν καὶ ἅμιλλαν ἔρωτος τῆι ψυχῆι παρέδωκε, §19).

The parallels between Gorgias' descriptions of the "working" or "shaping" of language and that of sculpture to "work" its effect in a soul are exact. In visual creations as in linguistic, there is an equivalence between the artisan's working up material elements into form—between "wrought sculptures" (ἡ τῶν ἀγαλμάτων ἐργασία) or paintings whose shapes and colors have been "wrought" into finished form (ἕν σῶμα καὶ σχῆμα τελείως ἀπεργάσωνται, §18)—and the "working" of a corresponding effect on the soul: stimulated by alluring images, the faculty of sight can "work" love and longing for "those bodies and things" from which the images emanate (ἔρωτα καὶ πόθον ἐνεργάζεται πραγμάτων καὶ σωμάτων, §18).[79]

Gorgias' apologetic task is done. We can draw these analogies together and get a coherent picture: Helen is off the hook because she was hooked into doing what she did by forces quite beyond her control. It matters little whether the motive impulse came from the gods, from Paris' main force, from his enrapturing appearance, or from his words: Helen's soul, like anyone's, was designed to be dominated by such impressions.

Gorgias' Art: "Training the Soul for Contests in Excellence"

Gorgias' argument, metaphors, and analogies concur in suggesting that composing an effective speech or an affecting poem is a process comparable to fashioning an attractive sculpture or painting: like stone or pigment, speech is raw material that may be shaped into a form that can override moral training or implant beliefs. The mechanistic implications of this

---

[78] Sicking 1963: 229. Cf. Empedocles B 23 DK, on painters mixing colors as an analogy for the combination of physical elements. Note that the analogy illustrates the imperceptibility of individual elements in a mixture rather than intimates some artistic structure in the cosmos, as is sometimes inferred (cf. 31 B 9, 35, 71 DK, and Aristotle *Politics* 3.11. 1281b10 ff.): see Wright 1981: 38–39.

[79] With §18, cf. §8: (λόγος) θειότατα ἔργα ἀποτελεῖ . . . δύναται χαράν ἐνεργάσασθαι; §11: ψευδῆ λόγον πλάσαντες; §13: ἡ πειθὼ προσιοῦσα τῶι λόγωι καὶ τὴν ψυχὴν ἐτυπώσατο ὅπως ἐβούλετο.

view do not rule out the possibility of an art of speech on matters of which (and these are many) we have no certain knowledge.[80] If sometimes we are affected by chance impressions, at other times it may be by (divine or mortal) design: the effect of Paris' body on Helen came "by the snares of chance, not the devices of intelligence, and by the compulsion of love, not the contrivances of art."[81] Even a skeptic about clear knowledge can allow that some people are better than others at stimulating the relevant receptive faculties to produce a desired effect in the mind, and *Helen* allows that certain arts of speech have been "discovered" (§10), in the sense that some people have found out in the course of time verbal formulas that produce certain effects.[82] Just as painters know how to blend colors and shapes to produce certain effects, and doctors mix drugs, experts in language would be able to select and arrange its elements with a view to the constitution of the recipient's body: sorcerers and magicians select and combine verbal phrases, and poets use meters as well as *logoi*. One other art has discovered how to produce "speeches written with art and not spoken with truth" (§13) that can persuade a throng of people.[83] This looks like a rhetorical art, and it is: as a physician observes the effects of drugs or the natural environment on a physical body, the new science of "speaking well" can prescribe how the forms and shapes of language may most potently be mixed and administered to a jury or assembly. But this *tekhnē* is decidedly not presented favorably: Gorgias refers to the unsavory profession of the logographer or professional speechwriter, constrained to write for the "compulsory contests" of the lawcourts to sell to litigants.[84] There is an elitist's disdain for success with a large mob (ὄχλου, §13)[85] in his suggestion that the will of the many can be duped

---

[80] Segal (1962: 119 ff). and MacDowell (1982: 12–16) are among those suggesting that the *Helen* (though not *On Not Being*) allows for rhetorical persuasion in realms of cognition in which we are not dominated by speech. But surely these would fall under Aristotle's category of things that no one debates about and that therefore lie outside the reach of rhetoric.

[81] §19: τύχης ἀγρεύμασιν, οὐ γνώμης βουλεύμασιν, καὶ ἔρωτος ἀνάγκαις, οὐ τέχνης παρασκευαῖς.

[82] For arts arising from experience, cf. the Hippocratic *On the Art* §9, *On Ancient Medicine* (§3, 20), and Democritus on the origin of human arts (B 144, 154 DK); for rhetoric: Gorgias' "pupil" Polus in Aristotle *Metaphysics* 981a3 (= B XIII 5 AS; cf. 4, 6). In *Gorgias*, Plato, of course, will adapt the analogy to degrade rhetoric to the level of "cookery" to philosophy's dietetics.

[83] Buchheim (1985: 425) derives Gorgias' idea of verbal "chemistry" from Empedocles.

[84] For this interpretation of *anagkaious agōnas* (§13), see Immisch 1927: 32, with the decisive parallel at Isocrates 15.1. Plato (*Theaetetus* 172ε) expresses a similar disdain for the "compulsions" to which philosophers are subject in the public arena.

[85] On the antidemocratic use of the one-many topos, see Segal 1962, who draws a different conclusion.

by a single person, working artfully behind the scenes.[86] Gorgias associates crafty writing with cunning manipulation, foiling simple, truthful oral discourse. It is a noteworthy contrast when Gorgias, master of the improvised discourse, goes on to speak of those who engage in on-the-spot oral debates, and only to these does he give the title "philosophers" (§13).

As far as we know, Gorgias never practiced the trade of logographer, and he does not seem to have been the sort of man one asked to write up a speech for a lawsuit. His most memorable performance in Athens occurred when he presented himself there as an ambassador from his native city in 427. He also addressed a panhellenic audience at Olympia on weighty themes (B 7–8 DK), and his Pythian Oration was so successful that it earned him the privilege of dedicating a gold statue of himself at the shrine (B 9; cf. A 1§4 DK). Gorgias could deliver a funeral oration or an encomium for the Eleans (B 10 DK). Accordingly, he eschews in *Helen* the role of cunning speechwriter and sympathizes more with the philosophers and their impressive oral debates. It might be thought that the role of "philosopher" or theoretician of speech would have appealed to Gorgias, but he speaks in *Helen* like a doctor rather than a literary theorist, which explains why he is often represented as a half-doctor in the testimonia.[87] Viewing language in material terms—as "a great potentate that, with an extremely small, quite invisible body, brings to accomplishment the most divine works"—comes easily in this perspective.[88] The calculated reasoning he brings to his subject (*logismos*, §2, cf. *Frogs* 973) is deployed to show language's hidden but material nature. In this he is like the author of *On Winds*, who makes a major theme of his prologue the distinction between the body, accessible to our senses, and the mind, unseen but accessible to reason: ἀλλὰ μήν ἐστί γε τῇ μὲν ὄψει ἀφανής, τῷ δὲ λογισμῷ φανερός (3.3). From this lofty perspective, Gorgias distinguishes his own discourse from the discussions of natural scientists, from the speeches

---

[86] There is a similar unflattering portrayal of mass deliberative assemblies, in Gorgias' *Palamedes* (B 11a 33 DK): "Lamentation and beseeching and the entreaties of friends are useful when the decision rests with a crowd (ἐν ὄχλωι μὲν οὔσης τῆς κρίσεως); but such things will not persuade you who are the first of the Greeks." Cf. Cleon in Thucydides 3.38.2, abusing greedy assembly orators who "toil away" at a "fine" speech to mislead their audience: κέρδει ἐπαιρόμενος τὸ εὐπρεπὲς τοῦ λόγου ἐκπονήσας παράγειν πειράσεται.

[87] Cf. Cole 1991: 146–47: Gorgias' praise of the power of *logos* is spoken from the position of "an experimenter in mind-altering drugs testifying on behalf of someone (Helen) who has committed a crime under their influence."

[88] See the parallel discussion of "invisible things" and the evolution of the arts in the Hippocratic *On Diet* (1.11–24), with the commentary of Joly (1960: 52–54) and Jouanna (1984). It is within this framework that I would account for the evidence compiled by Flashar (1956) on the influence of medical ideas on fifth- and fourth-century discussions of poetry's effects on the emotions.

written for the lawcourts, and from the "passionate contention (*hamillas*) of the philosophers." For him, as he says in closing, his own discourse is merely "play."

Much has been made of the close of *Helen*, where Gorgias says, "I have essayed to produce an encomium of Helen and a plaything of my own" (ἐβουλήθην γράψαι τὸν λόγον Ἐλένης μὲν ἐγκώμιον, ἐμὸν δὲ παίγνιον, §21). There have been attempts to see this as undoing the seriousness of the preceding argument in line with a radically skeptical Gorgias as construed from *On Not Being*.[89] But arguments that were useful in fighting off an Eleatic philosopher were not necessarily appropriate on all occasions, and in *Helen* the posture of seriousness mixed with levity (*spoudaiogeloion*) provides an appropriate conclusion to a wise man's epideixis. It is the tone to strike, for example, at the end of a clever speech at a symposium.[90] In the *Helen*, however, it may also be an apology for the rather earnest activity of producing a "publishable" text. One of the rhetoricians of the next generation, Alcidamas, concludes a written treatise (arguing against the use of speech-texts in teaching rhetoric) with a tone similar to Gorgias': if you want to influence people, he urges, practice improvisation, but regard writing "as a sport, practiced on the side, and you will be judged wise by those who think well."[91] Plato adopts this topos as a way of concluding his *Phaedrus*.[92] Following Cole's account of the function of such speeches, the metaphor of play may suggest that the sophist's written text is a plaything for students to use by memorizing but not taking too seriously.[93] The professional's text is called a plaything to

---

[89] So Wardy 1996: ch. 2, esp. 50–51; see Segal 1962: 139–40, 147–48 and nn. 24, 82. Buchheim (1989: xxiii–xxiv, 173) takes it as aimed not at the speech as a whole but at its character as encomium.

[90] Agathon concludes his encomium to love by dedicating it to Phaedrus: "Here it is, partly in play and partly in seriousness" (*ta men piadias, ta de sopudēs . . . metekhōn*, *Symposium*. 197E). Cf. Xenophon *Symposium* 2.26: Socrates prescribes moderate drinking to "make us more playful" (*paigniōdesteron*).

[91] Alicdamas *Sophists* §35: τοῦ δὲ γράφειν ἐν παιδίῳ καὶ παρέργως ἐπιμελόμενος εὖ φρονεῖν κριθείη παρά τοῖς εὖ φρονοῦσιν. So, too, Polycrates, to judge from Demetrius §120: "Polycrates was playing, not serious, and the weightiness of his writing is itself a *paignion*." *Paignia* is among the titles attributed to Thrasymachus by Suidas (B IX 1 *AS*). See O'Sullivan 1992: ch. 3, and, for a reversal of the *topos*, the conclusion to Athenaeus' own oeuvre (*Deipnosophistal* 15. *fin*, where Athenaeus cites Plato's (?) description of his dialogues as "the *paignia* of a Socrates young and fair": *Epistles* 2.314c).

[92] *Phaedrus* 278B–D, Cf. *Republic* 602B, where imitating is ranked as *paidia*, not serious pursuit (*spoudē*).

[93] Cole 1991: 78–79, while Gorgias is possibly here following his own advice to counter seriousness with levity, the text itself, being a compendium that packs as much model material together as possible, is "an educational toy" to be "played with" by being developed into full, and less outrageous, speeches. For metaphors of a "model" to be "played" with, i.e., "studied" (semantically, analogous with *skholē*), cf. Aristophanes fr. 699 *PCG*. παίγνια

show that he is not too earnest, that he is free and "playing" in a way that might amuse (free and playful) gentlemen of letters. This pose of amateurism did not prevent Gorgias from becoming the wealthiest of the sophists (Isocrates *Antidosis* §155). But in his *Helen* and in his high-flown theories of language, he presented himself as something loftier than a verbal artist, more philosophic and scientific. One of Gorgias' pupils (also a great-nephew, in fact) richly summed up the value of his teaching in an inscription he had placed on a statue of the sophist at Olympia: "Eumolpus dedicated this for two reasons: teaching and friendship. No mortal ever discovered a finer art to exercise (ἀσκῆσι) the soul for contests of excellence; his likeness (*eikōn*) stands in the soil of Apollo, a paradigm not of wealth, but of pious ways."[94]

Before concluding, it is worth pointing out that Gorgias' view of aesthetic response, though not the complete physiological system, persisted and constituted an important strand in thinking about poetry from Plato on. We should recognize Gorgianic themes, and can often recognize Gorgianic language as well, when Plato and others present poetry, rhetoric, and music as exercising an overmastering influence on the soul through the force of sheer sound. The absorption of these ideas in fourth-century rhetoric and poetics—as Gorgianic enchantment was domesticated into verbal charm once the properly scientific components of speech became syllables and sounds—established an inner conflict in classical criticism that has persisted in all its later adaptations. A separation between the two is implied in Gorgias' student Lycimnius, who seems to have broadened the inquiries opened up by Democritus into the study of words.[95] In his *Rhetoric*, Aristotle cites Lycimnius for the view that the "beauty of words" (κάλλος ὀνομάτων) is a combination of what they signify (σημαινόμενον) and their sound (ψόφοι); helpfully, Lycimnius and Polus (another associate of Gorgias) collected such ideal words for "eloquent composition" (*pros euepeias poiēsin*).[96] The classical approach to the split between

---

is associated with καναβευμάτα and κάναβοι, molds to be thrown away. *Meletē* would be working up a written text for transmission. Semantically similar is *athurma, athurein* for the text of a song or its realization: Pindar *Pythian* 5.23; Bacchylides 9.87, 18.57, *Epigrams* 1.3 S-M; for the rhapsodes' texts of Homer—Pindar *Isthmian* 3/4.57; *Homeric Hymn* 19.15; *Homeric Hymn to Hermes* 52, 485. Closer in meaning to *meletē* is a poets' word, *merimna*: see Barrett on Euripides *Hippolytus* 1428, *Rhesus* 550. Cf. Bacchylides 19.11 (= *meletē* in Pindar *Isthmian* 5.28).

[94] Gorgias A 7 DK. The text of the inscription: A 8 DK. Note Gorgias' use of *askein* for training both mind and body in his funeral oration: B 6 DK (as supplemented by Foss).

[95] So Wehrli 1948: 23. See Armstrong 1995 for the heritage of Democritean poetics in Philodemus and later criticism.

[96] Aristotle *Rhetoric* 1405b6–8; cf. Janko 1987: 180. On Lycimnius and Polus: Plato *Phaedrus* 267b–c (= B XIII 10 AS); for Polus' book, cf. *Gorgias* 462b.

sound and sense is, ideally, to harmonize the two (cf. *Cratylus* 387D); but at its limit, the scientific account of language reduced it to a substance that was properly manipulated by an art of sounds, not ethics. The tendency of this analysis was to isolate the power inherent in words as sound—as *psophos*, which we can translate with Barthes' "rustle of language" in mind. Already in Gorgias' heyday, Aeschylus was portrayed as incomprehensible because of his bombast—a "mountain-crag maker," full of "noise" (ψόφου, *Clouds* 1367)—and the admiration for his morals expressed in *Frogs* did not preclude joking about the "noise" of his language (τὸν ψόφον τῶν ῥημάτων, 492). Throughout ancient criticism, there remains a tension between its values, rooted in ethics, and its techniques, rooted in materialistic, even mechanistic, conceptions of language.

I hope to have shown compatibilities between Democritus and Gorgias as each attempted to account for the workings of language in the light of contemporary philosophies of nature. Without insisting on a direct or a single channel of influence, I have argued that each writer attests to the new formal, empirical, and scientific approach to language and applies it to poetry. But before materialism was installed in fourth-century poetics, it had to win a place in the market for sophistication about poetry that was consuming classical Athens. The next chapter considers how such higher speculations entered the flourishing literary culture there.

EIGHT

LITERARY CULTURE AND DEMOCRACY

POETS AND TEACHERS IN

CLASSICAL ATHENS

W E DO not know if Gorgias visited Athens before his famous
embassy of 427, and we do not know whether Democritus
ever did. But there is no doubt that wandering wise men from
all parts of Greece flocked to that increasingly prosperous and influential
capital once the Persian wars ended in 479. In the burgeoning Periclean
democracy, the arts and sciences were munificently supported, most conspicuously by Pericles and his circle of wise advisers, but also by citizens
of leisure as they met in their houses and their gymnasia, and as they sent
off their children for advanced education under "sophists," or professional wise men. The rest of the city also witnessed and, as far as their
means allowed, took part in the intellectual and scientific experimentation: schooling at all levels expanded throughout the century, and there
was always the agora, where Socrates found no shortage of people willing
to debate what a poem meant, even with the poets themselves (Plato *Apology* 22 A–C).

Thus, by 405, Aristophanes could address his audience as "veterans"
in the wars of criticism, and *Frogs* is only one among a number of comedies that attest to an interest on the part of the Athenian public in the most
innovative and startling new approaches to poetry.[1] The theater itself was
probably the most important single site for disseminating literary culture.
Dramatic festivals broadcast new ideas to more than 17,000 spectators
at a time, and many plays explored problems with language and representation—the very substances of drama. Aristophanes is replete not only
with parodies of higher criticism, but with paratragic imitations of tragic
song as well.[2] Nor did tragedians neglect the higher thought of the day in
depicting their heroes of old. Aeschylus' *Oresteia* of 458 probes deeply
into the powers of language, and many Euripidean plays delight in toying
with audience assumptions about illusion and reality; Euripides even went

---

[1] Other comedies on literary topics, now lost, are surveyed in Dover 1993: 25–28.

[2] For Aristophanes as a seminal influence on Hellenistic criticism, see Clayman 1977;
Cameron 1995: 328–31; and esp. O'Sullivan 1992.

so far as to compose metatheatrical passages such as the recognition scene in *Electra*, which unmistakably revises the improbabilities in the corresponding scene of Aeschylus' *Choephoroi*.[3]

The evidence of drama is obviously central to understanding Athenian musical culture, but I shall not take up the difficult task of reconstructing poetic theories for the major dramatists. This is not to deny that they were serious thinkers as well as artists, but criticism was to be a discourse of philosophers rather than of practitioners. In the critical tradition, the tragedians are remembered as dramaturges and stylists: critics turned to Euripides for his pathos-inducing diction and to see how he managed his plots; Aeschylus figures as an early innovator in the number of actors and as the embodiment of grand language and heroic values. Whatever Sophocles' *On the Chorus* was, there is not a trace of any critical idea it may have contained in later literature.[4] As original and influential as these thinkers may have been, there is no Aeschylean nor even Aristophanean position in ancient criticism. But the positions expressed in Aeschylus and Aristophanes can tell us much about the intellectual currents of the times.

To observe how Athens transfomed, as it appropriated and democratized, late archaic musical culture, I begin by picking up the symposium in the classical period. I shall first draw attention to the high value placed on musical and literary "sophistication" (*dexiotēs*) by the Attic-Ionic elite; then I indicate some ways in which refined musical culture was disseminated through the city. As *dexiotēs* spread among the populace, new teachers, with new exegetical techniques and new kinds of texts, changed ideas about the role of poets. A consideration of Athenian discussions of the nature and purpose of education in poetry will show that, although the old idea that poets were wise and worth learning was frequently voiced, the democratization of literary culture changed the meaning of certain texts: old poets who had been heard with pleasure by panhellenic elites now had to address the concerns of modern democratic cities. The poets, always teachers in some sense, began to teach new things when they were encountered in new textual forms and in new social spaces. These new perspectives, however, were not inclined to study poetry in isolation from its social and political values. Thus the theory and practice of literary discussion in the fifth century provided a necessary context, but only the context for the development of poetic theory in the fourth.

---

[3] On the *Oresteia*, see, e.g., Goldhill 1986; Walsh 1984: ch. 5. Euripides *Electra* 487–546; cf. *Choephoroi* 164–234. On this issue, see, e.g., Scodel 1990, Zeitlin 1990.

[4] It is solely attested in the *Suda* (testimonium 2.7 *TrGF*, cf. testimonia 52, 57, 100).

Dexiotēs at Dinner

Aristotle refers to an explosion of interest in the musical arts after the war, instancing a vogue among some gentlemen of taking up the *aulos*, an instrument necessary for symposia among other occasions, but usually left to professionals or slaves to wield (*Politics* 1341a26–b14). This proved to be a short-lived experiment, because playing the *aulos* was soon considered indecorous. (With urbanity suggestive of the culture of that age, Aristotle supports abandoning the instrument by allegorizing the myth that wise Athena invented the *aulos* but threw it away when she realized how playing it disfigured her face.) But cultural and intellectual experimentation continued among an elite dedicated to developing the late archaic "loving the fine" into a cosmopolitan ideal of civilized life (*habrosunē*).[5] Thucydides says that after the Persian wars, some Athenians retained the distinctive Ionic mode of dress and its luxurious style of life, and Heraclides Ponticus, a familiar of Plato and Aristotle, details the ways by which the "men of great spirit" among the Marathon victors represented themselves as intellectuals (*phronimoi*) and won a reputation for *sophia*: he mentions their purple cloaks, embroidered (*poikilous*) chitons, ornate rings, and gold "grasshopper" pins for their hair; slaves carried them in litters, "so they would not sit just anywhere."[6] Heraclides claims they cultivated pleasure as the greatest good, a view he endorses with a tag from Simonides, as they themselves may well have done: "What human life or position of absolute power is desirable without pleasure (*hadona*)? Without this, even the life of the gods is not worth envying."[7]

From around the 460's, sophists and other teachers brought the most advanced speculations about language and nature to an elite who prided themselves on their wisdom and leadership in the crisis just passed. By rare good luck, we happen to have a record from around the middle of the century of such gentlemen talking at table and showing what "sophistication" (*dexiotēs*) meant. Ion of Chios (ca. 480–421), a versatile poet and writer, belonged to the postwar international set. At noble houses in Athens and Chios, he met many notable figures of the time, including

---

[5] ἐρᾶν τὰ καλά, cf., e.g., Euripides *Antiope* fr. 198; Dover 1993: 24–37.

[6] Thucydides 1.6.3; cf. schol. ad *Iliad* 13.685; and Hornblower 1991: 25–26. Heraclides Ponticus 55 Wehrli. For *sophia* in this context, cf. Aristophanes *Clouds* 1024; on grasshopper pins and other forms of display: *Clouds* 984–85; Cratinus *PCG* fr. 257, cf. 256; Bowra 1970: 116–17; Geddes 1987.

[7] Simonides 584 *PMG*. Heraclides adds Pindar fr. 126 S-M (composed for Hieron), and Odysseus at Alcinous' table (*Od.* 9.5).

politicians like Cimon and Pericles and the ubiquitous Socrates; he even sat next to Aeschylus at the games (they talked sports). Ion recorded conversations he heard in his "Visits" (*Epidēmiai*), parts of which are quoted and excerpted by Plutarch and Athenaeus. In one extract, Ion records the literary conversation of a distinguished Athenian general who happened to be passing through Chios: this is none other than Sophocles, whom he recalls bantering about poetry over wine:

> I met Sophocles the poet when he stopped at Chios on his way to command the fleet against Lesbos,[8] and he showed himself to be an amusing and sophisticated man (*paidiōdei kai dexiōi*). At a party hosted by Hermesilaus, his friend and the political connection for Athenians on Chios, the boy pouring wine was standing before the fire; when he bade Sophocles, "Enjoy your wine," Sophocles replied, "I shall—if you take your time in serving me." As the boy blushed yet more furiously, Sophocles turned to the man reclining beside him and said, "How finely Phrynicus[9] spoke in the poem where he said, 'On his purple cheek (*parēisin*) there shone the light of love.'" To this the man, who was a letter-teacher from Eretria, replied, "You are doubtless wise about poetry, Sophocles, yet I am bound to say Phrynicus did not speak well when he called the fair boy's cheeks (*gnathous*) purple. For if a painter were to daub purple pigment on this boy's cheeks, he would not appear fair. It is quite unfair to liken (*eikazein*) what is fair to what is obviously unfair."
>
> At this Sophocles laughed aloud and said to the Eretrian, "I presume then, my good man, that you also disapprove of Simonides'[10] saying—'the maiden sending voice forth from purple mouth'—though it has quite a reputation among the Greeks as being well said, and of the poet when he said, 'Apollo of the golden hair,' on the grounds that a painter who made the god's hair gold rather than black would produce a contemptible picture. Nor does the one who said 'rosy-fingered' meet your approval, for if someone were to dip her fingers in red dye, the result would be a dyer-maid's hands and not those of a fair lady." Everyone laughed and the Eretrian was silenced by the riposte.[11]

Sophocles' opening remark shows his "playful sophistication" in several respects. First of all, to be able to pluck out a line from an estimable tragic poet of the previous generation suggests a mind richly stocked with

[8] In the Samian War of 441–440. On Sophocles' generalship, cf. Jacoby on 392 T 5(c) *FGrH*, and Jacoby 1941: 3–4.

[9] Cf. Atheneus 564f = Phrynichus 3 F 13 *TrGF* = 2 Bergk, who suggests it may be from a dithyramb (3.561).

[10] Simonides 585 *PMG* = 44 D.

[11] Athenaeus 13.603e–604f. I have translated Jacoby's text (omitting the conjectured lacuna) at 392 F 6 *FGrH*.

poetry.[12] Second, his quotation is perfectly adapted to the occasion: he captures the moment as the firelight illumines the boy's cheeks with what would be called the *kairos* in rhetorical theory. (The word is not used here, but Ion composed a "hymn" to *kairos*, which he mythologized as the youngest—that is, newest and freshest—offspring of Zeus.[13]) Finally, Sophocles shows adroitness in his subtle indirectness: ostensibly praising a poet's words, he manages at the same time to praise the boy's beauty and to suggest that he himself is inspiring this flush of love. Sophistication combines literary culture, muted self-praise, and seductive charm.

The unnamed schoolteacher (*grammatistēs*) seizes the opportunity to show himself equally quick on the uptake.[14] In a pretty speech of his own, he objects, with all due deference, to Sophocles' remark; in effect, he charges Sophocles with not playing the sympotic game of "drawing similes" (*eikazein*) well.[15] He concludes his rather pedantic and literal-minded performance (he glosses Phrynicus' poetic word for "cheek" with its prosaic name) with an epigram playing on the word "fair" (*kalos*).[16] But Sophocles counters with a flurry of quotations from widely admired poets that contradict the schoolteacher's view: the barrage includes wise Simonides,[17] an unnamed Doric poet who may be Pindar,[18] and finally Homer himself and his "rosy-fingered." The laughter of the group decides the issue in favor of the distinguished guest.

A general (who just happens to be a composer of Athenian tragedies) jostling for status with a fellow guest is sport, meant to be borne easily.

[12] Phrynichus, whose latest work seems to have been in the 470's, is favored by older men in Aristophanes (e.g., Philokleon in *Wasps* 219, 269; cf. *Birds* 748–51) and is rejected as old-fashioned by "Euripides" in *Frogs* 910.

[13] Pausanias 5.14.9 (= 742 PMG); Lesky (1966: 410) judges that *kairos* in this hymn "was not a creation of living religious feeling . . . but of the realm of ideal concepts"; cf. West 1985: 76.

[14] Unnamed, according to Diels (1910: 21), to characterize him as a *homo ignobilis*. Yet he is a guest of Hermesilaus, and it may be, as Jacoby supposes from the use of the article, that Ion had identified him earlier in an aside that is omitted by Athenaeus.

[15] On the sympotic game of "similes" (*eikones*), Epicharmus 87, 90 Kaibel; Aristophanes *Wasps* 1308–18, *Birds* 801–8, *Frogs* 906; Xenophon *Symposium* 6.8–7.1; Plato *Symposium* 214E, 215A, 216D–E, 221D–E, *Meno* 80A–C, *Laws* 933E. See, in general, Fraenkel on Aeschylus *Agamemnon* 1629ff. and 1244.

[16] Accepting, with Jacoby, Wilamowitz' οὐ κάρτα δὴ καλὸν; if reading οὐ γάρ δεῖ, "for one should not liken what is fair to what is not fair."

[17] Cf. the very similar use of Simonides by Polemarchus to confute a thesis of Socrates, and Socrates' ironic concession (*Republic*. 331D–E =642a PMG).

[18] Pindar uses the Doric *khrusokomas* substantively for Apollo several times (e.g., *Olympian*. 6.41, *Paean* 5.41 S-M). The epic form *khrusokomēs* is used of Dionysus in Hesiod *Theogony* 947, and of Apollo in one version of lines assigned to Tyrtaeus (Diodorus 7.12.6 = 14 Gentili-Prato), but not in Plutarch (*Lycurgus*. 6) as printed by West (4.2 IEG = 3 D).

The conversation happens to be about poetry, the plastic arts, and their conventions of representation, but theoretical rigor is less conspicuous than the desire to display a familiarity with the arts. According to both Plato and Xenophon, Socrates was also interested in the paradoxes of artistic representation, but he would not disdain to visit the workshops of painters and sculptors for technical discussions of these issues.[19] At the dinner party, by contrast, art is regarded from the point of view of the connoisseur, one who can praise and blame the products of artisans. The "aesthetic" observations here serve to establish social differences between general and schoolteacher, Athenian and Eretrian, and, by implication, between guest and servant, and indeed between the dyer-maid and one who can wear a purple cloak. These gentlemen regard the producers of art as a banausic class removed from "the fair." The wine-pourer himself is yet one more aesthetic object to be appraised and had, and, as it turns out, functions like a prize in the contest: in the sequel recounted by Ion, Sophocles went on to steal a kiss from the boy as the company roared its approval.[20]

As the schoolmaster's epigram made clear, the display of a sense for *ta kala* is what the game is about. The studied unseriousness of the game makes sense in a milieu in which Jan Bremer has discerned—noting that sympotic competition over boys comes increasingly to the fore through the classical age both in songs and on vase-paintings—aristocratic elites finding new spheres for competition in a world where they could claim less direct political influence.[21] In the spirit of the occasion, General Sophocles caps his performance with a war story having to do not with his battle skills, but with a clever trick he once played in dividing booty among allies; he closes with a self-effacing comment on his success with the slave: "I'm practicing my military tactics, gentlemen. For Pericles said that I know how to write poetry but not to be a general; yet this little stratagem of mine seems to have turned out well." Ion sums up: "Sophocles spoke and acted thus dexterously (*dexiōs*) on many other occasions when he drank. As for public affairs, he was neither particularly clever (*sophos*) nor dominant in politics, but just one of the good old, solid (*khrēstōn*) Athenians."

---

[19] Xenophon *Memorabilia* 3.10.1–8, Plato's Socrates reflects on the "dishonesty" of using purple paint, the fairest of colors, to signify dark eyes, "the fairest part of the animal" (Plato *Republic* 420C–D. Cf. *Hippias major* 290B–D. Poets are grouped with painters as deceptive by the author of the *Dissoi logoi* (3.17 DK).

[20] Cf. the challenge to a (singing) contest with a boy as prize in Theognis 993–96, and the competition for kisses between Socrates and Critoboulos at Xenophon *Memorabilia* 4.18–20, 5.1–10, with Guthrie [1969] 1971: 387–89. Erotic teasing in (sympotic?) elegiacs: Melanthius 3 *IEG* (= *Cimon* 4.9), Sophocles 4 *IEG*.

[21] Bremer 1990.

Earnest Plutarch criticized Ion's *idée fixe* that excellence (*aretē*) always had to have a humorous component, "like a tragic trilogy's always being followed by a satyr play" (*Pericles* 5.4). But a citizen of one of Athens' satellite cities was likely to find Athenian celebrities most attractive when they could be self-effacing. Ion's tastes in dinner companions follow his politics in other remarks he makes about notable figures of the time. When he expresses his opinions of Cimon (whom he admired) and Pericles (whom he found overbearing), his verdicts are backed up by an evaluation of their sympotic performances. Ion says Pericles' conversation (*homilia*) was impudent (*mothōnikos*) and smoldered with arrogance (*hupotuphon*); Cimon, by contrast, is praised for his "harmonious" temper (*emmelēs*) and smooth (*hugron*) and cultivated (*memousōmenon*) performance in good society (*sumperiphorais*).[22] Ion describes Cimon at a dinner given by a certain Laomedon in Athens (presumably before Cimon's fall in 461). There are libations, and when Cimon is called on (*parakaleomai*) to sing, he does so "not unpleasantly" and is hailed as more accomplished (*dexiōteron*) than Themistocles, who declared he "could not sing or play the lyre but knew how to make a city powerful and rich." "As is natural when drinking progresses," Ion went on, "people started to recall (*mnēmoneuomenōn*) the exploits of Cimon."[23] It was always hard to keep war stories from cropping up around the mixing bowl; but when smooth Cimon dwelt on his cleverest (*sophōtaton*) stratagem, it had to do, as with Sophocles, with a shrewd distribution of booty.

Anthologizing Culture

Ion makes clear that knowing how to deploy poetry dexterously had become a requirement for those who wished, as Pindar put it, "to give offense to no man at symposia and suffer none in return" (*Pythian* 4.294–97). This learned and literate elite included persons Aristophanes describes as collecting copies of certain poets and putting them in coffers along with their garments, "so they shall smell of cleverness" (*dexiotēs*, *Wasps* 1051). But *dexiotēs* came to be prized by a wider public in fifth-

---

[22] For Pericles: Plutarch *Pericles* 5.3 = 392 F 15 *FGrH*. An example of Pericles' poetasting boastfulness may have been his dictum that it had taken him only nine months to reduce Samos, the most powerful city in Ionia, whereas Agamemnon had taken ten years in conquering a barbarian city (Plutarch *Pericles* 28.7 = Ion 392 F 16): see West 1985: 73. Jacoby would take this as a garbled misremembering of Pericles' praising *Athens* in a funeral oration. For Cimon: Plutarch *Pericles*. 5.3 = 392 F 15 *FGrH*.

[23] Plutarch *Cimon* 9.1–6 = 326 F 13 *FGrH*.

century Athens.[24] The "sophistication in speech" of fifth-century symposia (Dionysius Chalchus 4.4 *IEG dexiotēs logou*, cf. *Wasps* 1307) was
represented to the mass audience in the theater, as when Aristophanes
shows a young man trying to teach his old-fashioned father how to speak
before "learned and sophisticated guests" (*Wasps* 1175: ἀνδρῶν
παρόντων πολυμαθῶν καὶ δεξιῶν). Aristophanes' audience clearly liked
to be flattered as "sophisticated" (*Knights* 233: *to theatron dexion*), even
while laughing as the comedian mocked the pretentious spectator
(*kompsos theatēs*).[25]

The sophists tend to dominate accounts of fifth-century literary culture,
but the elite learning they offered depended on, even as it reacted to, a
more wide-reaching expansion of musical education and culture. From
the end of the sixth century to the end of the fifth, the evidence suggests
a general increase in schooling throughout the Athenian citizen class and
a steadily wider dissemination of skill in reading and writing.[26] By the
century's end, what Plato calls "the traditional curriculum—gymnastic
for the body and *mousikē* for the soul" (*Republic* 376E)—was expanded
to accommodate a new subject, education in writing and recitation of
poetry under the *grammatistēs*.[27] As basic education expanded, the minimum level of "sophistication" rose. To meet the increasingly widespread
demand for *dexiotēs*, sophists and teachers of the later fifth century began
to supply anthologies that conveniently "selected from all the poets the
key sayings (*kephalaia*) and whole speeches (*rhēseis*) that had to be
learned by heart if one is to become good and wise" (Plato *Laws* 810E–
811A). The sophist Hippias advertised one such volume as containing
"some things said by Orpheus, others by Musaeus, in short, by this poet
here and that poet there, some things by Hesiod and some by Homer, and
by many others of the poets, and by prose writers, some Greek and some

<hr />

[24] Cf. Plato *Laws* 810E–811A (cf. 890A, "clever"), Aristotle *Nichomachean Ethics* 4.8 on
tactful and refined conversation as against boorish joking.

[25] Cratinus fr. 343 *PCG*; see Dover 1968 on *Clouds* 148 and 547; and Verdenius 1983:
24. For *kompsos*, see Chantraine 1945.

[26] Important recent discussions: Woodbury 1976; Harris 1989: chs. 3–4; Robb 1994: esp.
174–97; 197, and Morgan 1999, esp. 48, with nn. 9, 19, 58–59. Vase-paintings representing
reading and schooling have been collected, but it is hard to know how far to extend the
images on these objects, generally of high value, to the city at large: Immerwahr 1964: cf.
Lissarague 1987: 130, 132, with Webster 1973: 61.

[27] Though this tripartite schema is backdated in Plato's *Protagoras* 312A–B to sometime
ca. 430, Robb (1994) and Morgan (1999: esp. 50–51) place its arrival toward the end of
the fifth century. Robb is not quite accurate, however, to say (184) that "the 'letter-master'
(*grammatistēs*) . . . is not attested in Athenian literature of the fifth century": the *grammatistēs* mentioned by Ion of Chios has connections with prominent Athenians; Aristophanes'
schoolmaster in *Daitales* 233 *PCG* is teaching and glossing Homer.

foreign" (B 6 DK).[28] Havelock seems right to surmise that such books are referred to when Aristophanes says in *Frogs* that the audience will follow the poetry contest because everyone has a book (*biblion*) from which to con the "sophisticated passages" (*ta dexia*) of the poets.[29] It is from such books that his Euripides, a collector of neat little expressions (*stōmulio-sullektadē*, 841), has brewed the slimming "infusion" of neat phrases (*stō-mulmatōn*, 943) he administers to Aeschylus' bloated art.[30]

Anthologies offered widely usable texts for those wishing to round out or freshen up their primary educations. By selecting texts that were ripe for reuse and by juxtaposing them with others of a similar character, they prepared students to show they knew a little more about poetry than the *kalai dianoiai* of rhapsodes. Of course, some, like Niceratus, son of the great general Nicias, learned the entire *Iliad* and *Odyssey* by heart;[31] but Socrates was content to go through the "treasuries (*thēsauroi*) of wise men of old" with friends, picking out (*eklegometha*) what was good and "unraveling" it in hopes of becoming distinguished for wisdom.[32] An important consequence of this "publishing" innovation was that old songs could be deployed in new ways: a long narrative or a play that was received collectively by the citizens could be broken into small pieces to be reused and reinterpreted among smaller groups as a sign of familiarity with the arts.

This development can be observed in a passage from Xenophon's *Memorabilia* (1.2.56). Xenophon is responding to an anti-Socratic pamphlet, *A Condemnation of Socrates*, that had charged Socrates with picking out (*eklegō*) the most pernicious sayings from the esteemed poets as supporting witnesses (*martures*) in his corrupt teaching. One example of this practice is a seemingly unobjectionable line from Hesiod (*Works and Days* 311):

> ἔργον δ' οὐδὲν ὄνειδος, ἀεργίη δέ τ' ὄνειδος.
>
> Work is no reproach; but not working is a reproach.

According to the accusation, Socrates rather extraordinarily took the first half of the line as advice to refrain from no deed of daring that may lead

---

[28] On this work, see Snell 1944: 178–79 (= Classen 1976: 489).

[29] *Frogs* 1113–14. Havelock 1982: 302, 312, 288 n. 62; for anthologies, cf. Barns 1951: esp. 3–8. See Dover 1993: 34 for a different view. An anachronistic suggestion is that these were books of poetics: A. W. Verrall, *CR* 22 (1908): 174–75; Radermacher 1954: 303–4.

[30] On this family of words, see O'Sullivan 1992: 130–32.

[31] Xenophon *Symposium* 3.5; possibly the same Niceratus who was bested in a rhapsodic competition by Pratys (Aristotle *Rhetoric* 1413a6ff.): cf. Reincke, "Nikeratos (1)," and Diehl, "Nikeratos (2)," in *RE* 17 (1937): 312–13 and 313–14.

[32] Xenophon *Memorabilia* 1.6.14; "unraveling" nicely combines manipulating the papyrus roll with "interpreting" a dense saying (*anelissō*, "read, interpret," LSJ s.v.).

to profit, apparently taking *ouden* with *ergon* to mean, "There is not any deed that is reprehensible." This is perverse syntax, but it creates a phrase that could have served as the motto of an Alcibiades or Critias.[33] The *Condemnation* cited other, Homeric verses that, it says, Socrates "often" cited and interpreted (*exhegeisthai*) in an antidemocratic way, all of which Xenophon counters by giving a positive, democratic reading of the same texts.

Snippets extracted from song to be reused in a variety of situations become general maxims about life, and it is perfectly credible that Socrates had his favorite all-purpose verses.[34] Xenophon calls Socrates an "admirer" (*epainetēs*) of a certain line of Hesiod's ("according to your powers (*kad' dunamin*) perform the rites of the gods," *Works and Days* 336: *Memorabilia* 1.3.3). Socrates interpreted the phrase *kad' dunamin* broadly as "as your means will allow," and said it this was "fine advice" (*kalēn . . . parainesin*) not only for dealing with the gods but in all dealings of life. The little tag, with its Hesiodic piety and memorable Aeolic inflection, apparently came in very handy for the barefooted philosopher on a number of occasions.

Anthologizing supported the belief in the worthiness of traditional musical culture while making it possible to acquire without so much leisure and means. It also involved a reutilization of poetic traditions for a democratic city. As quotable phrases, Hesiodic agricultural saws or Homeric heroic lines were imbued with a universal and timeless wisdom. Exploiting this flexibility, teachers were able to claim that old poetry remained meaningful and authoritative in changing times.

Poets as Teachers and Teachers of Poetry

Singing was connected with education in Greece from very early times, but actual attestations of the idea that poets are teachers are less early than one might think, and they show profoundly different conceptions of what poets teach. The poets who taught adolescents to dance and sing for civic festivals, for example, were said in classical Greek to "teach" (*didaskalos*) them, and this included more than words and steps: choral training was a form of acculturation, and it could be said that through the chorus, the poet taught the city the myths and values that bound them

---

[33] The same line is subjected to sophistic (characterized as "Prodicean" 163D) hairsplitting by Critias in Plato *Charmides* 163B to separate banausic "labor," which may bad, from "doing" one's own thing, which is always good. See Ford 1999b: 237–39 on the subsequent (Xenophon *Memorabilia* 1.2.58) political interpretations of *Iliad*. 2.188–91, 198–202, in which Odysseus restrains the kings and subdues the troops.

[34] Halliwell 1988: 120, 152.

together and connected them to the gods.[35] The chorus in *Frogs* is referring to itself when it says, "It is right that the sacred chorus advise and teach things that are beneficial and useful for the city" (686–87). Elsewhere in that play, "teaching" can refer both to the poet's shaping the moral character of his audience (1019, 1069) and to his training the chorus to perform the play (1026).

Epic had a different role and place in civic life, but it was often claimed that its stories of the deeds of gods and heroes were educative. In support of the idea that spreading fame was always a form of teaching, it may be argued, after Havelock, that the role of the oral poet was above all to preserve, formulate, and convey social norms.[36] Heroic stories are recounted by the heroes to each other as moral examples: in the *Iliad*, Phoenix tells Achilles the story of Meleager from "the fames of long ago" to try to dissuade him from his wrath, and Mentes/Athena stirs a disconsolate Telemachus into action in the *Odyssey* by recounting the famous exploits of another great man's son, Orestes.

Yet there is nothing explicit in the epics about an educational role for song; rather, the pleasure song gives is stressed, as is its ability to banish care.[37] Leonard Woodbury is right to observe that "no one from the pre-Sophistic period speaks of teaching as the function of poetry,"[38] and that "the idea that teaching is rather a function, though not the sole or principal function of poetry, begins to occur in elegy." W. J. Verdenius has collected the evidence for the idea of Homer as "educator of the Greeks," but his compendious survey makes clear that before the classical period, explicit claims that poets teach are very few and far between. The first characterization of epic poets as teachers comes with Xenophanes, who was polemicizing when he said, "From the beginning all mortals have learned from Homer."[39] Heraclitus called Homer "wiser than all other Greeks" before going on to show his ignorance (B 56 DK); in the same way, he called Hesiod "the teacher (*didaskalos*) of the vast majority of people," despite his fundamental ignorance of cosmology (B 57 DK). Xenophanes and Heraclitus have been understood as providing the first clear articulation of the didactic function of poetry,[40] but their statements may

---

[35] LSJ s.v. *didaskalos* II. See Herington 1985: 24–25; cf. Calame 1977, 1:386 ff.

[36] Havelock 1963: 61–86, esp. 61: "The warp and woof of Homer is didactic, and . . . the tale is made subservient to the task of accommodating the weight of educational materials which lie within it."

[37] Dover 1993: 10–14 and 16, on the "strong archaic tradition of delight as the aim of the poet"; cf. Maehler 1963: 15, 25–31; Harriott 1969: 121–25. On Hesiodic and Homeric passages, Heath 1987: 5–7; Ford 1992: 49–52. The bard whom Agamemnon installed at home to watch over Clytemnestra (*Od.* 3.267) has been viewed as something of a tutor.

[38] Woodbury 1986: 247–48.

[39] Xenophanes B 10 DK; see Lesher 1992: 80–81.

[40] Lanata 1963: 113, very strongly: Untersteiner 1956.

have been intended to point out an unrecognized fact rather than to repeat a cultural commonplace, as when cultural critics oppose widespread notions that video games or television are harmless entertainment and argue that they provide powerful models for behavior. Very similar is Herodotus' pronouncement that Homer and Hesiod have taught the Greeks about the gods (2.53). This is not praise of the poets' omniscience (in which Herodotus does not believe), but part of a historical argument that Greek images and conceptions of divinity derive from them and not from poets thought to be earlier.

Russell subtly suggests that "the 'didacticist' view is perhaps always a product of a situation in which poetry appears to need defense."[41] Claims for the authority of poetry are polemical as far back as we can see (e.g., Hesiod *Theogony* 26–28), and Xenophanes, Heraclitus, and Herodotus may be exaggerating the authority of poets only to show that it belongs to themselves instead. We should regard both the educational view and its opposite as contentious assertions rather than as mirrors of cultural fact. It may be significant that Xenophanes and Heraclitus coincide with our first references to formal schooling in literacy in Greece. Herodotus reveals that children were "learning their letters" in the capital city of Chios in the first decade of the fifth century, and very likely the texts would have included epic (note that "schoolteacher" is one sense of *didaskalos* that Heraclitus applies to Hesiod).[42] Xenophanes and Heraclitus may be reacting to a new way of acculturation through reading traditional songs, supplementing both choral education, in which the poet was teacher for various age-classes, and rhapsodic performance, which was declaimed before a wider public.[43]

The latter third of the fifth century provides a second clustering of testimony to the idea of poets as teachers, and this coincides with another educational revolution—the establishment of sophistical, higher education in Athens. Aristophanes often airs the view that poets should teach men and make them better. One of the key passages is the catalog in *Frogs* that presents Homer as a teacher of "marshaling (*taxeis*), acts of courage (*aretas*), and the arming of men" (*Frogs* 1036) in the company of Or-

[41] Russell 1981: 86.

[42] Herodotus 6.27.2. On the relative paucity of schools outside of urban centers, Harris 1989: 96–102; on the dubious "Solonian" laws regulating schools in Aeschines (1.9–11), see Ford 1999b: 242–43.

[43] Herodotus 6.27.2 also mentions 100 Chiote youths who were sent as a chorus to Delphi; cf. Pausanius 5.25.2–4, with Herington 1985: 186; Nagy 1990: 407–9. According to Athenaeus 456f, Simonides was reputed to have taught in the *choregeion* of the port city of Ceos; the "chorus-building" was near a temple of Pythian Apollo and had a painting on the wall depicting Epeius drawing water for the Atreidae before Athena inspired him to make the wooden horse, a theme that figured in the *Iliou persis* and Stesichorus 200 *PMG*.

pheus, Musaeus, and Hesiod. But we have seen that this passage reflects not so much venerable tradition as an enlightened reinterpretation of musical history in which old singers are assigned a role in the progress of civilization. In another passage from the *Frogs* (1008–12), Aeschylus asks, "Why do we marvel at a poet?" and Euripides replies, "For cleverness and advice (*dexiotētos, nouthesias*); we make men better citizens (*beltious en polesin*)." In an illuminating discussion, Dover calls these "the most important lines in the play," but Dover does not persuade when he glosses the words as a rhetorical opposition between form (*dexiotēs*) and content (*nouthesia*).[44] The contrast here is ethical and stylistic at once: *dexios* characterized a speaker or saying as striking, memorable, bold, and witty: Aristophanes uses it especially of Euripides (71, 1009, sarcastically at 1121), and his Dionysus uses *dexios* for the "fecund" (*gonimos*) poet who is capable of producing "noble" (*gennaion*) and "bold" (*parakekinduneumenon*) expressions.[45] *Nouthesia*, a word made by compressing old gnomic formulas for "putting a wise thought in the heart," implied gravity, moral authority, concern for the other's well-being.[46] Aristophanes is combining two styles of using poetry; the one offers sophistication, diversion, and wit—for example, the ridiculous but modern "Aether, Zeus' bedroom (*dōmation*)"; the other promises moral soundness. The opposition between *nouthesia* and *dexiotēs* is between "the time-honored, traditional" education bent on inculcating courage and moderation, and the new, based on science and sophistication.[47] Euripides claims to offer both, and Aristophanes neglects neither in boasting of his own worth: he offers "novel concepts and sophisticated wisdom" (*dexias sophizomai, Clouds* 548), and he takes on in many passages the traditional posture of the choral, festival poet who advises his city.[48]

Of course, the jokes would not be funny unless all these ideas were current, and no doubt many Greeks in the fifth century took the view that the purpose of old poetry was to educate.[49] But I suggest that it was

[44] Dover 1993: ad loc.

[45] *Dexiotēs* has affinities with what Aristophanes dubbed "subtle-speaking" (*leptologein* in *Frogs* 876, 828, *Clouds* 320, 1496; cf. *Knights* 100, Hermippus 21 *PCG*).

[46] Cf. *noutheteseis* in *Protagoras* 326A for the "many admonitions" in "the works of good poets."

[47] See the definition of *nouthetētikēn* at Plato *Sophist* 229E–230C, with Nussbaum 1980: 43–44.

[48] For passages representing the comic poet as teacher of useful things to the city, see Dover 1974: 29–30, and the discussion of Henderson 1990.

[49] So Heath 1987: 41. Isocrates explains that "our ancestors" enshrined Homer in education so that, "hearing his verses *over and over*, we might learn to hate the barbarians and desire to emulate the excellent deeds of his warriors" (*Panegyricus.* 4.159). Aeschines affirms the usefulness of boys "learning the *gnōmai* of Homer by heart" (*ekmanthanein*) when young to use in later life (*Against Ctesiphon* 135).

especially teachers of poetry who advanced the claim that poets were teachers. The idea that a poet is a teacher is likely to have appealed to teachers, whether the schoolmasters who introduced the young to these improving works or the professors who showed young adults hidden depths in the common texts. A teacher in Plato says that a reason for young Athenians to learn "the works of good poets" is that they contain "many admonitions, admiring descriptions, and encomia of good men, with the result that the child may desire to emulate their deeds" (Plato *Protagoras* 325E–326A).[50] A closer look at what fourth-century educators actually found in Homer shows that, when new claims for the educative value of poetry followed the rise of sophistry in Athens, a new Homer followed in their wake.

Homer and the Generals

It is usually assumed that Plato attacked Homer and the poets[51] because of their immense influence as teachers and cultural authorities for the Greeks. He says as much himself (*Republic* 598D–E, 599A):

> We must examine tragedy and its leader Homer, since we hear from some that these men understand all the *tekhnai*, and all matters having to do with human virtue and baseness, and indeed divine affairs. . . . Is there something in what they say, and do good poets in fact know those things *about which they seem to the many to speak well*?

The wide dissemination of epic in this culture cannot be doubted.[52] But the *Republic* is set in the most sophisticated and cosmopolitan city in Greece a full century after Xenophanes' and Heraclitus' attacks (attacks that had been rebroadcast from the Athenian stage by Euripides).[53] Even the poets' professors, the sophists, could be rather cavalier in revealing Homer's inadequacies as they brought their novel approaches to bear on

[50] There was an educational potential in the "Trojan oration" of the sophist Hippias (A 9 DK), which he performed in schools; its pretext is that a young man asks an old hero what pursuits will lead him to becoming "highly reputed" (*eudokimōtatos*).

[51] I shall often follow Plato and use "Homer" as emblematic of the poetic tradition. This key linkage is established at *Republic* 595C, 598E, 607A, *Theaetetus* 152C (Epicharmus of comedy, Homer of tragedy); cf. Aristotle *Poetics* 1448b34–49a2.

[52] E.g., P. Murray 1996: 20–21: "Knowledge of Homer's poetry could impart technical expertise, but it was also essential for the cultivated man since it provided him with the moral and ethical examples on which he should model his own behavior." By contrast, Herington (1985: 71) characterizes the Homerolators in Plato as "the desperate and confused cries of a rear guard in the final retreat of a song culture."

[53] See Xenophanes "C" fragments (Imitations) in DK, and Dodds 1957: 182, 197 nn. 20, 21.

this staple of basic literary education. And they were quite prepared to assume for the purpose of argument that poetry was intrinsically deceptive and that its aim was pleasure rather than truth.[54] It is true that many fifth-century philosophers and sophists cited Homer along with other old poetry to support their theories, but these passing nods to tradition are usually accompanied by such strong mis- or re-readings as to give the impression that it is the writer's virtuosity rather than Homer's wisdom that is being displayed.[55] Rhapsodes may well have commanded large audiences at poetic exhibitions, but the upper classes could regard them as stupid, and Plato's *Ion* denied enthusiasts of Homer any pretension to expertise.[56] The educated classes in Athens continued to imbibe their Homer along with their letters, but seem to have had only a moderate view of its benefits: in *Protagoras* it is admitted that one studies poetry "for education (*paideia*), as befits (*prepei*) a nonprofessional and a gentleman (*idiōtēn kai eleutheron*)," and that parents charge lyre- and letter-teachers with instilling into their children "good" or decorous comportment (*eukosmia*) more than anything else (312B, 325D–E).

Sophistic and other higher education supplied elites with a more sophisticated familiarity with songs than they had acquired in youth from letter- and lyre-teachers (*grammatistēs* and *kitharistēs*). Among sophisticates, it was amusing to hear one who was "extraordinarily insightful" into Homer (*deinoi peri Homērou*), one who could analyze, rationalize, and often etymologize his myths so as to restore them, cleverly and often paradoxically, to respectability among well-educated but modern-minded men.[57] For this reason, when we hear that Homer knew important things, we may be hearing attempts to cloak contemporary practices and innovations with the authority and prestige of tradition. The declaration attributed to Protagoras (*Protagoras* 316D) that the ancient poets were really sophists and teachers of virtue in disguise cut two ways: it afforded sophists a certain sanction for their profession by suggesting that they were a continuation, in prose as it were, of traditional training in *aretē*; and at the same time, it placed Homeric poetry among the highly valued "useful" discourses of the day, and converted the heroic poet into an expert in such things as concerned the sophists and their audiences: "man-

---

[54] E.g., Gorgias B 23 DK; *Dissoi logoi* 3.17; Plato *Gorgias* 502B.

[55] See Ford 1997a: 94–96.

[56] Plato's figure of "10,000" for a rhapsode's audience in *Ion* is only notional, meant suggest the theatricality of rhapsodic performance: see Boyd 1994.

[57] For the term *deinos peri Homērou*, cf. Plato *Cratylus* 407A–B, *Protagoras.* 339A (= Protagoras A25 DK). Cf. Aristotle on the *Homērikoi* (*Metaphysics* 1093a27), who notice small differences but overlook great ones.

aging one's domestic affairs and being eminent in the city" (*Protagoras* 318E).[58]

This can be seen by taking one specific issue on which ideas had changed since Homer's times and looking at how Homer's classical champions supported him from specific texts. Of the many spheres in which traditional reverence for Homer's expertise needed to be adjusted to democratic realities, I choose one that was allowed to be among the "most important," his knowledge of military affairs.[59] This topic was the one Homer seemed *prima facie* to say the most about, for military tactics and leadership are the special expertise given to him in *Frogs*. But analysis will show how it was necessary to reinterpret ancient verses to make them applicable to contemporary realities.

On Plato's picture of Homer as an educator, quoted above, J. M. Adam comments suggestively:

> It is by no means extravagant to suppose that such views [i.e., that the poets know many valuable things] were actually maintained in Plato's time, though Pericles, for example, had a different criterion for strategic ability when he told Sophocles that he knew how to compose poetry but not how to command an army.[60]

Adams' example is telling, for anecdotes from the fifth century reflect a realization that the traditional forms of education, especially *mousikē*, were not after all necessary prerequisites for leadership. We have noted that Themistocles was said not to have learned how to play the lyre but knew how to make a city great, and Stesimbrotus says the youthful Cimon had an unsupervised early upbringing and so acquired neither *mousikē* nor any of the other liberal arts practiced by the Greeks.[61] These stories reveal a separation between the traditional aristocratic education in *mousikē* and fitness for leadership of the naval empire.

The separation of musical and military skill reflects a complex change in the office of general (*stratēgeia*) after Pericles, when the old elite could no longer expect to be the sole group from which generals were elected. Wealth was still important for the office, for no other reason than that a

---

[58] Cf. *Republic.* 600C–D: Protagoras and Prodicus and many others persuade students "that will they be able to manage neither their household nor their city (οὔτε οἰκίαν οὔτε πόλιν τὴν αὐτῶν διοικεῖν οἷοί τ' ἔσονται) unless they understand their *paideia*." Cf. *Symposium* 209A; Xenophon *Symposium* 4.6; and Ford 2001: 99.

[59] Generalship is among the "most important" things Homer has to teach at *Republic* 599C and at Xenophon *Memorabilia* 4.2.10 ("among the finest and most important").

[60] Adam 1965 on 598E.

[61] Ion of Chios F 13 (= Plutarch *Cimon* 9.1), cf. Plutarch *Themistocles* 2.3. Stesimbrotos 107 F 4 *FGrH* (= Plutarch *Cimon* 4).

wealthy general could provision troops as needed, but toward the end of the fifth century, comic poets complain that common scapegraces are being elected to the post.[62] The incursion of the power of sheer wealth into what had been a vocation of the cultured elite could suggest that the traditional education by which the old families had raised their children was no longer an essential formation.[63] Hence to claim Homer as a teacher of military leadership had strong implications for the democratic city, even if our sources are unwilling to state it baldly: if Homer teaches generalship, then those who have learned a good deal of Homer are most suited for the office.

The problem with this idea was that military command was an office for which democratic practice had to allow for real expertise, even to the extent of circumventing safeguards against excessive influence by one individual: unlike most administrative positions, which were filled by lottery and were held for a limited period of time, the generals were elected by the assembly and could be re-elected as many times as the people wished.[64] As the century went on, generals were no longer chosen from each of the tribes, and at its end, the office could even be given to a foreigner, as Socrates maliciously points out to the Ephesian Homerist Ion (*Ion* 541C–D).[65] The office of general thus made the question of competence urgent, and Pericles' denial of the skill to Sophocles was a joke with a serious side. Because Plato was aware of this, he returned to the example of the general in harassing praisers of Homer. Whether the poet can teach generalship is the capping argument in *Ion* (esp. 541B–C), and it figures prominently in *Republic* 10 (599). In Xenophon, too, Socrates quizzes generals and would-be generals about Homer's military ideas.[66]

---

[62] So Eupolis fr. 384 *PCG* (Stobaeus 4.1.9); cf. *Frogs* 718–37, with Dover 1974: 36 and Davies 1981: 128. A good example of the type is the high-toned, well-educated general who lectured the court on poetry in Aeschines 1, *Against Timarchus*: see Ford 1999b: 251–52.

[63] On these complex developments, see Davies 1981: 122ff. and app. 2.

[64] See Dodds 1959: 209 on *Gorgias* 455D. *Protagoras* 319 suggests Athenians listened to experts.

[65] See Moore 1974: 433–36. The issue frames the *Ion*: its opening reminds us that Ion is from Ephesus, which, we are reminded near the end, is under Athenian control, and Athens "will not elect Ion a general" (541D). Ion's name may encapsulate his rootless existence: Socrates asks him why, foregoing any chance to make his city great, he "wanders around (*periiōn*, 541B8) Greece rhapsodizing." Cf. *Republic* 600D: if Homer or Hesiod were really able to help men toward virtue, their followers would never have suffered them to "go around (*periiontas*) rhapsodizing" (600D), but would have ensured that they stayed with them.

[66] Cf. Davies 1981: 129, who discusses Xenophon *Memorabilia* 3.4, Socrates' conversation with Nicomachides ("Victor Von Battle"), a veteran who had just lost an election as

This was a field, then, in which pieties toward old traditions would be hard pressed against current realities. What was there really in Homer to meet the needs of fifth-century armies? Taking a specific Homeric phrase having to do with generalship shows how Homer had to be re-read in the light of fifth-century notions of leadership.

Xenophon's Socrates asks a man who has just been elected general, "But why on earth does Homer praise (*epainese*) Agamemnon by calling him 'both a good king and a mighty spearman, too'?"[67] Socrates is puzzled about what being a "mighty spearman" (*Iliad* 3.179) has to do with being a leader, heroic single combat having little relevance in modern warfare. Although Socrates is eventually able, with a good deal of ingenuity, to discover the ideal Socratic leader in Homer's phrase ("For the people have chosen [elected!] him general not so that he should do well in his own interests, but so that they should fare well under him," *Memorabilia* 3.2.3), there is an observable strain as readers try to hold both Homer and modern military science on the same high level.

In some contexts, such as elite sympotic conversation, the idea of practical benefits from Homer could be given a wild ride, acknowledging that the game was played with less than complete seriousness. Xenophon recounts a dinner-party discussion in which each guest proclaimed the greatest benefit he could confer (*Symposium* 4.3.3). Niceratus, memorizer of whole epics, naturally claims to make men better (*beltious esesthe*) through his familiarity with Homer, "the most wise," and offers to instruct the company on "skill in household economy, in public speaking, or in generalship." At this, the savant and expert on Homer Antisthenes immediately wonders if Niceratus knows generalship because "Homer praised (*epainēsenta*) Agamemnon in calling him '*both* a good king and a mighty spearman, too.'" (*Iliad* 3.179 is the same line that Socrates has discussed with the general; there were evidently favorite passages from Homer's big poems to use in debate.) Niceratus does not shrink from the challenge, but it is really a challenge in quoting Homer. Hence no one objects when he playfully shifts his ground from generalship to the art of chariot-driving: "Yes, I do know, and I know that in driving a chariot you have to guide it around the turning point"; he goes on to paraphrase Nestor's advice to Antilochus at *Iliad* 23.323 and 334 before reciting three of Nestor's difficult verses (*Iliad.* 23.335–37).

---

general to the militarily undistinguished but wealthy Antisthenes (a *chorēgos*, 3.4.3–4). Equally rich is *Memorabilia* 3.1 on Dionysiodorus, a sophist from Chios who, with his brother Euthydemus, taught generalship and rhetoric (cf. Plato *Euthydemus* 271c). Socrates quotes a tag from Homer (*Iliad.* 3.170) to tease one of his students.

[67] Xenophon *Memorabilia* 3.2.2: = *Iliad.* 3.179 (*basileus te . . . agathos karteros t' aikhmētēs*), Alexander's favorite verse, according to Plutarch.

Expertise in charioteering was another irrelevant skill for fifth-century generals, but this old chestnut of a text—also quoted in the *Ion*—was a perfect bit of technical-sounding lore to be found in Homer.[68] That this is all in sport becomes very clear as Niceratus goes on (4.7): "Besides this, I know something we can put into practice right away; for Homer says somewhere 'an onion too, a relish for the drink.' If someone brings an onion you will have benefited (*ophelēmenoi esesthe*) and you will drink more pleasantly (*hēdion*)." With agreeable self-irony, Niceratus offers another chestnut, from the poet's "Nestor's cup" passage, as his ultimate piece of "useful" Homeric knowledge.[69] This—unlike his knowledge of generalship or charioteering—it is actually possible to test in present circumstances, and so Antisthenes' challenge is met by sidetracking it into a call for drink. With equal tact and sophistication, Socrates seconds the change of topic, allegorizing the Homeric line about relish (*ospon*) as a warning against self-indulgence.[70] Nobody in this select company takes Homer very seriously, even as all are adroit at playing with him. The implication of Niceratus' performance is that the real benefit of knowing Homer was that it was a way to add "relish" to sympotic conversation.

These considerations make it hard to believe that old verse carried an unquestioned acceptance among at least those Athenians who could read the *Republic*. We must realize that proclamations of Homer's massive authority are often a fantasy of the good old days or a polemical exaggeration. The claims for Homer's wisdom cited by Plato must be analyzed as ideological constructs within a highly complex nexus of assertions and counterassertions. If they appear simply to carry on an established tradition of the poet's authority, they actually are reconstructing it, repositioning Homer yet again within contemporary ways of viewing the world. And heroic Homer came to look very different when he was read and recited in democratic Athens.

Other forms of song were also affected by the democritization of musi-

---

[68] *Iliad.* 23.335–40 is quoted by Ion (his first chance to perform in the dialogue) at Socrates' request as an example of the *tekhnai* Homer knows: *Ion* 537A–B. For the small textual differences, see Labarbe 1949: 90–101, Van der Valk 1963–64, 2: 315.

[69] *Iliad.* 11.630: *epi kromuon potōi opson*. Stesimbrotus of Thasos discussed the passage (107 F 23 *FGrH*). *Iliad.* 11.630 is also quoted at *Ion* 538C, along with two lines conflating *Iliad* 11.639–40, 630 to test Homer's medical knowledge. The passage is referred to again in *Republic* 405E–406A, where it is taken (surely ironically, as Glaucon admits that it seems bizarre medical lore, 406A1) as testimony of the severe medicine of the good old days. (For the apparently accidental substitution of Eurypulus and Patroclus for Machaon and Hecamede, see Labarbe 1949: 101–8.)

[70] On the ethics of "relishes" (*opson*), cf. *Republic* 372C–D; Xenophon *Cyropaedia* 6.2.28.

cal culture. As musical culture steadily expanded, Athenian symposia developed more elaborate singing games to display an ever more elusive musical distinction. While everyone was still obliged to sing the paean and to contribute a short lyric when the myrtle branch came his way, in the second half of the fifth century, the "most discerning" (sunetōtatoi) and "wisest" among the company would perform more difficult songs from the likes of Stesichorus, Simonides, or Pindar to their own accompaniment on the lyre.[71] But we can see the incursion of new forms of cleverness with the generation that would fight the Peloponnesian Wars. Eupolis complained that "it's out of date to sing the songs of Stesichorus and Alcman and Simonides, when one can listen to Gnesippus [a tragic poet], who discovered songs for adulterers to sing at night and woo women from their homes" (148 PCG). And he lamented that the works of Pindar were being consigned to silence, "because the masses fail to appreciate beauty" (ὑπὸ τῆς τῶν πολλῶν ἀφιλοκαλίας, 398 PCG).

The fact that Eupolis used Pindar's own trope of silence for obscurity (katasesigasmena, if this word be restored from Athenaeus 1.3a) indicates that he exaggerated, but a change in styles of philokalia is not to be doubted. A famous passage in Clouds shows a nouveau-riche father trying in vain to coax a show of dexiotēs from his wastrel son: he first requests that the boy take up a lyre and "sing" a lyric (melos) of Simonides, a custom the young man finds "archaic" and suitable for dinners of "grass-hoppers."[72] The father fares no better when he proposes the easier feat of taking up the myrtle branch and reciting a snatch of Aeschylean verse (lexai, cf. rhēsin lexai, Acharnians 416); finally he descends to asking for a recitation (1370) from the younger, clever (sophoi) poets, like Euripides, we understand.[73]

In the democracy, the trend was increasingly against old and, once decontextualized, obscure lyric songs and toward the collections of metrically simple but clever "little sayings" of Euripides, himself seen as a collector of sayings (stōmuliosullektadē). Of course, lyre-playing remained one of the accomplishments of liberally educated men, and refined musical culture continued to be sought among the leisured, as we shall see the next chapter. In these circumstances, the texts of old lyric songs

---

[71] Cf. Dicaearchus 88 Wehrli and Artemon of Cassandreia apud Athenaeus 694a–c, with Harvey 1955: 162–63, Reitzenstein 1893: 24–43.

[72] Clouds 1355–70. (ὡσπερεὶ τέττιγας ἑστιῶντα), with Dover 1968: lix–lxiv, 252; Morrow 1960: 341.

[73] This is possibly the background against which to understand the story of the Sicilian captives who saved themselves by their knowledge of Euripides in Plutarch's Nicias (29).

survived as rare cultural objects; those aspiring to *dexiotēs* clung to songs that they were no longer likely to meet frequently in social life of the late fifth century. But musical fashions continued to change, and in the generation that read Plato and Isocrates, yet a further revolution would replace singing songs with talking about them as the most refined form of leisure.

NINE

LITERARY CULTURE IN PLATO'S *REPUBLIC*

THE SOUND OF IDEOLOGY

AS A BRIDGE between the fifth and fourth centuries, this chapter takes up the representation of literary culture in Plato, dramatizations of sophisticated conversation about poetry of the late fifth century that were offered to fourth-century readers. In particular, I consider the parts of the *Republic* that precede Plato's critique of the poets, for this work contains not only an unforgettable if idiosyncratic rejection of art, but also a broader sketch of how poetry has influence in society. Plato's position, which will be illuminated with reference to the materialist poetics described previously, was not simply that old poetry is morally unsound and that all imitations are deceptive, but that human nature precludes the possibility that any nonphilosophical discourse can guide us to moral and scientific wisdom. Understanding Plato's views on this question goes far toward explaining why he did not participate, except as an irritant, in the fourth-century establishment of poetics.

Plato's attacks on poetry in the *Republic*—radically rejecting most traditional educational texts in Books 2–3, and banishing virtually all public forms of song from the ideal state in Book 10—are so well known as to require little comment beyond observing that we should not extract these books from the whole as an essay in aesthetics or pure literary criticism. The first and persistent question of the book is ethical, an inquiry into the nature of justice and the rewards of living justly; censoring poetry only comes into the discussion when this problem is pursued through an analogy between soul and state, and when this in turn raises questions about the optimal education of citizens.[1] This framework entails that the aesthetics of song, to which Plato was acutely sensitive, is always discussed in terms of a social psychology and in relation to political goals. Plato takes poetry in hand because he held it to be powerfully influential in shaping the souls of young citizens and in confirming the habits of those no longer young. It is for precisely the same reasons Aristotle takes up poetry and

---

[1] On this analogy, see most recently Lear 1992; on the broad argument, Kraut 1992. From the first, the "justice" that the interlocutors seek includes relations with the gods: the first definition of justice (331B), extracted by Socrates from Cephalus, is (a) not cheating or lying, and (b) not owing (b1) sacrifices to gods or (b2) money to men. The gods figure also in the speeches of Glaucon (362C) and Adeimantus (364B).

mousikē in *Politics* 7–8, a closely comparable and barely more liberal discussion of how to use the musical arts to habituate young citizens to virtue. Aristotle's *Poetics* is usually taken to be his response to Plato and a justification of poetry as a kind of moral education in the state. But Plato is never mentioned in that work, and a sufficient reply to the more outrageous aspects of the Platonic program is provided by the argument of *Politics* 8 (which makes several specific critiques of Plato's regime): Aristotle finds that state-sponsored musical performances do no harm and can provide a useful form of recreation. Aristotle's views will be taken up in chapter 12.

Because Plato's foray into questions of poetry is an aspect of his attempt to put politics on an ethical basis, censorship of schoolbooks and of civic song must be seen as part of a larger political art of managing public speech and thought (*logos*). This is the political scientist's dream of ensuring that all tales and representations in the city arouse a willing compliance on the part of its citizens with the principles on which the society is based. The insistence that *logos* management is necessary for a just and stable city is one of the more troublingly illiberal features of this work, but one that Plato hardly conceals. As Giovanni Ferrari observes in an excellent discussion, the treatment of poetry in the *Republic* is based on the idea that the majority of citizens, perhaps even all, are to be fed a diet of beneficial fictions. It is with a criterion of "truth" that melds into "what is useful for future citizens to believe"[2] that Plato goes through Homer and other verse, "striking out" or rewriting passages that give harmful representations of the nature of the gods, the deeds of ancestral heroes, and the purposes of human life.[3] The illiberal implications of this are well brought out when Ferrari contrasts such lies with our Santa Claus myth, which may be thought to inculcate worthwhile attitudes in the young but which we are expected to outgrow. By contrast,

> it seems that no one in Plato's ideal society would . . . ever grow out of a literal belief in Santa Claus; and this offends (as it should) our liberal belief that at some stage people must be sufficiently adult to be left as the best judges of whether the poetry to which they expose themselves does them harm or not.[4]

Ferrari's analogy is just; but Plato has more of a point if we realize that in the *Republic* he is finally not talking about poetry but about what we should call *ideology*: poets are prominent tellers of tales, but poetry is no

[2] Ferrari 1989: 112. Cf. *Laws* 663D–664A.

[3] How we are to emend *logoi* about this last topic is suggestively postponed at 392A–C; but what the "poets and prose writers" say on this topic—that many good men suffer and the unjust are often happy—is effectively replaced by the myth of Er (and, implicitly, the Platonic corpus).

[4] Ferrari 1989: 114.

more dangerous in principle than the fairy tales rehearsed to the young by mothers and nurses. As in his examination of individual justice through the larger and clearer example of justice in the state, Plato's discussion of poetry uses a conspicuous discourse in the city to show how people uncritically cobble together from what they read and hear beliefs about the nature of the world. Well aware that poetry often served as a badge status and that Homer's great authority was often only notional, Plato's attacks purposefully reach beyond poetry to intend the entire system of ideological representations in the city.

The ideological effects of poetry are dramatized early in the *Republic*, in the conversation at Cephalus' house that begins just after the opening scene in the Piraeus; talk about justice and poetry connects the introduction to the work with the discussion of education in Book 2. To approach Plato on poetry through this stretch of text is not so oblique as it may appear, for much of the work of Books 2–3 is accomplished indirectly here. In the speeches of Cephalus and Polemarchus in Book 1, and in those of Glaucon and Adeimantus in Book 2, we are shown how poetry has an ethical effect in the city, and specifically how poetry can sow moral confusion even among a well-educated elite. This opening aporetic discussion lays most of the groundwork for the subsequent censoring and banishing of poets. It shows that poetry is an important influence on moral belief, but also that it is only a part of a wider set of influences that mold young citizens and affect older ones in the way that a Hippocratic doctor would say an environment shapes and nourishes bodies.[5] Hence it is hardly surprising that Plato thinks people never become adults, for it is no more likely that people could emerge from ideology than that they could decide to breathe a different air than the one that envelops them.

Poetry *chez* Cephalus

As soon as Socrates steps in the door of Cephalus' house, poetic tags and quotations begin to be tossed back and forth. They lead to the framing of the book's main question, and thereafter quotations and discussions of poetry recur in the speeches by Cephalus' son Polemarchus and by Glaucon and Adeimantus. Following the discussion in the previous chapter of poetry in democratic Athenian culture, we are in a better position to see what goes on in the conversations in the early part of the *Republic*. Cephalus is not Callias, and this is not the *Protagoras*, where a company of super-experts shows off in dissecting a poetic text on *aretē*. The opening

---

[5] Cf. the discussion of climate and character at *Republic* 435E–436A, *Laws* 747D–E. See Lloyd 1987: 28–30, and below on the Hippocratic *Airs* ch. 15. On the general idea, cf. Euripides *Medea* 824 ff., with Page's commentary.

of the *Republic* rather shows the graceful, playful exchange of literary culture by gentlemen accustomed, no doubt through symposia, to use song to talk about ethical issues. In this preliminary scene, Plato shows the kind of moral discussion that traditional education in poetry could, at best, prepare the citizens to engage in.

In his opening conversation with his aged host, Socrates drops a phrase from the poets, asking Cephalus how it feels to be "at that time of life the poets call 'the threshold of old age'" (328E).[6] Cephalus himself is not unmusical and responds by quoting Pindar for having "charmingly expressed" his own view: when an old man is conscious of having done no evil in his life, "he always has hope, agreeable and good, to be his 'nurse of old age' (*gērotrophos*), as Pindar says."[7] Prodded by Socrates, Cephalus admits that his views are not acceptable to the many who think that money is all (329E). But Cephalus insists it all comes down to men's individual characters (*tropos*, 329D3, 329E3, cf. 368B2): those of an orderly and even-tempered nature (the *kosmioi* and *eukoloi*)[8] will use their money to achieve serenity and so will find old age only "moderately difficult" (*metriōs epiponon*).[9] Money in fact is not useful to "just anybody"; it requires a "forbearing" and moderate or "orderly" man (the *epieikēs* and *kosmios*) to use it to meet his obligations to men and gods (331A–B).[10] Cephalus' quality is reflected in his way of quoting poetry: coming from old money, his taste is for a high-minded, if somewhat *démodé*, poet, and what he admires in Pindar is the exquisite phrase; his highest approbation is *kharientōs*—"wonderfully well said, charming."[11] Socrates responds to

---

[6] Early attestations in Homer (*Iliad* 22.60, 24.487; *Od.* 15.246, etc.), Hesiod (*Works and Days* 331), *Homeric Hymn to Aphrodite* 106, and Herodotus 3.14.10. The meaning of "threshold" in this phrase was problematic for the Greeks: schol. *Iliad* 22.60.

[7] Fr. 214 S-M at 331A. My translation puts a comma before *gērotrophos* with Adam (1965), taking *agathē* as added to make a contrast with the preceding *kakē elpis* of the evil man. Otherwise, Jowett: "Hope is present to cheer him (*hedeia*) and to be his kindly (*agathē*) nurse in old age." Cf. *Isthmian* 8.15a (χρὴ δ᾽ ἀγαθὸν ἐλπίδ᾽ ἀνδρὶ μέλειν).

[8] 329D: ἂν μὲν γὰρ κόσμιοι καὶ εὔκολοι ὦσιν, καὶ τὸ γῆρας μετρίως ἐστὶν ἐπίπονον. Adam (1965) points out that Aristophanes (*Fro.* 82) called Sophocles "*eukolos* here in Hades as he was there above"; cf. *Frogs* 359, where the chorus bans from the comic feast anyone who stirs up strife and is not "even-tempered to his fellow citizens" (*mēd᾽ eukolos esti politais*). Dover (1993) on *Frogs* 82 notes the word is in no other play of Aristophanes. Plato *Hippias minor* 364D combines *praos* and *eukolos*. Cf. Anaxandrides fr. 54 PCG. *Metrios* (a moral term in Theognis 964) was "applied to the man who behaves as law and honor require," Dover 1974: 56 n. 18.

[9] Cf. Pindar *Pythian* 3.82–83: fools do not bear the ills sent by Zeus as gracefully (so Race [1997] translates *kosmōi*) as the *agathoi* who manage to display *ta kala*.

[10] Reading with Burnet, at 331B1: οὔ τι παντὶ ἀνδρὶ ἀλλὰ τῷ ἐπιεικεῖ καὶ κοσμίῳ. Cf. *Hippias major* 298E. For *epieikēs*, Dover 1974: 61, 191.

[11] For the force of *kharientōs*, cf. Isocrates *Antidosis* §62, where it is a term critics use for "prettily" (as Norlin translates) in lieu of committing themselves to calling it "well-

the speech as "very finely done" (*pankalōs*, 331c1) and does not trouble the pious old man too much.

Right from the start we learn that the group is elite, and consciously contrasts its values with those of "the many." They are educated, free men at leisure; they are disinclined to talk about money, and find those who talk about it insufferable (330c); they pride themselves on not being enslaved to pleasure, and are fond of stimulating discussions.[12] Where there is civilized discussion, there is poetry. But in this exchange of poetic tags, Cephalus has raised for the first time the question of what justice is, and so an interpretation of poetry has provoked the main question of the *Republic*.

Cephalus' son Polemarchus inherits the argument, but his tastes run to Simonides, a more challenging text to play with since he could be construed either as a sage or as the greedy consort of tyrants.[13] Polemarchus quotes Simonides in defining justice as "giving each man what is owed him" (331D = 642a *PMG*), and his defense of that position aims less to praise Simonides' charm and eloquence than to interpret the poet "correctly" (*orthōs*). Apparently, like many sons of the rich at the time, Polemarchus has had at least a passing acquaintance with the sophistic study of "correct speech" (*orthoepeia*). As usual, Socrates is anyone's match; and in a "transparent misinterpretation"[14] of the Simonidean text, he manages to subvert it. Socrates' counterexample (that it would not be just to return a borrowed sword if the lender had gone insane) evokes the kind of ethical riddle that sophists had taken over from symposia.[15] Socrates also manages to draw in Homer, exploiting his application of the epithet "noble" to the trickster-cheat Autolycus (*Od.* 19.395, quoted at 334A–B) to arrive at the delicious paradox that Simonides' dictum enjoins theft. For all his inventiveness, Socrates is just playing at explaining the poets: with mock reverence for Simonides, "that wise and godlike man" (*theios*, 331E), he confesses, "Though you may know what he means, I don't." As Plato says elsewhere, the problem with using poetic texts as guides to morality

---

spoken." The Pindaric "hope" Cephalus nurtures may have some affinity with Eleusinian mysteries, cf. Richardson 1974: 312, Mikalson 1983: 81–82.

[12] Cf. *Symposium* 173c, where the *logoi* of *philosophia* are called delightful and those of the "wealthy and money-makers" burdensome.

[13] See the excellent study by Bell (1978). In Plato, Simonides has a place among the Seven Sages (*Republic* 335E) and is enrolled along with Homer and Hesiod as a proto-sophist by Protagoras (*Protagoras* 316D); Hippias of Elis had a set lecture on the poet (*Protagoras*, 347B).

[14] Reeve 1988: 8.

[15] The author of *Dissoi logoi* (3.10–11 DK) quotes Cleoboulina's riddle on stealing and deceiving by force to argue, "on the evidence (*marturion*) of the older poems," against conventional notions of justice. Socrates' "borrowed sword" example is close to that at *Dissoi logoi* 3.4 DK.

is that the words in themselves impose no limits on interpretation: it will be hard to make progress in a moral argument with a poet who can speak in riddles (*ēinixato*, 332B14) and use one word when he meant another (332c). Socrates does not in the end find it worthwhile to dispute what the formula given by Simonides means; all one can say is that if it suggests an immoral or impossible meaning, then whoever said it is not wise (335E–336A).[16] This is practical literary criticism for Plato.

These displays of elite culture, whether admirably conventional or sophistically ingenious, do not get the speakers very far in their quest for the meaning of justice, and this is because, as the conversation shows, there is no limit on what poets may be taken to mean: a given interpretation can be confounded by bringing in apparently contradictory passages from the same or other poets, or a text can be radically reoriented by supposing the poet to have been "riddling." This poetasting seems to have reached an impasse, and the brash and ill-mannered Thrasymachus wants to sweep it all away. He alone of the speakers in this book quotes no poetry in his starkly realistic account of justice as the interest of the stronger.[17] But the poets return in force when Glaucon and Adeimantus take up the case Thrasymachus abandons.

As devil's advocate, Glaucon turns from the high-minded sentiments of poets to what "the many" (*hoi polloi*, 358A) actually believe, which is that justice is burdensome (*khalepos*) and, except for the rewards it may bring, to be avoided.[18] As champion of what "everyone believes," Glaucon overturns a verse of pious old Aeschylus in praise of the straightforward and noble man who "wishes not to seem but to be good" (*Seven against Thebes* 592, quoted at 361B6–8). Having argued the benefits of injustice when undetected, he comes back to say that Aeschylus would more properly have said of the *unjust* man that he "wishes not to seem unjust but to be it" (362A). Glaucon's radical rewriting is lent ironic support when he adds the two following lines from the play, which suddenly take on a sinister purport: "Reaping the fruit of the deep furrow of his mind, from which shrewd (*kedna*) counsels spring" (*Seven against Thebes*. 593–94). So little control do the words of Aeschylus impose that a little cleverness can make them imply shrewdness and deceit instead

---

[16] Cf. *Theaetetus* 152A and Ford 1994: 206–7.

[17] The significance of this is unclear to me. The equally radical Callicles cites poetry frequently in *Gorgias*, though he alludes to Pindar on *nomos* (169a S-M) by admitting, "I don't know the poem, but it says that . . ." (484B); Aristophanes in *Frogs* condemns those who chatter pretentiously with Socrates, "rejecting *mousikē* and neglecting the finest parts of the tragic art" (1494–95).

[18] Cf. *Protagoras* 340D–E for the (Protagorean) objection to an interpretation of Simonides' poem on the grounds that it flies in the face of what "everyone thinks," that *aretē* is very difficult (*khalepōtaton*).

of the trustworthiness and profundity Amphiareus commended in context. As Glaucon sees it, the "shrewd counsels" are stratagems for success—for making a profit in ruling, marrying, making compacts, competing, helping friends and harming enemies, and even cultivating the gods. Any words of any poet, no matter how admired, would be grist for Glaucon's mill.

Complementing Glaucon's effort, Adeimantus offers a critique of conventional praisers of virtue for focusing on its rewards rather than on virtue in itself. The distinctive feature of this performance is its comprehensive sweep: Adeimantus marshals Hesiod, Homer, and Musaeus along with other religious authorities, and insists that prose writers are in accord with them in speaking of the painfulness of virtue.[19] Adeimantus in fact is a speaking anthology of the kind that Hippias composed with Orpheus, Musaeus, Hesiod, Homer, and many prose writers (B 6 DK). When he speaks about the young "winging their way" among such sayings (ἐπιπτόμενοι, 365A), he suggests the image of bees gathering nectar that was already being applied to anthologies (*florilegia*).[20]

Adeimantus' closing argument brings us back to Pindar, as Cephalus had begun with him, but this time with a far darker view: he imagines a youth asking himself a question out of Pindar, "By which way will I scale the higher tower?" (fr. 213 S-M at 365B). With yet another glance at tricky Simonides ("Seeming overmasters even truth," 598 *PMG*), Adeimantus concludes with feigned cynicism but real literary culture: one should imitate the crafty ways of an Archilochus while adopting the outward appearance of an admirer of lofty Pindar.

In this final speech, setting Socrates a challenge, Adeimantus illustrates the many strands composing the city's discourse on justice, the account to be found most commonly and among its most prestigious authorities.[21] His praisers of conventional virtue include poets from Hesiod and Archilochus to Simonides and Pindar, and he notes that the same message is to be found in prose writers (363E, 366E). Adeimantus goes even further and looks past what poems people may commend to the beliefs they endorse in what they actually do. For all that "the many" may be willing to pay lip service to the value of the old poets, a deeper *logos* about justice

---

[19] 363B quoting from *Works and Days* 232–33; 364C–D quoting *Works and Days* 287–89; 363B–C quoting *Od.* 19.109–13; 364D–E quoting *Iliad* 9.497–500; 363D cites Orphic ideas. For "prose writers," cf., e.g., Prodicus' "Choice of Heracles," which stresses the theme of the burdensomeness (but worthiness) of virtue. Accordingly, Socrates' subsequent censorship campaign intends both prose and verse traditions: 380C ("in meter or without"), 390A ("in *logos* or in *poiēsis*"), 392A (*poiētai* and *logopoioi*).

[20] Cf. Barns 1951.

[21] 366B: τῶν πολλῶν τε καὶ ἄκρων λεγόμενος λόγος. Cf. Verdenius 1987 on Pindar *Isthmian* 2.10, where he refers to *Olympian* 11.19 (*akrosophon*).

is revealed in what "the greatest cities declare" in their official cults and rites (366B). Socrates' ideal of justice is opposed by an enormous consensus, which can be mapped in a literary tradition that stretches from "the most ancient speeches of the heroes that have been preserved" to the present day (366D–E). The conceit in part establishes the *Republic* as an essay "unattempted in prose or rhyme," as Adeimantus makes clear when he challenges Socrates (366D–367A): "No one in poetry or prose has ever adequately blamed injustice or praised justice" (366E). But he has also prepared us for an analysis of justice that uncovers ideological beliefs not just in the poets, but throughout the city.

The preliminary scenes of *Republic* 1–2 thus illustrate the unreliability of taking poets as founts of wisdom or sources of technical knowledge. The real sources of people's beliefs about justice are deeper and more pervasive. The modern term for all this would be "ideology," the beliefs about the world and about value that govern, invisibly, the lives of the citizens. Poets have contributed conspicuously to ideology, and may be cited to support ideological positions, but they are only part of what Plato is up against. The exercise of Books 1–2 lets us see the larger target Plato has in view. The city's discourse about justice includes anything that anybody with influence over the young says is fine or disgraceful.[22] The topic of censorship takes up the poets (377C–D) only as instances of "greater" tales (*muthoi*) that help us see the "smaller ones," too, since they both come from the same molds (*tupoi*, 377C).

But if this is so, why bother to censor poetry? Why not simply dismiss it, along with all faulty conceptions of justice? Plato has serious reasons for censoring the contents of poems, but these only emerge if we consider how far he entertains and adapts the materialist poetics of the fifth century.

Ideology and the Body

Ferrari's analysis of the *Republic* on poetry is especially valuable for stressing Plato's attack on poetry as *performance* even more than as bearer of ethical doctrines. For Plato, "imitation" certainly has a philosophically abstract aspect that can be analyzed as "representation" versus original, and poetic "imitations" are so analyzed in Book 10.[23] But the attack on "imitation" in Books 2 and 3 is directed at its more immediate,

---

[22] Adeimantus: 363E. Hence Socrates' educational survey joins poets and storytellers: 392D, 394B, etc.

[23] For an excellent discussion of the issues raised in Plato's metaphysical critique of poetry for the status of the *Republic* itself as imitation, see Reeve 1988: 220–31, esp. 226–27.

noncognitive influence on the soul. The word *mimēsis* had a root connotation of "miming" behavior, and the dangers of copying unsuitable models are stressed throughout Plato's critique. The viewer of poetic imitations undergoes an almost physical change, as directly and inevitably as gymnastic exercise shapes the body.[24] In the light of materialist poetics, one understands Ferrari's emphasis on how often Plato conceives of the influence of poetry and music in sheerly physical terms and presents them as an assault on the physical constitution of the auditor. The spectator "imitates" (mimes) in his soul what the performer imitates (represents or externalizes): the "original" is presented as sounds, sights, and gestures that bypass the intellect and "sink" into the soul: *mimēseis* practiced from youth shape the moral character and the physical body (*ethē, phusis, sōma*); patterns of feeling and action deposited there will be repeated in the sounds and thoughts that later emerge (*phōnai dianoiai, Republic* 395D). The reflexive, automatic nature of our response to the charms of poetry and music, especially when our characters are being formed in youth, is why Plato is so relentless—and so literal-minded—in censoring them.[25]

The "miming" aspect of Platonic *mimēsis* is an archaism resurrected with the support of the most advanced scientific outlook of his day. This outlook has complex conceptual debts, partly to the materialism of Democritus and the materialist rhetoric of Gorgias; it also takes from contemporary medical speculation the idea that the natural environment determines the health and function of living things. The key terms of this kind of thinking—nature, stamping, shaping, shape, and form (*phusis, tupoō, plassein, rhuthmos, skhēma*)—pervade Plato's discussion of poetry and operate as proofs at turning points of the argument. They make it clear that Plato found the materialist outlook, if not absolutely true and complete, at least a useful vocabulary for telling his story about poetry's potent effects.

The first image Socrates gives of the influence of imitations is a botanical one: in *Republic* 377B–C, he says that the beginning stages of growth are critical for the development of children as for plants; for a young child, like a shoot, is particularly flexible and able to be "shaped" (*plassesthai*) in various ways. At this time, children receive impressions from the outside world like a "stamp" (*tupoō*), and the shape thus left will persist through later growth.[26] *Logoi* are a direct way of shaping the soul of the

[24] Correspondingly, mechanical occupations warp souls: *Republic* 495D–E.

[25] Hence the importance for both Plato and Aristotle of education as habituation: *Laws* 653A–C, Aristotle *Nichomachean Ethics* 1104b8–12, *Politics* 7.15, 8.5 (esp. 1339a21–25).

[26] On Plato's use of the "stamp" image, Jaeger 1961, 2:258–59. Cf. Gorgias on artfully composed speeches "stamping" the soul (τυποῦν, *Helen* §13), and objects of sight "stamping the soul, even in its character" (ἡ ψυχὴ κἂν τοῖς τρόποις τυποῦται, §15), pp. 181–82

young, as the young body was thought to be shaped by massage.[27] Hence, analyzing the *logoi* to be used in education is a matter of asking, as Ferrari puts it with literal exactness, "what should be allowed to reach the ears of the impressionable young." Socrates says we will not let young children hear stories that are fashioned (*plasthentas*) by just anyone: for mothers and nurses "shape" the soul with tales (*muthoi*) no less than they shape the body with their hands.[28] In *Republic* 2–3, Plato "dumbs down" poetry because of his conviction that poetry literally "shapes" young souls. Poets have a "natural" ability (605A) to please the lowest and first developing parts of the soul.

Hence legislators will have to know the "patterns" (*tupous*)[29] on which poets must compose or shape (*poiein, plassein*) their fables (379A). Fictions are first shaped themselves, and then shape souls accordingly. The canons of what is admissible in poetry in Books 2–3 are a series of "molds" of stories that will form flexible young souls in the best way. The basic purpose of primary education in the *Republic* is to form character, not knowledge (522A).[30] The attitude to education (*paideia* is perhaps better translated "rearing" in these contexts) is as a training of habits: the curriculum is designed to follow nature, to help the *skulax* ("puppy"), whose philosophic "nature" Plato discovers in what we should call its instinctual responses to friend and foe, grow up into an even-tempered *phulax* (375E).[31] With a thoroughly controlled education, Plato hopes to produce a man who has been "born and bred" to be good (φύς τε καὶ τραφείς, 396C), and who will not willingly imitate unworthy men but will actively resent "modeling himself" (*ekmattein*, 396D7) to fit the *tupoi* of base characters. (Except, he adds, for the sake of "sport," leaving a place for sympotic play in life, 396D–E.) *Logoi*, whether mere tales or speeches of a truer sort, shape the soul to take on their shapes.

This is not to deny that Plato is concerned with poetry's cognitive influence in the sense that traditional tales may serve as paradigms of behavior.

---

above. On "shoots" and education, cf. *Laws* 765E and the comparison of education to soil in the Hippocratic *Canon* 3, Aristotle *Nichomachean Ethics* 1179b26.

[27] With 377C, cf. *Airs* ch. 15, which speaks of "shaping" (*anaplassein*) a baby's head to make it grow, cf. 12, 16, 23. A favorite Platonic idea: cf. *Gorgias* 483E (of whelps), *Timaeus* 88C ("shaping" the body corresponding to shaping the soul with intellectual exercises such as mathematics), *Laws* 671C (*paideuein* associated with *plattein*); cf. 789E on massage.

[28] 377C3–4. Cf. 381D–E, 449D; and Adam 1965, 1:114. Called Democritean in inspiration by Delatte (1934).

[29] Cf. *tupos* in *Republic* 380C7, 383A2, 383C6, 387C1, 396D–E, 398A, 398B, and cf. 412B. See a similar use of the trope in *Laws* 801C, cf. 800E; Aristotle adopts the term in *Politics* 1341b29–32, as he takes up the same concerns as *Republic* 3.

[30] See Gill 1985b.

[31] The right music and gymnastics reinforce the honor-loving part of the psyche: *Republic* 411E–412A, 424C–D.

Socrates worries, for example, that the tale of Zeus and Kronos may lead a young person to think he is doing nothing unjust in punishing his father (378B); when the young hear Zeus' lament for Sarpedon in the *Iliad* (388D), they may consider public grieving a not-unworthy activity. But such easy analogies are on the level of a pedagogue's preachments, and were already mocked by Aristophanes, who suggested an adulterer could excuse his conduct by referring to Zeus' many mythic *amours*.[32] Plato is rather concerned with poetry's earliest and most profound influence on young souls, a direct imprinting that bypasses intellection. Ferrari (1989: 111) well observes how objectionable heroic stories are assigned a detrimental physical impact on young constitutions: "shuddering along" with Achilles at death leads to future guardians *softening* themselves (387C); "weeping unabashedly" for Patroclus *saps* endurance at grief (388D); laughter *shakes up* the system (*metabolē*, 388E). The very names of the underworld rivers, the guttural-rich Kokytus and Styx, send a "shiver" through us (*phrittein*, 387B–C) that may disturb the guardians' temperament.[33] Even old Cephalus can speak in such accents when he describes his current frame of mind to Socrates. By no means an advanced intellect, Cephalus is yet accustomed to speak of his character and personality as affected by physiological forces: he finds that in old age, his desires (*epithumiai*) have ceased to "strain and slacken" (329C), and he suggests that his recent susceptibility to anxieties about the afterlife has to do with the increasing feebleness of his physical frame (330D–E).

Only this point of view explains why Plato rejects the tradition of allegorical interpretation as a way of reforming offensive poetry. This is surprising, since in moments of pious skepticism Socrates realizes how often we tell ourselves myths that may contain some truth but that, taken literally, are false (377A). All education, he admits, must contain some falsehoods; what poets are to be blamed for is not "lying well" (377E).[34] It would in principle be possible for him to deal with offensive tales allegorically, by assigning their evil aspects to the surface and discovering the good beneath them. But Socrates rejects this approach: he holds that even

---

[32] *Clouds* 1079–82, where Dover notes that Helen so excuses herself at Euripides *Trojan Women* 948–50, and that Isocrates (10.59) speaks of Zeus as "morally weak before beauty" (*pros to kallos tapeinos*). Cf. Euripides *Hippolytus* 451–58; Plato *Republic* 391E and *Laws* 941B. For Zeus' violent rise to power in the fifth century, cf. Aeschylus *Eumenides* 641; Aristophanes *Clouds* 904–6; Euripides *Hercules furens* 1314–21; and Plato *Euthyphro* 5E–6A (where Euthyphro's *katepinen* seems to refer to *Theogony* 459). Further, see Verdenius 1943: 254–55.

[33] Ferrari 1989: 111. Adam (1965) compares the "shuddering" (*phrikē*) produced by sight in *Phaedrus* 251A.

[34] 377D. Ferrari (1989: 113) makes the important observation that in speaking of "useful" lies, Plato is not "isolating the fictionality of poetic myth; rather he emphasizes that it is speculative."

if a worthy "under-meaning" (*huponoia*) be found in an old myth, the young will not detect it and will be harmed (378D). Not the last critic willing to censor literature in the name of the young, Socrates rejects allegory because the mere surface of the text will misshape the hearer. But for a very small and select group of people, Plato leaves open the possibility that the castration of Ouranos by Kronos may be told. In this, Plato recognizes that stories about such things as theogony will inevitably be fictions about things beyond human knowledge,[35] but that a very rare nature (not necessarily a wealthy one, since the sacrifice is not merely costly but "hard to obtain") can avoid being warped by the tale. For the rest, and this includes not only children but older people, too, such tales as theomachies and the binding of Hera are simply not to be told (378D).

Images in the City

Plato's "shaping" imagery extends beyond the effects of poetry and includes the effects of music, which was the paradigm for the ability of sensory input to move and form the soul. Music "pours into the soul through the funnel of the ears" (411A), and the power of rhythm and harmony is named as the strongest influence on the character of the soul (401D–E). Like many musicologists in the fourth century, Plato's Socrates regards different modes and rhythms as stirring up automatic resonances in the soul, unreflective harmonic responses as it were (398B–400E). Socrates illustrates with another physical analogy, this time from metallurgy: when poured through the ears, music softens spirits like iron being tempered; this can prevent them from becoming too harsh, but too much music "melts" and "dissolves" the hard part of the soul (410C–411E).[36] It is through, and not in spite of, its nature as sound that music educates the characters of guardians, "transmitting by harmony a certain harmoniousness, not knowledge, by rhythm a certain rhythmicalness" (522A).

All of Socrates' poetic and musical proscriptions aim at creating an ideal physical environment for nurturing (*trophē*) young spirits and main-

---

[35] 382C–D (on the tales told to children about gods): "In our ignorance of antiquity, we liken the false to the true as far as we may and make it useful." Cf. *Laws* 886C–D: "Your [Cleinias', i.e., Spartan] excellent institutions prevent what we have, literary narratives of the gods in verse or prose." Still, the Athenian holds that myth is less harmful than scientific atheism: on myths that place primitive realities like sky before the genesis of gods, "Now whether these ancient tales ultimately hurt or help is not lightly to be decided, but they are certainly bad models for our relations to parents. The ancient stories can be left alone, *let them be told any way heaven pleases*; but these modern tales of enlightened men, that gods are stones and hear not, are despicable."

[36] Cf. 387C4–5: "hotter and softer." *Laws* 666C, 671B: like iron in a furnace, drinking makes the spirit softer.

taining older ones. This emerges quite clearly when he moves on from music to censor the visual environment. For sights no less than sounds affect souls: when censoring tales of Gigantomachy, he says such stories must neither be told to children nor embroidered into fabrics, as indeed the ceremonial *peplos* presented to Athena was embroidered with scenes of theomachy.[37] Statues and other products of the crafts, such as houses and furniture, are to be made by those with a sense for the truly "fine and graceful" (401A–D).[38] At this most far-reaching reform (it is simply impractical, rather than undesirable, to go on and legislate manners, dress, business, and so on, 425B), Socrates makes a powerful and revealing analogy: allowing young people to be surrounded by base images is like letting them "graze in a place of bad pasturage; cropping a little here and there each day, they end up by taking great evil into their souls unawares." Conversely, he adds, the young surrounded by ennobling images, "dwelling as it were in a healthy place, will be benefited by everything; and from that place something of the fine works [i.e., a physical emanation] will strike their vision or their hearing, like a breeze bringing health from good places . . . and will, without their being aware, lead them to fair accord."[39] Here, as in the Hippocratic *Airs Waters Places*, a materialist *logismos* connects the environment to its flora and fauna. Plato is not being merely figurative when he says poetry "waters and makes grow" the passions of the soul (τρέφει γὰρ ταῦτα ἄρδουσα, *Republic.* 606D).

Plato's physicalist understanding of culture as an environment has several political implications. It first of all opposes what he calls the popular view that counts freedom the finest thing (*kalliston*, 562c1). If the most common cry in a democratic city is the phrase "free by nature" (*phusei eleutheros*),[40] Plato holds that we are constrained by nature, not liberated by tossing off convention. A further implication is that the formation of character will be determined, constrained by cause and effect, by the surrounding political climate. But to this powerful materialist outlook, Plato adds a saving element of unpredictability, the divine. His world picture does not leave out the divine, just as the divine survived in Democritus

---

[37] Cf. again Socrates' objections to the impiety of these images on the *peplos* or in the poets at *Euthyphro* 6c.

[38] Cf. Asmis 1992: 349. On the power of sight, cf. the proposal to fortify children by making them watch battles, *Republic* 466E–467A; presumably this is to immunize them from the disorienting shock (*ekplēxis*) the sight of enemy arms may arouse, a phenomenon discussed in Gorgias' *Helen* §16.

[39] 401c–D, trans. Allan Bloom. Socrates may be picking up Adeimantus' image of education as bees gathering nectar (365A).

[40] Adam (1965) cites Euripides *Ion* 669–75, Thucydides 2.37.2, Plato *Menexenus* 239a, Aristotle *Politics* 1310a29, 1317a40.

and the doctors, and this will leave an outlet for the production of higher, truer images of reality than poets provide.

The determining natural environment that surrounds growing souls needs an exception to account for just souls emerging in an unjust city like Athens. Democratic institutions produce democratic men; the courts and assemblies of the city are in effect sound boxes, amplifying mass ideology and projecting it to the citizens. As he surveys the democracy, Plato can only account for someone's choosing justice by attributing it to a sort of divine dispensation, the lucky chance of possessing a favored nature (*phusis*).[41] It is a matter of divine dispensation that some people manage even in the democracy to preserve philosophic natures.[42] The idea is adumbrated at 366C–D, where Adeimantus argues in summation that people are usually just out of fear, old age, weakness, or incapacity; the only way he can imagine someone being willingly just is "by some divine nature" (*theiai phusei*) that either makes injustice unappealing to him or gives him knowledge (*epistēmē*) of justice.[43] This suggestion is expanded on by Socrates by reading quite seriously a piece of encomiastic poetry that had once been composed for the Adeimantus and his brother.[44] He responds to the scandalous speeches of Glaucon and Adeimantus with praise of their noble natures: "Oh children of that man," he says, "the beginning of the elegiacs composed for you after the battle of Megara was right: you are descended 'from famed Ariston of godlike race' (*theion genos*). For you have experienced something quite out of the ordinary (*panu theion*) in being able to discourse about the superiority of injustice, all the while not believing it" (368A). The reference to the pair as children of a famous man may at first suggest Thrasymachus, for Glaucon and Adeimantus have inherited his argument as Polemarchus inherited that of his father Cephalus.[45] But they are actually sons of the aptly named Ariston, "Best" (they are Plato's own brothers), and they have from Ariston "the best kind" of inborn natures (*tropoi*), which have "inspired" them to value

---

[41] On the divine as being naturally inspired with learning, courage, magnificence (e.g., 494B), cf. 486A–C, 496C–497A, 499B–C. Cf. also 492A. This is fundamentally aristocratic view: cf. Pindar's use of the demonic to explain success, e.g., *Olympian* 6.8–9, 9.28, 110, *Nemean* 1.9.

[42] Cf. Aristotle's conflation of "the divine" with a favorable endowment as a cause of virtue in *Nichomachean Ethics* 1179b21–31.

[43] 492E. Cf. *Meno* 99E ("arriving via a *theia phusis*, without *nous*") *Laws* 642C; and Aristotle *Nichomachean Ethics* 1.9, 7.1, etc., on whether virtue is a divine gift. At *Republic* 595B, knowledge of the way things are can be an antidote to the damage to reason (*dianoia*) caused by imitative poetry.

[44] Anon. eleg. 1 *IEG*. Schliermacher conjectured it was by Critias, but see Bergk 2: 283–84.

[45] Cf. Adam's note (1965) on 368A1. On *theion genos*, cf. *Laws* 951B.

virtue and not to be corrupted by common beliefs. The proof—and any proof of divine favor is welcome—is in their military valor at Megara. Divine influence alone can explain why, though they have been born into the world of radical sophists like Thrasymachus and can impersonate proponents of such ideas, their natures have somehow escaped being corrupted by the discourses they know how to mimic. The little piece of encomiastic song as well appears to have escaped the fate of most poetry and to have encapsulated, in this case at least, a truth.

The effect of the environment on the nurture of the philosopher, and the need of some divine chance to preserve it, are expounded more fully in Socrates' discussion in Book 6 of how "philosophic natures" are so often corrupted, leading to philosophical impostors taking their place. A natural philosophic endowment (*phusis*) is rare enough to begin with (491A), and only a few grow up unscathed (490D–E). "We know," says Socrates, "that every seed or thing that grows, whether plant or animal, when they do not chance to find their proper nutrition, or climate or locale, feels the lack of these things more strongly to the extent that they themselves are more robust"; as a consequence, the best nature turns out the worst when deprived of proper nutrition (491D). So when the "naturally best" souls (*euphuestatas*, 491E) chance to meet with bad rearing (*paidagōgia*), their perverted strength makes them the worst of men. On the other hand, if a philosophical nature "chances to find the appropriate learning, it will inevitably grow up to reach every virtue" (492A: ἂν μὲν οἶμαι μαθήσεως προσηκούσης τύχῃ, εἰς πᾶσαν ἀρετὴν ἀνάγκη αὐξανομένην ἀφικνεῖσθαι). But if it is not sown, planted, and nourished in what is proper, it will reach every vice—"unless some god chances to be there to aid it" (492A5). This is the way that Glaucon and Adeimantus have turned out well in Athens. The possibility remains for other youths endowed with a philosophic nature (*philosophēi phusei*, 494A) to avoid being corrupted by the *dogmata* of the many at Athens: such souls may respond to protreptic speech (494D) because of an inborn affinity for such speeches (*suggenēs tōn logōn*, 494E1) and can be bent toward philosophy (cf. 495A).

This reflection on protreptic speech is connected to the immense question of the function of the *Republic* itself, what value this imitation of Socratic conversation may have. In the end, what is Plato's defense against the intense "charm" of rhythm and harmony that assaults and affects even those reared to be the best among us (607E)? It is of course the "argument we are making," the *Republic*. The imitation he submits to us as a replacement for those of the poets he is taking away, his "argument" in this book, is significantly characterized in Book 10 as a "countercharm" to be repeated each time we are confronted by the charm of poetry.[46] Plato's desire to rival the poets as a maker of images is well known.[47] We can understand this passage in the light of the ambition of Plato the writer to replace poetry as the basis of education. But calling his own work a counter-charm concedes a sort of equality to the poet, or at least confesses to a stand-off in which it is recognized that both finally are purveyors of *logos* to tender human nature. This passage, like Socrates' repeated return to the question of how his "city in words" may ever come to be,[48] is a daring acknowledgment that he is giving us a "story that might save us if we believe it" (or "are obedient to it," *Republic fin*). As a strategy, the story of the *Republic* has much in common with the "noble lies" Socrates would like to see disseminated throughout the citizenry.[49] Designed partly as "medicines" to temper the natural weakness of youth (377B, 378A), and partly as sheer "myths" to fill the place of human ignorance about "what the truth about ancient things actually is" (382C–D), these stabs at the truth must contain ethically and politically useful meanings.[50] They are dangerous and should only be administered by experts, as drugs by doctors (389B).

For all its rigor and care in reasoning, the *logos* of the *Republic* is no less a spell, a story, words; the whole discussion is a tale (*muthologein*) told at leisure (376D). It resembles the discussion of divine love in *Phae-*

---

[46] Precisely the same conceit in *Laws* 659D–E, where "charms" will educate the young to feel pleasure and pain in accord with the wisdom of the old (cf. the "charms for the soul" at *Laws* 665C); it emerges at 664B that what will form the "tender" (*hapalas*) souls of the young are "the noble things we have said and will say [in *Laws*]."

[47] It is clear in *Laws* that Plato sees his own work as rivaling that of the poets in representing life (cf. *Laws* 811, for replacing school texts with the *Laws* itself, and 817B where "we are the tragic poets of the finest life"; cf. *Phaedo* 61A). The *Republic* also presents "images" of men from the time Glaucon "polished up two paradigms like statues" of happy injustice and miserable justice. The speakers have been looking for a *paradeigma* of justice, like a good painter who creates a perfect paradigm of a beautiful man without worrying if he exists (472C; cf. 540B). Cf. n. 23 above.

[48] 369C; cf. 369A, 472A–E. The city will not come into being until kings philosophize or philosophers are kings: 592A–B.

[49] Esp. 382A–383C, 414B–415D; cf. 389B–D, 458B–460B. Other forms of deception, 459A–460A. As a good example of a useful myth about something beyond our ken, Ferrari (1989: 113) compares *Timaeus* 29C–D, 48D–E. In an otherwise valuable discussion, Reeve (1988: 208–13) splits hairs to defend Plato, arguing that the producer class will not be victims of "false ideology," although their ideology is "falsely sustained."

[50] Socrates censors stories about gods "so that our guardians may be god-fearing and divine insofar as a human being can possibly be" (383C). This requires that they "honor gods and ancestors and take their friendship with each other seriously" (386A), thus avoiding strife (*eris*); hence censoring stories of battles and disputes of gods (378C–D) and Socrates' discussion of the evils of *stasis* with Thrasymachus at 351D–E. He censors stories about Hades as "neither true nor beneficial" in fostering courage (386A–387B). Babut (1974: 107) notes that Plato's "neither useful nor true" (380C, 381E, 386C) combines the double criteria of Xenophanes: the stories are not true (*plasmata*) and not useful (*khrēston*).

drus 246C, where the immortal is not named by reasoned speech; yet, having neither seen nor conceived the god, we *fashion* some immortal *zōon*. But it may be that works of words can be so constructed, so made, as to exert a beneficent "charm" over the souls they reach.[51] Human nature being what it is, Plato could find no better way to bring about the best possible life for those who have been raised as we have been raised, who are constituted as we are.

To sketch the informing context of Plato's critique of poetry and culture is not to endorse his repressive measures; but it does bring out his far-reaching view of the nature of poetic authority. However illiberal Plato may be, his strictures on popularly circulated images and stories about reality stem from a powerful conception of the pervasiveness of ideological messages in the city: like some modern cultural critics, he believes we get ideas about what human beings are and how best to live not only from the official, authoritative discourses in society, but also from images produced by poets along with sculptors, painters, and even those who make household furniture. Plato holds that the entire visible and audible environment shapes our beliefs about our relations to those around us and to whatever gods there be. This insight makes more compelling his further suggestion that the harmful representations of his day cannot be overcome except by the substitution of other, more salutary representations. Plato declared himself a philosopher and not a poet; but when a philosopher has to do with mere mortals, the best one can do is to supply representations of reality that reason suggests are most useful for life.

As a critic of ideology influenced by materialist science of the fifth century, Plato on poetry appears as a kind of cultural materialist. Whether we find his descendants in the Marxian cultural tsars who set out rigid molds for literature and the arts in society's best interest, or in the attempt by Freud to foster individual happiness by regulating brute and unthinking forces in the psyche, Plato's dictatorial demand for politically salutary representations in his city is in fact offered as a humble *pis aller*, the best

---

[51] Cf. *Laws* 659D–E, 665C (where it is clear that the sheer repetition of incantations is the source of their effect), 670E, 812C. Philosophers will not want us to get carried away here: cf. Janaway 1995: 181; J. Smith 1986; and Belfiore 1980, who, for example, argues that "usually" Plato urges the value of dialectic as an "anti-magic" that logically drives out false beliefs. But in such passages (e.g., *Phaedo* 114D; see Belfiore pp. 134–35 for other examples) Plato is usually touching on matters worth believing but beyond dialectical demonstration. Note that in Belfiore's concluding illustration of the "limits" of this metaphor (from *Symposium* 216–22), when we penetrate through the exterior of Socrates' arguments to their heart, what we discover there are *images* (*agalmata*, 216E6) of virtue. I agree with Gill (1985b) that Plato has not been entirely clear about the connection of early training through habituation to advanced education of the reasoning faculties. For recent studies of Plato's use of myths, see P. Murray 1996: 135 on 377A1; Gill 1993: 66–69.

we can do with our recalcitrant natures. Thus for all of Plato's concern with defining the nature of poetry and its cultural force in the city, a knowledge of poetry in itself, poetics, had little interest for the philosopher. It was not instructive to sort out when poets may have chanced to say good things, because we would have to know the good already to discern them. It might be informative to undertake a technical study of the special linguistic and musical means by which poets seduced us into accepting their falsehoods; but such knowledge would not make our natures any less susceptible to those forces. It remained possible, however, for others to argue that, within the limitations of human nature, a non-philosophical verbal art might afford a pleasing and valuable experience with unique benefits in comparison with those provided by other forms of making. But this argument was carried out by less-idealistic philosophers, and it was first broached in thinking about prose texts.

PART IV

LITERARY THEORY IN THE FOURTH CENTURY

TEN

THE INVENTION OF LITERATURE

THEORIES OF PROSE AND THE

THEORY OF POETRY

THE ADVANCED thinking about poetry familiar to Socrates' interlocutors viewed it in enlightened terms as normal speech in elaborate form. As the rhetorical critic would say, strip away poetry's meter and other embellishments and you are left with *logos*.[1] Sophists like Protagoras and Prodicus held poetry to technical standards of linguistic correctness, but the *tekhnē* in question was the sophist's own, not that of poetry. Such a perspective left little scope for poetics proper, beyond the study of poetry's special adornments, the nature of rhythm and melody or the meaning of its traditional expressions. For a more than rhetorical poetics to arise, it was necessary that poetry be viewed as a special kind of discourse (*logos*) with its own values and ends. This conception is what Aristotle established in the opening of the *Poetics*: there, poetry is defined in formal terms—its "media of imitation" are *logos* with admixtures of rhythm and melody; but the use of these and other "seasonings" must be directed toward the poet's essential task, which is not versification but the "representation" (*mimēsis*) of human action (*Poetics* 1447a18–47b23; cf. 1451a37–b5, 1451b25–32). As a "representation," poetry had a unique truth-status; the "mimetic art" in words excluded the versified physics of Empedocles but would include any representation of human action, regardless of its metrical form (1447b17–20).[2] What a poet says may well be untrue, but it has been so structured and worked

---

[1] Gorgias (*Helen* §9), Plato (*Gorgias* 502c, *Republic* 601b), and Isocrates (*Evagoras* 11) all speak of "stripping away" the formal aspects of poetry, especially the rhythm and music, to reveal its essential *logos*. The idea is implicit in fifth-century tropes of language as clothing, as in *Frogs* 1059–61, where Aeschylus' words must be grand, "just as the clothes of demi-gods must be larger than ours." Cf. dress and diction in *Thesmophoriazusac* 148, 163, with Cole 1991: 35–36. A most suggestive version is ascribed to Epicharmus 23 B 6 DK; it is defended by Demand (1971) but may be post-Platonic: Webster in Pickard-Cambridge 1962: 245–47; Bucheim 1989: 166.

[2] House (1956) made the point; cf. Halliwell 1986: esp. 113–14, though he finds antecedents in Aristophanes and contemporary dramatic theory. Cf. R. Janko, review of Halliwell, *CP* 84 (1989): 154. Taking a cognitive-ethical view of catharsis, Gill (1993: 74–79) argues that not even Aristotle acknowledged fictionality. Cf. Halliwell 1997: 317–22.

out in language as to produce a special response in us that no other form of discourse can.

This chapter tracks down the earliest statements that ascribe to verbal composition a special value and truth that art alone can confer. I look for explicit statements, since the historical change of importance was the articulation of such ideas rather than their implicit adumbrations in early literature. Because from the very beginning Greeks produced works that serve us well as literature, scholars have been inclined to attribute at least an implicit awareness of literariness or "fictionality" to early poets. Such histories vary in their emphases according to their definitions of fictionality. Some have seen an implicit notion of fiction surfacing with fifth-century sophists, or among "self-conscious" archaic lyric poets, or even in Hesiod and Homer.[3] The Greeks always knew that make-believe was fun and were aware of gradations between the poles of truth and falsehood as far back as Hesiod's "lies like the truth" (*Theogony* 27) or the shrewd and diverting lies of Homer's Odysseus.[4] But nothing like a conception of fiction is evident in the handling of poetic texts by the keenest minds of the archaic and early classical periods. Neither Xenophanes nor Heraclitus pauses in reading Homer and Hesiod to consider possible fictional meanings beneath their tales. Herodotus does allow poets to choose stories appropriate to their songs, and it was widely assumed in the fifth century, as by Gorgias and the *Dissoi logoi*, that poets lied and deceived to give pleasure. But we do not find a sense of fiction as a story or poem that, though not true, provides a special form of knowledge or a uniquely valuable experience. Both the attacks on and defenses of poetry in *Frogs* (1006–72) assume that poets "make men better citizens" by teaching true and useful things.[5] If sophists like Protagoras closely observed and critiqued passages from the poets, it was to understand and appropriate their rhetorical power. For Gorgias, it was not poetry but

---

[3] For Finkelberg (1998), fictionality is in question when the poet, rather than the muse, is held responsible for his tales; this she locates in the fifth century, though she finds anticipations in Homer and Hesiod. For Bowie (1993b), it is when the poet knows he is making things up, which he locates in Stesichorus and probably in Homer and Hesiod. In defining fiction, I follow Janaway (1995: 187 ff), who holds to the Kantian idea that the aesthetic must be irreducible to other experiences.

[4] The question has been reopened by Rösler's (1980a, 1983) argument that fictionality was unknown to the ancients before the close examination of versions that written texts made possible; a similar case is made by Detienne (1981) on the rise of the concept of "myth." For an implicit idea of fiction already in Homer (with Odysseus as model fabulist) and in Hesiod (*Theogeny* 27), cf. Thalmann 1984: 172; Walsh 1984: 20; Goldhill 1991: 67; Pratt 1993: 55–94, esp. 85 ff.; Bowie 1993b. *Contra*: Finkelberg 1998: ch. 4, esp. 129; Gill 1993: 70–73.

[5] Note Euripides' defense of his *Phaedra* on the ground that he didn't make the story up (1051–52). Cf. Gill 1993: 73, Cole 1991: 62–63.

language in general that "cannot be evaluated by using ordinary standards of truth and falsehood."[6]

The Greek word that corresponds semantically to "fiction," *plassein* (equivalent to Latin *fingere*), is applied to poetry by Xenophanes and Gorgias, but in neither case do the emotionally powerful and persuasive "made-up things" belong to a special realm of literary discourse that is distinct from ordinary lying. The Greek word that can be said to express a concept of fiction is Aristotle's *mimēsis*. Plato never dropped the demand for truth from poets, but he provided a photographic negative, as it were, of a concept of fiction in speaking of poets "not lying well" (*Republic* 377D: ἐάν τις μὴ καλῶς ψεύδηται); an implication could be that lying well or "noble lies" might be useful and necessary in matters beyond human knowledge.[7] Aristotle's ideal poet knows "the right way to lie" (*Poetics* 1460a18–25) and produces a work that is not necessarily true (nor necessarily false) but presents the kinds of things that tend to happen, something "more philosophical than history" (ch. 9, esp. 1451b5–7).

If we begin with Aristotle's formulations and search backward, the first texts to adumbrate the position occupied by *Poetics* come from the first half of the fourth century. These are the theories of artistic prose formulated in the generation of Alcidamas, Isocrates, and Plato. Prompted by developments in rhetorical education of the early fourth century, these philosophers and rhetoricians debated the nature and uses of prose texts and defined, each in his own way, a kind of artistic prose with its special value. Whatever may be postulated about an implicit Greek awareness of fictionality, it was their attempts to isolate a unique value in good writing that provided the prototype for a notion of literary art, of a form of writing that, while answerable, as always, to standards of truth and goodness, yet possessed as well a distinctive artistic value.

The contexts in which such statements were made show that their sense of fictionality or literariness was provoked by a flood of new forms of written texts claiming a place in the cultural and educational life of Athens. The specific issue that sparked the debate was the question of the role model speeches should play in the training of orators. The importance of improvisational skills had been championed by sophists like Hippias (*Hippias minor* 363B), and Gorgias juxtaposed courtroom speeches "written with skill rather than spoken with truth" with the *viva voce* debates that show the "swiftness of intellect" of "philosophers." To inculcate this skill, Gorgias and others circulated sample speeches for their

---

[6] Cf. Finkelberg 1998: 177. On sophistic studies of poetry, Ford 2001.

[7] Cf. Gill 1993: 51–56, and p. 219 above. Gill (ibid.: 42–51) also argues that in treating poetry and the arts, Plato has no equivalent to our distinction between factual and fictional disourse but views them in veridical terms.

students to memorize and reuse in their own compositions.[8] With the fourth century came pitched battles about the usefulness of studying rhetoric this way. The debate between champions of improvisation and those urging the study of carefully crafted texts was a disciplinary war, though real concerns were at stake. Audiences resented a too-well-polished speech, and those who were better at polishing texts in their studies than at standing up and speaking in public were not admired.[9] In addition, Antiphon of Athens had been one producer of model court speeches in the later fifth century, and he was connected with the rise of professional speechwriting, which seemed to threaten the democratic balance of power.[10] At first, such texts as Antiphon's *Tetralogies* or Gorgias' *Helen* may have been more dazzling than worrisome, but by the beginning of the fourth century, teachers were expressing concerns about their use in education. The popularity and the controversy surrounding such pamphlets forced those who wished to defend written prose, like Isocrates, or those who, like Plato and Alcidamas, wished to continue writing without making excessive claims for its benefits, to theorize about its nature.

The language and metaphors that carry the argument in these texts allow us to trace an unexpected prehistory of their views back to the polemics of Pindar and Simonides against statues. In debating the usefulness of written prose, Alcidamas, Isocrates, and Plato took up and revived images and arguments that had been developed by the poets to discuss the value of verbal artifacts.[11] The same tropes and antithetical images appear as all three stigmatized "fixed" and "silent" writing in comparison with their own preferred form of speech: Alcidamas adapted the oppositions between speech and silence and between motion and immobility to valorize improvisational skill against teachers of rhetoric who based everything on fixed texts. Plato, taking up a set of Simonidean cudgels, abused all writing as mute and inflexible, though he suggested that an ideal written text might capture the vitality of living animals; for the first time, he stated clearly the idea that organic form may confer a certain

---

[8] On the nature of these exercises, Cole 1991: ch. 5. This work argues, persuasively in my view, that the increasing availability of written speeches for close study and comparison was crucial for the development of rhetorical theory.

[9] Cf. Ober 1989: 173, on Demosthenes 19.246–50, and Ober and Strauss 1989: esp. 250–55. A revealing text in this connection is Aeschines 2 *On the Embassy* §§34–35. Cf. Kennedy 1963: 210.

[10] On Antiphon as described by Thucydides, see Ostwald 1986: 360–65.

[11] For the sake of convenience only, I will discuss these authors in the order named. We lack sufficient evidence, but Isocrates' *Against the Sophists* is generally put in the late 390s (during his stint as a logographer), and Alcidamas is taken to respond to it: cf. Eucken 1983: 130. Yet it is possible to claim that Alcidamas and the *Phaedrus* (generally put in the 360s) belong together: Friemann 1990; Cole 1991: 173 n. 4. For a close comparison of the passages, see Eucken 1983: 120–40.

life on a text, but his irony left little room to take any text very seriously. In Isocrates, Pindar and others are used to claim the virtues of song for his own writings; unlike Plato, Isocrates contrived a nonironic defense of his own prose, which is the first claim for a status like that of literature: his ideal writing is well made, captures otherwise inexpressible truths about its subject's life, and rewards repeated study and careful formal analysis. The notion of verbal art that emerged from these debates created the possibility for poetry to shed its definition as versified speech and assume the status of literary composition par excellence. But that will be a subject for the following chapter.

Alcidamas against the Sophists

Alcidamas objected to teachers of rhetoric who relied too much on the production of specimen orations in his *On the Writers of Written Discourses* or *On the Sophists* (B XXII AS). He held that teachers should sharpen their students' ability to argue extemporaneously, since the skills needed to produce a piece of polished writing were of little use. Alcibiades gives a contemptuous picture of the writer who works at leisure, with premeditation, collecting thoughts from earlier writers and revising and deleting passages upon reflection or consultation with others (§4). Those who lavished such attention on their texts (much like Isocrates) Alcidamas dismissed as mere "poets of speeches" (ποιητὴς λόγων), an illustration of the lower, less desirable connotations of craft "making." In contrast, the speaker who can improvise is "awe-inspiring" (δεινός) and dominates any occasion.[12] Alcibiades allows written speeches some uses: they can be left behind as "memorials" for those ambitious for honor, and—a new theme struck in the debate—they make it possible to study progress in eloquence: as "mirrors of the soul," written speeches fix one's fluent thoughts and so permit comparison more easily than do two orations held in the memory (§§31–32).[13] But even with these allowances, written discourse is a pale reflection of the oral (§27):

ἡγοῦμαι δ᾿ οὐδὲ λόγους δίκαιον εἶναι καλεῖσθαι τοὺς γεγραμμένους λόγους, ἀλλ᾿ ὥσπερ εἴδωλα καὶ σχήματα καὶ μιμήματα λόγων, καὶ τὴν αὐτὴν κατ᾿ αὐτῶν εἰκότως ἂν δόξαν εἴχοιμεν, ἥνπερ καὶ κατὰ τῶν χαλκῶν ἀνδριάντων καὶ λιθίνων ἀγαλμάτων καὶ γεγραμμένων ζῴων.

---

[12] Alcidamas *On the Sophists*. §34; cf. Plato *Euthydemus* 305B, *Phaedrus*. 234E; Isocrates *Against the Sophists* §15, *Antidosis* §192 for "poet of speeches."

[13] Another text is a mirror in Alcidamas (the *Odyssey* is "a fine mirror of human life," a metaphor Aristotle found excessive: *Rhetoric* 1406b13). Song is a "mirror for noble deeds" in Pindar *Nemean* 7.14.

In my opinion, written speeches have no right even to be called speeches, but, as it were, copies and outlines and imitations of speeches. We should have the same attitude toward them as we have toward bronze statues of men or carved stone statues or painted figures.

Written speeches are mere derivatives in the same way that statues or paintings are inferior to their living originals. The immobility and inflexibility of these "copies of true bodies" make texts useless for actual speaking. In real life, shifting rhetorical debates, written compositions "keep a single posture and shape" and stand "unmovingly, without responding to the *kairos*" (§28: ἑνὶ σχήματι καὶ τάξει κεχρημένος . . . ἐπὶ δὲ τῶν καιρῶν ἀκίνητος).

Once the parallel of the plastic arts was introduced, it was predictable that written speeches would lack dynamism and flexibility. Correspondingly, the virtues Alcidamas goes on to claim for extemporized speech are that it is "ensouled" and "alive" (§28):

ὁ μὲν ἀπ᾽ αὐτῆς τῆς διανοίας ἐν τῷ παραυτίκα λεγόμενος ἔμψυχός ἐστι καὶ ζῇ καὶ τοῖς πράγμασιν ἔπεται καὶ τοῖς ἀληθέσιν ἀφωμοίωται σώμασιν, ὁ δὲ γεγραμμένος εἰκόνι λόγου τὴν φύσιν ὁμοίαν ἔχων ἁπάσης ἐνεργείας ἄμοιρος καθέστηκεν.

Now the speech that comes on the spur of the moment directly from the mind is ensouled, and lives, and is able to follow events and act like real bodies. But a written speech is by nature something like an image of a speech, and is so constituted as to be deprived of any kind of motion.

Extemporized speech has a soul that makes it capable of movement in the sense that it can "follow" events as real bodies do. Written texts are as motionless as statues, and equally lacking in vitality.[14]

Like the choral poets, Alcidamas first defines statues as static derivatives of living bodies, and then carries the prejudicial terms over to suggest that writing is essentially lifeless. The silence poets had reproved in sculpture may also be discernible in Alcidamas' indictment of the meticulous writer who, when forced to improvise, is barely able to produce a sound (μηδὲν διαφέρειν τῶν ἰσχνοφώνων, §16). A practiced writer who attempts oral improvisation is like a prisoner just released from chains: writing makes the progress of the mind slow (§17: ἡ βραδείας τὰς διαβάσεις τῇ γνώμῃ παρασκευάζουσα). The champion of oral improvisation values strong voice, fluency, and rapid movement, all said to be what a writer lacks.

---

[14] Behind Alcidamas may stand rhetorical doctrines of Theramenes, if these can be detected in *Frogs* when the shifty Dionysus is praised for his "going with the flow" politically (μετακυλινδεῖν αὑτόν, 536) rather than just "standing there like a painted image, taking a

Alcidamas concludes by taking up the question of why he has committed his condemnation of writing to writing (§§29-34), and here he picks out the advantages writing can provide. Writing outlasts a performance, and he admits that his text is in part a bid for fame that will allow him to reach those who have never heard him extemporize (§§29, 31); written orations can also be fruitfully studied, and he affirms that his text will withstand comparison with those by others, showing how easily an improviser can turn out prose essays when he cares to (§30, 32). But Alcidamas' final argument is concerned with establishing a socially acceptable position for the writer that is distinct from that of the professional writers who were tarred with the term "sophists": writing is all very well as an ancillary discipline, he says, but only those who study it "as an amusement and a pastime (*en paidia kai parergōi*) will have a reputation for sound thinking among those who think rightly." A professional teacher and public performer, Alcidamas is concerned that he not be taken for a sophist hawking his texts. As popular as such writings evidently were, producing them was regarded as an unsavory occupation for a gentleman. For all writers about speech at this time, and for their students, defining the role of such texts required tact. As a whole, *On the Sophists* functions not only as an essay in pedagogy but as an outline of the position a gentleman might take if he were a devotee of this form of literature but did not wish to descend to the class of professional wordsmith.

Isocrates against the Sophists

In Isocrates, these topics will develop into a significant defense of prose literature, as artistic speech that makes no claims to the charm of poetry but is yet worth writing down and preserving so it may be read, studied, and discussed among readers now and in the future. Isocrates carried the "mirror of the soul" idea in a new direction: defending his prose encomia, he argued that artistically polished texts can capture the inner lives of their subjects better than poetry and so are no less "useful to spend time with" (*Evagoras* §74).

Either in conjunction with Alcidamas or in anticipation of him, Isocrates touched on the same themes in his own *Against the Sophists*, though he could not afford to trivialize writing. His carefully written "speeches" were intended to be circulated as texts among friends (pupils and patrons), to be studied and compared with other written speeches as a way

---

single posture" (μᾶλλον ἢ γεγραμμένην / εἰκόν᾽ ἑστάναι, λαβόνθ᾽ ἐν σχῆμα): Süss 1911; Radermacher 1951: 219–20; and cf. McCall 1969: 4–7.

to make progress in the art (*Busiris* §34, *Antidosis* §78).[15] At times his speeches even contain instructions for how they are to be used, as when he apologizes for the many thousands of words of his *Panathenaic Oration* (§136) and advises readers to go through it in pieces, taking up "only as much of it as they want" at a time. A sort of teach-yourself text is the long dramatization in his *Panathenaic Oration* of how he and a student went over and critiqued a draft of the speech (§§200–264).[16]

Like Alcidamas, Isocrates acknowledges a distinction between "successful competitors" in speaking and those he calls "good poets of speech" (§15). Although the phrase fits Isocrates very well, for him it is faint praise: his school was based on the principle that technical perfection in style is not admirable in itself, nor does it benefit the city unless it be further developed by "philosophical" education.[17] The antithesis recurs in *Antidosis* §192, which contrasts improvisers who have the "boldness" one needs to speak in court with the mere "poet of speeches" who can produce pleasant texts if he has mastered such forms of speech as can be taught with exactness. Isocrates presented his "philosophical" education as a necessary supplement to rhetorical education: without it, rhetoric was only a rigidly "fixed" (*tetagmenēn*) art that could not "move" (*akinētos*, §§12–13) in response to events. Turning from this early polemic to Isocrates' encomiastic writings shows how he developed the poets' topoi into a new defense of his own works of verbal art. His strategy will be to take charges like those of Alcidamas and reverse them.

Isocrates was in a position not unlike an epinician poet's when he composed his *Evagoras*, a memorial to a Cyprian king (who died in 374/3) written for his son Nicocles (for which he was paid twenty talents, according to the Plutarchan life of Isocrates 838A), and indeed, he strikes many themes from Pindar. He begins by opining that Evagoras would prefer to be commemorated not by splendid material offerings but by a speech that might "go through his deeds in a fine way and make Evagoras' excellence always remembered among all men" (ὁ δὲ λόγος εἰ καλῶς διέλθοι τὰς ἐκείνου πράξεις, ἀείμνηστον ἂν τὴν ἀρετὴν τὴν Εὐαγόρου παρὰ πᾶσιν ἀνθρώποις ποιήσειεν, §4). The theme is extended later in the oration in a key passage giving three reasons for the superiority of commemorative texts to statues: "These [speeches] I prefer to statues first because serious men value them likewise, and second because memorials stay in one place, whereas the speeches can pass through Greece; there is the third advantage that one can imitate the manners and virtues as revealed

---

[15] On publishing: *Antidosis* §69. Cf. Kennedy 1980: 109–19.

[16] On Isocrates' instructions on how to use his texts, see Hudson Williams 1949.

[17] On the flexible meanings of "sophist" and "philosopher" at this time, cf. Ford 1993b: 33–41.

in speeches but cannot press the body to be like admirable statues" (§74).[18] The first reason derives from the old *sophos*-athlete debate we saw in Xenophanes 2 *IEG*, where the "inner" virtue of *sophia* was declared more worthy of admiration than physical excellence. Isocrates' second point expands on such texts as Pindar *Nemean* 5, noting that the "stamped images" (*tupous*) of a man are compelled to stay in one place and must address whatever company chance may bring; by contrast, his own speeches can pass through Greece and will have entrée into the best society (τοὺς μὲν τύπους ἀναγκαῖον παρὰ τούτοις εἶναι μόνοις παρ' οἷς ἂν σταθῶσιν, τοὺς δὲ λόγους ἐξενεχθῆναί ⟨θ'⟩ οἷόν τ' ἐστιν εἰς τὴν Ἑλλάδα καὶ διαδοθέντας ἐν ταῖς τῶν εὖ φρονούντων διατριβαῖς ἀγαπᾶσθαι).[19] The third advantage is new, though the idea that a soul can copy heroic narratives more easily than a body can assume sculptural form owes much to a contemporary tendency to oppose physical training of the body (*gumnastikē*) to education of the soul through song (*mousikē*). Drawing on these different repositories of imagery and ethical belief, Isocrates supports a claim that has not been made so far for the work of verbal art (§73):

κἀλὰ μνημεῖα καὶ τὰς τῶν σωμάτων εἰκόνας, πολὺ μέντοι πλείονος ἀξίας τὰς τῶν πράξεων καὶ τῆς διανοίας, ἃς ἐν τοῖς λόγοις ἄν τις μόνον τοῖς τεχνικῶς ἔχουσιν θεωρήσειεν.

Fair are memorials and bodily likenesses, but far more worthy of esteem are the intentions behind the actions, which can be discerned only in speeches that are composed with art.

Logoi, if artfully composed, can represent the subject's "inner" qualities, while works of plastic art can only copy external features.[20] Only a narrative can express the *actions* of a life and the actor's state of mind; moral qualities such as courage or intelligence are revealed in actions (*praxeis*), which are inaccessible to the arts of sculpture or painting.[21] Provided *logoi*

---

[18] Cf. δίαιταν μανύει ("to make his way of life known") in Pindar *Pythian* 1.93. The topos is important to Plutarch's *Lives*, e.g., *Cimon* 479E–480A.

[19] See Race 1987: 150, who notes that Isocrates' διαδοθέντας has the same force as Pindar's διαγγέλλοισ' (*Nemean* 5.3).

[20] What the "inner" qualities are may be seen from *Evagoras* §65: καίτοι πῶς ἄν τις τὴν ἀνδρίαν ἢ τὴν φρόνησιν ἢ σύμπασαν τὴν ἀρετὴν τὴν Εὐαγόρου φανερώτερον ἐπιδείξειεν ἢ διὰ τοιούτων ἔργων καὶ κινδύνων; "Dangers" refers to crises that reveal character: cf. *To Philip* §152 (Heracles' *aretē* revealed through his *kindunoi*, i.e., labors).

[21] Aristotle's *Poetics* provides the best gloss on the Isocratean terms when he discusses how to represent inner character: tragedy, which is an imitation of an action (*praxis*), uses *logoi* to reveal what the characters are thinking (*dianoia*) about the situations they find themselves in; upon their *dianoia* depends whether their actions are judged fair or foul (1450b4–12, 1456a34–b8).

rise to the level of the "artistic" or "technically accomplished," they are capable of getting at and setting down a vital dimension of their subjects that will escape plastic arts.[22] Turning the tables on Alcidamas (and on Plato, as we shall see), Isocrates reappropriates for his texts the mobility (to circulate) and vitality (to capture and communicate the inner man) that Alcidamas would have denied him. In so doing, he articulates a conception of the well-made text as *objet d' art*:[23] far from being in any material way inferior to sculpture, a text can "embody" the inner, ethical qualities of its subject in its own unique way.

If Pindar and others argued for the durability of song and for its power to broadcast fame, Isocrates goes beyond them with the claim that works of verbal art can capture something in the subject that is inaccessible to the sculptor or painter. In this he appears to have profited from contemporary discussions of the limits of various artistic media to represent invisible things like character. Xenophon's Socrates discussed with a famous painter how color and shape might express the soul's character (τὸ τῆς ψυχῆς ἦθος, *Memorabilia* 3.10.1–5); he turned to a sculptor known for "psychagogic" works that appear to be alive (τὸ ζωτικὸν φαίνεσθαι) to discuss how sculptors use postures and gestures to create "visible semblances of the soul's actions" (τὰ τῆς ψυχῆς ἔργα εἴδει προσεικάζειν, 3.10.6–8). Socrates' questions were profound for aesthetics, but hedging in the power of artistic illusionism was the old religious view expressed by the poets that all human works of art are limited. Xenophon's Socrates uses the poets' terms in an argument from design to convince a young man that the gods exist (*Memorabilia* 1.4.2–4). He opposes examples of mortal "making" that include epic, dithyramb, tragedy, sculpture, and painting to the divine art that produced man: "Who seems more admirable, those who produce unintelligent and immobile copies or who produce ones that are endowed with mind and are active and alive?" (Πότερά σοι δοκοῦσιν οἱ ἀπεργαζόμενοι εἴδωλα ἄφρονά τε καὶ ἀκίνητα ἀξιοθαυμαστότεροι εἶναι ἢ οἱ ζῷα ἔμφρονά τε καὶ ἐνεργά; (1.4.4). Here the categories the poets had used to distinguish poetry from sculpture are redeployed to set divine fabrication above human imitative art.

---

[22] Isocrates again insists on art (*tekhnikōs*) at *Panathenaic Oration* §271; cf. *Panegyric* (§§11–14), which opposes the simple (*halpōs*) speeches of nonprofessionals to Isocrates' own epideictic orations, which are "exceedingly closely worked (*akribōn*) and are intended for an audience that is irritated when it finds things said in a haphazard (*eikēi*) manner."

[23] Isocrates' focus on artful composition to make virtue last through time differentiates him from Pindar, for whom, e.g., speech "*lives*" longer than deeds/works (ῥῆμα δ' ἐργμάτων χρονιώτερον βιοτεύει, *Nemean* 4.6–8) *when it chances to meet with the Graces*. Artisanal skill is not sufficient; one must meet with a graceful acceptance (of poet by the Muses, of the Muses by the poet, and of the song by victor and community).

For the professional rhetorician, there is likely to have been an economic as well as a theoretical impulse to argue that fine speeches are better than sculptures, as there is when Isocrates urges Evagoras' son to "prefer to leave images of your excellence rather than of your body as your memorial" (*To Nicocles* §36). Xenophon himself used the inner/outer opposition in his encomium of Agesilaus (*obit* 359 B.C.E.) not to explore representation but to endorse a social opposition between nobles and craftsmen: "Though many wished for one, he refrained from setting up any replica of his body (τοῦ μὲν σώματος εἰκόνα στήσασθαι), but never ceased perfecting the memorial of his soul (τῆς δὲ ψυχῆς οὐδέποτε ἐπαύετο μνημεῖα διαπονούμενος), considering the former a job for statuaries, but the latter for himself, the former for the wealthy to pursue, the latter for the good" (*Agesilaus* 11.7). Xenophon's next topic is Agesilaus' liberal use of money.

The Isocratean passages are the first attempt to define a class of prose literature that is worth preserving and passing from hand to hand, at least in part because of the art that has been lavished on it. Because he has "organized" Evagoras' virtues and "adorned" them with his language, *Evagoras* is a text that deserves to be studied and re-read (εἴ τις ἀθροίσας τὰς ἀρετὰς τὰς ἐκείνου καὶ τῷ λόγῳ κοσμήσας παραδοίη θεωρεῖν ὑμῖν καὶ συνδιατρίβειν αὐταῖς, §74). By "artistic" or "technically accomplished," Isocrates appears to mean nothing more subtle than an account of a great man's deeds and states of mind that is orderly and attractive (*kalōs*); but the conveniently loose formulation goes beyond the common assumption that admirable deeds are worth recounting by locating the inspirational power of *Evagoras* in the composer's artistry and mode of presentation. It is as vain to expect efficacious moral instruction from a text that lacks this deeper dimension as it is to press one's body to resemble a fine statue or painting.

The art that allows Isocrates to give a specially penetrating representation of his subject, to capture his active life, grounds a new and complex sense of the text as literary artifact, as a plastic creation with the power not only to endure and to circulate, but to embody a special ethical content, a fixed portrait that is yet a dynamic guide to the conduct of life.[24] In finding this distinctive value in artistic prose, Isocrates finds a new reason for preserving such works—not for inscribing the ultimate truths of the world (as the many writers *On Nature* had), nor for setting down

---

[24] On this humanistic power of the word for Isocrates, cf. Eucken 1983: 167–68. Cf. *Panegyricus* §9, where the true test of a philosophical writer is not to speak on abstruse topics but to take the common inheritance of the culture and deploy it as the occasion demands (*en kairōi*), adding appropriate (*prosēkonta*) general statements and decking them out finely in words (*tois onomasi eu dithesthai*).

a recurring truth of human action (as Thucydides had). For Isocrates, artistic prose was valuable for being well told, for using technique to transcend mere depiction and construct a representation that reaches the inner character and motives of its subject.[25]

This idea of the artfully written speech as a special sort of artifact, an "image of the mind," was applied by Isocrates to the great self-portrait that is his *Antidosis*. Early on in this *apologia pro vita sua*, he describes it as a special sort of artifact that can mirror the subject's intentions as well as his acts: "This speech is as it were a likeness of my thought and of the events of my life" (λόγος ὥσπερ εἰκὼν τῆς ἐμῆς διανοίας καὶ τῶν ἄλλων τῶν [ἐμοὶ] βεβιωμένων, §7). The *Antidosis* is like an icon in that it is well-wrought and enduring; but it goes beyond what are normally called icons because it has captured the "motives" of its subject, the thoughts that have governed his deeds and words. The "life" that Pindar and Simonides wished to withhold from the unvoiced text of a poem is recaptured by Isocrates and made to inhere in his well-made prose artifacts. Hence, in defining artistic prose, he can boast, somewhat like the Midas monument, to have produced a special kind of object for making its subject "always-remembered" (ἀείμνηστον, *Evagoras* §4) among men.

Plato on Structure

All these texts on the relation of the wordsmith to the painter or sculptor converge in Plato's *Phaedrus*, but with a new purpose. Here Plato's thesis is the opposite of Isocrates': no writing is worth much in comparison with living, philosophical interchange. The traditional tropes are now summoned to claim for dialectic the vital dynamism previously associated with poetry as against statuary. Like Alcidamas, Plato first defines artworks as inferior derivatives of living bodies, and then carries the prejudicial terms over to the opposition of written texts to philosophic speech. Although Plato affects to regard writing as ultimately a trivial occupation, one implication of his argument is that good writing, like good speech, can be vital and alive, a point he will illustrate with a powerful analogy between the structure of a text and that of an animal. The idea first enunciated here—that texts should be organically composed—derived from a tradition that had said that a living, moving animal or a seeing, speaking

[25] Very close is *Panathenaic Oration* §§136–37, where he apologizes for the long account of virtuous men and well-governed states that may not please many, but will enable those who take time to read it little by little to pattern their lives upon his examples so as to enjoy good repute and benefit their cities (λόγου διεξιόντος ἀνδρῶν ἀρετὰς καὶ πόλεως τρόπον καλῶς οἰκουμένης, ἅπερ εἰ μιμήσασθαί τινες βουληθεῖεν καὶ δυνηθεῖεν, αὐτοί τ' ἂν ἐν μεγάλῃ δόξῃ τὸν βίον διαγάγοιεν καὶ τὰς πόλεις τὰς αὐτῶν εὐδαίμονας ποιήσειαν).

person is preferable to a fixed representation of one, however permanent the latter may be.

Like Simonides, Plato weighs in with his own criticisms of the Midas epitaph, and this is significantly in a discussion of what makes good writing. His Socrates demands of any writing that it not be "poured out" at random (like ink or paint), but rather that it exhibit a "logographic necessity" that binds each part of the text to the others and to the whole. The term is a bit beyond Phaedrus (264B–C), so Socrates offers an analogy between an animal and a well-composed text:

ἀλλὰ τόδε γε οἶμαί σε φάναι ἄν, δεῖν πάντα λόγον ὥσπερ ζῷον συνεστάναι σῶμά τι ἔχοντα αὐτὸν αὑτοῦ, ὥστε μήτε ἀκέφαλον εἶναι μήτε ἄπουν, ἀλλὰ μέσα τε ἔχειν καὶ ἄκρα, πρέποντα ἀλλήλοις καὶ τῷ λῳ γεγραμμένα.

But this much I think you would assent to, that every speech must be constituted like an animal with a sort of body of its own, so that it does not lack a head or feet, but has its middle parts and extremities composed so as to be fitting with each other and with the whole.

This is the first clear statement in Greek of the principle of organic unity: the parts of a text should "stand together" (συνεστάναι), that is, that they should have a structure in which the beginning, middle, and end "stand together"[26] in a "fitting" (πρέποντα) relation. In context, the demand for organic unity applies only to written texts ("logo-*graphic*" means "characteristic of written language") because of their inherent limitations, which will be discussed below. But the doctrine—along with the analogy and a number of Plato's terms—was taken over by Aristotle in recommending that the plot of a tragedy be unified "like an animal" (*Poetics* chs. 7-8). From this demand, one may generate all the other demands made on poets in the *Poetics*, since the "appropriate" use of diction, character, and all the elements of a drama depends on their functioning as subordinate parts to the ideally unified plot-structure. Halliwell rightly insists that for Aristotle, structured plots are structured *contents*, and that the events, actions, and motives composing this whole will be understood in ethical and social terms. This is to say yet again, and rightly, that classical criticism never sought to divorce itself from ethical norms. But installing organic unity as a central virtue in the poet's work as "maker" or

---

[26] Plato is quite aware of the metaphor behind the term σύστασις, cf. *Phaedrus* 268D: "The tragedians would laugh if someone thought that tragedy was anything other than the structuring (σύστασιν) of such things [scil. dramatic speeches], their standing together (συνισταμένην) so that they fit with each other and with the whole." It is possible to discern a forerunner of the idea in the charge that Aeschylus' plays are "unstructured" (ἀξύστατος, *Clouds* 1367); see Dover 1993 on *Frogs* 862, where *ta neura* (the "sinews") of tragedy have been glossed this way.

composer of plots meant that poetics, *qua* "art" of making, centered on the "necessity" that bound a work's internal, rhetorically analyzable elements together. For the critic of poetry, assessing organic unity was primarily a matter of analyzing structure and coherence rather than theology or ethics. Accordingly, for Aristotle (and not Plato), organic unity is a virtue that is specific to poetic composition: the *Rhetoric* does not advise artful public speakers to design their speeches in this way.[27]

To return to Plato's text: given the profound implications of the demand for logographic necessity in good writing, it is noteworthy that Plato has given no reason for texts to be structured like animals. And indeed, there is no binding reason. Here the poetic tradition plays its most significant role, for it is imagery that in the end motivates the acceptance of this claim by associating formal unity with life and power.

The emphatic position of γεγραμμένα at the end of the sentence quoted above calls attention to its ambiguity between referring to the ideal "written" or "painted" composition. The verb γράφω originally meant "to scratch," and so was used for both writing and painting or drawing. Here, even on a second glance, it is not clear whether Socrates is saying that the parts of a *speech* must be *written* in an artistically unified way, or that the naturally defined parts of an *animal* must be so *painted*. Plato exploits this ambiguity to superpose the antithesis written/spoken (γεγραμμένον / λεγόμενον) upon the inherited and heavily weighted opposition painted/living (γεγραμμένον / ζῷον). Writing a text thereby becomes like painting an animal: each is the attempt to capture active life in fixed form. In an animal, parts must "stand together" so the animal can do its "work"; in a speech or representation, the parts must be placed and proportioned so that the whole will not disintegrate and cease to exist.[28] There is a further implication: the written text (*gegrammenos logos*) stands in the same relation to its living subjects (*zōia*) as painted animals (*gergrammena zōia*) stand in relation to living animals (*zōia*). This suggests that the components of the well-written text or picture are like the parts of a well-developed animal. Because neither a text nor a painting is alive, logographic

---

[27] Heath 1989 valuably highlights the many nonunifying, rhetorical canons of good writing that pervade much ancient criticism, though I find he minimizes too much the importance of the idea to Plato and Aristotle: Ford 1991.

[28] This analogy between painting and writing may already be suggested at the beginning of this discussion, when the poor organization of Lysias' oration is condemned as "spilled out" without reason (χύδην, 264в3). The opposite of reasoned structure is not called "random" (εἰκῇ), as in the *Gorgias* (503ε2), but "poured" or "spilled," a metaphor appropriate to painting. So Aristotle returns to the same word and comparison in *Poetics* 1450b2 to illustrate the importance of structuring plot: the most beautiful colors "poured out" will give less pleasure than some discernible figure (*eikōn*), even if this be drawn in black and white.

unity consists in their parts "standing together" (264c3). Against the archaic epigrapher's conceit, which claimed that the solidity of bronze or
marble made any text on it endure, for Plato the formal structure of a
text is what bestows "some kind of body" on writing. And this body is
that of a living animal.[29] This analogy of a verbal composition with an
animal becomes in Aristotle's *Poetics* the structure of a work of verbal
art that remains timeless, even as it may be reread in varying situations.

Plato provides further clarification of logographic necessity when he
turns back to Lysias' speech, which, it will surprise no one, lacks organic
structure. But to illustrate this, Plato does not keep up the analogy with
an organism and say, for example, what Horace says in the *Ars poetica*
(1 ff.), that Lysias has constructed a body with feet sticking out of its neck.
Instead, he turns to the Midas epigram as an example of a text whose
elements are assembled at random. He thus moves from comparing a text
to a living body to dissecting a text about a dead body. Before he is done,
inartistic writing will be as dead as Midas.

Socrates chooses as his prime exemplar of inorganic writing the boastful text that Simonides complained had been too sure of its own stability
(264c–d):

> SOCRATES: Now if you examine whether your friend's speech is like this
> [lographically unified] or not, you will find that it is no different from
> the epigram that some say is carved over Midas the Phrygian.
> PHAEDRUS: Which inscription is this, and what is wrong with it?
> SOCRATES: It's this one,
>
>> I am a maiden of bronze and I rest upon Midas' tomb.
>> So long as water shall flow tall trees bloom,
>> Remaining on this very spot, over this much-lamented tomb
>> I will announce to those who pass that Midas is buried here.
>
> I presume you notice that as far as one can see it makes no difference
> which line is said first and which last.
> PHAEDRUS: You are making fun of our speech, Socrates.

Socrates quotes a shorter version of the epigram (lines 1, 2, 5, and 6 of
the poem as quoted in Diogenes Laertius: his game would not work on the
six-line version) and seems to be making a different point from Simonides.
Whereas the poet charged the stone and text with hubris for presuming
to resist natural change, Socrates faults it for lacking the adamantine (necessary) structure that alone can guarantee permanence: switch head and

---

[29] At *Phaedrus* 265E: division proceeds by dividing things in two at their natural articulations, "just as from *one single* body (ὥσπερ δὲ σώματος ἐξ ἑνός), one divides the limbs into
left and right." See Svenbro 1984b on the comparison between correct dialectical analysis
and carving up an animal along the "natural" articulations that produce its *eidē*.

feet, first and last lines, and it still makes much the same sense; there is no internal check against change of form.[30]

Though Simonides is not mentioned here, his oppositions endorse the value assumed for living being over lifeless imitation, for vital organism over sterile monumentality. Plato's adduction of the Midas poem is congruent with the outlook of Simonides' poem and borrows its terms to establish the value of organic composition that may be otherwise impossible to prove. Why should the interchangeability of the lines of the Midas epigram poem be a bad thing? Why should speeches be like animals? Here the hidden terms of Simonides' indictment of inscribed statues play a key role: Plato can assume we prefer the organically structured text to the indifferently written epigram because his ruling assumption is that mere material stability is deadly. So, too, we prefer a "living thing" (the root sense of *zōion*, "animal") to an artificial thing, because mere fixedness is no sign of continuing life. Both are arguing in favor of the primacy of oral performance, even as their culture finds more and more powerful uses for writing. Simonides' terms recur more explicitly later in the dialogue, when Plato generalizes his attack on Lysianic and all rhetorical composition to declare that there is something very strange and wrong with writing in itself.

Writing and Painting

In the deprecation of writing that concludes the *Phaedrus*, Plato illustrates its limitations by bringing in painting (275D–E):

δεινὸν γάρ που, ὦ Φαῖδρε, τοῦτ᾽ ἔχει γραφή, καὶ ὡς ἀληθῶς ὅμοιον ζωγραφίᾳ. καὶ γὰρ τὰ ἐκείνης ἔκγονα ἕστηκε μὲν ὡς ζῶντα, ἐὰν δ᾽ ἀνέρῃ τι, σεμνῶς πάνυ σιγᾷ. ταὐτὸν δὲ καὶ οἱ λόγοι· δόξαις μὲν ἂν ὥς τι φρονοῦντας αὐτοὺς λέγειν, ἐὰν δέ τι ἔρῃ τῶν λεγομένων βουλόμενος μαθεῖν, ἕν τι σημαίνει μόνον ταὐτὸν ἀεί. ὅταν δὲ ἅπαξ γραφῇ, κυλινδεῖται μὲν πανταχοῦ πᾶς λόγος ὁμοίως παρὰ τοῖς ἐπαΐουσιν, ὡς δ᾽ αὕτως παρ᾽ οἷς οὐδὲν προσήκει, καὶ οὐκ ἐπίσταται λέγειν οἷς δεῖ γε καὶ μή. πλημμελούμενος δὲ καὶ οὐκ ἐν δίκῃ λοιδορηθεὶς τοῦ πατρὸς ἀεὶ δεῖται βοηθοῦ· αὐτὸς γὰρ οὔτ᾽ ἀμύνασθαι οὔτε βοηθῆσαι δυνατὸς αὑτῷ.

There is this uncanny quality about writing, Phaedrus, that makes it very much like painting. For the offspring of that art also just stand there as if they were alive, but maintain a lofty silence if you ask them anything. The

---

[30] In addition, it seems that Plato has changed the use of a basic term in Simonides' scheme: if motion was for Simonides and Pindar a figure for poetry's true persistence as opposed to mere solid fixity, here the written text seems to exhibit too great a mobility. If

same goes for [written] speeches: you might suppose that they are full of mind and intelligence and are saying something; but if you wish to understand what they say and ask them a question, they always signify the same thing. And once any speech is written down, it is tossed about everywhere and addresses both those who are full of understanding and those whom it ought not, and it does not know how to speak to those whom it should and to be silent before those it should not. And being bandied about like this, it is reproached unfairly and always needs its father to come running to help it; for on its own it is incapable of fighting off attacks or defending itself.

Plato alludes to Simonides' dictum about silent poetry without naming him (275D). Using the etymological connection between painting, literally "figure-drawing" (zō-graphia), and "writing" (graphē), Plato says that writing, like painting, just stands there in silence, pretending to be alive. It is not only silent but inflexible, repeating the same thing each time you ask it a question, each time you re-read the text. Socrates assimilates written texts to paintings and then levels against both the charges Pindar and Simonides had laid against statues: such objects are incapable of living speech or independent action. Though the written text may appear to be saying something, it is little better than silence; if it gives the impression of an active mind behind the words, it only says the same thing over and over again, much like a grave marker that promises to "say the same thing always."[31]

Writing also just "stands there" (ἕστηκε), and this raises the poets' charge against fixed icons.[32] As in Socrates' discussion of the Midas epigram, motion may be treated either as a sign of life or as a form of material disintegration in an object. Like the Midas epigram, writing moves, but with the wrong kind of motion: any written text is "tossed about" in every direction (κυλινδεῖται μὲν πανταχοῦ πᾶς λόγος) or circulates, as we say, among anybody and everybody.[33] Pindar's boast that his song will sail on every skiff or merchant ship means for Plato that it is undiscrimi-

---

Simonides had put the flow of song and the flux of elements above stone, in Socrates, oral performance and reperformance disturb the text.

[31] Cf. 286.1–2 CEG: πᾶσιν ἴσ' ἀνθρόποις ηυποκρίνομαι ηόστις ἐροτᾶι / ηός μ' ἀνέθεκ' ἀνδρõν. The tropes recur in Protagoras 329A, where sophists and most public speakers are said to resemble books: unable to ask or answer questions, they just keep on ringing like bronze (n.b.) cymbals when questioned.

[32] Plato also denies that writing is bebaios, "well on its base," in the sense of reliable or certain (275C6, 277D8). The same metaphor from "solidly planted" to "certain in the mind" seems to be used in Parmenides B 4.1 DK: λεύσσε δ' ὅμως ἀπεόντα βεβαίως.

[33] Phaedrus 275E. Κυλινδεῖται is often used of being "rolled" or "tossed" on the sea (LSJ) and may remind us not only of Pindar's sea-voyaging songs but also of his use of that term at Olympian 12.5–7 and Pythian 1.24. Cf., too, Clouds 375 and note 14 above.

nating and can't address an audience selectively.[34] There is also the lack of dynamic strength in writing's need of its father, living speech, to defend it and speak up for it when it is abused.[35]

Conversely, as we would expect, good writing has the virtues that Simonides and Pindar had claimed for poetry (276A):

> Τί δ'; ἄλλον ὁρῶμεν λόγον τούτου ἀδελφὸν γνήσιον, τῷ τρόπῳ τε γίγνεται, καὶ ὅσῳ ἀμείνων καὶ δυνατώτερος τούτου φύεται;
>
> Τίνα τοῦτον καὶ πῶς λέγεις γιγνόμενον;
>
> Ὃς μετ' ἐπιστήμης γράφεται ἐν τῇ τοῦ μανθάνοντος ψυχῇ, δυνατὸς μὲν ἀμῦναι ἑαυτῷ, ἐπιστήμων δὲ λέγειν τε καὶ σιγᾶν πρὸς οὓς δεῖ.

SOCRATES: Now what about the other kind of speech, the legitimately born brother of this one: how does it come into being, and in what way is it naturally superior and more capable than the other?

PHAEDRUS: What speech is this and how does it arise?

SOCRATES: The one that is written with intelligence in the soul of the student, being capable of defending itself and knowing which people it should address and before whom it should remain silent.

Good writing takes place in the soul; it is legitimate offspring of oral speech, noble, dynamic, and discreet. It only remains for Phaedrus to add the traditional approbative metaphors:

> Τὸν τοῦ εἰδότος λόγον λέγεις ζῶντα καὶ ἔμψυχον, οὗ ὁ γεγραμμένος εἴδωλον ἄν τι λέγοιτο δικαίως.

You mean the speech of the one who knows, the living and ensouled speech of which the written could be justly called the image.

This kind of writing manages to be "alive" and "ensouled." Marks on stone or scroll are but an image of true discourse.

---

[34] The worry that writing indiscriminately addresses itself to anyone (shared to some extent by Isocrates, *Evagoras* §74) is new. Here the exclusivizing strategies of archaic sects are carried over to underwrite a sense of social distinction and elitism. In effect, Plato and Isocrates agree with the Pythagorean dictum that not everything is to be disclosed to everybody (μὴ εἶναι πρὸς πάντας πάντα ῥητά), a thesis kept alive by Antisthenes: Aristotle fr. 192 Rose; see Burkert 1972a: 178–79. Plato often alludes to the desire among some Pythagoreans to transmit the master's doctrines only orally and speaks to the inadequacy of exoteric, written accounts. Similarly, Plato would restrict true speech to those initiated to philosophic conversation.

[35] On the trope of the orphan text, cf. *Theaetetus*, where a quotation (i.e., a short text) of Protagoras proves impossible to interpret because "the father of the story" (πατὴρ τοῦ . . . μύθου) is not alive to "ward off attacks" (ἤμυνε) against it, and the guardians of this "orphan"—the avowed Protagoreans—will not defend it (βοηθεῖν) and stop its unjust abuse (164E). Further in Ford 1994: 205, 210 n. 20.

Behind Plato's analysis we can discern some of the issues raised by Simonides' discussion of the Midas poem, for writing is as much like that bronze statue as it is like a painting. Indeed, what Plato writes in the *Phaedrus* about the difference between writing and speech is a dilation of a poetic theme of the superiority of song to plastic artifacts. Whereas poets had used statues as a foil to their resounding and mobile choruses, Plato's ideal and truly immortal human activity is dialectical philosophy, a dynamic conversation that occurs and changes in time. On Plato's view, the written *logos* is like the boastful monument: it is an *eidōlon*, a duplicate of the true *logos*, a counterfeit of what was once alive.[36] Writing belongs on the side of painting and sculpture, as an enduring representation of a living thing that is fatally condemned by its fixity, silence, and lifelessness.

Plato introduces one further implication when the curse of writing is expanded to include barrenness (277A). The opposition of fecundity and sterility was perhaps suggested by the poets' praise of "flourishing" (θάλλειν).[37] In Plato, the theme is first adumbrated when paintings are described as the "offspring" of the painter's art (275D5) and writings are said to need their "father," their author, to defend them (275E).[38] This double evocation of a false birth, from the painter or the writer, also fits Midas' metallic maid, who will never have ensouled offspring, however long she may go on talking, and Phrasikleia, who is forever fixed as a maid. Socrates has juxtaposed his ideal of the text as living being with a text that begins "bronze maiden"; he has juxtaposed a sign of life with a sign of death, a living thing with a grave marker. Thus he characterizes them respectively as living/dead, favoring the animal against what cannot change and move (as Simonides would say), or against what cannot move without being harmed or killed, and so was never alive.[39] Unchanging and enduring though the maiden claims to be, she is actually too easily changed; in fact, were she an animal, Socrates' analysis would be a dismembering, a "cutting up" of the joints with the skill of a carver, as he

---

[36] Democritus has a suggestive description of images that are "resplendent in their clothing and adornment, but devoid of liveliness [heart]" (εἴδωλα ἐσθῆτι καὶ κόσμωι διαπρεπέα πρὸς θεωρίην, ἀλλὰ καρδίης κενεά, B 195.1 DK). Diels-Kranz suggest that he is thinking of "Götter, Frauen," but with nothing in Democritus' language for support.

[37] Cf. the quest in the *Frogs* 97 for a γόνιμος ποιήτης. Denniston (1927: 113) says this term was taken over from medicine.

[38] Cf. *Symposium* 209 D2, where Diotima speaks of the "offspring" that Homer and Hesiod and other good poets "have left behind" to provide *kleos* and *mnēmē*.

[39] In this connection, Aristotle's language in describing organic unity is striking (*Poetics* 1451a 34): "The parts must stand together so that if any part is taken away or removed, the whole is dislocated and put out of joint" (διαφέρεσθαι, κινεῖσθαι). The medical terms παρατείνειν and διαστρέφειν occur in a similar context at 1451b38–1452a1.

himself figures it (265E).[40] Undying though her message would like to be, it is only a sign of death. As Socrates says, no written discourse deserves to be treated very seriously (277E).

It is not paradoxical that the theory of poetry as literature should have arisen in connection with prose, and indeed, with rhetorical compositions that are ranked rather low as literary objects today. The fourth-century figures who most influentially theorized about writing and language were involved perforce in some way with rhetoric; all those discussed above produced, either by profession or by avocation, written prose texts, and all were eager to define their positions as writers by distinguishing their texts from other popular forms of writing. Thucydides had opposed his eternally valid text to oral performances of no enduring value, but the fourth century had thrown up enough new forms of prose writing that it became necessary to sort them out, assess them in relation to old song traditions, and ask which were worth reading and keeping and why. For professional teachers of speech like Alcidamas and Isocrates, the target was the flood of rhetorical model texts; for Plato, it was these and their philosophizing critics.

These writers borrowed from the poets a claim for a special quality in their creations that was in some way more than the words on a page. Alcidamas had it both ways, rejecting the fixed text but exhibiting his skills in a text against rhetorical texts. It was left to Isocrates to defend artistic prose texts in relation to a broader conception of value. Reversing the themes in which singers had sought to affirm their contribution to civic life, he contrived a justification for prose that set the pattern for all classically inspired conceptions of literature as works of art worth preserving and circulating for close and repeated study. Isocrates' "icons" of the soul are a paradigm for literature as writing that is valuable not only for its wisdom and learning but also for being executed in a specially artistic way. Plato continued an aristocratic pose of disdain toward the profession of writing and deprecated any attempt to leave behind something useful in a text, whether this be Homer's poems, Solon's laws, or Lysias' orations. With his ironies, Plato tried to leave readers ever-restless in the quest for perfection of form so that they would not stop before turning to philosophy. For all the fertility of his organic image of the text, Plato's *tour de force* in *Phaedrus* returns readers to his characteristic insistence that poetry and all writing are interesting only insofar as they attain philosophical discourse. But Isocrates contented himself with a well-wrought humanistic meaning as the best we could do. His strategy for defending verbal art was new: it was not poetry's ancient posture of

---

[40] Here again, see the excellent study of Svenbro 1984b.

the sacral *vates* who claimed access to metaphysical truth and transcendental fame; nor was it the suggestion of the master of *ainoi* that his stories and songs contained valuable knowledge in code. It developed rhetorical perspectives on song to claim that artful composition could impose a special quality on language, but a virtue that transcended the mere formalization of speech and bestowed a unique life on it. It was this special quality that placed verbal works of art above statues and paintings and accompanied those works as they traveled through Greece.

In this way, the artful prose text was the prototype for a kind of writing that gives meaning in a unique way, the prototype for the notion of literature. In the next stage, the new ideal of an artfully made text was to be transferred back to poetry, viewed no longer as speech with meter but as an art of imaginative composition. For this deeper conception of poetry to supplant its common identification with versified prose, a system of literary, mimetic genres was required. This final step from rhetoric to poetics is the subject of the next chapter.

ELEVEN

LAWS OF POETRY

GENRE AND THE LITERARY SYSTEM

THE PREVIOUS chapter traced to the fourth century the first clear expressions in Greek of an idea of literature as artful writing with a special and permanent value. It was partly a humanist and ethical notion, but partly technical, too—to the extent that "artful" composition was thought to "build" into texts meanings that could not be expressed so well in any other form. The impulse to articulate this notion seems to have been connected with a burgeoning rhetorical and philosophical prose literature that mixed a display of technical power with promises to improve their readers. Writers inclined to take up and modify these forms were obliged to explain that their texts offered something new and different, but Greek song had needed no such notion as literature to justify its preservation and study. From time immemorial, song had been granted its claims to be an invaluable gift of the Muse, and the belief was confirmed by observation: the vast body of songs preserved from one generation to the next proved by its very repetition that song was that which survived and deserved to survive (changes and losses of songs being invisible to the oral tradition). When fifth-century intellectuals challenged the singers' hieratic pretensions and suggested that poetry was only verbal flim-flam, poetry's defenders reasserted its didactic and civilizing functions more insistently and ambitiously than previously; but the new defenses remained within the tradition of claiming a divine source for the powers of song. Song's defenders could not permit its reduction to an art, to being mere language embellished by linguistic tricks. But this was the view taken by rhetoricians and philosophers, who needed not only to define their writings against their competitors in prose but also to urge their merits in comparison to poetry's traditional benefits. The invention of (prose) literature needed to define poetry as well.

In this chapter, I shall follow up the trail and see how the conception of literature was broadened to accommodate poetry. In this process, texts from Isocrates will provide the clearest illustration of how and why poetry became defined as a formal derivative of prose; but Plato will contribute an important new way of unifying the category "poetry" by insisting on the mimetic character of all its forms and on their close relation to other illusionistic arts. This prepared for Aristotle's *Poetics*, which marks the full arrival of literary criticism as a systematic map of all forms of literature (mimetic arts in words) and a technical account of how each achieves its peculiar effects. As said in the introduction, the specifically literary or "poetic" approach to song relied on transforming genre from social to formal requirements. The delineation of clear functional and formal distinctions between poetry and prose and the identification of distinct forms within each enabled songs to be assessed intrinsically, bracketing all considerations of performance and *mise en scène*. For fourth-century readers of song texts, poetics offered a set of principles (Plato will actually insist on "laws") governing poetic form. These principles, and the rules derivable from them, were properly literary because they were based on the place of each kind of poem within a system of genres defined in their reciprocal formal relations.

Genres thus became literary in the sense that their nature and authority derived from their place in a comprehensive classification that dictated to each form, as a condition of being that form and not another, that it treat certain topics and employ a specified range of linguistic and musical devices to achieve specific emotional and cognitive effects. The new approach was both reductive and enriching. Though deploring the artificiality and oppressiveness of generic constraints has become a Romantic topos (indeed, a small "genre" of critical writing in itself), generic notions always offer a framework facilitating communication and a road map for literary innovation.[1] In fourth-century Greece, the elaboration of generic forms and rules enabled educated readers to value and find meaning in works that textualization had removed from the public contexts that had originally informed them with meaning. It is Romantic to think of some fall from pure unstructuredness into genres: what the fourth-century literary theorists did was transform traditional religious and social structures that had had implications for form into literary and formal structures that had implications for society and religion.

To trace this development, I shall examine conceptions of genre in the three most influential fourth-century writers about literature. I shall begin with Isocrates and highlight the role genre plays in his reading and writing of texts, stressing its difference from later fifth-century concerns by examining his analysis of Gorgias' *Helen*. I then note how genre informs Plato's critiques of poetry, which suggests the distance traversed since archaic times while showing a return of religious concerns that formalist approaches were displacing. Finally, I point out the centrality of genre to the fully demythologized analysis of the *Poetics* and draw some of its implications for how we are to understand Aristotle's criticism.

---

[1] See the excellent treatment by Fowler (1982).

Isocrates on Genre

In the last decade of Gorgias' long and prosperous life and in the first decade of what was to be his own equally successful career, Isocrates wrote an encomium to Helen of Troy. It was obviously important for the young rhetorician and philosopher to show that he knew how that sort of speech ought to be done (Isocrates *Helen* §69), even as he affects distaste for his task. In introducing his work, he deplores the current fad among rhetoricians of writing up defenses of "eccentric and paradoxical" propositions so as to demonstrate their own skill (§§1, 14). Isocrates pronounces this a trivial pursuit, and one that "the old sophist," whom Isocrates certainly knew well, had done better than anyone anyway.[2] But it was only by finding some deficiency in Gorgias that Isocrates could justify offering yet another model speech on the topos, and he significantly chose rules of genre as his ground: "Now [Gorgias] says that he has written an encomium of Helen; but as it turns out he has delivered a speech in defense (*apologia*) of her actions; but a [defense] speech employs a quite different set of technical building-blocks (*ideai*), and it concerns itself with different sorts of action. Making defense speeches (*apologēsasthai*) is appropriate (*prosēkei*] in cases where people are accused of injustice, while praise is for those who are distinguished for some good quality" (§§14–15). For Isocrates, Gorgias' *Helen* misfires in generic terms because it does not execute the tasks its form requires.

If we look back at Gorgias' *Helen* in these terms, Isocrates' strictures may seem to have some grounds, but in fact, his demands for generic purity are misplaced. It is questionable whether Gorgias would have cared to define his speech any more precisely than calling it *On Helen*, which is indeed how Isocrates first refers to the work (§14). But Gorgias planted the seeds for confusion among later rhetorical theorists when he described the discourse in a final flourish:

ἀφεῖλον τῶι λόγωι δύσκλειαν γυναικός, ἐνέμεινα τῶι νόμωι ὃν ἐθέμην ἐν ἀρχῆι τοῦ λόγου· ἐπειράθην καταλῦσαι μώμου ἀδικίαν καὶ δόξης ἀμαθίαν, ἐβουλθην γράψαι τὸν λόγον Ἑλένης ἐμὸν δὲ ἐγκώμιον, ἐμὸν δὲ παίγνιον. (§21)

I have used *logos* to remove the woman's bad repute and have abided by the law that I set for myself at the beginning: I have tried to demolish unjust blame and the ignorance behind common assumptions; I wished to write what would be an encomium for Helen and a plaything for me.

---

[2] Doubts once raised as to whether it is Gorgias' *Helen* that Isocrates has in view are hypercritical: see the discussion in Buchheim 1989: 159.

The concluding rhyming antithesis, "an *enkōmion* for Helen, but a *paignion* for me*," is probably the reason Isocrates, along with most ancient manuscripts, assigned the *Helen* to the genre "encomium." But Gorgias is clear that the "law"[3] he followed in his speech is one he set up himself. His chosen subject, after all, necessarily required a good deal of "defense speech" (*apologēsasthai*), as he avers at one point, glossing the term as "demolishing blame" (§8). His prologue, to which his conclusion refers us, strongly suggested that his project was to be a generic hybrid: "It is the duty of the same man," he said, "to say in the right way what ought to be said (*ta deonta*) and to refute those who cast [false] reproaches" (§2). The program thus combines defending against false accusation with affirming the truth—in Helen's case, apology and encomium.[4] His twofold agenda may appear a hybrid to Isocrates, but it afforded Gorgias ample opportunity to defend shocking, paradoxical, and attention-getting propositions. The true "genre" here, as Isocrates probably knew, is the speech that displays oratorical talent.[5] Gorgias would have given a truer description of the work if he had reversed his final antithesis and called it "an encomium of Gorgias and a toying with the Helen legend"; but that, of course, was not a gentlemanly thing to say in earnest.

Isocrates' quibble with the *Helen* suggests that the generation of Gorgias' successors was more strongly attached than their master to a literary system of distinct prose genres, each requiring its own forms (*ideai*) of thought and expression.[6] His own *Helen* highlights his scrupulous observance of such rules, as when he apologizes for his magniloquence in praising Helen's beauty by pleading that hyperbolic language "befits" an extraordinary topic (§52); the apology manages to combine exalting his subject and displaying his rhetorical control. Again, when he worries (§29) that he has bypassed "the right degree" (*kairos*) in going on so long about Helen's connections with Theseus, the apology is disingenuous in a text aimed primarily at an Athenian audience; this is in fact a perfectly kairotic adaptation of an old hymnic topos in which the subject's inex-

---

[3] I have followed Diels-Kranz and others in reading νόμωι in §21; cf. Buchheim 1989: 160.

[4] He goes on to reiterate his double task chiastically, "to free from blame this woman with such a bad reputation while showing her accusers liars, both to reveal the truth and to put an end to ignorance" (§2). The hybrid quality of Gorgias' *Helen* can be seen from Immisch's (1927: 7–8) informative, if procrustean, analysis in Aristotelian generic terms: he labels §§3–5 as encomium and §§6–20 defense.

[5] Isocrates seems to recognize this when he introduces Gorgias: "*Of those who wished to speak finely on a topic* I most praise the one who wrote about Helen because he brought such a remarkable woman to mind" (§14).

[6] On *ideai* in Isocrates, see Lidov 1983. An idea of the kinds of technical rhetorical terms popular at this time may be gleaned from Socrates' mock-admiring survey in *Phaedrus* 266D–268A. See Ford 2001: 104.

haustible goodness is tactfully affirmed.[7] These instances, which could be multiplied in this cunning text, illustrate how genres with well-defined requirements supplied a way to analyze and judge written texts. In scenes of actual *viva voce* debate, *kairos* should mean what is appropriate to the fast-moving and particular circumstances; but here it concerns the permissible length of digressions in a well-composed text.[8] So, too, the rhetorical notion that speakers should suit their words to their characters and their subjects is already developed in Aristophanes, but in Isocrates this decorum refers rather to an internal relation of diction (gorgeous) to theme (Helen's beauty), form to content.

Isocrates relies on generic guidelines again to justify a display piece in honor of Busiris, an Egyptian tyrant who had been the subject of numerous anti-encomia (*Busiris* §5). This speech begins by picking a quarrel with another notable teacher of rhetoric, Polycrates of Samos, who had made a splash with his *Defense Speech for Busiris* and *Prosecutor's Speech against Socrates*. Here again, Isocrates charges his predecessor with violating generic rules, "falling short of what is required" (*to deon*, §4). The regrettable lapse from generic correctness once again impels him to descend to writing up a specimen to show "from what elements the encomium and the court speech ought (*edei*) to be composed" (§9).

Isocrates' conception of distinct prose forms was not intended to be novel; the difference between defense speeches and encomia was, as he says, patent to anybody (*Busiris* §4).[9] But genre provided him with more than a toehold for taking on prominent rhetoricians: the system of literary genres was finally central to Isocrates' ideas of what good writing should be. Throughout his career, the notion that rules and forms keep poetry from being prose and keep one kind of prose from being another was a fruitful point of departure for defining the value of his own works against "poetry" and for seeking out new possibilities for eloquence outside the established genres of prose. A short passage from the *Evagoras* will epitomize this.

Isocrates agrees with Plato that most of their contemporaries who teach rhetoric, those whom they label "sophists," are engaged in a trivial enterprise when to display their wares they produce speeches on such nonserious topics as the virtues of salt or death, or encomia for figures

[7] For the topos in Isocrates and its antecedents, Race 1978, and Heath 1989: 30–31 with n. 1. On Isocrates' conventional notion of the *kairos*, see 15.74 and 13.14–15, where he follows Gorgias in insisting that it is not reducible to an art. Cf. Plato *Phaedrus* 267B and Kennedy 1963: 66–68.

[8] See Vallozza 1985.

[9] See Plato *Phaedrus* 267A on the apology as a genre, and *Protagoras* 326A on encomia being especially suited to men of former times.

from myth.[10] To elevate himself above this unsavory company, he sometimes stresses that his works belong to a new genre, encomia that are not in poetry but in prose, and do not treat trivial topics or legendary figures but real people and their actual deeds. In the prologue to *Evagoras* (§§8–11), he justifies "encomizing the excellence of a man through speech (*dia logōn*)," that is, putting his virtues on display in prose rather than verse:

> To the poets many adornments (*kosmoi*) are allowed. For it is possible for them to make gods mixing in with mortals, speaking with and struggling alongside anyone they like; and they can reveal these things not only through conventional expressions but with some common ones, some new, and some metaphors, omitting none [of the forms of speech], but thoroughly embroidering (*diapoikilai*) their poetry with all the various forms (*eidē*). But for those concerned with *logoi* [bare prose], none of these is permitted. They must use [words] precisely and use only the ones in common use,[11] and they have to select arguments (*enthumēmata*) that actually bear on the issue.
>
> In addition, the poets make everything with meters and rhythms, but prose writers do not share in these things, which have such appeal (*kharis*) that even if the speech is poor in expression (*lexis*) and argument, nevertheless the smooth rhythms themselves and the symmetries move the souls (*psukhagagousin*) of their hearers. For if one took from the most esteemed poems their meter and left only their thought (*dianoia*) and words, they would have a far inferior reputation than they now enjoy.

These distinctions between what is allowed in poetry and what in prose are quintessentially rhetorical in their conception and their organization.[12] Artistic "ornament" is divided into content (admitting "mythical" confrontations between immortal and mortal) and style.[13] Style is subdivided into diction (further broken down into figures of speech and figures of thought) and arrangement, that is, rhythm and meter. Classical rhetoric had a prescribed place for the musical effects of language as an addendum to style (*lexis*). So Aristotle's *Rhetoric* discusses what to say in Books 1 and 2, and then talks about "style" in Book 3, where prose rhythm is treated as an aspect of style (3.8–9).

---

[10] On the literature of praising small things: O'Sullivan 1992: 84; Lausberg 1998: 104; Pease 1926.

[11] *Politikos*, i.e., in city-wide use, versus *rhētorikōs*; cf. *politikēs kai rhētorikēs*, *Poetics* 1450b6.

[12] Cf. Richardson 1981: 8. For some very interesting observations on the superficiality of Isocrates' relation with poetry, see Blass 1887–93, 2:46–52.

[13] Cf. *Rhetoric* 1405a7–8. On "the fabulous" (*to muthōdes*) as a license granted to poets, cf. Thucydides 1.21.1, Plato *Republic* 522A; Aristotle *Metaphysics* 1074b1–14. Cf. Isocrates *To Nicocles* §49.

In this passage, the heart of Isocrates' formalism is on display: there are different "forms" (here called *eidē*) of thought and speech that convention has unfairly distributed so that more of the "ornamental" ones are allowed in poetry. Most importantly, the orator (Isocrates' disguise as a writer of serious prose) has no share at all in poetry's most potent ornament, its enchanting rhythm and harmonies. Isocrates endows rhythm and meter—which to this formalist count as the most distinctive feature of poetry—with a quasi-magical power to "bewitch" (*psukhagōgein*) souls.[14] The intense psychological effects of "logos with meter" had been noted by Gorgias, and Plato was happy to agree: "meter, rhythm, and harmony" have "some sort of enchantment" (*kēlēsis*) about them that makes poetry compelling even to those who know poets lie (*Republic* 601A–B). The incantatory power of poetic language to reach "even the best of us" is the last and crucial argument for Plato's dismissing it from the state (see esp. 606A–B). But in *Evagoras*, Isocrates stakes out a position between Gorgias and Plato: for Gorgias, "psychagogic" power inhered in all *logos*; the "meter" of poetry was an augmenting but inessential ornament. Plato turned Gorgias' term against him and his ilk when he defined *rhetoric* as "swaying the mind (*psukhagōgia*) through words" (*Phaedrus* 261A8; cf. 271C10). Isocrates takes the psychagogy that Gorgias had attributed to language and that Plato had associated with rhetoric and confines it to poetry, and specifically to the sonorities of poetic language.[15]

The rhetorical view of genre had several advantages for Isocrates. Poets could be defined, *qua* poets, as abusing their audience, and the orator was allowed to borrow at least some of their verbal fireworks: elevated diction and figures of thought were properly employed by those ambitious enough to essay in prose the high themes that demand high language. By scapegoating the pure music of language, its ability to enchant and deceive, Isocrates assumed the poets' function as wise and pleasing teachers of a nation.

Rhetorical distinctions of genre enabled Isocrates to present his orations as a higher kind of prose than sophistic display, and yet not poetry. This is spelled out in his *Antidosis*, that innovative "verbal icon" whose prologue I have discussed. *Antidosis* also contains Isocrates' explanation of how his works should be placed generically. He begins by listing existing prose genres, which he asserts are no fewer than the genres of po-

---

[14] *Psychagogia* belongs to the realms of sorcery and necromancy, as in Aeschylus *Persians* 687. See Burkert 1962 and Faraone 1996 on Nestor's cup.

[15] Cf. *To Nicocles* §49. Süss (1910: 79) argues for the Gorgianic provenience of these ideas in Isocrates; cf. De Romilly 1975: 15. On psychagogy in fifth- and fourth-century discussions of poetry (and painting), Halliwell 1986: 64 n. 24, 188–89. Cf. *Poetics* 1450a33, 1450b16.

etry; balancing the two realms of *logos* in this way suggests they are equivalent.[16] The prose genre he claims to have developed is the sort of speech that is given at panhellenic assemblies; this genre, he says, is allowed a "more poetic and more embroidered style" and uses "the more splendid forms of thought and speech" (§47).[17] The payoff is that "all men take pleasure in such discourses no less than they do in poetry, and many wish to become students of such orators, thinking that they are wiser and more helpful than those who speak well in court" (ibid.). Just because he does not write verse, Isocrates need not be a logographer; nor need he forfeit the role of teaching and pleasing with fair speech. His rhetorical analysis of what makes poetry (the fabulous, meter, ornament in general, hypnotic music) manages to leave a space for a careful writer like himself (and no one lavished more care on his prose than Isocrates) to appropriate its ornaments in the service of teaching. Isocrates' literary system wins him a position above forensic rhetoricians and "sophistical" writers as a "sage" (§49).

To point out the strategic advantages of Isocrates' formalism, however, should not be to dismiss its importance as a map of a literary system. His well-defined conception of uncrossable lines between genres oriented his writing and helped him make the value of that writing comprehensible to his city. The high civic role he claims for artistic prose belongs to a larger, humanistic vision of the role of speech in society, a theme he repeated several times in his works.[18] In opposition especially to Plato, Isocrates' sense of "philosophy" did not aspire to advance beyond common reason; *doxa* was not Plato's "opinion," but the collective judgments people make about things that are impossible to know or difficult to decide. On Isocrates' view, after getting as close to an understanding of realities as human nature permits (*Antidosis* §§184, 271), society must construct its morality and wisdom somewhere between pure skepticism and pure idealism. And it is just here that *logos* plays its crucial role. Nature has given us no other instrument than language to ensure our survival and self-realization. Language enables human beings to communicate with each other, to articulate values and organize societies, and ultimately to become civilized. A capacity bestowed equally on all by nature, *logos* yet distinguishes human

---

[16] *Antidosis* §§45–47. He declines to name all genres of prose, but lists antiquarian genealogies, scholarly inquiry into poets, history, especially of wars (a genre he thinks is worthy of admiration), and finally eristics.

[17] Cf. *Panathenaic Oration* §§2, 271, 135 for a contrast between such speech and railing at assemblies or encomizing trivial subjects.

[18] *To Nicocles* §§5–9, reprised in *Antidosis* §§253–57; cf. *Panegyric* §48. On this tradition, stemming from the sophists, see Solmsen 1932: 151 ff. On Isocrates' encomia to *logos*, see the analysis of De Romilly 1975: 52 ff., esp. 54–55, where she points out that "logos is indeed a decisive substitution for the *dikē* of Protagoras' pattern."

beings from other animals, and its artistic employment may distinguish the true sages among men. Such a wise artisan will harness the resources of language to the good of the polity: its harmonious symmetries can charm citizens into reasonable accord.[19] For all its strategic advantages, Isocrates' literary formalism derives not from a fetishism of technique, but from an enlightened, humanistic view of language as a natural endowment that art may perfect to serve human ends.

Plato: Pure Forms

Conceptions of genre also play a key role in Plato's arguments with poets. Already in *Ion*, the fact that rhapsodes/critics tend to specialize in one genre and not another (as Socrates puts it, that Ion responds to Homer but not to Archilochus) suggests that there is no unitary art (*tekhnē*) of poetry (*Ion* 530D–532B). The divide between Homer and Archilochus (praise and blame) provides the crucial first step in the dialogue's argument that poets and rhapsodes have no art of their own. The defeat of the rhapsode in fact begins when he agrees with Socrates that "there is, I suppose, an art of poetry as a whole?" (ποιητικὴ γάρ που ἐστιν τὸ ὅλον; 532C). Ion's seemingly benign admission establishes that there is a knowledge of poetry as a whole that understands each of its forms; it follows that the epic specialist who is indifferent to iambus cannot be said to possess a technical expertise even in epic.[20]

Plato was concerned to define the art of poetry in a systematic way, but not because a knowledge of "poetics" had any serious value. The concept of poetics usually enables him lump together all forms of *mimēsis* and indict them under a single charge. When Plato makes Homer "the father of tragedy," this is not only a literary historical insight into an ethical affinity between two genres (an idea Aristotle shared);[21] Plato is constructing a unified poetic art whose principles the philosopher, as expert on dialectic and definition, will best understand. This allows Plato to subject all poets, Aeschylus beside Homer and Hesiod, to a single philosophical critique. Genre theories appear to play little role in the practical criticism of poetry of *Republic* 2–3. Yet Plato's censoring of the poets is organized in the standard sequence of rhetorical categories: Socrates begins by looking at *what* poets say (their *muthoi*: 376E) and then *how* they

---

[19] De Romilly (ibid., 53) well observes, "We are very far from Gorgias' magic used to create emotions."

[20] On *Ion*, see Kahn 1993. Other notable statements on this theme: *Apology* 22A–C, *Symposium* 223D, *Republic* 395A.

[21] Cf. chapter 8, note 51 above.

say it (his idiosyncratic division of poetry into three modes: dramatic/imitative, diegetic/narrative, and a mixture of the two, 392c); finally, he turns to a discussion of rhythms and melodies (398b). By the end of the work, his agglomeration of all songs into the "imitative arts" sponsors the metaphysical argument against poetry in Book 10.

Perhaps the most revealing generic distinction in the *Republic* comes late in the work, when Socrates formally exiles poets. In a much-discussed phrase, he says, "Our city only admits those kinds of poetry that are hymns to the gods and *enkōmia* to good men."[22] Attempting to read some mitigation of Plato's hostility to art misses the point of the phrase. The one generic distinction Plato will not do without is between mortal and divine song. To reduce all permissible poetry to these two kinds lays bare his fundamentally metaphysical approach to genre: even when reduced to a minimum, his sense of poetic forms affirms an unbreachable gulf between humanity and the divine from which all other considerations must follow.

Plato is the first Greek author to use the word *humnos* in the specific sense of "song for a god," and it may be that he changed the meaning of an old word for "song" just to make this distinction with songs for mortals.[23] I suspect this is so, for I think we can see Plato cloaking his innovation with the mantle of antiquity in a revealing passage from *Laws* (700A–701B).[24] It is one of Plato's many complaints about the decadence of musical styles in his day, but it is unique in offering a kind of natural history of genres.[25] In this account, once upon a time before the fall from aristocracy to democracy, the pure forms of song existed unmixed. In this pristine world, hymns were distinct from *thrēnoi*, which is to say, songs of divinity had no trace of songs of death, mortality, humanity. Within the class of hymns, dithyrambs were kept distinct from paeans because Dionysus was not Apollo (700B). The divine authority of genres was maintained in cities first of all by the silence and calm that "the cultured classes"[26] assumed when listening to music; but for children and pedagogues, it was enforced by the rod (*rhabdos*), like the rods still carried

---

[22] 607A: ὅσον μόνον ὕμνους θεοῖς καὶ ἐγκώμια τοῖς ἀγαθοῖς ποιήσεως παραδεκτέον εἰς πόλιν. At *Republic* 468D, he allowed "hymns" as part of cult for great warriors, as Ajax in Homer gets the chine. Adam compares Aristophanes' opposite proposal at *Ecclesiazusae.* 680.

[23] On *humnos*, see the introduction, p. 12.

[24] Cf. *Laws* 657c ff., 669c ff.

[25] E.g., at *Republic* 424B–D. Nagy (1990: 109–10) places such responses in the context of the infusion of panhellenic lyric genres into the theater.

[26] So England (1921) takes τοῖς γεγονόσι περὶ παίδευσιν at 700c5. The opposition to "pedagogues" militates against "those involved with education," as Ast and others take it. For *paideusis* as culture, see *Protagoras* 349A3, *Timaeus* 53c2.

by ushers "for the massive mob" in the theater.[27] So, at least, Plato imagines things must have been like before the radical democracy, before he was born.

"With the passage of time," decline set in (700D), and generic restraints slackened. Portraying the history of music as one of increasing lawlessness, Plato counters progressivist notions that had been used in defense of the "new" music.[28] In his pessimistic but natural history ("time" is the prime mover), the leaders of "unmusical lawlessness" (*amousou paranomias*, 700D) were poets, those "naturally endowed" with the ability to please through music.[29] Because a knowledge of music is, strictly speaking, only a knowledge of rhythms and melodies, poets were "ignorant about what is lawful and just to the Muse" (700D); wrongly assuming that there is no other "correctness" (*orthotēs*) in music than the pleasure of the listener, poets set out to cater to this figure and, in their zeal to multiply pleasure, set about to "mix" the genres.[30] The first example Plato gives of the fall is the most fundamental one—hymns were mixed with dirges (700D). Once singers had brought together these metaphysically antithetical kinds (700B), other basic distinctions soon fell: they confounded Apollo and Dionysus by mixing paeans and dithyrambs, and mixed the ecstatic modes of the *aulos* with the Dorian restraint of the kithara. It is no surprise in a book so named that what is needed to remedy the situation is a return to the basic "laws" of genre.[31]

Genre is important to Plato, but not as a literary concept. Song types are ultimately rooted in the absolute separateness of the divine from the

---

[27] Plato seems to be imagining a real use for what were in his day no doubt largely symbolic rods carried by the ushers or "beadles" (*rhabdoukhoi*) at musical and other contests: see Aristophanes *Peace* 734 with scholia, Plato *Protagoras* 338A.

[28] Progressivist accounts of musical history were frequently debated in the *libretti* of the very "new" music that Plato despised, such as Timotheus 796 *PMG* (progress) and Pherecrates fr. 155 *PCG* (decline); for good introductions to this very complex development, see Barker 1984: 93–98; West 1992: 356–72.

[29] Poetical natures arose just naturally: ποιηταὶ ἐγίγνοντο φύσει μὲν ποιητικοί, ἀγνώμονες δὲ περὶ τὸ δίκαιον τῆς Μούσης καὶ τὸ νόμιμον, 700d. Cf. *Republic* 605A, where the mimetic poet is "framed by nature" (πέφυκέ . . . πέπηγεν, cf. 530D) to be able to please the lowest parts of the soul. Plato thus agrees with the naturalistic account Aristotle gives for the rise of poetry in *Poetics* 4.

[30] 700c: βακχεύοντες καὶ μᾶλλον τοῦ δέοντος κατεχόμενοι ὑφ᾽ ἡδονῆς, κεραννύντες δὲ θρήνους τε ὕμνοις καὶ παίωνας διθυράμβοις, καὶ αὐλδίας δὴ ταῖς κιθαρῳδίαις μιμούμενοι, καὶ πάντα εἰς πάντα συνάγοντες. The paean composed to Lysander (Plutarch *Lysander* 18) may have been part of Plato's provocation.

[31] On *nomos* (also the word for musical mode) as "law" of genre, see esp. *Laws* 799E–800A, and cf. 722E1, 700B5, 734E, and [Plutarch] *De Musica*. 1133b–c. The Peripatetics proposed a different etymology: [Aristotle] *Problems* 19.28 (919b38) says musical nomes were so called because in ancient times laws used to be sung.

mortal and all that this entails. Looking back at *Republic* 2–3 from this point of view, we can see that Plato's theocratic agenda was subtly present all along. Ostensibly a thematic survey organized around the virtues he wished to inculcate through story, Socrates begins with the earliest poets, Homer and Hesiod, and with the earliest events they recount: the castration of Ouranos by Kronos, and then the battles of the gods (377E–378E). Such a "first things first" approach allows him to adapt the Xenophanean social and political demand for purified song to his own theology and ontology (*theologia*, 379A5–6). The pure image of divinity on which he insists is subtly affirmed by the way his discussion is organized—proceeding forward in mythical time and downward in metaphysical value. Marking each step of the way, Socrates follows his account of "stories concerning the gods" with those about death and the underworld (the transition at 386A makes clear that, unlike "modern" musicians, Socrates will keep death and the gods well apart); only then does he take up the behavior of heroes (387D).[32] The progression becomes more apparent once he has treated "the gods, the daemons, and heroes as well as what goes on in Hades" (392A), and breaks off before he can take up the expected account of how normal human beings (*anthrōpoi*) should be represented. Socrates decides that other questions need answering first, but, with typical coyness, Plato suggests that the *Republic* itself may provide the best paradigm for representing a mortal (392A–C).

Although Plato was a shrewd critic of rhetorical theories and a genius in inventing and parodying Greek prose forms, the divisions that matter in his philosophy are not the forms (*ideai*) of speech elaborated by sophists and rhetoricians, but the fundamental distinctions in reality that dialectic alone could reveal.[33] His insistence in the *Phaedrus* (269C–272B) that rhetoric must know all the kinds of speech and match them to receptive kinds of souls is less a realistic program for Aristotle's *Rhetoric* (though that work goes some way toward reformulating this program in practical terms) than a demand that any aspiring rhetorician first master Platonic philosophy. On poetics, Plato could agree with archaic Sappho that "it is not right that here should be a dirge in the house of the Muses' attendants," but the Muse is now philosophy, and the rules for "what befits us" to sing are not derived from social practices or even from literary conventions, but from Plato's philosophical vision of reality and his determination to refer all distinction to the divine.

---

[32] Once mortality is under discussion, he can add that gods like Thetis should not be depicted lamenting for their mortal offspring: 388A–B. The same applies to all-too-human laughter at 389A.

[33] See Svenbro 1984b: 231–32.

Genre in Aristotle's *Poetics*

A comprehensive system of genres enabled Aristotle to offer the first systematic account of poetry "in terms of the art of poetry, and not another art" (words to be weighed below). The first three chapters of the treatise are dedicated to defining the place of the "poetic art" within the larger class of "mimetic arts" and delimiting the genres of poetry. Aristotle works inductively, beginning with objectively determinable properties of imitations, such as the media in which they are executed. Thus is Aristotle able to combine the recognized forms of poetry in his day under a single category, imitations using language, and set them apart from other mimetic arts. Within the imitative arts, each genre can be defined on the basis of the same considerations—how far it avails itself of music and rhythm, the content (the "objects of imitation") it addresses, and the mode in which the imitation is presented (i.e., whether by pure narrative, by direct impersonation of characters, or by some mixture). To understand a play of Sophocles, one has to place it in relation to Homer (similarly serious and noble, but epic) and Aristophanes (similarly dramatic but comic).

Why Aristotle must begin with genre is indicated in the opening sentence of the work:

> Let us speak about the art of poetry, both in itself and in its distinct kinds, specifying what is the function of each kind, and how plots should be constructed if the composition is going to turn out *kalos*, and further let us specify the parts constituting each kind, their number and nature, as well as such other matters as belong to this field of inquiry; let us begin, taking up the subject with first principles, as is natural.

A *tekhnē* must intend a single subject, so Aristotle must define poetry itself, that is, as a whole.[34] He must also know poetry's particular kinds to determine the "potential" or "capacity" (*dunamis*) of each. Only if we know this can we decide that a given poem is such a thing as can be called "fine" (*kalōs ekhei*).[35] In general, each species or "genre" within the imitative arts will have its own end, and the "finest" form for each must be that which best conduces to its end.[36] For example, once tragedy

---

[34] *Tekhnê* is the key concept to this chapter, cf. 1447a21, 1447b29. On Aristotle's logical method here, see Hutton 1982: 9–10, Janko 1987: 66, cf. Hubbard in Russell and Winterbottom 1972: 106 n. 1.

[35] So a "plot that is fine" (*ton kalōs ekhonta muthon*, 1453a12–13) effects the proper ends of tragedy. *Kalōs* is the standard compliment of good singing and dancing (e.g., *Laws* 654B), used pregnantly by Plato in *Republic* 331E4.

[36] It is just in its greater concentration and compactness that tragedy excels over epic, for tragic unity is "not watered down" with irrelevant episodes (1462b3–11).

has been distinguished from other poetic forms, Aristotle can arrive at a definition of tragedy in chapter 6 that stipulates, among other things, that its specific goal is a catharsis of pity and fear. This end entails, for example, that "the tragedy that is most excellent (*kallistos*) in respect to the art" will have a change of fortune from good to bad (1453a22–23). If tragic poets compose plots in which the good end happily and the evil suffer, their works forfeit full endorsement as *kalos* because the kind of pleasure (*hēdonē*, 1453a36) they afford more properly belongs to a different genre, comedy, which has different ends (1453a30–39). If one knows the genre of a poem, one knows in principle how it ought to be constructed (poetry is fundamentally an art of "making"); absent whimsical audiences, a "fine" poem will do what poems of that kind are designed by their nature to do. Because genre provides the criteria for calling a poem technically "fine," the system of literary genres is the foundation that makes writing an "art" of poetry, a *Poetics*, possible.

The most profound change here from archaic ways of judging song is that ethical and religious criteria are replaced by technical appropriateness. This formal, ostensibly objective approach was especially fruitful for evaluating song as text removed from context. For Aristotle, a tragedy can be evaluated by reading it; there is no need to go sit in the theater. Like anything else that is made, poems can be understood intrinsically by considering how well their form follows their function. Readers can evaluate poems without reference to the contexts and occasions where they first appeared, and texts of plays that had first been produced before the author was born (for example, Aristotle's beloved *Oedipus the King* by Sophocles) can be examined, analyzed, and pronounced logically coherent and structurally sound.

Aristotle's opening survey of the forms of mimesis is indebted to materialist poetics in its vivid sense of the physical media of art—whether shapes, pigments, or the human body and voice. That imitations produced by painters or sculptors should have different capacities from those produced by poets is inevitable given the natural differences in the way we respond to colors or shapes or melodies or words.[37] The same natural distinctions will exist within a given class of art: poetry that avails itself of the natural powers of music will be capable of effects not available to that which confines itself to rhythmical language. The implication is that each branch of imitation is defined and in some respects limited by the materials it deploys. For example, to say that one way that tragedy differs

---

[37] In *Republic* 373B, imitation using "colors and shapes" is distinguished from *mousikê*. For this conventional dyad in Plato, see Gudeman 1934: 81 and Bywater 1909: 102. Aristotle's key discussion of the different imitative capacities (*dunamis*) of the visual and verbal arts is *Politics* 1340a1–b19, on which see Ford forthcoming.

from epic is in including the elements of "spectacle" and "music" is to say more than that tragedies conventionally were performed onstage and regularly had four odes: it points to two media that can make powerful appeals to the senses.

The inductive opening of the *Poetics* is followed by what may be called a natural history of poetry in chapter 4. Here Aristotle accounts for the origin of poetry and its genres as forms of human speech that evolved in historical social contexts. He begins in enlightened fashion by asserting that poetry has arisen naturally and not from some divine gift. Its sources lie in readily observable capacities of *homo sapiens*: people are natural imitators, as is seen by the fact that imitating is how we "first" learn (1448b8, *mathēseis prōtas*, an important qualifier that indicates imitating itself is not learned behavior). A second cause is needed, since imitation only becomes an art when an audience assembles; accordingly, taking pleasure in imitations must be natural too, a thesis Aristotle justifies by identifying the pleasure from imitations with our innate pleasure in learning. When one adds our natural (but not specifically human) affinity for rhythm and melody, the possibility existed for certain people, "naturally" inclined that way, to "give birth to poetry" by improvising imitations in language, rhythm, and melody (1448b20–23).[38] Genres arose with further help from nature, as innately serious people tended to imitate noble actions, while more common types took up the actions of lower sorts, as in satirical abuse. Like Plato, Aristotle settles on two fundamental kinds of poetry, but his dyad is social rather than theological: hymns and encomia are folded together into the poetry of praise (1448b27), and this is complemented by the poetry of blame (the source of parody and the ancestor to comedy). The two types arose from the "impulses" (1449a3) of individuals to pursue either the socially admirable or the base in accordance with their natures.[39] In the course of time, these two basic genres evolved, as trial and error showed that certain forms of speech and music best produced the satisfactions potential in the form. The genres themselves mutated and multiplied as tragedy succeeded epic as a way to represent serious imitation, just as comic drama derived from mock-heroic poetry.

[38] A poet must have a certain nature: *Poetics* 1455a30–34. Skill in metaphor, a poet's chief linguistic weapon, cannot be taught, "it is a sign of genius," 1459a6–7. So *Rhetoric* 1405a8; cf. 1394a5, 1412a10.

[39] A path to deconstructing the "natural" history of the *Poetics* lies in its conception of "proper natures" of individuals (1449a3–4: κατὰ τὴν οἰκείαν φύσιν). The adjective *oikeios* (literally, "being at home") introduces an aesthetic operator into his ostensible natural process, since there would be no fixed genres if poets were not bound by a (presumably natural) "suitability" to the kinds of poetry they produce. What is notable here is not simply Aristotle's assumption that serious people will not be "at home with" frivolous art, but that kinds of art have the same accord with individual character as that which governs what is "at home" within a given work of art.

The natural history of poetry in *Poetics* chapter 4 retroactively converts its opening diaresis into an "anatomy" of the arts, and some scholars have stressed Aristotle's biological approach to poetry. It has been protested that such an outlook should not be exaggerated, for both poetics and biology can be expected to reflect Aristotle's larger logical and teleological conceptions about how parts relate to wholes.[40] Certainly it is not necessary to remember that Aristotle collected marine specimens on the shores of Asia Minor to comprehend his literary system. But he does accord a central place to the analogy between poem and animal in explaining the relation of literary form and function. In recommending unity in composition, Aristotle follows Plato and compares the form of good poetry to the composition of living bodies, wherein each part fits with the others to constitute an optimally functioning whole. The previous chapter considered the *Phaedrus'* unprecedented image of the well-written text as an animal with all its parts in the right places. It clearly influenced Aristotle, for he rewrites the passage very closely in his own description of organic unity; the ideal tragic plot represents a "complete [or fully grown] and whole action of a certain size" (τελείας καὶ ὅλης πράξεως . . . ἐχούσης τι μέγεθος, 1450b24–25). Aristotle goes on to define "whole" as having a beginning, middle, and end (1450b25–27), and illustrates the importance of proper magnitude by saying that if a text or an animal is too big, "one can't consider it all at once and its unity and wholeness are lost from the spectator's view" (1450b39–51a2: οἴχεται τοῖς θεωροῦσι τὸ ἕν καὶ τὸ ὅλον ἐκ τῆς θεωρίας).[41] Like an animal, a poem is an object that, to be "fair," must have a certain size and arrangement (1450b34–37: τὸ καλὸν καὶ ζῷον καὶ ἅπαν πρᾶγμα ὃ συνέστηκεν ἐκ τινῶν οὐ μόνον ταῦτα τεταγμένα δεῖ ἔχειν ἀλλὰ καὶ μέγεθος ὑπάρχειν μὴ τὸ τυχόν· τὸ γὰρ καλὸν ἐν μεγέθει καὶ τάξει ἐστίν). There is, then, a strong biological cast to Aristotle's exposition of the "parts" of plays and how they work together. In part, this cast of thought lends poetics an empirical, objective tone, the high-minded disinterestedness of science. But Aristotle's conception of organic composition had a payoff for critical practice as well: if we place the arts within a teleological nature that "does nothing in vain," good poets might be held to similar standards; critics are then justified in examining each perceived detail of a literary text and asking what role it plays in the overall design.[42] It is apt that the most profoundly Aristotelian theory of literature in the twentieth century is called *The Anatomy of Criti-*

[40] E.g., Ress 1981, with the qualifications of Halliwell 1986: 98 n. 24.

[41] Compare 1459a32–34, where Aristotle says that an overly large epic plot will be "hard to perceive as connected" (οὐκ εὐσύνοπτος), and one of constricted length will be "overly complex because of its variety" (καταπεπλεγμένον τῇ ποικιλίᾳ). The use of εὐσύνοπτος in *Politics* 1326b24 is worth comparing.

[42] See good remarks in *GGL* 1: 133, 164.

cism. (Though here, of course, the naturalizing image for Frye's major discriminations ["modes"] is of the seasons.)

Social forces also shape poetry profoundly, but that some features of a developed genre are conventional does not mean that they may be discarded or ignored at will. The poetician's knowledge of the form and function of a genre will have prescriptive force as long as human societies have similar expectations about what is high and low behavior and respond similarly to the musical and verbal forms in which these are represented. One important gain from this naturalizing view of generic conventions is that the distinctions a good critic makes in "carving up" a text will express natural articulations. Thus poetics teaches a dispassionate and empirical analysis that is at least as valid and verifiable as whether an expert butcher has found the real joints of an animal with his knife. The organicism that Aristotle took from Plato and adapted to his formal and teleological view of poetry gave poetic criticism something of the objectivity of anatomy.

Learning from Poetics

To understand poetry as an art, then, is not to evaluate the moral or ethical value of particular poems, but to derive from an examination of all forms of poetry the principles governing each kind and determining its proper pleasure. This knowledge makes poetry into a *tekhnē*: with it, one will be able to specify in advance the kinds of procedure that will produce the "best" poems of each genre. The *Poetics* is for readers and critics rather than for writers of poems: it is clearly not a handbook, since Aristotle allows that poets may succeed through a knowledge of the principles of art or simply because they have picked up or been born with the knack for making successful plays.[43]

The auditor of Aristotle's lectures on poetics also got a different sort of knowledge of it than the spectator at a play. A confusion between these two social positions has, I believe, misled commentators into thinking that Aristotle thought poetry taught its audience profound truths about human life. In support of that view, much has been read into the reason Aristotle gives in chapter 4 for thinking we take pleasure in imitations:

> Images of things that we look upon with pain give us pleasure to contemplate when they are very precisely rendered, for example, the shapes of rather dis-

---

[43] This is indicated compendiously in the first chapter when Aristotle traces the forms of imitation to people experimenting, "some through art, others through a knack" (*sunētheia*, 1447a19–20). It is confirmed in his invocation of Homer as an excellent epic poet, "whether by art or naturally" (1451a24).

gusting animals and of corpses. And the reason for this is that learning is not only extremely pleasant for philosophers, but for others, too, though they share in it only to a little extent. For this reason, people are pleased when they look at images, because it is possible for them to learn something as they contemplate them, and to deduce (*sullogizesthai*) what each thing is, for example that this man is that man. [This is true] since, if someone happens not to have seen [the thing represented] before, the imitation will not please *qua* imitation, but on account of its fine workmanship or coloring or some other cause such as this. (1448b10–19)

If imitations please us because they afford a kind of learning, it might follow that the true aim of the imitative arts is to teach. When one adds that the difference between poetry and history is that poetry represents not particular facts but the *kinds of things* that happen (ch. 9), the pleasure tragedy gives its audience may be that of learning (even "deducing," on a narrow construction of *sullogizesthai*) patterns of human behavior from the structured plots of plays. This is a widespread current understanding of the *Poetics*.[44] A passage from Aristotle's *Parts of Animals* appears to support this view by offering a model of the pleasurable learning tragedy affords.[45] In that work, Aristotle urges that animals that give no pleasure to our perceptions (*aisthēsis*) can yet provide boundless delight for "those who can recognize causes and are by nature philosophers." "Indeed," he continues, "it would be paradoxical and strange, if we should take pleasure in studying *images* of unpleasant animals, because we are at the same time studying the graphic or shaping skill that fashions them, and yet we should not love still more the study of the originals put together by nature, at least when we can discern their causes" (645a7–17).

The text from *Parts of Animals* obviously casts light on *Poetics*, but both are far from identifying learning with the pleasure afforded by poetry. The pleasure in learning in *Poetics* 4 is illustrated at a very low level

[44] See, e.g., House 1956, revived by Janko 1984: esp. 139–42, 1987: esp. xvi–xx; Halliwell 1986: esp. 190–98, 353–54; and Kennedy 1989: 537; Nussbaum 1986: 378–94; Belfiore 1992: 345–53; Golden 1992: 5–29; and the contributions of Golden, Halliwell, Janko, Nehemas, Nussbaum, Kosman, and Freeland in Rorty 1992. They are followed by Gill 1993: 74–79; Janaway 1995: 197–98; and Finkelberg 1998: 14–17, 189–90. My view (Ford 1995 and forthcoming) is compatible with Lear 1988; cf. his debate (1995) with Halliwell (1995); and Hutton 1982: 11; Russell 1981: 91, 159–61.

[45] On this passage as a paradigm for learning from poetry, see esp. Sifakis 1986, and Gallop 1990. Though I take a different view from professor Gallop, I must note that I have benefited greatly both from his elegant and thoughtful paper and from happy conversations with him. Aristotle disagrees with a key Platonic passage (*Laws* 669A), where the common ability of people to recognize the original of a representation is distinguished from knowing that a representation is *kalon*; the passage is discussed in the next chapter.

("That man is Socrates"), and it is only adduced to establish the subordinate point that an instinctive pleasure in imitations is one of the natural causes of poetry. It is hardly necessary to infer that Aristotle considered learning the "essential" or sole pleasure that imitations may afford an adult in the theater.[46] This argument might go on a long time, but I would note that both *Poetics* 4 and *Parts of Animals* make a distinction between the common, popular pleasure in learning and the rarer pleasures taken by those who are "by nature" philosophers. To look dispassionately at a distressing corner of nature and infer a general truth by observing the relations of parts to wholes is indeed a "very great" pleasure, but it is one restricted to few. So, too, in *Poetics* ch. 4, "learning is not only extremely pleasant for philosophers but to others too, though they share in this pleasure only to a small extent" (1448b13–15).[47] A "small extent" of love of learning is all that is needed for spectators to assent to a mimetic illusion and say, "That's Agamemnon!"; only a slight interest in the "causes" of their response will make them open to tragedy's proper pleasure of arousing pity and fear through imitation. The philosopher's pleasure in poetry goes beyond evaluating the causes of Agamemnon's downfall to discern the causes of a well-constructed play. The cited passages describe not a pleasurable learning that poets ought to offer festival audiences but the pleasure offered by poetics to Aristotle's readers and auditors: for those equipped by nature to "share in" the pleasure of discovering and contemplating causes, Aristotle offers a scientific understanding of this cultural phenomenon; this knowledge allows them the great pleasure of looking at these stories, which made mass audiences wail and weep, with an analytical eye, recognizing yet again the orderly workings of nature. The *Poetics* offers a properly philosophical knowledge of the *causes* of poetic excellence; it can assess "the *skill* that fashions likenesses," just as natural science can discern how nature achieves its aims. Aristotle's students go beyond the natural pleasure people take in imitations to that "extreme" pleasure that is a knowledge of its workings.[48]

On the view of *Poetics* presented here, Aristotle was not defending poetry as morally instructive against Plato's attack. His views of poetry's

---

[46] Among commentators, Golden (1992) is the most insistent in this view. The best support for thinking audiences may learn patterns of life from plays seems to me the thesis of *Posterior Analytics*, that universals are more knowable causes than particulars (86a5–88a5).

[47] Janko 1987: 75 deals with Aristotle's observation in *Ethics* 1.5 that "most people" (1095b14) regard enjoyment, not learning, as the highest good, with the argument that man is by nature a rational animal, and so tragedy must ultimately satisfy reason. But *Politics* 8, discussed in the next chapter, militates against this optimism.

[48] On Socrates' portrait, note that we can only measure how well the aim has been achieved by first discovering what that aim is, i.e., by knowing what the imitation is an

benefits are quite different, and will be discussed in the next chapter. But dropping this common misreading of the *Poetics* makes the true significance of the work clear: in the mere fact of writing a poetics, Aristotle differed from Plato's view that poetry is only a knack or an innate talent some people have for entertaining with music and meter.[49] The *Poetics* says in contrast that tragedy and other forms of poetry work according to generalizable principles—this is what the *tekhnē* in the work's title means—and that these principles are specific to that activity and its particular ends. In this way, the *Poetics* inaugurates literary criticism as a technical appreciation of poetry that was distinct from the abundant moral, social, and religious critiques that we have sampled in this book. Poetics deserves to be classified as an autonomous intellectual enterprise among the sciences because its data and explanatory principles are independent of those in any other domain of inquiry.

Here we should consider the one sentence in *Poetics* in which Aristotle comes closest to defending the autonomy of art. In its penultimate chapter, Aristotle is discussing the standards that should be used in criticizing and defending poets. It is rather a grab bag, but it intends a real social phenomenon: Aristophanes and Plato show that debating the merits and demerits of poets had been popular in the salons frequented by sophists and among intellectuals generally; the game continued to be popular in the fourth century, as instanced by such writers as Zoilus of Amphipolis, the "scourge of Homer." In this context, Aristotle boldly states that "correctness in the poetic art is not the same as that in politics or other arts."[50] Though this sentence has been isolated as an aestheticist defense of poetry as an independent activity of the mind, in context it only responds to the sometimes trivial objections to a poem's historical or factual correctness that were exploited by sophistical critics out to make a score. It has been pointed out that Aristotle claims only a limited autonomy for poetry, for "representations of humans acting and faring well or ill" are simply unintelligible without some ethical framework.[51] But neither should Aristotle's dictum be underinterpreted as if it posed no problem for those who as-

---

imitation of. It is this latter distinct (and prior) learning that *Poetics* 4 says is pleasant for all and is to be assimilated to what Aristotle calls "easy learning" (*Rhetoric* 1410b10).

[49] Cf. *Gorgias* 502 and note 29 above.

[50] 1460b13–15: οὐχ ἡ αὐτὴ ὀρθότης ἐστὶν τῆς πολιτικῆς καὶ τῆς ποιητικῆς οὐδὲ ἄλλης τέχνης καὶ ποιητικῆς. For the distinction, cf. 1456b8–19, where Protagoras' *skhēmata lexeōs* are dismissed as belonging to another art and not the art of poetry. On the background to ch. 25, see in general Carroll 1895.

[51] For aestheticism, e.g., the long-influential Butcher 1907: 115: "The first clear conception of fine art as a free and independent activity of the mind . . . having an end distinct from that of education or moral improvement"; cf. 230–35. *Contra*, see Halliwell 1989: 339–47, 1988: esp. 25 n. 36; and the important study of Fortenbaugh (1975).

cribe to him a theory of poetry as moral education.[52] One must judge poetry by its own laws, and what might be an error in relation to another field of inquiry—Aristotle mentions politics, which he held to encompass educating citizens—is not an error in poetry if it contributes to the poem's end.[53] Accordingly, the *Poetics* insists on plausible, widely recognizable, and coherent plots, but never on edifying resolutions. Aristotle's basic idea of pleasures proper to each genre makes him less close to Plato than to Gorgias and the sophist who argued that "poets do not make their poems for truth but for the pleasures of men" (*Dissoi logoi* 3.17, cf. 3.10–11). This is limited autonomy, to be sure, but it also protects another domain—that of the critic. For the student of poetics will best know the ways in which poetry should be faulted "in terms of the art itself" and which charges are extraneous. The chapter as a whole amounts to a set of ground rules for conducting debates on whether a poem can be called *kalos* or not. In such discussions, Aristotle insists, the laws to which poetry can be held accountable are those deriving from its formal and final definition within the literary system—in short, from its genre. The limited autonomy being claimed here is not for poetry but for discoursing about poetry. Poetics is established as a field of expertise and an independent academic discipline.

In defining their prose against a notion of poetry as versified *logos*, fourth-century writers put the question of the nature of poetry on the agenda again. Isocrates' system of prose and poetic genres stressed formal harmony over performative context as determining the "fineness" of a composition. After Plato's searching, provocative, and finally impossible demands for producing writings worth reading, it was left to Aristotle to study poetry in the way Isocrates had recommended for his prose icons. Aristotle profited from Plato in defining poetry as "imitation" that uses language among its media, while "representation" allowed him to account for the brute appeal of poetry's form without reducing its task to sonorous psychagogy. The fact that "representing" must be strategic, must select and structure elements with only a limited concern for literal truth, made poetry literature, a discourse about something other than what has happened or what is the case. In addition, Plato's postulate of artificial organic wholes was the founding move in treating poetry as literature, as fiction that, while indeed capable of having educational and moral influence in society, is made in accordance with an art that is not

---

[52] C. Lord (1982: 91–92), who argues that the "aesthetic pleasure" to which Aristotle alludes at 1448a17–19 cannot be supposed to be exclusive of the pleasure of learning that Lord discerns at *Politics* 1339a36–38. Cf. Golden 1992: 7 n. 4.

[53] 1460b13–23; cf. Halliwell 1986: 132–37 and Finkelberg 1998: 13, with references.

the art of politics, nor of the sciences, nor of history, but the art of poetry. If some of the laws of poetry are independent of other laws, they must nevertheless have had some sanction for Aristotle, and he found that sanction in a postulate about poetry that has remained central to academic criticism to the present day: all its elements, though not directly answerable to the world of politics or philosophy, or to the real world, must answer at least to each other, and poetics best knows how to discern form and function in an artistic composition.[54] Synthesizing these ideas with the language-centered approaches to discourse (*logos*) that had been pioneered in the fifth century, Aristotle developed a method of analyzing poetry for readers who had begun to exploit the inner, verbal dynamics of song texts removed from their original contexts. My concluding question is what the critic gained by this knowledge.

[54] Halliwell, in a study that minimizes the autonomy of art for Aristotle, yet observes (1986: 96), "The concept of unity, in one version or another, is one of the most pervasive and arguably indispensable criteria in the understanding of art."

TWELVE

THE RISE OF THE CRITIC

POETIC CONTESTS FROM

HOMER TO ARISTOTLE

I F POETICS, in its most comprehensive and rigorously argued form, was first articulated as a topic for students of philosophy, the consolidation of such knowledge in itself changed the standards for expertise in poetry. For Aristotle's interlocutors inside and outside the Lyceum, and for the teachers and advisers they would come to support, a knowledge of how poetry worked as poetry was now added to the ethical and social wisdom that had traditionally been expected of commentators on song. This hybrid skill, combining technical expertise with a broader vision of social harmony, was expressed by the Greeks through the metaphor of "judging" (*krinein*) poetry, a metaphor we still use when we recognize such a thing as "literary *criticism*." It was only after the death of Aristotle, in the period of intensive literary scholarship from the third to the first centuries B.C.E., that we find professional experts in literature claiming to be "judges" or "critics" (*kritikoi*) of poetry. Antiquity remembered Crates of Mallos, a scholar attached to the royal library in second-century Pergamon, as having adopted the word *kritikos* to name his conception of the true literary expert.[1] Forged in opposition especially to the Alexandrian "scholars of letters" (*grammatikoi*), whom Critias considered too narrowly concerned with lexicography and meter, and in competition with such titles as "language-lover" (*philologos*), *kritikos* was taken up as a title for specialists providing advanced instruction in literature or claiming patronage from a Hellenistic king.[2] After him, *kritikos* was another name for the minister of culture who could authenticate,

---

[1] Athenaeus 490e. On *kritikoi* and *grammatikoi*, Pfeiffer 1968: 157–59, 206–07, 238; Schenkeveld 1968: 177–79; Russell 1981: 7–8, 11; and Porter 1992: esp. 85–86 on Crates. Longinus associated "literary judgment" (*logōn krisis*) with achieving a genuine understanding of true sublimity: *On the Sublime* 6.1.

[2] Alfred Gudeman, ("*kritikos*," *RE* 11 1922: 912–15, and "Grammatik," *RE* 7 1912: 1808) notes that the word is first used in connection with literature in a text from the end of fourth century or later, [Plato] *Axiochus* 366E. There *kritikoi* are ranked with geometers and teachers of military tactics, all of whom provide advanced education for boys who have finished with teachers of reading and writing (*grammatistai*).

edit, and rank in a canon those texts from the past that were worth preserving and studying.[3]

If literary critics today owe their title to academic rivalries of the post-classical age, the idea of the critic as a specially qualified "judge" (*kritēs*, pl. *kritai*) of literature ultimately goes back, via an anfractuous route, to a very ancient and distinctive site of Greek criticism, namely contests. Long before poetic texts entered Hellenistic academies and schoolrooms, singers had performed before judges at competitions throughout the Greek world, judges who at Athens were called *kritai*. Nagy has rightly stressed that, from archaic times, song contests were occasions for "selecting" or "judging" (both expressible by *krisis*) what works were to be preserved, and so criticism is as old as canon formation.[4] As a way of concluding this study, I propose to look at how poetic contests were managed at three major points in the history recounted above. Bringing out the criteria of judgment in each case will support my thesis that only with the generations of Plato and Aristotle was the case made that poets should be judged on the basis of criteria specific to their art. My sampling is also designed to show why, in Athens, the technical analysis of poetry could only be consolidated into an art by removing it from the city's public displays.

Histories of Greek criticism usually mention contests only in passing since they are poorly attested in the early period and not fully understood even in classical times.[5] It is also true that, as Simon Goldhill has put it, "We cannot expect to know how an Athenian audience would react to any tragedy, and more importantly, it is an intolerably naive idea to suppose that an audience for a drama has only a uniform, homogeneous or collective response, or that such a response should be the sole proper object of criticism."[6] Yet we can recover some of the ways that the Greeks ran their poetry contests, and this can tell us much about what they expected from songs. Contests always occured in a social space, and a principal function of Greek poetic contests at all periods was to declare, in the name of the group, that a performance was pleasing, acceptable, and commendable under a certain description: a public declaration of who was the best performer was also a proclamation of the values of the group sponsoring the event. A look at some ways in which singing contests were organized and at a few of the verdicts that have been preserved shows

---

[3] On this perspective on Hellenistic literary activity, Gentili 1988: 171–76. On the "writerly" conception of poetry, Bing 1988: esp. 15–20; reservations about making Hellenistic culture too distinctive in these regards, Cameron 1995: 24–70.

[4] Nagy 1989: 2, 13, 20; 1990: ch. 2, esp. 62–63, and 162–63, 402.

[5] Sikes 1931: 10, 17; Atkins 1934: 12; Grube (1965: 7–8) suggest that contests must have educated popular taste. More searching are Nagy 1990 and Griffith 1990, discussed below.

[6] Goldhill 1990: 115.

that Greek poetic contests were about more than judging literary merit. In addition, asking who was entitled to judge allows us to trace important changes in Greek ideas about expertise in the Muses' arts.

In what follows, I propose three chronologically successive "models" for poetic contests. The first is what I call the "heroic" model, one suggested by descriptions in the poems the Greeks assumed to be their oldest, epics. Derived partly from the evidence of epics themselves and partly from later antiquarian reconstructions, the heroic model is to be recognized whenever the contest is decided by a single (usually royal) judge or an elite body of officials in virtue of their political and social preeminence. A quite different model was employed at the festivals of democratic Athens, where an elaborate set of procedures for selecting judges placed the decision literally in the hands of the people's representatives. Finally, fourth-century philosophers, especially Plato and Aristotle, disparaged the verdicts of mass audiences and sought, each in his own way, to define the correct bases upon which to judge poetry. They were the first to theorize what judging poetry should be, and the first to urge that it be based on a special affinity for the musical arts rather than political authority or the chances of democratic voting. Plato offered an alternative to what he called the Athenian "theatocracy" in arguing that the true judge of art would be found among very few men, or even only in one supreme judge. Aristotle took a more tolerant view of popular Athenian culture, but he thought that education could and should provide all citizens with the ability to judge the *kalon* in poetry. Aristotle's scheme to produce citizens of discernment in public performances outlined the expertise required to be a connoisseur of literature and art; he paved the way for Crates by using the term *kritikos* for one whose education had equipped him with this special competence.

Heroic Contests

Our earliest explicit reference to Greek poetic contests comes from around 700 B.C.E, when Hesiod, as he tells us himself, won a tripod at funeral games held in honor of Amphidamas, a nobleman from Chalcis in Euboea (*Works and Days* 654–58):

> There [Euboea] I went to the games for wise Amphidamas
> crossing over to Chalcis, and the sons of that great-hearted man
> had announced many contests and set out prizes. And there I declare
> that I gained the victory with my song and carried off an eared tripod,
> which I dedicated to the Muses of Helicon.

Hesiod mentions that Amphidamas' sons publicized the games and managed them (665–66), and I take it that these men, locally influential and evidently skilled in the arts of communication, awarded the prizes as well.[7] Such is the case at the (exclusively athletic) games for Patroclus' funeral that Achilles administers in *Iliad* 23 (cf. 257–61), and when we next hear of musical contests, in the sixth century, they show signs of being directed by leading local families: as tyrant of Sicyon, Cleisthenes undertook to cancel its old epic contests and to revise its choral celebrations (Herodotus 5.67); the Peisistratids clearly controlled the rhapsodic contests and other musical performances at the Athenian Panathenaia.[8] In these cases, it seems a safe assumption that winners were not picked in complete indifference to the wishes of the leading men on the scene.

In what we may call the heroic model of poetic competition, the verdict is rendered by a single noble personage or his effective delegates. There were doubtless other models for archaic Greek contests, but we do not know why one rhapsode was proclaimed the "sweetest" of wandering singers by the Delian maiden's chorus (*Homeric Hymn to Apollo* 169), nor can we determine what Plato's Ion did to win "first prize" from the Aesclepiadae of Epidarus and hope for a crown from the Sons of Homer of Chios (Plato *Ion* 530A, D).[9] Nevertheless, the heroic model was clearly an influential way of managing such events. A ripely archaic, or perhaps merely archaizing, version is mentioned by the Athenian historian Philochorus at the end of the fourth century. Philochorus says that it was an old custom among Spartans on campaign for men to sing the (elegiac and martial) poems of Tyrtaeus at their messes and for the war-king to bestow a choice cut of meat on the winner.[10] This contest is archaic and heroic in its setting (a ritualized *Männerbund*, rather than a civic festival), in its prize (not tripods, crowns, or money, but a choice cut of meat, the same reward Odysseus gives an admired singer in *Od.* 8.473–81), and not least in placing the right to judge in the hands of the king.

We may unpack some of the implications of the heroic model by considering a late and fictional account of one such match recorded in the *Con-*

---

[7] Cf. the games given by the sons of Amarunkeus, recounted by Nestor at *Iliad* 23.630–45.

[8] Perhaps indeed with the advice of "cultural advisers": among Peisistratus' courtiers were Lasus of Hermione, who seems to have had a hand in the way the city celebrated dithyrambs, and Onomacritus, an expert in purportedly ancient oracular verse; see D'Angour 1997.

[9] The slender evidence for archaic poetic contests is surveyed in Herington 1985: 8, 161–66, and discussed, especially for lyric contests, by Barker 1995.

[10] Philochorus *FGrH* 328 F 216 = Athenaeus 630. For defenses of the antiquity of the custom, Nagy 1985b; Bowie 1990: 224–28, against the suggestion of Jacoby 1918, and on Philochorus *FGrH* 328 F 215, 216, that it was an archaizing reform after Leuctra.

test of Homer and Hesiod. Without entering into the attempt to delineate the contributions of Alcidamas and others, we can read the core narrative in the *Contest* as a picture of heroic contests that seemed appropriate and plausible for the classical age.

This contest is set at the funeral of the same Amphidamas of Chalcis, thus removing any suspense about its outcome (announced in advance at 70–72).[11] The interest of the story lies rather in the way the contest is run and how it arrives at its foregone conclusion. The deceased is now styled "king of Euboea" (64), and the leading Chalcidians are installed as judges (*ekathezonto kritai*) along with the king's brother, Paneides (68–69). They and "all the Greeks" (176) look on as the poets engage in an archaic kind of verbal duel more reminiscent of folktales than of the formal presentation of epic at festivals.[12] For example, Hesiod first throws out epic-style hexameters that make peculiar or no sense in themselves and challenges Homer to cap them with a line that restores meaning to them. Hesiod then poses ethical and political questions reminiscent of the climax of *Frogs*, such as, "How are cities best managed and with what character of men?" (161).[13] To these Homer gives versified replies, and the panhellenic audience clamors for him to be crowned (176–78). But Paneides forestalls a decision by issuing a final challenge for each poet to recite "the finest" piece from his poems (*to kalliston idiōn tōn poiēmatōn*, 168). Homer gives a cento from the *Iliad* describing the two Ajaxes standing firm against a ferocious onslaught of Trojans (12.126–33, 339–44), while Hesiod offers a bit of meteorological lore for the use of farmers and sailors (*Works and Days* 383–92). Although Homer is said to have met every one of Hesiod's challenges (cf. 90–96, 103, 138, 148–50), and although at the end the people clamor for him yet again (205), Paneides crowns Hesiod the winner: "It is right," he says, "that the one who calls the people to farming and peace should win, not the one who narrates wars and slaughter" (207–10).

Although "the verdict of Paneides" eventually became proverbial for a foolish decision, the *Contest* gives no hint that he has decided wrongly, and his name, "All-Knowing," suggests the opposite.[14] In giving the prize

---

[11] Cited by lines from Allen 1946: vol. 5. *Works and Days* 666–67 is taken up at *Contest* 213–14; cf. Hesiod fr. 357 M-W.

[12] Griffith 1990: 192. Cf. West 1967: 440. Janko (1982: 259–60) compares *Contest* 75–89 with the duel of seers recounted in Hesiod's *Melampodia* frs. 273–74 M-W and *Contest* 140–75 with fr. 278 M-W.

[13] So Radermacher 1954: 336–38 on Dionysus' climactic quizzing of the tragedians about Alcibiades at *Frogs* 1420 ff. Cf. West 1967: 443 n. 1, adding Alcidamas *On the Sophists* §§9, 26, 27; Isocrates *To Nicocles* §43.

[14] Richardson (1981) takes the conclusion as a story pattern of a surprising intervention by a clever fellow. For "the verdict of Paneides," West 1967: 443 and 439 n. 5.

Cleisthenic divisions of the *dēmos* was represented. The importance of representative judging is clear from one occasion when normal procedures were suspended: Plutarch (*Cimon* 8.7–9) recounts that in the heated competition of 468 B.C.E., the arkhon at the last moment decided to impanel the city's ten Generals; their prestige made the exception palatable, and could be justified by the fact that at that time the Generals were selected from each of the tribes. It may be further suggested that the citizens as a whole had an opportunity to ratify the vote of their representatives. At the general assembly held in the theater right after the festival, one standing item of business was hearing "complaints (*probolai*) concerning the processions or the contests."[22] Since one attested complaint (decided by a thumbs-up or -down of all present) concerned the "unjust" judging of dithyrambic contests, it seems reasonable to suppose that any flagrant irregularity (e.g., bribery of judges) could have been cause for such action, and so this assembly gave those present a chance to stamp the festival awards implicitly with the people's acceptance.[23]

In all this, there is no mechanism to secure judges with any particular competence in tragedy or dithyramb. True, nothing prevented literary expertise and taste from playing a part at any point in the process, from the preliminary selection of candidates to the final casting of ballots.[24] And it must be remembered that citizens could attend such performances several times a year, and that literally thousands of them had direct experience of memorizing and performing dense and difficult songs. (The Dionysia alone called on 500 boys and 500 men to perform dithyrambs each year).[25] On such grounds as these, scholars have reassured themselves about the tastes of Athenian judges, pointing out that Aeschylus and Sophocles did well on the whole in competition, and devising explanations for Euripides' comparatively poor showing.[26] Still, the final lottery ensured that the influence of critical skill was haphazard, and one could not predict whether the palm for a comedy, for example, would go to the

---

[22] The law is cited and interpreted at Demosthenes 21 *Against Meidias* 8–10. MacDowell 1990: 13–16. On the meeting, see Pickard-Cambridge 1988: 68–70.

[23] Cf. Aeschines 3 *Against Ctesiphon* 232, which says "the people" could punish judges of the dithyrambs for judging unfairly, with Pickard-Cambridge 1988: 64, 68–70, 98.

[24] There was also an important but little-understood prior event, the "pre-contest" (*proagōn*), held a few days before the City Dionysia (and the Lenaia) in which plays to be produced at the festivals were previewed in some fashion to an audience: Pickard-Cambridge 1988: 64–68.

[25] For the number of citizens involved in public choruses, Herington 1985: 96 with n. 83. Beyond this, citizens learned to march or row to music in their military training.

[26] The mixed verdict of Pickard-Cambridge (1988: 98–99, 272–78) is that "the general level of education among the audience should not be rated too highly" (275), though the audience "must have possessed on the whole a high degree of both seriousness and intelligence" (277). A less optimistic view is Römer 1884.

funniest or the wisest play: Aristophanes speaks of the judges of comedy as including both those who could appreciate his wisdom (*sophia*) and those who simply enjoyed a good laugh (*Ecclesiazusae* 1154–60). There was also a passionate audience response to reckon with. We know that theatrical audiences vociferously showed their preferences both during the performances and at the moment of voting.[27] But in the documented cases of audience attempts to influence judging, the motives are hardly aesthetic: to curry favor with Alcibiades when he was *chorēgos*, or to attack the choruses of rivals out of jealousy.[28] In comparison with the impassioned chivvying for personal or tribal supremacy, subtle assessments of artistic merit were bound to carry little weight. Plato repeatedly says that what Greek audiences at tragedy or epic recitations especially liked was a good emotional workout: the rhapsode in *Ion* says that if he can make his audience cry, he will laugh all the way to the bank, whereas if they laugh, it will be he who cries (535E); in the *Republic*, Socrates takes it for granted that the epic or tragic poet who wins the most praise is the one who puts the audience in the strongest state of mourning, making them beat their breasts and wail (605C–D). Plato is a hostile but not dishonest witness.[29] The whole proceeding thus seems designed to decide something other than the literary excellence of the winner.

The ability to conduct these contests successfully, to accept the judges' verdict however heated the competition may have been, in itself enacted a fundamental requirement of political community, the consensus (*homonoia*) of citizens. That reaching a common evaluation of poets was felt to be an important expression of civic *homonoia* can be inferred from one fourth-century text. Xenophon's Socrates agrees with a sophistical political theorist that *homonoia* is the greatest good for cities, but his reasons are his own: he says *homonoia* is valuable because it makes people abide by the laws, "not so that the citizens may judge (*krinôsi*) the same choruses the best, nor that they may praise (*epainein*) the same musicians and prefer the same poets, nor that they may take pleasure in the same things" (*Memorabilia* 4.4.16). The view Socrates rejects was, I venture to say, a popularly acceptable interpretation of the civic value of musical

---

[27] On the audience attempting to influence the verdict, see Wallace 1997; Csapo and Slater 1995: 286–305; Pickard-Cambridge 1988: 97–99.

[28] [Andocides] 4 *Against Alcibiades* §21; Demosthenes 21 *Against Meidias*, esp. §§14–18; and the discussion in MacDowell 1990: 241–42, for Meidias' attempts to disrupt and defeat the hated Demosthenes' chorus in the men's dithyramb. Cf. Csapo and Slater 1995: 163 on Lysias 3 *On the Premeditated Wounding*, which assumes that a judge at the Dionysia would be partisan toward friends and fellow tribesmen.

[29] For pleasure in tragedy, cf. [Plato] *Minos* 321A, cited by Herington 1985: 98, on tragedy being, like film nowadays, "the most pleasing and hypnotizing form of poetry"; and Gorgias *Palamedes* (B 11a 33 DK) and note 40 below.

contests as showing that the people can agree on who are the best poets and musicians. On this view, a show of *homonoia* would have been given each time the people crowned a poet in the theater of Dionysus.[30]

The Athenians' belief that the right to pronounce on poetry belonged to every citizen made it suspicious when the possibility of assessing artistic merit on more objective, technical grounds was propounded by sophistic critics. Aristophanes' literary scenes usually present advanced criticism as high-falutin' nonsense. Popular resentment at technical experts regularly surfaces when Aristophanes speaks of poetic expertise, for the ambition to measure poetry precisely is a pretension Aristophanes mocked in any wise man. No comment is needed to make Socrates ridiculous as he is introduced in *Clouds* (148–52) engaged in an ingenious but absurd project for casting flea legs in wax to determine exactly their jumping power.[31] Later in the play, a metrical approach to poetry is mocked as Strepsiades becomes the plain-talking everyman whose only use for "metrics" is as it may to apply to dry measures. In *Frogs* the contest between the poets is introduced with mock awe at genius at work (796–802): when the tools of criticism are brought on stage—the measuring-sticks (*canones*, whence our "canon"), cubit-measures, and squares that will be brought to bear on the poets' language—the deflating response is that the wise men must intend to make bricks.[32] The joke is not simply in misunderstanding technical tropes, but in the demotion of scientific expertise to the level of the working man. Hearing that the art of music will be "weighed out" on a scale, the slave is amazed that they will treat tragedy as if it were meat (798, cf. 1364–413).

It is hardly surprising that comic poets would flatter the mass audience (*homilos*) as the best judge of poetry,[33] but *Frogs* reveals a blend of pride and mockery toward the democratic process of judging art. Dionysus is certified as an "expert in the art" of tragedy (*tēs tekhnēs empeiros*, 811), but this is a joke referring to the god's presumed presence in the front row at Athenian dramatic festivals. The contest between Aeschylus and Euripides ridicules discussions of linguistic and dramatic technique, and turns for its conclusion to political and social questions: Dionysus' final

---

[30] Plato also associates shared musical tastes with civic harmony at *Laws* 816C–D. The imperative to reach *homonoia* would have been the more important to the extent that Greek tragedy was, as Vernant and many others have argued, dedicated to exposing the tensions and ambiguities of Athenian democracy. Future discussions should take note of the definitions in Goldhill 1990: esp. 114–15; cf. Said 1998 for further discussion.

[31] Cf. Dover 1968: lx.

[32] "Canons" would begin an influential second career in Alexandria to describe those works judged (*enkrithentes*) to be worthy models or standards against which to measure new works of verbal art. See Pfeiffer 1968: 207.

[33] Cratinus 360 PCG; cf. Plato Comicus 96 PCG, Isocrates *Panegyricus* §§45–46.

challenge is for each poet to offer advice on the charismatic but dangerous Alcibiades (1420–23).[34] In *Frogs*, as in the *Contest of Homer and Hesiod*, the issue is settled by an almost arbitrary (1469) decision of the presiding figure. Though Dionysus is introduced as a passionate reader of Euripides and an "expert" in poetry, in the end he in fact exemplifies the old heroic model of king as critic: having come down to Hades in search of a "potent" poet who can "give birth" to the "wellborn" phrase,[35] he brings him back to provide "salvation" for the city (1501, cf. 1419).

The ambivalence in *Frogs* emerges most clearly in the scene in which Dionysus is installed as judge. As the butler to the underworld tells it, the contest between the poets began in populist passion: upon his arrival, Euripides displayed his talent in public (*epedeiknuto*, 771), winning over the riff-raff, petty thieves, and criminals "who constitute the majority (*plēthos*) in Hades" (774). When the mob went mad for his poetry and songs and proclaimed him "wisest" (*sophētatos*), Euripides was encouraged to challenge Aeschylus for the underworld chair of poetry (774–78). There ensued an angry dispute about who would judge this contest, "for the two poets found a want of wise men in the underworld" (806). Aeschylus was in a bind: anecdotes surrounding his removal late in life to Sicily are exploited to suggest that he got on badly with the majority of Athenians; and yet he considered everyone outside Athens worthless in recognizing (*gnōnai*) the true nature of poets (807–10). In the end, they turned the matter over to Dionysus on account of his experience in the art (*tēs tekhnēs empeiros*, 811), with all the irony that choice entailed.

Other observers on the scene also felt a "want of wise men" in democratic voting, for the parallel between political and musical verdicts was obvious. So Thucydides' Cleon compares Athenian assemblies to "badly run contests" where the spectators care only for the "pleasures of the ear" (3.38). In the fourth century, other conservative writers retreated from the democratic model of musical judging in favor of some expertise in art. These discussions make clear the connection between the politics and aesthetics of judging, even as the possibility of an artistic, purely technical appreciation of poetry was raised.

Plato: The Problems with Theater

Plato shows an interest in who speaks well about poetry from his earliest writings: the *Apology* says that bystanders in the agora could "speak better" (*beltion elegon*) about tragedy, dithyramb, and other poetry than

---

[34] Cf. Griffith 1990: 189–91.

[35] *Frogs* 96, on which see Segal 1994: 101; for the metaphor (*goinmos poiētēs, gennaion rhēma*), Taillardat 1965: 428; Denniston 1927.

the poets themselves, and *Ion* refutes a rhapsode's pretensions to be a "competent judge" (*hikanon kritēn*) of Homeric or any poetry.[36] In the *Gorgias*, musical performers can be assumed to "aim at nothing other than gratifying the mob (*okhlos*) of spectators, with no concern for whether they are being harmed or improved" (501E–502A). Poetic performances—explicitly including tragic competitions—are characterized as demagoguery in which speech (*logoi*) is decked out with rhythm and music to appeal to a motley public (*dēmos*) composed of "children, men and woman all together, slaves and free alike" (502D).[37] This orientation toward a mass audience figures in the *Republic*'s condemnation of theater because the mixed character of theatrical audiences—"all types of people gathered together" (604E, cf. 493C–D)—entails that a poet can only succeed by saying "what seems to be fine and beautiful (*kalon*) to the many, though they do not know" (602B).

Plato makes the political implications of theater explicit. Although theatrical audiences were actually more diverse than the assembly or courts (which were restricted to adult male citizens), Plato found all such settings corrupted by the dynamics of mass psychology. The *Republic* condemns the noisy turbulence (*thorubos*) of democratic assemblies (492B7), where "thronged multitudes" shout out praise and blame so loudly that the din (*thorubos*) overwhelms those of a philosophic nature (492C);[38] the same word is used of the theater in *Laws*, where the "clamor" (*thorubos*) of the "uneducated crowd" roaring and clapping carries the day, even though the judges have sworn to vote justly (700D). Music is a major issue for *Laws* because of Plato's argument, examined in the previous chapter, that politics in Athens have followed music in allowing a "base theatocracy" to supplanted its inherited "aristocracy of music" (701A–B). With disarming irony, the speaker concludes his account of the decline of musical standards by saying that the corruption of musical standards is no grave matter in itself; but the problem is that the supposition (*doxa*) that everyone has wisdom (*sophia*) in music leads to the effrontery of men thinking they are wise in everything, and this is the corruption of the state.

Whereas *Republic* simply banished most professional musical performances from the ideal city, in *Laws* Plato retains but revises them to re-

[36] *Apology* 22A–C. *Ion* 532B; cf. *krinein* in the sense of "judging" what is "rightly" or correctly said by poets at 538D5, 539D3.

[37] Cf. *Laws* 817C: tragedy "demagogues youths, women, the whole mob." On the vexed question of whether women were admitted to theatrical performances in the fifth century, there is a strong argument that they were in Henderson 1991, and strong reservations are expressed in Goldhill 1994. At least as regards the fourth century, I believe the Platonic evidence for their presence is credible (so Pickard-Cambridge 1988: 263–65): the theatrical comparison is useful to Plato precisely to the extent that its audience was more evidently *mixed* than the all-male citizen bodies of the assembly and courts.

[38] On shouting in courts to influence the verdict, see Hall 1995: esp. 43–44.

store the musical aristocracy.[39] In the course of this discussion, he formulates a significant description of the ideal judge of musical art. Plato's "wise judge" will, unsurprisingly, judge art in philosophical and moral-social terms, but he will also have a special expertise in music (*empeiros*, *Laws* 765A–B).

Plato begins by conceding the popular idea that "in our festivals we should consider and judge most wise (*sophōtatos*) the one who produces in us the greatest delight" (*Laws* 657D–E).[40] His crucial proviso is that this should not be "just anyone's pleasure," but "what pleases the best men and best educated, and indeed the single man who is supreme in his moral and intellectual qualities" (659A). Such a man must have the courage to withstand the clamor of a mob audience and the wisdom to act as a kind of teacher to the audience of what is good in art (659B). The argument is clearly aimed at contemporary Athens, though Plato speaks rather of an allegedly "current practice (*ho nomos nun*) in Sicily or Italy" by which the whole audience awards dramatic prizes by a show of hands (659B). Against this radically democratic model he sets an alleged "ancient and Hellenic" *nomos* by which a single judge was installed (*kathizei*), ready to oppose performers who pandered to the mob with inappropriate or incorrect pleasures.[41] In this courageous and wise judge opposing popular pleasure, Plato may be thinking of scenarios like the *Contest* (perhaps even Alcidamas' version), where, as noted, Paneides resists the popular clamor for Homer.

Plato goes on in *Laws* to spell out three things that ideal judges, "those who are seeking the finest song and Muse" (668B), must know:

> The man who would be a sound and rational (*emphrōn*) critic of any likeness (*eikōn*), whether in painting or in music or whatever, must have first a knowledge of the nature of the original; next, a knowledge of the correctness of the copy; and third, a knowledge of how well (*hōs eu*) the copy is fashioned in words and melodies and rhythms.[42]

[39] Dithyramb would fall under the ritual choirs regulated in 800C–802E. Comedy is to be retained in the city, so one can learn about the good through its opposite; but only practiced by foreigners and not taken seriously: 816D–E.

[40] 655C–D. The popularity of the idea is by no means a Platonic construct, but the basis against which he frames his arguments: cf. *Gorgias* 501D–502C with Dodds 1959: 321; *Laws* 657E, 658E; *Gorgias* B 8.18, B 23 DK; *Dissoi logoi* 3.17 DK; Thucydides: 2.41.4; and the papyrus (P. Oxy. III 414) sometimes ascribed to Antiphon and discussed in Lanata 1963: 214.

[41] Inserting Winkelman's *ou* at 659B6 as in Burnet's Oxford text. The phrase is bracketed by England (1921), but the passage, with its otherwise unattested "ancient and Hellenic" custom nicely balancing the "current Italic or Sicilian" custom, seems more like a Platonic than a scholiastic invention.

[42] *Laws* 669A–B: "in words and melodies and rhythms" is bracketed by England as inapplicable to the other arts named, but Plato is anticipating his immediate return to judging

The first and most important requirement is a sort of dialectical knowledge of the nature and composition of any object imitated; in the case of judging a painting of an animal, this means understanding the parts and form of actual animals as well as their superficial features. Knowing all this allows the judge to pronounce on the "correctness" (orthōtēs) of a representation (668D). But Plato adds a final component to artistic judgment that goes beyond previous notions in distinguishing "how well" artists deploy their media. He thus recognizes a strictly technical aspect to imitative art (e.g., how song deploys words, rhythms, and melodies), even as he subordinates it to the demand for moral utility and intellectual truth. No previous Greek statement on criticism is so clear that one can judge the *how* as well as the *what* of an imitation. Plato is so relentless in charging poets with ignorance about what they represent that it can escape notice that he concedes them an expertise in their own art. That some imitations were more gripping than others was obvious, and Plato grants that some people are particularly good at producing effective imitations, whether this be ascribed to their inborn capacity (719C) or to divine gift (682A).[43] Plato's aesthetics recognizes, even as he seeks to control, the natural "capacity of poets and *mousikoi* for poetry" (802B).

Over and above artistic "correctness," Plato sets a further quality, the beauty or fineness (*kallos*) of a work. A "correct" rendering of a morally corrupting original could not be judged *kalon* or *eu*: "If we know that a painting or sculpture is a man," the Athenian stranger goes on to argue, "and we know that all his parts, color, and shape have been rendered artistically, then do you necessarily know whether the work is *kalon* or whether it falls short of beauty and fineness (*kallos*)?" (669A). Cleinias finds this an absurd proposition: "Then practically all of us would know what is *kalon* in artistic representations (*zōia*)."[44] A poet is expected to have knowledge of rhythm and harmony, but not to be able to assess whether an imitation is fine or not (670E). There is no better reason for this assumption than the Athenian's certainty (one that Cleinias shares) that "the many cannot judge what is truly fine" (*to kalon*, 700D). It is axiomatic for Plato that the many, lacking a philosophic foundation, cannot know "the fine itself," just many particular "fine" things (*Republic* 493E–494A). Knowledge of *to kalon* is thus separate from the common

---

songs, which has been his main concern and which he generalized to include other representations at 668C–D.

[43] The *Republic* points out this knowledge while dismissing it: like a good painter, "the poet, understanding *nothing except how to imitate* (οὐκ ἐπαΐοντα ἀλλ᾽ ἢ μιμεῖσθαι), gives colors to certain crafts with his words and phrases," *Republic* 601A).

[44] The correct rendering of *zōia* (not "animals") is explained by Saunders (1972: 10–11), who observes that the thrust of 668E–669A is that beauty in art is more than fidelity to the model and is not something that can be judged by every viewer.

response to art. The presence of beauty or fineness is not signaled by pleasure but by a separate emotion called "charm" (*kharis*, see *Laws* 667B–D); this subtle feeling is concomitant upon a competent critic's perception of a work's "correctness" and "utility" (*ōpheleia*, a salutary moral effect, see 669A–B).[45] To those who have been initiated into the higher mysteries of music (669D: "those who have reached the full flower of pleasure," a tag from Orpheus), current musical practices are "boorishness" (*agroikokia*, 669E), and the pretensions of the "great mob" (*polus okhlos*, 670B) to understand these things are dismissed as ludicrous.

Plato's unabashedly elitist conception of artistic judgment underscores the political importance of the question of who has the right to pronounce a musical performance *kalon*. The ideal judge responds to poetry as an imitation of objects and acts whose true nature and worth only he understands. The criticism of poems or paintings is subordinated to the Platonic demand for a dialectical (parts and wholes) knowledge of reality. But Plato also includes in judging an appreciation of "how well" the work is done. Aristotle will extend this capacity beyond Plato's elderly choirs and select civic judges and have it taught to the citizen class as a whole. Through an early training in discerning what is "correct" in music, Aristotle's educated class will be prepared to sit in judgment on any public performance. In describing this education, Aristotle outlined a prototype of the literary critic, the possessor of a developed critical faculty and a musical sensibility that lent his verdicts of *kalon* a greater weight than those of the ordinary spectator.

Aristotle: The Birth of the Critic

Aristotle's views on both the nature of poetic excellence and the politics of judging are more complex than Plato's, but in the end he, too, denies true aesthetic discrimination to the mass audiences of Athenian festivals. Aristotle's *Politics* most directly confronts the musical regime of *Republic* and *Laws*, but his *Poetics* merits brief consideration at this point to underscore its ambivalence about theatrical audiences.

Given the fact that the tragedy Aristotle regarded as supremely well constructed, Sophocles' *Oedipus the King*, did not take first prize when

---

[45] Plato actually intimates the idea of aesthetic pleasure when he allows that pleasure in its gross sense is a criterion for judging objects that are incapable of affording utility or correctness (667D–E), but the *imitative* arts are by definition excluded from this class of objects.

it was produced, we can understand what one critic has called his "general reluctance to appeal to the mentality of audiences as a standard of poetic practice."[46] The *Poetics* enunciates the principles that entitle a poem to be called *kalon*, but Aristotle's research in the records of the contests would have made clear to him that following the dictates of theory did not always result in success. He thus distinguishes between deciding certain questions "in terms of the art itself" and "in respect to its audiences" (1449a9), and in a number of places allows for the fact that composers will neglect the principles of art and seek victory by fawning on debased audience tastes. For example, we have observed that the definition of tragedy in chapter 6 entails that "the tragedy that is most excellent (*kallistos*) in respect to the art" will have a change of fortune from good to bad, since the reverse does not even arouse pity and fear (1453a22–23). Nevertheless, in their "weakness," audiences may prefer plots in which the good end happily and the evil suffer, and sometimes tragic poets will cater to their wishes (*akoulouthountes kat' eukhēn*, 1453a34–35). An audience thus catered to may be expected to demonstrate its approbation, but even a prize-winning melodrama would not be *kalon* in respect to the art if it is tragic in form but comic in the pleasure it affords (1453a35–36). Again, from the definition of tragedy, Aristotle deduces in chapters 8–9 (1452a1–11) that poets should compose plots linked by a probable or necessary sequence of events; but he observes that poets compose "episodic" plots (1451b33–52a1) either because they're bad poets or to show off the actors and win competitions (cf. *agōnismata*, 1451b37).[47] Aristotle's many prescriptive rules for good composition may help a playwright avoid being laughed off the stage, but they cannot guarantee victory.

Aristotle's rejection of popular appeal as a criterion of artistic excellence comes out most clearly in the final chapter of the extant *Poetics*, where he enters a debate on whether tragedy or epic is the superior art (esp. 1461b26–62a12). One view held that epic was superior because it appealed to a superior audience, while tragedy was inescapably vulgar because its dramatic form in itself encouraged exaggerated, apelike delivery to drive the message home.[48] Aristotle defends tragedy, but without defending theatrical audiences. He concedes that acting can be exceedingly vulgar, but argues that it is an inessential adjunct to the tragic art

---

[46] Halliwell 1986: 103, cf. 296.

[47] At *Rhetoric* 3.12.1413b9–12, it is said that famous actors sought out plays that were rich in character and dramatic incident ("ethical" and "passionate"), and that poets obliged.

[48] The imagined contest of genres in *Laws* 658D (where old men prefer Homer or Hesiod, boys comedy, and young men, educated women, and the crowd generally vote for tragedy) suggests Plato would have shared the pro-epic view, but Aristotle clearly addresses a widely debated question.

since nothing prevents a tragedy's dispensing with these accouterments and being declaimed like an epic (1462a4–14).[49] This remarkable intimation of closet drama is in line with another famous and telling observation, that tragedy should produce the same effect when one reads or hears the story as it does when seen (1453b3–7). Both show Aristotle removing himself from the hubbub of theater to the Lyceum in order to discern the true character of the art and the principles that entitle a specimen of it to be called *kalon*.[50]

Aristotle returns to the theater in his *Politics*, where he differs from Plato in not thinking Athenian festival arrangements politically dangerous. His general approach to managing musical culture in an ideal state is to leave popular spectacles in place but to secure by education a general appreciation among citizens of good and bad in art. If Plato wanted to restore to the musical judge some of his imagined archaic power and authority, Aristotle aims to make each educated citizen a *kritikos*, a man of general discernment who is, among other things, a good judge of musical performances and a connoisseur of the arts.

Aristotle does not share Plato's absolute distrust of mass audiences. In fact, at one point he flatly declares that large groups are better judges of musical contests than any single individual. The statement arises in a discussion in Book 3 (1281a42–b9) of whether political supremacy ought to be vested in the few best men or in the many: in favor of the many, Aristotle says that, even if the individuals in a mass assembly be comparatively inferior ("not *spoudaios*") in character and intellect, yet collectively they may make better decisions than a single man. "This is why," he goes on, "the general public (*plēthos*) is a better judge [than the individual] of

---

[49] Aristotle's treatment of acting is exactly parallel to his discussion of delivery in the *Rhetoric*: just as actors good at delivery generally win prizes at the dramatic contests, so dramatic orators succeed "because of the low character of the citizens" (*tēn mokhthērian tōn politōn*, 1404b34–35). In both works Aristotle detaches the art of performance from the true core of the art. Rhetorical delivery is effective because of the low character of the auditor (*tēn tou akroatou mokhthērian*, 1404a7–8), but is an inessential add-on to the art. These prejudices inform Aristotle's history of rhetoric: the first part of the rhetorical art to be studied was what was "naturally first"—the sources of conviction (1403b18–19); style was explored next, relatively late (1404b36); finally, delivery has yet to be systematically treated in Aristotle's own day, "though it has the greatest capacity" to influence the audience. Delivery is rightly thought to be vulgar, but rhetoric is for the real world, and since persuasion depends on *doxa*, one cannot confine oneself to the dispassionate use of demonstrative proof. See Fortenbaugh 1986 for a general discussion.

[50] Aristotle goes some way here to removing the tragic aficionado from the theater and putting him in a library, as at 1453b17–11 (arguing that the arts of scene-making and production are dispensable) and 1450b18–20 (the *dunamis* of tragedy does not depend on the production or actors). See Halliwell 1986: appendix 3.

musical and poetic compositions (*erga*), for some judge one part, others another, and collectively they judge the whole."[51] Although each member of the audience may lack the philosopher's synoptic vision of the whole, this is potentially a powerful defense of democratic musical judgment. It remains so even with Aristotle's subsequent qualifications that such a multitude (*plēthos*) should not be "excessively slavish" (1282a14–18) and that it should be "composed of freeborn persons acting in accord with the laws" 1286a36–37). Still, for Aristotle, all this remains on a theoretical level: "It is not clear whether this superiority of collective to individual judgment applies to every democracy (*dēmos*) and every multitude (*plēthos*), and in some cases this is manifestly not so . . . but nothing prevents what has been said from being true in the case of a particular mass audience" (1281b16–21). What Aristotle thought about actual Athenian audiences emerges in the discussion of the musical education of citizens in Books 7 and 8, and is hardly complimentary.

Fundamental to Aristotle's outlook is an old idea about music that was supported by certain respected "philosophers of music" in his day (1341b28). This view held that certain rhythms and harmonies have an inherent power to corrupt and vulgarize young bodies and souls, while others foster virtue (1340a14–19). For this reason, Aristotle recommends that legislators ensure that only improving melodies and rhythms are employed in the education of future soldiers and citizens. This is clearly distinct from the music offered by professionals in festival contests, which appeal "to slaves, children, and even some animals" (1341a12–17). In the theater, professional musicians aim not at moral excellence but provide the audience with a "vulgar" pleasure; they fawn on the spectator, "who tends to be vulgar" too (*ho gar theatēs ōn phortikos*, 1341b10–18).

Thus far, Aristotle exhibits no higher an opinion of Athenian musical audiences than Plato and is only more liberal in allowing such spectacles to continue provided their music is kept out of the classroom. His reasons for allowing nonimproving kinds of music in the theater are starkly clear:

> Those who undertake to provide music as contestants in the theater should be permitted to employ such [noneducational] rhythms and melodies; for the audience is, after all, double, composed partly of the free and educated but partly, too, of the vulgar—tradesmen and laborers and other such—and these people, too, must be granted spectacles as a relaxation. Just as their minds are, as it were, perverted from their natural condition, so, too, the music to

---

[51] διὸ καὶ κρίνουσιν ἄμεινον οἱ πολλοὶ καὶ τὰ τῆς μουσικῆς ἔργα καὶ τὰ τῶν ποιητῶν 1281b7–8). Newman (1902) takes this passage as aporetic.

which they naturally respond is distorted. Hence those competing before a spectator of this sort must be permitted to employ the corresponding [low] kind of music. (1342a17–22.)[52]

This double audience is divided primarily by education; Aristotle had earlier indicated that workers and tradesmen will not have the same education as full citizens (1328b24–29a39). But neither is the free and "educated man" (*ho pepaideumenos*) a professional musician, an occupation Aristotle regards as menial and unsuitable for free men because providing a pleasure to vulgar spectators deforms the professional musician until he becomes vulgar himself in character and bodily comportment.

What will these "free and educated" people have studied? Not necessarily works like the *Poetics*, since Aristotle has also made it clear that not every citizen will be required, or indeed able, to pursue philosophical studies (1333a16–30). What the educated spectators will have learned must be the musical curriculum Aristotle had outlined earlier in the book. Aristotle lays out in detail how, with proper musical instruction and a proper upbringing (sheltered in youth from slavish companions, lewd paintings, comedy, drinking parties, and riotous music), citizens can develop the ability to respond to music on a level above "its common pleasure, which appeals to all characters and ages" (1340a1–5). The goal here is to produce citizens who are, among other things, good "judges" or critics (*kritai*) of music (1340b25). If citizens are trained in youth to "delight in music correctly," they will be able "to judge it correctly and to take pleasure in [music representing] admirable characters and actions" (1340a17–18: τὸ κρίνειν ὀρθῶς καὶ τὸ χαίρειν τοῖς ἐπιεικέσιν ἤθεσι καὶ ταῖς καλαῖς πράξεσιν). Being a "judge" in this sense is a matter of training, temperament, and social position, as can be seen clearly from how Aristotle tackles the disputed question of whether citizen-critics should learn to play instruments themselves (ch. 6). The danger is that such a pursuit can be banausic and degrading. But Aristotle recommends the practice because "to be a good judge of anything one needs to have engaged in that activity" (1340b23–25).[53] Although citizens may if they wish take up an instrument themselves when "drunk or having fun" (1339b10), the young should learn to play so as to be able to judge later. Like Aristophanes' Dionysus or Plato's civic judges, they will be "experienced" in the art.

[52] Against the trend among recent commentators on *Poetics*, my interpretation in Ford 1995 is in line with the view of the *Politics* in Anderson 1966: 138: "Music for public performance should be no better than the type of audience which enjoys it. There can be no doubt that Aristotle believed attendance at tragic performances to be an important experience in adult life, but he saw the goal of such attendance as purgation rather than purification." *Contra*, C. Lord 1982, 1996; Salkever 1986; Depew 1991.

[53] Cf.*Nicomachean Ethics* 1181a11–17.

But the mythic paradigm Aristotle offers for the musical critic is Zeus himself, who does not play an instrument himself but listens while others perform. Judgment always takes place in a hierarchical setting: like sculptors, painters, and furniture-makers, professional musicians and singers ranked as banausic workmen who had to turn over their productions for others to judge and enjoy. The model is the king who has the leisure to listen to poetry and music provided by others.

Elsewhere Aristotle uses the term *kritikos* for the man of general education and reliable discernment. The *kritikos* is able to form a fair judgment of the goodness or badness of an exposition on virtually any subject, without having particular expertise on the topic (*Parts of Animals* 639a1–11). The kind of person he has in mind also appears in his ethical treatises as "the good man," the standard to aim at.[54] Such a person is superior to the common run of men chiefly in his ability to judge "correctly" what is noble and pleasant, while others are often misled by pleasure.[55] In practice, being a *kritikos* will be confined to a subset of the population. True, Aristotle thinks that the ability to recognize *to kalon*, while not a universal endowment, is widely attainable through education and training to anyone whose soul is not corrupt. But he also says that "it is not possible to turn the majority of men (*hoi polloi*) to the ways of a gentleman (*kalokagathian*). They pursue their own [suitable] pleasures and the means of getting them . . . of the truly pleasant and noble (*alēthōs hēdus*) they have not even the idea, never having tasted them."[56]

This looks like the "double" audience in *Politics*, which contains the lower sorts whose sole criterion is pleasure and whose debased tastes will be satisfied by theatrical music; there will also be the educated, whose training from youth will have rendered them "immune" from the corrupting aspects of the performance and who will judge rightly of the nobility of the actions and characters represented (*Politics* 7.17. 1336b22–23). But the *kritikos* claims no special authority in the theater. He takes his place beside the uneducated as just another member of the audience, while "others" perform. If he has no special authority, he knows the right demands to make of music and reserves the right to pronounce on what is *kalon* because education has given him a special familiarity with the art.

In theory, nothing prevents a mixed audience from judging rightly, provided that the whole does not have a predominantly slavish character and comports itself in an orderly way. In an ideal state, in which all the citizens

---

[54] On the excellent person as standard, cf. *Nichomachean Ethics* 9.4 and 10.5 esp. 1176a15–22, where Aristotle adds that the excellent person finds objectionable what pleases those whose taste has suffered corruption and damage.

[55] *Nicomachean Ethics* 3.4 (esp. 1113a25–b2).

[56] *Nicomachean Ethics* 1179b10–15.

are men of complete excellence (and in which farmers, laborers, and merchants are not citizens at all), this will be so.[57] In the meantime, the *Politics* is a book for legislating the uses of music in an education designed to produce citizens who will judge "correctly" of art, even as they will pronounce rightly on other questions that are presented to them as citizens. The *Poetics* offers more than this: it is a complete theory of the causes of excellence in poetry, not necessarily available to all natures, nor strictly needed to be a good citizen.

On the whole, then, Aristotle's view of mass art is more nuanced than Plato's: he recognized, at least in theory, that a large group of decent people behaving decently were better judges of musical works than individuals. And he is happy to leave theatrical verdicts in the hands of their audiences, since he thinks they afford a useful diversion and no great harm will come of them.[58] But he will not neglect educating all his citizens in the arts to a certain degree. Responding equally to Plato and to the practices of his adoptive city, Aristotle gives us the first clear portrait of the literary critic as man of letters and a sketch of the special expertise in the art that he applies to poetry. A man of trained sensibility and some experience the critic will not need to understand the reasons for his trained judgments. This knowledge is provided by Aristotle's *Poetics*, which is intended for philosophers, those few who are equipped by nature to study the causes of things. Aristotle's idea of the citizen-*kritikos* foreshadows the professional literary critic as one whose judgments in musical works command assent because of his special sensibility in the arts, shaped by training and informed by a certain amount of experience, though not necessarily a theoretical or philosophical knowledge.

Understanding, interpreting, and appreciating works of literature as literature was not what early Greek contests aimed at. The judge was at first a political authority and spokesman for social order, and remained so even in Athenian festivals, where the sovereign people exalted one poet as "wisest" until the time came around for the people to vote again (cf. Aristophanes *Knights* 518). This is why many verdicts seem, in the words of Mark Griffith, "curiously arbitrary, even unfair."[59] Griffith suggests

---

[57] *Politics* 1328b33–92a2, cf. 1293b1 ff. On the conflict, Ober 1989: 164 n. 21; Kraut 1997: 104.

[58] This is the enlightened view of Thucydides' Pericles (2.38.1): We have provided for the mind (*gnōmē*) very many refreshments from toil (*ponōn pleistas anapaulas*), with games (*agōsi*) and sacrifices throughout the year, and distinguished (*euprepesin*) private furnishings, of which things the pleasure (*terpsis*) drives away sadness (*to lupēron ekplēssei*). On leisure and culture, see E. Koller 1956 and Solmsen 1964; cf. Carter 1986: esp. ch. 1, and Balme 1984.

[59] Griffith 1990: 188–89, for this and the following quotation.

that what was at stake at archaic poetic contests was a broad, undifferentiated concept of poetic "wisdom" (*sophia*) that could comprise, without explicit differentiation, "the accuracy or truth of what the poet sang, its moral and educational force, and even its technical skill, formal control and emotional impact." The differentiation of technical skill and formal control as praiseworthy in themselves was facilitated by fifth-century rhetorical approaches to poetry, but even in *Frogs* it is hard to find a clear example of poetry being praised simply on the basis that it was well expressed or well made.[60] Early evaluations of poets tended (like poets' own boasts of their worth) to focus on whether they were socially or morally useful. This is not to say that aesthetic power went unappreciated before the fourth century, but we have seen that contests were not designed to discover and reward these qualities. Fundamentally, Greek poetic contests served as occasions to articulate the community's conception of itself and to demonstrate, by the very conduct of the event, its cohesiveness and order.

A break set in with Plato and Aristotle, who in different ways isolated a specifically literary discrimination as essential to correct judging. Plato's approach to singing contests was framed by a strong sense of their political implications, but he distinguished more clearly than previously between judging poetry by what it says and judging it by how it says it. Aristotle's *Poetics* systematized a way of judging poetry on a higher level of understanding than prevailed in the theater; but it was the *Politics* that articulated a role for criticism as part of the equipment of the educated citizen and spelled out the intellectual and moral discipline needed to produce a *kritikos*. Aristotle's ideal state was not to be realized, though it was something much like Aristotle's *kritikos* that Crates revived when he claimed the word as a title under which to seek patronage from the Hellenistic kings. As combined minister of literary antiquities and master decoder of difficult books, the word and profession went to Rome, and then beyond to us.[61]

---

[60] The earliest example of technical skill as a criterion listed by Griffith 1990: 193 is Pratinas fr. 3 *TGrF*.

[61] Cf. Brink 1963–82, 3: 414–19, on the *critici* at Horace *Epistles* 2.1.150.

EPILOGUE

WE PAUSE in the history of Greek criticism on the verge of the Hellenistic age and the first academies devoted to professional literary study and research. The *Poetics* can mark the arrival of criticism because that work fully synthesized a conception of poetry and a method for analyzing it in terms taken from the art of poetry "and not from another art." At the same time, the curious fact that the *Poetics*, along with most of Aristotle's library, seems to have disappeared from sight until the Renaissance is a good reminder that classical critical theory and practice was not the product of a single genius: many of Aristotle's assumptions and methods were shared by other writers of the time, including the influential and long-read Isocrates and Plato; and Theophrastus, his successor as head of the Lyceum, carried on and extended his studies of rhetoric and poetics for the next generation of scholars.[1]

This collective work of intellectual synthesis had for a number of reasons more historical impact than theories of literature usually do. In its immediate context, the formal and grammatical methods of poetics suited an education centered on reading and writing and made it a great aid to rhetorical training. Its historical view of poetry made it effective in analyzing old texts, and also suited the classicizing tendencies of the later fourth century. In the next generation, the categorization of song in terms of genre and form helped literary scholars collect and classify song texts that had become separated from performative contexts. Classical literary theory also provided postclassical (as they thought of themselves) scholar-poets with a synoptic vision of poetry as a system within which they could recreate and continue the traditions of Greek song in new circumstances. There is thus a certain amount of truth in Strabo's remark that Aristotle taught the kings of Egypt how to organize the library.[2]

Perhaps most importantly, the internalization and formalization of poetic value made classical criticism exportable and applicable to works composed in other languages and for other cultures. Thus criticism could follow Greek philosophy as well as Greek letters as both were absorbed

---

[1] Among representative transitional figures, one could name Demetrius of Phaleron (born ca. 350); an associate of Theophrastus, he advised Ptolemy I about the Alexandrian library: Pfeiffer 1968; 95–102, esp. 99 ff.; Fraser 1972, 1:315, 321–22. Ptolemy's son, the future Philadelphus, was tutored by Philitas of Cos (b. ca. 340), poet, *grammatikos*, and *kritikos*, and associate of Zenodotus of Ephesus, the first librarian at Alexandria: Fraser 1972, 1:308–9, 556; cf. Pfeiffer 1968: 88–93; Hunter 1996: 17 n. 47.

[2] Strabo 13.608; cf. Fraser 1972, 1:320 and 2a: 473 n. 100, on the fate of Aristotle's library.

by a culture-hungry Rome in the third century. In the event, these ideas and values, together with their panoply of technical terms and methods of exegesis, shaped Latin literary culture and have informed Western literary study ever since. Hence it was that, though the Greeks were far from the first or only ancient society to subject their old texts to close scrutiny and to use them in educating the young, the specific form that this activity took in classical Athens set the pattern for Western literary study to the present day.

The continuing influence of Greek criticism obviously depended on many historical contingencies, but in thinking about these, we may ask of criticism what Janaway asks of art: "What institutional theories do not tell is whether institutions which are called 'art' arise or persist *because* things of genuine value are produced or discovered in them."[3] I have focused on recovering social contexts in this study, both of song and of criticism, because Greek criticism achieved technical status precisely by suppressing their influence. But this is not to imply that the rise of literary criticism can be adequately explained as an elitist mystification of poetry for the purpose of amassing cultural prestige. It is clear from its subsequent history that poetics supplied a common language, a kind of *koinē* for carrying on the traditions of Greek song. Poetics was a theory for Aristotle, an answer to the omnivorous human appetite to understand (*Metaphysics* A.1), but the "tissue of definitions" he offered could also serve as a set of ground rules, as it were, for debating the merits and demerits of poems. This potential becomes explicit in the treatment of "challenges and solutions" in *Poetics* 25, but a group of like-minded discussants is already being assembled in the first sentence: "Let *us* discuss poetics," says Aristotle, "beginning that field of inquiry (*methodos*) from its natural first principles."[4]

" 'Natural' for whom?" one must ask. To the extent that the audiences of the *Poetics*, removed from the theater to the lecture hall and thence to the court, the schoolroom, or the salon, still formed a community within other communities, criticism may be regarded as only a further refinement in the methods by which elites had long distinguished themselves in their sport with song. Doubtless critical theory often was, as it still may be, a means of appropriating cultural objects held in common, and its terminology lends itself to being used as a sort of Pythagorean watchword, a secret token exchanged among those "in the know." But critical terminology can succeed by expressing, compendiously, axioms of a common discussion, and the scientific vocabulary of classical criticism expressed its up-

---

[3] Janaway 1995: 189.

[4] 1447a11–13: ὅσα τῆς αὐτῆς ἐστι μεθόδου, λέγωμεν ἀρξάμενοι κατὰ φύσιν πρῶτον ἀπὸ τῶν πρώτων. For "tissue of definitions," Hutton 1982: 5 ff.

to-dateness, its need to place songs, old and new, within their best under-standing of the world. The aspirations of poetics to the status of material-ist science inclined it to becoming a science of sounds; but this was checked by the key role afforded to "the appropriate," a matter not to be precisely measured but to be arrived at by discussion among those shar-ing, as ever, an interest in "the fine" in life. Finally, in limiting the reach of its *tekhnē* in this way, classical criticism respected ancient piety for "measure" in human ambition. When restored to its place within Greek social life, classical criticism is more than a fruitful if conflicted method of investigation; in its abstract and theoretical way, it took up the old tasks of recalling old songs and performing new ones, and of translating both into present concerns. In these regards, little had changed since ar-chaic times. In the Lyceum and often thereafter, there was a need for both "memory and straining after excellence," as Xenophanes, among many others, had said.

BIBLIOGRAPHY

Periodicals are abbreviated as in *L'Année philologique*.

Adam, James. 1965. *The Republic of Plato*. 2 vols. Cambridge: Cambridge University Press.

Adkins, A.W.H. 1985. *Poetic Craft of the Early Greek Elegists*. Chicago: University of Chicago Press.

Allen, T. W. 1924. *Homer: The Origins and Transmission*. Oxford: Clarendon Press.

———, ed. 1946. *Homeri opera*. 5 vols. Corrected reprint of 1912 edition. Oxford: Clarendon Press.

Anderson, Øvind. 1987. "Mündlichkeit und Schriftlichkeit im frühen Griechentum." *A&A* 23: 29–44.

———. 1989. "The Significance of Writing in Early Greece." In *Literacy and Society*, ed. Karen Schousboe and M. T. Larsen, pp. 73–90. Copenhagen: Akademisk Forlag.

Anderson, Warren D. 1966. *Ethos and Education in Greek Music*. Cambridge, Mass.: Harvard University Press.

Annas, Julia. 1982. "Plato on the Triviality of Literature." In Moravcsik and Temko 1982: 1–28.

Apicella, G. R. 1980. "Orfismo e intrepretatizione allegorica." *BollClass* 3.1: 116–30.

Ardizzoni, Anthos. 1953. *ΠΟΙΗΜΑ*. Ricerche sulla teoria del linguaggio poertico nel l'antichità. Bari: Adriatica.

Armstrong, David. 1995. "The Impossibility of Metathesis: Philodemus and Lucretius on Form and Content in Poetry." In *Philodemus and Poetry*, ed. D. Obbink, pp. 210–32. Oxford: Oxford University Press.

Asmis, Elizabeth. 1992. "Plato on Poetic Creativity." In *The Cambridge Companion to Plato*, ed. R. Kraut, pp. 338–64. Cambridge: Cambridge University Press.

Atkins, J.W.H. 1934. *Literary Criticism in Antiquity*. Cambridge: Cambridge University Press.

Babut, Daniel. 1974. "Xénophane critique des poètes." *AC*. 45: 83–117.

Baker, W. W. 1904. "De comicis Graecis litterarum iudicibus." *HSPh* 15: 121–240.

Balme, M. 1984. "Attitudes to Work and Leisure in Ancient Greece." *G&R* 31: 14–52.

Barker, Andrew. 1984. *Greek Musical Writings: The Musician and His Art*. Vol 1. Cambridge: Cambridge University Press.

———. 1995. "Gli agoni musicali." In *Musica e mito nella Grecia antica*, ed. D. Restani, pp. 257–70. Bologna: Il Mulino.

Barker, Andrew, and M. Warner, eds. 1992. *The Language of the Cave*. Nottingham: Academic Publishers.

Barnes, Jonathan. 1982. *The Presocratic Philosophers*. 2d ed. London: Routledge and Kegan Paul.

Barns, John. 1951. "A New *Gnomologium*: With Some Remarks on Gnomic Anthologies II." *CQ* 45: 1–19.

Barrett, W. S. 1964. *Euripides: Hippolytus*. Oxford: Clarendon Press.

Bartol, Krystyna. 1992. "Where Was Iambic Poetry Performed? Some Evidence from the Fourth Century B.C." *CQ* 42: 65–71.

Battisti, Daniela. 1990. "*Sunetos* as Aristocratic Self-Description." *GRBS* 31: 5–25.

Becker, Andrew S. 1995. *The Shield of Achilles and the Poetics of Ekphrasis*. Lanham, Md.: Rowman and Littlefield.

Belfiore, Elizabeth. 1980. "Elenchus, Epode and Magic: Socrates as Silenus." *Phoenix* 34: 128–37.

———. 1985. "Pleasure, Tragedy and Aristotelian Psychology." *CQ* 35: 349–61.

———. 1992. *Tragic Pleasures: Aristotle on Plot and Emotion*. Princeton: Princeton University Press.

Bell, J. M. 1978. "*Kimbix kai sophos*: Simonides in the Anecdotal Tradition." *QUCC* 28: 29–86.

Benediktson, D. T. 2000. *Literature and the Visual Arts in Greece and Rome*. Norman: University of Oklahoma Press.

Benseler, G. E., and F. Blass. 1879. *Isocratis orationes*. 2 vols. Leipzig: Teubner.

Bernabé, A. 1988. *Poetae epici Graeci: Testimonia et fragmenta*. Leipzig: Teubner.

Bernadini, A. 1967. "Linguaggio e programma poetico in Pindaro." *QUCC* 4: 80–97.

Bers, Victor. 1994. "Tragedy and Rhetoric." In Worthington 1994: 176–95.

Bicknell, P. J. 1969. "Democritus' Theory of Precognition." *REG* 82: 318–26.

Bielohlawek, K. 1924–27. "Μέλπεσθαι und μολπή." *WS* 44: 1–18, 125–43, and 45: 1–11.

———. 1940. "Gastmahls- und Symposionslehren bei griechischen Dichtern: Von Homer bis zur Theognissammlung und Kritias." *WS* 58: 11–30.

Bing, P. 1988. *The Well-Read Muse*. Göttingen: Vandenhoeck and Ruprecht.

Blank, R. 1988. "Socratics vs. Sophists on Payment for Teaching." *Cl Ant* 4: 1–49.

Blass, Freidrich. 1887–93. *Die Attische Beredsamkeit*. 2d ed. 3 vols. Leipzig. (Reprint, Hildesheim, 1962.)

Blumenberg, H. 1957. "'Nachahmung der Natur': Zur Vorgeschichte des schöpferischen Menschen." *Studium generale* 10: 266–83.

Boedeker, Deborah, and K. A. Raaflaub, eds. 1998. *Democracy, Empire and the Arts in Fifth-Century Athens*. Cambridge, Mass.: Harvard University Press.

Boegehold, Alan L., and Adele Scafuro, eds. 1994. *Athenian Identity and Civic Ideology*. Baltimore and London: The Johns Hopkins University Press.

Bourdieu, Pierre. 1967. "Systems of Education and Systems of Thought." *International Social Science Journal* 19: 338–58.

———. 1984. *Distinction: A Social Critique of the Judgement of Taste*. Translated by Richard Nice. Cambridge, Mass.: Harvard University Press.

———. 1990. "Reading, Readers, the Literate, Literature." In *In Other Words*, trans. M. Adamson, pp. 94–105. Stanford: Stanford University Press.

———. 1993. *The Field of Cultural Production*. Edited by Randal Johnson. New York: Columbia University Press.

Bowie, E. L. 1986. "Early Greek Elegy, Symposia and Public Festivals." *JHS* 106: 13–35.

———. 1990. "*Miles Ludens?* The Problem of Martial Exhortation in Early Greek Elegy." In Murray 1990: 221–29.

———. 1993a. "Greek Table-Talk before Plato." *Rhetorica* 11: 355–71.

———. 1993b. "Lies, Fiction and Slander in Early Greek Poetry." In Gill and Wiseman 1993: 1–37.

Bowman, Alan K., and Greg Woolf, eds. 1994. *Literacy and Power in the Ancient World*. Cambridge: Cambridge University Press.

Bowra, C. M. 1941. "Xenophanes, Fragment 3." *CQ* 35: 119–26.

———. 1952. *Heroic Poetry*. London: Macmillan.

———. 1953. *Problems in Greek Poetry*. Oxford: Clarendon Press.

———. 1961. *Greek Lyric Poetry*. 2d ed. Oxford: Clarendon Press.

———. 1964. *Pindar*. Oxford: Clarendon Press.

———. 1970. "Xenophon on the Luxury of Colophon." In idem, *On Greek Margins*, pp. 109–21. Oxford: Clarendon Press.

Boyancé, P. 1937. *Le culte des Muses chez les philosophes grecs*. Paris: E. De Boccard.

———. 1974. "Remarques sur le Papyrus de Derveni." *REG* 414: 91–110.

Boyd, Timothy. 1994. "Where Ion Stood, What Ion Sang." *HSPh* 96: 109–21.

Braswell, Bruce K. 1992. *A Commentary on the Fourth Pythian Ode of Pindar*. Berlin and New York: Walter de Gruyter.

Braun, A. 1938. "I verbi del fare nel greco." *SIFC* 15: 242–96.

Bremer, Jan N. 1983. *The Early Greek Concept of the Soul*. Princeton: Princeton University Press.

———. 1990. "Adolescents, *Symposion*, and Pederasty." In Murray 1990: 135–48.

———. 1991. "Poets and Their Patrons." Ed. H. Hofmann and A. Harder. In *Fragmenta dramatica*, pp. 39–60. Göttingen: Vandenhoeck and Ruprecht.

Brink, C. O. 1963–82. *Horace on Poetry*. 3 vols. Cambridge: Cambridge University Press.

Brown, Peter. 1992. *Power and Persuasion in Late Antiquity*. Madison: University of Wisconsin Press.

Browning, R. 1958. "Greek Abstracts in *-sis*." *Philologos* 102: 60–72.

Bruns, Gerald. 1992. *Hermeneutics Ancient and Modern*. New Haven and London: Yale University Press.

Buchheim, Thomas. 1985. "Maler, Sprachbildner: Zur Verwandschaft des Gorgias mit Empedocles." *Hermes* 113: 417–29.

———, ed. 1989. *Gorgias von Leontini: Reden, Fragmente und Testimonien*. Hamburg: Felix Meiner Verlag.

Buffière, F. 1956. *Les mythes d' Homère*. Paris: Belles Lettres.

Bundy, E. L. 1986. *Studia Pindarica*. Berkeley and Los Angeles: University of California Press.

Burkert, Walter. 1960. "Platon oder Pythagoras. Zum Ursprung des Wortes 'Philosophie.'" *Hermes* 68: 159–77.

———. 1962. "ΓΟΗΣ. Zum Griechischen 'Schamanismus.'" *RhM* 105: 36–55.

———. 1968. "Orpheus und die Vorsokratiker." *A&A* 14: 93–114.

Burkert, Walter. 1969. "Das Proömium des Parmenides und die Katabasis des Pythagoras." *Phronesis* 14: 1–30.

———. 1970. "La genèse des choses et des mots: Le Papyrus de Derveni entre Anaxagore et Cratyle." *Les études philosophiques* 25: 443–55.

———. 1972a. *Lore and Science in Ancient Pythagoreanism.* Translated by E. L. Miner Jr. Rev. ed. Cambridge, Mass.: Harvard University Press. Originally published as *Weisheit und Wissenschaft* [Nürnburg: Hans Carl, 1962].)

———. 1972b. "Die Leistung eines Kreophylos: Kreophyleer, Homeriden und die archaische Heraklesepik." *MH.* 29: 74–85.

———. 1976. "Das Hunderttorige Theben und die Datierung der Ilias." *WS.* 10: 5–21.

———. 1977. "Air-Imprints or Eidola: Democritus' Aetiology of Vision." *ICS* 2: 97–109.

———. 1979a. "Kynaithos, Polycrates, and the *Homeric Hymn to Apollo.*" In *Arktouros: Hellenic Studies Presented to Bernard M. Walter Knox,* ed. G. Walter Bowersock, Walter Burkert, and M.C.J. Putnam, pp. 53–62. Berlin and New York: Walter de Gruyter.

———. 1979b. *Structure and History in Greek Mythology and Ritual.* Berkeley and Los Angeles: University of California Press.

———. 1980. "Craft Versus Sect: The Problem of Orphics and Pythagoreans." In *Jewish and Christian Self-Definition,* ed. B. F. Myers and E. P. Sanders, pp. 1–23. Philadelphia: Fortress Press.

———. 1983a. "Itinerant Diviners and Magicians: A Neglected Element in Cultural Contacts." In Hägg and Marinatos 1983: 115–19.

———. 1983b. "Oriental Myth and Literature in the *Iliad.*" In Hägg and Marinatos 1983: 51–56.

———. 1985. *Greek Religion.* Translated by J. Raffan. Cambridge, Mass.: Harvard University Press.

———. 1986. "Der Autor von Derveni: Stesimbrotos ΠΕΡΙ ΤΕΛΕΤΩΝ." *ZPE* 62: 1–5.

———. 1987a. "The Making of Homer in the Sixth Century B.C.: Rhapsodes versus Stesichoros." In *Papers on the Amasis Painter and His World,* pp. 43–62. Malibu, Calif.: Getty Museum.

———. 1987b. *Ancient Mystery Cults.* Cambridge, Mass.: Harvard University Press.

———. 1991. "Oriental Symposia: Contrasts and Parallels." In Slater 1991: 7–24.

———. 1992. *The Orientalizing Revolution.* Translated by M. E. Pinder and W. Burkert. Cambridge, Mass.: Harvard University Press.

Burnett, A. P. 1983. *Three Archaic Poets: Archilochus, Alcaeus, Sappho.* Cambridge Mass.: Harvard University Press.

———. 1985. *The Art of Bacchylides.* Cambridge, Mass.: Harvard University Press.

Burns, Alfred. 1981. "Athenian Literacy in the Fifth Century B.C." *JHI* 43: 371–87.

Burnyeat, M. F. 1999. "Culture and Society in Plato's *Republic.*" *The Tanner Lectures in Human Values* 20: 215–324.

Bury, J. B. 1965. *The Nemean Odes of Pindar.* Amsterdam: Hakkert.

Burzachechi, M. 1962. "Oggetti parlanti nelle epigrafi Greche." *Epigraphica* 24: 3–54.

Butcher, S. H. 1907. *Aristotle's Theory of Poetry and Fine Art.* 4th ed. London: Macmillan.

Bywater, I. 1909. *Aristotle on the Art of Poetry.* Oxford: Clarendon Press.

Cairns, F. J. 1972. *Generic Composition in Greek and Roman Literature*: Edinburgh: Edinburgh University Press.

Calame, Claude. 1974. "Réflexions sur les genres littéraires en Grèce archaïque." *QUCC* 17: 113–28.

———. 1977. *Les choeurs des jeunes filles en Grèce archaïque.* 2 vols. Rome: Ateneo and Bizzarri.

———. 1993. "Rhythme, voix et mémoire de l' écriture en Grèce classique." In Pretagostini 1993, 2: 785–99.

———. 1995. "Variations énonciatives, relations avec les dieux et fonctions poétiquies dans les *Hymnes Homeriques.*" *MH* 52: 2–19.

———. 1998. "La poésie lyrique grecque: Un genre inexistant?" *Littérature* 111: 87–110.

Calder, W. M., and J. Stern, eds. 1970. *Pindaros und Bakchylides.* Wege der Forschung 134. Darmstadt: Wissentschaftliche Buchgesellschaft.

Cambiano, Giuseppe, Luciano Canfora, and Diego Lanza, eds. 1992. *Lo spazio letterario della Grecia antica.* 3 vols. Rome: Salerno.

Cameron, Alan. 1995. *Callimachus and His Critics.* Princeton: Princeton University Press.

Campbell, David. 1967. *Greek Lyric Poetry.* London and New York: St. Martins.

———. 1982–93. *Greek Lyric.* 5 vols. Loeb Classical Library. Cambridge, Mass.: Harvard University Press.

Cantarella, R. 1967. "Omero in occidente e le origini dell' omerologia." *PP* 22: 5–28.

Cantor, Paul. 1991. "Aristotle and the History of Tragedy." In *Theoretical Issues in Literary History,* Harvard English Studies 16, pp. 60–85. Cambridge, Mass.: Harvard University Press.

Carroll, M. 1895. *Aristotle's* Poetics *c. XXV in the Light of Homeric Scholarship.* Baltimore: John Murphy.

Carson, A. 1992. "Simonides Painter." In Hexter and Selden 1992: 51–64.

Carter, L. B. 1986. *The Quiet Athenian.* Oxford: Clarendon Press.

Cartledge, Paul, Paul Millett, and Stephen Todd, eds. 1990. *Nomos: Essays in Athenian Law, Politics, and Society.* Cambridge: Cambridge University Press.

Càssola, F. 1975. *Inni omerici.* Milan: Fondazione Lorenzo Valla.

Cerri, G. 1976. "Frammento di teoria musicale e ideologia simposiale in un distico di Teognide (v. 1041 ss.): Il role paradossale dell' auleta. La fonte probabile di G. Pascoli, *Solon.* 13–15." *QUCC* 22: 25–39.

Chantraine, Pierre. 1945. "Grec κομψός." *REG* 58: 90–96.

———. 1956. *Études sur la vocabulaire grecque.* Paris: Klincksiek.

———. 1968–77. *Dictionnaire étymologique de la langue grecque.* 2 vols. Paris: Klincksiek.

———. 1979. *La formation des noms en Grec ancienne.* Paris: Klincksiek.

Chase-Greene, W. 1950. "The Greek Criticism of Poetry, A Reconsideration." *Harvard Studies in Comparative Literature* 20: 19–53.

Cherniss, H. F. 1935. *Aristotle's Criticism of Presocratic Philosophy.* Baltimore: The Johns Hopkins University Press.

Christ, G. 1941. *Simonidesstudien.* Freiburg: Pualusdruckerei.

Cingano, Éttore. 1985. "Clistene di Sicione, Erodoto e i poemi del Ciclo tebano." *QUCC* 20: 31–40.

Classen, C. J. 1959. "The Study of Language amongst Socrates' Contemporaries." *Proceedings of the African Classical Association.* 2: 33–49. (= Classen 1976: 215–47.)

———, ed. 1976. *Sophistik.* Wege der Forschung 187. Darmstadt: Wissenschaftliche Buchgesellschaft.

Clayman, D. L. 1977. "The Origins of Greek Literary Criticism and the *Aitia* Prologue." *WS* 11: 27–34.

Cobet, Justus. 1977. "Wann wurde Herodots Darstellung der Perserkriege Publiziert?" *Hermes* 105: 2–27.

Cole, A. T. 1967. *Democritus and the Origins of Greek Anthropology.* Chapel Hill, N.C.: Western Reserve University. Reprinted Atlanta: Scholar's Press, 1990.

———. 1986. "Writing in a Readerless Society: Topos and Text in the Age of Plato." *Sewanee Review* 94: 186–95.

———. 1991. *The Origins of Rhetoric in Ancient Greece.* Baltimore and London: The Johns Hopkins University Press.

———. 1992. *Pindar's Feasts, or the Music of Power.* Rome: Ateneo.

———. 1993. "Le metamorfosi della saggezza: *Sophia* fra oralità e scrittura." In Pretagostini 1993, 2: 753–63.

Collingwood, R. G. 1938. *The Principles of Art.* Oxford: Clarendon Press.

Commellback, F. M. 1987. "The λύσις ἐκ τῆς λέξεως." *AJPh* 108: 202–19.

Cook, R. M. 1971. "'Epoiesen' on Greek Vases." *JHS* 91: 137–38.

Cooper, John. 1993. "Rhetoric, Dialectic and the Passions." In *Oxford Studies in Ancient Philosophy,* vol. 11, ed. C.C.W. Taylor, pp. 175–98. Oxford: Clarendon Press.

Croally, N. T. 1994. *Euripidean Polemic: The* Trojan Women *and the Function of Tragedy.* Cambridge: Cambridge University Press.

Csapo, Eric, and W. J. Slater. 1995. *The Context of Ancient Drama.* Ann Arbor: University of Michigan Press.

Culler, Johnathan. 1981. *The Pursuit of Signs.* Ithaca, N.Y.: Cornell University Press.

Cunliffe, R. J. 1986. *A Lexicon of the Homeric Dialect.* Norman: University of Oklahoma Press.

Curtius, E. R. 1953. *European Literature and the Latin Middle Ages.* Translated by Willard R. Trask. Princeton: Princeton University Press.

D'Alessio, G. B. 1997. "Pindar's Prosodia and the Classification of Pindaric Papyrus Fragments." *ZPE* 118: 23–60

Dalfen, Joachim. 1974. *Polis und Poiesis.* Munich: Fink.

D'Angour, Armand. 1997. "How the Dithyramb Got Its Shape." *CQ* 47: 331–51.

Davies, J. K. 1981. *Wealth and the Power of Wealth in Classical Athens*. Salem, N.H.: Ayer.

Davies, Malcolm, ed. 1988. *Epicorum Graecorum fragmenta*. Göttingen: Vandenhoeck and Ruprecht.

———, ed. 1991. *Poetarum melicorum Graecorum fragmenta*. Vol. 1. Oxford: Clarendon Press.

Davison, J. A. 1968. *From Archilochus to Pindar*. London: MacMillan.

Dawson, David. 1992. *Allegorical Readers and Cultural Revision in Ancient Alexandria*. Berkeley and Los Angeles: University of California Press.

Defradas, J. 1962. "Le Banquet de Xénophane." *REG* 75: 344–65.

Delatte, Armand. 1915. *Études sur la littérature Pythagoricienne*. Paris: Champion.

———. 1934. *Les Conceptions de l' enthousiasme chez les philosophes présocratiques*. Paris: Les Belles Lettres.

Delgado, J.A.F. 1990. "Orakelpoesie, mündliche Dichtung und Literatur im Homerischen *Hermes Hymnus*." In Kullmann and Reichel 1990: 199–226.

Demand, Nancy. 1971. "Epicharmus and Gorgias." *AJPh* 92: 453–63.

Denniston, J. D. 1927. "Technical Terms in Aristophanes." *CQ* 21: 113–21.

———. 1934. *The Greek Particles*. Oxford: Clarendon Press.

Depew, D. J. 1991. "Politics, Music and Contemplation in Aristotle's Ideal State." In *A Companion to Aristotle's Politics*, ed. D. Keyt and F.D.R. Miller, pp. 346–80. Oxford: Blackwell.

DeRomilly, J. 1973. "Gorgias et le pouvoir de la poésie" *JHS* 93: 155–62.

———. 1975. *Magic and Rhetoric in Ancient Greece*. Cambridge, Mass.: Harvard University Press.

———. 1992. *The Great Sophists in Periclean Athens*. Translated by Janet Lloyd. Oxford: Clarendon Press.

Derrida, Jacques. 1972. "La Pharmacie de Platon." In *La Dissémination*, pp. 69–196. Paris: Seuil. (Originally published in *Tel Quel* 32–33 [1968]); trans. B. Johnson as "Plato's Pharmacy" in *Dissemination* [Chicago: University of Chicago Press, 1981].)

Detienne, Marcel. 1962. *Homère, Hesiode et Pythagore: Poésie et philosophie dans le pythagorisme ancien*. Collection Latomus 57. Brussels: Universa.

———. 1967. *Les maîtres de vérité dans la Grèce archaïque*. Paris: François Maspero.

———. 1981. *L' invention de la mythologie*. Paris: Gallimard.

———, ed. 1988. *Les savoirs de l'écriture en Grèce ancienne*. Cahiers de Philologie 14. Lille: Presses Universitaires de Lille.

Detienne, Marcel, and J. -P. Vernant. 1974. *Les ruses d' intelligence: La mêtis des grecs*. Flammarion: Paris. English translation by J. Lloyd, *Cunning Intelligence in Greek Culture and Society*. Sussex: Harvester Press; New York: Humanities Press Inc., 1978.

De Vries, G. 1973. "Mystery Terminology in Aristophanes and Plato." *Mnemosyne* 26: 1–8.

Dickson, K. M. 1990. "Voice and Sign in Pindar." *Ramus* 19: 109–29.

Diehl, E. 1940. "Fuerunt ante Homerum Poetae." *RhM* 89: 81–114.

———. 1949–52. *Anthologia lyrica Graeca*. 2 vols. 3d ed. Leipzig: Teubner.

Diels, Herman. 1910. "Die Anfänge der Philologie bei den Griechen." *Neue Jahrbücher*: 1–25.

Diels, Herman, and W. Kranz. 1952. *Die Fragmente der Vorsokratiker*. 6th ed. 3 vols. Berlin: Weidmann.

Dimas, Marian. 1999. *Lyric Quotation in Plato*. Totowa, N.J.: Rowman and Littlefield.

Diller, Hans. 1956. "Der vorphilosophische Gebrauch von ΚΟΣΜΟΣ und ΚΟΣΜΕΙΝ." In *Festschrift Bruno Snell*, 47–60. Munich: C. H. Beck.

Dodds, E. R. 1952. "The Alcidamas-Papyrus Again." *CQ* 2:187–88.

———. 1957. *The Greeks and the Irrational*. Berkeley and Los Angeles: University of California Press.

———. 1959. *Plato: Gorgias*. Oxford: Oxford University Press.

Donlon, Walter. 1985. "*Pistos Philos Hetairos*." In Figueira and Nagy 1985: 223–44.

Dornseiff, F. 1921. *Pindars Stil*. Berlin: Weidmann.

Dover, K. J. 1964. "The Poetry of Archilochus." In *Archiloque*, ed. J. Pouilloux et al., Entretiens sur l' Antiquité Classique 10. Vandoeuvres-Geneva: Fondation Hardt.

———. 1968. *Aristophanes: Clouds*. Oxford: Clarendon Press.

———. 1974. *Greek Popular Morality in the Time of Plato and Aristotle*. Oxford: Blackwell. Reprinted 1994 with corrections, Indianapolis: Hackett.

———. 1978. *Greek Homosexuality*. London: Duckworth.

———. 1980. *Plato: Symposium*. Cambridge: Cambridge University Press.

———. 1987–88. *The Greeks and Their Legacy*. 2 vols. Oxford: Blackwell.

———. 1993. *Aristophanes: Frogs*. Oxford: Clarendon Press.

Downing, E. 1990. "*Apate, Agon* and Literary Self-Reflexivity in Euripides' *Helen*." In Griffith Mastronarde 1990: 1–16.

Duchemin, J. 1955. *Pindare: Poète et prophète*. Paris: Les Belles Lettres.

———. 1970. "Essai sur le Symbolism Pindarique: Or, Lumière et Couleurs." In *Pindaros und Bakchylides*, ed. W. M. Calder III and J. Stern, pp. 278–89. Darmstadt: 1970. Reprinted from *REG* 65 (1952): 46–58.

Dunbar, Nan. 1995. *Aristophanes: Birds*. Oxford: Clarendon Press.

Dupont, Florence. 1999. *The Invention of Literature*. Translated by Janet Lloyd. Baltimore and London: The Johns Hopkins University Press.

Dupont-Roc, R., and J. Lallot. 1980. *Aristote: La Poétique*. Paris: Seuil.

Durante, M. 1976. *Sulla preistoria della tradizione poetica greca. Parte seconda: risultanze della comparazione indoeuropea*. Incunabula Graeca 64. Rome: Editore d' Ateneo.

Eagleton, Terry. 1983. *Literary Theory: An Introduction*. Minneapolis: University of Minnesota Press.

———. 1984. *The Function of Criticism*. London: Verso.

Ebert, Joachim. 1972. *Griechische Epigramme auf Sieger an gymnischen und hippischen Agonen*. Abhandd. Sächischen Akad. Wiss. Phil-Hist. Klasse 63.2. Berlin: Akademie Verlag.

Eden, K. 1986. *Poetic and Legal Fiction in the Aristotelian Tradition*. Princeton: Princeton University Press.

Edmunds, Lowell. 1985. "The Genre of Theognidean Poetry." In Figueira and Nagy 1985: 96–111.

———. 1994. "Thucydides and the Act of Writing." In Pretagonistini 1994: 831–52.

Edmunds, Lowell, and R. W. Wallace, eds. 1997. *Poet, Public, and Performance in Ancient Greece*. Baltimore and London: The Johns Hopkins University Press.

Edwards, Mark J. 1991. "Notes on the Derveni Commentator." *ZPE* 86: 203–11.

Egger, Émile. 1886. *Essai sur l'histoire de la critique chez les Grecs*. 3d ed. Paris: Pedone.

Ehrenberg, Victor. 1952. *The People of Aristophanes*. 2d. ed. Oxford: Blackwell.

Eisenberger, H. 1970. "Demokrits Vorstellung von Sein und Wirkung der Götter." *RhM* 113: 141–58.

Else, G. F. 1958. "Imitation in the Fifth Century." *CPh* 53: 73–90.

———. 1967. *Aristotle's Poetics: The Argument*. Cambridge, Mass.: Harvard University Press.

———. 1972. *The Structure and Date of Book X of Plato's* Republic. Heidelberg: C. Winter.

England, E. B. 1921. *The* Laws *of Plato*. Manchester: The University Press.

Eucken, Christoph. 1983. *Isokrates: Seine Positionen in der Auseindersetzung mit den zeitgenössischen Philosophen*. Berlin: De Gruyter.

Fantuzzi, M. 1980. "Oralità, scrittura, auralità. Gli studi sulle techniche della communcazione nella Grecia antica (1960–1980)." *Lingua e stile* 15: 593–612.

Faraone, C. A. 1996. "Taking the 'Nestor's Cup Inscription' Seriously: Erotic Magic and Conditional Curses in the Earliest Inscribed Hexameters." *Cl Ant* 15: 77–112.

Färber, Hans. 1936. *Die Lyrik in der Kunsttheorie der Antike*. Münich: Neuer Filser-Verlag.

Farinelli, Caterina. 1995. "Le citazioni omeriche in Herodoto II, 116–117." *Annali dell'Istituto Orientale di Napoli* 17: 5–29.

Feeney, D. C. 1991. *The Gods in Epic: Poets and Critics of the Classical Tradition*. Oxford: Clarendon Press.

Fehling, D. 1965. "Zwei Untersuchungen zur Griechischen Sprachphilosophie." *RhM* 108: 212–29.

———. 1989. *Herodotus and His "Sources": Citation, Invention and Narrative Art*. Translated by J. G. Howe. Leeds: Francis Cairns.

Fehr, B. 1990. "Entertainers at the *Symposion*." In Murray 1990: 185–95.

Ferrari, Franco. 1988. "*P. Berol*. inv. 13270: I canti de Elefantina." *Studi classici e orientale* 31: 181–228.

Ferrari, G.R.F. 1987. *Listening to the Cicadas: A Study of Plato's* Phaedrus. Cambridge: Cambridge University Press.

———. 1989. "Plato and Poetry." In Kennedy 1989: 92–149.

Festugière, A. J. 1948. *Hippocrate: L' Ancienne médecine*. Paris.

Figueira, T. J., and G. Nagy, eds. 1985. *Theognis of Megara: Poetry and the Polis*. Baltimore: The Johns Hopkins University Press.

Finkelberg, Margalit. 1998. *The Birth of Literary Fiction in Ancient Greece*. Oxford: Clarendon Press.

Finley, M. I. 1965. *The World of Odysseus*. Rev. New York: Viking.

————. 1975. "The Heritage of Isocrates." In idem, *The Use and Abuse of History*, pp. 193–214. London: Chatto and Windus.

Finnegan, Ruth. 1977. *Oral Poetry: Its Nature, Significance and Social Context*. Cambridge: Cambridge University Press.

Flashar, H. 1956. "Die medizinischen Grundlagen der Lehre von der Wirkung der Dichtung in der griechischen Poetik." *Hermes* 84: 12–48.

Fletcher, Angus. 1964. *Allegory: The Theory of a Symbolic Mode*. Ithaca, N.Y.: Cornell University Press.

Forbes, P.R.B. 1933. "Greek Pioneers in Philology and Grammar." *CR* 47: 105–12.

Ford, Andrew. 1985. "The Seal of Theognis: The Politics of Authorship in Archaic Greece." In Figueira and Nagy 1985: 82–95.

————. 1988. "The Classical Definition of ΡΗΑΨΩΙΔΙΑ." *CPh* 83: 300–307.

————. 1991. "Unity in Greek Criticism and Poetry." *Arion*, 3d ser. 1: 125–54.

————. 1992. *Homer: The Poetry of the Past*. Ithaca, N.Y.: Cornell University Press.

————. 1993a. "The Price of Art in Isocrates: Formalism and the Escape from Politics." In *Rethinking the History of Rhetoric: Multidisciplinary Essays on the Rhetorical Tradition*, ed. T. Poulakos, pp. 31–52. Boulder, Colo.: Westview Press.

————. 1993b. "Platonic Insults: 'Sophistic.'" *Common Knowledge* 1: 31–47.

————. 1993c. "L' inventeur de la poésie lyrique: Archiloque le colon." *Métis. Revue de l' anthropologie grecque* 8: 59–73.

————. 1994. "Protagoras' Head: Interpreting Philosophic Fragments in *Theatetus*." *AJPh* 115: 199–218.

————. 1995. "Katharsis: The Ancient Problem." In *Performativity and Performance*, Papers from the English Institute, ed. Andrew Parker and Eve Sedgwick, 108–32. London and New York: Routledge.

————. 1997a. "The Inland Ship: Problems in the Performance and Reception of Early Greek Epic." In *Written Voices, Spoken Signs: Tradition, Performance, and the Epic Text*, ed. E. Bakker and A. Kahane, pp. 83–109. Cambridge, Mass.: Harvard University Press.

————. 1997b. "Epic as Genre." In *A New Companion to Homer*, ed. Barry Powell and Ian Morris, pp. 398–416. Leiden: E. J. Brill.

————. 1999a. "Epic and the Earliest Greek Allegorists." In *Epics and the Contemporary World*, ed. M. Beissinger, J. Tylus, and S. Wofford, pp. 33–53. Berkeley and London: University of California Press.

————. 1999b. "Reading Homer from the Rostrum: Poetry and Law in Aeschines, *In Timarchus*." In Goldhill and Osborne: 231–56.

————. 1999c. "Odysseus after Dinner: *Od*. 9.2–11 and the Traditions of Sympotic Song." In *Euphrosune: Studies . . . Dimitrios Marinatos*, ed. A. Rengakos and John Kazazis, pp. 109–23. Stuttgart: F. Steiner.

————. 2001. "Sophists without Rhetoric: The Arts of Speech in Fifth-Century Athens." In *Education in Greek and Roman Antiquity*, ed. Y. L. Too, pp. 85–109. Leiden: Brill.

Ford, Andrew. Forthcoming. "Catharsis: The Power of Music in Aristotle's *Politics*." In *Music and the Muses: Song, Dance, and Word in Classical Athenian Culture*, ed. Penelope Murray and Peter Wilson. Oxford: Oxford University Press.

Fortenbaugh, W. W. 1975. *Aristotle on Emotion*. New York: Barnes and Noble.

———. 1986. "Aristotle's Platonic Attitude toward Delivery." *Philosophy and Rhetoric* 19: 242–54.

Fowler, Alastair. 1982. *Kinds of Literature*. Cambridge, Mass.: Harvard University Press.

Fowler, R. L. 1987. *The Nature of Early Greek Lyric*. Toronto: University of Toronto Press.

Fraenkel, E. 1920. "Zur Form der AINOI." *RhM* 73: 366–70.

———. 1950. *Aeschylus: Agamemnon*. 3 vols. Oxford: Clarendon Press.

Fränkel, Hermann. 1975. *Early Greek Poetry and Philosophy*. Translated by Moses Hadas and J. Willis. New York and London: Harcourt Brace Jovanovitch. From *Dichtung und Philosophie des frühen Griechentums*, 2d ed. (Munich: C. Hermann, 1973).

Fraser, P. M. 1972. *Ptolemaic Alexandria*. 3 Vols. Oxford: Clarendon Press.

Friedel, W. Otto. 1873. "De Philosophorum ac Sophistarum qui fuerunt ante Platonem studiis Homericis: I. De Sophistis." Diss., Halle.

Friedländer, P., and H. Hoffleit. 1948. *Epigrammata: Greek Inscriptions in Verse*. Berkeley and Los Angeles: University of California Press.

Friemann, S. 1990. "Überlegungen zu Alkindmas' Rede über die Sophisten." In Kullmann and Reichel 1990: 301–16.

Frisk, H. 1960–70. *Griechisches Etymologisches Wörterbuch*. 2 vols. Heidelberg: Carl Winter.

Frontisi-Ducroux, F. 1975. *Dédale: Mythologie de l' artisan en Grèce ancienne*. Paris: Maspero.

Frye, Northrop. 1957. *Anatomy of Criticism: Four Essays*. Princeton: Princeton University Press.

Fuhrmann, M. 1973. *Einführung in die antike Dichtungstheorie*. Darmstadt: Wissenschaftliche Gesellschaft.

———. 1992. *Dichtungstheorie der Antike*. Darmstadt: Wissenschaftliche Gesellschaft.

Furley, David J. 1956. "The Early History of the Concept of the Soul." *Bulletin of the Institute for Classical Studies* 3: 1–18. (= Irwin 1995: 190–26.)

Gadamer, H. G. 1976. *Philosophical Hermeneutics*. Berkeley: University of California Press.

Gallagher, Catherine, and Stephen Greenblatt. 2000. *Practicing New Historicism*. Chicago: University of Chicago Press.

Gallop, David. 1990. "Animals in the *Poetics*." In *Oxford Studies in Ancient Philosophy*, vol. 8, ed. J. Annas, pp. 145–71. Oxford: Clarendon Press.

Geddes, Anthony. 1987. "Rags and Riches: The Costume of Athenian Men in the Fifth Century." *CQ* 37: 307–31.

Gentili, Bruno. 1988. *Poetry and Its Public in Ancient Greece: From Homer to the Fifth Century*. Translation and introduction by A. T. Cole. Baltimore: The Johns Hopkins University Press.

Gentili, Bruno, and G. Cerri. 1988. *History and Biography in Ancient Thought.* Amsterdam: Gieben.

Gentili, Bruno, and G. Paioni, eds. 1985. *Oralitá: Cultura, letteratura, discorso.* Atti del convegno internazionale, Urbino, 21–25 luiglio 1980). Rome: Ateneo.

Gentili, Bruno, and C. Prato, eds. 1979. *Poetae elegiaci I.* Leipzig: Teubner.

Gera, D. L. 1993. *Xenophon's Cyropaideia: Style, Genre and Literary Technique.* Oxford: Clarendon Press.

Gerber, D. E. 1970. *Euterpe.* Amsterdam: Hakkert.

———. 1982. *Pindar's Olympian One: A Commentary. Phoenix* suppl. 15. Toronto: University of Toronto Press.

———, ed. 1997. *A Companion to the Greek Lyric Poets.* New York: Brill.

Gernet, Louis. 1981. *The Anthropology of Ancient Greece.* Translated by J. Hamilton, S. J. Nagy, and B. Nagy. Baltimore: The Johns Hopkins University Press.

Giangrande, Giuseppe. 1968. "Sympotic Literature and Epigram." In *L'épigramme grecque*, Entretiens sur l' Antiquité Classique 14, pp. 91–177. Vandoeuvres-Geneva: Fondation Hardt.

Giannantoni, G. 1983. *Socraticorum reliquiae.* 4 vols. Rome: Bibliopolis.

Gianotti, G.-F. 1975. *Per una poetica pindarica.* Torino: Paravia.

Gill, Christopher. 1985a. "Ancient Psychotherapy." *JHI* 46: 307–26.

———. 1985b. "Plato and the Education of the Character." *AGPh* 67: 1–26.

———. 1993. "Plato on Falsehood—Not Fiction." In Gill and Wiseman 1993: 38–87.

Gill, Christopher, and T. P. Wiseman, eds. 1993. *Lies and Fiction in the Ancient World.* Austin: University of Texas Press.

Giuliano, F. M. 1991. "Esegesi letteraria in Platone: La discussione sul carme simonideo nel *Protagora*." *Studi classici e orientali* 41: 105–90.

Gladigow, B. 1965. *Sophia und Kosmos.* Spudasmata 1. Hildesheim: Olms.

Golden, Leon. 1992. *Aristotle on Tragic and Comic Mimesis.* Atlanta: Scholars Press.

Goldhill, Simon. 1986. *Reading Greek Tragedy.* Cambridge: Cambridge University Press.

———. 1990. "The Great Dionysia and Civic Ideology." In Winkler and Zeitlin 1990: 97–129.

———. 1991. *The Poet's Voice: Essays on Poetics and Greek Literature.* Cambridge: Cambridge University Press.

———. 1994. "Representing Democracy: Women at the Great Dionysia." In Osborne and Hornblower 1994: 347–69.

Goldhill, Simon, and Robin Osborne, eds. 1999. *Performance Culture and Athenian Democracy.* Cambridge: Cambridge University Press.

Gomperz, Heinrich. 1912. *Sophistik und Rhetorik.* Stuttgart: Teubner.

Goodell, Thomas D. 1914. "ΧΡΗ and ΔΕΙ." *CQ* 8: 91–102.

Goody, Jack, and I. Watt. 1968. "The Consequences of Literacy." In *Literacy in Traditional Societies*, ed. J. Goody, Cambridge: Cambridge University Press.

Goold, Thomas. 1991. *The Ancient Quarrel between Poetry and Philosophy.* Princeton: Princeton University Press.

Grafenhan, A. 1843. *Geschichte der klassischen Philologie im Alterthum*. Bonn: König.

Graff, Gerald. 1987. *Professing Literature: An Institutional History*. Chicago: University of Chicago Press.

Graziosi, Barbara. 2002. *Inventing Homer: The Early Reception of Epic*. Cambridge: Cambridge University Press.

Green, P. 1979. "Strepsiades, Socrates and the Abuse of Intellectualism." *GRBS* 20: 15–25.

Greenberg, N.A.S. 1961. "The Use of *Poiema* and *Poiesis*." *HSPh* 65: 263–90.

Greenblatt, Stephen J., ed. 1981. *Allegory and Representation*. Selected Papers from the English Institute, 1979–80. Baltimore and London: The Johns Hopkins University Press.

Griffith, Mark. 1975. "Man and the Leaves: A Study of Mimnermus fr. 2." *California Studies in Classical Antiquity* 8: 73–88.

———. 1977. *The Authenticity of the* Prometheus Bound. Cambridge: Cambridge University Press.

———. 1983a. "Personality in Hesiod." *ClAnt* 2: 37–65.

———. 1983b. *Aeschylus: Prometheus Bound*. Cambridge: Cambridge University Press.

———. 1990. "Contest and Contradiction in Early Greek Poetry." In Griffith and Mastronarde 1990: 185–207.

Griffith, Mark, and D. Mastronarde, eds. 1990. *Cabinet of the Muses. Essays on Classical and Comparative Literature in Honor of Thomas G. Rosenmeyer*. Atlanta: Scholars Press.

Griffiths, Alan. 1995. "Non-Aristocratic Elements in Archaic Poetry." In Powell 1995: 85–103.

Griffiths, J. G. 1967. "Allegory in Greece and Egypt." *JEA* 53: 79–103.

Groningen, B. A. van. 1960. *Pindar au banquet*. Leiden: Sythoff.

Grube, G.M.A. 1965. *The Greek and Roman Critics*. London: Methuen and Co.

Gudeman, A. 1934. *Aristoteles: ΠΕΡΙ ΠΟΙΗΤΙΚΗΣ*. Berlin and Leipzig: De Gruyter.

Guillory, John. 1993. *Cultural Capital: The Problem of Literary Canon Formation*. Chicago: University of Chicago Press.

Gundert, H. 1935. *Pindar und sein Dichterberuf*. Frankfurt am Main. Reprinted Utrecht: HES, 1978.

Guthrie, W.C.K. 1965. *The Presocratic Tradition from Parmenides to to Democritus. A History of Greek Philosophy*, vol. 2. Cambridge: Cambridge University Press.

———. [1969] 1971. *The Sophists. A History of Greek Philosophy*, vol. 3, part I. Cambridge: Cambridge University Press.

Hägg, R., and N. Marinatos, eds. 1983. *The Greek Renaissance of the Eighth Century B.C.: Tradition and Innovation*. Proceedings of the Second International Symposium at the Swedish Institute in Athens, 1–5 June 1981. Stockholm: Aströms Förlag.

Hall, Edith. 1995. "Lawcourt Dramas: The Power of Performance in Greek Forensic Oratory." *Bulletin of the Institute for Classical Studies* 40: 39–58.

Halliwell, Stephen. 1986. *Aristotle's* Poetics. Chapel Hill: University of North Carolina Press.

———. 1988. *Plato*: Republic *10*. Warminster: Aris and Phillips.

———. 1989. "The Importance of Plato and Aristotle for Aesthetics." *Proceedings of the Boston Area Colloquium in Ancient Philosophy* 5: 321–48

———. 1990. "Aristotelian Mimesis Reevaluated." *Journal of the History of Philosophy* 28: 487–510.

———. 1995. "Tragedy, Reason and Pity: A Reply to Johnathan Lear." In Heinaman: 85–95.

———. 1997. "The *Republic's* Two Critiques of Poetry." In *Platon: Politeia*, ed. O. Höffe, pp. 313–32. Berlin: Akademie.

———. 2000. "The Subjection of Muthos to Logos: Plato's Citations of the Poets." *CQ* 50: 94–112.

Handley, E. 1953. "*-Sis* Nouns in Aristophanes." *Eranos* 51: 129–42.

Hansen, P. A. 1983. *Carmina epigraphica Graeca saeculorum vii-v a. Chr. n.* Texte und Kommentare 12. 2 vols. Berlin and New York: De Gruyter.

Harriott, R. 1969. *Poetry and Criticism before Plato*. London: Methuen.

Harris, W. V. 1989. *Ancient Literacy*. Cambridge, Mass.: Harvard University Press.

Harvey, A. E. 1955. "The Classification of Greek Lyric Poetry." *CQ* 49: 157–75.

Häussler, Reinhard. 1974. "λίνος *ante* Λίνον?" *RhM* 117: 1–14.

Havelock, E. A. 1963. *Preface to Plato*. Cambridge, Mass.: Harvard University Press.

———. 1982. *The Literate Revolution in Greece and its Cultural Consequences*. Princeton: Princeton University Press.

Heath, Malcolm. 1985. "Hesiod's Didactic Poetry." *CQ* 35: 245–63.

———. 1987. *The Poetics of Greek Tragedy*. Stanford: Stanford University Press.

———. 1988. "Receiving the κῶμος." *AJPh* 109: 180–95.

———. 1989. *Unity in Greek Poetics*. Oxford: Clarendon Press.

Hedrick, Charles W. 1994. "Writing, Reading and Democracy." In Osborne and Hornblower 1994: 157–74.

Heiden, Bruce. 1991. "Tragedy and Comedy in the *Frogs* of Aristophanes." *Ramus* 90: 95–111.

Heinaman, Robert, ed. 1995. *Aristotle and Moral Realism*. Boulder, Colo.: Westview.

Heinimann, Felix. 1945. *Nomos und Physis*. Basel: Friedrich Reinhardt.

———. 1961. "Ein vorplatonische Theorie der *technē*." *MH* 18: 105–30. (= Classen 1976: 127–69.)

Heitsch, Ernst. 1994. *Xenophanes und die Anfange kritischen Denkens*. Mainz Akademie der Wissenschaften und der Literatur. Stuttgart: F. Steiner.

Heldmann, K. 1982. *Die Niederlage Homers im Dichterwettstreit mit Hesiod*. Hypomnemata 75. Göttingen: Vandenhoeck and Ruprecht.

Henderson, Jeffrey. 1990. "The Demos and the Comic Competition." In Winkler and Zeitlin 1900: 271–313.

———. 1991. "Women and the Athenian Dramatic Fesitvals." *TAPhA* 121: 133–47.

Henrichs, Albert. 1972. "Toward a New Edition of Philodemus' Treatise *On Piety*." *GRBS* 13: 67–98.

———. 1975. "Two Doxographical Notes: Democritus and Prodicus on Religion." *HShP* 79: 93–123.

———. 1984. "The Sophists and Hellenistic Religion." *HSPh* 88: 139–58.

Henry, Madeline. 1986. "The Derveni Commentator as Literary Critic." *TAPhA* 116: 149–64.

Herington, C. J. 1985. *Poetry into Drama: Early Tragedy and the Greek Poetic Tradition*. Berkeley: University of California Press.

Herter, H. 1956. "Das *Symposion* des Xenophanes." *WS* 69: 33–48.

Heubeck, Alfred. 1979. *Schrift*. Archaeologia Homerica, Band III X. Göttingen: Vandenhoeck and Ruprecht.

Heubeck, Alfred, et al., eds. 1988–92. *A Commentary on Homer's* Odyssey. 3 vols. Oxford: Clarendon Press.

Hexter, Ralph, and D. Selden, eds. 1992. *Innovations of Antiquity*. New York and London: Routledge.

Hofmann, H., and A. Harder, eds. 1991. *Fragmenta dramatica*. Göttingen: Vandenhoeck and Ruprecht.

Hornblower, Simon. 1991. *A Commentary on Thucydides*. Vol. 1, *Books I–III*. Oxford: Clarendon Press.

House, H. 1956. *Aristotle's* Poetics. London: Rupert Hart-Davis.

Howald, E. 1910. "Die Anfänge der literaischen Kritik bei den Griechen." Diss., Zurich.

———. 1919. "Eine vorplatonische Kunsttheorie." *Hermes* 54: 187–207.

Hubbard, T. K. 1985. *The Pindaric Mind: A Study of Logical Structure in Early Greek Poetry*. Leiden: E. J. Brill.

———. 1991. *The Mask of Comedy: Aristophanes and the Intertextual Parabasis*. Ithaca, N.Y.: Cornell University Press.

Hudson Williams, H. L. 1949. "Isocrates and Recitations." *CQ* 43: 65–69.

Humphreys, S. C. 1975. " 'Transcendence' and Intellectual Roles: The Ancient Greek Case." *Daedalus* 104: 91–118.

Hunter, Richard. 1996. *Theocritus and the Archaeology of Greek Poetry*. Cambridge: Cambridge University Press.

Hurst, A., ed. 1984. *Pindare*. Entretiens sur l' Antiquité Classique 31. Vandoeuvres-Geneva: Fondation Hardt.

Hutton, J. 1982. *Aristotle's* Poetics. New York: W. W. Norton.

Huxley, G. L. 1968. "Glaukos of Rhegion." *GRBS* 9: 47–54.

———. 1969. *Greek Epic Poetry*. Cambridge, Mass.: Harvard University Press.

Immerwahr, H. R. 1960. "*Ergon*: History as a Monument in Herodotus and Thucydides." *AJPh* 81: 261–90.

———. 1964. "Book Rolls on Attic Vases." In *Classical, Mediaeval, and Renaissance Studies in Honor of Berthold Louis Ullman*, ed. Charles Henderson, Jr., pp. 17–48. Rome: Edizioni di storia e letteratura.

Immisch, O., ed. 1927. *Gorgiae Helena*. Berlin and New York: Walter de Gruyter.

Irwin, Terence. 1985. *Aristotle: Nichomachean Ethics*. Indianapolis: Hackett.

Jacoby, Felix. 1918. "Zur ältgriecher Lyriker. I Tyrtaios." *Hermes* 53: 1 ff.

———. 1933. "Homerisches I: Der Bios und die Person." *Hermes* 86: 1–50.

Jacoby, Felix. 1941. "The Date of Archilochus." *CQ* 35: 97–109.

Jaeger, Werner. 1947. *The Theology of the Early Greek Philosophers*. Translated by E. S. Robinson. Oxford: Clarendon Press.

———. 1961. *Paideia*. Translated by Gilbert Highet. 3 vols. New York: Oxford.

Janaway, C. 1992. "Craft and Fineness in Plato's *Ion*." *OSAPh*. 10: 1–23.

———. 1995. *Images of Excellence: Plato's Critique of the Arts*. Oxford: Oxford University Press.

Janko, Richard. 1982. *Homer, Hesiod and the Hymns: Diachronic Development in Epic Diction*. Cambridge: Cambridge University Press.

———. 1984. *Aristotle on Comedy: Towards a Reconstruction of Poetics 2*. Berkeley and Los Angeles: University of California Press.

———. 1987. *Aristotle: Poetics I*. Indianapolis: Hackett.

———. 1997. "The Physicist as Hierophant: Aristophanes, Socrates and the Authorship of the Derveni Papyrus." *ZPE* 118: 61–94.

Jedrkiewicz, Stefano. 1996. "Gudizio 'giusto' ed alea nei concorsi drammatici del V secolo ad Atene." *QUCC* 54: 85–101.

Jeffery, L. H. 1990. *The Local Scripts of Archaic Greece*. Revised with a supplement by A. W. Johnston. Oxford: Clarendon Press.

Joly, R. 1960. *Recherches sur le traité pseudo-hippocratique Du Régime*. Paris: Belles lettres.

Jouanna, Jacques. 1984. "Rhétorique et médicine dans la collection Hippocratique." *REG* 97: 26–44.

———. 1988. *Hippocrate*. Vol. 5, pt. 1, *Des Vents, De l' Art*. Paris: Belles lettres.

Kahn, Charles. 1960. *Anaximander and the Origins of Greek Cosmology*. Cambridge: Cambridge University Press.

———. 1993. "Plato's *Ion* and the Problem of *technē*." In Rosen and Farrell 1993: 369–78.

Kannicht, R. 1988. *The Ancient Quarrel between Philosophy and Poetry: Aspects of the Greek Conception of Literature*. Canterbury: University of Canterbury.

———. 1989. "*Thalia*: Über den Zusammenhang zwischen Fest und Poesie bei den Griechen." In *Das Fest*, ed. Walter Haug and Rainer Warning, Poetik und Hermeneutik 14, pp. 29–52. Munich: Wilhelm Fink.

Käppel, Lutz. 1992. *Paian: Studien zur Geschichte einer Gattung*. Berlin and New York: Walter de Gruyter.

Karuzos, Chr. I. 1972. "*Perikalles Agalma*: Empfindung und Gedanken der archaischen Greichen um die Kunst." In Pfohl 1972: 85–152.

Kassel, R., and C. Austin, eds. 1983–. *Poetae comici Graeci*. Berlin and New York: De Gruyter.

Katz, J. T. and Katarina Volk. 2000. "'Mere Bellies?' A New Look at *Theogony* 26–9." *JHS* 120: 122–31.

Kennedy, G. A. 1963. *The Art of Persuasion in Greece*. Princeton: Princeton University Press.

———, ed. 1989. *The Cambridge History of Literary Criticism*: Vol. 1, *Classical Criticism*. Cambridge: Cambridge University Press.

Kenyon, F. G. 1897. *The Poems of Bacchylides*. London: The British Museum.

Kerferd, G. B. 1950. "The First Greek Sophists." *CR* 61: 8–10.

———. 1976. "The Image of the Wise Man in Greece in the Period before Plato." In *Images of Man in Ancient and Medieval Thought*, ed. F. Bossier et al., Louvain: Leuren University Press.

———. 1981. *The Sophistic Movement*. Cambridge: Cambridge University Press.

Kermode, F. 1979. *The Genesis of Secrecy*. Cambridge, Mass.: Harvard University Press.

Kingsley, Peter. 1995. *Ancient Philosophy, Mystery and Magic: Empedocles and the Pythagorean Tradition*. Oxford: Clarendon Press.

Kinkel, G. 1877. *Epicorum Graecorum fragmenta*. Leipzig: Teubner.

Kirk, G. S. 1954. *Heraclitus: The Cosmic Fragments*. Cambridge: Cambridge University Press.

Kirk, G. S., et al., eds. 1985–93. *The* Iliad: *A Commentary*. 6 vols. Cambridge: Cambridge University Press.

Kirk, G. S., J. Raven, and M. Schofield. 1983. *The Presocratic Philosophers*. 2d ed. Cambridge: Cambridge University Press.

Kleingünther, A. 1933. *ΠΡΩΤΟΣ 'ΕΥΕΡΤΗΣ*. Untersuchung zur Geschichte einer Fragestellung. *Philologus* suppl. 26.

Knox, B.M.W. 1985. "Books and Readers in the Greek World." In *The Cambridge History of Classical Literary Criticism*, vol. 1, *Greek Literature*, ed. B.M.W. Knox and P. E. Easterling, pp. 1–16. Cambridge: Cambridge University Press.

Koller, E. 1956. "Musse und musische Paideia: Über die Musikaporetik in der aristotelischen *Politik*." *MH* 13: 1–37, 94–124.

Koller, H. 1954. *Die Mimesis in der Antike*. Orbis Antiqui 1.5. Bern: Francke.

Koster, S. 1970. *Antike Epostheorien*. Palingenesia 5. Wiesbaden: F. Steiner.

Koster, W.J.W. 1975. *Scholia in Aristophanem*. Pt. 1, bk. 1A, *Prolegomena de Comoedia*. Groningen: J. B. Wolters.

Kotsidu, Haritini. 1991. *Die musischen Agone der Panathanaen in archaischer und klassischer Zeit*. Frankfurt am Main: tudv.

Kranz, W. 1924. "Das Verhältnis des Schöpfers zu seinem Werk in der althellenischen Literatur." *Neue Jahrbücher*. 53: 65–86.

———. 1955. *Kosmos*. Archiv für Begriffsgeschichte 2.1. Bonn: Bouvier.

Kraus, W. 1955. "Die Auffassung des Dichtersberufes im frühen Griechentum." *WS*. 68: 65–87.

Kraut, Richard. 1992. "The Defense of Justice in Plato's *Republic*." In *The Cambridge Companion to Plato*, ed. R. Kraut, pp. 311–37. Cambridge: Cambridge University Press.

———. 1997. *Aristotle*: Politics, *Books VII and VIII*. Oxford: Clarendon Press.

Kristeller, P. O. 1951–52. "The Modern System of the Arts: A Study in the History of Aesthetics." *JHI* 12: 496–527 and 13: 17–46.

Kube, J. 1969. Τεχνή *und* ἀρετή. *Sophistisches und Platonisches Tugendwissen*. Berlin: De Gruyter.

Kuhlmann, Gustav. 1906. *De poetae et poematis Graecorum appellationibus*. Inaugural dissertation, Marburg.

Kullmann, W. 1990. "Hintergrunde und Motive der platonischen Schriftkritik." In Kullmann and Reichel 1990: 317–34.

Kullmann, W., and Jochen Althoff, eds. 1993. *Vermittlung und Tradierung von Wissen in der griechischen Kultur*. Tübingen: Gunter Narr.

Kullmann, W., and M. Reichel, eds. 1990. *Der Übergang von der Mündlichkeit zur Literatur bei den Griechen*. Tübingen: Gunter Narr.

Kurke, Leslie. 1991. *The Traffic in Praise: Pindar and the Poetics of Social Economy*. Ithaca, N.Y.: Cornell University Press.

———. 1992. "The Politics of ἁβροσύνη in Archaic Greece." *ClAnt* 11: 91–120.

———. 1999. *Coins, Bodies, Games and Gold: The Politics of Meaning in Archaic Greece*. Princeton: Princeton University Press.

Labarbe, J. 1949. *L' Homère de Platon*. Paris.

Laks, André 1997. "Between Religion and Philosophy: The Function of Allegory in the Derveni Papyrus." *Phronesis* 42: 121–42.

Laks, André, and Glenn Most, eds. 1997. *Studies on the Derveni Papyrus*. Oxford: Clarendon Press.

Lamberton, R. 1986. *Homer the Theologian: Neoplatonist Allegorical Reading and the Growth of the Epic Tradition*. Berkeley: University of California Press.

Lamberton, Robert, and John J. Keaney, eds. 1992. *Homer's Ancient Readers*. Princeton: Princeton University Press.

Lambin, Gérard. 1988. "Ἔλεγος et ἐλεγεῖον." *RPh* 62: 69–78.

Lanata, G. 1956. "La poetica dei lirici Greci arcaici." In *Antidoron. Hugoni Henrico Paoli oblatum*, pp. 168–282. Milan: Varese.

———. 1963. *Poetica preplatonica*. Florence: La Nuova Italia.

Lanza, Diego. 1979. *Lingua e discorso nell' Atene delle professioni*. Naples: Liguori.

———. 1988. "Le comédien face à l' écrit." In Detienne 1988: 359–86.

Lardinois, André. 1996. "Who Sang Sappho's Songs?" In *Reading Sappho: Contemporary Approaches*, ed. Ellen Greene, pp. 151–72. Berkeley: University of California Press.

———. 1997. "Modern Paroemiology and Gnomai in Homer's *Iliad*." *CP* 92: 213–34.

Lasserre, François. 1962. "La condition du poète dans la Grèce antique." *Études des lettres* (Faculté de l' Université de Lausanne), 2d ser., 5: 3–28.

———. 1976. "L' historiographie grecque à l' époque archaïque." *Quaderni di storia* 4: 113–42.

Lasserre, François, and P. Mudry, eds. 1983. *Formes de pensée dans la collection Hippocratique*. Actes du IVᵉ Colloque International Hippocratique, Lausanne, 21–26 September 1981. Geneva: Droz.

Latacz, J. 1990. "Die Funktion des Symposions für die entstehende griechische Literatur." In Kullmann and Reichel 1990: 227–64.

Latte, K. 1925. "Glossographica." *Philologus* 80: 136–75.

Lausberg, Heinrich. 1998. *A Handbook of Literary Rhetoric*. Translated by M. T. Bliss et al. Leiden: Brill.

Lear, Johnathan. 1988. "Katharsis." *Phronesis* 33: 327–44.

———. 1992. "Inside and Outside the *Republic*." *Phronesis* 37: 184–215.

———. 1995. "Testing the Limits: The Place of Tragedy in Aristotle's *Ethics*." In Heinaman 1995: 61–84.

Ledbetter, Grace M. N.d. "Poetics before Plato: Interpretation and Authority in Early Greek Theories of Poetry." Unpublished manuscript.

Lee, R. W. 1977. *Ut Pictura Poiesis: The Humanistic Theory of Painting*. New York: Norton.

Lefkowitz, M. K. 1963. "Τὼ καὶ ἐγώ: The First Person in Pindar." *HSPh* 67: 177–253.

———. 1981. *The Lives of the Greek Poets*. Baltimore and London: The Johns Hopkins University Press.

———. 1984. "The Poet as Athlete." *SIFC* 77: 5–12.

———. 1995. "The First Person in Pindar Reconsidered—Again." *Bulletin of the Institute for Classical Studies* 40: 139–50.

Lesher, J. H. 1978. "Xenophanes' Scepticism." *Phronesis* 23: 1–21. (= Irwin 1995: 285–306.)

———. 1992. *Xenophanes of Colophon: Fragments. A Text and Translation with a Commentary*. Toronto: University of Toronto Press.

———. 1994. "The Significance of *kata pant' a(s)tē* in Parmenides Fr. 1.3. " *AncPhil* 4: 1–20.

Lesky, Albin. 1966. *A History of Greek Literature*. Translated by J. Willis and C. de Heer. New York: Crowell.

Levine, Daniel. 1985. "Symposium and the Polis." In Figueira and Nagy 1985: 176–96.

Lewis, Sian. 1995. "Barbers' Shops and Perfume Shops: 'Symposia without wine.'" In Powell 1995: 432–41.

Lexicon des frügriechischen Epos. 1979–. Edited by B. Snell et al. Göttingen: Vandenhoeck and Ruprecht.

Lidov, J. B. 1983. "The Meaning of ἰδέα in Isocrates." *PP* 38: 273–87.

Lissarague, François. 1987. *Un flot d' images: Une esthétique du banquet grec*. Paris: Biro.

Lledo Íñigo, Emilio. 1961. *El concepto "Poíesis" en la filosofía Griega*. Madrid: Instituto Luis Vives.

Lloyd, A. B. 1986. *Herodotus Book II*. Leiden: Brill.

Lloyd, G.E.R. 1966. *Polarity and Analogy: Two Types of Argumentation in Early Greek Thought*. Cambridge: Cambridge University Press.

———. 1979. *Magic, Reason and Experience*. Cambridge: Cambridge University Press.

———. 1987. *The Revolutions of Wisdom: Studies in the Claims and Practices of Ancient Greek Science*. Berkeley: University of California Press.

Lloyd-Jones, H. 1990. *Greek Epic, Lyric and Tragedy*. Oxford: Clarendon Press.

Long, A. A. 1968. *Language and Thought in Sophocles*. London: Athlone.

———. 1992. "Stoic Readings of Homer." In Lamberton and Keaney 1992: 41–66.

Longo, Oddone. 1978. "Scrivere in Tucidide: Communicazione e Ideologia." In *Studi in onore di Anthos Ardizzoni* 1, ed. E. Livrea and G. A. Privitera, pp. 519–54. Rome: Ateneno e Bizzari.

Longrigg, J. 1963. "Philosophy and Medicine: Some Early Interactions." *HSPh* 67: 147–75.

———. 1983. "[Hippocrates] *Ancient Medicine* and Its Intellectual Context." In Lasserre and Mudry 1983: 249–56.

Lonie, I. M. 1983. "Literacy and the Development of Hippocratic Medicine." In Lasserre and Mudry 1983: 145–61.

Loraux, Nicole. 1986. *The Invention of Athens*. Translated by A. Sheridan. Cambridge, Mass.: Harvard University Press.

Lord, A. B. 1995. *The Singer Resumes the Tale*. Ithaca, N.Y.: Cornell University Press.

Lord, Carnes. 1982. *Education and Culture in the Political Thought of Aristotle*. Ithaca, N.Y.: Cornell University Press.

———. 1996. "Aristotle and the Idea of Liberal Education." In Ober and Hedrick 1996: 271–88.

Lucas, D. W. 1968. *Aristotle: Poetics*. Oxford: Clarendon Press.

MacDowell, D. M., ed. 1982. *Gorgias: Encomium of Helen*. Bristol: Bristol Classical Press.

———. 1990. *Demosthenes: Against Meidias*. Oxford: Clarendon Press.

Maehler, Herwig. 1963. *Die Auffassung des Dichterberufs im frühen Griechentum bis zur Zeit Pindars*. Hypomnemata 3. Göttingen: Vandenhoeck and Ruprecht.

———. 1982. *Die Lieder des Bakchylides*. Vol. 1, *Die Siegeslieder*. Leiden: Brill.

———. 1997. *Die Lieder des Bakchylides*. Vol. 2, *Die Dihyramben und Fragmente*. Leiden: Brill.

Maguire, J. P. 1964. "The Differentiation of Art in Plato's Aesthetics." *HSPh* 68: 389–410.

Marcovich, M. 1978. "Xenophanes on Drinking-Parties and Olympic Games." *ICS* 3: 1–26.

Marg, W. [1957] 1968. *Homer über die Dichtung*. Reprint. Münster: Aschendorff.

Markwald, G. 1986. *Die Homerischen Epigramme*. Königstein/Ts.: Anton Hain.

Martin, Josef. 1931. *Symposion: Die Geschichte einer literarischen Form*. Paderborn: F. Schöningh.

Martin, R.P.M. 1993. "The Seven Sages as Performers of Wisdom." In *Cultural Poetics in Archaic Greece*, ed. C. Dougherty and L. Kurke, pp. 108–28. Cambridge: Cambridge University Press.

McCall, Marsh. 1969. *Ancient Rhetorical Theories of Simile and Comparison*. Cambridge, Mass.: Harvard University Press.

McKeon, R. 1946–47. "Aristotle's Conception of Language and the Arts of Language." *CPh* 41: 193–206 and 42: 21–50.

Meier, Christian. 1989. "Zur Funktion der Feste in Athen im 5. Jahrhundert vor Christue. In *Das Fest*, ed. W. Haug and R. Warning, 569–91. Munich: Wilhelm Fink.

Meijering, R. 1987. *Literary and Rhetorical Theories in Greek Scholia*. Groningen: Forsten.

Merkelbach, R. 1952. "Die pisistratische Redaktion der homerischen Gedichte." *RhM* 95: 23–47.

Merkelbach, R., and M. L. West. 1967. *Fragmenta Hesiodea*. Oxford: Clarendon Press.

Mikalson, Jon D. 1983. *Athenian Popular Religion*. Chapel Hill: University of North Carolina.

Miller, A. M. 1983. "*N*. 4.33–34 and the Defense of Digressive Leisure." *CJ* 78: 202–20.

Momigliano, Arnaldo. 1971. *The Development of Greek Biography*. Cambridge, Mass.: Harvard University Press.

Montoneri, L., and F. Romano, eds. 1985. *Gorgia e la Sofistica*. Atti del convegno internazionale (Lentini—Catania, 12–15 Dec. 1983). Lentini: Universitá di Catania. (= *Siculorum Gymnasium* 38.)

Moore, J. D. 1974. "The Dating of Plato's *Ion*." *GRBS* 15: 421–40.

Moravcsik, J., and P. Temko, eds. 1982. *Plato on Beauty, Wisdom and the Arts*. Totowa, N.J.: Rowman and Littlefield.

Morgan, Kathryn. 1999. "Literate Education in Classical Athens." *CQ* 49: 46–61.

Morris, Ian. 1996. "The Strong Principle of Equality and the Archaic Origins of Greek Democracy." In Ober and Hedrick 1996: 19–48.

Morrow, Glenn R. 1960. *Plato's Cretan City*. Princeton: Princeton University Press.

Most, G. W. 1984. "Rhetoic und Hermeneutic: Zur Konstitution der Neuzeitlichkeit." *A&A* 30: 62–79.

———. 1986. "Sophistique et hermeneutique." In *Positions de la sophistique*, ed. B. Cassin, pp. 233–45. Paris: J. Vrin.

———. 1994a. "Die früheste erhaltene griechische Dichterallegorese." *RhM* 136: 209–12

———. 1994b. "Simonides' Ode to Scopas in Contexts." In *Modern Critical Theory and Classical Literature*, ed. Irene J. F. De Jong and J. P. Sullivan, pp. 127–52. Leiden: Brill.

———. 1997. "The Fire Next Time: Cosmology, Allegoresis, and Salvation in the Derveni Papyrus." *JHS* 117: 117–135.

Mourelatos, A.P.D. 1985. "Gorgias on the Function of Language." In Montoneri and Romano 1985: 607–638.

Muecke, Frances. 1982. "Portrait of the Artist as a Young Woman." *CQ* 32: 41–55.

Mullen, William. 1982. *Choreia: Pindar and Dance*. Princeton: Princeton University Press.

Müller, Dietram. 1974. *Handwerk und Sprache. Die sprachlichen Bilder aus dem Bereich des Handwerks in der griechischen Literatur bis 400 v. Chr.* Beiträge zur Klassischen Philologie 51. Meisenheim am Glan: Anton Hain.

Müller, Eduard. 1834–37. *Geschichte der Theorie der Kunst bei den Alten*. 2 vols. Breslau: Joseph Mar.

Murray, Oswyn. 1980. *Early Greece*. Glasgow: Fontana-Collins.

———. 1983a. "The Greek Symposium in History." In *Tria Corda. Scritti in onore di A. Momigliano*, ed. E. Gabba, pp. 257–72. Como: Ed. New Press.

———. 1983b. "The Symposium as Social Organisation." In Hägg and Marinatos 1983: 195–99.

———, ed. 1990. *Sympotica*. Oxford: Clarendon Press.

———. 1991. "War and the Symposium." In Slater 1991: 83–104.

———. 1995a. "Histories of Pleasure." In Murray 1995b: 3–16.

———, ed. 1995b. *In Vino Veritas*. Oxford: The Alden Press.

Murray, Penelope. 1981. "Poetic Inspiration in Early Greece." *JHS* 101: 87–100.

———. 1992. "Inspiration and *mimesis* in Plato." In Barker and Warner 1992: 27–46.

———. 1996. *Plato on Poetry*. Cambridge: Cambridge University Press.

Murrin, Michael. 1980. *The Allegorical Epic*. Chicago: University of Chicago Press.

Nagler, M. 1990. "Ethical Anxiety and Artistic Inconsistency: The Case of Oral Epic." In Griffith and Mastronarde 1990: 225–39.

Nagy, Gregory. 1979. *The Best of the Achaeans*. Baltimore and London: The Johns Hopkins University Press.

———. 1985a. "Theognis and Megara: A Poet's Vision of his City." In Figueira and Nagy 1985: 22–82.

———. 1985b."On the Symbolism of Apportioning Meat in Archaic Greek Elegiac Poetry." *L' Uomo* 9: 45–52.

———. 1989. "Early Greek Views of Poets and Poetry." In Kennedy 1989: 1–77.

———. 1990. *Pindar's Homer: The Lyric Possession of an Epic Past*. Baltimore and London: The Johns Hopkins University Press.

Nails, Debra. 1995. *Agora, Academy, and the Conduct of Philosophy*. Dordrecht: Kluwer Academic Publishers.

Nehemas, Alexander. 1982. "Plato on Imitation and Poetry in *Republic* 10." In Moravcsik and Temko 1982: 47–78.

———. 1992. "Pity and Fear in the *Rhetoric* and the *Poetics*." In *Essays on Aristotle's Poetics*, ed. A. O. Rorty, pp. 291–314. Princeton: Princeton University Press.

Nestle, Wilhelm. 1911. "Spuren der Sophistik bei Isokrates." *Philologos* 70: 1–51.

———. 1936. "Die Horen des Prodikos." *Hermes* 71: 151–70. Reprinted in Classen 1976: 425–51.

———. 1942. *Von Mythos zum Logos*. 2d ed. Stuttgart: Kröner.

Nethercut, W. 1969. "Dionysus' Vote for Aeschylus." *Classical Bulletin* 44: 81–84, 89–94.

Neville, James W. 1977. "Herodotus on the Trojan War." *G&R*: 1–12.

Newman, W. L. 1902. *The* Politics *of Aristotle*. 4 vols. Oxford: Clarendon Press.

Nightingale, A. W. 1995. *Genres in Dialogue: Plato and the Construct of Philosophy*. Cambridge: Cambridge University Press.

Nisetich, Frank J. 1975. "*Olympian* 1.8–11: An Epinician Metaphor." *HShP* 79: 55–68.

———. 1977. "Convention and Occasion in *Isthmian* 2." *California Studies in Classical Antiquity* 10: 133–56.

———. 1989. *Pindar and Homer*. Baltimore and London: The Johns Hopkins University Press.

Norden, Eduard. 1913. *Agnostos Theos. Untersuchungen zur Formengeschichte Religiöser Rede*. Leipzig and Berlin: Teubner.

———. 1958. *Die antike Kunstprosa*. Darmstadt: Wissenschaftliche Buchgesellschaft.

North, Helen. 1952. "The Use of Poetry in the Training of the Ancient Orator." *Traditio* 8: 1–33.

Nünlist, Rene. 1998. *Poetologische Bildersprache in der Frügriechischen Dictung.* Stuttgart and Leipzig: Teubner.

Nussbaum, Martha C. 1980. "Aristophanes and Socrates on Learning Practical Wisdom." *YCS* 26: 43–97.

———. 1986. *The Fragility of Goodness: Luck and Ethics in Greek Tragedy and Philosophy.* Cambridge: Cambridge University Press.

Ober, Josiah. 1989. *Mass and Elite: Rhetoric, Ideology and the Power of the People.* Princeton: Princeton University Press.

Ober, Josiah, and Charles Hedrick, eds. 1996. *Dêmokratia: A Conversation on Democracies, Ancient and Modern.* Princeton: Princeton University Press.

Ober, Josiah, and Barry Strauss. 1990. "Drama, Political Rhetoric and the Discourse of Athenian Democracy." In *Nothing to Do with Dionysus: Athenian Drama in its Social Context,* ed. John J. Winkler and Froma Zeitlin, pp. 237–70. Princeton: Princeton University Press.

Ong, W. J., S.J. 1982. *Orality and Literacy.* London: Methuen.

Osborne, R., and S. Hornblower, eds. 1994. *Ritual, Finance, Politics: Athenian Democratic Accounts Presented to David Lewis.* Oxford: Clarendon Press.

Ostwald, Martin. 1986. *From Popular Sovereignty to the Sovereignty of Law.* Berkeley and Los Angeles: University of California Press.

O'Sullivan, Neil. 1992. *Alcidamas, Aristophanes and the Beginnings of Greek Stylistic Theory.* Hermes Einzelschriften Heft 60. Stuttgart: Franz Steiner Verlag.

Page, Denys. 1934. *Actors' Interpolations in Greek Tragedy.* Oxford: Clarendon Press.

———. 1955. *Sappho and Alcaeus.* Oxford: Clarendon Press.

———, ed. 1962. *Poetae melici Graeci.* Oxford: Clarendon Press.

———, ed. 1974. *Supplementum lyricis Graecis: Poetarum lyricorum Graecorum fragmenta quae recens innotuerunt.* Oxford.

———. 1981. *Further Greek Epigrams.* Cambridge: Cambridge University Press.

Pagliaro, A. 1963. *Saggi di critica semantica.* 2d ed. Messina and Florence: G. d' Anna.

Palmer, D. J. 1965. *The Rise of English Studies.* London and New York: Oxford University Press.

Palmisciano, Riccardo. 1996. "Simonide 531 P. Testo, dedicatario e genere letterario." *QUCC* 54: 39–53.

Papillon, Terry L. 1996. "Isocrates on Gorgias and Helen: The Unity of the *Helen.*" *CJ* 91: 377–91.

Parke, H. W. 1945. "The Use of Other than Hexameter Verse in Delphic Oracles." *Hermathena* 66: 58–66.

Parke, H. W., and D.E.W. Wormell. 1956. *The Delphic Oracle.* 2 vols. Oxford: Blackwell.

Parker, Robert. 1995. "Early Orphism." In Powell 1995: 483–510.

Patey, D. L. 1988. "The Eighteenth Century Invents the Canon." *Modern Language Studies* 18: 17–37.

Patzer, Andreas. 1986. *Der Sophist Hippias als Philosophienhistoriker.* Munich: Alker.

Pavese, C. O. 1972. *Tradizione e generi poetici nella Grecia antica*. Rome and Bari: Laterza.

Pease, Arthur S. 1926. "Things without Honour." *CPh* 21: 27–42.

Pellizer, Ezio. 1990. "Sympotic Entertainment." In Murray (1990: 177–84).

Pépin, J. 1958. *Mythe et allégorie*. Aubier: Montaigne.

Peppler, C. 1916. "The Suffix -*ma* in Aristophanes." *AJPh* 37:459–65.

Perkins, David, ed. 1991. *Theoretical Issues in Literary History*. Cambridge, Mass.: Harvard University Press.

Péron, Jacques. 1974. *Les images maritîmes de Pindare*. Paris: Klinksieck.

Pfeiffer, Rudolph. 1968. *History of Classical Scholarship: From the Beginnings to the End of the Hellenistic Age*. Oxford: Clarendon Press.

Pfligersdorfer, G. 1943–47. "*Logioi* und die *logioi anthropoi* bei Demokrit." *WS*. 61–62: 5–49.

Pfohl, G., ed. 1972. *Inschriften der Griechen: Grab- Weih- und Ehreninschriften*. Darmstadt: Wissentschaftliche Buchgesellschaft.

Philipp, Hanna. 1968. *Tektonon Daidala*. Quellen und Schriften zur bildenden Kunst 2. Berlin: Hessling.

Pickard-Cambridge, A. W. 1962. *Dithyramb, Tragedy and Comedy*. 2d ed., revised by T.B.L. Webster. Oxford: Clarendon Press.

———. 1988. *The Dramatic Festivals of Athens*. 2d ed. with addenda, revised by J. Gould and D. M. Lewis. Oxford: Clarendon Press.

Pinte, Daniel. 1966. "Un classment des genres poétiques par Bacchylide." *AC* 35: 459–67.

Plebe, A. 1959. "Origini e problemi dell' estetica antica." In *Momenti e problemi di storia dell' estetica, I: Dall' antichità classica al barocco*, pp. 1–80. Milan: Marzorati.

Podlecki, A. J. 1968. "Simonides: 480." *Historia* 17: 257–75.

———. 1980. "Festivals and Flattery: The Early Greek Tyrants as Patrons of Poetry." *Athenaeum* 58: 371–95.

Pohlenz, M. 1920. "Die Anfänge der griechischen Poetik." *Nachtrichten von der Gesellschaft der Wissenschaft zu Göttingen* 2: 142–78.

———. 1933. "To *prepon*: Ein Beitrag zur Geschichte des Griechischen Geistes." *Nachtrichten von der Gesellschaft der Wissenschaft zu Göttingen* 16: 53–92.

Pöhlmann, E. 1990. "Zur Überlieferung griechischer Literatur vom 8. bis zum 4. Jh." In Kullmann and Reichel 1990: 11–30.

Pollitt, J. J. 1974. *The Ancient View of Greek Art*. New Haven: Yale University Press.

Pomeroy, Sarah B. 1994. *Xenophon: Oeconomicus*. Oxford: Clarendon Press.

Pope, Maurice. 1986. "Athenian Festival Judges—Seven, Five or However Many." *CQ* 36: 322–26.

Porter, James I. 1992. "Hermeneutic Lines and Circles: Aristarchus and Crates on the Exegesis of Homer." In Lamberton and Keaney 1992: 67–114.

———. 1993. "The Seductions of Gorgias." *ClAnt* 12: 267–99.

Powell, Anton, ed. 1995. *The Greek World*. London and New York: Routledge.

Powell, Barry. 1991. *Homer and the Origins of the Greek Alphabet*. Cambridge: Cambridge University Press.

Pozzi, Dora C., and John M. Wickersham, ed. 1991. *Myth and the Polis.* Ithaca, N.Y.: Cornell University Press.

Pratt, Louise H. 1993. *Lying and Poetry from Homer to Pindar.* Ann Arbor: University of Michigan Press.

Preminger, A., and T.V.F. Brogan, eds. 1994. *The New Princeton Encyclopaedia of Poetry and Poetics.* Princeton: Princeton University Press.

Pretagostini, Roberto, ed. 1993. *Tradizione e innovazione nella cultura Greca da Omero all' eta ellenistica. Scritti in onore di Bruno Gentili.* 3 vols. Rome: Gruppo Editoriale Internazionale.

Prier, R. A. 1976. "Some Thoughts on the Archaic Use of *Metron.*" *CW* 70: 161–69.

Pritchard, J. B. 1954. *Ancient Near Eastern Texts Relating to the Old Testament.* Princeton: Princeton University Press.

Pucci, Pietro. 1977a. *Hesiod and the Language of Poetry.* Baltimore and London: The Johns Hopkins University Press.

———. 1977b. "Euripides: The Monument and the Sacrifice." *Arethusa* 10: 165–95.

———. 1980. "The Language of the Muses." In *Classical Mythology in Twentieth-Century Thought and Literature,* ed. W. M. Aycock and T. M. Klein, pp. 163–86 Lubbock: Texas Tech Press.

———. 1988. "Inscriptions archaïques sur les statues des dieux." In Detienne 1988: 480–97.

Puelma, Mario. 1977. "Der Dichter und die Wahrheit in der griechischen Poetik von Homer bis Aristoteles." *MH* 46: 65–100.

Raaflaub, Kurt. 1988. "Homer and the Beginnings of Political Thought in Greece." *Proceedings of the Boston Area Colloquium in Ancient Philosophy* 4: 1–25.

Race, William H. 1978. "*Panathenaicus* 74–90: The Rhetoric of Isocrates' Digression on Agamemnon." *TAPhA* 108: 175–85.

———. 1980. "The End of *Olympian* 2: Pindar and the Vulgus." *California Studies in Classical Antiquity* 12: 251–67.

———. 1981. "The Word Καιρός in Greek Drama." *TAPhA* 111: 197–213.

———. 1987. "Pindaric Encomium and Isocrates' *Evagoras.*" *TAPhA* 117: 131–55.

———, ed. and trans. 1997. *Pindar.* 2 vols. Cambridge, Mass.: Harvard University Press.

Radermacher, Ludwig. 1951. *Artium Scriptores. Reste der voraristotelischen Rhetorik.* Vienna: Rohrer.

———. 1954. *Frösche.* 2d ed. by W. Kraus. Vienna: Rohrer.

Raubitschek, A. E. 1968. "Denkmal und Epigram." In *L'épigramme grecque,* Entretiens sur l' Antiquité Classique 14, pp. 1–37. Vandoeuvres-Geneva: Fondation Hardt.

Reden, Sitta Von. 1995. "Deceptive Readings: Poetry and Its Value Reconsidered." *CQ* 45: 30–50.

Redfield, J. 1975. *Nature and Culture in the Iliad.* Chicago: University of Chicago Press.

Reeve, C.D.C. 1988. *Philosopher Kings.* Princeton: Princeton University Press.

Reinhardt, K. 1916. *Parmenides und die Geschichte der griechischen Philosophie*. Bonn: Friedrich Cohen.

Reitzenstein, R. 1893. *Epigramm und Skolion. Ein Beitrag zur Geschichte der Alexandrinischen Dichtung*. Giessen. (Reprint 1970, Hildesheim: Olms.)

Ress, B. R. 1981. "Aristotle's Approach to Poetry." *G&R* 28: 23–39.

Reynolds, Dwight F. 1995. *Heroic Poets, Poetic Heroes: The Ethnography of Performance in an Arabic Oral Epic Tradition*. Ithaca, N.Y. and London: Cornell University Press.

Rhodes, P. J. 1993. *A Commentary on the Aristotelian Athenaion Politeia*. Oxford: Clarendon Press.

Richardson, N. J. 1974. *The Homeric Hymn to Demeter*. Oxford: Clarendon Press.

————. 1975. "Homeric Professors in the Age of the Sophists." *PCPhS* 21: 65–81.

————. 1981. "The Contest of Homer and Hesiod and Alcidamas' *Mouseion*." *CQ* 31: 1–10.

————. 1985. "Pindar and Later Literary Criticism in Antiquity." *Papers of the Liverpool Latin Seminar* 5: 383–401.

Riedweg, Christoph. 1997. " 'Pythagoras hinterliess keine einzige Schrift'—ein Irrtum?" *MH* 54: 65–92.

Risch, E. 1974. *Wortbildung der Homerischen Sprache*. Berlin: Walter de Gruyter.

Rispoli, G. M. 1980. "Teagene o dell' allegoria." *Vichiana* 9: 243–57.

Ritoók, Zs. 1968. "The Epithets for Minstrels in the *Odyssey*." *AAntHung* 16: 89–92.

————. 1989. "The Views of Early Greek Epic on Poetry and Art." *Mnemosyne* 42: 331–48.

Robb, Kevin. 1994. *Literacy and Paideia in Ancient Greece*. Oxford: Oxford University Press.

Roberts, R. H., and J.M.M. Good, eds. 1993. *The Recovery of Rhetoric: Persuasive Discourse and Disciplinarity in the Human Sciences*. London: Bristol Classical Press.

Robertson, Noel. 1991. "The Betrothal Symposium in Early Greece." In Slater 1991: 25–8.

Römer, Adolf. 1884. "Die Homercitate und die Homerischen Fragen des Aristoteles." *Sitzungsberichte der königlichen bayerische Akademie von Wissenschaft*, Phil.-Hist. Klasse 264–314.

————. 1905. *Ueber den litterarisch-aesthetischen Bildungstand des attischen Theaterpublikums. Akademie der Wissenschaft München*, Phil.-Hist. Klasse Abhandlungen 22.

Romer, F. E. 1982. "The *Aisumneteia*: A Problem in Aristotle's Historical Method." *AJPh* 103: 25–46.

Rorty, A. O., ed. 1992. *Essays on Aristotle's Poetics*. Princeton: Princeton University Press.

Rose, V., ed. 1886. *Aristotelis qui ferebantur librorum fragmenta*. 3d ed. Leipzig: Teubner.

Rosen, Ralph, and Joseph Farrell, eds. 1993. *Nomodeiktes: Greek Studies in Honor of Martin Ostwald.* Ann Arbor: University of Michigan Press.

Rosenmeyer, T. G. 1955. "Gorgias, Aeschylus and Apate." *AJPh* 76: 225–60.

———. 1985. "Ancient Literary Genres: A Mirage?" *Yearbook of Comparative and General Literature* 34: 74–84.

Rösler, Wolfgang. 1980a. *Dichter und Gruppe: eine Untersuchung zu den Bedingingen und zue historischen Funktionen früher griechischer Lyrik am Beispiel Alkaios.* Theorie und Geschichte der Literatur und der schönen Künst 50. Munich: Fink.

———. 1980b. "Die Entdeckung der Fiktionalität in der Antike." *Poetica* 12: 283–319.

———. 1983. "Schriftkultur und Fiktionalität. Zum Fiktionswandel der griechischen Literatur von Homer bis Aristoteles." In *Schrift und Gedächtnis. Beiträge zur Archäologie der literarischen Kommunikation,* ed. A. and J. Assmann and Chr. Hardmeier; pp. 109–122. Munich: W. Fink.

———. 1990. "Mnemosune in the Symposium." In O. Murray 1990: 230–37.

———. 1995. "Wine and Truth in the Greek *Symposion.*" In Murray 1995: 106–12.

Rossi, L. E. 1971. "I generi letterari e le loro leggi scritti e non scritti nelle letterature classiche." *Bulletin of the Institute for Classical Studies* 18: 69–94.

Rostagni, A. 1922. "Un nuovo capitolo nella storia della *Retorica* e della *Sofistica.*" *SIFC* 2: 148–201. (= Rostagni 1955: 1–59).

———. 1945. *Aristotele*: Poetica. Turin: Chiantore.

———. 1955. *Scritti minori I: Aesthetica.* Turin: Erasmo.

Russell, D. A. 1981. *Criticism in Antiquity.* Berkeley and Los Angeles: University of California Press.

Russell, D. A., and N. G. Wilson, eds. 1981. *Menander Rhetor.* Oxford: Clarendon.

Russell, D. A., and M. Winterbottom. 1972. *Ancient Literary Criticism: The Principal Texts in New Translations.* Oxford: Oxford University Press.

Rusten, J. S. 1985. "Interim Notes on the Papyrus from Derveni." *HShP* 89: 121–40.

Said, Suzanne. 1998. "Tragedy and Politics." In Boedeker and Raaflaub 1998: 275–95.

Saintsbury, George. 1908. *History of Criticism and Literary Taste in Europe.* 3 vols. London: Blackwood.

Salkever, S. G. 1986. "Tragedy and the Education of the *Dêmos*: Aristotle's Response to Plato." In *Greek Tragedy and Political Theory,* ed. J. P. Euben, pp. 274–303. Berkeley and Los Angeles: University of California Press.

Saunders, Trevor J. 1972. *Notes on the* Laws *of Plato. Bulletin of the Institute for Classical Studies,* suppl. vol. 28.

Schadewaldt, W. 1970. "Furcht und Mitleid? Zur Deutung des Aristotelischen Tragödiensatzes." In *Hellas und Hesperien,* vol. 1, 2d ed., 194–236. Zurich: Artemis Verlag.

———. 1973. "Der Umfang des Begriffs der Literatur in der Antike." In *Literatur und Dichtung,* ed. H. Rüdiger; pp. 12–25. Stuttgart: Kohlhammer.

Schäfer, Christian. 1996. *Xenophanes von Kolophon. Ein Vorsokratiker zwischen Mythos und Philosophie*. Stuttgart and Leipzig: Teubner.

Schaper, Eva. 1968. *A Prelude to Aesthetics*. London: Allen and Unwin.

Scheid, John, and Jesper Svenbro. 1996. *The Craft of Zeus: Myths of Weaving and Fabric*. Translated by Carol Volk. Cambridge, Mass.: Harvard University Press.

Schenkeveld, D. M. 1968. "*Hoi kritikoi* in Philodemus." *Mnemosyne* 21: 176–214.

Schiappa, E. 1990. "Did Plato Coin *Rhêtorikê?*" *AJPh* 111: 457–70.

Schibli, H. 1990. *Pherecydes of Syros*. Oxford: Clarendon Press.

Schmid, W., and O. Stählin. 1929–34. *Geschichte der griechischen Literatur*. 2 vols. Munich: Beck.

Schmitt, Rudiger. 1967. *Dichtung und Dichtersprache in indogermanischer Zeit*. Wiesbaden: Harrassowitz.

Schmitt-Pantel, Pauline. 1990. "Sacrificial Meal and Symposium." In Murray 1990: 14–33.

———. 1992. *La cité au banquet*. Rome: École Française.

Schneider, H. 1989. *Die griechische Technikverständnis*, Impulse der Forschung 45. Darmstadt: Wissentschaftliche Gesellschaft.

Schraeder, Herman. 1880. *Porphyrii Quaestionum Homericarum ad* Iliadem *pertinentium reliquias*. Leipzig: Teubner.

Schröder, Stephan. 1999. *Geschichte und Theorie der Gattung Paian*. Leipzig: Teubner.

Schweitzer, Bernhard. 1963. *Zur Kunst der Antike: Ausgewählte Schriften* Vol. 1. Tübingen: Ernst Wasmuth.

Scodel, Ruth. 1987. "Literary Interpretation in Plato's *Protagoras*." *AncPhil* 6: 25–27.

———. 1990. "Euripides and *Apate*." In Griffith and Mastronarde 1990: 75–87.

Seaford, Richard. 1976. "On the Origins of Satyric Drama." *Maia* 28: 209–21.

———. 1977–78. "The *Hyporchema* of Pratinas." *Maia* 29: 81–94.

———, ed. 1984. *Euripides: Cyclops*. Oxford: Clarendon Press.

———. 1994. *Reciprocity and Ritual*. Oxford: Clarendon Press.

Sedgwick, W. B. 1948. "The *Frogs* and the Audience." *C&M* 9: 1–9.

Segal, C. P. 1962. "Gorgias and the Psychology of the Logos." *HSPh* 66: 99–155.

———. 1970. "Protagoras' *Orthoepeia* in Aristophanes' 'Battle of the Prologues' (*Frogs* 1119–97)." *RhM* 113: 158–62.

———. 1974. "Arrest and Movement in Pindar's Fifth *Nemean*." *Hermes* 102: 397–411. (Shorter version in Segal 1998: 167–84.)

———. 1982. "Tragédie, oralité, écriture." *Poétique* 50: 131–54.

———. 1984. "Greek Tragedy: Writing, Truth, and the Representation of the Self." In *Mnemai: Classical Studies in Memory of Karl K. Hulley*, ed. Harold D. Evjen, pp. 41–67. Chico, Calif.: Scholars Press.

———. 1985. "Messages to the Underworld: An Aspect of Poetic Immortalization in Pindar." *AJPh* 106: 199–212. (= Segal 1998: 105–32.)

———. 1986. *Pindar's Mythmaking: The Fourth Pythian Ode*. Princeton: Princeton University Press.

———. 1989. "Song, Ritual and Commemoration in Early Greek Poetry and Tragedy." *Oral Tradition* 4: 330–59.

———. 1994. "Classical Criticism and the Canon, or, Why Read the Ancient Critics?" In *Reading World Literature: Theory History and Practice*, ed. Sarah Lawall, pp. 87–112. Austin: University of Texas Press.

———. 1996. "Catharsis, Audience and Closure in Greek Tragedy." In Silk 1996: 149–72.

———. 1998. *Aglaia: The Poetry of Alcman, Sappho, Pindar, Bacchylides and Corinna*. Lanham, Md.: Rowman and Littlefield.

Sengesbusch, Maximillian. 1855–56. *Dissertatio Homerica*. Vols. 1 and 2. Leipzig: Teubner.

Shapiro, H. Alan. 1990. "Oracle-Mongers in Peisistratid Athens." *Kernos* 3: 335–45.

———. 1994. *Myth into Art: Poet and Painter in Classical Greece*. London: Routledge.

Shorey, P. 1909. "Φύσις, Μελέτη, ᾿Επιστήμη." *TAPhA* 40: 185–201.

Sicking, C.M.J. 1963. "Organische Komposition und Verwandtes." *Mnemosyne*. 16: 225–42.

Sifakis, G. M. 1986. "Learning from Art and Pleasure in Learning: An Interpretation of Aristotle *Poetics* 4 1448b8–19." In *Studies in Honor of T.B.L. Webster, I*, ed. J. H. Betts, J. T. Hooker and J. R. Green, pp. 211–22. Bristol: Bristol Classics Press.

Sikes, E. E. 1931. *The Greek View of Poetry*. London: Methuen.

Silk, M. S., ed. 1996. *Tragedy and the Tragic: Greek Theater and Beyond*. Oxford: Clarendon Press.

Simon, Bennett. 1978. *Mind and Madness in Ancient Greece*. Ithaca, N.Y.: Cornell University Press.

Skiadas, A. D. 1972. "ΕΠΙ ΤΥΜΒΩΙ: Ein Beitrag zur Interpretation der griechischen metrischen Grabinschriften." In Pfohl 1972: 59–84.

Slater, W. J. 1969. *Lexicon to Pindar*. Berlin and New York: Walter de Gruyter.

———. 1976–77. "Doubts about Pindaric Interpretation." *CJ* 72: 193–208.

———. 1981. "Peace, the Symposium and the Poet." *ICS* 6: 205–14.

———. 1990. "Sympotic Ethics in the *Odyssey*." In Murray 1990: 213–20.

———, ed. 1991. *Dining in a Classical Context*. Ann Arbor: University of Michigan Press.

Smith, Janet. 1986. "Plato's Use of Myth in Education." *Phoenix*.40: 20–34.

Smyth, H. W. 1906. *Greek Lyric Poets*. London. (Reprinted Biblo and Tannen, N.Y., 1963.)

Snell, Bruno. 1938. *Leben und Meinungen der Sieben Weisen*. Munich: E. Heimeran.

———. 1944. "Die Nachrichten über die Lehren des Thales und die Anfänge der Griechischen philsophie und Literaturgeschichte." *Philologus* 96: 170–82. Reprinted in Classen 1976: 478–90.

———. 1953. *The Discovery of the Mind*. Translated from the 2d ed. (Hamburg: Claassen und Goverts, 1948) by T. G. Rosenmeyer. Cambridge, Mass.: Harvard University Press.

———. 1961. *Poetry and Society*. Bloomington: Indiana University Press.

Snell, Bruno. 1973. "Wie die Griechen lernten was geistige Tätigkeit ist." *JHS* 93: 172–84.

Snodgrass, Anthony. 1998. *Homer and the Artists: Text and Picture in Early Greek Art*. Cambridge: Cambridge University Press.

Solmsen, F. 1932. "Drei Rekonstruktionen zur Antiken Rhetorik und Poetik." *Hermes* 67: 133–54.

———. 1964. "Leisure and Play in Aristotle's Ideal State." *RhM* 107: 193–220.

Sommerstein, A. H., ed. 1994. *Aristophanes: Thesmophoriazusae*. Warminster: Aris and Phillips.

Sörbom, Goram. 1966. *Mimesis and Art: Studies in the Origin and Early Development of an Aesthetic Vocabulary*. Upsala: Svenska Bokforlaget.

Sperdutti, A. 1950. "The Divine Nature of Poetry in Antiquity." *TAPhA* 81: 209–40.

Stanford, W. B. 1958. *Aristophanes: The Frogs*. 2d ed. London: Macmillan.

Stehle, Eva. 1997. *Performance and Gender in Ancient Greece*. Princeton: Princeton University Press.

Steiner, Deborah. 1986. *The Crown of Song: Metaphor in Pindar*. London: Duckworth.

———. 1993. "Pindar's 'Oggetti Parlanti.'" *HSPh* 95: 159–80.

———. 1994. *The Tyrant's Writ*. Princeton: Princeton University Press.

Steiner, W. 1982. *The Colors of Rhetoric: Problems in the Relation between Modern Literature and Painting*. Chicago and London: University of Chicago Press.

Steinruck, Martin. 2000. *Iambos: Studien zum Publikum einer Gattung in der frügriechischen Literatur*. Spudasmata 79. Hildesheim: Olms.

Stocks, J. L. 1936. "ΣΧΟΛΗ." *CQ* 30: 177–87.

Striker, Gisela. 1996. *Essays on Hellenistic Epistemology and Ethics*. Cambridge and New York: Cambridge University Press.

Süss. W. 1910. *Ethos*. Leipzig: Teubner.

———. 1911. "Theramenes der Rhetor und Verwandtes." *RhM* 66: 183–89.

Svenbro, Jesper. 1984a. *La parola e il marmo: Alle origini delle poetica greca*. Turin: Boringhieri. Revised and corrected edition of *La parole et le marbre: Aux origines de la poètique grecque* (Lund: Studentlitteratur, 1976).

———. 1984b."La découpe du poème. Notes sur les origines sacrificielles de la poétique grecque." *Poétique* 58: 215–32.

———. 1993. *Phrasikleia: An Anthropology of Reading in Ancient Greece*. Translated by Janet Lloyd. Ithaca, N.Y. and London: Cornell University Press.

Svoboda, K. 1927. *L' esthétique d' Aristote*. Brno: Tiskem.

Taillardat, Jean. 1965. *Les images d' Aristophane*. Paris: Belles lettres.

Taplin, Oliver. 1977. *The Stagecraft of Aeschylus*. Oxford: Clarendon Press.

———. 1980. "The Shield of Achilles within the *Iliad*." *G&R* 27: 1–21.

———. 1983. "Tragedy and Trugedy." *CQ* 33: 331–33.

Tate, J. 1927. "The Beginnings of Greek Allegory." *CR* 41: 214–15.

———. 1934. "On the History of Allegorism." *CQ* 28: 105–14.

Tedeschi, G. 1982. "Solone e lo spazio della communicazione elegiaca." *QUCC* 10: 33–46.

Thalmann, W. G. 1984. *Conventions of Form and Thought in Early Greek Poetry*. Baltimore and London: The Johns Hopkins University Press.

Thayer, H. S. 1975. "Plato's Quarrel with Poetry: Simonides." *JHI* 36: 3–26.

Thomas, Rosalind. 1989. *Oral Tradition and Written Record in Classical Athens.* Cambridge: Cambridge University Press.

———. 1992. *Literacy and Orality in Ancient Greece.* Cambridge: Cambridge University Press.

———. 1993. "Performance and Written Publication in Herodotus and the Sophistic Generation." In Kullmann and Althoff 1993: 225–44.

———. 1995b. "The Place of the Poet in Archaic Society." In Powell 1995: 104–29.

Tigerstedt, E. N. 1970. "*Furor Poeticus*: Poetic Inspiration in Greek Literature before Democritus and Plato." *JHI* 31: 163–78.

Too, Yun Lee. 1998. *The Idea of Ancient Literary Criticism.* Oxford: Clarendon Press.

Trédé, Monique. 1993. *Kairos: L'á-propos et l' occasion.* Paris: Klinksieck.

Treu, M. 1968. *Von Homer zur Lyrik.* Zetemata 12. Munich: C. H. Beck.

Trimpi, Wesley. 1983. *Muses of One Mind.* Princeton: Princeton University Press.

Trumpf, Jurgen. 1973. "Über das Trinken in der Poesie der Alkaios." *ZPE* 12: 139–60.

Tsirimbas, Basilios. 1936. *Die Stellung der Sophistic zur Poesie im V. und IV Jahrhundert bis zu Isokrates.* Munich: Pilger-Druckerei.

Turner, E. G. 1975. "I libri nell' Athene del V e IV secolo a. C." In *Libri, editori e pubblico nel mondo antico*, Historical and Critical Survey, ed. G. Cavallo Rome: Laterza. Revised edition of *Athenian Books in the Fifth and Fourth Centuries B.C.* (London, 1952).

Untersteiner, M. 1954. *The Sophists.* Translated by Kathleen Freeman from *I sofisti* (Turin, 1949). Oxford: Blackwell.

———, ed. 1956. *Senofane: Testimonianze e frammenti.* Florence: La Nuova Italia.

Vallozza, Maddalena. 1985. "Καιρός nelle retorica di Alcidamante e di Isocrate, ovvero nell' oratoria orale e scritta." *QUCC* 50 (n.s. 21): 119–23.

Van der Valk, M. H. 1963–64. *Researches on the Text and Scholia of the* Iliad. 2 vols. Leiden: Brill.

Van Wees, Hans. 1995. "Princes at Dinner." In *Homeric Questions*, ed. J. P. Crielaard, pp. 147–82. Amsterdam: Gieben.

Veneri, Alina. 1995. "La cetra di Paride: L'altra faccia della musica in Omero e nei suoi interpreti antichi." In *Mousike: Metrica, ritmica e musica greca in memoria di Giovanni Comotti*, ed. B. Gentili and F. Perusino, pp. 111–32. Pisa: Instituti Editoriali e Poligrafici Internazionali.

Verdenius, W. J. 1943. "L' *Ion* de Platon." *Mnemosyne* 11: 233–62.

———. 1970. *Homer, the Educator of the Greeks.* Amsterdam: North Holland Publishers.

———. 1981. "Gorgias' Doctrine of Deception." In *The Sophists and Their Legacy*, ed. G. B. Kerferd, *Hermes* Einzelschriften 44, pp. 116–28. Wiesbaden: Steiner.

———. 1983. "The Principles of Greek Literary Criticism." *Mnemosyne.* 36: 14–59.

———. 1987. *Commentaries on Pindar.* Leiden: Brill.

Vernant, J.-P. 1982. "La belle mort et le cadavre outragé." In *La mort, les morts dans les sociétés anciennes*, ed. G. Gnoli and J.-P. Vernant, pp. 45–76. Cambridge: Cambridge University Press.

———. 1991. *Mortals and Immortals: Collected Essays*. Edited by Froma I. Zeitlin. Princeton: Princeton University Press.

Vetta, M. 1977. "Un nuovo capitolo di storia di poesia simposiale (per l' esegesi di Aristoph. *Vesp.* 1222–48)." *Dialoghi di archaeologia* 9–10: 242–66.

———, ed. 1983. *Poesia e simposio nella Grecia antica: Guida storica e critica*. Rome and Bari: Laterza.

Vine, Brent. 1999. "On 'Cowgill's Law' in Greek." In *Compositiones indogermanicae in memoriam Jochem Schindler*, ed. H. C. Luschnützky and H. Eichner, pp. 555–600. Prague: Enigma Corp.

Vitali, Luca. 1990. "Le biografie di Omero tra immaginazione e realità: Spunti di critica letteraria." *RAL*. 43: 131–41.

Voigt, E.-M., ed. 1971. *Sappho et Alcaeus*. Amsterdam: Polak and Van Gennep.

Von Blumenthal, Albrecht. 1939. *Ion von Chios: Die Reste seiner Werke*. Stuttgart and Berlin: W. Kohlhammer Verlag.

Von der Mühl, P. 1976. "Die Griechische Symposion." In *Ausgewählte Kleine Schriften*, pp. 483–505. Basel: F. Reinhardt.

Von Reden, Sitta. 1995. "Deceptive Readings: Poetry and Its Value Reconsidered." *CQ* 45: 30–50.

Wade-Gery, H. T. 1952. *The Poet of the Iliad*. Cambridge: Cambridge University Press.

Walker, Jeffrey. 2000. *Rhetoric and Poetics in Antiquity*. Oxford: Oxford University Press.

Wallace, R. W. 1997. "Poet, Public, and 'Theatocracy': Audience and Performance in Classical Athens." In Edmunds and Wallace 1997: 97–111.

Wallace, R. W., and Bonnie MacLachlan, eds. 1991. *Harmonia mundi: musica e filosofia nell' antichita*. Rome: Ateneo.

Walsh, G. B. 1984. *The Varieties of Enchantment: Early Greek Views of the Nature and Function of Poetry*. Chapel Hill: University of North Carolina Press.

Wardy, Robert. 1996. *The Birth of Rhetoric*. New York: Routledge.

Weber, L. 1917. "Steinepigram und Buchepigram." *Hermes* 52: 536–45.

Webster, T.B.L. 1939. "Greek Theories of Art and Literature Down to 400 B.C." *CQ* 33: 166–79.

———. 1956. *Art and Literature in Fourth Century Athens*. London: University of London.

———. 1973. *Athenian Culture and Society*. Berkeley: University of California Press.

Wehrli, Fritz. 1928. "Zur Geschichte der allegorischen Deutung Homers im Altertum." Diss., Basel.

———. 1948. "Der erhabene und der schlichte Stil in der poetisch-rhetorischen Theorie der Antike." In *Phyllobolia für Peter von der Mühl*, ed. O. Gigon et al., pp. 9–34. Basel: Benno Schwabe.

———. 1957. "Die Antike Kunsttheorie und die Schöpferische." *MH* 14: 39–49.

———. 1967–78. *Die Schule des Aristoteles*. 2d ed. 10 vols. and 2 suppl. Basel: Schwabe.

Weil, Henri. 1900. "L' origine du mot 'poète'." In *Études sur l' antiquité grecque*, Paris: Hachette.

Weinstock, Stephan. 1927. "Die platonische Homerkritik und ihre Nachwirkung." *Philologus* 82: 121–53.

Wersdoerfer, Hans. 1940. *Die Philosophia des Isokrates im Spiegel ihrer Terminologie*. Harrassowitz: Leipzig

West, M. L., ed. 1966. *Hesiod: Theogony*. Oxford: Clarendon Press.

———. 1967. "The Contest of Homer and Hesiod." *CQ* 17: 433–50.

———. 1971. *Early Greek Philosophy and the Orient*. Oxford: Clarendon Press.

———. 1974. *Studies in Greek Elegy and Iambus*. Berlin and New York: Walter de Gruyter.

———, ed. 1978a. *Hesiod: Works and Days*. Oxford: Clarendon Press.

———. 1978b. "Phocylides." *JHS* 98: 164–67.

———. 1978c. "An Unrecognized Fragment of Archilochus?" *ZPE* 32: 1–5.

———. 1983. *The Orphic Poems*. Oxford: Clarendon Press.

———. 1985. "Ion of Chios." *Bulletin of the Institute for Classical Studies* 32: 71–78.

———, ed. 1989–92. *Iambi et elegi Graeci*. 2d ed. 2 vols. Oxford: Clarendon Press.

———. 1990. "Archaische Heldendichtung: Singen und Schreiben." In Kullmann and Reichel 1990: 33–50.

———. 1992. *Ancient Greek Music*. Oxford: Clarendon Press.

———. 1993. "Simonides Redivivus." *ZPE* 98: 1–14.

———. 1995. "The Date of the *Iliad*." *MH* 52: 203–19.

———. 1997. *The East Face of Helicon: West Asiatic Elements in Greek Poetry and Myth*. Oxford: Oxford University Press.

West, Stephanie. 1988. "The Transmission of the Text." In Heubeck et al. 1988–92, 1: 33–48.

Whitman, Jon. 1987. *Allegory: The Dynamics of an Ancient and Medieval Technique*. Oxford: Clarendon Press.

———. 1994. "Allegory, Western." In Preminger and Brogan 1994: 31–36.

Wickersham, John M. 1991. "Myth and Identity in the Archaic Polis." In Pozzi and Wickersham 1991: 1–31.

Wilamowitz-Moellendorff, Ulrich von. 1893. *Aristoteles und Athen*. 2 vols. Berlin: Weidmann.

———. 1907. *Einleitung in die Griechische Tragödie*. Berlin: Weidmann. (Extract from idem, *Euripides Herakles I*, chs. 1–4.)

———. 1913. *Sappho und Simonides*. Berlin: Weidmann.

———, ed. 1929. *Vitae Homeri et Hesiodi*. Berlin: Walter de Gruyter.

———. 1931–32. *Die Glaube der Hellenen*. Berlin: Weidmann.

Wilson, J. R. 1980. "Kairos as Due Measure." *Glotta* 58: 177–204.

Wilson, P. J. 1996. "Tragic Rhetoric: The Use of Tragedy and the Tragic in the Fourth Century." In *Tragedy and the Tragic: Greek Theater and Beyond*, ed. M. S. Silk, pp. 310–31. Oxford: Clarendon Press.

———. 1997. "Leading the Tragic *Khoros*: Tragic Prestige in the Democratic City." In *Greek Tragedy and the Historian*, ed. Christopher Pelling, pp. 81–108. Oxford: Clarendon Press.

———. 1999. "The *aulos* in Athens." In Goldhill and Osborne 1999: 57–95.

———. 2000. *The Athenian Institution of the Khoregia.* Cambridge: Cambridge University Press.

Wimsatt, W. K., Jr., and C. Brooks. 1957. *Literary Criticism: A Short History.* New York: Vintage.

Winkler, John J., and Froma Zeitlin, eds. 1990. *Nothing to Do with Dionysus: Athenian Drama in its Social Context.* Princeton: Princeton University Press.

Wolf, F. A. 1795. *Prolegomena ad Homerum.* Edited by R. Peppermüller [1884]. Halle: Waisenhaus. (Reprinted Hildesheim: G. Olms, 1963.)

———. 1985. *Prolegomena to Homer.* Translated by A. Grafton, G. W. Most, and J. G. Zetzel. Princeton: Princeton University Press.

Woodard, Roger D. 1997. *Greek Writing from Knossos to Homer.* New York: Oxford.

Woodbury, Leonard. 1961. "Apollodorus, Xenophanes, and Massilia." *Phoenix* 15: 134–55. (= Woodbury 1991: 96–117.)

———. 1968. "Pindar and the Mercenary Muse." *TAPhA* 99: 527–42.

———. 1976. "Aristophanes' *Frogs* and Athenian Literacy." *TAPhA* 106: 349–57.

———. 1986. "The Judgement of Dionysus: Books, Taste and Teaching in the *Frogs*." In M. J. Cropp, E. Fantham, and S. E. Scully, eds. *Greek Tragedy and its Legacy: Essays Presented to D. J. Conacher,* pp. 241–57. Calgary: University of Calgary Press.

———. 1991. *Collected Writings.* Edited by C. G. Brown, et al. Atlanta: Scholars Press.

Woodman, A. J. 1988. *Rhetoric in Classical Historiography.* London: Croon Helm.

Worthington, Ian, ed. 1994. *Persuasion: Greek Rhetoric in Action.* New York: Routledge.

Wright, M. R. 1981. *Empedocles: The Extant Fragments.* New Haven and London: Yale University Press.

Wyatt, William. 1969. *Metrical Lengthening in Homer.* Incunabula Graeca 35. Rome: Ed. d'Ateneo.

Young, D. C., ed. 1961. *Theognis.* Leipzig: Teubner.

———. 1983. "Pindar, Aristotle, and Homer: A Study in Ancient Criticism." *ClAnt* 2: 156–70.

Yunis, Harvey. 1996. *Taming Democracy: Models of Political Rhetoric in Classical Athens.* Ithaca, N.Y., and London: Cornell University Press.

———. 1998. "The Constraints of Democracy and the Rise of the Art of Rhetoric." In Boedeker and Raaflaub (1998: 223–40.

Zeitlin, Froma I. 1990. "Playing the Other: Theater, Theatricality and the Feminine in Greek Drama." In Winkler and Zeitlin 1990: 63–96.

Ziegler, K. 1965. "Xenophanes von Kolophon, ein Revolutionär des Geistes." *Gymnasium* 72: 289–302.

INDEX OF PASSAGES DISCUSSED

GENERAL INDEX

feasts: categorization of, 35n. 34; and festival customs, 140n. 34

Feeney, D. C., 68n. 5, 74n. 28

Fehling, D., 167n. 23, 170n. 39

Fehr, B., 33n. 28

Fera, Maria Cannata, 15n. 14

Ferrari, Giovanni, 33n. 29, 210, 216–17, 218, 219, 219n. 34, 224n. 49

festival of the Carnea, 139

fictionality, 230–31, 230nn. 3 and 4. See also *mimēsis*

Finkelberg, Margalit, 95n. 7, 131n. 1; dismissal of Tigerstedt's thesis, 168n. 29; on early Greek criticism, 2n. 4; on Gorgias' fictionality, 173n. 50; on Homer's fictionality, 156n. 94, 230nn. 3 and 4; on *metron*, 18n. 40

Finley, M. I., 8n. 18, 94n. 1

Flashar, H., 184n. 88

Fortenbaugh, W. W., 269n. 51, 288n. 29

Fowler, Alastair, 10n. 22, 251n. 1

Fränkel, Hermann, 56n. 48, 59nn. 65and 67, 106–7, 107n. 54, 111n. 66, 124; on the Midas epigram, 108n. 55

Fraser, P. M., 294n. 2

Frogs (Aristophanes), 3, 13, 62–63, 65n. 84, 163, 188, 196, 199–200; chorus in, 198; implications for Athenian literacy, 153n. 85; inventor catalogue in, 144; on judging art, 20, 281–82; language as clothing in, 229n. 1; poetic contest in, 64; presentation of Homer, 203; view of poetry in, 230, 293

Frye, Northrop, 265–66

funeral: games, 277n. 15; orations, 128–30

Furley, David J., 164n. 10

Gadamer, Hans Georg, 81, 81n. 61

Gallop, David, 267n. 45

genres: archaic, 10–13; Cairns on, 8n. 16; classical, 17–22; as literary, 251; rhetorical view of, 256; Romantic perspective on, 251; Rossi's "unwritten laws of," 10n. 21. *See also* Isocrates, on genre; Plato, on pure forms; *Poetics*, on genre

Gentili, Bruno, 9, 9n. 20, 14n. 32, 32n. 26, 57n. 54, 76n. 42, 95n. 7, 98, 155n. 91; on Hellenistic literary activity, 273n. 3; on *logoi* and *muthoi*, 55n. 47; on *stasis*,

56n. 50; stress on embeddedness of archaic song in performative context, 8

Gerber, D. E., 60n. 70, 108n. 54, 111n. 65

Gernet, Louis, 117n. 16

Giants, 46, 56, 56n. 49, 57, 221; Pindar's use as foil, 64

Gill, Christopher, 225n. 51, 229n. 2, 231n. 7

Giuliano, F. M., 154n. 88

Glaucus of Rhegium, 139–40, 144; history of music, 140–42

glōssai, 70, 170n. 36

Gnessiups, 207

gnōmai, 4, 41, 72, 83

Golden, Leon, 268n. 46

Goldhill, Simon, 35n. 35, 281n. 30; on Athenian audiences, 273; on the Dionysia, 278; on fiction in Homer and Hesiod, 230n. 4; on Odysseus' poetic "performance" at Phaeacia, 30n. 18; on the *Oresteia*, 289n. 3; on poetry and social praise, 2n. 4; on Simonides 531 *PMG*, 111n. 66; on teleological narrative, 46n. 1; on women admitted to theatrical performances, 283n. 37

Gorgias (Plato), 20, 283

Gorgias of Leontini, 94–95, 135, 137, 172–75, 217, 230–31; art of, 182–86; association of piety and fear, 176n. 58; influence on poetry from Plato on, 186–87; on *logos*, 229n. 1, 256; on magic spells, 178; and model speeches, 231–32; on poetry, 177–78; and "the present occasion," 19n. 43; as representative of sophistic rhetoric, 174; self-praise, 19n. 43; speeches given by, 184. See also *Helen; On Not Being; Palamedes*

Graff, Gerald, 4n. 8

grammatikoi, 272

grammatistēs, 192, 195, 195n. 27, 202, 272n. 2

graphas, 154, 154n. 90

graphein, 134, 138, 155

Graziosi, Barbara, 71n. 17

Griffith, Mark, 87n. 78, 153n. 84, 273n. 5, 292–93, 293n. 60

Grube, G.M.A., 2n. 4, 273n. 5

Gudeman, Alfred, 136n. 17, 263n. 32, 272n. 2

Guillory, John, 4n. 8

gumnastikē, 237

salon, 81

Sappho of Lesbos, 13–14, 54, 66, 145, 147, 261; house of, 14n. 32; as Muses' "minister," 134n. 6

Saunders, Trevor J., 285n. 44

Schadewaldt, W., 177n. 63

Schäfer, Christian, 59n. 62

Schenkeveld, D. M., 272n. 1

Schiappa, E., 161n. 2

Schibli, H., 69n. 6, 74n. 29, 94n. 1

Schmitt, Rudiger, 2n. 4

Schmitt-Pantel, Pauline, 35, 35n. 34, 36n. 37

Schröder, Stephan, 8n. 16, 11n. 26

Schweitzer, Bernhard, 94n. 1

Scodel, Ruth, 149n. 71, 154n. 88, 189n. 3

Scopas, 59n. 63

sculpture: and songs/poems, 98; and speeches, 239. *See also* Pindar, on statuary; Simonides of Ceos, on statuary

Seaford, Richard, 14n. 32, 52n. 36, 140n. 34, 142n. 39, 278n. 20

Sedgwick, W. B., 153n. 84

Segal, Charles, 96n. 10, 107n. 50, 116, 154n. 89, 178n. 68; on epicinian, 119; on Gorgias, 173n. 50, 177n. 61, 183n. 80; on Pindar, 111n. 67, 118, 118–19n. 24, 121n. 34, 122, 122nn. 38 and 44; on tragedians as producers of written texts, 153n. 84

sēma/sēmeia, 102, 104, 129, 130

sēmainein, 75, 75n. 35

Semonides, 134

Sengesbusch, Maximillian, 68n. 5

Seven Sages, 41, 106, 108n. 54

"shaping," 134, 218, 218n. 27, 231

Shapiro, H. Alan, 52n. 36

Sifakis, G. M., 267n. 45

Sikes, E. E., 2n. 4, 273n. 5

Simonides of Ceos, 41–42, 49, 78, 79, 85, 96, 119, 122, 127, 135, 147, 190, 192, 207; on the arts, 96–101; on "ever-flowing" fame and Thermopulae (531 *PMG*), 110–11; on the Midas epigram, 105–9; "plastic" style, 97n. 14; in Plato, 213n. 13; singing at symposia, 25n. 4; on statuary, 106–8, 112, 121, 232, 243, 244; use of by Alcidamas, Isocrates, and Plato, 232–33. See also *Protagoras*

singer, 131; as craftsman, 132; epithets for, 113; Homer's classification of, 113

singing, 9, 133; archaic lexicon for, 131; craft metaphors for (*see* Bacchylides, craft metaphors for song in; Pindar, craft metaphors for song in); development of into poetry, 9; distinguished from "making" or "poetry," 131; history of (*see* music, history of); as "play," 39

-*sis* abstracts, 137, 137n. 21

Sisyphus (Critias), 167n. 24

skhēma, 44, 51, 166, 217

skolion. See song, *skolion*

Slater, W. J., 29nn. 15 and 17, 36n. 37, 277n. 16, 278n. 17, 280nn. 27 and 28

Smyth, H. W., 11n. 26

Snell, Bruno, 15n. 35, 47n. 9, 107nn. 50 and 54, 109n. 61, 114

Snodgrass, Anthony, 78n. 49

Socrates, 188, 191, 193, 196–97; attendance at symposia, 26; in *Clouds*, 164, 281; in the *Iliad*, 205; in *Ion*, 258; in the *Minos*, 59–60; in *Phaedrus*, 86, 242, 243–44, 245, 247–48, 253n. 6; in the *Republic*, 72–73, 86–87, 193n. 19, 219–21, 223, 224, 224n. 50, 225, 258–59, 263; and selecting from "treasuries," 196–97; in the *Theatetus*, 87; in Xenophon, 73, 64n. 81, 238, 280–81

Solmsen, F., 257n. 18, 292n. 38

Solon, 18, 36, 42, 46, 106, 108, 127, 132, 145, 147; listing of occupations, 50; and the "remaking" of verse, 154; on *sophia*, 47n. 9; view of banqueting, 36n. 37

Sommerstein, A. H., 156n. 95

song, 9, 93; as *agalma*, 115–19; archaic lexicon for, 131; assignment to a god, 14; and buildings, 123–27; as "chariot," 121; and context-derived obligations, 9, 11; cult, 145; definition of, 4; dependence of on religious ideas, 15; development into poem, 9; dirge, 13; dithyramb, 10–11, 15, 140, 140n. 35, 142, 143, 259, 284n. 39; elegy, 25, 34, 35–36; epinician, 100n. 28; etymology of, 12n. 27; "goat-song," 11; Greek texts on, 4; group processional song, 11; *humnos*, 12, 12n. 27, 43n. 69, 131, 259, 260; *iambos*, 10, 18, 25; *kōmos*, 11, 32; lament, 10, 14, 16, 18, 52, 140nn. 34 and 35, 259; lyre-song, 52, 141; lyric, 145; male prerogative in pronouncing on, 7; martial, 34–35, 52; *melos*, 131; metaphors for composing, 113; paean, 10,